DEVIL'S FIRE, SOUTHERN CROSS

OSPREY
PUBLISHING

JEFFREY R. COX

DEVIL'S FIRE, SOUTHERN CROSS

THE CONCLUSION OF THE GUADALCANAL-SOLOMONS CAMPAIGN, OCTOBER 1943–FEBRUARY 1944

OSPREY PUBLISHING
Bloomsbury Publishing Plc
Kemp House, Chawley Park, Cumnor Hill, Oxford OX2 9PH, UK
Bloomsbury Publishing Ireland Limited,
29 Earlsfort Terrace, Dublin 2, D02 AY28, Ireland
1385 Broadway, 5th Floor, New York, NY 10018, USA
E-mail: info@ospreypublishing.com
www.ospreypublishing.com

OSPREY is a trademark of Osprey Publishing Ltd

First published in Great Britain in 2025

A catalog record for this book is available from the British Library

ISBN: HB 978 1 4728 6448 2; PB 978 1 4728 6447 5; eBook 978 1 4728 6446 8;
ePDF 978 1 4728 6451 2; XML 978 1 4728 6450 5

25 26 27 28 29   10 9 8 7 6 5 4 3 2 1

Plate section image credits and captions are given in full in the List of Illustrations (pp. 6–7).

Maps by www.bounford.com
Index by Kate Inskip
Typesetting by Six Red Marbles India
Printed and bound in Great Britain by Clays Ltd, Elcograf S.p.A.

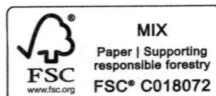

FSC
www.fsc.org

MIX
Paper | Supporting
responsible forestry
FSC® C018072

Osprey Publishing supports the Woodland Trust, the UK's leading woodland conservation charity.

To find out more about our authors and books visit **www.ospreypublishing.com**. Here you will find extracts,
author interviews, details of forthcoming events and the option to sign up for our newsletter.

For product safety related questions contact productsafety@bloomsbury.com

CONTENTS

LIST OF ILLUSTRATIONS

The destroyer USS *Spence* in San Francisco Bay, July 24, 1943. (Naval History and Heritage Command)

USS *Charles Ausburne* off Boston, Massachusetts, on March 6, 1943. (Photograph from the Bureau of Ships Collection in the US National Archives)

VMF-214 (Marine Fighting 214 or Marine Fighter Squadron 214) ("the Black Sheep") pilots run to their Vought F4U-1 Corsair aircraft on call, September 11, 1943, at Turtle Bay air base, Espiritu Santo Island, New Hebrides. (US National Archives)

Douglas SBD Dauntless dive bombers take off from Munda airfield, October 28, 1943. (US National Archives)

Rear Admiral Frederick C. Sherman (center, in cap), Task Force 38 commander, gets good news from Commander Joseph C. Clifton (far right), *Saratoga*'s fighter group commander concerning the air attack on Rabaul's Simpson Harbor, on board flagship USS *Saratoga*. With Admiral Sherman are (left to right): Captain Robert C. Sutliffe, Commander Robert E. Dixon and Lieutenant Albert F. Howard. Commander Clifton's fighters escorted the strike. The two strikes on Rabaul occurred on November 5 and 11, 1943. (US National Archives)

Admiral William F. Halsey, Commander, South Pacific Force/3rd Fleet (left) enjoys a joke with Commander Clifton (right) at a party given for *Saratoga* officers at Espiritu Santo, New Hebrides, following the carrier's November 1943 Rabaul raids. (Official US Navy Photograph, now in the collections of the US National Archives)

Rear Admiral A. Stanton Merrill, Commander, Task Force 39, on board flagship *Montpelier* in December 1943. (Official US Navy Photograph, now in the collections of the US National Archives)

The Japanese heavy cruiser/seaplane carrier hybrid *Chikuma* under attack by US Navy carrier planes in Simpson Harbor, photographed from a USS *Saratoga* SBD scout bomber's gun camera during the November 5, 1943 raid on Rabaul. (Official US Navy Photograph, now in the collections of the US National Archives)

The aircraft carrier USS *Saratoga* arrives at Pearl Harbor from the US West Coast, June 6, 1942. Laid up with torpedo damage during much of the Guadalcanal campaign, she played a key role in the neutralization of Rabaul in November 1943. (Official US Navy Photograph, now in the collections of the US National Archives)

Curtiss SB2C Helldivers flying in formation off Norfolk, VA, December 1943. (Photograph by Lieutenant Horace Bristol, USNR. US National Archives)

At Yokosuka, September 6, 1945. These appear to be largely experimental models of standard Japanese combat aircraft types, including two G4Ms (Betty); one J1N (Irving); and two D4Ys (Judy). (US National Archives)

Admiral Ozawa Jisaburo. Although voted the ugliest admiral in the IJN, Ozawa was highly respected by friend and foe alike. He took over command of a reduced and renamed *Kido Butai* in November 1943 after Admiral Yamamoto sacked Admiral Nagumo, and many believed Ozawa should have held this command all along. (Naval History and Heritage Command)

Admiral Koga Mineichi became commander-in-chief of the Combined Fleet of the IJN following the death of his predecessor Admiral Yamamoto over Bougainville. Before he was killed, Yamamoto recommended Koga for the position. (Naval History and Heritage Command)

The light carrier USS *Princeton* during her shakedown cruise. (US National Archives)

The South Pacific on November 1, 1943

Combat range of Japanese aircraft
Combat range of Allied aircraft

Ki-61   Ki-43   P-39 P-40   D3A   SBD   PV/TBF/F4U/P-38   F6F   B5N / Ki-45   SB2C   Ki-48 / D4Y1 / J1N1   Beaufighter   Ki-21 / A6M2 / A6M3   G3M / G4M: range beyond this map   B-24/B-25

Legend:
- Allied air bases
- Allied naval ports
- Japanese air bases
- Japanese naval ports
- Japanese sea plane port

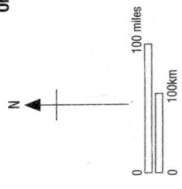

ADMIRALTY ISLANDS

Manus

NEW HANOVER

Emirau (May 1944)

Kavieng

BISMARCK ARCHIPELAGO

NEW IRELAND

Rabaul complex (Lakunai, Vunakanau, Tobera, Rapopo, Keravat)

St. George's Channel

Bismarck Sea

Talasea

NEW BRITAIN

Gasmata

Arawe/ Cape Merkus

Cape Gloucester

Dampier Strait

Vitiaz Strait

Finschhafen

Lae

Salamaua

Wau

Tsili-Tsili

NEW GUINEA

Port Moresby

Dobodura

TROBRIAND ISLANDS

Kiriwina

WOODLARK ISLANDS

Woodlark

Solomon Sea

Green Is (Mar 1944)

Buka

Bonis

Piva (Jan 1944)

Kieta

Torokina, Dec 1943

Kara

Buin/Kahili

Ballale

BOUGAINVILLE

TREASURY ISLANDS

Barakoma

VELLA LAVELLA

Ondonga

NEW GEORGIA

Munda

Sergi Point

RUSSELL ISLANDS

Banika

SOLOMON ISLANDS

The Slot

Rekata Bay

SANTA YSABEL

Renard

Henderson Field

GUADALCANAL

N

0   100 miles

0   100km

The Invasion of Bougainville (Operation *Cherryblossom*), November 1, 1943

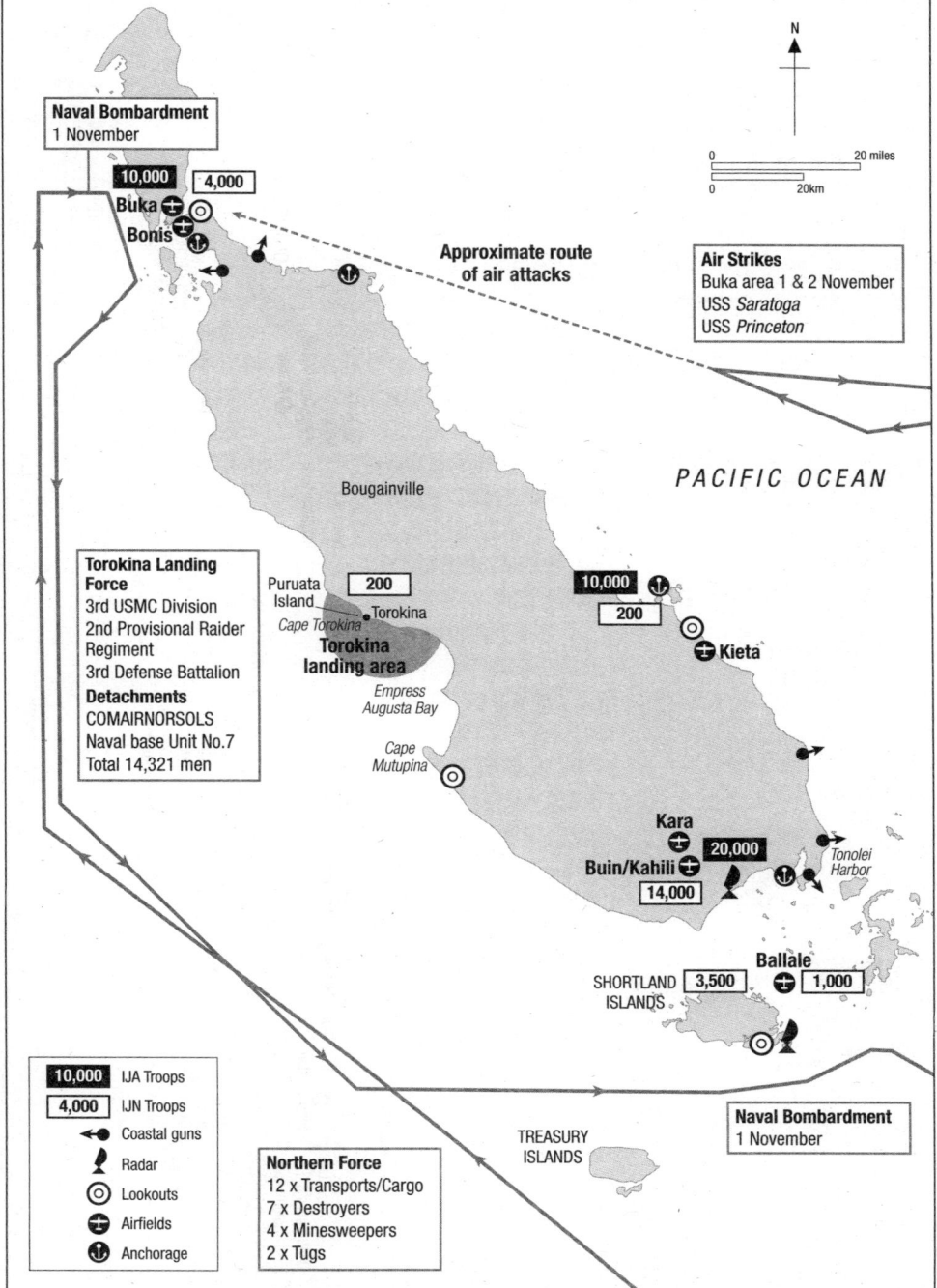

N

Naval Bombardment
1 November

0   20 miles
0   20km

10,000   4,000

Buka

Bonis

Approximate route
of air attacks

Air Strikes
Buka area 1 & 2 November
USS *Saratoga*
USS *Princeton*

Bougainville

PACIFIC OCEAN

**Torokina Landing
Force**
3rd USMC Division
2nd Provisional Raider
Regiment
3rd Defense Battalion
Detachments
COMAIRNORSOLS
Naval base Unit No.7
Total 14,321 men

Puruata
Island
Cape Torokina
**Torokina
landing area**

200

Torokina

*Empress
Augusta Bay*

*Cape
Mutupina*

10,000

200

Kieta

Kara

Buin/Kahili

20,000

*Tonolei
Harbor*

14,000

Ballale

SHORTLAND   3,500   1,000
ISLANDS

10,000   IJA Troops
4,000   IJN Troops
Coastal guns
Radar
Lookouts
Airfields
Anchorage

Northern Force
12 x Transports/Cargo
7 x Destroyers
4 x Minesweepers
2 x Tugs

TREASURY
ISLANDS

Naval Bombardment
1 November

The Battle of Empress Augusta Bay, November 2, 1943

Torpedo attack
Gunfire attack

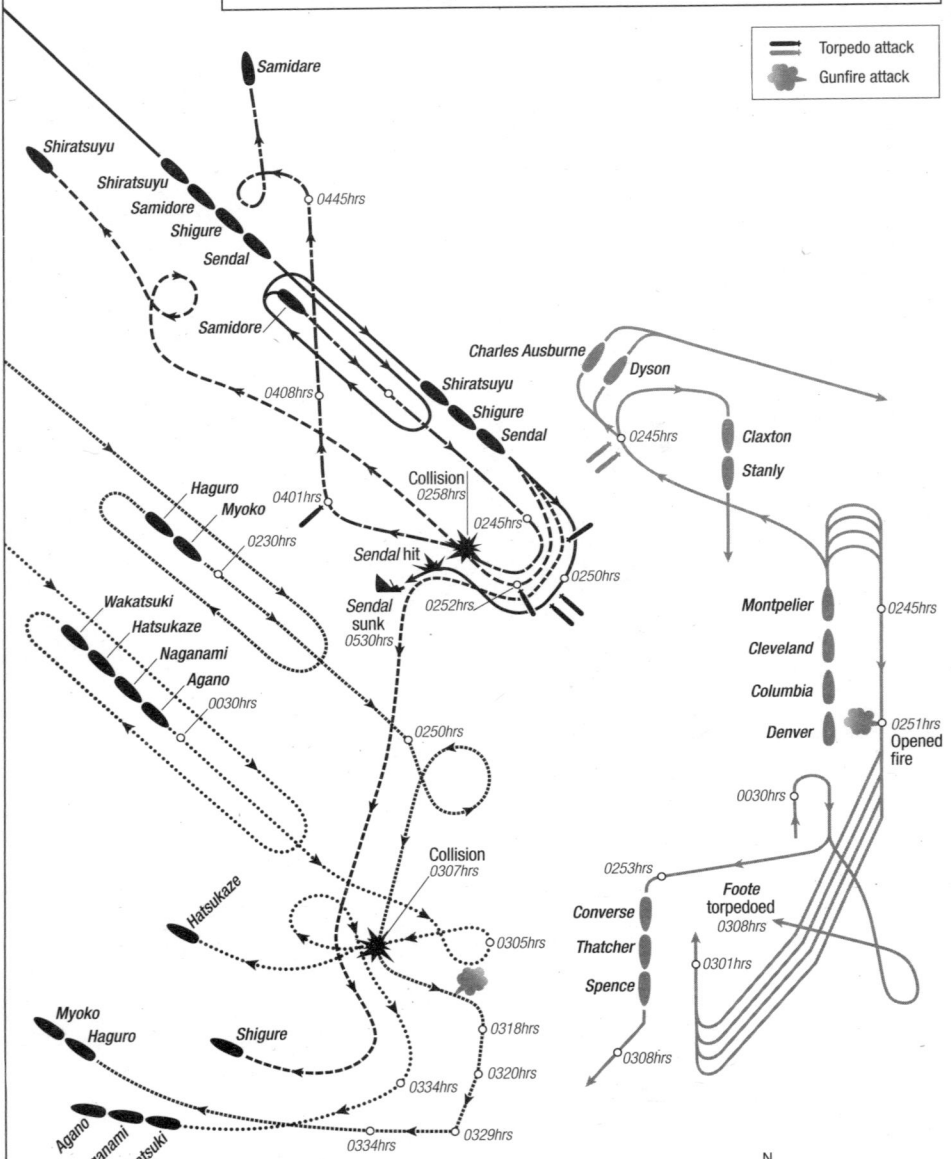

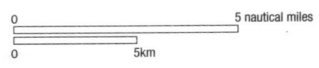

Samidare

Shiratsuyu
Shiratsuyu
Samidore
Shigure
Sendal

Samidore

0445hrs

0408hrs

Charles Ausburne
Dyson
0245hrs
Claxton
Stanly

Shiratsuyu
Shigure
Sendal

Collision
0258hrs

0401hrs

Haguro
Myoko
0230hrs

Sendal hit

0250hrs

Sendal
sunk
0530hrs

0252hrs

Montpelier
0245hrs
Cleveland
Columbia
Denver
0251hrs
Opened
fire

Wakatsuki
Hatsukaze
Naganami
Agano
0030hrs

0250hrs

0030hrs

Collision
0307hrs

0253hrs
Foote
torpedoed
0308hrs

0305hrs

Converse
Thatcher
Spence

0301hrs

Hatsukaze

0318hrs

0320hrs

Myoko
Haguro
Shigure

0308hrs

Agano
Naganami
Wakatsuki
0334hrs

0329hrs

0334hrs

N

0   5 nautical miles
0   5km

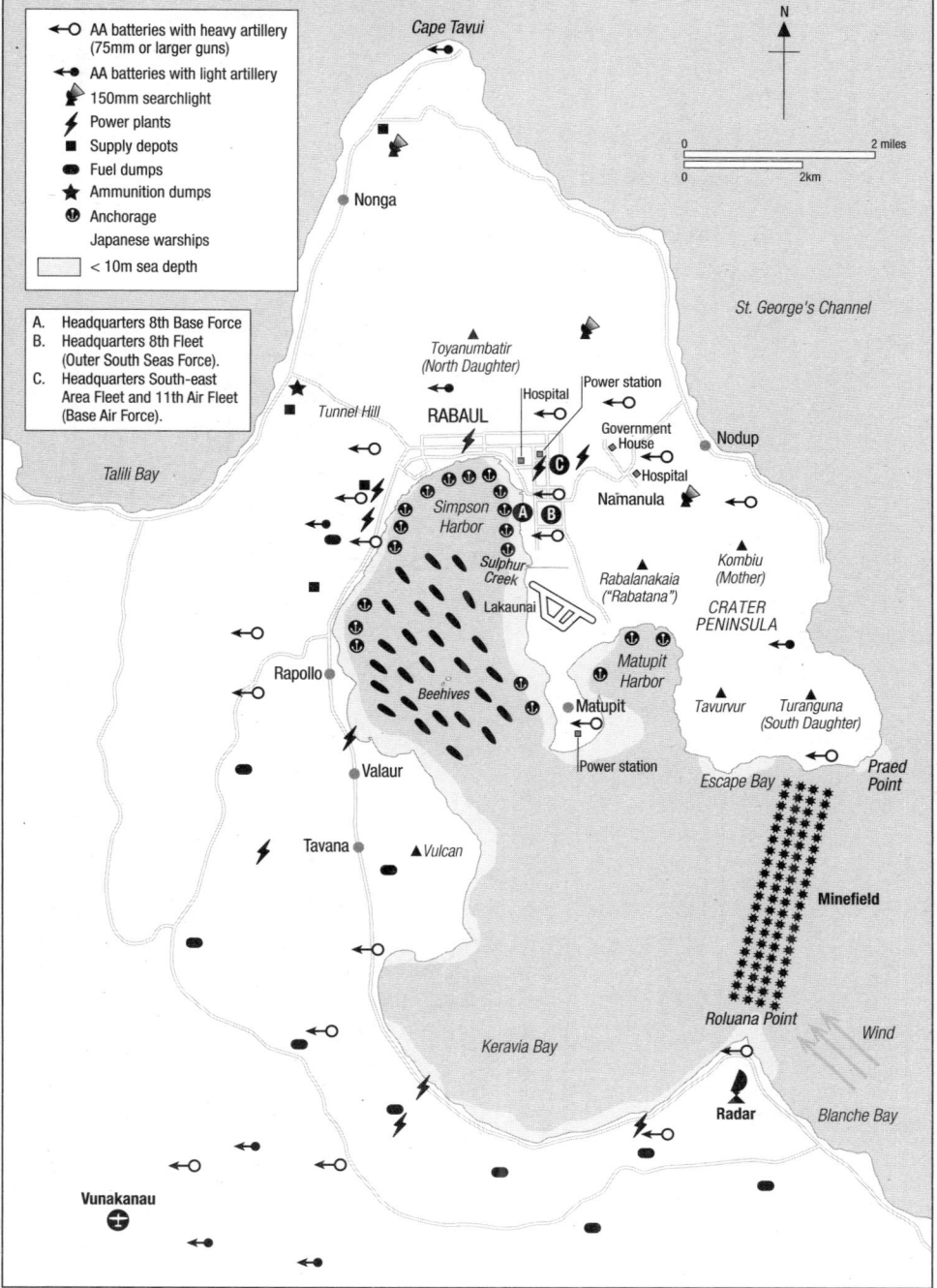

Rabaul Caldera Defenses, November 5, 1943

N

Cape Tavui

0   2 miles
0   2km

Nonga

St. George's Channel

Toyanumbatir (North Daughter)

Power station

Hospital

RABAUL

Tunnel Hill

Government House

Nodup

Hospital

Talili Bay

Naimanula

Simpson Harbor

Kombiu (Mother)

Sulphur Creek

Rabalanakaia ("Rabatana")

CRATER PENINSULA

Lakaunai

Matupit Harbor

Rapollo

Beehives

Matupit

Tavurvur

Turanguna (South Daughter)

Valaur

Power station

Escape Bay

Praed Point

Tavana

Vulcan

Minefield

Roluana Point

Wind

Keravia Bay

Radar

Blanche Bay

Vunakanau

The Battle of Cape St George, November 25, 1943

Dyson

Yugiri
0328hrs

Charles Ausburne
Claxton
Dyson

Converse
Spence

Amagiri

Uzuki

0225hrs

0230hrs

0255hrs

0225hrs

0240hrs
0222hrs

0254hrs
Onami
Makinami

2000hrs
0156hrs
0215hrs

0210hrs
0220hrs

0145hrs

0156hrs

0158hrs

0201hrs

Onami
Makinami
Screening
Group (Kagawa)

Destroyer
Division 45
(Burke)

Charles
Ausburne

Claxton

Dyson

Converse

Spence

Destroyer
Division 46
(Austin)

N

Amagiri
Yugiri
Uzuki
Transport Group
(Yamashiro)

0	5 nautical miles
0	5km

PROLOGUE

Admiral William F. Halsey, Jr, stood looking over a map of the South Pacific in his headquarters in Nouméa, New Caledonia, contemplating his next move, his next battle. Or what he planned to be his next battle. Down here, what was planned to be the next battle and what ended up being the next battle were usually not the same thing. Just getting this building for his headquarters had been a battle with French colonial authorities, who, like many in the Free French establishment, forgot that the liberation of their mother country from the Nazis depended on the goodwill of the United States, in whose Navy Halsey served, and Great Britain.[*]

Admiral Halsey was in charge of all Allied forces in the US Navy's South Pacific Area. That was the old name, anyway. The South Pacific Area had been renamed the 3rd Fleet, but Halsey seemed loathe to call it that. He was not the first commander of the South Pacific Area. That honor had gone to Vice Admiral Robert L. Ghormley. Ghormley had not considered it much of an honor, however, nor did he consider it an honor to be the first US Navy commander to be given the task of unraveling the various threads of the defensive web Japanese Admiral Yamamoto Isoroku, commander-in-chief of the Combined Fleet of the Imperial Japanese Navy, had assembled during the so-called "Centrifugal Offensive" with which Imperial Japan had started the Pacific War. The thread Ghormley had been assigned started at the southeastern end of the double line of islands called the Solomons at an airfield on Guadalcanal. As part of a strategic operation called *Pestilence* – an entirely appropriate name given the Solomons' veritable cornucopia of diseases – the Allies were to unravel the Solomon Islands' thread through the Japanese naval anchorage in the Shortland Islands and the Japanese air bases on and just off Bougainville all the way to Rabaul, the great Japanese fortress of the South Pacific, where the Solomons' thread intersected with threads from Papua New Guinea, the Admiralty Islands, Kavieng, and Truk.

But Admiral Ghormley did not like that offensive. It was not so much that Ghormley thought the operation was going to fail, but that he thought the operation had already

---

[*] Judging by the World War II exhibit in the *Hôtel des Invalides* in Paris in 2022, the French establishment has forgotten that fact once again.

failed, so he needed to salvage what he could for a new line of defense. To put it bluntly, Ghormley crippled the Allied efforts on Guadalcanal more than the Japanese did.[1] Eventually, Admiral Chester W. Nimitz, commander-in-chief of the US Pacific Fleet, and Admiral Ernest J. King, commander-in-chief of the US Fleet and chief of naval operations, decided more aggressive, less teary-eyed leadership was needed, and replaced Ghormley with Halsey.

Admiral Halsey then led a faltering Allied offensive to take Guadalcanal to victory through energy, confidence, daring, and no small amount of luck. True, it was not as complete a victory as he had wanted, but it was a victory nonetheless, with the primary strategic objectives completed. Guadalcanal and its air base could now be used to unravel that Solomons thread.

In a rather convoluted command arrangement that had him answering to the commander of the South-West Pacific Area, General Douglas MacArthur, Admiral Halsey had taken *Pestilence*, now renamed *Cartwheel*, and rolled up that thread into the central Solomons, moving on to take the New Georgia island group. That move started with the rather rare feat of a fairly excellent execution of a lousy operational plan. The offensive bogged down until more of that energy and daring were tossed in, along with acquisition of some real estate on Vella Lavella at the northwestern end of that island group. The result was another victory, with the primary strategic objectives completed, albeit, again, not as complete a victory as Halsey had wanted.

Now Admiral Halsey had the unenviable task of figuring out how to deal with what everyone knew would be the next major target in the unraveling Solomons thread. That target was the giant cork at the northwestern end of the double line of islands: Bougainville.

Named after – and by – the French explorer and mathematician Louis-Antoine, Comte de Bougainville, Bougainville from overhead looks like a filet mignon. Which isn't saying much; most islands from overhead look like a cut of meat of some sort. Bougainville is a microcosm of the twisted, dishonest nature of the Solomon Islands. At 125 miles long from northwest to southeast, and 30 to 48 miles wide, it was the largest of the Solomon Islands, though today it is not part of the political entity called "The Solomon Islands" but is instead a restive part of Papua New Guinea.[2] It is split longitudinally by a mountain range called "the Emperor" in the northwest and "the Crown Prince" in the southeast. Such bizarre names should make apparent how a major bay of Bougainville could be called "Empress Augusta Bay." It was named after Augusta Viktoria of Schleswig-Holstein, wife of Wilhelm II and thus the Queen of Prussia and later German Empress. It is typical of the twisted, topsy-turvy nature of the Solomon Islands that an island named after and by a French admiral would have its major bay named after German royalty.

Be that as it may, as part of that Emperor mountain range, Bougainville boasts (at least) two stratovolcanoes, 10,000-foot Mount Balbi and 8,000-foot Mount Bagana, which could impress anyone unless they were from Rabaul. Bagana is fairly active at spewing gas and ash, though it is not explosive like Vesuvius or Krakatoa. There were few reports of the Japanese having issues with Bagana like they did in Rabaul with Vulcan and, especially, Tavurvur. Most importantly, Bagana just looks like your stereotypical volcano – a tall cone – and overlooks Empress Augusta Bay.[3]

The mountain range ends toward the southern part of the island, where there is a coastal plain on which the Japanese had built airfields at Kahili – the Japanese called that airfield "Buin" – and Kara. The placement of the coastal plain was fortunate because it was next to one of the few anchorages available to Bougainville – the anchorage formed by the Shortland Islands. The Buka Passage was another such anchorage. What few harbors Bougainville had, such as Kieta and Tonolei, were suitable only for small craft, not warships. Empress Augusta Bay, spanning from Cape Torokina to the northwest to Mutupina Point and Gazelle Harbor to the southeast, is an open bay sheltered only from southeast winds, but was deep enough for warships with eight to 24 fathoms of water.[4]

As much effort as it took to write that, as much as it took to read that, this information wasn't nearly enough for a combat operation. According to the 3rd Marine Division History, "Virtually nothing was known of the hydrography, terrain conditions inland from selected beaches, and location of enemy defenses in the immediate area."[5] Even so, the Americans were under no illusions as to the difficult nature of the geography of Bougainville and its outlying islands. The Marine Corps Aviation history called Bougainville, "as forbidding and inhospitable as the Devil's furnace room [...]."[6]

The Americans were also under no illusions as to the importance the Japanese placed on that furnace room and the Hell's fire they were willing to use to defend it. Increasing Allied air superiority meant more reconnaissance flights that could keep the door open and the lights on in that furnace room.

But there was a lot to watch in that furnace room. The number of aircraft and ships varied, but estimates of the number of Japanese troops were troubling. The Imperial Japanese Army was believed to have positioned about 37,500 troops of the 17th Army under Lieutenant General Hyakutake Harukichi.[7] The Imperial Navy had added some 20,000 "Special Naval Landing Force" troops, which are often mistermed "Marines," though they weren't even all that special, but were just sailors on shore duty. Most of these shore-duty sailors were around Buin and in the Shortland Islands around the southeastern end of Bougainville, but they were static troops that could not be moved. Of the Imperial Army troops, it was believed that more than 25,000 were in southern Bougainville and the Shortland Islands, where they joined the 20,000 Special Naval Landing Force troops to form what was essentially one army. A second army was the 5,000 Imperial Army troops around the Buka Passage guarding the air base on Buka Island and the twin air base at Bonis on the mainland. A third army consisted of 5,000 troops around the Kieta air base on the northeast coast. That left maybe 2,500 strung out along the southwest coast.[8]

Halsey looked at his map. The admiral was charged with invading a territory with three sizable armies defending it. If he wanted to capture the island, he would have to defeat all three armies. But if those armies combined, they would outnumber any force he could land on Bougainville. As it was, the army in the south alone outnumbered his own force. If he landed troops to face only one of those armies, there was no guarantee he could defeat that army before the others could reinforce it. There was no guarantee his troops would not be pinned in place, unable to advance, unable to even move …

The Japanese had packed Bougainville with soldiers and naval infantry, grouped into three armies. General Hyakutake dared the Allies to attack even one of them.

Admiral Halsey had other ideas.

CHAPTER 1

CALDERA OF DAMOCLES

A long time ago on an island half a world away, there was a rather unpleasant man named Dionysius.[1] Dionysius was the tyrant of the Greek city of Syracuse on the east coast of Sicily. While in modern usage, "tyrant" is something of a pejorative, in antiquity it merely described a ruler with absolute power. It was how he used that power that determined whether his tyranny was good or otherwise.

Dionysius' tyranny was otherwise, to say the least. Indeed, Dionysius was one of the reasons the word "tyrant" became a pejorative. He was regarded by his contemporaries as the worst kind of despot – cruel, suspicious, and vindictive.[2]

The bad kind of tyrants tended to keep their courts full of sycophants. One of these courtiers in Dionysius' retinue was a man named Damocles. One day, Damocles was commenting on Dionysius' armies, his wealth, his power, the plenty he enjoyed, the grandeur of his royal palace, ending with the statement that no one could be happier than Dionysius. The tyrant reportedly replied, "Since this life seems so appealing to you, Damocles, do you want to taste it yourself and make a trial of my fortune?"

Damocles answered in the affirmative. Who wouldn't? So, Dionysius had Damocles sit on a golden couch covered with a beautiful woven rug, embroidered with splendid works; he adorned many sideboards with chased silver and gold. Beautiful servants were ordered to wait on Damocles and to observe his gestures, in order to serve him what he wanted. There were ointments, garlands, perfumes, and tables piled high with the choicest foods. Damocles thought himself very fortunate indeed.

In the middle of this luxury, Dionysius ordered a shining sword to be suspended from the ceiling by a single hair from the tail of a horse tied to the pommel. The tyrant instructed his servants to lower the sword until the point of its blade dangled over the head of the fortunate courtier.

Damocles' demeanor suddenly changed. He looked neither at those beautiful servers nor the gold and silver table settings nor even at the food; nor did he reach for the food.

The room was silent for several moments. Finally, Damocles begged Dionysius to let him leave. He no longer wanted to be so fortunate.

And this event became known as the "Sword of Damocles," even though the sword was not Damocles' but Dionysius'. This ancient story, told by the Roman senator and orator Cicero, is more than likely apocryphal. For one thing, a horse hair is not long enough to tie around both the pommel of a sword and a hook in the ceiling. For another, this description makes Dionysius sound like a fount of understated wisdom when he was more like an ancient Vladimir Putin.

But the term "Sword of Damocles" has become a popular idiom nonetheless. While the story can have multiple interpretations, in general it has come to mean an ongoing, imminent threat. Like the Rabaul caldera. Anyone who lives under an active volcano knows about feeling under the Sword of Damocles. At any time you could be shaken by earthquakes, buried in ash, suffocated by gas, incinerated by lava, crushed by lava bombs, vaporized by pyroclastic flows, even drowned in tsunamis, or all of the above.

The Japanese air bases around the Rabaul caldera were capable of wrecking catastrophic damage on Allied forces. Lakunai, the fighter base at the base of Rabalanakaia and closest to Tavurvur. Vunakanau, the main bomber base and closest to Vulcan. Tobera, another fighter base, and Rapopo, used by the Imperial Army Air Force. General MacArthur and his air commander General Kenney, and Admiral Halsey, were very familiar with the enemy air bases around the Rabaul caldera and what they could do to any Allied units that came within their range. Enter that range, and you sense the Sword of Damocles over you. And as both vectors of *Cartwheel* closed in on Rabaul and each other, MacArthur, Kenney, and Halsey could sense the Sword of Damocles. But what to do about those air bases? There were so many of them. With so many aircraft and so many antiaircraft guns. It was the veritable Caldera of Damocles. Something had to be done. But resources in the South-West Pacific and especially the South Pacific were slim, with reinforcements and replacements directed to the central Pacific. They could not just bludgeon their way into Rabaul. There had to be some finesse. But what?

It was in the face of the Caldera of Damocles that the more mundane yet deadly operations of war continued. On October 3, the destroyer *Reid* was leading her tincanmates *Smith* and *Henley* in a column heading north off Cape Ward Hunt. At 6:15pm or so, just before sunset, Commander Carlton R. Adams on the *Henley* saw the *Smith* ahead of him sheer out of line to starboard. They were going to form a scouting line abreast at sunset for an offensive antisubmarine sweep, so Adams interpreted the *Smith*'s move as starting to form that scouting line to starboard of the *Reid*. He had the *Henley* increase speed to 25 knots and turn to port to form that line on the *Reid*'s port side …

That's when he saw the real reason the *Smith*, that survivor of the Battle of the Santa Cruz Islands, had turned to starboard: two torpedo wakes were approaching from port.

Commander Adams ordered a hard port turn to try to comb the wakes. He succeeded in passing between them, one passing 30 yards ahead, the other 10 yards astern.

Then he saw a third one coming between the tracks of the first two. That's when you know it's really, really not your day.

Adams had no chance. The Japanese torpedo embedded itself into the *Henley*'s port side in her Number 1 boiler room, destroying her boilers, so she had no power. Additionally, her keel was broken and her bow was bent 30 degrees from her longitudinal axis. The *Henley* was finished.

Commander Adams ordered the destroyer evacuated, and at about 6:30pm the *Henley* broke in two and sank. One officer and 14 sailors were killed; eight officers and 44 sailors injured. The *Reid* and *Smith* spent the next seven hours making depth charge attacks, but the *Henley*'s assailant, Lieutenant Arai Jun's six-month-old submarine *Ro-108*, made her escape.[3]

That bit of good news would have to last Vice Admiral Ryunosuke Kusaka Jinichi, commander of the Imperial Navy's land-based 11th Air Fleet – given the operational title "Base Air Force" – for a while. On October 8, 1943, the Japanese Naval Air Force's 204 Air Group was pulled back from Buin to Rabaul. Just in time, in a manner of speaking, anyway.[4]

On October 12, just before 9:00am, a dozen B-25 Mitchells of Major Raymond H. Wilkins' 8th Bombardment Squadron, 3rd Bombardment Group, roared low over a ridge in a V-formation, just like the old Base Air Force had done over the mountains northwest of Clark Field, except these were south of the Rapopo air base 14 miles southeast of Rabaul on the other side of Simpson Harbor. Also, unlike Clark Field, Rapopo had absolutely no warning whatsoever.[5]

Like a scythe the dozen Mitchells swept the runway from south to north with all 96 of their .50-cal. machine guns blazing. Antiaircraft guns were unmanned, their barrels still with their protective covers, many pointing the wrong way. Later on, one crewman saw "a dozen Japs standing on the porch of a house and looking with amazement at the approaching planes." Japanese mechanics and other personnel were seen "standing around planes lined up on the ground" as if nothing unusual was happening. And, in a sense, nothing was. Indeed, Rabaul had seen many air attacks. But nothing like this.[6]

As they shot up everything on or near the runway with some 30,000 rounds of .50-cal. ammunition, the B-25s released hundreds of little bombs with parachutes attached, called "parafrags." To land softly and explosively once the B-25s had safely passed. Not that the B-25s were finished gunning. When Major Wilkins' squadron arrived, six twin-engine Mitsubishi Ki-21 Type 97 Heavy Bombers from the Japanese Army Air Force's 14th Air Regiment were trying to take off for a scheduled stage into Alexishafen for a mission. Four succeeded and escaped just before the Americans arrived. The fifth was caught by gunfire soon after it cleared the runway; it pitched over and crashed, killing pilot Captain Kurano Teruo and his five crew. The sixth wisely aborted its takeoff and was damaged on the ground.[7]

In 30 seconds, Rabaul had gotten its first real taste of the B-25 gunship. And it did not like it. The B-25 had been a mediocre bomber until Major Paul "Pappy" Gunn modified it in the field by putting eight .50cal machine guns in the nose and pioneered the practice of low-level bombing at sea, which after their incredible success at the Battle of the Bismarck Sea became the norm for the rest of the Pacific War. The modified B-25s became known as "commerce destroyers" or "gunships."* These particular low-level gunship attacks were:

> [...] devastating to maintenance personnel, aircrews, gun crews, and support staff. One can only imagine the psychological effect of being caught in the open as a dozen gunships approach just above the treetops, their noses ablaze with the muzzle blasts of a hundred machine guns. A few seconds after tens of thousands of bullets have scythed the airdrome, hundreds of explosions ripple across the ground as the parafrags detonate. But the attack is not yet over. Thirty seconds later, the nightmarish experience repeats – twice.[8]

Because next came 14 gunships of the 13th Bombardment Squadron under 3rd Bombardment Group commander Major Donald P. Hall to give another 30,000 .50-cal. rounds and 693 parafrags. Watching from about a mile behind Hall's gunships, war correspondent Lee Van Atta was more than an interested observer to the action. "We struck in split formations of three, each echelon sweeping across the airdrome and dispersal bays in beautiful waves," he later wrote. "[B]ombs and machine-gun fire from Hall's lead ship could be seen pummeling down on the airdrome installations; in seconds the whole path in front of us was a holocaust." Perhaps not the best word choice in this war, but he could not have known that yet.[9]

"Us" was a reference to the crew of the B-25 *Notre Dame de Victoire*, from where Van Atta was watching the action behind pilot Major John P. "Jock" Henebry, who was leading another dozen gunships, these from his own 90th Bombardment Squadron, who came in about a mile and 30 seconds behind the 13th. By this time, some of the antiaircraft guns were manned, and Van Atta would later call their gunfire "uncomfortably fierce," but the evidence they left was only a few bullet holes. Radio towers proved to be more dangerous. Lieutenant Clifford L. Wonderly was lining up a radio station for a strafing run when "a tall steel tower suddenly appeared dead ahead." He rolled to the right, hoping to stay in formation. The strike photos later revealed "a maze of wires" to the left of the tower.[10]

With that, the 3rd Bombardment Group's attack on Rapopo was over. But Rabaul's day was just beginning. The Mitsubishi A6M Type 0 (called the "Zero") carrier fighters of the 204 Air Group at Lakunai and the 253 Air Group at Tobera were probably ordered to scramble.[11] But they may not have had time to get into the air ...

---

*The narrative wanted to call the B-25 Mitchells modified to Pappy Gunn's specifications "Gunships" to call attention to and honor in an admittedly small way Gunn's massive contribution to winning the war in the South Pacific and ultimately the Pacific War with his modifications, but certain editors would not allow it.

Before 9:00am, more B-25 gunships from the 38th and 345th Bombardment Groups, along with their P-38 Lightning fighter escort, appeared uninvited over the big bomber base at Vunakanau. Despite taking place five minutes after the first attack at Rapopo (because the Mitchells had to fly 12 miles further than the first attack), Vunakanau was almost just as unprepared – antiaircraft positions unoccupied, gun barrels covered and pointing the wrong way; Bettys of the 751 Air Group were even practicing takeoffs and landings – and was treated just as harshly as Rapopo was. The first three waves of 44 gunships, all from the 345th, scythed down Vunakanau's mile-long concrete runway. Somehow during this attack, a single Zero from the 253 Air Group managed to take off only after its pilot, 18-year-old Flying Seaman 1st Class Kawato Masajiro, who had been doing paperwork, yelled at and browbeat two terrified mechanics into starting his fighter. The last wave of the 345th's Mitchells, these from the 500th Bombardment Squadron, could see Zeros taking off in the distance from the Tobera airfield. Trouble was coming, as the Japanese defenders slowly recovered from their shock and started fighting back.[12]

The 345th was followed by two squadrons of the 38th, starting with the 71st Bombardment Squadron. The 71st's 11 Mitchells formed a wide line abreast and strafed 10–15 bombers and 8–10 fighters, as well as supply dumps, fuel trucks, and other targets of opportunity, with 19,000 rounds of .50-cal. ammunition and released 642 parafrag bombs. A Zero was caught trying to take off and was set afire before it could do so, but the 71st counted five Zeros airborne, though none of them pressed the issue with the 71st.

At least not like they did with the 405th that followed, whose 12 gunships formed a half-mile-wide front and raked, again, the air base with 96 .50-cal. machine guns and dropped an additional 759 parafrag bombs. But as they pulled away, the six B-25s on the right side of the formation were jumped by nine Zeros, probably from the 18 Zeros that the 253 Air Group reportedly scrambled from Tobera at 9:25am local time. One of them was probably Flying Seaman 1st Class Kawato. Another 22 Zeros of the 204 Air Group took off from Lakunai ten minutes later.[13] Whoever they were, they sank their teeth into the 405th and would not let go.

Indeed, not for another 14 minutes as they slashed at the withdrawing Mitchells, getting their pound of flesh and steel. As the US Army Air Force formation got out over the water, the Zeros, including Kawato, damaged the B-25 flown by 2nd Lieutenant Edsal J. Crews. Kawato and his cohort swarmed it, shooting off the starboard engine. In return, Kawato's fighter took several punishing hits. He briefly considered ramming Crews' Mitchell, but thought better of it and ducked under the B-25. Or maybe he did not and instead rammed or just plain collided with Crews' Mitchell. With Kawato, it's hard to tell what is fiction and nonfiction. In any case, Kawato was compelled to bail out; he was later rescued. Crews and his men would not be that lucky. He radioed his chilling last words: "I'm going in." Witnesses said turret gunner Staff Sergeant James J. Patrick "kept his guns blazing at pursuing Zekes until the end." The Mitchell crashed into the water.[14]

As undeniably tragic as the fate of Crews and his crew was, theirs was the only gunship shot down of the 113 that attacked Rapopo and Vunakanau. The next Allied attack was not nearly so fortunate.

That was by a dozen Bristol Beaufighters from the Royal Australian Air Force's No. 30 Squadron. A baker's dozen had taken off from Dobodura, but they had taken off late because they literally had to wait for the dust to settle after all the B-25s had taken off ahead of them. One of the Beaufighters had to turn back because an oil leak had shut down its port engine. Because they were late, they missed the rendezvous with their escort of P-38 Lightnings who had staged into Kiriwina to escort this early morning attack, and so had to go on alone. According to one of the Beaufighters' crew, "As usual our team was late and a bit of misunderstanding crept in." They ran into two squadrons of Mitchells from the 3rd Bombardment Group heading the other way, at least one of whom opened fire after mistaking the Beaufighters for Japanese Army Air Force Ki-27 "Sally" bombers before Wing Commander William T. M. Boulton could establish their bona fides.[15]

The delay would prove especially unfortunate. The Beaufighters' target was the aforementioned Tobera airfield. If the Beaufighters had been on time, they might have caught the 253 Air Group's Zeros on the ground. As it was, Boulton and his aviators were almost two hours late – and all alone.

No. 30 Squadron was not bothered by that, however. These were veteran aircrews who were confident in themselves and their tough Beaufighters. Approaching from the southeast, No. 30 Squadron caught the Zeros of Tobera air base in the process of landing, some with their wheels down, but not landed yet. Quickly, the landing gear was retracted and 19 Zeros, most of which were from the 253 Air Group but at least one from the 204, all led by the veteran Lieutenant Oshibushi Takashi, were ready to face the Australians. Not intimidated, the Beaufighters wheeled to the right to keep formation, avoid dogfights, and carry out their mission. They were only partially successful. They saw no aircraft on the ground at Tobera. What happened next is not clear. At around this time, with the base alerted, its antiaircraft guns in action, and Zeros blocking the way, Boulton apparently aborted the attack and radioed everyone "to get out for 'Home and Mother.'" After that, the formation started to fray. Pilot Flying Officer Alfred "Alf" Catt went in over Tobera anyway and seems to have strafed it; a building at Tobera was reportedly set on fire. Catt's navigator told him Zeros "were firing at us from astern, so I told him to use the gun in his cupola and fire right back at them. He told me that it didn't work, so I told him to poke his tongue out at them." That seemingly worked, and the Zeros broke off after about 15 minutes. Meanwhile, Wing Commander James Emerton turned to shoot at one of the Zeros – it is called a Beau*fighter*, after all – but as he did so, Rapopo came into view, so he roared down the Rapopo runway firing his machine guns while being chased by three Zeros led by Lieutenant Hayashi Yoshishige, who reported engaging an "A-20A." Emerton was able to use superior speed to pull away. The rest of No. 30 Squadron tried to do the same and were mostly able to do so after a 30-minute running battle, but Flight Lieutenant Derrick R. "Dick" Stone disappeared after climbing to take on a Zero. Perhaps not coincidentally, while it was fighting off Zeros trying to escape the area, the 405th Bombardment Squadron saw an unidentified aircraft being chased by Zeros south of Rapopo. The aircraft was seen to burst into flames. This may have been Stone's Beaufighter. His aircraft is believed to have been overwhelmed by Zeros from the 204 Air Group led by Lieutenant (jg) Fukuda Sumio and crashed two miles east of Tobera near the village of Ganai.[16]

That was it. For the morning attacks, anyway. Five minutes after midday 62 B-24 Liberators of the 43rd and 90th Bombardment Groups, escorted by 47 P-38s from the 39th Fighter Squadron of the 35th Fighter Group and the 80th Fighter Squadron of the 49th Fighter Group, showed up uninvited over Simpson Harbor.[17]

It was supposed to be a much larger strike. Taking off from the Port Moresby airfield complex that morning were 87 Liberators, each carrying six 1,000lb general purpose bombs. Perhaps in part because the bombers were so heavy, 25 of them had to turn back. As it was, the entire flight had to fly around the tip of the Papuan peninsula rather than try to carry all that weight over the Owen Stanley Mountains. They hooked up with their Lightning escort near the Kiriwina fighter staging field before heading to Rabaul.[18]

This airstrike was led by Lieutenant Colonel Arthur Rogers, commander of the 90th Bombardment Group, flying at the head of the 400th Bombardment Squadron. The target of Rogers' Liberators this day was no airfield, but the ships in Simpson Harbor.

The Liberators separated into six-plane elements, each assigned specific targets based on overhead photographs taken the previous day. This is where problems, which had started with the 30 percent abort rate, really started piling up. Apparently as part of the plan of attack, the leader of the 39th Fighter Squadron dropped his 16 P-38s back to protect the bombers' exit. The remaining 28 Lightnings could not protect the now-enlarged formation of B-24s. Finally, the Liberators were bombing the ships in the harbor from altitudes of 21,000 to 23,000 feet.[19]

In the face of heavy but ineffective antiaircraft fire, the B-24s of the 90th Bombardment Group dropped their big bombs just as ordered and headed out. As the Liberators headed out, Rogers' bombardier Captain George P. "Ace" Dunmore stated that he had "hit the target, sir"; he believed the target to be a big destroyer tender, but it's now believed to have been the *Tsukushi*, an armed hydrographic survey ship. Rogers did not hear him. "I was amazed and flabbergasted," he later wrote, "to see just ahead the biggest swarm of enemy fighters I had ever seen in the air at one time."[20]

Rogers had obviously missed Pearl Harbor, Darwin, and Midway, but he did not miss the 34 Zeros of the 204 and 253 Air Groups, who positioned themselves ahead of the retreating Liberators to make coordinated attacks from the front in another running gun battle. Lieutenant Colonel Rogers took a 20mm shell in his left outboard fuel tank, just behind the Number 1 engine. Like most American combat aircraft, the Liberators' fuel tanks were self-sealing. Allegedly. Rogers could see high-octane aviation fuel leaking close to the hot exhaust outlets. And he remembered the Liberator had a bad reputation for catching fire.[21] Between catching fire and breaking up when it hits the water, it's not entirely clear how the Liberator was an improvement over the Boeing B-17 Flying Fortress, which could lose all four engines, both wings, the vertical stabilizer, the hull, the hydraulics, the radio, the air conditioning, the cigarette lighter, and the lower lumbar support, and still return safely.

Lieutenant Colonel Rogers called for help from the escorting P-38s. He got none. One Lightning of the 80th Fighter Squadron shot down one clipped-wing Zero, probably from the 204 Air Group. That was it. As they had done earlier with the 38th Bombardment Group, the Zeros sank their teeth into the 90th and would not let go. All six of the leading Liberators were damaged by 20mm cannon fire. "From radio conversations," noted Rogers, "the other flight commanders were all having their difficulties and I began to wonder if any of us would get back. The Japs had followed us out seventy-five miles and were still attacking us as fiercely as if the fight had just begun."[22]

And they got their pound of flesh and steel. The Liberator flown by Lieutenant Hampton E. Rich of the 321st Squadron lost three engines. Rich radioed that he would try to ditch. He succeeded, only for several Zeros to strafe the floating aircraft until it exploded. Given its previous activity that included strafing parachuting pilots, the Zeros responsible were probably from the 204 Air Group. Another B-24, piloted by Flight Officer Donald K. McNeff of the 400th, was "shot up" but "did not appear to be in trouble," only to disappear at some point after it was last seen at 1:30pm.[23]

The Zeros were still chasing Lieutenant Colonel Rogers' 90th Bombardment Group, so they almost completely missed the following 43rd Bombardment Group. As Rabaul historian Bruce Gamble pointed out, "Free from distractions, the 43rd Group's bombardiers had a rare opportunity to conduct textbook bombing."[24] The 43rd claimed the destruction of "between six and a dozen large and small watercraft," with an equal number damaged.[25]

So ended what Lieutenant General George C. Kenney, commander of the US 5th Air Force under MacArthur, called, "the biggest attack so far in the Pacific," which it was. "Everything that I owned that was in commission, and could fly that far, was on the raid." Kenney claimed to have "destroy[ed] at least 100 airplanes on the ground and badly damage[ed] another fifty-one."[26] Well, not quite. In addition to the Japanese Army Air Force aircraft already mentioned, Base Air Force admitted to nine Mitsubishi G4M Type 1 land attack planes ("Bettys") destroyed – six of which were from one squadron of the 751 Air Group – and 36 damaged. Even worse, 20 skilled aviation mechanics assigned to the 751 Air Group were killed and more than 50 wounded.[27]

Be that as it may, Allied intelligence officers were shocked when they got the results from cameras carried by the bombers as well as four photographic Lightnings, including one that took color photographs, the 8th Photo Reconnaissance Squadron sent over Rabaul. As the 8th's "unofficial war diary" put it:

When all the pictures were developed, the observed damage wasn't nearly what was expected, and all afternoon generals and colonels were calling the [reconnaissance] pilots, pleading with them to say that they personally observed 5 warships rolled over and sunk, etc. – they had to, damn it – didn't 80 B-24s bomb the harbor? Next morning's A-2 report from the bomber crews substantiated the fact that they can't even see to work a bomb sight, let alone observe direct hits from 23,000. According to the heavies, they sank everything in the harbor; according to 8th Photo's pictures, they're damn lucky if they sank a total of five good-sized ships.[28]

It was true. As if confirmation was needed, an internal summary published by the 5th Air Force revealed that of 36 bombs dropped by Lieutenant Colonel Rogers' lead element, only three hits were scored: a ratio of 8 percent.[29] Despite such evidence, MacArthur issued a communiqué that announced, "[T]he enemy has sustained a disastrous defeat from air attack at Rabaul." It alleged, "[O]ur heavy bombers with 1,000lb bombs sank or destroyed three destroyers, two merchant ships of 5,800 tons each, and one of 7,000 tons, forty-three seagoing cargo vessels ranging from 100 to 500 tons, and 70 harbor craft. In addition they hit and severely damaged a submarine and its 5,000 ton tender, a 6,800 ton destroyer tender, and a 7,000 ton cargo ship." Ignoring the apparent duplication of losses, MacArthur declared, "[T]his operation gives us definite mastery in the air over the Solomon Sea and adjacent waters, and thereby threatens the enemy's whole perimeter of defense."[30]

There were three fairly obvious issues with the attack. One was the "textbook bombing" of the ships in Simpson Harbor conducted by the B-24s. "Textbook bombing" ships in the US Army Air Force meant bombing ships from high altitude. Which was almost always ineffective, and was the primary reason for the development of skip-bombing and low-level bombing that had been used to destroy the Lae convoy the previous March. It was as if Generals Kenney and Ennis Whitehead had forgotten the lessons about low-level bombing. As if they thought the laws of physics had changed since March. In fairness, one of the major rationales for high-altitude bombing was that it was near or above the maximum altitude for antiaircraft fire, and Rabaul had almost 400 antiaircraft guns, so resorting to high-level bombing over Rabaul was understandable. But the bottom line is, it was not effective.

Captain Hara Tameichi, commodore of the Imperial Navy's Destroyer Division 27 who watched the attack from his command destroyer *Shigure*, was certainly unimpressed. "The high-altitude bombing was not very accurate, however, and only one transport was sunk." One significantly sized transport was lost: the Imperial Navy's 5,879-ton *Keisho Maru*.[31] Also sunk were Imperial Army seatrucks *Wakamatsu Maru No. 1* and *Mishima Maru*, each of about 600 tons. Damaged ships included the destroyer *Mochizuki* having her Number 2 4.7-inch mount disabled by a near miss, the destroyer *Minazuki* with her Number 1 and 2 4.7-inch mounts temporarily disabled by another near miss, and the *Tachikaze* who suffered minor damage. Also damaged were submarines *I-177*, *I-180*, and *Ro-105*; the aforementioned *Tsukushi*, tanker *Naruto*, and auxiliary sailing vessels *Tenryu* and *Koan Marus*.[32]

A second issue was the delay in sending up the Australian No. 30 Squadron. While it was understandable that Boulton and his Beaufighters would want to wait until the dust had literally settled from the takeoffs of the B-25 gunships so his squadron could take off with better visibility, it resulted in a delay of almost two hours. It was a critical delay because of the three air bases that were to be hit by strafers – Rapopo, Vunakanau, and Tobera – Tobera was the only one that was primarily a fighter base, and not just a fighter base, but a fighter base for the Japanese Naval Air Force, who had the primary responsibility for the air defense of Rabaul. The Beaufighters' delay in taking off meant the Zeros of the 253 Air Group at Tobera were not caught on the ground as the aircraft were at Rapopo and Vunakanau. While their entry was late, they did enter the battle and cause serious problems for the 38th and 90th Bombardment Groups' attacks as well as that of No. 30 Squadron itself. There were and are ways of suppressing dust kicked up at air bases, including just wetting down the runway; they should have been used at Dobodura.

The third major problem is related to the second. The first objective of any air attack is to neutralize any air defenses, including and especially fighters. That is why Tobera should not only have been attacked on time, but should have been a higher priority than Rapopo and Vunakanau. Yet an even higher priority should have been what had been the primary fighter base at Rabaul ever since the Japanese took over: Lakunai air base, where the 204 Air Group was based. In this surprise air attack, the first in months, Lakunai was completely ignored. Exactly why is unclear. It might simply have been that Lakunai was next to downtown Rabaul in the center of all those air defenses, while Rapopo, Vunakanau, and Tobera were more on the periphery. Merely getting to Lakunai would require flying through those air defenses, thus possibly losing the element of surprise. Then again, considering the quality work by General MacArthur's intelligence officer General Charles Willoughby, it may simply have been that MacArthur did not even know about Lakunai.

Be that as it may, some drama queens decided to call the October 12 attack on Rabaul "Japan's Pearl Harbor." Commanding General Henry "Hap" Arnold of the Army Air Forces (AAF) went so far as to cable congratulations to General Kenney and his American and Australian units for this "Pearl Harbor in reverse."[33]

The October 12, 1943, Simpson Harbor attack and the Pearl Harbor attack were both air attacks that took place in harbors. That was about the extent of their similarities.

As Samuel Eliot Morison commented, "The raid was widely publicized as having 'knocked out' Rabaul; but the Bismarcks base was not even leaning on the ropes."[34] Perhaps that was tacitly admitted in the wee hours of October 13, when a dozen Australian Beauforts of No. 8 Squadron, led by Wing Commander Geoffrey Nicoll, made two torpedo attacks on shipping in Simpson Harbor, with no results observed.[35]

Whatever the failings of the October 12 attack, it was a shocking scene for the Japanese. "So huge a raid on a main Japanese base was very impressive," Captain Hara admitted, "and it shocked Truk headquarters."[36]

So much so that fears of an imminent invasion of Rabaul became very real. Which was part of the idea. This was just the beginning. The two prongs of the Allied advance in New Guinea and the Solomons had rolled up the Japanese to the point where continued operations, let alone advancing further, were under that Caldera of Damocles – Lakunai,

Vunakanau, Tobera, Rapopo, and the various seaplane bases in Simpson Harbor. Whether that horse hair was really long enough or strong enough to suspend that sword or not, General MacArthur, General Kenney, and Admiral Halsey did not want to depend on the strength of that horse hair. The Caldera of Damocles was foreboding in its volcanoes and air bases. The Allies knew they could do something about only one of those threats.[37] If they could not remove that sword, they would at least try to get it to fall when no one was seated under it. If they did it repeatedly, after every time the Japanese reattached that sword to the ceiling, that sword would be blunted, dented, scratched. Less effective even if it did strike flesh.

Their opposite number, Admiral Kusaka, determined to strike flesh with that sword, tried a counterattack on October 15: 15 Aichi D3A (Allied reporting name "Val") dive bombers of the 582 Air Group, escorted by 39 Zeros (24 from the 204 Air Group, 15 from the 253), went after shipping in Oro Bay south of Dobodura that the Japanese apparently believed were essential to any invasion. The Japanese were met by seven Lightnings of the 9th Fighter Squadron, 16 from the 431st, apparently 18 from the 432nd, and 17 from the 433rd; plus eight Warhawks of the 7th Fighter Squadron. The Japanese claimed five transports "sunk or damaged"; Kenney said the ships "suffered no damage." Conversely, Base Air Force admitted 14 D3As and five Zeros "failed to return" (three from the 204 and three from the 253; apparently one more Zero was declared a writeoff on its return to base). The attack was another disaster for Base Air Force, as Kusaka likely expected it to be.[38]

With the 582 Air Group down to exactly one Aichi D3A Type 99 Carrier Bomber, Admiral Kusaka decided to try a fighter sweep over Dobodura on October 17. The 204 Air Group sent 32 Zeros while the 253 sent 28. They were met by 43 Lightnings (12 from the 9th; 13 from the 431st; 18 from the 433rd); and three Warhawks from the 7th. The result was an aerial tussle over Oro Bay that scared off four squadrons of B-25s who were trying to stage into Dobodura for another attack on Rabaul. Four Lightnings and one P-40 were downed in exchange for eight (five from the 253 and apparently three from the 204).[39]

During this period, General Kenney was trying to follow up on his October 12 attack on Rabaul that had so traumatized the Japanese, but the weather would not cooperate. The next day, 70 Liberators took off and rendezvoused with 100 Lightnings from Kiriwina, only to be driven off by a storm 150 miles from Rabaul. The fighters turned back; three were lost in the storm and one crashed in landing. Gradually the bombers gave up and turned back, with 27 attacking alternate targets in western New Britain. The weather did not seem to stop Base Air Force, however, though whether that actually benefitted Base Air Force given the combat losses it was incurring is open to question.[40]

General Kenney's next chance for weather that was forecast to be even "marginal" was October 18. Eight squadrons of Liberators (for a total of 77) and two groups of Mitchells (for a total of 54) took off to hit Vunakanau, Lakunai, and Tobera. The hope was for the Liberators to draw off the Zeros, then when the Zeros returned to the one intact airfield, Rapopo, to refuel, the gunships would hit them. Over Kiriwina, the bombers picked up their escort of Lightnings, as was the practice now. And they ran into another storm.

All the fighters turned back while the Liberators felt their way along the coast of New Britain looking for an opening in the clouds. Not finding one, 15 Liberators hit alternate targets in western New Britain. Again. Six hit Sio in New Guinea. The rest jettisoned their bombs and headed back, but four never made it and ran out of fuel. Three of the crews bailed out over New Guinea and all survived; the fourth ditched off Port Moresby and seven of the crew drowned.[41]

Yet the gunships kept going. They were led by Lieutenant Colonel Clinton V. True, commander of the 345th Bombardment Group. He had not heard the fighters announcing they were going to abort, or so he later said. And he kept going with all his Mitchells following him, hugging the water to get through the storm.

The gunships made it to the coast of New Britain all right, and split off for their assigned airfield targets. The 498th, 499th, and 501st Squadrons (345th Bombardment Group) under Lieutenant Colonel True hit Rapopo while the 71st and 405th Squadrons (38th Bombardment Group) hit Tobera. Surprise was again achieved. Or so they thought. A lookout on New Britain had in fact alerted Base Air Force of an incoming air strike. In response, the 204 Air Group sent up 26 Zeros while the 201 Air Group, in the process of being withdrawn from Buin to Rabaul, contributed 16.[42] While the 38th Bombardment Group gunships escaped from Tobera largely unscathed, Lieutenant Colonel True's B-25s faced a fight for their lives. The gunships hit the deck and tightened their formation to benefit from their defensive guns. Some of the Zeros made runs at the Mitchells, only to crash into the water after misjudging their altitude. Many of the Japanese lost interest and looked for other prey.

Meanwhile, the Mitchells of another squadron of the 345th, the 500th, were each armed with two 1,000lb bombs, so they went after some ships off Vunapope. They damaged two vessels with near misses, and blew the bow off the subchaser *Ch-23*, who had to beach herself in sinking condition.[43]

Only for the 500th to run afoul of 20 Zeros from the 253 Air Group. Again, the B-25s had to hit the deck, again they had to tighten their formation to mass their defensive firepower. But soon the Zeros of the 253 were joined by the Zeros of the 201 and the Zeros of the 204. Somehow, only two of the B-25s were shot down; one of these had ditched, only to be shot to pieces by vengeful pilots of the 253 who had evidently been taking lessons from the 204. A third made it to Kiriwina, where it would remain for months having its damage repaired.[44]

Lieutenant Colonel True and his remaining gunships were proud of themselves. The six squadrons from the 38th and 345th Bombardment Groups claimed 41 enemy aircraft destroyed on the ground, 38 fighters shot down, and three ships sunk. They were a little off. Actual reported Japanese losses: three ships damaged, one of which was beached in sinking condition; five aircraft destroyed or badly damaged at Tobera, three burned or severely damaged at Rapopo, and three Zero fighters failed to return, probably from cartwheeling into the sea diving on the retreating Mitchells. The missing were Reserve

Ensign Aizawa Yoshio and Petty Officer 1st Class Mogi Yoshio of the 201 Air Group and Chief Petty Officer Yokoyama Yuji of the 204.[45]

Though the actual damage was bad enough for the Japanese, the claimed Japanese losses were taken at face value, which allowed Lieutenant Colonel True to turn a possible court martial into a Distinguished Service Cross. He had not disobeyed a direct order, but rather a standing instruction that bombers were to abort if the fighter escort aborted. True had "walked a fine line," but he probably figured that Kenney, who fostered aggressive leadership, would not punish him. And he was right. According to Kenney:

> After congratulating him on the success of his mission, I said, "Now that it's all over, tell me, True, didn't you hear the P-38s say that they were going home?" The rascal looked me in the eye, grinned, and said, "General, I didn't hear a word."[46]

While the bad weather between New Guinea and Rabaul allowed the 5th Air Force to get in some badly needed attacks on places like Wewak to keep them suppressed, photographs taken of the Rabaul air bases on October 19 suggested the Japanese had rebuilt their fighter strength to 211 – or that it had not been as whittled down by the air attacks of October 12 and 18 as everyone thought it was, though that second option didn't seem to have been seriously considered outside the 8th Photo Squadron yet. A forecast of decent weather on October 23 meant the 5th Air Force could get another swipe at Rabaul.

October 23 was going to be about heavy bombers. The 90th Bombardment Group would hit Lakunai – finally – while the 43rd would hit Vunakanau. Six squadrons of Lightnings would join the Liberators. Three P-38 squadrons would sweep ahead just before the attack, one squadron would be assigned to each bomb group, while the last squadron would provide top cover. With that in mind, 57 Liberators hooked up with 100 P-38s near Kiriwina and together they headed for Rabaul.

Where they found Lakunai and Vunakanau socked in by clouds up to 20,000 feet. That high-altitude bombing again. No secondary target was assigned, so on the fly the group commanders decided to bomb Rapopo, which was relatively clear. But because Rapopo had not been planned, they had to work out their approaches on the fly so as to not get in each other's way or collide. The result: Rapopo was plastered by two bomb groups. The groups claimed that 20 planes were destroyed on the ground and four in the air, but it's not clear how much damage was actually done. The Lightnings claimed 13 shot down for one loss: the P-38 of the 431st Fighter Squadron's Lieutenant Edward J. Czarnecki. The defending 15 Zeros of the 201 Air Group, who had completed their pullback to Rabaul on October 22, claimed four P-38s at a cost of one Zero damaged. The 204 Air Group apparently sent up five Zeros, losing three with two pilots killed, one of whom was Reserve Ensign Moriyama Hidemichi, while claiming nine enemy aircraft shot down. The 253 contributed 22 (one flight of 15 and another of seven) and lost one while claiming 14 shot down.[47]

Admiral Kusaka decided two could play this game and sent an airstrike of his own to hit shipping off Finschhafen. The attack comprised 20 Zeros escorting all of four Aichi D3A carrier bombers, yet another example of the deterioration of Base Air Force's strike capability. Giving them a reception was the job of 23 P-47 Thunderbolt fighters of the 348th Fighter Group. The Zeros bounced the Bolts but the Vals claimed only two near misses on destroyers. Worse, one carrier bomber did not return even though the P-47s never touched them. The entire day seems to have been a wash.[48]

But there's always tomorrow to start over again. For the Allies, October 24 was supposed to be gunships hitting Tobera, Rapopo, and Vunakanau, but their takeoff was delayed and the formation fragmented and had to be reformed – off the coast of New Britain, no less – and the Japanese had ample warning of their approach.[49] Moreover, Base Air Force had a new toy. Well, a different toy, anyway.

An advance group of the 501 Air Group had arrived with 14 of a sleek, beautiful dive bomber the Japanese called the Yokosuka D4Y1 Type 2 Carrier Bomber, which they nicknamed "Suisei" (Comet). While it was new as a dive bomber, it was not exactly a new aircraft. In its previous iteration (i.e., while the structural flaws in its design as a dive bomber were being corrected), it was called "Yokosuka D4Y1-C Type 2 carrier reconnaissance plane." It was in this role that the D4Y showed an extremely high speed, a penchant for locating an enemy force when no one else could, and an equal if not greater penchant for suffering a radio failure immediately after locating said enemy force so that it was unable to inform anyone of it in time to do any good. Like, say, when one found all the US Navy aircraft carriers off Midway, but because its radio had failed had to fly all the way back to Japanese Carrier Striking Force *Kido Butai* to make its contact report, by which time half of *Kido Butai* was in flames. Or when it found another US Navy carrier off the Santa Cruz Islands, but its radio failed again, so it had to fly all the way back to *Kido Butai* again to make its contact report, by which time two thirds of *Kido Butai* was in flames. The Allies had given it the recognition name "Judy." Exactly two of these Type 2 carrier bombers were in the air this day, each carrying one of those Type 3 aerial burst bombs that are supposed to explode among enemy aircraft formations and shred them with shrapnel and phosphorus. Those things never worked, but the Japanese were determined to keep trying them.[50]

They would not work this day, either. The interceptors this time were led by 253 Air Group ace Chief Petty Officer Nishizawa Hiroyoshi leading 13 of his group's Zeros; they would claim three B-25s and 13 P-38s shot down for the loss of two aircraft, with one pilot killed, the other badly wounded. The 26 Zeros sent up by the 201 Air Group claimed six P-38s, while 204 Air Group's 26 pilots claimed 11 victories but lost seven Zeros, with six of the pilots killed, including ace Chief Petty Officer Ishi-i Shizu-o, a two-year veteran with 29 victories, Petty Officer 1st Class Tanaka Tsuyoshi; and Petty Officers 2nd Class Kubo Masaru and Kobayashi Masakazu. In actuality, "[i]n the hottest battle yet encountered," no P-38s are known to have been shot down, though one disappeared for no apparent reason and two crash-landed on Kiriwina with no injury to the pilots. Two Mitchells were shot down; the crew of one rescued. The gunships claimed 21 destroyed on the ground at Rapopo; 5th Air Force seems to have been oddly obsessed with Rapopo, despite the fact that it was a Japanese Army Air Force base in an area where the Japanese Naval Air Force was responsible for air defense. Maybe it was just professional courtesy. The Mitchells claimed 27 destroyed on the ground at Vunakanau; the Japanese admitted that 27 G4Ms were "hit"; seven more "[were] set afire or suffered great damage," which would seem to account for almost every attack plane at Vunakanau.[51] Despite the Americans' claims, it seems little damage was done to any of the airfields themselves, especially Tobera, where only four aircraft were observed on the tarmac, and two of those were already disabled. But Base Air Force suffered heavy losses, not just among the bombers at Vunakanau, but especially among the irreplaceable fighter pilots.

However much of an Allied victory the attack of October 24 represented, it had its critics. A 5th Air Force summary later explained:

> One complaint asserted that the Japanese had been expecting the attack, and that the time of the attack and route to the target should have been different from previous strikes. It was also argued that coconut groves surrounding Rapopo and Tobera concealed the airdrome so well from low-flying planes that that type of attack was impracticable. In any case, the 13th Squadron was convinced that the Tobera mission had been merely a waste of effort in view of the few planes based there.[52]

Captain Hara would have smiled. Nevertheless, there was likely more than a repetitive pattern involved. By this time, the Japanese seem to have developed an analog of the air warning system at Henderson Field, where Allied coastwatchers and radar gave enough warning for interceptors to be up and attack planes to be sent off to ride out the attack.[53]

But there's always tomorrow to start over again. Despite "pessimistic" weather forecasts, General Ennis Whitehead sent out another strike on October 25. The plan called once more for a two-squadron fighter sweep to be followed by a two-group heavy bomber attack. This time there would be one primary target: the ever-elusive Lakunai air base. A secondary target would be the ships in Simpson Harbor. General Whitehead was determined to get that main fighter base at Lakunai, maybe because he was increasingly aware of how much his inexplicable neglect of that base during the first surprise attack of October 12 was costing the 5th Air Force. For 61 Liberators meeting 81 Lightnings near Kiriwina, it was Lakunai or bust.[54]

And it was bust. Once again, the weather would not cooperate. With storms taking over again, the fighters announced over the command frequency that they were turning back. Once again, the leader of the bombers, in this case Colonel Harry J. Bullis, deputy commander of the 90th Bombardment Group – *ahem!* – did not hear the message and all but 11 of the Liberators kept going, flying on instruments. Major Charles H. MacDonald and his flight of eight Lightnings of the 432nd Fighter Squadron did not want the bombers to go on by themselves, so he kept his unit going as well. But what could eight fighters do against Rabaul?[55]

Give Major MacDonald credit for resourcefulness and maybe a good knowledge of history. He led his flight up to 27,500 feet, above the weather, and then weaved back and forth over the lead element of Liberators, and probably in and out of the clouds, too. This made it look like there were a lot more than eight fighters. To some, anyway. The 25th Air Flotilla reported: "At 1020 [10:20am Japan Standard Time] about 40 P-38s and 50 B-24s attacked Rabaul." On the other hand, another Japanese report said 40 B-24s and 12 P-38s.[56]

Yet deception can only take you so far. Eventually, you need to start disbursing your munitions, and that's when the deception usually falls apart. Rabaul needed no deception, especially in Simpson Harbor, where two heavy cruisers, the *Myoko* and *Haguro* of the 5th Cruiser Division, and six destroyers (including *Shigure*, *Samidare*, *Shiratsuyu*) were parked. The warships added significantly to Rabaul's already serious antiaircraft artillery, and caused problems for the Liberators even though the bombers were above 20,000 feet. "Ack-ack was heavy and accurate," observed Captain William M. Waldman, one of Major MacDonald's pilots. "Heavy and medium caliber was shot at not only the bombers but at P-38s, too."[57]

To add injury to injury, 45 Zeros (ten from the 201 Air Group, 19 from the 204, and 16 from the 253) and two of those Type 2 carrier bombers were waiting for them. Some of the Zeros tried to mix it up with the leading Liberators, but when Major MacDonald sent one Zero, apparently from the 204 Air Group, to a fiery death, they backed off and seemed reluctant to press their advantage. Sheep led by lions are more dangerous than lions led by sheep and all that.[58]

But the crews of the B-24s were well aware of the importance of Lakunai air base and were determined to put it down. First the Liberators of the 90th Bombardment Group literally unloaded on Lakunai, then the 43rd did the same. Big general-purpose bombs to destroy buildings and crater runways; fragmentation bombs to shred vehicles and people. The 43rd even bragged, "We gave Lakunai drome at Rabaul a first-class plastering today in a daylight raid without fighter cover." They were not wrong.[59]

The Japanese were not entirely consistent in their reporting concerning this attack. According to one report, more than 20 parked aircraft were burned or severely damaged, including five twin-engine Mitsubishi Ki-46 Type 100 command reconnaissance aircraft ("Dinahs") of the Japanese Army Air Force's 10th Flying Regiment. Five more sustained lesser damage. The Imperial Navy said 13 fighters and bombers were "set afire" and the airfield was "out of use." A postwar summary stated that "about 10 petrol or oil wagons, machine guns, ammunition dumps and the greater part of the airfield installations were destroyed." To top it off, eight ships anchored in Matupit Harbor, that little body of water wedged in between the air base and Tavurvur, were damaged.[60]

As the Liberators turned away to return to base, the Zeros lashed at the rear ranks, again hesitant to press their advantage. The B-24 piloted by Lieutenant John W. Carlson of the 403rd Bombardment Squadron took the brunt of it for 15 minutes, staying in the air until the Zeros lost interest and headed back. But shortly thereafter it lost its two remaining engines and had to ditch. The Liberator, as usual, broke up on impact with the water. Carlson and his co-pilot Lieutenant Oscar M. Williams were trapped in the crushed cockpit and were lost – the only aviators lost that day. The surviving crew spent only an hour in the water before a PBY Catalina flying boat set down to pick them up. Theirs was the only Liberator that did not return.[61]

General Whitehead had scheduled a low-level attack on shipping for the next day, October 26, but the weather exercised its veto once again. The next major attack was on October 29, with 46 Liberators hitting Vunakanau in a high-altitude attack. The 43rd Bombardment Group led with 6lb fragmentation bombs, which the 90th followed with 500lb bombs. One report has at least seven aircraft destroyed on the ground, while another has three fighters and two medium bombers suffering heavy damage. The Japanese scrambled 75 Zeros, but, well, as the returning aviators described them: "The eager pilots were not experienced; and the experienced not eager." Four of the Zeros "failed to return," including the 201 Air Group's Petty Officer 1st Class Noguchi Yoshinori.[62]

Every effort was made to keep the pressure on Rabaul, both its air base complex and its anchorage in Simpson Harbor. General Whitehead assigned the "Washing Machine Charlie" and "Louie the Louse" roles to PBY Catalinas and No. 70 Wing of the Royal Australian Air Force at Kavieng and Rabaul, respectively. Bristol Beauforts from No. 8 Squadron armed with torpedoes were sent to harass shipping at the mouth of Simpson Harbor just outside the area of antiaircraft coverage.[63]

But the big air attacks? Those had to wait until the weather gave its approval.

By the time it did, the situation in the South Pacific had been completely upended.

Koga Mineichi, the Commander-in-Chief of the Combined Fleet in place of the dearly departed Admiral Yamamoto, was a good Japanese naval officer. Not necessarily a good leader or a good tactician or a good strategist, mind you, but a good Japanese officer. That means he thought the way a Japanese officer was supposed to think, planned the way a Japanese officer was supposed to plan, fought the way a Japanese officer was supposed to fight.

That meant that the ultimate objective of everything he did was to bring about that "Decisive Battle," that one big battle that would decide the Pacific War in favor of the Japanese. Just as Tsushima had in 1905.

And just like the Imperial Japanese Army with its banzai charges, the Imperial Japanese Navy was held back, if not shackled by its devotion to the Decisive Battle. Every tactical, operational, or strategic problem was not viewed on its own merits, but in the context of bringing about that Decisive Battle – at least as the Japanese thought of that Decisive Battle.

And the Imperial Japanese Navy thought that Decisive Battle would be fought in the Central Pacific, with battleships and cruisers. Especially battleships.

The Guadalcanal Campaign had two engagements – Eastern Solomons and Santa Cruz, both actually north of the Solomon Islands – that came about because the Japanese were trying to force that Decisive Battle, other objectives be damned. They failed, not just at bringing about that Decisive Battle, but at other objectives, such as bringing Imperial Army troops to Guadalcanal or suppressing that bothersome Lunga airfield, that might have been more beneficial in the long run.

Except for Eastern Solomons and Santa Cruz, nothing in the Guadalcanal Campaign looked like what the Imperial Japanese Navy thought the Decisive Battle was supposed to look like. So the Imperial Japanese Navy did not treat the Guadalcanal Campaign like the Decisive Battle so battleships were, for the most part, held back. The *Kongo*s that had been sent into the Solomons had left two of their kind behind as permanent residents, but they were considered not quite the battleships to fight the Decisive Battle. Their guns were too small, their armor too thin.

Even cruisers were not usually committed to the Guadalcanal Campaign. When they were, again except for a few occasions, they were the oldest cruisers in the Japanese inventory, like the 6th Cruiser Division, the *Tenryu*, the *Yubari*. The more modern cruisers like the *Mogami*s, the *Takao*s (except for the *Chokai*, which was usually a fleet flagship) were also held back.

Consequently, much of the campaign was fought by destroyers, destroyers who were tasked with things they were never intended to do on a regular basis, like running in troops and supplies. Those destroyers had suffered disproportionate losses. In a way, that made the most sense. Of all the men-of-war, destroyers were the smallest, the cheapest, and the easiest to build, and as a consequence, the easiest to replace.

But the destroyers' constant running of troops and supplies was costing the Japanese destroyers faster than those destroyers could be replaced.

Admiral Koga was a good Imperial Japanese naval officer. And good Japanese officers always look for that Decisive Battle. In his eyes, the central Pacific still looked like a better bet than the Solomons for the new Tsushima the Combined Fleet brass had always dreamed of. And he thought he had found it.

On September 18, a Pacific Fleet task force centered on three US Navy aircraft carriers (fleet carrier *Lexington* and light carriers *Princeton* and *Belleau Wood*) staged air attacks on Tarawa, Makin, and Abemama in the Gilbert Islands. An excited Admiral Koga decided to make this the big one. Sortieing from Truk on September 18 to Eniwetok (or Brown) in the Marshall Islands was what was called the First Section. It consisted of the fleet carriers *Shokaku* and *Zuikaku*, joined by light carrier *Zuiho* a day later; superbattleship *Yamato*, battleship *Nagato*, 5th Cruiser Division's *Myoko* and *Haguro*; 7th Cruiser Division's *Mogami*, just converted from a powerful heavy cruiser into a weird heavy cruiser/seaplane hybrid; 8th Cruiser Division's *Tone* and *Chikuma*, who were already heavy cruiser/seaplane carrier hybrids; new light cruiser *Agano* with her 10th Destroyer Flotilla; and new light cruiser *Noshiro* leading her 2nd Destroyer Flotilla. This First Section was commanded by Vice Admiral Ozawa Jisaburo, who also commanded the entire force.

There was also the Second Section, commanded by Admiral Kurita. It consisted of the 4th Cruiser Division's *Atago* and *Takao*, and that was about it. Admiral Koga himself remained at Truk in the Combined Fleet flagship and most powerful battleship *Musashi*, with old battleship *Fuso*, and fast battleships *Kongo* and *Haruna*. How exactly this weird arrangement was supposed to bring the Americans to battle is not clear, but you can be sure it involved some decoy or bait or diversion. In any event, they never found the Americans, so the Japanese went back to Truk, arriving on September 25.

On October 5–6, six US Navy carriers (fleet carriers *Essex*, *Yorktown*, and *Lexington*; and light carriers *Independence*, *Belleau Wood*, and *Cowpens*) bombed Wake Island. Analysis of US Navy radio traffic suggested to the Japanese that the Americans were going to bomb Wake Island again or maybe the Marshall Islands. This had to be the big one, Admiral Koga thought. On October 17, out came the Combined Fleet again: fleet carriers *Shokaku* and *Zuikaku*; light carrier *Zuiho*; superbattleships *Yamato* and *Musashi*; battleships *Nagato*, *Fuso*, *Kongo*, and *Haruna*; the 4th Cruiser Division's *Atago*, *Takao*, *Maya*, and *Chokai*; 7th Cruiser Division's *Suzuya* and *Mogami*; 8th Cruiser Division's *Tone* and *Chikuma*; light cruiser *Agano* leading her 10th Destroyer Flotilla; light cruiser *Noshiro* leading her 2nd Destroyer Flotilla; and new light cruiser *Oyodo* leading nothing.

This time, Admiral Koga led the fleet personally to Eniwetok again before moving to a point some 250 miles south of Wake Island. Again, the Japanese found nothing. Again, the fleet returned to Truk, arriving on October 26. How disappointing.

While Admiral Koga was running hither and yon to respond to Allied incursions both real and imagined, Admiral Kusaka was rapidly running out of places to run. What had begun as an inverted "V" with two widely divergent prongs – one in New Guinea, the other in the Solomons, both pointed at and meeting in Rabaul – was not so divergent any more. General Kenney's bombers were regularly attacking Rabaul itself now. In the Solomons, if anything, the situation was even worse.

The loss of the Munda air base on New Georgia was felt relatively quickly. As a general rule, the Japanese Imperial Navy and the Imperial Japanese Army did not retreat, did not even have the concept of retreat, so they did not prepare to retreat. Therefore, such ideas as destroying confidential documents, destroying whatever supplies they could not take with them, rendering whatever equipment and installations they had to leave behind unusable by the enemy were rarely considered because they would only be required should the Japanese retreat, which they did not do. As a result, the Munda airfield was not damaged as much as the Allies had feared, and what damage there was, was repaired fairly quickly – much more quickly than the Japanese would have – and the field was even expanded. As Marine Dauntless pilot LeRoy Smith described it:

When the Seabees got through with Munda they just flattened the mountain and you could have landed four B-24s side-by-side. It was huge: You could come back dragging your ass in the water all shot up and you had something to come back to. They ran right up to the water.[64]

Munda was now an operational air base. Even worse, after the Allies landed on Vella Lavella, they promptly built an all-new air base from scratch at Barakoma. The airfield was operational in late September.

The Japanese completed a new airfield of their own in late September, at Kara, northwest of Buin.[65] They hoped to take the pressure off of Buin. The result was that air attacks by AirSols (the joint command of Allied aircraft in the Solomons) in the Bougainville and Shortlands sector had intensified. In mid-October, those attacks had become downright relentless, starting with October 15.

That day, it was 21 Army Air Force Liberators escorted by 12 Lightnings of the 339th Fighter Squadron and 16 Marine Corsairs of Marine Fighting 214 attacking installations at Buin. Base Air Force sent 22 Zeros from the 201 Air Group – by this time the last Imperial Navy fighter group remaining at Buin – to meet them. The Japanese thought they had shot down two bombers and two Lightnings, but none were lost. One Zero, that of Lieutenant (jg) Arai Tomokichi, did not return to base. The Liberators reported causing "four explosions" and "several fires," with the runway being heavily cratered.[66] Later that evening, six Mitchells from the 42nd Bombardment Group made a low-level attack on Buka, causing "a large explosion and numerous fires."[67]

Just before dawn on October 16, six Mitchells made a low-level bombing and strafing run on Ballale, their 72 parafrag bombs landing with a "good bomb pattern" on the runway, meaning the craters left by the bombs were spaced as to render the runway unusable, at least temporarily. A weather front caused a planned attack by 23 Liberators on Buin and Kara to go awry, leaving only eight to bomb both complexes from high altitude through a cloud layer that obscured results.[68]

On October 17, it was 21 Marine Corsairs of Marine Fighting 214 on a late afternoon fighter sweep over Ballale. The Marines estimated 14 fighters shot down with two more damaged. The Japanese admitted two Zeros were set afire in the air; these would have been the Zeros of Petty Officers 2nd Class Yamauchi Yoshimi and Ito Shunji. Upon return to base one Corsair had to make a belly landing.[69]

On October 18, it was 28 Liberators, 32 Dauntlesses, and a dozen Avengers escorted by 339th Fighter Squadron P-38s hitting Ballale; Base Air Force sent up 22 fighters to meet them.[70] The bombers deposited 29 tons of bombs, getting "many hits." The Japanese claimed eight Corsairs shot down, which overstated the number shot down by only eight. Late that afternoon, 19 Corsairs of Marine Fighting 214 and 221 made a fighter sweep over Buin but were bounced over Ballale by 15–20 Zeros. The Americans claimed eight Japanese fighters shot down with two damaged. It's not clear how many the Japanese lost in this attack, but for the day 201 Air Group admitted five Zeros were shot down, including those of Reserve Ensign Aizawa Yoshio and Petty Officer 1st Class Mogi Yoshio, with one pilot managing to bail out. Ominously, while this skirmish was taking place, 18 Dauntlesses, 14 Lightnings, and 11 of the US Navy's new front-line carrier fighter, the Grumman F6F Hellcat, bombed and strafed Japanese positions near Kakasa on Choiseul.[71]

In the predawn darkness of October 19, four US Navy Vega PV-1 Ventura bombers made an attack on Ballale, bombing antiaircraft positions, causing four explosions and fires; they reported the runway unusable. At the same time, four other Venturas attacked Kara, causing a large explosion and fire, but one of their own failed to return. Before the noon hour it was 24 B-24s bombing Buin from high altitude escorted by 14 P-38s of the 339th Fighter Squadron. The attack started "5 large fires," but at the expense of two pilots, whose Lightnings collided in the clouds. While that was going on, a dozen Avengers – the TBF Avenger was proving itself to be a very good glide bomber as well as a torpedo carrier – joined 20 Dauntlesses, escorted by 20 fighters, in another attack on Kara, scoring "many hits on the runway" as well as buildings northeast of the runway and antiaircraft positions. Late that afternoon, two Corsairs made a strafing attack on Kara as well, claiming five fighters destroyed on the ground.[72]

After dawn the next day, four Navy Venturas bombed Japanese positions near Kakasa on Choiseul, dropping eight tons of bombs, causing "a large explosion and heavy smoke." A little before noon, two dozen Corsairs made a fighter sweep over Buin, tangling with 20 Zeros. The Marines claimed three Zeros shot down – the Japanese admitted only one "failed to return" – while two of their own were damaged by antiaircraft fire and crash-landed at Barakoma. A follow-up fighter sweep 80 minutes later by two dozen P-40s failed to find anything worth hitting. In the middle of the afternoon, two of the Navy PV-1s that had bombed Kakasa that morning returned to check out their handiwork. They reported the village of Kakasa was badly damaged by the first attack. That was apparently not good enough for AirSols, who sent in seven Dauntlesses who bombed Kakasa, causing two explosions and "considerable smoke" before heading back. The SBDs escorting fighters then strafed the village, which was attracting a lot of attention all of a sudden.[73]

Kakasa was hit again just before noon on October 21, this time by three Navy Venturas, who dropped two tons of bombs but did not see the results. A dozen B-25s escorted by 36 US Navy fighters swept over Kara at midmorning, dropping seven tons of bombs, scoring 15 hits on the runway and destroying several buildings.[74]

It would prove to be the relative lull before the storm of October 22. The day started with ten Liberators escorted by 20 Hellcats from Fighting 40 who dropped 33 tons of bombs on Buin, but did not see the results. They were watched by some 18 Zeros, who did not engage. A second attack at noon involved a dozen Liberators escorted by 16 Warhawks from the 12th, 68th, and 70th Fighter Squadrons. Nine Zeros showed up and "made several half-hearted attacks." The Japanese admitted, "Three fighters failed to return" while nine more "suffered great damage or (were) set afire." Less than an hour later, 24 Avengers and 48 Dauntlesses escorted by 68 fighters relieved themselves of their bomb loads over the beleaguered base. The strike planes dropped 32 tons of explosives, claiming 15 hits on the base, including the destruction of several antiaircraft guns and two Bettys. The Japanese reported two Zeros shot down, their pilots killed, while seven more fighters "suffered great damage or (were) set afire." Buin was pretty much useless for the rest of the day. About a half hour later, two dozen more AirSols fighters made a strafing sweep over the Kara air base, claiming 16 aircraft destroyed out of an estimated 30 parked on the ground. The attacks coming several times each day as well as at night had now pushed 201 Air Group to the breaking point. While some of its Zeros had already staged into Rabaul, Admiral Kusaka yanked back the rest of the unit from the Bougainville sector.[75]

In the midst of this bedtime for Buin, there were two more attacks on Choiseul. One featured nine Liberators escorted by a dozen of those new Navy Hellcats, dropping 36 tons of explosives on the beach at Pora Pora. A dozen Zeros tried to intervene but accomplished nothing with no loss to either side. Another attack by nine Liberators escorted by eight Hellcats bombed the Choiseul coast but did not see results. Eight Zeros attempted to intervene, shooting down one Hellcat while another had to crash land at Segi.[76]

The next day, October 23, saw 16 Lightnings of the 339th Fighter Squadron escort 11 Liberators to Buin, where 44 more tons of bombs were dropped on the unfortunate air base. That was followed by a half dozen more Liberators, escorted by 16 fighters, with 24 more tons of bombs. "[M]any craters" were seen on the runway. Nearby Kara was also visited twice, first by two dozen Dauntlesses, 18 Avengers, and 60 fighters from AirSols. The second strike was by two dozen Dauntlesses, 18 Avengers, and 36 fighters from AirSols. Together, they dropped a total of 59 tons of bombs on the base, including antiaircraft guns, supply caches, and the runway. One AirSols aircraft was shot down.[77]

This would become a very unpleasant marathon for the Buin air base. Just after 9:00am on October 24, nine Liberators escorted by 13 fighters dropped 36 tons of bombs on Buin, which despite the retreat of the 201 Air Group was not completely empty. Two hours later 47 Dauntlesses and 22 Avengers, escorted by 28 fighters, dropped 45½ tons of bombs on the runway and antiaircraft positions at Buin. Less than an hour later it was 19 Liberators escorted by 14 fighters dropping 26 tons of bombs. Late that evening, 36 Mitchells of the 42nd Bombardment Group escorted by 39 fighters dropped 44 tons of bombs on the runway and revetment areas, starting several fires and leaving the runway cratered. Base Air Force did not even attempt a fighter interception, in part because Rabaul was also under heavy air attack this day. While a few Allied aircraft were damaged by antiaircraft fire, none were lost. AirSols was operating at will over the former Japanese fortress of the Shortlands.[78]

As was shown the next day, when 31 Dauntlesses and 18 Avengers escorted by 30 fighters dropped 33 tons of bombs on Ballale, then strafed the runway. Again, Base Air Force did not even attempt a defense, as Rabaul was again under heavy air attack.[79]

Rabaul was not under heavy attack on October 26, and the marathon resumed around 7:30am when seven US Navy Liberators (PB4Ys) escorted by 15 Lightnings attacked Buin yet again. At 9:00am, it was 69 AirSols fighters escorting 22 42nd Bombardment Group Mitchells, 49 Dauntlesses, and 36 Avengers giving Buin yet another drubbing, this time with 88 tons of bombs. One aircraft was lost to antiaircraft fire and seven others damaged. About 90 minutes later it was 20 Liberators escorted by 16 Corsairs.[80]

Buin finally got a break that afternoon. At 2:43pm, eight P-38s of the 339th Fighter Squadron bombed and strafed the new-ish Bonis Plantation airstrip on Bougainville on the opposite side of the Buka Passage from the Buka airfield, which was also bombed and strafed. The strafing at Bonis was so bad that an estimated 300 construction workers (out of an estimated 2,500) were killed working on the field itself or in their tents. It sounds brutal to be killing construction workers, especially since most of those workers were little more than slave labor, but the fewer workers, the more slowly the damage would be repaired. At Buka itself, five Zeros were destroyed on the ground, and a bomber was hit on the runway. There was no fighter interception or even antiaircraft fire. That changed about an hour later, when six gunships and 15 escorting Lightnings worked over Buka with strafing and 216 parafrag bombs. The control tower was hit, another bomber was destroyed on the ground, and four other aircraft were destroyed. This time, there was moderate antiaircraft fire, but all AirSols planes returned to base.[81]

Late than afternoon, 30 Dauntlesses and 18 Avengers, escorted by 42 fighters, returned to Bougainville to drop 33 tons of bombs on Kara, ruining the freshly repaired runway. At around the same time, rather curiously, five US Navy Venturas bombed the south shore of Mono Island in the Treasury Island group.[82]

Curious or not, this was getting ridiculous. "[T]he Buin and Ballale airfields, in particular, [were] put out of operation by repeated raids over a period several days," the Japanese later admitted. "It appeared that the enemy was planning a new operation in the area. After the 18th it became impossible to use the Ballale airfield for hours at a time, and the same situation prevailed at Buin after the 21st; for all practical purposes, the airfields on Bougainville were useless as operational bases."[83]

Useless, perhaps, but the Japanese were still going to defend them. Lieutenant General Inamura Hitoshi's 8th Area Army was trying to prepare for the Allied offensive, whenever that would be. The 18th Army was still trying to reposition itself on New Guinea after the loss of Finschhafen. In the northern Solomons, it was the 17th Army under Lieutenant General Hyakutake Harukichi. When last we saw Hyakutake, he was busy screwing up the Guadalcanal Campaign for the Japanese. And, no, he had not gotten much better since then.

These days, General Hyakutake's assignment was seemingly to mess up the Solomons Campaign for the Japanese. His 17th Army had some 20,000 troops, mostly of the 6th Kumamoto Division, whose most famous accomplishment was the Rape of Nanking. And, no, the 6th had not gotten much better since then, either, as those 517 British prisoners who disappeared after they had constructed the Ballale airfield discovered. Some 15,000 of these troops were positioned in southern Bougainville.[84]

Also available to General Hyakutake were a considerable number of naval infantry. Some elements of the 8th Fleet headquarters remained after Vice Admiral Baron Samejima Tomoshige pulled it back to Rabaul. There were also 6,800 naval infantry of the 1st Base Force, mostly at Buin; and some 5,000 men of the 4th South Seas Garrison Unit who were positioned on the outer islands of the Shortlands. Most of these naval troops were static and could not be moved, but they could still fight in defense.[85]

So the good general had a substantial number of toys to play with, even if more than a few of them could not be moved. Most of the 1st Base Force was deployed to defend the Buin air base complex, including Buin itself, Kara, and blood-drenched Ballale. Most of the 4th South Seas Garrison Unit was placed on a perimeter of islands defending the Shortlands anchorage. Also defending the Buin–Shortlands area was a formidable battery of naval artillery, including eight 140mm guns, three 120mm guns, 21 80mm guns, 70 25mm machine guns, and 40 13mm machine guns. Dedicated antiaircraft guns included ten 120mm, seven 80mm, and 27 70mm. Topping it off were 16 searchlights.[86]

The other major area General Hyakutake had covered was the Buka Passage, with the air base on Buka Island the principal area of defense. Some 6,000 troops (5,000 army; 1,000 navy) were positioned to defend the Buka sector. To this General Inamura was adding four infantry battalions and one artillery battalion of the 17th Division from New Britain, who were due to arrive in November; the remainder of the 17th, which had just arrived from China, was sent to western New Britain to defend the Dampier Strait area opposite Finschhafen.[87]

With this deployment, General Hyakutake had covered the important Japanese bases in both the south and the north of Bougainville, but those 6,000 troops guarding Buka Passage were not just there for the air bases. They were there to also guard against "island hopping," a bitter taste of which the Japanese had gotten when the Allies landed on undefended Vella Lavella, which cut off and practically nullified all those Japanese troops on Kolombangara. The way the Allies could hop over Bougainville was to land on Buka, and Hyakutake had made certain that Buka was far from undefended. Even from a position of numerical inferiority, the Japanese had sufficient forces on Buka to at least fight any Allied landing there to a stalemate long enough for Japanese reinforcements from Bougainville to arrive to maintain the stalemate for the foreseeable future, maybe even eke out a victory. There would be no island hopping over Bougainville. No way these decadent Americans were going to outsmart Hyakutake Harukichi.

Elsewhere on Bougainville, at the port of Kieta on the east coast were 4,000–6,000 Imperial Army troops and some 200 naval infantry. The naval troops were equipped with two 80mm guns and one 13mm machine gun. Around Gazelle Harbor near the southern end of Empress Augusta Bay on the west coast were 2,000–3,000 soldiers and some navy lookouts.[88] These troops were at Empress Augusta Bay mostly for what might be called due diligence. The area around the bay was generally swampy and heavily wooded, with the central mountains limiting access to and from the interior, while the bay itself was windy and unprotected. In short, it was not an attractive site for an amphibious landing, which, Rabaul pointed out, might make it the perfect place to land, because it would be so unexpected. Nevertheless, Hyakutake and his friends at Buin believed that the unhospitable nature of the Empress Augusta Bay area meant there would be no enemy landing there.[89]

General Hyakutake's 17th Army had worked with Admiral Samejima's 8th Fleet to craft a strategy that might be called complementary. The 8th Fleet would ideally stop an invasion fleet before it could land, but if it did land, Plan B would be to cut off its seaborne supply routes behind it while Hyakutake's troops would destroy any force that did manage to land. That would be a tall order, the general knew, because he would be outnumbered and outgunned. However, he was a true believer in the superior "spiritual power" of the Japanese soldier that would overcome any numerical or technological advantage on the part of the enemy.

"The battle plan is to resist the enemy's material strength with perseverance, while at the same time displaying our spiritual strength and conducting raids and furious attacks against the enemy flanks and rear," Hyakutake ordered. "On this basis we will secure the key to victory within the dead spaces produced in enemy strength, and, losing no opportunities, we will exploit successes and annihilate the enemy." That superior "spiritual strength" had not worked on Guadalcanal, it had not worked on New Georgia, it had not worked on Vella Lavella, but Hyakutake believed it had to work eventually.[90]

Making it work required reinforcements to be sent to the Bougainville and western New Britain sectors, which was rapidly becoming an adventure. Just after midnight on October 21, while Admiral Koga was obsessed with the Central Pacific, the light cruisers *Kiso* and *Tama* and the destroyer *Uzuki* were 53 miles from Cape St. George on the way out from Rabaul after bringing in about 1,000 troops of the 2nd Battalion of the 54th Infantry Regiment of the Imperial Army's 17th Division. At the same time, Beauforts from No. 9 Group of the Royal Australian Air Force (seven from No. 6 Squadron under Flight Lieutenant A.J.R. Oates; 11 from No. 8 Squadron under Wing Commander Geoffrey Nicoll; and nine from No. 100 Squadron under Flight Lieutenant Clifford Ernest Tuttleby) were doing some night prowling carrying torpedoes and 250lb bombs. After a torpedo attack achieved nothing, there was a low-altitude bombing attack in which one of those bombs detonated in the *Kiso*'s starboard engine room, disabling her. The *Tama* moved in to help her sister ship, but about 30 minutes later she attracted Beauforts of her own. She was not hit, but four near misses ruptured some hull plating. The *Samidare* came out to assist, and with the *Samidare* and *Uzuki* screening them, the *Tama* apparently had to tow the *Kiso* back into Simpson Harbor. The Beauforts seem to have lurked in the darkness and returned to attack two more times between 2:00 and 3:00am, but they caused no further damage. The Beaufort flown by Flight Lieutenant Geoffrey H. Vincent did not return to base, having been hit and forced down at sea. *Kiso* would be stuck in Rabaul for another week while making emergency repairs to enable her to get back to Japan. Vincent and two others of his crew would be stuck in Rabaul until their decomposing corpses were dug out of a mass grave on Matupit Island, where they had been murdered.[91]

Two days later it was Captain Hara's Destroyer Division 27, now new and improved with the addition of the destroyer *Shiratsuyu* to go along with the *Samidare* and Hara's own *Shigure*, though, according to Hara, the *Shiratsuyu* "was manned almost completely by inexperienced sailors and I doubted that *Shiratsuyu* would prove much of an asset to my division." Maybe not as inexperienced as Hara had thought, however, because skipper Lieutenant Commander Matsuda Kuro and the crew of the *Shiratsuyu* had already been through something of a baptism by fire, or at least by a lit cigarette. On October 15, she had left Truk escorting the transports *Hakusan* and *Tokyo Maru*s as Convoy No. 1152. Just before noon on October 17, they were some 80 miles from Kavieng strolling along at 10 knots when they were greeted by a US Navy PB4Y Liberator flying alone and carrying five 300lb bombs. The Liberator dove, then roared over the largest ship in the convoy, the 10,380-ton *Hakusan Maru*, at masthead height. Then the Liberator turned around and repeated the maneuver. Except this time, at least one of the bombs planted itself in the transport's deck near the bow: two, maybe three more were near misses. The *Hakusan Maru* was set afire, with thick black smoke pouring from the hole in her deck, and 36 men were killed. The Liberator, flown by Lieutenant Commander Whitney Wright of AirSols' Patrol Bombing 104, escaped, having just completed the first successful low-level bombing attack by a US Navy Liberator. The transport did not sink, however. Within ten hours the fires were extinguished, and the ships made Simpson Harbor.[92]

Now, all three of Captain Hara's destroyers were going on a run to Iboki, about 50 miles east of Cape Gloucester. That way, Hara's ships missed the air attack on Rabaul that day, but they got a consolation prize of an attack all their own, as they were harassed by aircraft, probably more "Black Cat" Catalinas, in the predawn darkness. This "warm reception" caused Hara to order his ships to scatter, but the attackers gave up at dawn with the Japanese destroyers undamaged. Hara completed his mission in good order and returned to Rabaul.[93]

That good order would not extend to others. The *Uzuki* would be a busy ship. Later that day the *Uzuki* and sister ship *Mochizuki* went on what the Japanese called "rat transportation" to Jacquinot Bay on New Britain. They arrived around midnight on October 24 and began disembarking their troops. It seems to have been during this activity at a little after 1:00am that the *Mochizuki*, already damaged during the October 12 air attack on Rabaul, suffered an explosion in her engineering spaces amidships and caught fire. The damage may have left her without power to fight the fires. In any event, she sank at 1:16am with ten killed and 23 injured. The *Uzuki* picked up survivors, including Captain Sawamura Seiji, commanding officer of Destroyer Division 30, and skipper Lieutenant Commander Iwabuchi Goro. The reinforcement mission was aborted and the *Uzuki* returned to Rabaul. The explosion had been caused by a bomb from a prowling bomber, reportedly another Catalina flying boat from Patrol Squadron 101 operating out of Port Moresby.[94]

Not even the night, long the ally of the Japanese, was safe any more.[95]

It was still enough of an ally, however, to allow Captain Hara to make another troops transport run, this one to Garove Island, a highly volcanic island north of the Willaumez Peninsula on the north coast of New Britain, with his *Shigure*, *Samidare*, and *Shiratsuyu* on October 26. He seems to have made another such run on October 29, with just the *Shigure* and *Shiratsuyu*. Despite his misgivings about the *Shiratsuyu*, she seems to have impressed Hara somewhat. For now.[96]

But Captain Hara and his destroyers would soon have much more dangerous work. At 4:20am (probably 6:20am local time) on October 27, a reconnaissance seaplane (from either the 938 or 958 Air Groups), reported a large convoy composed of 15 transports and three cruisers proceeding north at a point ten nautical miles southeast of Mono Island in the Treasury Island group. The 8th Fleet headquarters, in Rabaul only a few days after moving back from Shortland, immediately ordered an alert.[97]

That alert included the Mono Island Garrison Unit of 190 naval infantry. At 7:20am (Japan Standard Time), it radioed, "Enemy landings commenced 0340 hours [3:40am Japan Standard Time]. We have engaged them." That was the last they heard from the garrison.[98]

In a raging downpour, the US Navy destroyers *Pringle* and *Philip* kicked off the invasion of the Treasury Islands at 5:45am local time by bombarding the south shore of Mono Island, the northern and by far the larger of the two principal islands in the Treasury group. The two destroyers, along with the destroyer *Eaton* who was covering them from both surface and air attacks courtesy of her embarked fighter director, stayed outside the western entrance to Blanche Harbor but did not enter the harbor itself, which separated Mono and Stirling Islands, because it was too narrow.[99]

The bombardment seems to have been relatively ineffective, due in part to the weather, in part to communications issues with the spotter plane. Then again, it may have been because the invasion force was under the command of Rear Admiral George Fort. Fort was last seen personally directing the landings at Wickham on New Georgia, which took place with what was described as "impressive disorganization." Before that, his main claim to fame was, as senior Navy officer on Guadalcanal, needlessly delaying the departure of the US Navy oiler *Kanawha* in the face of an imminent Japanese air attack that prevented her escape and ultimately sank the ship. And, no, he too had not improved much since then.

Even so, the bombardment "gave confidence to the boats" full of landing troops.[100] These landing troops were mostly from the reinforced 8th New Zealand Brigade (part of the 3rd New Zealand Division) under the command of Brigadier Robert A. Row. These Kiwis were tough veteran troops who had fought the *Wehrmacht* in Greece and North Africa and were anxious to take on the *Wehrmacht*'s Axis partners in the Pacific.

The destroyer transport *McKean* landed a small party of some 200 men on Mono's north shore to set up a radar station. The rest of the fast destroyer transports – *Stringham*, *Talbot*, *Waters*, *Dent*, *Kilty*, *Crosby*, and *Ward* – also stayed outside the harbor as they loaded troops onto landing boats. Two infantry landing craft that had been modified with 3-inch guns to serve as gunboats escorted the boats headed for Mono Island.[101]

The transport units for this invasion were divided into five groups. This first group was under the direction of Commander John D. Sweeney. But Admiral Fort was in charge of this entire operation, so, naturally – and intentionally – these groups got mixed up, which made the divisions essentially meaningless. The two landing craft gunboats were actually part of the second transport group, but they had moved up during the night.

Good thing, too, because despite the destroyers' preparatory bombardment as well as the bombing by the Navy Venturas, the approaching boats were fired on by a number of Japanese machine guns, some mortars, and a particularly bothersome twin-mount 40mm automatic gun at Falamai. The two gunboats had arrived from Nouméa just in time to be thrown into this operation without any kind of training for the guns. Nevertheless, they made short work of the 40mm weapon and helped to counter the machine guns.[102]

The Kiwis landed right on time at 6:26am, exactly three minutes after the bombardment stopped and 26 minutes after their air cover of 32 fighters provided by AirSols arrived on station. This first wave consisted of 16 landing craft carrying 640 troops. The landing craft gunboats, which had been part of the Second Transport Group, stayed in the area all morning. For their part, the fast destroyer transports, which had been part of the First Transport Group, landed about 1,600 men and at least 80 tons of supplies. They left at 8:00am, escorted by the destroyers *Conway* and *Renshaw*, who were in the Third Transport Group. At this point, it's fair to wonder what exactly was so important about dividing the invasion force into five transport groups if Admiral Fort was just going to mix and match them all.[103]

Nevertheless, the Second Transport Group, under Captain Jack E. Hurff – minus the two gunboats – came on the scene with its eight large landing craft escorted by the destroyers *Waller*, *Cony*, and *Saufley*, and minesweepers *Adroit*, *Conflict*, and *Daring*. The minesweepers led the way as the large landing craft headed for the beaches under enemy fire, which was not as strong as it might have been because much of it was directed at those two gunboats. In spite of this opposition, the landing craft debarked another 1,600 troops and 150 more tons of supplies within 35 minutes. With no casualties among the naval personnel, the landing craft left at 7:30am – before the fast destroyer transports – escorted by the destroyers *Pringle*, who had been in the first group, *Waller*, and *Saufley*.[104]

At 7:15am, the Third Transport Group arrived. Under Commander James R. Pahl, it consisted of two tank landing ships screened by the destroyers *Conway* and *Renshaw* and yard minesweepers *197* and *260*. With no one to tell them where to go, the skippers of the tank landing ships just picked their own landing beaches. This was a bad thing. Both tank landing ships landed on schedule at 7:35, and were then pounded by Japanese mortar fire. One landing ship, *LST-399*, had beached herself maybe eight yards from an enemy pillbox. When she lowered her landing ramp, the pillbox shot the first three who tried to step off. The landing ship's crew was unable to bring their own guns to bear and had to take cover themselves. Their request to leave the beach was denied. They were pinned down.[105]

That is, until a resourceful Kiwi mounted a bulldozer that was on the landing ship. He raised the blade to protect himself from enemy fire and rolled angrily down the ramp. Though he had covering fire from some soldiers with Bren guns, Japanese bullets clanked off the thick blade. He worked his way behind the problematic pillbox, then lowered the blade, and charged at the back of the bunker. Even more effectively than plowing snow or dirt, he plowed the pillbox and its seven occupants under the earth, "tamping it down well all around, effectively silencing its fire."[106]

Now the landing could resume, though after another fashion. Both landing ships had to unload by hand, about which the Kiwis were decidedly not happy. The mortars that had caused much of this trouble managed to quiet themselves when Admiral Fort's destroyer *Eaton* came around trying her hand at counterbattery fire. The destroyer *Philip* was ordered to take over the counterbattery fire and fired five salvos. The mortar remained quiet until the late morning, when it managed two hits on the struggling *LST-399* and one hit on an ammunition dump, which caused a spectacular explosion and fire that damaged the *LST-399* yet again. The *Philip* reappeared and the mortar disappeared again, never to return. Maybe because the Kiwis had captured it.[107]

In fact, before noon, the Kiwis had captured two 75mm guns and one 90mm mortar. The Japanese defense, though deadly, had been disjointed, likely because about 24 hours before the landing, an advance party of New Zealand noncommissioned officers and some local inhabitants had landed on Mono to cut communication lines between the observation post at Laifa Point and the radio station, which would explain the very sluggish notification of the attack to Rabaul. The advance work was a critical element of an excellent if chaotic performance in which the Allies had landed 2,500 men – 252 Americans of the 198th Coast Artillery and a few other detachments, the rest Kiwis. Tiny Stirling Island was secured by a single battalion, aided by the complete lack of Japanese on the island. The 87th Construction Battalion promptly began construction of an airfield there. The 8th Brigade set up a perimeter around the Mono Island beach and began to advance. Resistance to the landing itself was eliminated as the Japanese fled inland.[108]

The Japanese Special Naval Landing Force troops were now stuck. Once again, they had lived up to their reputation of never surrendering. Once again, they had done so by fleeing into the jungle, which is technically not surrendering. The problem for them was that there was nowhere to run. Mono Island was not that big. They were hemmed in.

By November 12, the Brigade had completely eliminated all resistance on Mono Island at a cost of 40 New Zealanders and 12 Americans killed; 145 New Zealanders and 29 Americans wounded. The Allies counted 205 Japanese corpses, which was odd since the Japanese themselves later said there were only 190 naval troops on the island.[109]

That was still in the future. For now, the Allies were in effective control of the Treasury Islands. The 2,500 troops were a tenth of what the Japanese had in the Shortlands, only 25 miles away. The Allied landings were not, from the Japanese standpoint, a good thing. But General Hyakutake did not panic. He had this all figured out.

The landings in the Treasuries, Hyakutake believed, were just a preliminary to a much larger operation. The Allies would build an airfield on the Treasuries, take Choiseul, and after intensified air and surface operations, would land three divisions on southern Bougainville in late November. He felt that they might invade Buka; that whole island-hopping thing. To Hyakutake, it meant that the defenses in southern Bougainville needed to be further strengthened. How troops in southern Bougainville were to help defend Buka was something he never quite explained, but this was his story and he was sticking to it.[110]

Admiral Kusaka had a bit of a different story. Among his early responses to the Allied seizure of the Treasuries was to send the submarine *Ro-105* on patrol near Mono Island. Reportedly, Kusaka organized a "combined assault force" of the light cruiser *Nagara* and ten destroyers, "which were in the Rabaul area, in preparation for a night raid against the invasion forces." The *Nagara* arrived in Rabaul that very day, and, reportedly, promptly turned around and headed back to Truk. There would be no night raid, no Savo Island for the time being.[111]

But there would be an air attack. With his once-widely divergent fronts in New Guinea and the Solomons now not so divergent, Admiral Kusaka decided to switch his offensive emphasis, such as it was, from New Guinea back to the Solomons. He recalled the 501 Air Group with its Yokosuka D4Y Comets from Kavieng to Rabaul.[112] At 12:30pm local time, 39 Zeros and ten Aichi D3A carrier bombers took off from Rabaul.[113] They arrived over the Treasuries to find very little worth bombing, at least in the water. Most of the big stuff had departed, leaving the two tank landing ships and two destroyers, the *Cony*, who was handling fighter direction, and the *Philip*.

The *Cony*'s radar detected the incoming Japanese strike and vectored in AirSols fighter coverage protecting the invasion beaches. First up were 16 P-38 Lightnings from the 339th Fighter Squadron in two groups of eight, one at 20,000 feet, the other at 25,000 feet. Also on station were 16 P-40s and eight Airacobras at 10,000 feet. Eight of the Lightnings and eight of the P-40s were loitering 15 miles northeast of the Treasuries, the rest were 15 miles northwest.

The conglomeration of AirSols aircraft was not enough to stop the carrier bombers from getting through. Several D3As came in out of the sun in an attack that the *Philip* described as "the best coordinated and severest this ship had experienced." The *Philip* did some *fouettés* at high speed, trying to keep the bombers at bay with antiaircraft fire. Approximately 12 bombs landed from 15 to 100 yards off the starboard side, but none of them hit the *Philip*.

The *Cony* was not so lucky. The destroyer pirouetted just as the *Philip* was doing, but unlike the *Philip*, the *Cony* was attacked from multiple directions. Maybe six bombs fell within 100 yards of the *Cony* before she was hit by two bombs at 3:34pm. They both struck her main deck aft on opposite sides of the Number 4 5-inch mount. One of the bombs hit the starboard main deck at frame 163 and detonated on contact, but the other penetrated the port main deck at frame 157, eight feet inboard, angled through bulkhead 157, and exploded. The after engine room was flooded and had a dangerous steam leak that forced its abandonment. A fire was reported aft, so the after magazines were flooded; the Number 3, 4, and 5 5-inch mounts were disabled anyway. Four men were killed, four more mortally wounded, and ten more wounded.

After the attack ended, the *Cony* informed the *Philip* that her damage was serious enough that she had to leave at once, so the *Philip* had to take over fighter direction. The *Cony* began crawling away on one engine. Overhead, a vengeful AirSols fighter cover whacked away at the retreating Japanese, engaging them near Kahili. One Zero was shot down, but four or five Aichis were shot down as well, a big loss considering Base Air Force did not have a lot of dive bombers to begin with.[114]

For their part, the Zero pilots claimed one Allied fighter shot down and one probable; AirSols losses, including those from a late morning attack by 17 unescorted Liberators on Buin and Kara, were zero. The Japanese claimed two transports and two cruisers sunk.

They had not even attacked the tank landing ships, and there were no cruisers off Mono Island. All they had managed to do was damage one destroyer. And while the damage to the *Cony* was heavy, it was manageable. And it was being managed. The fires were brought under control by 7:00pm. An hour later, she joined the destroyer *Waller* and the tug *Apache* heading down The Slot.* Good thing, because the next morning, after the fires had been put out and the after engine room pumped out, the *Cony* wiped a spring bearing and had to be towed by the *Apache* to Purvis Bay.[115]

The landing on Mono Island was completed with all the organization for which Admiral Fort was famous. The Fifth Transport Group, consisting of one coastal transport, six "mechanized" landing craft, and an aircraft rescue boat all under the command of Lieutenant James E. Locke, arrived off the western entrance to Blanche Harbor at about 6:30pm. About 20 minutes after the Fifth Transport Group arrived, the Fourth Transport Group, with one coastal transport, three tank landing craft, and two PT boats, arrived. Both groups were ordered to report to the new Commander Naval Base, Treasury Islands, for beaching and unloading assignments.[116]

That was much more direction than the Third Transport Group had received, which contributed to their nasty experience on the beaches of Mono Island. Both tank landing ships had left at 7:43pm. They were treated to reports of "bogies" on radar, the sound of aircraft engines overhead, and a big explosion on the beach where the heretofore unlucky *LST-399* had been. Seven Japanese "reconnaissance seaplanes" had dropped six to eight bombs on the beach.

But the Japanese seaplanes were not finished with the *LST-399*. At 8:24pm, she and the *LST-485* were heading back under the escort of the destroyer *Philip* when several flares and floatlights appeared nearby. The *Saufley* joined their little group. At 10:57pm, a floatplane dropped two bombs and a floatlight off the port side of the *LST-399*. The bombs missed, but the tank landing ship was severely shaken, with shrapnel cutting into the conning station. The single floatplane responsible for this attack "suffered great damage" and crashed during its return.[117]

These were not the only nocturnal developments. At 11:10pm, a Japanese plane made an unsuccessful bombing attack on Allied ships between Vella Lavella and Choiseul. At 1:45am, a Navy Type 0 Reconnaissance Seaplane (Allied reporting name "Jake") – possibly the same aircraft who made the earlier attack – dropped two bombs off the port quarter of an American destroyer off Voza, Choiseul. Despite making at least one and possibly two bombing attacks, the aircrew apparently reported "no signs of enemy activity" in the central Solomons. Admiral Kusaka decided the Treasury Islands landings could wait for a solution and switched the emphasis of Base Air Force back to New Guinea.[118]

It was a curious decision that evinces some dysfunction in the Japanese command arrangements. Because that same day, October 28, Admiral Koga put the emphasis back

* "The Slot" was the nickname for the New Georgia Sound – the area between the double line of the Solomons that looked like a slot.

on the Solomon Islands. He activated a contingency plan called the "RO" Operation or "Ro-Go." This involved rapid reinforcement of the Southeast Area Fleet with – you guessed it – aircraft from *Kido Butai* to help Base Air Force overwhelm the Allied aircraft and, at least at this point, destroy Allied shipping in the New Guinea area. Koga alerted Vice Admiral Ozawa to prepare to send his 173 carrier planes from the *Shokaku, Zuikaku,* and *Zuiho* – 82 Zeros, 45 Aichi D3A carrier bombers, 40 Nakajima B5N carrier attack planes, and six Yokosuka D4Y reconnaissance planes – to Rabaul. Again. This would be the third time the Japanese had sent their carrier planes to Rabaul in an effort to overwhelm the enemy. It had not worked the previous spring, and even played an indirect role in the death of Admiral Yamamoto. It had not worked the previous summer. But Koga figured it had to work eventually.[119]

You've read that before. Not even two years into the Pacific War – a war they had started – the Japanese were simply out of ideas. They were reduced to insanity, trying the same things over and over again, expecting a different result. And when they did not get it, they would act as if they did, sometimes even convince themselves they did.[120]

It would take some time to get the carrier planes of *Kido Butai* to Rabaul. In the meantime, the Allies were running rampant over the Japanese bases on Bougainville. A little after 7:30am, 19 Avengers and 29 Dauntlesses, with an escort of 46 fighters, bombed and strafed the runway at Kara. Two hours later it was 19 Liberators paying Kara a visit with no fighter escort. At 12:45, 21 Avengers and 38 Dauntlesses, escorted by 32 fighters bombed and strafed Ballale. No Japanese Zeros or fighters of any kind were seen the entire day. Antiaircraft fire was damaging, with one TBF forced to ditch off Barakoma; the aircrew was rescued.[121]

The next day, October 29, AirSols gave Base Air Force a morning of mayhem for its bases around Buka. At 8:30am or so it was a squadron of Mitchells, escorted by 23 Corsairs, bombing and strafing both Buka and Bonis. Some 15 minutes later, nine B-25s dropped 648 parafrag bombs on Buka, then proceeded to strafe it. A little more than an hour after that it was 21 B-24s. Some 15 minutes later it was 11 Mitchells escorted by 24 Corsairs bombing Buka at the same time a dozen US Navy Venturas and one Mitchell dropped three tons of delayed action bombs and 354 parafrags on Bonis.[122]

Yet that was hardly the only excitement for the Japanese that day. On Choiseul, US Marines attacked a barge staging point at Sagigai. The Marines chased the Japanese off and then destroyed the barges and supplies. Just before 7:00 that morning, 12 TBF Avengers escorted by 26 fighters attacked those Japanese near Sagigai, some eight miles from Voza.[123] Voza was where that Japanese scout plane had found a US Navy destroyer the other night and unsuccessfully bombed it. What had that destroyer been doing?

Landing Marines on Choiseul, obviously. Just as General Hyakutake had foreseen it; he was two for two so far. The Americans would busy themselves securing Choiseul and then land in southern Bougainville, where Hyakutake would be ready for them.

The Marines on Choiseul were moving toward Vagara, but that was not to be the big battle. Southern Bougainville would be the big battle. Or maybe Buka. Didn't matter, because General Hyakutake had prepared for both. But probably southern Bougainville – Buin, Kara, and the like. Speaking of which, just after 9:30am on October 30, 16 unescorted Liberators bombed the airfield at Kara. They were followed ten minutes later by 68 SBDs, 27 TBFs, and 50 fighters. The afternoon was about Kieta, as six 42nd Medium Bombardment Group Liberators bombed and strafed the air base there, while their 32 escorting Corsairs strafed shipping offshore. Three of the fighters were brought down by antiaircraft fire, but two of the pilots were rescued. About an hour later, at 2:05pm, a dozen Airacobras and four Kiwi Venturas from the newly arrived No. 1 Squadron paid the Kieta airfield a visit and left the runway cratered and unusable. One of these attacks on Kieta – it's not clear which one – apparently sank the sea truck *Ujigawa Maru*. At 3:10 AirSols made a return to the Shortlands, as two dozen Corsairs and a dozen Airacobras strafed shipping in Tonolei Harbor. One Airacobra was damaged by antiaircraft fire but managed to return to base, while a second was compelled by damage to ditch, but the pilot was rescued.[124]

The next day, October 31, was short but deadly, as three waves of attackers hit the Kara airfield within 15 minutes, starting at 9:00am. First was 19 Liberators, followed by 34 Dauntlesses, 24 Avengers, and 54 fighters, then finally 23 Mitchells and 16 fighters. Photographs showed 65 craters in the runway.[125]

Those craters were simple dimples compared to the report that came in from a Mitsubishi G4M on a special scout mission over the central Solomons, one with an aircrew that was apparently more capable than the previous reconnaissance seaplane: at 7:50am, a large convoy of three cruisers, ten destroyers, and 30-odd transports of various types was sighted 20 miles off Gatukai Island in the New Georgia group heading west at a speed of 10 knots.[126]

A convoy of that many transports is not out there for fun. Well, it could be, but probably not, and it was not the reason here. It had to be the big invasion convoy everyone was waiting for, the one headed for Bougainville. And Admiral Kusaka knew it.

The first thing the admiral did was to reactivate the interception operation he had activated after the invasion of the Treasuries and then deactivated after the aircrew of one reconnaissance plane said there were "no signs of enemy activity" in the central Solomons despite its bombing at least one group of US Navy ships. Kusaka reoriented Base Air Force's operations back from New Guinea to the Solomons. Moreover, he tried to organize an air attack on the convoy.[127]

Admiral Kusaka also ordered formation of another "Combined Assault Force," this time consisting of the 5th Cruiser Division with the heavy cruisers *Myoko* and *Haguro* under Rear Admiral Omori Sentaro and the 3rd Destroyer Flotilla with the light cruiser *Sendai* under veteran Rear Admiral Baron Ijuin Matsuji. The Combined Assault Force's mission would be to intercept the invasion convoy that night near Mono Island.[128]

In short, this was to be a complementary strategy. Base Air Force would attack the convoy from the air, 8th Fleet would attack it from the sea. Whatever survived would be wiped out by General Hyakutake's troops, either at Buka or, more likely, southern Bougainville.

Updates on the convoy's progress continued throughout the day. At 1:30pm a reconnaissance plane reported the convoy had split into two parts. One consisted of eight destroyers and 19 transports of various types, the second of four cruisers and nine "special transports." Both elements were southwest of Rendova heading northwest at 10 knots.[129] Three hours later, the four cruisers and eight destroyers had formed their own group and were northwest of Ganongga Island heading northwest.[130]

The problem for Admiral Kusaka was that his forces could not get their act together. It was partly due to the incessant air attacks that had left the Buin, Ballale, Kara, Kieta, Bonis, and Buka air bases with a total of 31 aircraft between them. With respect to Base Air Force, that was Kusaka's responsibility, but also his fault. His hasty cancelation of the Solomons air counterattack had left what strike aircraft he had ready to strike land targets in New Guinea, not ship targets at sea.[131]

At 10:00am, Admiral Omori received orders to sortie to intercept the Americans. It was 3:00pm when his Combined Assault Force left Simpson Harbor. Slapped together on short notice, it consisted of his own flagship *Myoko* and her sister ship *Haguro*; the 3rd Destroyer Flotilla's flagship light cruiser *Sendai*; one other light cruiser that Omori later identified as the *Nagara*, which had supposedly left Rabaul on October 27; and two unidentified destroyers who may or may not have been the *Samidare* and *Minazuki*. They maneuvered down St George's Channel toward Mono Island, where they hoped to intercept the Americans, either the cruisers or, preferably, the transports. The *Myoko* launched two floatplanes, the *Haguro* one. All three scout planes fanned out ahead of the Combined Assault Force to search for the Americans. The night was overcast, however, and the floatplanes found nothing, so they headed for Buka while Omori's ships made for Rabaul.[132]

Their quarry were soon located. At 12:21am local time on November 1 (10:21pm October 31 Japan Standard Time), that enemy force of four cruisers and eight destroyers showed up off the west coast of Buka. This was Rear Admiral Aaron Stanton "Tip" Merrill's task force centered on the light cruisers *Montpelier*, *Cleveland*, *Columbia*, and *Denver*. Leading the cruisers in this column were three destroyers of Destroyer Division 45 under Captain Arleigh A. Burke: *Charles F. Ausburne*, *Dyson*, and *Claxton*. A fourth destroyer of the division, *Stanly*, was positioned seaward of Merrill's force to guard against any interference from surface forces. Also in front of the cruisers were two destroyers of Destroyer Division 46 under Commander Bernard L. "Count" Austin: *Spence* and *Thatcher*. Behind the cruisers in column were the other two destroyers of Destroyer Division 46: *Converse* and *Foote*. When the time came, the *Stanly* would bring up the rear, keeping herself between the task force and any possible Japanese naval interference from Rabaul.[133]

With the help of spotters on Black Cats overhead, Merrill's ships sailed by Buka and Bonis at 20 knots and proceeded to lob 300 6-inch and 2,400 5-inch shells at both airfields. The shelling reportedly started large fires at both air bases, but especially at Buka, where at 12:30am a fire started and "grew rapidly in intensity until it lighted up the area for miles around." Captain Burke called the gunfire from the six-mile-long American column "impressive," while one of the spotter planes called it "beautiful." Truly, beauty is in the eyes of the beholder.[134]

The Japanese did not take this lying down, at least not literally. The destroyer *Stanly* had to deal with what she believed were Japanese motor torpedo boats. Whether they were or not is anyone's guess, but no US Navy ships suffered torpedo hits. Shell hits from Japanese shore batteries were a slightly different story. Their response was merely "gun flashes from the beach" until 12:37am, when two Japanese planes appeared on the scene – probably Admiral Omori's floatplanes – and backlit the American column with parachute flares. Then the Japanese gunfire became more intense and accurate. One shell even struck close to Admiral Merrill's flagship *Montpelier*, drenching the exposed gunners and wrecking his favorite typewriter. The bastards. Then the American ships sped off, harassed by the floatplanes until shortly after 2:00am, though no bombing or torpedo attacks were made. The fires at Buka were reportedly so bad that they could be seen when Merrill's ships were 60 miles away at 3:00am.[135]

At 12:30am, while heading northwest toward Rabaul, Admiral Omori had received a report that the American cruisers were off Buka. His Combined Assault Force appears to have initially overshot Admiral Merrill's cruisers in their quest to catch them off the Treasury Islands. Omori turned his own cruiser force to the north to try again to catch them. But as he approached Buka he received no updates as to their location, so he turned back toward Rabaul once again. While the Americans had not been intercepted, the bombardment suggested that the target of the invasion fleet was indeed Buka.[136]

Or not. At 6:19am (4:19 Japan Standard Time) – six minutes after sunrise – the coast defense batteries on Shortland saw that force of enemy cruisers and destroyers off the island's southwest coast and opened fire at a range of 13,000 yards. The enemy ships were, once again, Admiral Merrill's cruisers and destroyers. Like a bus that performed a drive-by shooting at each stop, they had shot up Buka and Bonis, then sped southeast 192 miles in order to reach Shortland around 6:30am, at which time they would attempt to shoot up Shortland, Ballale, and other bases in the Shortlands. But there was a catch: this would be the first bombardment of an enemy base in broad daylight in the South Pacific.[137]

Oh, well, someone's gotta be first. Might as well be Admiral Merrill and his men. It was not like they had not bombarded these same targets before. They had, back on the night of June 29–30. That was at night. In a thunderstorm. When no one could see you. This bombardment would be no different. Except it was not in a thunderstorm. And it was during the day. When the enemy could see you. And could shoot at you. Like they were now.

And the Japanese gunfire, as Captain Burke put it, was "unexpectedly heavy." With his ships moving at the high speed of 30 knots, Admiral Merrill ordered his destroyers to return fire and silence the Japanese guns. The cruisers were allowed to return fire at their discretion. Shell splashes made it plain that the Japanese were targeting the entirety of the American column, but generally they were well short. As the admiral had expected. His cruisers'

6-inch guns outranged the Japanese coast defense guns that he believed were also 6-inch. He was not far off; the biggest the Japanese actually had was 5.5-inch. The problem for him was that he would need to come within their range for his guns to hit their assigned targets, so those Japanese guns had to be silenced. As if to emphasize the point, the leading destroyers started taking the brunt of the gunfire, with Burke's own *Charles Ausburne* straddled repeatedly. Accordingly, the *Cleveland* opened fire at 6:23, followed a minute later by Merrill's flagship *Montpelier*. The rest of the ships opened fire moments later.[138]

The gun duel continued, but for only a few minutes. The Japanese stopped firing at about 6:24. The cruisers had their own scheduled bombardment to conduct – with no aerial spotting as they had at Buka just hours earlier. Admiral Merrill's column came to course 90 degrees True – due east – for the first leg of the bombardment. They were to enfilade the reverse slope of Poporang Island – one of the Shortland Islands, this one a little island just east of Shortland, serving as a seaplane base – by indirect fire; and to hit the eastern end of Shortland and Faisi Islands, the latter a very tiny island off Shortland north of Poporang. They would need to hit everything, because at 6:29 the Japanese opened fire again, especially a battery of coastal artillery on Morgusaia Island just south of Shortland.[139]

Two minutes later, the cruisers officially began their bombardment of the Shortlands. That was also the time the *Charles Ausburne*'s fantail was showered with fragments (with no casualties) by a near miss off her stern. Two minutes later a "very ragged" 5.5-inch salvo straddled the *Montpelier*, with one shell passing between her smokestacks and landing some 50 yards to starboard, a second landing 50 yards astern, and an instant later a third splashed just short of her port beam. One more minute and the *Dyson* was straddled.[140]

It was getting dangerous, but Admiral Merrill had prepared for this. He would signal immediate turns for his ships; rapid and radical maneuvering that kept his ships in the same order and facing the same direction, even if they were not always in column. The exception was Captain Burke's destroyers in front, who were under heavier fire and were free to perform individual maneuvers in addition to those ordered by the admiral. The evasive maneuvering and counterbattery fire were mostly effective in frustrating the Japanese aim.[141]

At 6:36, Captain Burke's *Charles Ausburne* turned 40 degrees to port to course 50 degrees True – roughly northeast – to start the column turn that would begin the second phase of the bombardment. It would be another ten minutes or so before Admiral Merrill's cruisers behind him reached the point where they would follow, with an order for "4 turn." This second leg was mainly to hit the Ballale air base with 6-inch gunfire via direct fire in which the results could be seen – assuming the smoke from the guns and explosions did not obscure the targets.[142]

Admiral Merrill's flagship *Montpelier* was not able to open fire for this second phase until 6:50. At a range of 22,000 yards, the first three salvos fell short, but the fourth started a plastering of the air base. The destroyers were still pouring on the counterbattery fire, as were some of the secondary batteries on the cruisers, but Japanese gunfire remained very heavy. Captain Burke was mystified at the continuing level of resistance. "It did not seem possible that the enemy could continue to fire with the volume of fire poured at him from our ships," he later wrote.[143]

The Japanese fire not only continued, but got more dangerous. It was apparently during this leg that four "six inch" guns on the ridge of Poporang Island opened fire. These were not just any "six inch" guns; these were .50-cal. 3rd Year Type 14cm (5.5-inch) guns, the same gun that was on almost all Japanese light cruisers, who despite being relatively old (and the 3rd Year Type gun older still) and very ugly had consistently punched above their weight. These were dangerous guns, especially to the US Navy destroyers.[144]

As if to emphasize the point, the *Charles Ausburne* was straddled again. The other destroyers continued their evasive maneuvers, which were not enough to keep the *Dyson* from taking a 5.5-inch shell in her bow above the water line that resulted in minor damage. Instead of pressing their advantage, when Admiral Merrill's cruisers came into range, the 5.5-inch guns switched targets to them, but it took time for the guns to acquire these targets. In the meantime, their shots were consistently short. The counterbattery fire may have had an effect. Two of the problematic pistols stopped firing, whether from damage or (more likely) crew casualties is unclear. Behind the ridge on Poporang was the small village of Nila, home to a Roman Catholic mission and hospital built by the Society of Mary (Marist) order – three priests who requested to be left behind were sent to Vunapope – but also elements of that seaplane base. Large fires were reported in Nila after the bombardment.[145]

It all had to end; the Americans had overstayed their welcome. Pursuant to their original plan, at 6:50am, the *Charles Ausburne* turned to starboard and course 115 degrees True – roughly east southeast – for the run back to safer waters and, hopefully, a fueling rendezvous for the always-thirsty destroyers. Shortly after 7:00am, the last shots of the bombardment were fired, and Admiral Merrill had his tired, hungry men "piped down to coffee and eggs." Two of the Japanese 14cm guns on Poporang defiantly continued shooting at the withdrawing Americans.[146]

As far as the Japanese were concerned, however, the bombardment, while damaging, was more evidence their predictions would come true. OK, maybe the Allies were not going to invade at Buka, as it had appeared in the wee hours of the morning, but they had just blasted the Shortlands, including the virtually empty airfield at Ballale. This had to mean that the invasion convoy would land around southern Bougainville.

General Hyakutake was ready. Ready for either Buka or southern Bougainville, but especially southern Bougainville. While he had some 6,000 troops around Buka and Bonis, he had some 25,000 troops around Buin and the Shortlands. As far as ground troops, the Japanese were ready.

Buka or Buin, General Hyakutake thought. They may outnumber us, but we are dug in. Buka or Buin. It doesn't matter. We will beat them. At 7:00am or so, the Japanese got word that the Americans had landed.[147]

At neither.

CHAPTER 2

"JAPAN WILL TOPPLE IF BOUGAINVILLE FALLS"

The preparation for the invasion of Bougainville had started the previous summer. Much of it was intelligence gathering, not at all an easy task on Bougainville since the Japanese had been successful in turning the locals against the Allies and had thus been able to drive the coastwatchers off the island earlier in 1943.

Although that intelligence picture was limited, the Americans were also under no illusions as to the difficult geography of Bougainville and its outlying islands, nor the importance the Japanese placed on that Devil's furnace room and the resources they were willing to use to defend it. Allied intelligence estimated the Japanese had about 37,500 troops of the 17th Army and 20,000 sailors and naval infantry. The number of aircraft and ships varied, but the increasing Allied air superiority meant more reconnaissance flights, enabling Allied intelligence to keep tabs on most of them.[1]

All of this information had to factor into planning the Bougainville operation. The final version of General MacArthur's *Elkton* plan, known as *Elkton III*, had called for the invasion of southern Bougainville that General Hyakutake and the Japanese were expecting to take place during the fifth month after the beginning of *Cartwheel* (a.k.a "Your simple plan for conquering Rabaul in only 13 easy steps") into which *Elkton III* had been incorporated, and simultaneously with the seizure of New Georgia.[2]

Admiral Halsey had altered the plan by starting the invasion of New Georgia on June 30. General MacArthur prayed he would not alter the plan any further. Because MacArthur had alterations of his own. In ordering the offensive against Lae, Salamaua, and the Huon Peninsula in June, MacArthur had directed Admiral Halsey to be ready to take southern Bougainville on his orders. Halsey had planned to use the 3rd Marine

Division and the 25th Infantry Division for this purpose; and use the 2nd Marine Division and the New Zealand 3rd Division later on against Rabaul. But that did not work. The 2nd Marine Division was sent to the central Pacific, while the 25th Infantry Division had to be used on New Georgia, where it was chewed up.[3]

So, Admiral Halsey altered the plan again. He understood that the objectives of the Bougainville operation were denying the use of airfields and anchorage to the Japanese and, conversely, securing airfields and anchorages for the Allies as a step toward the capture of Rabaul. Furthermore, the Bougainville operation was going to be big and costly because the Japanese had made the area a fortress and forward base protecting Rabaul. So, near the end of July, Halsey suggested that they not invade Bougainville at all, but instead seize the Shortlands and Ballale. There they would place big-time artillery to interdict the Japanese use of the Kahili air base; the Japanese had likely considered this possibility in their construction of the Kara air base inland from Buin. The Allies could build air bases on the Shortlands and use the Shortlands anchorage. That last one was probably not a good idea. Resting ships so close to a shore the enemy holds – especially a shore the enemy holds in strength like southern Bougainville – was a bad idea. The rest of it seemed workable, and it would save lives, war assets, and time. MacArthur approved the plan.[4]

Then Admiral Halsey altered the plan again. This was in the aftermath of the very successful invasion of Vella Lavella that had successfully driven the Japanese off of Kolombangara entirely, the only downside being that almost all of the Japanese troops had escaped. Nevertheless, it proved the feasibility and potential of "island hopping." Moreover, even taking just the Shortlands was going to be an expensive operation, requiring two divisions of troops, or exactly half the available troops (the US Army's 37th Infantry and Americal Divisions; the US 3rd Marine Division, and the New Zealand 3rd Division) in the South Pacific. Securing the Shortlands would mean no offensive operations would be possible for months afterward while the two divisions recovered, their place in the Shortlands being taken by the other two divisions. And the Shortlands were not good for building air bases anyway, which was why the Japanese had conspicuously left the Shortlands relatively air base-free except for the one crammed onto Ballale and the seaplane base that did not require runways.[5]

So, on September 10, the South Pacific Commander proposed a recommendation from Vice Admiral Aubrey Fitch, commander of South Pacific aircraft; Rear Admiral Theodore Wilkinson, commander of the South Pacific Amphibious Force; Lieutenant General Millard Harmon, Commander of Army Forces in the South Pacific; and Major General Charles D. Barrett, commander of the I Marine Amphibious Corps, that "the concept of the attack on Shortland should be abandoned" and that "the following alternate plan should be placed in effect":

Step 1 – Complete projected airfields in New Georgia and Vella Lavella.

Step 2 – Continue and increase air effort to neutralize by air enemy airfields in the South Bougainville Area, and to put heavy pressure on airfields in the Buka Area.

Step 3 – On D-Day simultaneously seize and occupy Treasury Islands and Choiseul Bay Area; install long range radar at both of these positions, construct airfields at one or both positions as found feasible, establish motor torpedo boat advance bases and staging points for landing craft at both positions; all in order to contain and strangle Southern Bougainville.

Step 4 – By air action, neutralize airfields in the Buka area.

Furthermore, after accomplishing Step 4, the Allies would advance up the axis of either Choiseul to Kieta on the east coast of Bougainville or that of Treasury Island to Empress Augusta Bay on the west coast, depending on the Japanese reaction to the original attack. That is, if establishment of positions on the mainland of Bougainville was required.[6]

The rapid success of the Vella Lavella operation was the gift that kept on giving, as it again caused the plan to be re-evaluated yet again, with the idea of neutralizing the Bougainville air complex without actually invading the Japanese strongpoints in the Buin and Buka sectors. Halsey started seeing his immediate mission as the neutralization of Buka, which, he believed, could be accomplished if airfields were constructed on the northern tip of Choiseul Island or in the Treasury Islands or both.

The idea of invading Choiseul and the Treasuries in lieu of invading Bougainville was too much for Douglas MacArthur, and understandably so. Neutralizing Buka from the Treasuries and Choiseul as a way of avoiding the Japanese defenses in Buka and Buin was fine, but then what? Buka's land defenses would still be in a blocking position for Rabaul. There was no way to get closer to Rabaul without going onto Bougainville. MacArthur wanted air bases from which fighters could reach Rabaul. Choiseul did not qualify; Bougainville – and only Bougainville – did. He had a counterproposal:

1. October 15–November 1: Southwest Pacific air forces would make heavy attacks against Japanese aircraft, air installations, and shipping at Rabaul;
2. October 20–25: South Pacific forces would occupy the Treasuries and positions on northern Choiseul in order to establish radar positions and PT boat bases;
3. November 1: South Pacific forces would occupy Empress Augusta Bay on the west coast of Bougainville in order to establish airfields within fighter range of Rabaul;
4. November 1–6: the Southwest Pacific would continue air attacks on Rabaul and would assist in the neutralization of Buka;
5. December 25, 1943–1 January 1, 1944, Southwest Pacific forces would seize Cape Gloucester and Saidor in order to gain control of Vitiaz and Dampier Straits and to secure airdromes for the neutralization of Kavieng. During this period South Pacific forces would neutralize Rabaul.

As to whether to land on the east or the west coast of Bougainville, MacArthur said, "[T]hat is entirely as Halsey decides. To me it makes no difference."[7]

As a result, on September 22, Admiral Halsey issued warning orders which placed Admiral Wilkinson in charge of the upcoming invasion and canceled Halsey's many, many earlier plans. The new plan was multiple choice, at least for Phase I: (1) "Seize and hold Treasury Islands and northern Empress Augusta Bay area, Bougainville Island, and construct airfields in the vicinity of Empress Augusta Bay;" or (2) "Seize and hold Treasury Island and Choiseul Bay Area, install radars, PT bases and staging points thereat, and construct airfields in the vicinity of Choiseul Bay Area in preparation for Phase 2." During the latter part of December, a second phase to either alternative was to take place involving seizure of a largely unused Japanese single-runway airfield about 30 miles northwest of Kieta on the east coast of Bougainville at a place called Tenakau.[8]

That did not help Admiral Wilkinson much. Two widely separated possibilities. How are you supposed to plan for that? They were quickly narrowed down, however. On September 22 or so, exasperated by the continuing staff discussions about where to land on Bougainville, Halsey abruptly announced: "It's Torokina. Now get on your horses!"[9]

Horses would be an … interesting way of getting to Empress Augusta Bay. As Admiral Halsey described it:

> The conception was bold and the probability of provoking a violent air-land-surface action was accepted and welcomed on the premise that the by-products of enemy destruction would, in themselves, greatly further the over-all Pacific plan. Enthusiasm for the plan was far from unanimous, even in the South Pacific, but, the decision having been made, all hands were told to "Get going."[10]

Be that as it may, there was a very basic reasoning for choosing Torokina: information provided by the few coastwatchers able to operate on Bougainville for any length of time had indicated that Cape Torokina "was going to be completely undefended."[11] Halsey informed MacArthur of his decision on October 1. MacArthur was impressed with the plan and promised maximum air support. The invasion would be launched on November 1.[12]

On October 12, Admiral Halsey issued the basic orders for the operation, code-named "Cherryblossom," which sounded a lot better than the New Georgia invasion's name *Toenails*. In terms of ships, Halsey did not have a lot to work with because Admiral Nimitz had stripped most of his naval resources for his own central Pacific offensive with the 5th Fleet. Organizationally, Halsey set up five task forces. Task Force 31 under Admiral Wilkinson was the invasion force; Task Force 33 under Admiral Fitch was the land-based aircraft component; Task Force 38 was the force of aircraft carriers under Rear Admiral Frederick Sherman; Task Force 39 was Admiral Merrill's force of light cruisers and destroyers – the last and only such force remaining in the South Pacific. Captain James Fife's submarines in Brisbane comprised Task Force 72.[13]

Cherryblossom would include the reappearance of significant carrier operations in the South Pacific, albeit of a small group. Admiral Sherman's Task Force 38 consisted of the fleet carrier *Saratoga*, the sister ship to his own *Lexington* that had been sunk at Coral Sea; and the new light carrier *Princeton*. Escorting them were the light antiaircraft cruisers *San Diego* and *San Juan*; and a seriously veteran group of destroyers: *Lardner*, *Farenholt*, *Woodworth*, *Buchanan*, *Lansdowne*, *Grayson*, *Sterett*, *Stack*, *Wilson*, and *Edwards*.[14] This was the extent of the carrier support *Cherryblossom* was to receive, although Admiral Nimitz promised that the 5th Fleet carriers positioned for the central Pacific offensive would be close enough to help if things went south – well, more south than necessary – on Bougainville.

As part of that October 12 order, Admiral Halsey ordered Admiral Wilkinson to seize the Treasury Islands on October 27. It had occurred to someone that Empress Augusta Bay was rather far from the closest Allied base, which was Barakoma on Vella Lavella, and even further from the Allied staging areas on New Georgia and Guadalcanal. Moreover, there were those Japanese bases at Buin and the Shortlands between the Kaiserin's Bay and those Allied bases. The Treasuries would help secure that supply line. In an operation code-named "Goodtime," the Treasuries were to be secured by that 8th Brigade of the New Zealand 3rd Division, to be landed by Admiral Fort's amphibious force, as already described.

The ground forces for *Cherryblossom* would come from the I Marine Amphibious Corps, which was every bit a mix and match of services and nationalities as AirSols, consisting of the 3rd Marine Division, the US Army's 37th Infantry Division, and the New Zealand 8th Brigade Group of the New Zealand 3rd Division.[15] The problem was that the commander of the I Marine Amphibious Corps, General Barrett, had died under mysterious circumstances in Nouméa.[16] The only officer in the South Pacific who could immediately replace him was General Alexander Vandegrift, of Guadalcanal fame. But he had recently left for Washington to take up his well-earned new position as Commandant of the Marine Corps. Admiral Halsey requested his return and Vandegrift agreed.

But Vandegrift could not run it forever. The I Marine Amphibious Corps needed a permanent replacement. Admiral Halsey discussed the matter with his War Plans officer, Marine Brigadier General William E. Riley. Riley told Halsey he would go to his room and think it over. Halsey told Riley he would go to his room and think it over. A few minutes later, Halsey burst out of his office to head for Riley's office. Riley met him halfway. His first words were, "I have the very man!"

With feigned nonchalance, Admiral Halsey replied, "You mean Roy Geiger, of course." General Riley was flabbergasted. "Right! How did you know?"[17]

Major General Roy Geiger was another old friend from Guadalcanal; he had headed the precursor to AirSols: the Cactus Air Force. Geiger was currently in Washington as head of Marine Corps Aviation. Admiral Halsey requested his transfer, which was quickly approved. But it would take him time to get to the South Pacific. Vandegrift would run it in the interim.[18] Vandegrift, Geiger, Wilkinson, Halsey, and their staffs would make *Cherryblossom* the first amphibious operation to benefit from planning by a staff with wartime experience. As Marine infantry officer and historian David C. Fuquea put it, "Seasoning at all levels meant competence and innovation to a high degree."[19]

The whole I Marine Amphibious Corps would not be landing on Bougainville. Not yet. The total number of men landing was to be 14,321, which is a rather suspiciously precise number when you think about it. The landing force was centered in the 3rd Marine Division under Major General Allen H. Turnage, less the 21st Regiment. The 3rd Marine Division was well-trained – better prepared for the jungle than the 1st Marine Division had been on Guadalcanal or, especially, the Army troops who landed on New Georgia – but it was untested in battle. Joining them was the 2nd Provisional Raider Regiment; the 3rd Defense Battalion (less detachments); elements of the I Marine Amphibious Corps headquarters; and elements of a subgroup of AirSols called "Air Command Northern Solomons," or "AirNorSols," which doesn't sound like a disinfectant so much as a brand of shoes.[20]

Also part of that October 12 order, Admiral Wilkinson was to be prepared to establish a PT boat base on northwestern Choiseul on five days' notice. Like the Santa Cruz Islands during the Guadalcanal operation, it was generally agreed that *something* should be done with Choiseul, but nobody was quite sure what. Unlike the Santa Cruz Islands, Choiseul was not off the beaten path, nor did it have its own virulent strain of cerebral malaria. Ultimately, General Vandegrift and his staff, specifically Staff Secretary Major James C. Murray, came up with a better reason to land on Choiseul than building a PT boat base. The Treasury Islands were on a direct line to the west coast of Bougainville, including Empress Augusta Bay. *Goodtime* might tip off the Japanese as to the location of the *Cherryblossom* landing. A landing on Choiseul might at least muddy the waters a bit and keep the possibility of the pincer attack on Shortland or a landing on the east coast of Bougainville in the Japanese mind.[21]

With that settled – for now – everyone got to work. General MacArthur had promised maximum air support. And he made as good as he was able. That promise of maximum air support was the basis for the intense series of air attacks against the Rabaul air bases by MacArthur's 5th Air Force that began in mid-October. At the same time, AirSols and the 13th Air Force began their intense series of air attacks against the air bases at Kahili, Kara, Ballale, Buka, and Bonis. On October 21, Air New Georgia was dissolved – it never developed a decent acronym – and AirSols commander Major General Nathan Twining moved up AirSols headquarters from Guadalcanal to Munda to be closer to the new front. Allied intelligence believed that by the end of October, Japanese air power had been largely, if not entirely, suppressed. *Magic*, the Allied cryptoanalysis project, had intercepted a message from Admiral Kusaka to Admiral Koga revealing that Base Air Force's "disposable" force numbered 71 fighters and ten dive bombers. A subsequent series of messages discussed how to rectify this lack of combat power. In short order, the Allies detected movement of a number of fighter and bomber squadrons and a "possible" staging of the carrier planes of *Kido Butai*.[22]

Working from Guadalcanal, Admiral Wilkinson had to get his very limited and scattered transport ships and escorts together for three amphibious operations to take place over a period of less than one week. The 3rd Fleet area had been denuded of most of its transport ships so Admiral Nimitz could have them for his central Pacific offensive. Wilkinson would have to get creative. General Vandegrift had his troops train and practice as much as possible.

That creativity would be shown in something of a postscript to that seizure of the Treasury Islands. As already described, Admiral Fort's amphibious force successfully landed the New Zealand 8th Brigade on the Treasuries, in the first Kiwi contested landing since Gallipoli.

And, also as already described, the invasion of the Treasuries turned out a lot better than Gallipoli. Most of the ships assigned to Admiral Fort raced back toward Guadalcanal to be under the protective umbrella of Allied fighters before any Japanese air strikes could reach them, but a part of Fort's force made a slight detour. With the destroyer *Conway* as escort, Commander Robert H. Wilkinson in the fast destroyer transport *Kilty* led the fellow fast destroyer transports *Ward*, *Crosby*, and *McKean* in splitting off from the convoy and going through the Gizo Strait to Juno River on Vella Lavella, where they arrived at 6:30pm. A large number of loaded boats were already off the beach and able to come alongside as soon as the transports stopped.[23]

Those boats were carrying 725 men of the 2nd Marine Parachute Battalion, 1st Marine Parachute Regiment, with their commander, "the diminutive and pugnacious" Lieutenant Colonel Victor H. "Brute" Krulak, as well as Sub-Lieutenant C. W. Seton of the Royal Australian Navy, who served as a coastwatcher on Choiseul. They were about to start Operation "Blissful." When they were all loaded aboard the destroyer transports, at 7:21pm, the versatile former four-pipers fell in column behind the *Conway* and crossed The Slot with all the ease of crossing a street, at least if there are no cars. After they crossed, they slowed down and turned toward the west of Zinoa Island, off Choiseul, though the charts of the area were so inaccurate that they had trouble finding Zinoa at first.[24]

And things started getting more interesting. At 11:10pm an explosion was heard coming from the port quarter of the rear transport, *McKean*.[25] A few minutes later a plane was heard overhead, though it was not otherwise detected visually or on radar. The Marine paratroopers on the transport thought the ship was firing her guns. "What are they shooting at?" one of them asked.

"My boy," answered one of the battalion's officers, "you have just been bombed."[26]

At 11:22pm, the transports stopped some 2,400 yards off the village of Voza, behind Zinoa on the southwest coast of Choiseul. Some 25 minutes later, a scouting party under Lieutenant Rea E. Duncan left the *Ward* and made its way to shore to meet some 80 Melanesian locals recruited by Sub-Lieutenant Seton. As that took place, the *Conway* stood off about 3,000 yards to seaward. The first wave of boats started heading to shore at 12:19am on October 28. With the help of the Melanesians, the paramarines and most of their supplies were landed by 1:20am.[27]

While the transports were getting ready to leave, at 1:45am a Japanese Jake floatplane flew over the *Conway* at an altitude of about 200 feet and dropped two bombs which exploded off the port quarter. A night fighter had been assigned to guard this little flotilla, but it never saw the Jake, who did not continue its attack and disappeared about ten minutes later. Clearly, the Japanese had found the Americans off Choiseul.[28]

But that was okay with the Americans. The objective of *Blissful* was to make the Japanese believe the Allies were trying to seize Choiseul as a prelude to an attack on the south or east coast of Bougainville or the Shortlands. Simply put, Lieutenant Colonel Krulak and his paramarines were to cause as much trouble and make as much noise as possible in order to make their force appear much larger than it actually was. General Vandegrift specifically instructed Krulak, "Make sure they think the invasion has commenced."[29]

That was fine with "Brute" Krulak. He set out to deal with a problematic Japanese barge base at Sangigai, some eight miles from Voza. His attack got off to a bad start on October 30 when TBF Avengers, intended to support his attack, mistakenly attacked and disabled some of the boats he was planning to use for it. On the fly, Krulak changed his plan and would now attack Sangigai from the west with one company under Captain Robert R. Manchester and the east with another company under Captain Spencer H. Pratt. Upon meeting Manchester's men, the Japanese proceeded to abandon the village and base. Manchester's company occupied Sangigai and its base without opposition. This war thing was getting easy – until Pratt's men, still moving through the jungle to get at Sangigai from the east, found that the Japanese who had abandoned the base were now facing them in prepared defensive positions. A nasty engagement followed at around 2:30pm on October 30 and lasted almost an hour. The paramarines were outmanned, but the Japanese were outgunned. "The outcome appeared to be in question," Lieutenant Colonel Krulak later wrote, "until the Japs destroyed their chances by an uncoordinated banzai charge which was badly cut up by our machine guns. Seventy-two Japs were killed an[d] an undetermined number wounded. Marine losses were 6 killed, 1 missing and 12 wounded." Among the wounded were Krulak, who was hit in his face and arm by shrapnel, and Captain Pratt. About 40 Japanese survivors managed to escape and were seen running southward "in most non-Samurai fashion."[30]

This small action was a big success because Captain Manchester's company had captured that annoying barge base. Using demolition charges, the paramarines destroyed everything that could conceivably ever be used by the Japanese, including administrative buildings, a field hospital, bunkers, and all the supplies (about 180 tons). They even found a relatively new barge, which was immediately sunk. Even better from the Allied standpoint and worse from the Japanese standpoint, before the administrative buildings were destroyed, Sergeant Vernon Hammons found a large cache of secret documents, maps, and charts. Once again, before abandoning a base, the Japanese had not secured their secret materials, simply because they could not conceive of retreating – did not technically even have a word for "retreating" – and so did not know how to handle such materials.[31]

One of these charts caught Lieutenant Colonel Krulak's eye:

The one that fascinated me was a chart that portrayed the minefields around southern Bougainville. When I reported this, the night after the Sangigai attack, I saw my first flash message. I had never seen one before. It came back and said, "Transmit at once the coordinates of the limits of the minefields and all channels as shown going through it." So we laboriously encoded the critical locations and sent them off. To an armada going into that area this is not incidental information. This is necessary information. Halsey in true Halsey fashion was not satisfied to know where the minefields were; he, before the Torokina landings, sent in a minelayer there and dropped mines in the entrance ways to those channels and they got two Japanese ships.[32]

So important were these documents that included a chart of the local barge routes that when a Dumbo rescue PBY Catalina pulled up near the Voza beachhead to drop off supplies and evacuate wounded, the documents were also loaded aboard to be taken straight to Admiral Halsey.[33]

Though there would be other attacks on Choiseul by the 2nd Marine Parachute Battalion, the Sangigai raid was the big highlight and the big achievement because of both destroying a base for those annoying barges and capturing the trove of secret documents. The Japanese on Choiseul did manage to get themselves organized for a counterattack. Some 800–1,000 Japanese troops reportedly reoccupied the Sangigai area, which was being turned into a marshaling area for troops coming from further east on the island. General Vandegrift ordered Lieutenant Colonel Krulak to beat a brave retreat. Leaving their food behind for the locals who had helped them so much, the paramarines took 12 minutes to board three infantry landing craft in the early hours of November 4 and moseyed away, arriving at Vella Lavella at 7:30 that morning. The raid cost 11 Marines dead, 14 wounded; 143 Japanese were estimated to have been killed.[34]

The response of General Hyakutake, General Inamura, and Admiral Kusaka is not recorded. Whether the raid actually accomplished its mission of convincing the Japanese that the imminent Bougainville landing would take place in the east or south of the island is debatable. Hyakutake had predicted a landing of some sort on Choiseul in preparation for a landing on southern Bougainville, so a Choiseul landing was already baked into the proverbial Japanese cake. What is clear, however, is that no forces were moved out, which was part of the purpose of the exercise. Hyakutake believed the invasion would be in southern Bougainville or the Shortlands in late November, and the Choiseul raid did nothing to disavow him of that belief.[35]

While the Choiseul raid was going on, Allied intelligence was furiously trying to get information on the area around Empress Augusta Bay area. Not just the enemy forces located there – the coastwatchers' reports of a "completely undefended" area were mostly accurate, albeit not totally – but the bay itself. An aerial photographic survey revealed the coast line to be eight to ten miles out of positions indicated by Hydrographic Office charts, which were known to be only approximations. The southwest coast of Bougainville is somewhat like the southern coast of New Georgia in that it is fronted with islets and reefs, though some of the reefs off Bougainville were as much as 17 miles off shore. The submarine *Guardfish* was sent in to check the place out and found two uncharted shoals less than four fathoms deep.[36]

Eleven landing beach sites had been selected, which began at Torokina Point, the northern end of Empress Augusta Bay, and extended approximately 3½ miles up the coast to the northwest, with a twelfth beach on the eastern shore of Puruata Island, northwest of Torokina Island and Cape Torokina. By comparison, the *Watchtower* landing on Guadalcanal had only two. A dozen landing beaches meant the maximization of combat power being landed and the rapid unloading of supplies. "The landing plan," Marine historian David Fuquea opined, "was a work of art that only staffs such as Halsey's and Vandegrift's, with a major amphibious assault behind them, could have conceived and successfully executed."[37]

But there was a catch: "There remained the question as to the exact geographical location of Cape Torokina, upon which the approach was to be made." And that was by no means the worst: an aerial survey showed not just the coast, but the entirety of Bougainville Island to be eight to ten miles northeast of its charted position.[38] Oh, well. Details. Only the entire *Cherryblossom* landing force was to go there. They would find it eventually. Or they would land in the wrong place. But when has that ever happened?

It was with this air of complete confidence in the preparations that everyone moved into position for *Cherryblossom*. Admiral Halsey moved the headquarters of the South Pacific Area, 3rd Fleet to a place called "Camp Crocodile" on Guadalcanal.[39] There he met with Admiral Wilkinson and General Vandegrift one last time. Meanwhile, Wilkinson's transport groups left their widely scattered ports. Leaving Efate late in the afternoon of October 28 was Transport Division Baker under Captain George B. Ashe, with the "attack transports" *American Legion*, *Fuller*, *Crescent City*, and *Hunter Liggett*, all veterans of the *Watchtower* landings on Guadalcanal and the *Toenails* landings on New Georgia. They were carrying 6,103 men of the reinforced 9th Marine Regiment. The transports were joined by destroyers *Fullam*, *Bennett*, *Guest*, *Hudson*, and *Conway*. They headed for a point 20 miles south of San Cristobal, where, just before dark on October 30, they were joined by Transport Division Charlie, who had left Guadalcanal that morning. Transport Division Charlie was commanded by Captain Henry E. Thornhill with the "attack cargo ships" *Alchiba* and *Titania* and just plain cargo ships *Alhena* and *Libra*. All four were veterans of the New Georgia landings; *Alhena* and *Libra* also veterans of the Guadalcanal landing. These cargo ships (attack and otherwise) were carrying 1,400 men of the reinforced 3rd Marine Defense Battalion along with their antiaircraft guns and other heavy equipment. Joining them was the tug *Sioux* – just in case – and a group of minesweepers under Commander Wayne R. Loud with his command ship *Hopkins*, and the *Hovey*, *Dorsey*, and *Southard*.[40]

Also leaving the New Hebrides late in the afternoon of October 28, albeit leaving Espiritu Santo, not Efate, was Transport Division Able under Captain Anton B. Anderson.

Able consisted of the transports *President Jackson, President Adams, President Hayes,* and *George Clymer*; all four veterans of the New Georgia landings, and all except *George Clymer* had been through the Guadalcanal landings. The transports, who were carrying 6,421 men of the 3rd Marine Regiment, picked up escorting destroyers *Anthony, Wadsworth, Terry, Braine, Sigourney,* and *Renshaw.* The transports arrived off Guadalcanal on October 30, where Admiral Wilkinson and General Vandegrift embarked on the *George Clymer.* The group left that night, and joined up with its groupmates at 7:40 the next morning at the rendezvous point south of San Cristobal.[41]

At that point, Commodore Lawrence F. Reifsnider – the rank of commodore was no longer just an informal title for non-admirals commanding more than one ship, but an actual rank re-established the previous April by Admiral King – took tactical command of the combined groups from his flagship *Hunter Liggett*. And all headed off – toward Shortland.[42]

Meanwhile, Admiral Merrill's cruiser force was moving as well. Merrill's ships had left Purvis Bay at 2:30am on October 31 for the run of 537 miles to Buka and their errand of malice to keep several of the Japanese air bases around Bougainville suppressed. They went well south of The Slot, south of the Russell Islands and New Georgia Islands and west of the Treasury Islands, and then looped to strike Buka from the north. The hope was to surprise the Japanese defenders at Buka and Bonis and catch aircraft on the ground. Strict radio silence was ordered, and a night fighter was assigned to prevent Japanese scouts from finding the task force.[43]

The effort to conceal Admiral Merrill's ships failed, as they were sighted during the afternoon. Inclement weather limited the effectiveness of the night fighter. Another bogey was detected just before 7:00pm who closed within five miles just after 7:00pm and acted as if it had found them and reported them to Buka. Merrill suspected the Japanese now knew his target. Whether they did or not, the bombardment of Buka and Bonis took place as described earlier, but the Japanese reported no aircraft destroyed. Merrill then sped southeast to bombard the Shortlands, as described earlier.[44]

While that was going on, Admiral Wilkinson's invasion force had kept heading for the Shortlands until after dark on October 31, at which time it turned northwest underneath a protective cover of specialized night fighters. Six Type 1 land attack planes of the 702 Air Group had been sent up from Vunakanau to poke around the Munda area in the hope of finding enemy ships. But overcast skies helped prevent them from finding any shipping targets, so they bombed land targets like Munda, mostly ineffectually. Mostly. Ten other G4Ms were sent up from the 751 Air Group. Four reported bombing a ship or two but could not confirm the results. What is known is *someone* ran into the US Navy's first night fighter squadron, Night Fighting 75, under the command of Lieutenant Commander William J. "Gus" Widhelm, famous as a dive bomber pilot at Santa Cruz. Lieutenant Hugh D. "Danny" O'Neill had taken off from Munda in a radar-equipped F4U Corsair and, in a "ground-controlled interception" directed by Major Thomas E. Hicks and Technical Sergeant Gleason of Marine Night Fighting 531 on Vella Lavella, scored the first kill by a radar-equipped night fighter of the Pacific Fleet by shooting down a Betty at

11:00pm. Exactly whose Betty is uncertain. The G4M piloted by the 702's Flying Chief Petty Officer Yoshimoto Yoshiaki was listed in Japanese records as "lost to weather," but he may have been the victim. The G4M commanded by the 751's Warrant Officer Shinohara Juzo also failed to return and may have been the target.[45]

That was not quite the end of the 702's mission, however. Unable to find maritime targets, two other G4Ms made a slight detour to bomb Barakoma on the way back to base. One of these land attack planes, that of Flying Petty Officer 2nd Class O'otaki Isuro, managed to drop six 60kg (132lb) bombs near the airfield. Little damage was done, but it did delay the efforts of ground crews to clear the runway of wreckage from the fatal crash of the Marine Fighting 212 Corsair of Lieutenant George W. Grill, Jr, which, while still on the runway trying to take off, went out of control for reasons unknown and crashed into a parked Ventura night fighter of Marine Night Fighting 531, who had started night patrols over Cape Torokina, and exploded. This was hardly the only tragedy facing the Barakoma air base. A Marine Fighting Corsair flown by 2nd Lieutenant Robert L. Keister lost power just after takeoff and had to ditch. Keister was never seen again. A similar accident happened to Lieutenant Edwin McCaleb of Marine Fighting 211 as he took off from Ondonga, but fortunately he was rescued.[46] Once again, in war, combat is hardly the only thing that can kill you.

Blissfully oblivious to this drama, the invasion convoy continued onward. At 4:32am on November 1, they changed course to 45 degrees True – northeast – to make a beeline for Cape Torokina. A half hour later, all ships went to battle stations. The destroyer *Wadsworth* was the tip of this particular spear, using her radar to pinpoint places like that slippery Cape Torokina. Behind the *Wadsworth* were the minesweepers, who were themselves leading the rest of the transport force for obvious reasons. At 5:47am, when the range to Cape Torokina was 7,900 yards, the *Wadsworth* opened fire with her forward guns. And the long-awaited invasion of Bougainville was on.[47]

The *Wadsworth* kept firing with her forward guns until just after 6:00am, when the range had closed to 3,000 yards and Cape Torokina was within the firing arcs of all five of her guns, at which time she used all five of her guns. One building was destroyed. Joining the *Wadsworth* in bombarding separate zones were the *Anthony*, *Terry*, and *Sigourney*.[48]

The *Anthony*, well to the seaward of the other destroyers, drew the interesting assignment of hitting Puruata Island, northwest of Cape Torokina. For more than an hour, the *Anthony* shelled the island with her 5-inch guns in two-gun salvoes. The gunfire was indirect, controlled from the firing plot, and spotted by aircraft.[49] Air superiority has its privileges. After that hour, the *Anthony* shifted her gunfire to the landing beaches.[50]

The *Sigourney* weaved her gunfire in her assigned areas successfully, but the *Wadsworth* and *Terry* drew the even more interesting assignment of bombarding the northwest side of Cape Torokina. The Japanese had created a small defensive network there that would have to be dealt with. It was understood that the two destroyers would have a difficult time making a dent in those defenses under even the best of circumstances, and with their firing options limited because of the activities of the transports and landing craft, these were far from the best of circumstances. The efforts of the *Wadsworth* and *Terry* largely failed, through no fault of their own. It was an expected failure, but it still meant the 1st Battalion of the 3rd Marine Regiment, who were on board the *President Adams* and who drew the assignment to attack this particular patch of ground, would have to face these defenses.[51]

Admiral Wilkinson was a thorough, detail-oriented commander who wanted to limit variables as much as possible. This was the reason why he chose to land just after dawn, which was at 6:14am. With little confidence in their nautical charts, Wilkinson wanted there to be enough light to see, for instance, where Cape Torokina was, and where Bougainville was, the issues related to which had kept Commodore Reifsnider up at night. The minesweepers went ahead, found no mines, and determined the water was deep enough for the transports. Which was fortunate for the Americans. When the skipper of one of the transports asked his navigation officer for the ship's position, the officer referred to the chart and answered, "About three miles inland, sir!"[52]

With that little hiccup, the transports began to enter the landing area about 5:45am, with veteran Commodore Reifsnider's just-as-veteran *Hunter Liggett* in the lead. Upon reaching a point about 3,000 yards off Cape Torokina, each transport executed a 100-degree turn to port, which put them on a course heading north northwest paralleling the coast, and shelled the cape with their 3-inch guns. As they passed Puruata Island, they swept her with 20mm cannon fire. These transports may have been fat and slow like transports tend to be, but they were far from defenseless. Their shooting on this occasion was completely ineffective, but that was not the point. Giving the crews a chance to shoot at the Japanese was the point. The crews cheered when they got the word. Morison called it "good clean fun that boosted morale no end." Although, as usual, it's good clean fun only until someone loses an eye. The term "attack transport" is ridiculous, but on this day all the transports tried to be attack transports, especially the *Hunter Liggett*, who was actually designated an attack transport ("APA").[53]

At 6:37am, Admiral Wilkinson announced that H-Hour would be 7:30. Eight minutes later, all the transports were anchored in a line about 3,000 yards from the beach, the attack cargo ships were in a parallel line some 500 yards to seaward of the transports. The signal came: "Land the landing force."[54]

Over the sides of the transports and into the landing craft went the US Marines – an unusually large number of US Marines. Counting a bit on surprise, Generals Vandegrift and Turnage expected slight resistance at the beach, so they planned on taking advantage by landing 7,500 Marines in the very first wave of boats. That way, unloading of supplies would be faster. The first heavy resistance, they expected, would come from air attacks. They wanted the supplies offloaded and the ships away as soon as possible. Admiral Wilkinson took precautions of his own, combat loading (another tough lesson learned) the transports and cargo ships below capacity; one half capacity for the transports, one quarter for the cargo ships. The hope – wish, really – was that they could be emptied in four to five hours. This was not *Watchtower*, not Guadalcanal, not makee learnee. Now it was makee doee. They had learned tough lessons on Guadalcanal and New Georgia. They were putting those lessons to work.[55]

One of those tough lessons, one that Admiral Wilkinson took to heart, was that the Japanese would launch an air attack. And while the air bases in the Bougainville sector had literally been rendered useless, the air bases around Rabaul, though they had been hit hard, were still functional. Evidently, unlike the Treasury Islands, the Japanese at Cape Torokina and around Empress Augusta Bay got off a warning message, because it was 7:18am – before the Marines had even stepped onto the beaches of Bougainville, even before the last landing boats had left the transports – that radar showed a large group of unidentified aircraft at bearing 305 degrees True – roughly northwest – at a distance of 50 miles. Admiral Kusaka and Base Air Force had been ready for this, or at least as ready as they could be, and had sent up 44 Zeros (24 from the 201 and 20 from the 204 air groups); eight Aichi D3A carrier bombers from the 582 Air Group; and one Yokosuka D4Y carrier bomber from the recently recalled 501 Air Group, all under the direction of the 204's Lieutenant (jg) Fukuda Sumio.[56]

The landing boats were still in the water headed for the beach when the transports and cargo ships were ordered to get under way, come to course 210 degrees by emergency turn, and move out into open water to gain maneuvering room in preparation for the air attack. The bombardment by the destroyers ceased at 7:21am, and the destroyers were ordered to move out to screen the transports. The softening up of the invasion beaches continued, however, with 31 Marine TBF Avengers from Marine Torpedo Bombing 143, 232, and 233 and Marine Scout Bombing 144 operating out of Munda who bombed and strafed the invasion beaches for five minutes. The Avengers were followed by seven SBD Dauntlesses from the Navy's Composite 38 who dropped smoke bombs to help conceal the invaders. Even so, the softening up operations did not leave the beaches that soft. According to the history of the 3rd Marine Division, "It was one of the first occasions in the Pacific where the amphibious assault troops encountered an occupied and organized immediate beach defense practically untouched by preliminary bombardment."[57]

While knowledge of this fact might have given the Marines pause, the knowledge of the imminent Japanese air attack may have done the opposite, because the 2nd Battalion, 3rd Marine Regiment from the *President Jackson* started hitting the beaches at 7:26am, four minutes early. The rest of the Marines landed in short order, and within about five minutes signals started coming from the invasion beaches that the landing was successful.[58]

Admiral Wilkinson would have to multitask, running the invasion while preparing for the air attack. Once again, the Japanese response had been completely expected. General Twining had committed to keeping 32 fighters over the invasion fleet and landing zone from dawn to dusk, and AirSols lived up to that commitment. According to the Japanese, their air strike first made contact with the defending Allied fighters at 8:05am (6:05am Japan Standard Time). That first contact was with eight P-40s of the Royal New Zealand Air Force's No. 18 Squadron flying out of Ondonga under Flight Lieutenant Robert H. Balfour some 16,000 feet over Cape Torokina. They had actually been watching the landing itself when they were vectored out by the destroyer *Conway*, carrying the fighter director team led by Lieutenant Reginald F. Dupuy, who was doing a good job. According to the Kiwis, the Japanese "were flying in three Vs in good formation and their steady direction suggested that they were not interested in, and possibly were not aware of, the landing in Empress Augusta Bay." The Kittyhawks swooped in and surprised the escorting Zeros, claiming to have shot down seven with no loss, though the P-40 flown by Flying Officer K. D. Lumsden was chased by two Zeros, damaged by antiaircraft fire and a US Marine Corsair, and forced to ditch. Above the Kiwis at 23,000 feet were 16 P-38s of the 339th Fighter Squadron led by Lieutenant Colonel John McGinn of the headquarters of the 347th Fighter Group, the 339th's parent unit. After the Kiwis were done, eight of the 339th's swooped in to take their place, later claiming to have shot down another seven with no loss. Lumsden would be rescued by an American barge, but only after nearly being machine-gunned by the crew, who mistook his red and white rescue flag as a Japanese one. This friendly-fire incident, combined with earlier incidents experienced by Kiwi Kittyhawks, convinced the Royal New Zealand Air Force to change its roundel insignia by adding horizontal white bars to each side of the blue and white disks.[59]

It was Base Air Force's bad luck to have arrived shortly after the Marine and Navy bombers had attacked the landing beach, because those bombers had their own escorts, many of whom hung around to join in cutting up the Japanese air strike. Eight Corsairs from the US Navy's Fighting 17 joined in, claiming to have shot down five Zeros. Marine Fighting 215 may have chimed in as well.[60] It was not enough, however, as the Japanese dive bombers got through to make their attacks.

Just not very well. A number of bombs were reportedly dropped in the transport area without causing harm, but several dive bombers glided out of the sun taking aim at the *Sigourney* and *Wadsworth*. The first bombs fell near the *Sigourney*, but it was the *Wadsworth* who seems to have drawn most of their attention. One bomb splashed 25 yards off the starboard quarter; five more landed from 100 to 500 yards away, causing no damage. Then one detonated 25 feet from frame 208 on the *Wadsworth*'s port side. The destroyer was sprayed with shrapnel that killed two, wounded five seriously, and caused light damage to the ship. Hull and superstructure were sprayed with fragments which caused minor damage. The Zeros strafed the beaches to little effect and then headed back to Rabaul. The *Wadsworth* claimed it shot down two bombers, while the *Bennett* claimed one. Ultimately, none of the claims made by the Allied fighter squadrons were correct, but it was still a very expensive breakfast for Base Air Force: 11 Zeros (eight from the 201 Air Group and three from the 204) and three carrier bombers (all Aichi D3As from the 582 Air Group) did not return to Rabaul, while two more Zeros from the 201 Air Group crash-landed and three more (two from the 201 Air Group and one from the 204) returned but were so damaged as to be written off. The Japanese claimed two transports, one cruiser, one destroyer, with another cruiser or destroyer set afire, and two "large landing barges" heavily damaged; one Lightning was claimed shot down as well.[61]

This first attack was closely followed by a second. So closely, in fact, that in many American accounts they were apparently combined into one, but Japanese records treat this as a separate attack. This second strike took place only 50 minutes after the first, when

16 Zeros from the 204 Air Group (two more apparently turned back because of mechanical issues) came in to do … something. Some have called it a fighter sweep, but it was supposedly directed at "small craft" and the landing beach. Eight Corsairs, apparently from the US Navy's Fighting 17, seem to have stayed over from the first morning air battle and moved in to intercept in what became an inconclusive contest. Though the Japanese claimed six destroyers "set afire" – how one would set fire to destroyers using only 20mm cannons is an interesting, albeit rhetorical, question – and four small craft "seriously damaged," the attack was completely ineffective, damaged nothing, and accomplished nothing. Though, in fairness, it cost nothing; while six Zeros were damaged, none were shot down, despite American claims to have shot down five.[62]

Because of these two attacks, the transports were unable to return to the landing area and resume unloading until about 9:30am. It was now that everyone experienced why Empress Augusta Bay was not a good place to land, even without opposition. The surf on the beach was bad, but in places the beach was very narrow and had a 12-foot bank immediately back of the surf line. The landing boats could not ground properly. Admiral Halsey pronounced the beach and terrain conditions "worse than anything ever encountered before in the South Pacific."[63]

The 3rd Fleet commander's melodrama aside, the offloading in the northern part of the landing area was, according to one officer, "almost a disaster." A total of 86 boats from the entire transport group were broached and stranded during the landing operations. When the surf grew worse late in the morning, the *Crescent City*, *American Legion*, *Hunter Liggett*, *Alchiba*, and *Titania* were shifted to beaches to the southeast. It was during this time that the *American Legion* grounded on an uncharted shoal in 4½ fathoms of water. The ship remained on even keel, but some damage was done by pounding on the reef. The tugs *Sioux* and *Apache* went to her aid. Between the loss of the landing boats, the shifting to different beaches, and the grounding of the *American Legion*, the offloading was delayed significantly, and would take much more than the four to five hours for which Admiral Wilkinson had hoped.[64]

And that was with few if anyone shooting at the Marines. It was far worse on the American right at the southern end of the landing area, where more than a few Japanese were shooting at the Marines. It was expected – feared, but expected – that the Marines on the *President Adams* would have to land in the face of heavy Japanese fire from Cape Torokina and Puruata Island. That is why both locations were subject to their own specific bombardment. But it was also expected that the bombardment would be ineffective. And it was.

And the Japanese did not disappoint. Dug in were maybe 240 Japanese soldiers of the 2nd Company, 1st Battalion, and 30 from the Regimental Gun Company, all from the 23rd Infantry Regiment, all under the command of one Captain Ichikawa. One platoon held Puruata Island, the rest were on Cape Torokina, where the Japanese had built a mini-Gifu: 18 camouflaged pillboxes built with coconut logs, sandbags, and dirt; each pillbox with two machine guns; mutually supporting, arranged in depth, and with connecting trenches. The

Japanese had also positioned a 75mm gun in an open-ended log-and-sand bunker with a spectacular view of a few of the beaches at the southern end of the landing zone. They had held their fire through the destroyer bombardments and the AirSols bombing.

But when the landing craft approached the cape, the 75mm gun opened fire, joined in short order by the machine guns. Many of the boats were damaged or even sunk; the men of the 3rd Marine Regiment had to disembark under heavy fire and start fighting the instant they were on the beach. Some 60 percent of the Marines had to be committed to reducing the Cape Torokina position. The combat and the resulting lack of personnel forced the unloading of the *President Adams'* 520 tons of supplies to be moved to other beaches.[65]

Again, however, the Marines put to use the costly lessons of Guadalcanal and New Georgia. The pillboxes were reduced by three-man fire teams, one shooting a Browning Action Rifle at the firing ports, the others flanking the bunker and dropping grenades down ventilation shafts. The 75mm gun position was a more difficult problem, but that was handled by Sergeant Robert A. Owens of A Company. Under cover from four riflemen who tried to suppress the two bunkers guarding the 75mm gun, Owens rushed the gun position itself. He quickly lost his covering fire as the four Marines were shot, and Owens himself was wounded multiple times. But he was able to enter the gun position through the fire port; kill some of the gun crew, who had just loaded another shell into the gun; and drive the remainder through the rear door, where they were killed. Owens then died of his wounds; he was posthumously awarded the Medal of Honor.[66]

By 11:00am, Cape Torokina was cleared. Of the Japanese, only 68 officers and men had been able to escape the American attack. Of the US Marines, 78 men were killed and 104 wounded. For the Americans, it was a lower casualty count than might have been expected after Gifu, New Georgia, and Buna. For the Japanese, it was a creditable performance by 270 men against 3,166 US Marines.[67]

But the fact that the only serious ground combat was 270 Japanese and one 75mm artillery piece defending against 3,166 US Marines underscores the brilliance of Admiral Halsey's decision to land at Cape Torokina. Here Halsey was facing three Japanese armies: the biggest one at and around Buin in the south of Bougainville, but also sizable forces at Buka Passage in the north and Kieta in the east. So Halsey landed in the west, where there were estimated to be 2,500 Japanese. The first wave of US Marines alone would outnumber the Japanese three to one. But barely 10 percent of those 2,500 were anywhere near the landing area. The rest were at the southern end of Empress Augusta Bay.

Cherryblossom was second only to *Watchtower* in its boldness, and second to nothing in its creativity. Just a masterstroke, a masterstroke that ultimately saved American, Australian, Kiwi, Japanese, and Melanesian lives.

But that masterstroke was not yet complete. At 12:48pm came another warning that radar had detected a large group of unidentified aircraft coming from the northwest. Again, landing operations were halted so all the ships could get under way and position themselves for air defense. This time it was 42 Zeros (12 from the 201 Air Group, 16 from the 204, and 14 from the 253) escorting seven dive bombers (six Aichi D3As from the 582 Air Group, and, again, one Yokosuka D4Y from the 501). The attack was led by Lieutenant (jg) Umasawa Kanekichi of the 253 Air Group.[68]

Once again, the transports hauled anchor and moved out to gain maneuvering room. Except for the *American Legion*. She was still stuck on that reef. The destroyer *Bennett* was assigned to guard her. The other destroyers moved to screen the transports.[69]

The small number of strike aircraft – seven "carrier bombers," as the Japanese called dive bombers – compared with an escort of 42 fighters had become an ongoing problem and was testimony to the shape Base Air Force was in. But the Imperial Navy's "Sea Eagles" carried on and arrived over the landing area at 1:45pm. The dive bombers were sighted making their attacks, some against the beach, some in the transport area. The Japanese claimed 30 destroyers and small craft "completely destroyed." Maybe they hit barges already grounded on the beaches, as the invasion force suffered no hits and few casualties.[70]

The defenders this time were the Corsairs of Marine Fighting 215 and 221 and the US Navy's Fighting 17. Except Marine Fighting 221 could not find the Japanese, so it was up to Marine Fighting 215 and Fighting 17, who took part in what seem to have been two separate dogfights, one between Fighting 17 under Lieutenant Commander Roger Hedrick and the 253 Air Group that ended only after one Zero had been shot down, the other between Marine Fighting 215 and the 201 Air Group that transitioned to pursuit of the amalgamated Japanese fighter formation as it retreated toward Rabaul, shooting down three Zeros from the 253 Air Group. Four carrier bombers were hit as well, two seriously enough to apparently be written off. The Japanese claimed three Corsairs shot down, but the Americans suffered no combat losses, though Lieutenant Robert M. Hanson had to ditch after his Corsair lost power, but he was picked up by the *Sigourney* and returned to duty a few days later.[71]

That was Base Air Force's last attack of the day. And it was only early afternoon. Not only were the Allies successfully defending the Cape Torokina landing beaches, they were launching air strikes of their own. Not just with AirSols, though AirSols had indeed been busy launching its attacks while the invasion was going on. At around 7:00am, five Corsairs had strafed the Shortlands, with one being damaged by intense antiaircraft fire and forced to ditch, with the pilot rescued. At the same time, four B-25 gunships raked the floatplane base near Poporang and Faisi in the Shortlands as well. Later that morning around 10:00, 21 unescorted Liberators hit Kahili with more than 60 tons of bombs, escaping without loss or even damage despite "[i]ntense, heavy AA fire."[72]

But none of these could compare to a little incident that took place a little before 8:00am local time (9:00am Solomon Islands time) some 30 miles east of New Ireland's Cape St George. The Japanese were struggling to get a sharper image of exactly what they were facing. To help in that effort, they started sending out specialized reconnaissance missions and shifting their reconnaissance assets around. As part of the latter, on the morning of November 1, Commander Terai Kunizo of the 938 Air Group ordered Lieutenant (jg) Nishiyama Terukazu to lead a detachment of Aichi E13A Type 0 reconnaissance floatplanes from the Shortlands to Buka.[73] Captain I'ida Rinjuro of the 958 Air Group, which was normally focused on antisubmarine patrols, also sent some float planes to Buka, where they would operate under the operational command of the 938. The nighttime reconnaissance and bombing missions by the annoying float planes the Marines on Guadalcanal had dubbed "Louie the Louse" would be making a comeback.[74]

As part of the former, however, a lone Type 1 land attack plane from the 702 Air Group had taken off from Vunakanau on a mission to find Allied shipping. Vunakanau never heard from it again, logging the cause of its demise as "unclear." Turns out that as it reached 25,000 feet it had an unpleasant encounter with the Lightnings of Lieutenant Darrell Cramer and Captain Joseph Restifo, part of a patrol of eight Lightnings led by a Captain V. Harter of 339th Fighter Squadron, 347th Fighter Group on their way back from "a shipping prowl." The full seven-man crew of the G4M may not have even known they were under attack; radio operator Flyer 1st Class Miyawaki Harunobu could not even get off a distress call before Cramer and Restifo ganged up to send it plunging into the waters below. Nevertheless, this was a momentous event: it was the first victory of Allied fighters based in the Solomons over New Ireland or New Britain.[75]

Even so, a perhaps even bigger event – a naval air event – took place east of Bougainville. Someone had noticed that the Pacific Fleet's aircraft carriers had, well, maybe not been pulling as much weight in 1943 as they had in 1942. So in comes Admiral Frederick Sherman with Task Force 38 centered on the (oldest) fleet carrier (in the US Navy), *Saratoga*, and the new light carrier *Princeton*.[76] Their job was to stage yet another attack on Buka and Bonis.

While this may sound like same old-same old, especially after Admiral Merrill's cruisers had just finished bombarding those same targets, it was no such thing. The bases had to be not just knocked down, but held down. In this case it would be performed by two aircraft carriers who would be the first to venture within the range of Rabaul since March 1942 and the first ever to venture into range of both the Rabaul air complex and Kavieng.[77]

As strange as it may sound to those not used to military life, Admiral Sherman and his men were excited:

> We on the carriers had begun to think we would never get any action. All the previous assignments had gone to the shore-based air. Admiral Halsey had told me that he had to hold us for use against the Japanese fleet in case it came down from Truk to interfere with our Guadalcanal and New Georgia operations. We were now to have our opportunity.[78]

The men of the *Saratoga* in particular were looking forward to the mission. The carrier had spent most of the first year of the Pacific War in drydock after being torpedoed by submarines on two separate occasions. She had finally returned in November 1942, only to be delegated minor operations. The sailors of the Pacific Fleet had given the *Saratoga* nicknames like "the Reluctant Dragon" (a rather unoriginal insult normally directed at powerful warships who display a talent for missing battle, such as the light cruiser *Boise* during the Java Sea Campaign); "the *Sara Maru*" (another unoriginal nickname); "the Pond Lily"; even "the Model Housing Project."[79]

For that reason, according to Admiral Sherman, "With smiles on their faces, the alert young pilots took off from our carrier decks [...]" Or tried to. Weather at the launching point was "unfavorable," inasmuch as it was "without a breath of wind." Sure, aircraft carriers usually have catapults – though the *Saratoga* did not – but the preferred method for generating the lift for takeoff is to move at high speed and turn into the wind; the latter is complicated when there is no wind. Add to that the predawn darkness and things did not go quite as planned.[80]

The strike started taking off at 4:27am, with 18 Grumman F6F Hellcats (nine from *Saratoga*, nine from *Princeton*), 15 SBD Dauntlesses (all from the *Saratoga*), and 11 TBF Avengers (two from *Saratoga* and nine from *Princeton*). On takeoff, two Avengers (the heaviest carrier plane in US Navy service) and one Dauntless from the *Saratoga* plopped into the water, killing one aviation radioman; two Hellcats from the *Princeton* also ended up in the drink, both pilots rescued. With all that, the strike did not leave until almost 6:30am. For some, that was more than two hours after takeoff; for all, that was after dawn, which kind of defeated the purpose of the predawn takeoff.[81]

Admiral Wilkinson's transports were well into their landing when Admiral Sherman's airstrike reached Buka and Bonis from the northeast. The Avengers and Dauntlesses placed three 1,000lb bombs on Buka's runway and 72 100lb bombs on dispersal and supply areas. The Hellcats swooped down to 50 feet making strafing runs. One freighter was set afire by strafing as were two small vessels that moved to its aid. But strafing damage to Bonis was hidden by palm trees. There was heavy and light antiaircraft fire of medium intensity, inaccurate as to deflection (mostly trailing) and altitude.[82]

It was 9:30am when the *Saratoga* and *Princeton* launched a second attack, this with 14 Hellcats (six from *Saratoga*, eight from *Princeton*), 21 Dauntlesses (all from *Saratoga*), and 11 Avengers (two from *Saratoga* and nine from *Princeton*). Because this was in daylight, there were no launch casualties. Except for that, it was a virtual repeat of the first strike. There was even another freighter set afire, along with two small launches sent out to aid it. This time, three 2,000lb bombs landed on the Buka runway, and another 72 100lb bombs spread over supply and revetment areas. Their work for the day done, the *Saratoga*, the *Princeton*, and their escorts ran off toward Ontong Java Atoll to the east of Bougainville to hopefully avoid any retaliation.[83]

Not even close to being done were Admiral Wilkinson's men. It was 3:00pm before the transports were back in position to resume unloading. With the help of the *Sioux* and *Apache*, the *American Legion* was able to back clear of the reef after three hours of bouncing on it. Her grounding had delayed the unloading operations, well beyond Admiral Wilkinson's expectations, to the point where they could not be completed that day.

But the *American Legion* was not alone in that regard. The Japanese, as could be expected, were the biggest reason. The three air attacks, two of which required all ships to suspend unloading operations and remain under way for maneuvering; the third merely keeping them that way. There was also Japanese gunfire, both from the Cape Torokina fortifications and also from snipers. The Marines had solved that first issue and were in the process of solving the second, with a new auxiliary that was proving very effective: the 1st Marine Dog Platoon.[84]

But those 24 specially trained dogs (mostly Dobermans) could not help with the unloading, and while the Japanese had a hand in throwing off Admiral Wilkinson's carefully crafted plan, Empress Augusta Bay and those inaccurate nautical charts played a big role. The surf that wrecked 86 landing craft. The narrow beaches that created congestion among the landed troops and unloaded cargo.

Even so, by 5:30pm, those eight transports had been almost emptied. Despite the air attacks, the bad charts, the narrow beaches, the *American Legion* grounding, in eight hours' time some 14,000 men and 6,200 tons of supplies had been landed on Cape Torokina and the beaches north of it. Admiral Halsey called it a record performance "accomplished in a most brilliant manner."[85] The transports could be sent out of harm's way. So they had that going for them. Which was nice.

And that was the good news. The bad news was: four ships – transports *Hunter Liggett*, *American Legion*, and *Crescent City*; and the cargo ship *Alchiba* – had barely been touched. This was a problem. Because the sun was going down, and when the sun went down the invasion force would lose most of its air cover, which would leave it vulnerable to another Savo Island-style disaster with these slow, fat, juicy ships vulnerable to slaughter by the Japanese. The solution was to withdraw all eight transports and four cargo ships.

General Vandegrift was not happy at that prospect. He remembered all too well what had happened on Guadalcanal when the transports and cargo ships were pulled with most of the equipment for his 1st Marine Division still in their holds.[86]

However, unlike certain flag officers involved in the Guadalcanal landings, Admiral Wilkinson was not unreasonable. He told Vandegrift he would pull all the ships back, but the *Hunter Liggett*, *American Legion*, *Crescent City*, and *Alchiba* would come back to complete their unloading tomorrow morning.[87]

With that decided, Admiral Wilkinson and Commodore Reifsnider took their ships back toward Guadalcanal. Aboard one of them was General Vandegrift. General Allen H. Turnage was now in command on Bougainville from Cape Torokina. The 3rd Marine Division had seized a beachhead that ran north from Cape Torokina for more than four miles, but was very shallow going inland. They would start setting up a defense perimeter and sending out patrols.[88]

And those patrols would quickly discover that the terrain of Bougainville did not get easier inland. The beaches were bad enough. The sand was bad enough. It's coarse and rough and irritating and it gets everywhere. But these beaches were so narrow that one Marine described them as "like running across 30 feet of the Sahara and suddenly dropping off into the Everglades," the "Everglades" being a swamp that ran for two miles behind those narrow beaches. Turnage would later say, "Never had men in the Marine Corps had to fight and maintain themselves over such difficult terrain as was encountered on Bougainville."[89]

The Cape Torokina area was not a fun place for an amphibious landing, true, but that was why General Hyakutake had left it undefended: who would be crazy enough to land there? Admiral Halsey.

From the landward side, the Cape Torokina area comprised a natural defensive region of approximately eight by six miles. It was almost equidistant from enemy installations to the north of Buka and to the south in the Buin–Shortlands area. It was astride enemy communications from that Buin–Shortlands area to Rabaul. And, as Admiral Halsey later explained, Torokina "was so inaccessible from established Japanese positions on Bougainville that an estimated three months would be necessary for organizing a strong Japanese ground counter attack."[90] Inland of those narrow landing beaches was that swamp, about which the Americans had not known.[91] It should be emphasized that on an island covered by rain forest with only two seasons – wet and really wet – this area was considered a swamp.

Further inland was the big mountain range. There were only a few ways through or around that mountain range, and those few ways could be sealed off. The Japanese could go over that mountain range, but that is difficult in even the best circumstances. And these would not be the best circumstances. Because the mountain range was topped by an active stratovolcano. Not that an active stratovolcano has always been a bar per se to movement, but most do not try to move past or through an active volcano while it's actually smoking, as Bagana normally did and was doing now.[92]

Conversely, with those kinds of natural defenses, the Cape Torokina area would be not only easy to defend, but difficult to attack out of. The Americans would be pinned in the Empress Augusta Bay area by those swamps, mountains, and active stratovolcanoes. Yet that was part of the beauty of Admiral Halsey's plan: he did not plan to attack out of the beachhead the 3rd Marine Division had just seized. He just wanted enough land to build an air base. And the Seabees had demonstrated such skill and ingenuity everyone knew that if they found driftwood at sea, the Seabees could build an air base on it.

With the approval of General MacArthur, Admiral Halsey had shown more tactical ability on land than 90 percent of the generals in history, including pretty much everyone in the Imperial Japanese Army. He had outfoxed three Japanese armies and attacked where they weren't. He had seized a beachhead that would be extremely difficult to reduce. That beachhead would soon hold an air base that would bring Rabaul within range of AirSols fighters. And he had come close to cutting off all those Japanese troops in Buin and the Shortlands. Astride their communications and supply lines, the Americans could just sit and wait those three months for the Japanese to attack. The Japanese could not sit. They would have to attack. Under very unfavorable conditions at a place chosen by their enemy.

In a Pacific War that had started with atrophy, inertia, incompetence, and selfishness from many of America's army, naval, and air officers, the seizure of Cape Torokina was an act of breathtaking brilliance.

Before that breathtaking brilliance could take final form, however, there would be the night of November 1–2. It would not be a restful night for pretty much anyone in the US Navy in the South Pacific. Probably as a result of the chart of the Japanese minefields around southern Bougainville Lieutenant Colonel Krulak and his men had captured during the Choiseul raid, the destroyer *Eaton* escorted the destroyer minelayers *Tracy* and *Pruitt* as they laid a two-row minefield across at the eastern entrance to the Shortlands. Such a tiny force operating so close to Japanese bases and a Japanese minefield had to be nerve-wracking.[93]

The *Eaton*, *Tracy*, and *Pruitt* could take some comfort in that American nerves would be wracked all over the South Pacific. A repeat of the disastrous Battle of Savo Island was the fear, and Admiral Wilkinson was determined to avoid it.

Some 15 miles northwest of Torokina was Cape Moltke.[94] It was thought that in order to move against the invasion beaches, a Japanese naval force would have to come by Cape Moltke. Wilkinson used this hypothesis to better fortify against another Savo. The destroyer *Renshaw* and the destroyer minelayers *Breese*, *Gamble*, and *Sicard* proceeded up to Moltke. The *Renshaw* kept watch as the converted destroyers set about laying three rows of mines offshore.[95]

But this tiny little flotilla had to hurry, lay the mines, and get out of there fast. And they knew it. Their clock was ticking.

The Japanese were coming.

Extreme consternation, disbelief, even outrage.

These feelings – the usual Japanese reactions when the Americans did not act as the Japanese had thought they would and had planned accordingly – were on full display in the *Musashi* at Truk, in Rabaul, and in the Shortlands when word came of the Cape Torokina landings.

The Americans were supposed to attack Buin, the Shortlands, or Buka. Not Cape Torokina. General Hyakutake had prepared such a warm reception for the Americans at Buin and Buka, and Americans go to Cape Torokina instead? How inconsiderate. So much so that Hyakutake, ensconced at his headquarters on tiny Erventa Island near Tonolei Harbor, refused to believe it was the real landing. Demonstrating that same tactical acumen that had been so beneficial to the Japanese on Guadalcanal, he thought the landings were a feint to draw attention from the real intended landing spot: Buin.[96]

Elsewhere in parts of the Greater East Asia Co-prosperity Sphere that were neither in Asia nor prosperous, some Japanese were trying to respond with alacrity. While General Hyakutake was content to wait for the real landing near Buin to take place, his superior General Inamura was not. Inamura ordered Hyakutake to destroy the American forces that had landed at Cape Torokina. And to help in that effort, Inamura arranged with

Admiral Kusaka a counterlanding operation to be conducted at Cape Torokina. The Japanese did love their counterlanding operations. Well, they loved planning those counterlanding operations, sometimes even ordering those counterlanding operations. Not necessarily actually following through with those counterlanding operations, but, as they say, two out of three ain't bad. A counterattacking force was designated from the 2nd Battalion, 54th Infantry Regiment, and the 6th Company, 2nd Battalion, 53rd Infantry Regiment, both from the 17th Okayama Division, who had been waiting to be shipped to western New Britain. They would be transported on six destroyers – more so-called rat transportation – escorted by two heavy cruisers, two light cruisers, and six destroyers under Admiral Omori.[97]

Admiral Kusaka did make these arrangements, but he likely was not happy about it. For one thing, the invasion of Cape Torokina changed the context of the staging of the air crews of *Kido Butai* into Rabaul, due to be completed that same November 1 as part of *Ro-Go*. It required 173 aircraft to fly the 700 nautical miles due south from Truk to the Rabaul air base complex. The first were the fighters: 36 Zeros from the *Shokaku* under Lieutenant Sakami Ikuro; 27 Zeros from the *Zuikaku* under Lieutenant Notomi Kenjiro; and 19 from the *Zuiho* under Lieutenant Sato Tomeo. They arrived at 10:50am after a flight of almost five hours over nothing but open sea. They were followed by 40 Nakajima B5N Type 97 carrier attack planes and 45 Aichi D3A Type 99 carrier bombers. The aircraft dispersed themselves between Lakunai, Vunakanau, and Tobera. Also staging into Vunakanau were six Comet reconnaissance aircraft. Though they were from all three carriers, they would operate as one dedicated reconnaissance unit, led by the *Shokaku*'s Lieutenant Kimura Satoshi.[98]

While the Sea Eagles of *Kido Butai* were staging into Rabaul, the Sea Eagles of Base Air Force were striking back at the unwanted intruders on Bougainville as best they could. While they had attacked the Allied landing zone three times that day, Admiral Kusaka's staff prepared several night attacks as well. The results ranged from negligible to disastrous. After dark, six Type 99 carrier bombers from the 582 Air Group took off from Vunakanau and headed southeast toward Torokina. Two of the Aichis carried flares; they were to illuminate targets, which were to be enemy destroyers hanging out off Torokina, for the following Aichis armed with bombs. But one dive bomber turned back with mechanical problems, and fickle weather, featuring clouds, rain, and intermittent thunderstorms, ensured none of the remainder reached their target area. Four more became lost in the crushing wet gloom and were lucky to make it back to Vunakanau. The fifth, one of the lead bombers carrying flares, was never seen again.[99]

A second strike was being prepared at Buka by Lieutenant (jg) Suma Osamu of the 582 Air Group. This time, the mission was to find US Navy ships – preferably the carriers that had attacked Buka earlier that day – that the Japanese estimated were operating east of Buka. Suma would command this strike of nine Aichi Type 99 carrier bombers from the back seat of one of said bombers. He would end up doing a lot of backseat flying, because the same unfriendly weather that had ruined the earlier attack would ruin this one as well. Once again, one Aichi turned back with mechanical issues, and the remaining eight, flying into darkness, clouds, rain, and lightning, became scattered. Three disappeared in the boiling blackness, and only five returned to Buka.[100]

It would be a long night for Base Air Force. In more ways than one. In the wee hours of November 2, two G4M land attack planes paid a visit to Munda. Six Type 0 reconnaissance seaplanes attacked Mono in the Treasury Islands at various times throughout the night. They were more a nuisance than anything else.[101]

The objectives of *Ro-Go* seem to have been murky and very, very flexible. It had started out as a campaign to overwhelm Allied air power on New Guinea in order to destroy Allied shipping there, which would in turn buy time for Japan to strengthen her defenses in the Southeast Area. With the invasion of Bougainville, that objective changed to overwhelm Allied air power in the Solomons – in other words, AirSols – in order to destroy Allied shipping in the Bougainville area. But because the invasion of Bougainville included large numbers of Allied fighters to protect the invasion fleet and beaches, the *Ro-Go* aircraft would have to overwhelm Allied air power at its strongest point, which right now was over those Bougainville beaches with the last of the trained, veteran aviators of *Kido Butai*. With the last of the trained, veteran aviators who had attacked Pearl Harbor. While Kusaka needed aerial reinforcements and he knew it, he certainly understood the grave risks involved.

The reasons for Admiral Kusaka's mood went far deeper than a sense of foreboding for the additional fliers now under his command. Admiral Koga was "determin[ed] to make an attack employing the entire mobile strength of the Combined Fleet […]." To that end he put the entire 2nd Fleet – that is, the battle fleet – at Admiral Kusaka's disposal. Furthermore, he ordered the 2nd Base Air Force (the 12th Air Fleet) sent to Kusaka's Southeast Area, except for flying boats and those forces in the Kuriles. Finally, the *pièce de resistance*, he ordered the tankers *Kamikaze* and *Nissho Marus* to the area.[102]

This was a big deal. One Japanese history points out that, with those aircraft of *Kido Butai* already en route to the Rabaul area, "this action of the commander-in-chief put the entire mobile surface and air strength of the Combined Fleet under the command, either direct or delegated, of the commander of the Southeast Area Fleet." That is, Admiral Kusaka.[103]

As a general rule, battlefield commanders always want reinforcements and always welcome them. The Guadalcanal-Solomons Campaign, however, had seen more than its share of instances where reinforcements were not welcomed. Admiral Ghormley had sometimes acted against his receipt of reinforcements, probably because once he got them he would be expected to use them. Another instance occurred before the Battle of Tassafaronga, when Admiral Halsey at the last minute assigned two additional destroyers to Admiral Carleton Wright's surface force. The two destroyers had not worked with any of Wright's ships, had no idea of the battle plan, could not be informed of the battle plan in the limited time remaining before combat commenced, basically just had to wing it, and, by their own admission, added nothing of value to the task force.

Now would be another instance. With the subtlety that was, well, typical of the Imperial Japanese Navy leadership, one Japanese history said, "Southeast Area Fleet

Headquarters apparently experienced some difficulty in deriving maximum effectiveness from its suddenly increased strength." Admiral Kusaka had made "strong protests" to Combined Fleet "against the use of surface ships south of New Britain, which lay within the area dominated by the enemy's light planes." He was overruled by Admiral Koga, who was "convinced that this was the last opportunity to take advantage of the strategic situation in the Southeast area, was firmly determined to strike a decisive blow at the enemy's surface strength and acted accordingly."[104] Like all good Imperial Japanese admirals, Koga was always looking for opportunities to force the US Pacific Fleet into that one "Decisive Battle."

But while Admiral Koga certainly had Tsushima in his mind somewhere, he had in the front of his mind a more recent battle: Savo Island. It does seem as if the victory of Vice Admiral Mikawa Gunichi, then commander of the 8th Fleet, at the "First Battle of the Solomon Sea" – the Japanese name for what the Allies call the Battle of Savo Island – just after the Allied landings on Guadalcanal had spoiled the Imperial Japanese Navy the way that Admiral Togo's victory at Tsushima had. Because of the decisive battle and victory at Tsushima, Imperial Navy strategic theory depended on recreating such a "decisive battle" and winning it. To the exclusion of everything else. Because of Mikawa's victory at Savo Island, Combined Fleet's response to, it would seem, every new Allied invasion was to send out a force of surface ships to recreate that victory.

Admiral Mikawa had indeed scored a brilliant tactical victory at Savo Island; it was natural that the Japanese would want to repeat it. With the Americans streaming ashore at Guadalcanal and Base Air Force reporting hordes of Allied warships and even more Allied transports, Mikawa determined he would attack that night and sink the warships and then go after the undefended transports.

With that idea in mind, he had slapped together every warship he could get his hands on – the luxurious heavy cruiser *Chokai* that would serve as his flagship, the four heavy cruisers of the 6th Cruiser Division, two old light cruisers, and one old destroyer. Mikawa then led this force in a single column down the New Georgia Channel to Guadalcanal. He had swept counterclockwise around Savo Island, where he sank or mortally damaged four of the five Allied cruisers screening the invasion transports that night, while suffering negligible damage to his own ships.

Then Mikawa had decided he did not have enough time before daylight to attack the now-defenseless transports, so he rounded up his now-scattered ships and returned to Rabaul, leaving the now-defenseless transports alone. The Japanese did not want to repeat that part of the victory.

Oh, well. Details. Admiral Koga had tried to recreate the Savo Island success after the invasion of New Georgia by sending in Rear Admiral Akiyama Teruo with the 3rd Destroyer Flotilla for a Savo Island-style surprise attack on the Americans. It had resulted in a Savo Island-style surprise attack on the jungle. Which probably did surprise the Americans, so at least Koga had gotten it half right. Now Koga wanted to get his recreation of Savo Island all right, right after the invasion of Bougainville. His surface reinforcements would take some time to get to Rabaul. For now, the only forces available were those aforementioned ships under Admiral Omori's command.

Having just returned that morning from the ineffectual attempt to intercept Admiral Merrill's cruisers who had blasted Buka and Bonis, Admiral Omori was faced with orders to go out again to both guard the counterlanding force and attack the invasion transports off Cape Torokina. Omori held a briefing conference that Hara described as "short" for his senior officers in the *Myoko*'s gun room. "We have never teamed together before, and this can be a serious detriment in battle," Omori admitted. "But Admiral Mikawa managed without a previously trained team, and so can we. I have firm trust and faith in the skill of each of you commanding officers and in the ability of your men. I believe we shall win."[105] Well, OK, then.

Some of his senior officers were less certain. As the meeting broke up, Admiral Ijuin tapped Captain Hara's shoulder. "Hara," he said, "this will be a tough one. I shall be relying on you."

The commodore laughed. "Let's be prepared for a swim and take along plenty of shark repellent," Hara joked. But Ijuin wasn't laughing.

The baron mumbled glumly, "I do not like cruiser *Sendai*. She is now nine years old, and so sluggish." The *Sendai* was actually 19 years old, but who's counting?

Nonetheless, Captain Hara understood Admiral Ijuin's complaint was not necessarily about the *Sendai*'s age. He had not used this cruiser in months, although she was the designated flagship of his 3rd Destroyer Flotilla and, indeed, was a veteran cruiser who had been fighting the Pacific War since literally before the Pearl Harbor attack, when she led the landings at Kota Bharu. Though most flag officers prefer to sail in big warships – historically, size has very much mattered in these things – Ijuin preferred to sail in destroyers. He had even fought his engagements off Vella Lavella from destroyers, which were faster and more maneuverable than the *Sendai*, or any cruiser, really.

"But then *Sendai* is younger than your *Shigure*," the baron added. She was not – by 12 years – but, again, who's counting?[106] "I am uneasy about this operation, and hope that the ships from Truk will do a fine job. Their crews, though inexperienced, are young and fresh. They are not as tired as we are."

If anything, Admiral Ijuin understated his "uneas[iness] about this operation." He had asked Admiral Kusaka to scrub the mission.[107] It seems that both Kusaka and 8th Fleet head Admiral Samejima were not down with this mission, but Kusaka had his orders from above.[108]

The baron and the commodore walked in silence to the ramp to leave the *Myoko* where Admiral Ijuin offered his hand and said, "Brooding will do us no good, Hara. We must fight and fight desperately.

"Japan will topple if Bougainville falls."[109]

CHAPTER 3
MIRROR, MIRROR

The ancient Carthaginian general Hannibal, given the appellation "Barca" (Lightning) that had belonged to his father Hamilcar even though there were no surnames in Carthage, was one of the titans of the ancient world, winning victory after victory against Rome throughout the early years of the Second Punic War. Much of Hannibal's early success was attributable to one thing: the refusal of the Roman military establishment to learn from its mistakes. Rome continued to follow its doctrine of: 1. Find the enemy; 2. Attack the enemy; and 3. Defeat the enemy. And Hannibal repeatedly used that doctrine against the Romans in actions at Trebia River, Lake Trasimenus, and Cannae that were disastrous defeats for Rome.

While a few select Romans – most notably Quintus Fabius Maximus Verrucosus – developed new tactics to deal with Hannibal – this was how Fabius got his nickname "Cunctator" (Delayer) – only one Roman was able to see through the institutional and, indeed, the cultural arrogance to see the advantages in Hannibal's tactics and adapt them for Rome. This was Publius Cornelius Scipio.[*]

Publius Cornelius Scipio had personally watched his father, also named Publius Cornelius Scipio (Roman names were very repetitive and confusing), lose to Hannibal, then had not only survived but rallied Rome's surviving troops after the devastating defeat at Cannae. The younger Publius had not witnessed the deaths of his father and uncle in battle against Carthaginian-led troops in Spain, but he basically volunteered to go there to rally the Roman survivors there, who had been chased up to the sliver of Spain north of the Iberus (Ebro) River. He had learned Hannibal's tactics and his penchant for confounding the Romans by doing the unexpected. And Scipio used those same tactics against the Carthaginians.

[*]Publius Cornelius Scipio, later "Africanus" and still later "Africanus Major," was the son of Publius Cornelius Scipio, who was the son of Lucius Cornelius Scipio. Publius Cornelius Scipio had another son, named Lucius Cornelius Scipio, later "Asiaticus," brother to Publius Cornelius Scipio.

Scipio saw three Carthaginian armies, each of which was the equal of his own – at least – roaming around Spain suppressing the ever-present restlessness of the Celt-Iberian tribes. The only good news was that these armies were widely scattered, at least ten days' march from him. Their commanders were not on good terms with each other, which, considering two were brothers of Hannibal, says all you need to know about the Barcids, as Hannibal's family became known. They obviously no longer considered the Romans a threat. If Scipio tried to engage one of these armies, there was no guarantee he could defeat it before the other armies arrived to overwhelm him. What to do?

After a week of marching and sailing, Scipio and his Roman legionaries and his supporting fleet were nowhere near any of the Carthaginian-led armies, but instead were outside the walls of a port the Romans called "Carthago Nova" – New Carthage.* This was the logistical, economic, and political center of Barcid Spain, where Hannibal and his family stored their silver used to pay their (mostly) mercenary troops, the supplies used for supporting their troops in Spain, and the hostages used to keep the Spanish tribes in line. Scipio had decided he would not attack any of the Barcid armies but would instead go after this relatively undefended capital of Barcid Spain.

Within a matter of days, New Carthage and everything in it were in the hands of Scipio. It was an abject catastrophe for the Barcids and Carthage. As Hannibal had done, Scipio had refused to play by the rules, had refused to stick to the script, had flipped the field, had upended the table, to mix metaphors. This was a revolting development for Carthage. Literally. Many of the Spanish tribes who had supported the Barcids started switching sides. With one stroke, Scipio had threatened the Carthaginians' hold on Spain, their armies, and the Barcids' base of operations …

While both generals were much more creative than their contemporaries, nothing Hannibal did during the entire Second Punic War had nearly the effect of Scipio's seizure of New Carthage. New Carthage was the shatterpoint for the Barcids in Spain, and to a lesser extent overall. Ultimately, Scipio finally won the war for Rome by defeating Hannibal in battle outside Carthage in North Africa at a place called Zama, earning Scipio the cognomen "Africanus."

Most officers study military history, want to learn that history, want to avoid making the same mistakes made back in the day. In all likelihood, not too many of the US Marines who waded ashore near Cape Torokina in Empress Augusta Bay knew about Scipio and New Carthage. It's not clear how much even Admiral Halsey knew about it. Douglas MacArthur certainly knew about it. Knew the lessons from it, not that he always followed them. But in this case, both Halsey and MacArthur followed those lessons.

---

*To make communication with the mother city easier, Hamilcar's son-in-law, Hasdrubal, called "The Fair," founded a port city that he called in the Phoenician language "QRT-HDST," which was, confusingly, the name of the mother city as well. "Qrt-hdst" is usually rendered phonetically as "Kart-Hadasht," which was Latinized as "Carthago" and Westernized as "Carthage." "Qrt-hdst" – Carthage – means "New City." Therefore, "New Carthage" would be "New New City."

Most officers also work to learn the enemy's tactics, in order to counter them. The US Navy had tried to determine the secrets of Japanese success during the Guadalcanal–Solomons Campaign. Tried to counter those secrets. With varying degrees of success.

Very few officers, however, work to learn not just the enemy's tactics, but how to use those tactics against the enemy. No matter which military or which service, there is a strong institutional, sometimes even a cultural, bias against using tactics pioneered by the enemy. It's a tacit admission that the enemy was right and you were wrong. Losing a lot of battles catastrophically tends to reduce these biases, but not always. It took Rome a long time to even be able to counter Hannibal's tactics.

One of those rare officers who was willing to not just learn enemy tactics, but use those same tactics against the enemy was Publius Cornelius Scipio Africanus.

Two more were Aaron Merrill and Arleigh Burke.

The Imperial Japanese Navy's Combined Fleet had a unit the Japanese called *Sentai 5*. "Sentai" means "squadron," so the literal translation of the unit's designation is "Squadron 5" or "5th Squadron."

That's not real descriptive, however. Is it a fighter squadron? A cavalry squadron? A battleship squadron? That last one is the most problematic because the Imperial Japanese Navy tended to use the word "sentai" to describe a squadron of battleships or cruisers, but a *sentai* generally did not contain both. So, most English-language histories of the Pacific War dispense with the literal translation, instead adding a descriptive word and maybe changing it for clarity. In these histories, it is usually called the "5th Cruiser Squadron" or the "5th Cruiser Division."

As the Pacific War approached, the Imperial Japanese Navy tended to put all the ships of the same class into one *sentai*. For instance, all of the *Takao*-class cruisers were put into *Sentai 4* – the 4th Cruiser Division; all of the *Furutaka*-class cruisers (technically the *Furutaka* and *Aoba* classes, the latter class being merely modified versions of the former) were put into *Sentai 6* – the 6th Cruiser Division; all of the *Mogami*-class cruisers were put into *Sentai 7* – the 7th Cruiser Division; all of the *Tone*-class heavy cruiser/seaplane carrier things were put into *Sentai 8* – the 8th Cruiser Division. *Sentai 5* – the 5th Cruiser Division – had the cruisers of the *Myoko* class: *Myoko*, *Ashigara*, *Nachi*, and *Haguro*.

But then life happened, or, in the case of war, death happened. The *Ashigara* was split off from her cruiser division so she could be a fleet flagship. The same thing happened to the *Chokai* with regularity; her exceedingly large bridge with a veritable greenhouse of glass windows was luxurious by warship standards, and, though a bit top heavy, safe enough so long as no one was shooting at you. The *Atago* was often designated as a fleet flagship as well, but she was able to keep her sister ship *Takao* with her. Of the 6th Cruiser Division, all were now sunk except the *Aoba*, who was under repair in a shipyard – again.

A similar fate had befallen the *Mogami*. She was severely damaged during the episode at the end of the Battle of Midway that saw her sister ship *Mikuma* sunk. *Mogami* spent a year in a shipyard being converted into a heavy cruiser/seaplane carrier thing like the *Tone*s, which were themselves reassigned to the 7th Cruiser Division as replacements for the *Mikuma* and *Mogami*.

The beginning of the Pacific War saw a 5th Cruiser Division with cruisers *Myoko*, *Haguro*, and *Nachi*. Its commander was Rear Admiral Takagi Takeo, who made the *Myoko* his flagship. Until early January 1942, when a bomb from a B-17 hit the *Myoko*. She had to go back to Japan for repairs, and Takagi shifted his flag to the *Nachi*.

That was basically where things stood until February 27, 1942. Admiral Takagi had the assignment of guarding the incredibly large Eastern Invasion Convoy headed for the northern coast of Java. Assigned to help him were two flotillas of destroyers: the 2nd under Rear Admiral Tanaka Raizo and the 4th under Rear Admiral Nishimura Shoji. Each flotilla consisted of a light cruiser serving as flagship, the *Jintsu* for the 2nd and the *Naka* for the 4th, for a flock of destroyers, eight in the 2nd, six in the 4th.

Except for the attack that scored the lucky bomb hit on the *Myoko*, the 5th Cruiser Division had seen almost no combat. It had escorted convoys to their invasion targets, but little else. Admiral Takagi thought today would be no different.

Takagi Takeo was, as described by historian Arthur Marder, "A stout, broad-shouldered, round-faced officer, friendly, down to earth, easy to work with, and morally courageous. He was a brilliant torpedo specialist and submariner, but not a naval tactician. Neither was he a leader – a commanding officer prepared to take the initiative."[1] Hara Tameichi, who was skipper of the destroyer *Amatsukaze* as part of the 2nd Destroyer Flotilla, would paint a very different picture of the admiral's personality – arrogant, overconfident, sloppy.

The 2nd and 4th Destroyer Flotillas were assigned to directly shepherd the invasion convoy to Java, the 2nd positioned in front, the 4th positioned just behind it. Admiral Takagi hung back some 200 miles behind the convoy he was supposed to be protecting, thinking he would not have to escort the convoy at all. A force of enemy cruisers and destroyers his floatplanes had been keeping under surveillance had been of concern to him as it headed in his general direction, but when those floatplanes reported the force had turned around and headed back toward Soerabaja, Takagi laughed. The enemy ships were just avoiding the daily Japanese air attacks on Soerabaja, he said, and were in no shape to fight. The Japanese ships would stick to their schedule. Then his floatplanes reported the force of enemy ships had turned around again and now were headed straight for him and assuming battle formation. Takagi stopped laughing.

The enemy force consisted of the battered, bruised, and exhausted ships of the Combined Striking Force: 14 American, British, Dutch, and Australian ships (two heavy cruisers, three light cruisers, and nine destroyers) that had been slapped together into a designated unit under Dutch Rear Admiral Karel Doorman and sent forward with orders to attack the Japanese "until the enemy is destroyed."

While on paper it matched up decently against Admiral Takagi's force of two heavy cruisers, two light cruisers, and 14 destroyers, in reality the Combined Striking Force was the proverbial house of cards. These ships from four different countries in three different navies whose crews spoke two different languages had never had time to train together or develop common communications code. The best they could do was a conference that lasted about an hour. The Americans, British, and Australians had little confidence in their commander Admiral Doorman, who for his part believed this was a suicide operation from which he would not return.[2] Many of the ships were damaged and all were in dire need of maintenance, but little of that could be addressed while the Japanese were regularly attacking their bases. Those attacks and continued operations had left the crews exhausted.

After racing as fast as possible to join his destroyers literally as the Allied force came into view, Admiral Takagi ordered the Japanese to deploy in three columns: the 5th Cruiser Division in the center, the 2nd Destroyer Flotilla on the left, and the 4th Destroyer Flotilla on the right.

Takagi's three-column formation might be better described as a three-group formation, because the destroyer flotillas seem to have occasionally grouped their destroyers in multiple columns behind the flagship light cruiser. Even so, this was a standard Japanese formation, relatively simple to execute, and good for the destroyer flotillas to launch massed torpedo attacks. With his limited communications, Admiral Doorman was only able to use a single-column formation and give very limited orders like "Counterattack" and, most famously, "Follow me," which left the Allied ships following him like segments of a centipede. After Takagi opened fire – at an excessive range, his many critics would point out – it was just a matter of time before a wobbly card caused the whole house to topple. That card was a single hit on Doorman's most powerful ship, the Royal Navy heavy cruiser *Exeter*, that caused it to lose speed, spew smoke that blinded the ships behind him, and shear out of that column, throwing the rest of the Allied ships into confusion. The house of cards collapsed; the segments of the Allied centipede were picked off one by one. Only four Allied ships from the Combined Striking Force – the four old US Navy destroyers – would survive the next 48 hours.

Admiral Takagi's performance at Java Sea was underwhelming – in addition to the issues listed above were a profligate use of torpedoes from long range and poor shooting angles; and stopping *in the middle of battle* to recover a floatplane – but enough to accomplish his mission. He got a promotion to vice admiral and, though he remained in direct command of the 5th Cruiser Division, he was kicked upstairs and ended up running the attempted Japanese seaborne landing at Port Moresby. That turned into the Battle of the Coral Sea, in which Takagi's performance was again underwhelming. After that failed effort, Admiral Yamamoto never trusted him with a major operation again, so Takagi was left in the uncomfortable position of being a vice admiral in command of a single cruiser division, now of only two cruisers because the *Nachi* was sent away to that all-important Aleutian front.

A cruiser division that became one cruiser when the *Haguro* was sent back to Japan for a refit. Admiral Takagi's last appearance in surface combat was with the *Myoko* when it joined with the *Maya* to bombard Henderson Field the night of October 15–16, right after the bombardment.[3] Takagi was relieved as commander of the 5th Cruiser Division shortly thereafter, replaced by Rear Admiral Omori Sentaro.

Omori Sentaro was an interesting character. Earlier in his career, he had been an instructor at what was called the "Torpedo School" three times, which might be one reason why Japanese torpedoes were the best in the world.[4] Omori had been commander of the 1st Destroyer Flotilla, which had accompanied *Kido Butai* on the Pearl Harbor attack and subsequent operations. After the foray into the Indian Ocean, the 1st was sent to that all-important Aleutian front. The flotilla spent its time moving between the Aleutians, the Ominato navy base on the northern tip of Honshu, and the base at Paramushiro (now Paramushir, Russia).

That would be some important experience for Admiral Omori. After his appointment to the 5th Cruiser Division, the 5th was sent to cover the withdrawal – er, turning around and advancing – from Guadalcanal, after which Omori was sent ... back to the Aleutian front with his command. Hot and cold. Whether the repeated trips between Arctic cold and tropical heat negatively affected Omori's health is unknown.

Described as "a quiet man with a somewhat shy demeanor," Admiral Omori was, in the words of historian John Prados, a "torpedoman par excellence."[5] However, as Hara Tameichi pointed out, he "had never been in a major naval action."[6] That's not necessarily a bad thing – everybody has to start somewhere – but being the officer in tactical command of a major force in a major battle is a lot different than being a unit commander serving under someone else who is the officer in tactical command. And Omori had not even been a unit commander serving under someone else who was the officer in tactical command. Omori had never been in a major naval battle, period; commanding the destroyer screen for *Kido Butai* at Pearl Harbor does not count. He was basically making the jump from classroom instructor to major battle commander with none of the normal steps in between. Hara, for one, could not understand how Omori could have been selected to lead this operation.[7] The answer was simple: Omori was there. He was there and already commanded the *Myoko* and *Haguro*, which were the most powerful ships at Rabaul and would be the nucleus of this task force.

In short, Admiral Omori was a theoretician. A very good theoretician, perhaps, but a theoretician nonetheless. And theory and practice perfectly overlap only rarely. As Prados opined, what Japan needed at this time "was a Blackbeard, a pirate destroyerman along the lines of the British Napoleonic hero Sir Edward Pellew. Omori Sentaro, well-informed and conscientious, better fit the mold of Alfred Thayer Mahan."[8]

At 4:20pm on November 1, Admiral Omori's ships left Simpson Harbor.[9] His was designated the "Combined Assault Force" – one of many uncomfortable parallels to the Battle of the Java Sea that started appearing about now – and now consisted of his own 5th Cruiser Division, with the heavy cruisers *Myoko* and *Haguro*; Admiral Ijuin's 3rd Destroyer

Flotilla with his unwanted light cruiser flagship *Sendai* followed by the destroyers *Shigure*, *Samidare*, and *Shiratsuyu*; and Admiral Osugi Morikazu's 10th Destroyer Flotilla, with his flagship, the new light cruiser *Agano* followed by the big antiaircraft destroyer *Wakatsuki*, the just plain destroyer *Hatsukaze* and, for good measure, the just plain destroyer *Naganami* from the 2nd Destroyer Flotilla.[10] The Combined Assault Force's assignment was twofold. First, it was to escort some 930 Imperial Japanese Army troops from the 17th Okayama Division loaded aboard five destroyers, the *Amagiri*, *Yunagi*, *Uzuki*, *Fumizuki*, and *Minazuki* to conduct a counterlanding operation near Cape Torokina on Bougainville.[11] Second, it was to make contact with and destroy enemy ships in the vicinity of Empress Augusta Bay.[12]

In short, half of the Combined Assault Force's mission was pretty much the same here as it was at Savo Island: to attack and destroy enemy ships in the vicinity of the landing zone. The other half was pretty much the same as the 5th Cruiser Division had at Java Sea: to escort transports full of troops for a landing in hostile territory.

And as soon as they had cleared Simpson Harbor, they went into what Hara calls "regular cruising formation." Admiral Omori's flagship *Myoko* followed by sister ship *Haguro* were in the center. To port and slightly ahead of the flagship was Admiral Ijuin's *Sendai* followed in a tight column by the destroyers *Shigure*, *Samidare*, and *Shiratsuyu*. On the flagship's starboard hand was Admiral Osugi's *Agano* followed in column by destroyers *Naganami*, *Hatsukaze*, and *Wakatsuki*.[13]

This is where things start getting a bit cloudy, especially with respect to the five destroyer transports. According to Omori, when the Combined Assault Force reached St George's Channel, he "received a despatch that there was a delay in loading the military personnel (aboard the destroyer transports)." As a result, his ships were compelled to loiter in submarine-infested St George's Channel until the destroyer transports joined him at 7:30pm, after sunset. Omori was disgusted at the delay, and even more disgusted by the relatively slow speed of the "old types" in the little convoy that limited the speed of his own ships. Omori had set course as 160 degrees True – roughly south southeast – at a speed of 26 knots.[14] According to Hara, the five destroyer transports followed the Combined Assault Force at a distance of "several miles."[15] The three scout planes Omori had launched the previous day that had landed at Buka returned overhead to perform scouting and antisubmarine duties.[16] The *Myoko*, *Haguro*, *Agano*, and *Sendai* were each equipped with a Type 21 air-search radar that was installed the previous summer, but Omori had little confidence in the radars or their operators.[17] He would be relying on his floatplanes and his lookouts with their oversized, polarized binoculars to gather information.

Admiral Omori's fears about enemy submarines proved prescient when an American submarine was sighted just after they had left St George's Channel. He was able to clear it by turning almost due south, but that delayed him further. The weather was the same that hampered the nocturnal dive bomber attacks: cloudy and drizzly with cool temperatures, limiting their visibility.[18]

But apparently not limiting the enemy's visibility. Hara was soon picking up enemy radio chatter from nearby; they were being tracked by enemy scout planes. SB-24s, radar-equipped scouting variants of the B-24 Liberator from AirSols' 394th Bombardment Squadron, 5th Bombardment Group.[19]

So much for surprising the enemy like at Savo Island.

The realization that their counterlanding and attack would not be a surprise spurred some reconsideration; by whom, exactly, is not clear. According to Omori:

> In view of the initial rendezvous delay, the additional delay due to avoiding the submarine, the limiting speed of the destroyer transports 26 knots [sic], and the fact that we were sighted by the American plane, I recommended that the counter-landing not be attempted, but that our combatant ships attempt to destroy the American transports unloading in the vicinity of Empress Augusta Bay.[20]

Knowing he had been sighted, Admiral Omori appears to have transmitted this request to Rabaul at 8:20pm.[21] Shortly after this time, one of Omori's cruiser floatplanes reported, "Three battleships, many cruisers and destroyers at Empress Augusta Bay near Torokina."[22] When your own scout plane describes the number of enemy ships as "many," that's a bad sign.

An even worse sign came at 8:45pm. One of the snooping Liberators poked through the clouds and made some harassing bombing runs on the *Sendai*. Admiral Ijuin's flagship was not damaged, but it was nerve-wracking knowing enemy bombers were watching and able to attack at any time.[23] Admiral Doorman and the Combined Striking Force had had to live with this fear, especially when facing the 5th Cruiser Division. Now it was that same 5th Cruiser Division and the rest of the Combined Assault Force having to live with this fear.

According to Omori, at 11:30pm he received Rabaul's approval of his idea to cancel the counterlanding operation that night.[24] That was his story and he was sticking to it. Oddly, other Japanese sources say:

> An enemy surface force made of up three battleships, six cruisers, and a number of destroyers had shelled Shortland at dawn on the 1st and was cruising in the area. This fact taken in conjunction with the activities of the enemy air force, led to the conclusion that it would be difficult to make a counterlanding that night; the commander of the Southeast Area Force decided to give up the attempt, send the transport division back to Rabaul, and let the Combined Assault Force concentrate on finding and destroying the enemy fleet first.[25]

For his part, Hara says Omori "consulted with Rabaul headquarters, where at [10:30pm] Admiral Kusaka ordered the transports to turn back."[26] Regardless of who ordered it or why – other reasons given include the late arrival of the destroyer transports and their slow speed; the 1,000 troops were pitifully few compared to the troops the Americans had landing at Cape Torokina; and that Omori just did not want to deal with the destroyer transports – the counterlanding operation was called off for that night and the destroyer transports went back to Rabaul, though the *Minazuki* was directed to reinforce Buka instead.[27]

Finally freed of his proverbial ball and chain, Admiral Omori increased speed to 32 knots and headed for a point south of Sand Island. That continued until at least 1:24am on November 2. That's when another of the SB-24 snoopers shadowing Omori's force made a bombing attack, this time on the *Haguro*. Omori says one bomb struck the cruiser amidships, opening up her side plating and reducing her speed to 30 knots, and, as commander of the 5th Cruiser Division, he should know.[28]

About 15 minutes later the *Haguro*'s floatplane reported in: "One cruiser and three destroyers spotted 50 miles, 330 degrees from Cape Mutupina."[29] The indicated position was only 20 miles away. Omori wanted better information, however, so he ordered the floatplane to continue searching. In the interim, Omori had the entire Combined Assault Force reverse course simultaneously to mark time, which consisted of running about ten kilometers in about ten minutes and then turning around again.[30]

None of these developments made Commodore Hara feel any more confident about this operation. He had left Rabaul with less than complete confidence in Admiral Omori and wondered why someone with so little (read "no") combat experience had been chosen to head this sortie.[31] Again, the obvious answer was convenience: the 5th Cruiser Division was the most powerful surface force available in Rabaul and Omori was its commander.

But Admiral Omori was playing the role of Admiral Doorman in a production that looked less like the Battle of Savo Island that the Japanese had wanted and more like the Battle of the Java Sea, but some weird mirror Battle of the Java Sea with the Japanese "Combined Assault Force" playing the role of the ABDA (American-British-Dutch-Australian Command) "Combined Striking Force." A task force that had just returned to harbor ordered to move out again. A task force adding ships who had just arrived from distant bases. A task force that had never trained or worked together. The only preparation for the mission being a short conference. A task force that did not have confidence in its commander. A task force under constant aerial surveillance and harassment. On the Japanese side, a task force using a formation of three columns, with the 5th Cruiser Division in the middle and destroyer flotillas on either side.

Captain Hara had been at Java Sea, but Java Sea was as far away from him now as its namesake. As he stared into the black bulk of Bougainville to port, Hara was developing more immediate concerns. He estimated that the continuing drizzle was limiting visibility to about 5,000 meters. At best. Because his destroyers were in Admiral Ijuin's column, which was the closest to the Bougainville coast, the dark land mass seemed to swallow everything on the port hand. It reminded Hara of the Kolombangara supply operation back in August, when the dark land mass of Kolombangara seemed to swallow everything to starboard – including the US Navy destroyers that were waiting to ambush his Japanese column.[32] Hara had been the only one to see the potential dangers hiding in the black shadow that was Kolombangara. The other three destroyers were ambushed and sunk, and even then his own *Shigure* had only been saved by the destroyer's own old engines that had not been able to keep up with the rest of the column; otherwise she would have fallen victim as well. As it was, an enemy torpedo had passed through the *Shigure*'s rudder without exploding.

But this would be no Vella Gulf. It was 2:25am, as the Combined Assault Force was resuming its course toward the enemy, when Captain Hara saw a dim red flare in the sky, maybe 70 degrees to port, 20 kilometers away. It was consistent with the position of the enemy force reported by the *Haguro*'s scout plane. The flare disappeared after two or three seconds.[33]

Deciding the flare must have been dropped by the *Haguro*'s scout planes to mark the enemy's position, Hara dictated an urgent message to all ships, "Enemy sighted 70 degrees to port." He ordered it prepared for transmission, but held off on sending it until he actually made visual contact. Sure enough, at 2:45 one of the lookouts yelled, "Four ships, 70 degrees to port!" Hara had the prearranged message sent.[34]

Captain Hara was still processing the information when the lookout called out again. "The enemy force has split into two groups," he said. "One going away, the other paralleling our course. They are destroyers! Distant [sic] 7,000 meters!"[35] One group was going away? That could only mean …

"Launch torpedoes! Hard right rudder!" Hara thundered. He had always held the ancient Japanese credo: *When in doubt, launch torpedoes.* The commodore had trained the crew of the *Shigure* well. The response was swift. All eight torpedoes were sent churning toward the enemy at two-second intervals as the destroyer heeled over away from her starboard turn. Hara watched the torpedoes speeding away, certain that his evasive maneuver had succeeded in avoiding the torpedoes he knew those destroyers headed away from him had launched.[36] That was close. Hara turned away from watching his torpedo wakes streaking into the dark, but quickly saw that in avoiding one danger he had placed himself squarely in the path of another.

The *Sendai* was coming straight at him.

The commodore had been too distracted by the flare and the dark Bougainville coast to notice how dangerously close the ships of the 3rd Destroyer Flotilla were, the result of those two course reversals. What had been a nice, neat column of the 3rd Destroyer Flotilla with ships at 500-meter intervals had turned into a compact blob with the *Samidare* off to starboard and the *Sendai*, though still leading, jumbled with the *Shigure* and *Shiratsuyu* within 300 meters of each other.[37] The *Sendai* had sighted a different group of enemy ships than the *Shigure* had, bearing 110 degrees, distance 9,000 meters. Admiral Ijuin had ordered a hard right to launch four torpedoes – evidently without telling the rest of his ships.[38] The light cruiser's turn, according to Hara, was executed in "an exceptionally fast and violent manner." But evidently a very efficient manner, as the old cruiser had turned more sharply than the *Shigure*. As a result, the *Sendai* was now speeding like a giant torpedo toward the *Shigure*'s port side.[39]

It took Captain Hara a moment to recover from his shock. "Full starboard helm!" he yelled. "Full speed!"[40]

According to Hara, as the *Sendai*'s "towering bows" plowed closer and closer to the sluggish *Shigure*, he held his breath and "icy sweat coursed down [his] back" – no small feat in the South Pacific. Hara braced for the collision, but the *Shigure*'s stern cleared the *Sendai* with ten feet to spare.[41]

Another crisis averted.

Or not. Because when Captain Hara looked back, he saw the *Sendai* continuing her crazy careen, compelling the *Samidare* to swerve hard to starboard to avoid the squadron flagship. In that effort, the *Samidare*'s skipper Lieutenant Commander Sugihara Yoshiro was successful, but in turning hard to avoid the squadron flagship, Sugihara turned into the destroyer *Shiratsuyu* and sideswiped her. The *Samidare*'s bow was crushed; the *Shiratsuyu*'s port side crumpled from the impact, wrecking her torpedo tubes and disabling her main battery director.[42]

"Newcomer *Shiratsuyu* had proved she was no asset to my division," Hara later wrote.[43] Why he blamed the *Shiratsuyu* for the collision is not clear. Evidently, he thought her skipper Lieutenant Commander Matsuda should have tried harder to avoid the *Samidare*. Regardless, both destroyers, now limited to about 15 knots, were useless for battle.[44]

Admiral Ijuin was shocked at the chaos and carnage his flagship had wrought, all on his own ships. They had barely engaged the enemy, and he was already down two destroyers. On the baron's orders, the *Sendai* swung back to the left …

And straight into the first salvo from their US Navy adversaries. Hara was stunned and impressed. "I had never seen such spectacular accuracy – a first salvo hit!"[45]

Hara's shock paled compared to that of Admiral Omori. When he received Hara's 2:45am sighting report, he could see no enemy ships anywhere. He nevertheless ordered a course change to 180 degrees True – due south. Five minutes later he saw the *Sendai* explode for no reason that he could see. Moreover, the *Sendai* was supposed to be about 1,000 meters off the port bow of Omori's flagship *Myoko* and on a parallel course, but now she was on the *Myoko*'s port beam, burning brightly and attracting enemy shells like a magnet.[46]

What the hell was going on?

The *Sendai* was not just the unhappy recipient of a first salvo hit, but second and third salvo hits, too.[47] Several of the shells detonated in her boiler rooms, starting serious fires. Then the aft engine room was hit and the *Sendai* went dead in the water. Still more hits jammed her rudder.[48] The *Sendai* gamely responded to this early pounding by loosing another four torpedoes "in the general direction of the bombarding ships."[49] The *Samidare* sent eight torpedoes of her own toward the US Navy ships at 2:52am.[50] The destroyer quickly took three hits that did not appreciably add to the damage she had already suffered. She was in better shape than the *Sendai*, who according to Hara, "flamed like a giant torch," destroying his night vision for the time being. He was "suddenly overjoyed" when one of his lookouts announced that the *Shigure*'s torpedoes had sunk two enemy destroyers, but for the moment Hara himself could not see enemy ships and could not get a grasp on the battle situation.[51]

Admiral Omori was even more confused. One of his ships was being destroyed by an enemy he could not see. That one ship was also badly out of position. Were any of his other ships out of position? Where were they? He did not know.

This was bad. Admiral Omori had been taken by surprise – taken by surprise even though he had left Rabaul expecting, even seeking combat – and he knew it. Though he had taught at the Torpedo School, Omori was apparently not a believer in the ancient Japanese credo: *When in doubt, launch torpedoes.* He had one of his own: *When in doubt, turn around.* No one seems certain of what Omori hoped to accomplish by turning around, and, likely, neither was he. Hara said Omori was trying "to adjust his formation to its original deployment," but even Hara does not seem completely sold on that reason, calling the maneuver "influenced by the 'conservation' idea so prevalent in command circles." Nor does Hara indicate exactly how turning around would accomplish this. Neither did Omori, who never discussed it.[52]

While Admiral Omori was turning around for no apparent reason, Admiral Osugi, so far left out of the night's festivities, thought he had a better idea than both launching torpedoes or turning around to reform the formation: *When in doubt, charge.* Osugi had his *Agano* lead the *Naganami*, *Hatsukaze*, and *Wakatsuki* on a full-speed charge at their tormentors.[53] No one knows what exactly Osugi hoped to accomplish by just rushing at the enemy like cavalry, and, likely, neither did he. There was a lot of that going around.

The Japanese were flailing madly. Admiral Ijuin was staggering. Admiral Osugi was charging. Admiral Omori was turning around. Ijuin was in a burning and disabled flagship. Osugi was charging at an enemy he could not see. Omori was turning away from an enemy he could not see. Captain Hara could see the enemy and had as a result made an incorrect presumption. None of them knew what they were dealing with.

But there was one thing they did know.

This was no Savo Island.

———————————— ◉ ————————————

If the engagement developing just outside what the Allies called Empress Augusta Bay and what the Japanese called Gazelle Bay was no Savo Island, neither was it Tassafaronga, Kula Gulf, or Kolombangara.

Although, to be sure, it was starting out like Tassafaronga (well, sort of), Kula Gulf, and Kolombangara. American cruisers were flinging prodigious amounts of shells into their first target. And, for the most part, hitting it. At Tassafaronga, that target had been the destroyer

Takinami, who stupidly opened fire when all the other Japanese destroyers restricted themselves to torpedoes. At Kula Gulf, that target had been the destroyer *Niizuki*. At Kolombangara that target had been the light cruiser *Jintsu*. On this night, it was the *Sendai*. "[T]he typical concentration of night radar-controlled gunfire," Morison would call it.[54]

But Admiral Merrill, while happy with the damage done to the *Sendai*, was hoping that was where the similarities ended, because those beginnings had been misleading. With the exception of the ambush of the Japanese destroyers *Murasame* and *Minegumo* off Vila-Stanmore the previous March, every naval surface battle in the Solomons directly involving men-of-war larger than a destroyer starting with Tassafaronga had developed the same way. The Japanese would try running a supply and/or reinforcement operation. They would encounter a superior force of Allied warships. They would run away, launching torpedoes as they did so. The Allied warships would blunder into the torpedoes, usually with disastrous results. Tassafaronga. Kula Gulf – twice. Kolombangara. The only reason Vila-Stanmore did not progress the same way was because the *Murasame* and *Minegumo* had been pinned against the coast of Kolombangara unable to run away and were overwhelmed with US Navy gunfire and torpedoes so quickly they were unable to launch torpedoes and were barely able to even fire their guns. Only when the Allies started using destroyers instead of cruiser-centric forces for interceptions would the pattern be broken.

What was happening off Empress Augusta Bay was very different from literally all of the other surface engagements in the Solomons in 1943. The Japanese were not running a supply operation. They were not running away. They had come to fight – poorly, if the battle so far was any indication. While Hara Tameichi had called the formation Admiral Omori used a "regular cruising formation" and other Japanese naval analysts would claim Omori "had not yet gone into battle formation," that formation had, in fact, been used successfully in combat, specifically by Admiral Takagi in the Battle of the Java Sea.[55] While Takagi's was perhaps not the best recommendation for such a formation, a much better one was on hand.

That recommendation belonged to Rear Admiral Aaron Stanton "Tip" Merrill.[56] If the Imperial Japanese Navy was given to flattery, it could have considered Merrill's battle plan the sincerest form. While Merrill was certainly versed in US Navy doctrine, he liberally borrowed from the Japanese many tactics that worked, and maybe a few that did not, in the process throwing away US Navy doctrine that had proven ineffective or at least not as effective as what the Japanese were doing.

The US Navy force facing the Japanese this night included two of its foremost theoreticians. One was Admiral Merrill. The Mississippi-born Merrill was, according to one history, "trim, soft-spoken, and shy."[57] Yet, as a sailor aboard Merrill's flagship light cruiser *Montpelier* said, "Everyone took to him the first time they saw him. They don't come any better than Admiral Merrill."[58] Robert B. "Mick" Carney, who had commanded the light cruiser *Denver* under Merrill, knew him as someone who had a magnetic personality and an infectious laugh.[59] Merrill's chief of staff, Commander Bill Smedberg, said, "He loves people and he'll drink with anybody who wants to drink with him."[60]

So Admiral Merrill was a gifted leader of men, but he was also a gifted commander who led his men with energy and intelligence. When Admiral Nimitz expressed his solution to the problems that created the defeat at Tassafaronga in December 1942 with the phrase: "[T]raining, TRAINING and M-O-R-E T-R-A-I-N-I-N-G," he found a willing adherent in Merrill.[61] As commander of a task force centered on his Cruiser Division 12, with the new *Cleveland*-class light cruisers *Montpelier*, *Cleveland*, *Columbia*, and *Denver*, Merrill drilled his men and drilled and drilled and drilled them some more. Well aware that most of the surface actions in the Pacific War had taken place at night, for which US Navy training and doctrine had been sorely lacking, as the disaster at Savo Island attested, Merrill placed a special emphasis on night combat.[62]

After such exercises, Admiral Merrill would gather his ship captains in the officers' club to talk cruiser-destroyer tactics. This is where he would get an earful from the other theoretician involved in this night's combat off Empress Augusta Bay: Captain Arleigh Burke, commander of Destroyer Squadron 23. The squadron was nicknamed the "Little Beavers" after an American Indian character from a comic strip that one of the sailors had painted on the torpedo tubes, a character the sailors loved and identified with.[63] Like most destroyer skippers, Burke would complain about "being tied to the cruisers' apron strings," that is, being bolted to the cruisers in formation and requiring the permission of the task force commander before firing torpedoes.

Burke had studied dozens of action reports and could easily back up these opinions. At night, if a surface engagement is in the cards, Burke argued, all the destroyers should be deployed in front of the cruisers so that they could fire their torpedoes without explicit orders from the task force commander and then get out of the way of the cruisers' gunfire. Why should the destroyers up front have to wait for permission from the task force commander once they have spotted the enemy? If the destroyer commodore knew his business, he should strike at the enemy at once.

That was asking a lot from the US Navy in general and from task force commanders specifically. In any military, wanting more control is instinctive. And Arleigh Burke knew it. He put the new destroyer doctrine in a memo titled "Employment of Destroyers." In the section titled "Use of destroyers with cruiser task force at night against enemy surface craft," he advocated the policy of immediate destroyer torpedo attack from the van (front). Such a policy required three things: 1. The destroyers must be ready for attack; 2. The destroyer commander must initiate the attack at the first favorable opportunity after contact; and 3. The task force commander must have confidence in the destroyer commander's ability to make a successful attack and retire with the least inconvenience to the cruisers. "The last of these is the most difficult," Burke admitted. "The delegation of authority is always hard and under such circumstances as these, when such delegation of authority may result in disastrous consequences if a subordinate commander makes an error, it requires more than is usually meant by confidence – it requires faith."[64]

While wanting more control is instinctive, it is not necessarily effective. It can slow down response times. The biggest and best example – and Captain Burke knew it – was the engagement off Tassafaronga almost a year earlier. Commanding a force of cruisers and destroyers, Admiral Wright had deployed his ships in a column and, like Burke suggested, put most of his destroyers at the front of that column. But when the destroyer commodore found Japanese ships on radar and requested permission to launch torpedoes, Wright hesitated. He seems to have momentarily forgotten that his destroyers were closer to the Japanese than he was and thus had a much better shot than he did. When Wright finally gave his approval, the time for the shot had passed. Arguably, Wright's hesitation was the difference in the battle, the difference between a possible American victory and a disastrous American defeat.

Captain Burke was very conscious of time. Burke firmly believed in the value of surprise and stressed the need to waste no time in opening fire. "It is necessary that [commanders] realize the value of time," he said. "It is the only commodity you can never regain."[65]

Admiral Wright never regained the time he lost spacing out on his destroyers' request to launch torpedoes. It may have cost him the battle; it certainly did not help. That hesitation, that delay, was on Captain Burke's mind a lot. In a conversation with a young ensign on his bridge, Burke asked, "Son, can you tell me the difference between a good officer and a poor one?" The ensign began a long explanation about dedication, leadership, and tactical skills. Burke listened, then said quietly, "The difference between a good officer and a poor one is about ten seconds."[66]

It was but one point of Arleigh Burke's combat philosophy:

- **Speed:** move quickly while the other fellow's trying to make up his mind.
- **Look for fights:** if you look for 'em you'll probably find 'em.
- **Be prepared:** if you're ready for a fight you should win your share.[67]

The use of destroyers in the way Burke advocated seems obvious in hindsight. Understanding just how big a change this doctrine represented also requires a bit of a digression and some unpacking.

First, something very similar to this doctrine had been used by the Imperial Japanese Navy since before the war. The US Navy had always been about big guns. Guns are better than torpedoes, the thinking went, and maybe it was true as far as US Navy torpedoes went. It was one reason why the torpedo tubes were removed from almost all US Navy cruisers. Guns fire first, then torpedoes come in to take care of cripples.[68] The Japanese had this reversed: torpedoes first, then guns. They saw what the US Navy refused to see: that torpedoes are better at putting big holes under the waterline of enemy ships than shells are (or, for that matter, bombs). While this seems rather basic, it came down to an even more fundamental difference: day and night.

The US Navy envisioned fighting in the daytime, with a decisive battle involving the big guns of battleships in the Central Pacific. The Japanese also envisioned a Decisive Battle – too much, as has been seen – decided by the big guns of battleships much like

Tsushima, except fought in the Central Pacific. However, due to what they knew would be their inferiority in materiel, Japanese naval planners had envisioned whittling the Pacific Fleet down to size in a series of nighttime ambushes as the fleet steamed across the Pacific to that Decisive Battle.

For that reason, the Imperial Japanese Navy had put a lot of thought and effort into developing their night fighting capability. The most obvious example was the Type 93 torpedo, which with its long range could be launched at the enemy before the enemy even knew the Japanese were there, and with its oxygen propulsion that, counterintuitively, did not leave a telltale trail of bubbles, would not be spotted until the last possible moment.

But there were other examples as well. Japanese illumination rounds burned brighter and for longer than American starshells. The Japanese specially trained sailors with the best eyesight to serve as lookouts and gave them oversized, polarized binoculars to spot the enemy at night; for most of the war these lookouts had even outperformed American radar. The Japanese even developed a flashless powder, so when Imperial Navy ships fired their guns at night, they showed little in the way of a gunflash.[69]

All of these developments were made with the idea of fighting at night, to enhance surprise and concealment while preventing the enemy from achieving the same. The US Navy, by contrast, had put very little effort into preparing for night combat. The reason was the Americans envisioned fighting in the daytime and put little thought into concealment and surprise. One example of this predilection was, in contrast to the Japanese flashless powder, the US Navy originally used a smokeless powder. In the days before radar, smoke could blind American lookouts and even give away the positions of ships at long range. The Americans did develop a flashless powder, but it was the opposite of smokeless powder in that it produced prodigious amounts of smoke, which, again, blinded American sailors, which might not seem like a big deal in the age of radar, but those radar operators and blinded lookouts managed to completely miss the sinking of the *Helena* at Kula Gulf – and she was in the center of their formation. Perhaps most damningly and damaging of all, American torpedoes did not have even remotely the range of the Type 93 and thus usually could not be in the water before the enemy even knew the Americans were there.

Torpedoes were a special issue with the US Navy and not just because of the Great Torpedo Scandal, though it is related. Torpedoes were and are big, cumbersome, temperamental – and expensive. The proximate cause of the Great Torpedo Scandal was inadequate testing of the torpedoes. They were not tested properly because the cash-strapped US Navy did not want to waste expensive torpedoes on testing – testing that might have discovered the faulty depth mechanism, the too-weak firing pin, or the impossibility of the magnetic influence feature of the Mark 6 detonator.

While most of the flaws of US Navy torpedoes had been fixed, the philosophy that allowed these flaws to develop was still in place. It was one reason why the US Navy had "guns first, torpedoes second," with the torpedoes used to dispatch ships already disabled by the big guns: a torpedo is much more likely to hit a disabled, motionless ship than it is a moving ship (though, to be sure, US Navy torpedoes had issues hitting even motionless ships; consider the scuttling of the original carrier *Wasp* and the attempted scuttling of the original carrier *Hornet*). It was one reason why task force commanders had kept tight reins on their destroyer squadrons: if they did not, the destroyers might launch these expensive torpedoes and not get a hit, which would waste the expensive torpedoes and denude the destroyers of torpedoes until they could get reloads from port or destroyer tenders.

The Imperial Japanese Navy, as has been seen, adhered to the ancient Japanese credo *When in doubt, launch torpedoes.* The Japanese were profligate in their use of torpedoes. Usually the first thing a Japanese commander did upon sighting the enemy was launch torpedoes, partly to take advantage of surprise. It's hard for an enemy ship to avoid torpedoes if it does not know the torpedoes are coming, even harder if the enemy ship does not know the Japanese are even there. Imperial Japanese Navy destroyers, uniquely among the big navies, also usually carried one set of torpedo reloads, which proved to be a nasty surprise for Allied forces. Thus, to an extent, the Japanese could afford to launch torpedoes willy-nilly.

What it all meant was that, in short, Arleigh Burke was advocating changing US Navy tactical doctrine to that of the Imperial Japanese Navy. In the middle of a war against that same Imperial Japanese Navy. Again, that change might seem obvious now, but the US Navy had invested a lot of time, effort, materiel – and egos – into its doctrine that had now been proven ineffective. It took a lot to convince the Army Air Force that its doctrine of bombing from high altitude did not work against moving surface ships, and it would take a lot to convince the US Navy that its prewar doctrine of guns first, torpedoes second did not work.

Arleigh Burke found a willing listener in Admiral Merrill. However, the only major surface engagement in which Captain Burke had fought in the Solomons, the only major surface engagement in which Admiral Merrill had fought as well, was in early March 1943 when together they ambushed the Japanese destroyers *Murasame* and *Minegumo* off Vila-Stanmore. It was, arguably, the best surface performance of the US Navy in the Pacific War to date, sinking two destroyers so quickly they could not launch torpedoes, could barely get a shell off. But it was not good enough for Burke because of his own momentary misjudgment. When his radarman reported enemy contacts, Burke asked him if he was certain. When the radar operator confirmed it, Burke hesitated for mere seconds, then ordered torpedoes launched. Burke would chastise himself for the delay of those seconds. It had no impact on the battle, but that was the high level of performance that Burke demanded of everyone, including himself.[70]

This would be the first major surface engagement Admiral Merrill and Commodore Burke had fought since Vila-Stanmore. Though the cruiser forces of Merrill and Rear Admiral Walden Ainsworth were supposed to be something of a tag team, Ainsworth's force had ended up fighting the major actions at the beginning of the New Georgia Campaign – with the result that all of Ainsworth's cruisers were laid up with heavy damage except for the *Helena*, which was sunk. That was when it was decided to have destroyers do most of the fighting in the central Solomons.

Except, in a continuation of the long US Navy tradition of reassigning its officers at the worst possible times (see, e.g., Santa Cruz and Tassafaronga), that was when then-Commander Burke was reassigned to another destroyer squadron that had convoy duty. Burke, however, made it more exciting by, without Admiral Halsey's permission, sending one of his destroyers, the USS *Saufley*, to Sydney to get badly needed repairs to its boilers – and to buy beer and whiskey for his overworked, exhausted men. Only when the destroyer was on its way back did he notify headquarters of his action.

Burke received an ominous message instructing him to meet Halsey the next time he was in Nouméa. Burke did so. In his office, Halsey waited before addressing the commodore. "Oh, Burke." Halsey looked at notes on his desk. "*Saufley*?" Halsey sat upright. "Why in God's name did you take it in your own hands to send *Saufley* to Sydney?"

"Sir," Burke began, "My boys haven't had any beer or whiskey for months …"

Halsey interrupted, shaking his head, "You mean you sent that ship down there for *booze*?"

"Yes, sir, the captain did pick up a lot of liquor. But …" Burke was about to explain the urgent need for boiler repairs.

Halsey smiled. "All right, Burke. You win. Your boys have been doing a great job, and I can't condemn you for going out on a limb for them. But don't do it again."

Halsey pointed his finger at Burke. "If you had told me you sent *Saufley* for *repairs*, I'd have had your hide."[71]

Needless to say, both Burke and Halsey were popular with their men, as was Merrill.

The *Saufley* was not in Burke's command any more. Burke was reassigned with a promotion in August, and later reassigned again to command Destroyer Squadron 23 under Admiral Merrill – which is exactly what both Burke and Merrill wanted. It was the rare occasion of a US Navy reassignment that was actually in time to do some good.

Both Admiral Merrill and Captain Burke were hoping to put some of Burke's innovative (for the US Navy) ideas to work on this night. They knew the Japanese were coming.

Which was why Admiral Merrill and his ships had to do some speeding. They had spent the night of October 31–November 1 bombarding the Japanese air bases at Buka and Bonis. Then they had sped down the west coast of Bougainville, looped around to the south of Shortland, and bombarded the Shortlands, too. After that, they had turned to course 115 degrees True – roughly east southeast – and sped away from the Shortlands until they were out of range of the Japanese shore batteries, especially those "6-inch" guns on Poporang Island. Then Merrill's ships slowed down to 20 knots.[72]

The reason was fuel. Admiral Merrill's ships had been running at "near maximum speed" for 766 miles. As has been said here before, destroyers do not get good gas mileage at highway speeds, and the fuel bunkers of Captain Burke's destroyers in particular were, in Merrill's words, "distressingly small for ships of their size." Now, the destroyers had only enough fuel for "a short engagement provided high speed was not necessary before or after the engagement. It was not enough for any margin of safety." In short, the destroyers were short of fuel.[73]

This problem had been anticipated, however. Admiral Halsey had ordered Admiral Merrill to keep his ships under way northwest of Vella Lavella in position to protect the withdrawal of the *Cherryblossom* invasion transports while he detached his destroyers by individual division to refuel in Hathorn Sound between Arundel and New Georgia in Kula Gulf. Merrill sent Captain Burke's Destroyer Division 45 first at 7:15am.[74]

Now began what Captain Burke christened "The Battle for Fuel." "[T]his interesting battle" began with this half of Little Beavers speeding southeastward to the north of Vella Lavella, then looping around the north and east of Kolombangara and sailing down the Kula Gulf to the Hathorn Sound and the waiting oil barge *YO-144*.[75] Maybe that was the fastest route; maybe it wasn't. If it wasn't, if, say, going through the Blackett Strait between Kolombangara and Arundel to the Hathorn Sound was faster, there was an explanation for taking the slower route that borders on an urban legend.

It seems that the US Army had some troops stationed on Arundel at the entrance to the Blackett Strait. In what was perhaps not among the best of decisions by the US Army, these soldiers had built Japanese-style outhouses on stilts at the water's edge. The result was entirely predictable. Ships going through the Blackett Strait made waves – the faster the ship was going, the bigger the wave. So, when destroyers went through the Blackett Strait at high speed, they sent "gigantic" waves to shore that sometimes knocked over the poorly anchored privies, to the confusion and aggravation of any occupants.[76]

For some of the destroyermen, it became a game, a "Battle of the Privies" the soldiers on Arundel deserved for adopting such a stupid design for their outhouses, and a Japanese design at that. In return, the angry army men turned their ire toward the most famous of the destroyermen: Captain Burke and his Destroyer Squadron 23. A story emerged that a senior admiral called Burke on the carpet and roared "Burke, if your ships don't stop knocking down those goddamn privies, I'll have your stripes!"[77]

According to Captain Burke, that story was a load of crap. The entire Battle of the Privies was a matter on which he repeatedly tried to defecate, including the identity of the responsible party, which was not Burke's Destroyer Squadron 23 – at least not primarily – but Captain Rodger W. Simpson's Destroyer Squadron 12. Simpson's ships went so far as to paint the symbol of a palm-thatched privy on their bridges, adding a hashmark beneath it for every such stilted structure knocked down by their wakes. Ever the party-pooper, Simpson ultimately ordered the practice stopped.[78]

On this day, Commodore Burke would happily knock down privies, public restrooms, even entire sewage treatment plants if it would get him and his men their gas more quickly. As exhausted as his men were, everyone knew that a report of an approaching Japanese surface force would come any minute now. At 7:50 that morning, shortly after Burke's Destroyer Division 45 had detached, a reconnaissance plane reported sighting a Japanese task force of four light cruisers and six destroyers southeast of St George's

Channel heading west northwest (300 degrees True) at a speed of 25 knots. In response, Admiral Wilkinson telegraphed Admiral Merrill, "Request interception as enemy may reverse course." Admiral Halsey and AirSols had been copied on that message. Perhaps feeling as if its manhood had been questioned, AirSols immediately chimed in, "Continuous search in area. Search planes tracking. Enemy cruisers and destroyers nearing St George's Channel at [9:15am]." It was being kept under continuous surveillance. AirSols' message ended with this promise: "If they reverse course, we will sink them before they reach Torokina."[79]

Maybe, maybe not. Hermann Göring had promised the Luftwaffe would destroy the Allied troops trapped at Dunkerque, and you see how that turned out. Yes, there was that whole "Bismarck Sea" thing, but General Kenney's 5th Air Force had many more aircraft to work with than AirSols. Nevertheless, six torpedo-armed Beauforts of the Royal Australian Air Force's No. 8 Squadron led by Squadron Leader Owen Price were sent on an antishipping sweep between Rabaul and Bougainville, but could not find the Japanese. Admiral Halsey was not taking any chances and ordered Admiral Merrill, "Take position to intercept and destroy if enemy force reported threatens our landing operations." Merrill asked AirSols for more information on this force and to track the approaches to Cape Torokina. He then signaled Admiral Wilkinson and copied Captain Burke that his task force would arrive west of the beachhead at 2:15pm but that he was down four destroyers who were refueling. Wilkinson came back informing Merrill that he expected the transports to leave the Torokina area at 4:00pm unless delayed by air attacks.[80]

Captain Burke was aware of these developments. Admiral Merrill's ships had to be ready to block the Japanese, or else it would hit the fan. To stop the Japanese they had to be together. To get back together, these Little Beavers had a long way to go and a short time to get there.

According to Captain Burke, after his destroyers arrived in Hathorn Sound at 11:15am, he and his skippers were overcome by "a fever of impatience" to complete fueling. The oil barge could only take two at a time, so the *Charles Ausburne* and *Dyson* went alongside to fuel first, while the *Stanly* and *Claxton* kept watch for submarines. "Everybody tried to get more capacity out of the barge fuel pumps than was in them," he wrote. Burke even had the *Stanly* and *Claxton* line up with the barge's pumps so as soon as the *Charles Ausburne* and *Dyson* left the barge, which they finally did at 1:05pm, they could zip in and start fueling.[81]

It was 4:30pm before the *Stanly* and *Claxton* could start moving again after getting their fill of bunker fuel.[82] They rejoined the *Charles Ausburne* and *Dyson* at around 6:00pm, and together they headed for the rendezvous with Admiral Merrill's force. But it was literally not smooth sailing. Shortly after leaving Kula Gulf, the *Dyson* struck a "submerged object" that caused "excessive vibrations."[83] On a ship, there are no good vibrations. At a minimum, vibrations can damage sensitive equipment like radios and radars. In worst case scenarios such as the battleship HMS *Prince of Wales* and the destroyer USS *Pope* during the Java Sea Campaign, the vibrations can even lead to the loss of the ship if they are caused by the ship's propeller shaft spinning off-center and thus destroying the glands that sealed the tunnel through which the shaft passed. The *Dyson* would have to deal with the vibrations, apparently caused by her starboard propeller, as best she could until she could make repairs.[84]

The *Stanly* was in considerable danger as well. The tubes to one of her boilers were threatening to blow out, an already serious danger made worse by a far bigger danger: fuel vapors were building in her boiler rooms. At Coral Sea, the carrier *Lexington* had showed that fuel vapors building up in your ship can be a bad thing. It could cause the ship to blow up and sink, as the *Lexington* did. And it can overcome your men in the boiler rooms. Calling the vapors "abnormally bad," the *Stanly*'s skipper, Cleveland-native Commander Robert Cavanagh, had to issue oxygen masks to her fireroom personnel. The *Stanly*, too, would have to make do.[85]

As this half of the Little Beavers sped northwest, Captain Burke's radio picked up hints of how the landings were going. The reported Japanese force had not turned around, had not headed back to Bougainville. Not yet, anyway. He picked up from Admiral Wilkinson that, because of air attacks and the grounding of the *American Legion*, the transports would not leave the Empress Augusta Area until 6:00pm. This report made Burke consider going north of the Treasury Islands to save time, but he decided against it, as Burke diplomatically put it, "in order not to confuse our Motor Torpedo Boats operating to the north of those islands."[86] Then he got word that after those transports left, four of them – the cargo ships – would turn around at 11:00pm to be back in the landing area the next morning to complete unloading. A request was sent to AirSols seeking fighter protection for these ships. Admiral Halsey gave new orders to Admiral Merrill's force to cover the transports from a position near Vella Lavella.[87]

Everything changed when an AirSols reconnaissance plane reported, "Sighted eight enemy vessels 04-50 lat., 152-40 long., at [8:50pm]." The Japanese force had reappeared just outside St George's Channel. That wasn't good. The plane announced it was planning to attack; this was apparently the SB-24 Liberator that later made the bombing run on the *Sendai*. Admiral Halsey immediately ordered Admiral Merrill to protect the returning transports against this enemy force. At 11:28pm, Halsey followed up that order with a second, clarifying order that canceled his earlier order that Merrill position his ships near Vella Lavella and instead "to cover from [the] west ships TF31 [Admiral Wilkinson's transports] landing troops Torokina at daybreak and DMs [destroyer minelayers] laying defense mines Cape Moltke."[88]

Captain Burke was thus keeping himself informed as his destroyers went as fast as they could to rejoin Admiral Merrill. At 10:22pm, the *Charles Ausburne*'s radar detected unidentified ships to the northwest. Upon the destroyer's voice radio contact report, Admiral Merrill broke in, saying those were the transports retiring from Cape Torokina and ordering Burke and his destroyers to join him southwest of the transports. It was now that Burke was informed that four of the transports were going to turn around and head back to Cape Torokina, so he wanted to stay well clear to starboard of the transport group. A turn to due west did just that.[89]

It was 11:15pm when Commodore Burke's destroyers were able to rejoin Admiral Merrill's task force. "The Squadron Commander and the Captains of Desdiv 45 were greatly relieved to have effected rendezvous with the Task Force before enemy contact was made," Burke later admitted.[90] It was undoubtedly true. It also signified defeat in the "Battle for Fuel." Only half of Burke's Destroyer Squadron 23 – the four tin cans of Destroyer Division 45 that were under his direct command – had been able to refuel. The other half – the *Spence*, *Thatcher*, *Converse*, and *Foote* of Destroyer Division 46 under Commander Austin – had not. Their fuel levels would hang over the full task force like a gas pump of Damocles. But while Burke may have been defeated in the Battle for Fuel, it must be said that only Arleigh Burke could make a refueling trip sound so dramatic.

A report came in from another scout plane. At 10:15pm it had attacked 12 ships at 05-18 lat., 153-07 long., course 145 degrees True – roughly south southeast – speed 20 knots. This may have been the attack on the *Haguro*. This report was immediately followed by another one, this apparently from the same SB-24 that had attacked the *Sendai*, that eight to 12 enemy ships were at 05-35 lat., 153-26 long., on course 125 degrees True – roughly east southeast. Burke determined that this position was as of midnight.[91] The Japanese were closing in on the Torokina beachhead.

Always ready to add more of an intellectual element to warfare, Captain Burke made his own intelligence estimate. He believed it possible that the enemy had assumed that: (1) there was only one US Navy cruiser task force in the South Pacific; (2) this task force had bombarded Buka at midnight on November 1 and the Shortland Islands at dawn the same day; (3) the same task force had covered unloading operations of the transports at Empress Augusta Bay; (4) that task force had left the landing area with the transports at dusk of November 1; (5) these operations must have left the destroyers and probably the cruisers low on fuel and ammunition; (6) these continuous operations must have caused fatigue among the task force personnel; and (7) as a result, the task force was retiring for fuel, ammunition, and rest. If he made these assumptions, Burke concluded, "the enemy probably believed the night of November 1–2 was an ideal time to clean-up on our landing force at Empress Augusta Bay without heavy opposition from our surface forces."[92] This analysis was well-thought-out, logical, and completely wrong.

Admiral Merrill had set 1:00am as the time when the crews would go to battle stations. By this time, the task force had settled into its approach formation. Instead of approaching the Japanese in one long line of ships (destroyers in front, heavier ships such as cruisers in back, maybe more destroyers bringing up the rear), his Task Force 39 was in a formation of three staggered columns bunched tightly together. In the center were four 6-inch-armed light cruisers of Merrill's Cruiser Division 12: his flagship *Montpelier* followed by the *Cleveland*, *Columbia*, and *Denver*. To starboard was Captain Burke commanding Destroyer Squadron 23 and, directly, Destroyer Division 45, consisting of his command destroyer *Charles F. Ausburne* followed by the *Claxton*, *Stanley*, and *Dyson*.

To port was Destroyer Division 46 under Commander Austin, with his command destroyer *Spence*, *Thatcher*, *Converse*, and *Foote*.[93] A three-column formation like Admiral Omori was using here and like Admiral Takagi had used at Java Sea.

There was still more than an hour of waiting and anticipating among the crews before, at 2:20am, the *Columbia* reported two radar contacts bearing 011 degrees, distance 13 miles.[94] "This sent preliminary thrills up and down many spines," Captain Burke later reported.[95]

Alas, as Admiral Merrill quickly confirmed, these contacts were the destroyer USS *Renshaw* leading the minelayers *Breese*, *Sicard*, and *Gamble* heading back south from their mission laying mines off Cape Moltke.[96] Their course would take them between Admiral Merrill's task force to the west and Empress Augusta Bay to the east. Something else Merrill had to protect. The *Renshaw* cheekily reported that she was "bringing her snooper down with her."[97] The snooper was the floatplane from the *Haguro*, stalking and dropping flares over the minelaying group. Its presence suggested the minefield the minelayers had just laid would be reported and swept in short order. Or not. At around 2:00am, the *Haguro* floatplane had in fact reported that the minelaying group was "many transports unloading troops."[98]

As the minelaying group was hustling off to the rear areas accompanied by their voyeur, things quickly started to get real. At 2:29am, Admiral Merrill's flagship *Montpelier* reported "Apple Gadgets," which was slang for surface radar contacts, in this case at bearing 306 degrees, distance 16 miles.[99]

Maybe a minute later, the *Charles Ausburne*'s radar picked up the same contact bearing 291 degrees, distance 30,100 yards. "This contact had to be real!" Burke wrote. "It must be the enemy! It could not be another rain squall!"[100]

It really could have been another rain squall, because rain squalls were in the area, but it was not. It was actually the enemy. Admiral Merrill immediately ordered a change of course to 000 degrees True – due north – speed 28 knots. His own three groups shifted from three separate, staggered columns to an east-west line of bearing; that is, the *Montpelier*, Merrill's flagship, was even with Captain Burke's *Charles Ausburne* leading Destroyer Division 45 to starboard and even with Commander Austin's *Spence* leading Destroyer Division 46 to port. They were in position between Empress Augusta Bay to the east and the incoming Japanese to the northwest.

Captain Burke radioed the admiral, "We have that contact and am [sic] heading for it." The *Charles Ausburne* "threw over her rudder," ultimately to course 311, almost a collision course with these radar contacts that were headed southeast. Admiral Merrill radioed back, "Attack with torpedoes, acknowledge." The commodore did so with a "Wilco." He considered the admiral's order "a reassurance and a friendly pat on the back as we went in."[101]

It was only one group of Japanese ships, the northernmost group, but shortly thereafter two more groups appeared, one to the south of the first, and a third group southwest of the second. Merrill later admitted he had initially misjudged the Japanese formation as two columns of four destroyers each flanking a column of four cruisers in the center "based on the way we ourselves would dispose them, i.e., by types with all heavy units in the center."[102] Instead, it was one light cruiser leading three destroyers of Admiral Ijuin's 3rd Destroyer Flotilla in the northernmost group; Admiral Omori's two heavy cruisers in the center; and another light cruiser leading another three destroyers, these of Admiral Osugi's 10th Destroyer Flotilla, to the southwest. Between Ijuin's to the north and Osugi's to the southwest, the three enemy groups were spread over more than eight miles.

Nevertheless, the American task force was in a good, if fortunate, position. "Our timing proved to be accurate to the point that we were almost in a 'capping' position when contact was first made," Admiral Merrill later reported.[103] That is, almost "capping the 'T,'" though in this case there were multiple verticals, so it would have been more like "capping the 'Π.'" But it was due more to Admiral Omori's earlier reversal of course to mark time while the *Haguro*'s floatplane gathered more information. Otherwise, the Combined Assault Force might have beaten Merrill to the battle site, which would have given it the chance to attack the "transports" found by the floatplane – actually the minelaying group – and maybe gotten around Merrill's force to attack the actual transports, who were only some 30 miles away. Might have. Even so, Merrill's calculations enabled the Americans to take advantage of what was arguably a bad call by Omori.[104]

With the minelaying group having just passed them heading toward the bay and the transports a further 30 miles beyond them, blocking entry into Empress Augusta Bay was a rather obvious necessity, and so was part of Admiral Merrill's plan. Merrill took it a bit further, however, and intended to push the Japanese further west. The battle site was the best that could be chosen under the circumstances, but it was too close to uncharted shoals known to surround Empress Augusta Bay, so he wanted to gain sea room for maneuvering. Fairly basic.

There were some interesting nuances, however. Writing in the third person, Admiral Merrill later reported, "As our four cruisers constituted the principal surface strength left in the South Pacific area to cover planned landing operations from night raids by enemy surface forces, the Task Force Commander felt that he should take every precaution against getting these ships torpedoed."[105]

For that reason, Admiral Merrill's plan here was very conservative. He was not under orders to attack the Japanese "until the enemy is destroyed," which gave Merrill much more flexibility than Admiral Doorman had at Java Sea. If he could annihilate the Japanese force, that would be great, but not "at the expense of losing several of his own cruisers out of action for the remainder of the current operations."[106] As a result, his objective was not to annihilate the Combined Assault Force, but to "decisively" repulse it while "retaining his force in condition to fight again tomorrow night."[107]

Repulsing the Japanese required blocking the entrance to Empress Augusta Bay. The primary responsibility for holding that line was with Admiral Merrill's light cruisers *Montpelier*, *Cleveland*, *Columbia*, and *Denver*. Merrill had done his homework. He and others in the US Navy had (finally) figured out that the Japanese Type 93 "Long Lance" torpedo had a range, speed, and explosive power far superior to that of American Mark 15s, even the new Mark 15s with Torpex.[108]

Admiral Merrill had put considerable thought into counteracting the Long Lance. He planned to keep his cruisers at something close to the maximum range of the Type 93 and no closer.[109] Moreover, although it is not mentioned in the battle plans or histories, Merrill seems to have intended to keep his cruisers on a particular course and speed for no longer than it would take one of the Long Lances to reach them. The cruisers would change course so often that any Japanese firing solution would be ineffective because once the torpedoes arrived, the cruisers would have already changed course and would be somewhere else.

In practice, Admiral Merrill would keep the cruisers in the blocking position while making a series of figure-eights. Yet, once again, Merrill would add some twists, at least more twists than are typical for a figure-eight. The cruisers would be in column when heading due north (000 degrees True) or due south (180 degrees True). All turns would be simultaneous line turns, which would change each cruiser's position and profile the most quickly. The order of the cruisers would always be, north to south, *Montpelier*, *Cleveland*, *Columbia*, and *Denver*.

For cruisers at high speed and in such close quarters, this would be a dangerous tactic, risking a catastrophic collision. But the Type 93s had already proven themselves far more dangerous than anything Merrill could put his cruisers through. Additionally, Merrill had repeatedly drilled everyone under his command, but especially his cruisers, over which he had direct command. In all probability, these maneuvers had been practiced and practiced again.

With the cruisers holding back in a standoff position, the destroyers would be the striking arms to the cruisers' torso. The destroyer divisions would charge at the enemy flanks and launch torpedoes off both bows. Just as Arleigh Burke wanted.

With his ships in position and the enemy forces detected on radar, Admiral Merrill went to work executing that plan. He was already executing that plan by sending Captain Burke charging at the northern group. Merrill radioed Commander Austin, leading Destroyer Division 46 in the *Spence*, "Do you have contact?"

"Affirmative."

"Attack with torpedoes, acknowledge." Just like he had with Burke.

But it was not just like Burke when Austin came back with, "I regret my answer should have been negative. My people have corrected their statement."

"Disregard my last transmission," the admiral replied.[110]

A 50-50 choice, and Commander Austin had gotten it wrong. Because the radarman on the *Spence* was wrong. It was going to be that kind of night for the good commodore, through little fault of his own. Though it seemed like a simple question – do you have them on radar or not? – nothing would be simple for Austin's destroyers this night.

At 2:36, Admiral Merrill radioed, "Execute to follow, turn 18, repeat, turn 18" and requested Commander Austin and the *Columbia*'s Captain Frank A. Beatty, Jr acknowledge. Both did.

Two minutes later, the admiral ordered Austin, "Execute countermarch." Merrill quickly followed that with an order to his cruisers. "Execute to follow, turn 18, repeat, turn 18, stand by, execute." All four cruisers immediately turned to starboard and headed south. They were still in column, but now the *Denver* was in front, followed by the *Columbia*, *Cleveland*, and *Montpelier*, in that order. Technically, this is a type of countermarch.

Within another two minutes, Commander Austin asked for clarification, "Just to clear up we are to stay in column[?]" An apparently annoyed Admiral Merrill answered, "You are correct. Out."[111]

When sending tactical orders in the midst of battle by voice radio, it was common to give warning that a particular order was coming, with a phrase like "execute to follow," followed by what the order itself would be. This is often called a "preparatory order." After that, the order will be officially given, maybe followed by "stand by" but always ending with the word "execute," as in, "execute this order right now." The process can be very quick, as with the "Turn 18" for the cruisers.

It was also common to employ shorthand. A "turn 18," for instance, was an immediate starboard turn of 180 degrees, as in, reversing course. An "18 turn" would be an immediate port turn of 180 degrees. The position of the number relative to the word "turn" indicated the direction of the turn. Clever.

So, what Admiral Merrill had done at 2:36am was warn his cruisers and Commander Austin that they were about to reverse course. They would not reverse course, however, until Merrill said the word, "Execute."

Then Merrill ordered Austin, "Execute countermarch." A "countermarch" can mean a number of things, all of which involve reversing the direction of the unit. In the context of Austin's destroyers, a countermarch meant a column turn, something like a "follow the leader" move. At the time "execute countermarch" was spoken, Austin's command destroyer *Spence* was leading the *Thatcher*, the *Converse*, and the *Foote*, in that order, due north. In this case, the countermarch would mean making a 180-degree turn to starboard to head due south. When "execute countermarch" was uttered, Austin and the *Spence* would immediately start to make the turn, but the *Thatcher* would not, instead waiting until she reached where the *Spence* had started her turn to start her own 180-degree turn, and complete the turn to follow behind the *Spence*. The *Converse*, in turn, would follow the *Thatcher*, and the *Foote* would follow the *Converse*. When the column turn was completed, the destroyers would be in the same order they had been heading north, with Austin on the *Spence* leading the *Thatcher*, the *Converse*, and the *Foote*, but heading south.

That was the intent. And it sounds simple. But as Carl von Clausewitz said, "Everything in war is very simple. But the simplest thing is difficult," for very good reasons.

Admiral Merrill's message "Execute to follow, turn 18" was, it would seem, a very understandable warning to Commander Austin's destroyers and his own cruisers that they were about to reverse course. But while Merrill had meant for Austin's destroyers to make a column turn to starboard, he meant for his cruisers to make an immediate turn to starboard. Merrill's message "Execute to follow, turn 18" used the terminology for an immediate turn. He did not use or include the term for a column turn, which was often the word "corpen." Thus, Merrill's message was literally warning them they were all about to make an immediate turn to reverse course.

Sure enough, when Admiral Merrill told Austin's destroyers, "Execute countermarch," the *Foote*'s skipper, Commander Alston Ramsay, understood it to mean the immediate turn that had been referenced by the earlier warning. And he immediately turned the *Foote* 180 degrees to starboard.

Now, instead of Commander Austin's *Spence* leading his destroyer division as it headed south, the *Spence* was far behind the *Foote*. Seeing the *Foote* make the turn first is probably what motivated Commander Austin to ask Admiral Merrill, "Just to clear up we are to stay in column[?]" Ramsay's action here has been termed a "gaffe," among other noncomplimentary things.[112] It was a mistake, to be sure, but an understandable one.

The simplest thing is difficult.

And was now made more difficult because the *Foote* had to get back to her proper position at the tail end of Commander Austin's column of destroyers. Specifically, she had to cross the *Spence*'s bow and sort of drift back to take station at the back of the column.[113] And Austin quickly ordered his tin cans to charge due westward, leaving the *Foote* even further behind.[114] She was like a member of a marching band who during the halftime show had missed a spot in the drill. Even though she was ahead of the column, she was now trying to catch up with what everyone else was doing to be where she was supposed to be. Except in a halftime show, it's only (very) embarrassing. In battle, it can be the difference between life or death.

Admiral Merrill ordered Commander Austin, "Report when you have contact and solution." Two minutes later at 2:45, Austin said he had a contact and a solution at bearing 298. "Does that check?"[115] Merrill confirmed it.

Then Commander Austin finally got to ask the magic words: "Request permission to go in."

"Attack with torpedoes [...]," the admiral replied.

"Follow me [...]," Austin ordered his destroyers. And Commander Austin and Destroyer Division 46 were off. In more ways than one.

Meanwhile, Captain Burke was having a ... thrill leading his four destroyers charging on a collision course at the northern group. Burke was so set on launching his torpedoes that he initially wanted to make his attack from the starboard bow of this group – that is, between Admiral Ijuin's group and the 5th Cruiser Division to its south. Citing a change of course on the part of his targets, Burke changed his mind to attack off the port bow. In actuality, Ijuin's group had not changed course quite yet. Either the radar return for Ijuin's ships had firmed up on Burke's radar, or Burke had thought better of charging between two groups of enemy ships when he knew Merrill's cruisers were planning to open a big can of 6-inch spray on them.[116]

Whatever the reason, at 2:45, when the range had closed to 5,600 yards, Captain Burke ordered, "Stand by to fire torpedoes. Fire half salvo." That meant each destroyer was to fire five of the ten torpedoes it carried in its tubes. Since, unlike the Japanese, the Americans did not carry torpedo reloads, Burke wanted to save some torpedoes for follow-up attacks. Within that minute came the order, "Execute firing torpedoes." Burke turned to radio Admiral Merrill, "My guppies are swimming."[117]

"Fine work," Admiral Merrill commented. Now Burke had to get his ships out of there. He quickly ordered a 90-degree turn to starboard to come to course 50 degrees True – just north of northeast. Probably right before his destroyer turned away, the *Claxton*'s skipper Commander Herald F. Stout apparently decided to combine General Vandegrift's battle cry of "Why not?" with the principle that it is better to ask for forgiveness than permission in a launch of his remaining five torpedoes against the biggest target in that northern group, which he estimated to be a cruiser. Keeping with evasive maneuvers, Burke ordered a "Turn 3" to a course of 80 degrees True – roughly east northeast.[118]

Even during all this maneuvering, "we lived years waiting for the torpedoes to explode[…]," Captain Burke later wrote. As it slowly became clear the torpedoes were not going to explode, Burke turned to the *Spence*'s skipper Commander Luther K. "Brute" Reynolds and groaned, "My God, how do you like that?"

"That, Commodore," replied Reynolds, "is what comes of a Swede expecting to have the luck of the Irish!"[119]

The commodore and the skipper started discussing "how [they] could possibly have missed with such an ideal set-up."[120] "[F]or the next two to three minutes, we regretted driving into such close range where the enemy might have sighted us as we fired."[121] That was exactly what had happened, but there was a limit as to how far off Burke could have launched torpedoes and still have had a reasonable chance of hitting the target. No matter how much the Bureau of Ordnance worked to fix the Mark 15, it could never give the Mark 15 anything approaching the range of the Type 93, which allowed the Japanese to launch torpedoes when their ships were little more than specks on the horizon.

It was an anticlimax, a disappointment to Captain Burke. Here he had been all excited to finally try his new destroyer tactics and the Japanese had completely foiled it. But the commodore was wise enough to know that this result did not mean his tactics would not work. Remember, the enemy always gets a say in what works and what does not. Burke would console himself with the idea that a set of explosions had been seen on the target at the time when the *Claxton*'s second half salvo of torpedoes was supposed to hit.[122] But those explosions were likely something else.

Because as soon as Admiral Merrill saw that the Japanese had turned away from Captain Burke's destroyers, he decided that Burke's torpedo attack would fail, so there was no point in waiting any longer. Seaman James J. Fahey, an antiaircraft gunner on the

Montpelier, wrote in his diary, "You sense a funny feeling as both task forces race toward each other." He continued, "It is very dark and heat lightning can be seen during the battle along with a drizzle. Our ship did not waste any time."[123] At 2:50am, Merrill said the magic words to his cruisers: "Dog execute."

Once again, no animals were harmed in the execution of this order, nor did any dogs execute anyone. "Dog" was code for "commence firing, main batteries." The *Montpelier* opened fire with her 6-inch main battery on the largest target in the Japanese northern group, the *Sendai*, at a range of 19,000 yards. The other three cruisers joined in within a few minutes, going to rapid fire as soon as they found the range. Admiral Merrill quickly ordered a 20-degree turn to starboard to close that range a bit, but the *Denver* had some problems complying because she had to dodge the *Foote*, who was in the way.[124] Even so, she continued with the other cruisers firing at the *Sendai*. Once again, as Morison called it, "[T]he typical concentration of night radar-controlled gunfire."[125]

And that typical concentration of night radar-controlled gunfire meant the *Sendai* was hit early and often. Within minutes the light cruiser was a blazing wreck, dead in the water, her rudder jammed. But she did fight back, launching those four torpedoes earlier, probably launching another four around this time, and probably opening fire with her main guns. Though Admiral Omori does not mention it, the *Myoko* and *Haguro*, after they turned south, probably opened fire with their main battery as well.

While it's not clear who was shooting at the Americans, it's certainly clear that *someone* was shooting at them. Admiral Merrill saw return fire almost immediately after his cruisers were unleashed, but the Japanese shells fell 2,000 to 3,000 yards short. The Japanese illumination rounds fell short as well. Some of the shell splashes were determined to have come from 8-inch shells.

That presented a dilemma for Admiral Merrill, one similar in nature to the one presented to Admirals Callaghan and Scott during the Friday the 13th Action. At that time, Callaghan and Scott had to face Japanese battleships with heavy cruisers, knowing that their heavy cruisers' guns normally could not penetrate the hull armor of a battleship. Whether by intent or accident, the *San Francisco* and *Portland* were able to close the range to almost potato-throwing distance, and even then the *San Francisco* was only able to penetrate the armor due to a lucky hit on a ventilation duct. That hit would ultimately prove fatal to the battleship *Hiei*, though it did not sink the battleship by itself, to be sure, but it was a lucky shot. Only the guns of another battleship or torpedoes could penetrate a battleship's armor. And the US Navy had taken the torpedo tubes off its cruisers. Stupid. Absolutely stupid.

Now, Admiral Merrill was facing Japanese heavy cruisers with light cruisers. His light cruisers could fire a lot of 6-inch ammunition very, very quickly, but none of that ammunition could penetrate the hull armor of the *Myoko* and *Haguro* at the long range at which Merrill intended to fight this action. To have a chance at penetrating that armor, Merrill would have to get up close and personal with the *Myoko* and *Haguro*, but in so doing he would expose his light cruisers to Japanese torpedoes he had decided to avoid at all costs.[126] Merrill decided that he did indeed want to repulse the enemy, not destroy them. He would keep fighting the battle at long range. As the US Navy destroyers did to the *Hiei* and the Japanese did to the *South Dakota*, he could still wreck their superstructures and make their lives very uncomfortable.

Admiral Merrill was certainly making the lives of Commander Austin's destroyers very uncomfortable. The *Spence* had led the *Thatcher* and *Converse* into such a position that they "began to run into the illumination intended for the cruisers." Not only that, Austin's squadron "was uncomfortably placed between the fires of both the enemy and our cruisers."[127]

With "[n]ear miss splashes [being] observed at this time and shells [being] heard passing overhead," Austin ordered a "9 turn" – a 90-degree turn to port. "Had to change course to keep from getting in your line of fire. Do you wish me to come in again[?]" he asked Admiral Merrill. "This group is being fired upon."[128]

"Press your attack," the admiral answered.[129] Which did not quite answer the question, but all righty then. With that, Commander Austin ordered a 90-degree turn to starboard to head due west again.[130] For his part, Admiral Merrill ordered another 30-degree turn to starboard, putting his cruisers on a course of 230 degrees – roughly southwest. Slightly after 3:00am, Merrill decided he had closed the range enough and ordered a 130-degree starboard turn to arrange his cruisers back in column with the *Montpelier* in the lead headed due north. [131]

Admiral Merrill asked Captain Burke if his ships had fired all of their torpedoes. Burke answered that he had a half-load left, as did all the others except for one, who had none. The *Claxton*'s Commander Stout interjected, "My mistake. I fired all my fish."[132] Better to ask forgiveness than permission.

But the admiral was asking a different question when, just after this exchange, he received from an unidentified source the note, "I have been rammed."[133] Such a tantalizing, cryptic note deserved follow up, but Admiral Merrill did not immediately respond.

The message, as it turned out, came from Commander Austin. It was reported in the *Spence*'s voice radio log as "Someone rammed this ship. Have not found out who, will keep informed." Commander Austin started querying.

"*Thatcher*, are you with me?"

"Yes," came the answer.

"Keep it coming. *Foote*, are you still with me?"

After a moment of silence, Austin continued, "*Converse*, are you still with me?"

"Affirmative," came the answer.

That wasn't good. Where was the *Foote*?

"We came left to avoid a can," the *Thatcher* added. That explained things.

The simplest thing is difficult. With three of his four destroyers heading south in line abreast, Commander Austin had ordered a simultaneous 90-degree turn to starboard to reform the column heading due west with his own *Spence* in the lead. What happened next is not entirely clear. There is some belief that the *Thatcher* turned early, either because she misinterpreted a preparatory order as an execute, or that she simply anticipated the order; exactly how one would anticipate that order in this situation was left ambiguous.[134] More likely, what happened is that the *Thatcher* turned too quickly, too sharply, while the *Spence* rounded her turn a bit.

Either way, as the *Spence* was making her turn, she saw the *Thatcher* approaching off the port bow on a collision course. For her part, the *Thatcher* saw the *Spence* approaching her starboard beam. The *Thatcher* feared a head-on collision with her division leader, which would have been no small feat. The head-on was averted when the *Thatcher* went hard to port and backed engines and the *Spence* swung hard to starboard, but collision remained inevitable. The two destroyers ended up side swiping, *Thatcher*'s starboard beam to *Spence*'s port beam. The *Thatcher*'s starboard side was bashed in, but her guns and engines remained functional. The *Spence* immediately swung her bow to port to clear her stern of the *Thatcher* and thus limit the damage, which the *Spence*'s damage control reported to be relatively minor.[135]

"We are OK," the *Spence* announced.[136] Was everyone else OK? Where was the *Foote*?

Ever since Commander Ramsay had misunderstood Admiral Merrill's easily misunderstood "countermarch" order, the *Foote* had been struggling to get back into her position in the halftime show. The *Foote* had to change course and speed to get to her proper position in Austin's column, but in so doing she got mixed up with the cruisers and nearly run down by the *Denver*. The cruisers' turn to starboard to close the range to the Japanese delayed the destroyer's attempt to clear them.[137]

The *Foote* was finally able to cross well in front of the cruisers, except at that point they proceeded to fire over the destroyer at the Japanese. She raced ahead and, because her division mates were headed south instead of west, cut enough off the corner to close to 850 yards off the *Converse*'s starboard quarter.[138] Almost there.

Over the voice radio, the *Montpelier* had a rather cryptic question: "We almost rammed you. Who are you?"[139] The question would go unanswered for the next few minutes. The *Columbia* quickly chimed in, reporting a destroyer on her port bow.[140]

That was … ominous. The explanation would come two minutes later at 3:08am. "Have been hit in the after engine room. Cannot maneuver."[141] That was the *Foote*, all right.

The *Foote*'s effort to get back to her station – Morison described it as "hot-footing it in Austin's direction […]" – abruptly ended at 3:01am, when a torpedo exploded "under" the *Foote*'s stern.[142] It is not entirely clear who was responsible for launching the offensive Long Lance, but it was either the *Sendai* or, more likely, the *Samidare*.[143] What was clear was the damage to the *Foote*. The entire stern aft of frame 185 – basically the stern aft of the after 5-inch mount – was literally gone. Without a stern, you can't move and you can't steer; neither could the *Foote*, with both engine shafts bent and probably broken. All radio and detection equipment were knocked out of commission. Not surprisingly since the destroyer no longer had a stern, the main deck was awash aft with a 4-degree list to port. The main deck was cracked and bent at frames 43, 170, and 180. The after 5-inch mount was jammed in train. Three 20mm antiaircraft guns, the chemical smokescreen generator, and all 600lb depth charges were missing. A few minutes later those missing depth charges made themselves felt by exploding very deep under the destroyer. They caused no additional damage.[144]

But other American weapons could cause additional damage, because the *Foote* had drifted to a stop in the path of Admiral Merrill's cruisers. The *Montpelier* had to swerve to port to avoid the crippled destroyer. The *Montpelier* broadcast a warning about the *Foote's* presence in the path of the cruisers, but the *Cleveland* did not receive it. A gunflash revealed the disabled destroyer almost under her bow, and the *Cleveland* had to use full rudder to avoid the *Foote* by a mere 100 yards. As the *Cleveland* passed the destroyer, the *Foote* used an Aldis lamp to identify herself and report that she had been torpedoed and disabled. The destroyer was emitting smoke and other fumes, including apparently chlorine, which set off the gas alarms in the *Cleveland*.[145]

Within another 10 minutes, the *Foote* had gotten the radar and voice radio functioning again. She quickly reported to Commander Austin and Admiral Merrill, "Have been hit in the steering engine room. Cannot move."[146]

With that settled for the moment, the *Foote* sat in between two columns of cruisers who were shooting at each other, looking for a chance to make herself useful, like by launching her torpedoes and firing her guns at the Japanese if any came within her firing arcs. Also looking for an opportunity to fire their guns was Captain Burke's group of destroyers. When we last left our hero, he was speeding away from the Japanese while lamenting that all 20 of the torpedoes he had just launched had missed, then celebrating that some of the extra five torpedoes the *Claxton* had launched had scored. They hadn't, but for the time being it did not hurt to let him live the fantasy. Burke continued speeding away from the Japanese longer than he had planned because his lookouts had reported faint flashes from their Japanese targets, indicating they had launched torpedoes at Burke's group. Then Burke received "[U]nconfirmed but persistent reports of torpedo wakes passing us [...]." How he proposed to "confirm" torpedo wakes had passed is open to speculation, but he did not see any, so it must not have happened.[147]

In any event, as his destroyers sped away from the Japanese, Captain Burke opened fire on the Japanese with his 5-inch guns. In all the talk of better use of destroyers' torpedoes, it might be forgotten that destroyers have guns, too. This was Burke's own take on the Parthian shot. His plan was to turn to course 320 degrees True – northwest – to put his division back in "normal order" and guard the Americans' northern flank against a Japanese end run, about which Admiral Merrill was concerned.

But as his destroyers neared the limit of their gun range, Captain Burke was presented with an odd dilemma. Two contacts had just appeared on radar in "fairly good position" to make a torpedo attack on Admiral Merrill's cruisers. That was odd; Burke and his staff were mystified as to how two Japanese ships had managed to get there so quickly. The commodore ordered a 90-degree turn to port, then he started getting the idea something was not quite right with his own ships.[148]

Captain Burke radioed the *Dyson*, who was immediately behind his own destroyer *Charles Ausburne*. "Do you have another ship behind you?"[149]

"Yes," came the answer. "I think it is the *Claxton*, though."[150] *Claxton*? Where was the *Stanly*? The *Stanly* was supposed to be ahead of the *Claxton* and behind the *Dyson*.

"*Claxton*, are you with us?" Burke asked.

"I'm with *Stanly*," Commander Stout replied, which did not answer the question.[151]

The battle had now reached the point where the commanders were misplacing their own ships. It was very common in night battles. Remember the *Helena* at Kula Gulf? Of course, she was not so much misplaced as lost. And no one had seen it, even though she was in the middle of the US Navy cruiser column.

"I'm coming to course 180 (degrees True)," Burke announced.

"I have you bearing 010, distance 2½," the *Stanly* chimed in.[152]

Captain Burke had gone a bit beyond merely misplacing a ship. He had tracked two radar contacts that he thought were Japanese ships. They turned out to be two wayward destroyers of his own division. The commodore had been "chasing his own tail."[153]

"If you will join us we will go back and give them some more," came the order from Captain Burke.

"We are coming around behind you now," the *Stanly* replied. "You got the report we have no more fish."

"That's right," Burke confirmed.[154] The commodore would reform his division before and make sure all his ships were together before resuming his attack on the Japanese, possibly including the use of his last ten torpedoes.[155]

If it seems obvious to readers that the two allegedly Japanese radar contacts were actually the missing destroyers *Stanly* and *Claxton*, there is one complicating factor to keep in mind, one that readers might not be able to deduce from the written word: the radar. No, there was nothing wrong with the radar, and after almost two years of war, US Navy crews were fairly up to speed on radar, so there was nothing wrong with them. The issue was that this engagement was, geographically, a large action.

Recall that the Japanese Combined Assault Force was so spread out that from the 3rd Destroyer Flotilla to the 10th Destroyer Flotilla spanned eight miles. Ten ships across eight miles. Admiral Merrill felt compelled to keep his cruisers at what was believed to be the maximum range for the Type 93 torpedo. And Captain Burke's and Commander Austin's destroyer groups had to move far out on the flanks to attack the spread-out Japanese.

The result was, as the *Stanly* put it, an engagement "so spread out that no one ship had all others on the PPI (radar) scope continuously, which added to the complexity of the problem."[156] Captain Burke said the radar scope "became very confused" and admitted that both he and the *Charles Ausburne*'s combat information center could not keep track of his own ships, Admiral Merrill's cruisers, Commander Austin's destroyers, and the three Japanese columns, especially as all these groups began to disintegrate, the ships scattering.[157] Just imagine trying to watch an ice hockey or soccer game if all the players for both teams were wearing the exact same uniform and only one quarter of the playing area was visible at any one time.

What was very visible to the rest of the playing area was the burning *Sendai*. Hanging around in the general area of the *Sendai* were the three destroyers of Admiral Ijuin's 3rd Destroyer Flotilla. The *Samidare* and *Shiratsuyu*, their speed limited to about 15 knots as a result of damage from their collision, did not really have much else they could do. The *Shigure* was still in fighting shape, but the enemy shelling of the *Sendai* and the fires resulting therefrom were so fierce that the destroyer could only get as close as 500 meters off the *Sendai*'s starboard beam.[158] The *Sendai* herself was in grave condition. By 3:05am her stern was down by 2 meters and she had a 10-degree list to starboard.[159]

Captain Hara "watched glumly" as the crippled *Samidare* and *Shiratsuyu* received Admiral Omori's permission to withdraw.[160] They began moseying northwest toward Rabaul. Then the *Shigure*'s bridge lookout reported there was a message for Hara. It was from the stern Aldis lamp of the *Sendai*:

"*Shigure*, approach me … *Shigure*, approach me … *Shigure*, approach me …"[161]

This was both an emotional and a command dilemma for Captain Hara. He described Admiral Ijuin as his "best friend," and that best friend was requesting and very clearly needed help. But by this time the *Sendai* was an inferno, dangerous to approach even if the enemy was not shooting at them. And the enemy was still shooting at them. And hitting them, or at least hitting the *Sendai*. They had not hit the *Shigure* yet, but that could and would change if Hara approached the flotilla flagship, especially if the *Shigure* had to slow or stop to take off the crew. While the enemy was shooting at them.

The *Shigure*'s skipper Lieutenant Commander Yamagami quickly made his feelings known by yelling, "Let's go, Captain Hara. Let's approach *Sendai*. The Squadron Commander has given us an order."

The skipper's "imploring tone and words" tugged at the commodore's heart strings, but Hara had made his decision. "No, Yamagami, I have decided not to. If we go to *Sendai*'s aid we too will be pinned down by enemy gunfire. We might take off a few crewmen, but all of us would perish."

Lieutenant Commander Yamagami was incredulous and angry. "But we have orders!" he shouted.

"Orders? You are right!" Hara shouted back. "And let's get on with them. Our primary orders are to strike at the enemy. In battle rescue is always secondary. Let's go!"

"But our friends are asking for help," pleaded Yamagami. "They are dying before our eyes."

A furious Captain Hara thundered, "Shut up! This is no place for sentiment or debate. This is my responsibility. Don't interfere with authority!"

But Hara was right. Openly disagreeing with a superior in front of the crew is bad form, to say the least. Doing so vehemently was bordering insubordination.

On the other hand, though still 500 meters from the *Sendai* and unable to "close for rescue operations" by Hara's own statement, the *Shigure* was already standing by the flagship and Hara obviously had been contemplating those rescue operations. Now, *after* Admiral Ijuin ordered those operations to begin, Hara decides it's too dangerous and their orders "to attack the enemy" take precedence over rescue? It did not make much sense. Under the circumstances, not taking off Ijuin and the crew of the *Sendai* was the right call, if a coldly calculating and personally painful one. Hara might have been more persuasive, avoiding the argument with his skipper altogether, if he had continued "to attack the enemy" instead of standing by the *Sendai*.

Be that as it may, with Lieutenant Commander Yamagami now "stunned into silence" and respecting the commodore's authority, Captain Hara gave his new orders, "Port helm! Full speed ahead! We attack!" The *Shigure*'s engines quickly built up speed to 30 knots and she went off toward the south looking to tag along with other Japanese ships still fighting.

In the meantime, however, a lot had happened with those other Japanese ships still fighting. Admiral Omori's 5th Cruiser Division had not just turned around, but turned itself around almost completely, a port turn of at least 340 degrees, settling on a southerly course. Aside from doing the "hokey pokey," what exactly Omori accomplished with this maneuver remains rather nebulous.

No matter. The *Myoko* and *Haguro* were now heading due south, 180 degrees True. They were under fire, but Admiral Omori still could not get the position of the American cruisers nailed down.[162] The *Myoko* fired some illumination rounds, but according to Omori, they were duds and no illumination resulted. In actuality, according to Admiral Merrill, they fell short of the US Navy cruisers, which may not have been seen by the lookouts because of the drizzly weather conditions.[163]

Meanwhile, Admiral Osugi and his 10th Destroyer Flotilla were still charging at the US Navy cruisers. By 3:05am, Osugi was about 13,000 yards west of Admiral Merrill's cruisers.[164] Osugi was also starting to draw their fire, specifically from the *Columbia*.[165] He didn't like that. Not. One. Bit.

So, under gunfire that was uncomfortably close, but not actually hitting anything, Admiral Osugi's *Agano* led his three destroyers on a turn to port and skedaddled northwest back the way they had come – without even launching torpedoes.[166] In the culture of the Imperial Japanese Navy and especially its destroyers and destroyer flotillas, Brave Osugi turned about and gallantly chickened out.

As they beat a very brave retreat, they had to take evasive action.[167] Each ship zigging and zagging on its own as it felt necessary while maintaining a base course to the northwest. The *Agano* zigging to the left and zagging to the right. The *Naganami* zigging to the right and zagging to the left. The *Hatsukaze* zigging to the left and zagging to the right ...

BAM!!!

With a loud, jarring impact from starboard, the *Hatsukaze* heeled over. The view from the destroyer's bridge suddenly went completely black as she was dragged along to port for a moment. Then, with groans, creaks, and the sound of metal snapping, the *Hatsukaze*'s bow tore away. The front of what remained of the destroyer was now open, the engines pushing her at what was supposed to be high speed, but instead only driving the ship into the side of a much bigger ship, Admiral Omori's flagship *Myoko*. As the heavy cruiser passed, the *Hatsukaze* scraped away at the *Myoko*'s hull on the port side with more creaks, groans, and fingernails on a chalkboard. The time was 3:07am.[168]

On board the *Myoko*, Admiral Omori and his staff and skipper Nakamura Katsuhei, just promoted to rear admiral, had to recover their balance before taking stock of what had just happened. Omori himself was aghast. As he looked to port and then astern, he could see no sign of the *Hatsukaze*. He believed she was sunk.[169]

She was not sunk – not yet, anyway – but what exactly did happen to the *Hatsukaze* as a result of the collision remains uncertain. "[C]ommitting the most serious error of the night," in the words of Hara Tameichi, Admiral Osugi's rash charge had led to an even more rash retreat. It is possible that one or more of the Japanese illumination rounds that fell short went between Osugi's ships and Omori's ships, so that either could have been screened from the sight of the other, but that is unlikely. More likely is that, in his mad dash for the rear, Osugi, in his first surface battle, was too focused on getting away from the Americans to notice his retreat was cutting across the path of Admiral Omori's *Myoko* and *Haguro*. The *Agano* and the *Naganami* got by in front of the *Myoko*, but the *Hatsukaze* did not; she was trying to regain her position in Osugi's column when the *Myoko* came knifing through.[170] Following the *Myoko*, sister ship *Haguro* just barely avoided colliding with the destroyer following the *Hatsukaze*, the *Wakatsuki*.[171]

For which the Japanese were very fortunate. While the collision between the *Samidare* and the *Shiratsuyu* is generally described as a side-swipe, most indications point to the collision between the *Myoko* and the *Hatsukaze* being one of the worst kinds: both ships at high speed, apparently neither making so much as an attempt to evade the other, colliding at something approaching right angles, maybe even a T-bone, a crossing of the T the Japanese would rather not have accomplished.[172]

While Hara says the *Myoko* "brushed the tender nose" of the destroyer, not mentioning a severance of the bow, there is general agreement that the *Myoko* sliced off the *Hatsukaze*'s bow. But what constitutes the "bow" is open to interpretation. Admiral Omori would later say the *Myoko* "apparently cut *Hatsukaze* in half." His description suggests that what is generally described as the "bow" in this case really means, at least, everything forward of the bridge.[173] Supporting this inference is the *Myoko*'s later return to port, where part of the *Hatsukaze*'s starboard bow was found wrapped around the cruiser's bow.[174] For her part, as the *Myoko* passed the wrecked destroyer, the jagged remainder of the *Hatsukaze* dragged down the cruiser's hull on the port side, damaging the main deck structure and tearing off two torpedo tubes.[175]

A "panic-stricken" Admiral Osugi led the remainder of his column on a turn to starboard, apparently trying to go back for the *Hatsukaze*, but either "[a] quick survey was enough to convince him that nothing could be done for her in the height of battle" or, more likely, he could not find the wrecked destroyer. He continued the starboard turn for almost 270 degrees to fall in on the starboard quarter of the *Myoko* and *Haguro*.[176]

If they could stop playing bumper ships, the *Myoko* and the *Haguro* still had to deal with those annoying US cruisers. Having pummeled the *Sendai* and chased off Admiral Osugi's group, the *Denver, Columbia*, and *Cleveland* were now sending shells toward the 5th Cruiser Division. Admiral Omori watched as the Americans' third salvo "walked right into the target." This would be the *Haguro*, who was hit by six 6-inch shells, only two of which exploded, killing one and wounding five, starting some minor fires but little real damage. The fourth salvo was over, and Admiral Omori maneuvered to keep the rest over as well.[177]

So far, the Battle of Empress Augusta Bay had consisted of wrecking the *Sendai*, disabling the *Foote*, and collisions. Three collisions, two by the Japanese. This was a bizarre, almost comical, and definitely poorly executed engagement by both sides so far. Yet it was about to get much more dangerous.

At around 3:12am, according to Admiral Merrill, the illumination rounds fired by the Japanese cruisers started becoming much more effective. "At this time the rain had ceased but a heavy bank of clouds hung over the formation at about 1,500 feet. As the enemy's brilliant star shells broke through, the ceiling of clouds acted as a reflector and enhanced the intensity of the illumination."[178] Captain Burke called it, "the most effective illumination that any of us had ever seen."[179] Think of it as shining a flashlight on the ceiling. There was a bigger problem, however. Japanese cruiser floatplanes that had been the bane of Allied naval forces since the beginning of the Pacific War would be so on this night. One floatplane, probably the one from the *Haguro* and probably the infamous Mitsubishi F1M Type 0 Observation Seaplane – the "Jake" – started dropping flares behind the US Navy cruisers, and even dropped some red flares to communicate to Admiral Omori that these ships were cruisers.[180] Merrill saw that the flares were falling on the disengaged port side and about to backlight his ships, so he ordered an immediate 30-degree turn to port to try to put the flares on the starboard side so they would not silhouette his ships.[181] Once he was able to put the flares between his cruisers and the Japanese, he had his cruisers resume the course due south.

Nevertheless, it was not until 3:13am that the Japanese finally saw the US Navy cruisers, when a lookout on the *Myoko* reported them at a bearing of 80 degrees True – roughly east northeast. Admiral Omori changed the course of his own cruisers from 180 degrees to 160 degrees True in order to close the range. Two minutes later both the *Myoko* and the *Haguro* opened fire with their 8-inch main batteries. Captain Hara derided the Japanese cruisers who, as far as he could tell, "opened fire blindly with their big guns, in the general direction of the enemy."[182] Admiral Merrill and the Americans would soon take issue with the "blindly" part.

At 3:18, five minutes after she had finally located the American cruisers and three minutes after she had opened fire with her 8-inch battery, the *Myoko* unleashed four of her deadly Type 93 torpedoes; the *Haguro* followed two minutes later with six.[183] According to Hara, the two cruisers "released a total of 24 torpedoes which were entirely wasted."[184]

While that assessment is harsh, the reality is that the action reports of Admiral Merrill and the US Navy cruisers do not mention having to dodge torpedoes.

It was at this point in the duel of the cruisers that Commander Austin's three remaining destroyers started making their presence felt. In more ways than one. At 3:11, the *Spence*, she later reported, saw a single ship pass down her port side. It was believed to be American, but it seems to have actually been Captain Hara's *Shigure* speeding south looking for friends to join, and somehow passing both Admiral Omori's 5th Cruiser Division and Admiral Osugi's 10th Destroyer Flotilla while seeing neither. Hara had then spent ten minutes in a "frantic search for targets." Then he tried to find targets by "following gunfire traces," but that did not work, either, though it might explain how he missed Austin's three destroyers, who were not yet using their guns. The skill level of the Japanese lookouts, so good – even better than American radar – for so long had deteriorated just as the skill level of pretty much everyone else in the Imperial Japanese Navy had. Austin may not have seen the *Shigure*, either, as he does not mention the sighting in his report. If he did see her, he ignored her, for he had bigger fish to fry. And launch.[185]

Commander Austin's destroyer division was closing in on the *Myoko* and *Haguro* from the east. This caused problems for both sides because, while Admiral Omori's heavy cruisers were in danger from the destroyers, by 3:20am on Admiral Merrill's radar the blips of Austin's destroyers had merged with those of the *Myoko* and *Haguro*. Merrill called it "a source of distress to the Officer in Tactical Command as from this time on there was doubt as to the identity of ships near this bearing."[186]

The admiral's distress may have been justified. Commander Austin's destroyer *Spence* was rocked by two near misses to starboard, then at 3:19am was hit by a third that left a diagonal gash four feet long and one foot wide in the hull near the starboard quarter at frame 157. This hit started what the *Spence* described as "[a] minor fire" that burned one mattress before it was put out.[187] The hole was plugged with shores, mattresses, and bags of beans.[188] Beans. Is there anything they can't do?

Indeed, there was. While beans have a reputation for giving gas, they could not give gas to the *Spence*. The hit pierced three compartments, causing seawater to mix with the destroyer's bunker fuel before the damaged part of the system could be isolated. As a result, the after fuel system was contaminated by seawater.[189] Because the *Spence* had not been able to refuel before coming to Empress Augusta Bay, she had very little fuel to spare. The seawater running in the fueling system would cause the *Spence* to basically stall repeatedly.

More curious was the hit itself, especially the question of exactly who landed it. The *Myoko* has been given credit for the hit in some histories.[190] The *Spence*'s skipper Commander Henry J. Armstrong did not identify the source of the shell, but he did believe it to be Japanese.[191] The shell did not explode, but rather, Armstrong believed, the high angle of the shell's trajectory caused it to glance off the hull, shattering in the process, and land in the water.[192] Little of the shell was recovered, but among the pieces recovered was "part of the nose of a common projectile, six inch."[193] Assuming Armstrong is correct, since the *Myoko*'s main battery is 8-inch and her secondary battery is 5-inch, that would seem to rule out the heavy cruiser as the source of the shell. Admiral Merrill would later write that the *Spence*, while "under fire from a ship of the northern group, received an enemy 6-inch shell hit [...]."[194] None of the ships in the northern group had 6-inch guns. The closest anyone could come was the *Sendai*, whose main guns fired 5.5-inch shells. The light cruiser *Agano* had 6-inch guns, but she seems to have been off the *Spence*'s port bow on the starboard quarter of the *Myoko* and *Haguro*, who themselves were dead ahead.[195] The hit was to the *Spence*'s starboard quarter and, if Armstrong is correct, from a high angle that suggests long-range fire. When these factors are added to the ongoing gun duel between the 5th Cruiser Division and Admiral Merrill's 6-inch-armed light cruisers who were to starboard and the merging of Austin's destroyers' blip with that of the *Myoko* and *Haguro*, it becomes difficult to rule out the disturbing possibility that the *Spence* was hit by 6-inch fire from the *Denver*, *Columbia*, or *Cleveland*. Fortunately, the hit caused no casualties, but it did increase the danger to the *Spence* with her very limited fuel now contaminated.

Be that as it may, Commander Austin continued his charge toward the *Myoko* and *Haguro*, the range now 6,000 yards and closing fast. It was time for his three ambulatory destroyers to unleash 30 new improved Mark 15 torpedoes (now with Torpex!) on two 8-inch-armed cruisers which had 55-gallon drums of Allied blood on their hands, starting with the Java Sea Campaign, and were starting to turn the tables on the US Navy's only remaining operational surface force in the South Pacific, a surface force that, while state-of-the-art and capable of rapid fire of 6-inch ammunition, was significantly outgunned. But plugging the *Myoko* and *Haguro* with torpedoes could turn the table back ...

Hold on, said a target evaluator in the combat information center, two decks below where Austin was located on the bridge. Those two big ships dead ahead were not Japanese heavy cruisers, but friendly ships – Captain Burke's destroyers.

Well, that was a buzzkill. With the range closing fast, Commander Austin had no time to evaluate the evaluator's evaluation. "[B]eing an aggressive leader who is capable of making decisions," as Admiral Merrill would describe him, Austin just swerved to starboard to head for the northern group of Japanese ships that was definitely enemy because they were shooting at him. Well, one of them was shooting at him and, as far as he could tell, had hit his ship.

Not shooting at him were three ships that the *Thatcher* reported passing down her port side at 3:22 at a range of about 3,000 yards.[196] These appear to have been Admiral Osugi's light cruiser *Agano* leading the *Naganami* and *Wakatsuki*. By this point, Admiral Osugi, in his first surface battle, does appear to have been "panic-stricken" (as Captain Hara said, despite his reputation for aggressiveness) by losing the *Hatsukaze* or simply by the enemy shooting at him. What remained of his 10th Destroyer Flotilla was now hanging out off the starboard quarter of the mighty *Myoko* and hefty *Haguro*. It was safer that way.

So Commander Austin passed all these ships that were not shooting at him to target the one that was shooting at him from a distance. That ship was the hapless *Sendai*. At one point, that ship had been stopped. She had started slowly circling.[197] Her engineers and damage control teams had managed to get one of her engines going, but with her rudder jammed the light cruiser was going nowhere. Even so, the old and ugly light cruiser was a veteran, with veteran gunners who lashed out like a wounded animal with her functional 5.5-inch guns, and remained "as dangerous as a wounded water buffalo."[198]

The *Spence* closed to about 6,000 yards and at 3:28 fired a half salvo of five torpedoes. Behind her, the *Converse* loosed three of her own. Two underwater explosions were felt at about the time the torpedoes were to have hit, but none of the lookouts saw any visible explosions.[199] With potentially larger targets on radar to the northwest, at 3:30 Commander Austin ordered a course change to 320 degrees True and speed to 34 knots to chase them down.[200]

The combat information center was a relatively new development in naval technology. It was a dedicated room into which all the sources of combat intelligence, especially the radars, are gathered and passed on to the people – especially skippers, commodores, and admirals – who could use it. Those two most important, intertwined facets of any combat operation, communications and information, were and are wedded to each other in the combat information center.

Today, the combat information center is considered the nerve center of any warship. It was not quite that during the Pacific War, because it was so new; the US Navy was just getting a feel for it, its potential, and its utility.

And this incident would be an example of getting a feel for it. Commander Austin had been in the combat information center so he could have all this intelligence at his fingertips, but when the *Spence* and the *Thatcher* had collided, he went to the bridge, two decks up. Without Austin in the combat information center, the radarmen and the evaluators became disoriented. Austin, on the bridge, could not correct them.

Admiral Merrill would later lament, "A golden opportunity to attack two Japanese heavy cruisers at close range, 4,000–6,000 yards, with thirty torpedoes, was lost because the Division Commander (Austin) was not able to easily to get into the Combat Information Center from time to time to check the decision of the evaluator. Had he been able to step directly into Combat Information Center from time to time and look at the plot, his experience would have told him immediately that this unit could <u>not</u> have been friendly." (Emphasis in original.)[201]

With a new lease on life, the *Myoko* and *Haguro* turned to unleash death. Thanks to the better visibility, the air-dropped flares, and the clouds that helped magnify those flares, the Japanese 8-inch gunfire, which had so far been heavy but inaccurate, started improving in accuracy and getting uncomfortably close to the US Navy cruisers. At 3:20, Admiral Merrill ordered, "Counter illuminate with starshells."[202] "Counter illuminate" is probably as military a word or phrase as they come, but here it had a specific context. Merrill wanted to fire starshells that would fall between the Americans and the Japanese, thus allowing his cruisers to hide behind their glare. It was another tactic the Japanese had used before, specifically during the night portion of the Battle of the Java Sea, and so may have been borrowed from them. The only problem was, "[p]erhaps due to the feebleness of our starshells compared with those of the enemy, this did very little good [...]."[203] Merrill also ordered a 20-degree turn to starboard to try to shake off the shells.[204]

The *Denver*, *Columbia*, and *Cleveland*, who had been targeting the center and southern Japanese groups, drew the bulk of the fire and were repeatedly straddled in range. According to the *Cleveland*, "[a]fter illumination was established, the enemy error in deflection was so small that, while they were not hitting, the ship steamed through the splashes before they had fallen away. This probably lead [sic] the enemy spotters to believe they were hitting."[205] Admiral Merrill made similar observations.[206] The *Myoko* and *Haguro* were observed to fire 10-gun salvos every 15 seconds or so, with the characteristically tight Japanese spread, in this case of 100–200 yards.[207]

Sure enough, the 5th Cruiser Division started hitting. At 3:20, as Admiral Merrill was trying to "counter illuminate," the *Denver*, now leading the line of light cruisers, was hit by an 8-inch shell that did not explode. There were more where that came from. At 3:22, the *Denver* was hit by an 8-inch shell that was far more damaging, passing completely through the ship from just below the main deck at frame 37 on the starboard side and exiting just below the third deck at frame 28 on the port side below the waterline, but, once again, failing to explode. Nevertheless, one compartment was completely flooded, three more were partially flooded, and bedding was set afire in a store room. A third 8-inch hit was received shortly thereafter at frame 6 near the bow, once again passing completely through the ship from starboard to port, and once again not exploding.[208]

Admiral Merrill was certainly impressed:

> [The enemy's] patterns were small and during the period of effective illumination, they were exceedingly accurate. [The enemy's] 10 gun [sic] salvos appeared almost as one enormous splash when seen from the line of fire and the pattern limits in range appeared to be as low as 200 yards. Had the enemy's luck been as good as his shooting we would have suffered severe casualties.[209]

With damage incurred from three different salvos, the *Denver* began independent evasive maneuvers to try to throw off the Japanese aim. The *Columbia* had watched one salvo land just short and another just over, so she resorted to basically chasing the salvos, moving toward where the last salvo landed so when the Japanese gunners corrected their aim, they would miss again.

The *Myoko* and *Haguro* were starting to make their gunpower advantage felt. Just as bad if not worse, the range between the Admiral Omori's heavy cruisers and Admiral Osugi's group, such as it was, on one hand, and Admiral Merrill's light cruisers on the other had dwindled to 13,000 yards – too close to Japanese torpedo territory for Merrill's taste. Moreover, his cruisers had been on the same course for six minutes – roughly the amount of time for Japanese torpedoes to reach him.

At 3:24, in a very unusual tactic for the US Navy, Admiral Merrill ordered his cruisers to immediately make smoke, both with funnels and dischargers.[210] For reasons known only to the US Navy, while it used smokescreens a lot during amphibious operations to cover landing troops, it had refrained from using smokescreens during surface engagements for pretty much the entirety of the Pacific War. The Japanese were fairly liberal in their use of smokescreens during surface engagements, including during the November 15 action off Guadalcanal. Even the Royal Navy used smokescreens during the Pacific War, especially in trying to protect the crippled cruiser *Exeter* during the Battle of the Java Sea.

Smokescreens had some reduced effectiveness against the Japanese, however, because of their very liberal use of cruiser floatplanes, which would fly over the smoke and spot the fall of gunfire. But that reduced effectiveness came with the caveat that gunfire dependent on forward spotters is generally not as effective as gunfire spotted from, say, the main battery director, especially against moving targets. The reluctance of the US Navy to use smokescreens in surface combat is a mystery, especially considering a smokescreen would block Japanese lookouts, no matter how great their training or their optics, while not inhibiting American radar. It may simply have been a lack of confidence in or understanding of early radar. But Admiral Merrill had confidence in his radar and knew how to use it. The smokescreen, while maybe yet another idea taken from the Imperial Japanese Navy, was a very logical play.

Admiral Merrill waited a few moments to give the smoke a chance to take effect. The low cloud ceiling had served to reflect the light from the Japanese flares, thus intensifying their illuminative effect. The smoke almost completely nullified that effect. It filled the space below the clouds around the American light cruisers and would have diffused the light. In the midst of this smokescreen, Merrill ordered a 160-degree turn to port to open the range. It brought the cruisers to course 40 degrees True – roughly northeast. A few minutes later, he ordered another 40-degree turn to port to reform the column, now with the *Montpelier* in the lead, heading due north.[211]

The gunfire from Admiral Omori's heavy cruisers started to fall off in volume, as, once again, his lookouts could not see their targets.

However uncomfortable the engagement was becoming for Admiral Merrill, it was more so for Admiral Omori. He did receive a report at 3:27am that one Japanese torpedo had hit the leading US Navy cruiser, two had hit the second, and two had hit the third. Gunfire hits were also reported.[212]

Yet immediately after that report, Admiral Omori changed course to 180 degrees True – due south – and away from the American cruisers.[213] He did not know the composition of the forces opposing him, but, as Omori later explained:

The analysis of reports indicated that there were at least 7 heavy cruisers and 12 destroyers opposing us. I had lost one cruiser by shell fire, one due to collision and two additional destroyers out of action due to collision. The *Myoko* had lost 30 percent of its torpedo tubes.

Our formation speed was reduced to 26 knots due to bomb damage of the *Haguro*. We had exhausted our supply of flares. Aircraft flares did not seem effective. The *Haguro* had received six 6" hits although four of them were duds. In addition I felt that I should retire by [3:00am] in order to be outside of the radius of dive-bombers by dawn. This radius was considered 250 miles.[214]

At 3:37am, Omori ordered the remaining ambulatory ships of the Combined Assault Force to break off and head back to Rabaul.[215] Three minutes later, Admiral Osugi's 10th Destroyer Flotilla launched eight Type 93s at Admiral Merrill's leading cruisers in a rather perfunctory attack before turning away. Though the range was extreme, about 15 minutes later, Osugi reported getting one hit on a cruiser as his squadron took position on the port side of the 5th Cruiser Division for the trek back to Rabaul.[216]

Already headed toward Rabaul were whatever Commander Austin's destroyers were chasing. The radar resolved into two (some said three) separate targets varying speeds between 15 and 25 knots. Austin's destroyers were roaring along at 34 knots, but it was still a stern chase and it took a while to close the range from the original 17,000 yards.[217] After some 20 minutes of chasing that included passing through an oil slick, the *Spence* had closed the range to about 3,000 yards and Austin ordered a torpedo attack. The *Spence* fired her remaining half salvo of five torpedoes to starboard, then turned away to port on a course of 220 degrees True – roughly southwest. The *Thatcher* followed after launching her full load of ten torpedoes, then the *Converse* with four; she could not launch a fifth due to "a misfunctioning of one torpedo firing key."[218] The *Thatcher* reported seeing explosions suggesting the torpedoes hit, the *Spence* saw no explosions but felt two underwater explosions, while the *Converse* saw and felt nothing.[219]

After opening the range back up to 7,000 yards, Commander Austin decided to try to cross the targets' "T" from astern, so he turned west and "executed Dog" at 3:58am.[220] Once again, no animals were harmed in the execution of this coded order to open fire with the 5-inch main battery. The only one injured was the target, the destroyer *Samidare*, who, with the *Shiratsuyu*, was hobbling as fast as she could away from the battle zone. They were still capable of defending themselves, however, and began returning the gunfire. The *Samidare* even loosed six torpedoes at her pursuers at 4:01am, which was the same time the bridge of the *Spence* reported both targets were set afire by the shelling.[221] The *Samidare* took two direct hits which knocked out her steering control, forcing her to resort to hand steering. Five men were killed and five injured. Her skipper Lieutenant Commander Sugihara Yoshiro reported, "We returned gunfire and launched six torpedoes at the enemy, and believe we inflicted as much damage as we received."[222]

Not quite. None of her pursuers were damaged, but one of them, the *Spence*, had already suffered damage that manifested itself at 4:10am, when she lost suction due to the saltwater contamination of her fuel. She turned off to port to drop out, but the *Thatcher* and *Converse*, not realizing what was going on, still followed her. At 4:15, Commander Austin radioed his two following destroyers, "Continue to pursue these two targets and try to finish them off." He then radioed Captain Burke, "*Spence* having to drop out [on] account [of] oil trouble, am telling my boys to finish off those two."[223]

Burke had, rather prudently, chosen to round up the scattered li'l doggies of his Destroyer Division 45 before charging at the enemy once again. He then led his destroyers on a course of 230 degrees True – roughly southwest – and later turned due west in an attempt to reach the closest of several contacts showing up on his radar. Roaring on at 33 knots, Burke noted that the skippers of his division "seemed to enjoy" running and maneuvering at full battle speed.[224] Whatever floats your boat. In this case, literally.

At 3:35am, Burke's *Charles Ausburne* led the *Dyson*, *Stanly*, and *Claxton* on a turn to 300 degrees True – roughly northwest. He was trying to close on two ships that appeared to be together on his radar, but one turned and fled to the north, in Burke's words, "abandoning his friend dead in the water to the fate which was about to overtake him." It was around this time that he received Commander Austin's message that the *Spence* had lost suction due to the contaminated fuel and that he had ordered the *Thatcher* and *Converse* to continue chasing enemy ships. Burke was somewhat concerned because he did not know where the *Spence* was, or, for that matter, where the *Thatcher* and *Converse* were.[225]

But that was not going to stop Captain Burke from dishing out its fate to the ship that was dead in the water. At 3:49am, the commodore's destroyers made a high-speed pass at a range of 7,000 yards firing their main guns at the disabled ship, which he described as "larger than a destroyer," meaning that it was not the *Spence*. Hopefully.[226]

Because Burke's division proceeded to score repeated hits on the ship, starting small fires all over, and possibly causing her to start to settle. He did not stop or even slow down for the target, and after inflicting "such terrific punishment" in this drive-by shooting, the destroyers ceased fire to save what little was left of their ammunition to "see if we could get a live one." He turned to the west northwest and moved on.[227]

Captain Burke turned to Commander Reynolds. "You know, Brute, that was a big fellow, and she couldn't have been a light hulled ship either, considering the gun punishment we gave her without sinking her. She must be a cruiser."[228] Indeed, she was the luckless *Sendai*. It's not clear what additional damage, if any, Burke's destroyers caused, but at 3:50 the starboard list had increased to 15 degrees and the flooding was getting worse. At 4:00am, the order to abandon ship was given.[229] With her accompanying destroyers gone, however, prospects for the rescue of her crew were bleak.

"But where the hell is Division 46?" the commodore continued. "They must be low on fuel; we're all running out of ammo, and I don't like this business of not knowing where Austin is or what he's up to."

"Well, I'll tell you how I figure it, Commodore," replied the skipper. "The Count, Heinie Armstrong, Ralph Lampman, and Ham Hamberger are all certain to do one thing. That's head for the enemy. I figure all we have to do is look around for a fight, head for it, and I dare say we'll pick 'em up!"[230]

Captain Burke did look for a fight. His next target was 21,000 yards away and making 34 knots. Burke started chasing it, but he quickly realized this was a stern chase and he was unlikely to catch the target unless it made a mistake or had some malfunction in its propulsion. He reported his status to Admiral Merrill, who responded by ordering him to send one of his destroyers back to identify the target they had just blasted. Burke told him he would not do that because he was already 8,000 yards beyond the disabled target and, more importantly in this area of scattered and unidentified contacts on radar, he wanted to keep his ships together.[231]

With the stern chase becoming a losing proposition as the target pulled away, Captain Burke and Commander Reynolds found their fight at 4:03am when gunfire was seen to port. The *Charles Ausburne* and the rest of the Little Beavers headed toward it. He suspected the *Spence* was somewhere around here and called out to her. Commander Austin reported the *Spence* was engaging two Japanese ships while trying to chase them down. Burke decided to join in and turned due west at 4:13, then to 260 degrees True at 4:15 in order to close the range. A few minutes later, the *Charles Ausburne* came across a ship that was "smoking badly." When the ship turned to port, Burke called up Austin and asked, "Are there any enemies coming toward me?"

"Don't really know where you are," Austin replied, which did not answer the question, for obvious reasons.

Burke admonished the four destroyers in his division. "Do not open fire on smoking ship, think it is ComDesDiv 46 (Austin)."

"We are east of you, I think," Austin clarified. Poorly.

"I am sure you are," Burke agreed. "We have a target smoking badly at range 7,000 yards and are going to open up."

"Oh-Oh, don't do it, that's us," came the reply from Austin.[232]

Sigh. How disappointing. Especially since it was not Austin's *Spence*, who was actually west of Burke's destroyers.[233]

That only took care of things for a little while. Because someone was shooting at the *Spence* from off her port quarter. There began another round of inquiry.

"I think you are about due west of us," Burke explained. "Will you check?"

"Group of ships due south of us which I think is you," Austin answered. Things quickly started getting a little more serious. "I think we just got another bad hit here. Hope you are not shooting at us."

"We'd like to," explained Burke, "but we can't find out where the hell you are."[234]

Moving on, Captain Burke's destroyers saw more gunfire at bearing 264 degrees True – roughly west southwest. At 4:30am, radar also showed two contacts to the northeast. Burke figured those contacts were the *Thatcher* and *Converse* of Commander Austin's group, so he headed west toward the gunfire. A frustrated Burke reported to Admiral Merrill at 4:38, "There's a hell of a lot of ships of both nationalities in one little huddle on our port bow. If we can identify one as enemy, we will take care of him!"[235] He had just missed two. Just before 4:30, the *Thatcher* and *Converse* had just passed Burke's group – to the south – on an opposite course – at a distance of less than 1,000 yards. The *Converse* appears to have fired a few shots at one of Burke's destroyers, but quickly stopped in the mistaken belief she was firing on the *Spence*. Otherwise, neither column even noticed the other. The *Thatcher* and *Converse* continued chasing those two ships to the northeast, who were the *Samidare* and *Shiratsuyu* scooching away.[236]

Oh, well. Closing in on the gunfire revealed a ship off the *Charles Ausburne*'s port beam. Captain Burke then radioed his skippers, "Does anybody have any doubt that the ship on port beam is enemy?"

Who said the military is not a democracy? No one objected. The *Stanly* even chimed in, "Think he is enemy."

That was what he was waiting for. Burke radioed, "Stand by to fire on ship on port beam. Does anyone know where the *Foote* is?" Not entirely damn the torpedoes, but he had to fight this war with no idea where Commander Austin's destroyers were. "Commence firing on target."

The *Charles Ausburne*, *Dyson*, *Stanly*, and *Claxton* opened fire with their main batteries. It was quick and accurate fire, straddling the target five times. That was when Commander Austin decided to interject.

"Cease firing. Cease firing. Goddamn it, that's me!"

"Were you hit?" asked Burke.

"Negative," replied the *Spence*, "but they aren't all here yet!"[237]

"Sorry, but you'll have to excuse the next four salvos. They're already on their way!" came the reply from Captain Burke. This line became an instant classic in the US Navy.[238] None of the voice radio logs show this line specifically, but those logs have been known to paraphrase or even omit.

This was getting ridiculous. Like no matter what Captain Burke did, he was just destined to shoot at Commander Austin's *Spence*. The *Spence* turned on her identification lights, always dangerous in a night battle, as Savo Island had made clear, but there seemed to be little choice here. "Just showed my fighting lights. Did you identify my lights?" asked Austin. "They're on now."

"They bear 200 degrees from us," Burke answered. That clarified things.

"I think you are the one who shot at us then," Austin announced.

Burke could only respond with, "I'm afraid so too."[239]

But the squadron commander was not as embarrassed or sheepish as his response would suggest. He turned to Commander Reynolds with a big grin, exclaiming, "Well now, by God, at least we know where *Spence* is!"[240]

With that finally settled, Captain Burke ordered the *Spence* to fall in behind the *Claxton* to keep his ships together and have no more problems of identification.

Problems of identification were not limited to Captain Burke's squadron of destroyers. Admiral Merrill's cruisers were having issues of their own. Still trying to shake the 8-inch gunfire, at 3:37am the cruisers had settled on a course of 300 degrees True – roughly west northwest – on a line of bearing with, as they had been the entire battle, the *Montpelier* in the north and the *Denver* in the south. It was not the nice and neat formation it had been earlier though. "Are you out of formation," Merrill asked the *Columbia*. "If so, what's the trouble?"

"We are in position unhit," came the *Columbia's* reply.

"Which one of us is out of formation?"

"We are," reported the *Denver*. It was the result of her maneuvering to evade the gunfire directed at her. Admiral Merrill told her to get back in formation.

At 3:54am, the *Montpelier* radioed the *Cleveland*, "You appear to have a light well forward."

Not the *Cleveland*, as the cruiser replied, "We think [the] ship showing light well forward is *Columbia*. We can see it, too."

Now it was time to ask the *Columbia*, "Do you have [a] light well forward?" Merrill asked. "Appears to be fire." There was no answer.

"You have a light showing low on your bow," the admiral asked four minutes later. Still no answer. He repeated his statement. Still no answer. Was the *Columbia* having issues with its voice radio? Maybe unable to hear him? One way to find out.

"Execute to follow: 3 turn." He even repeated the preparatory order; a 30-degree turn to port. "*Columbia* acknowledge."

"Wilco." No problem getting that message.

"Stand by, execute."

That was simple enough.

"Execute to follow: 210 turn." Again, he repeated it, a port turn to 210 degrees. "*Columbia* acknowledge."

"Wilco."

"Stand by, execute."

That was simple enough.

"You're still showing light forward. Very low," the *Cleveland* notified the *Columbia*. No acknowledgment of the message.

Now the *Columbia* got in on the act. "You are showing a light," she radioed the *Montpelier*.

"Where is the light? You still have a light near the waterline. Looks like it might be a shell hole," the flagship answered. "Where is our light? Yours is on the bow on the waterline."

"There is a mistake. There is no light showing. Out."

While Admiral Merrill's tactics were aggressive, it would seem the *Columbia's* Captain Beatty preferred tactics that were more passive-aggressive. Having not acknowledged any message telling him that his ship was showing a light that could reveal their position, even going so far as to accuse the flagship of showing a light, at 4:25, Beatty received word from the *Columbia's* damage control teams that there was, in fact, a shell hole near the bow at frame 9 about 7 feet above the waterline. As best as they could tell, an 8-inch shell had splashed short of the cruiser. In so doing the base plug ricocheted off the water, pierced the hull, and traveled almost completely through the ship to bounce off the interior of the hull at frame 10, leaving a large, unsightly dent, coming to rest in a sail locker. One compartment was flooded with about two feet of water. The light reported by the other cruisers was the *Columbia*'s interior light showing through the hole, which was patched with a mattress – mattresses and bedding seemed to be playing an outsized role this night – shored up with a wooden plank. The water was pumped out.[241] That took care of the offending light.

Not that anyone could tell from reading Captain Beatty's after-action report, which makes no mention of the light, though it does mention that an 8-inch shell nicked a radar antenna on the mainmast, not "affect[ing] measurably" performance except making the motion of the antenna "somewhat noisy and rough." But Admiral Merrill mentioned the light, noting, "[T]he light which showed through this hole caused considerable hard feelings between the Officer in Tactical Command and the *Columbia*."[242]

Ship identification was a constant problem in this engagement. At 4:45am, Admiral Merrill asked the *Montpelier*'s skipper Captain Tobin if he was ready to open fire on a target bearing 318 distance 19,000 yards. Tobin answered, "Affirmative." At 4:48, Merrill announced, "*Montpelier* will turn on battle [identification] lights for 10 seconds. Everyone take bearing. I want to identify."[243] Had to be done.

Because the admiral then called out, "Unknown ship, you bear 326, 17,000 yards from me. I am going to open fire unless you identify yourself."[244] Nothing. At 4:56, the *Montpelier* fired what was basically a warning salvo at the unknown ship, now bearing 330, distance 17,500 yards, but offset so that it missed but was close enough to get the ship's attention.

Or not. Still no response, no indication that it was a friendly ship. Admiral Merrill ordered Captain Tobin to open fire on the silent ship. After one minute of shooting, Merrill ordered cease fire. The ship had flashed its identification lights; it was Commander Austin's *Spence*, who was having a very unpleasant night.[245]

At 5:12 the *Montpelier*'s radar picked up a new contact, bearing 34 degrees True, distance 29,700 yards. The main battery fire control radar locked it in, and, when the range had closed to 22,000 yards, the fire director announced it was ready to open fire. Admiral Merrill did it again, "I have a target at 030 at 22,000 yards. Am going to open fire unless you identify."

"Don't shoot. It's me," pleaded the *Converse*.

"Turn on your fighting lights," Merrill ordered.

The destroyer complied. "Lights are on."

"We see your lights, who is with you?"

"*Thatcher* is with us," answered the *Converse*.[246]

It was a source of considerable frustration. The *Charles Ausburne*'s Commander Reynolds acidly noted, "From 0416 to until [sic] 0510 we were trying to distinguish our forces from the enemy, with little or no result."[247]

The results were mostly set. Mostly. Captain Burke had his destroyers turn north at 4:55am to pursue a target heading north, but its lead was too great, so he broke it off. At

4:57, Admiral Merrill brought the action to a screeching halt. Mostly. He ordered Burke to gather his Little Beavers and rendezvous with the cruisers to withdraw. The admiral expected heavy air attacks after dawn and he wanted his ships together for maximum antiaircraft effectiveness.

There were still two unidentified contacts on Captain Burke's radar. He determined one was a squall. The other one was moving at about 10 knots on a course of 345 degrees True – roughly north northwest. Commander Austin delayed his withdrawal and the *Spence* split off to 70 degrees True – roughly east northeast – to check it out. The *Spence* closed to about 4,000 yards and fired a salvo across the ship's bow, asking by radio if she was firing on a friendly unit. There was no answer, so she determined this was a group of three enemy ships. It was a rather curious determination inasmuch as the *Spence*, all by herself, chose to attack these allegedly three ships – one-on-three fast breaks rarely work.[248] Not only that, it was actually only one ship. Or, more accurately, half a ship.

Because this target was the short lost destroyer *Hatsukaze*. No one had physically seen the destroyer since the *Myoko* had turned her into a larger *PT-109*, though the American cruisers had been tracking her on radar since 4:08.[249] While perhaps their powers of observation left something to be desired, it was a testament to the skill and seamanship of her skipper, Commander Ashida Buichi, and her crew that the severely damaged destroyer had not yet joined the *PT-109* in the depths. And not only was the *Hatsukaze* still afloat, she was making at least 10 knots, maybe even 17.[250] That may have been the best speed her bowless hull could handle structurally, or the best speed her engines could generate having to work extra hard to overcome the drag from the open bow, or both. Whatever that maximum speed was, she knew she had to push it as fast as possible if she was to have any hope of even getting out of the battle area. After the collision, the *Hatsukaze* had drunkenly followed a wobbly course, first west, then north.[251] She likely did not expect a US Navy destroyer to chase her down from the west.

But, even with their contaminated fuel, Commander Austin and the *Spence* managed to do just that. At 5:12am, the destroyer opened radar-controlled fire on her shattered enemy counterpart on a bearing due east. And got a first salvo hit, the second of the day, or, more accurately, night.[252] The blast set the *Hatsukaze* on fire, giving the *Spence* a good point of aim, which she used to hit the Japanese destroyer consistently, starting more fires.

Yet it seems that the *Hatsukaze* put up a valiant fight. The blazing, bowless destroyer hobbled toward the northeast, possibly in a desperate effort to beach herself on Bougainville, while her two aft 5-inch mounts kept the *Spence* at bay with some relatively accurate gunfire. "I may need some help," Commander Austin radioed.[253] A few minutes later at 5:15, Austin reported that he "might be in a tight little fight right now because of a lack of ammunition."[254]

Have no fear. Arleigh Burke is here, and he will not be defeated by a single destroyer, let alone half of one. Commander Austin passed the *Hatsukaze*, who had gone dead in the water at 3:35, off to Burke, who arrived with all four of his division's destroyers. "I think a few will finish him off as he is stopped. And we are about out of bullets," Austin advised Burke.[255]

And all four of Burke's destroyers – *Charles Ausburne*, *Dyson*, *Stanly*, and *Claxton* took out their frustrations on the hapless *Hatsukaze*. Then again, maybe not so hapless. The Japanese destroyer used whatever hap she had left to turn her remaining 5-inch guns on her new tormentors. But the issue was no longer in doubt. What had remained of the *Hatsukaze*'s bridge after the collision was now completely demolished. Three separate explosions were observed, two amidships and one aft. The explosion near the stern was apparently the aft magazine; so tremendous that it blew the 5-inch mount into the air, end over end. It did not shoot after that.[256]

The explosion may have blown the stern off the already bowless destroyer, for almost immediately thereafter, at 5:38am, the *Hatsukaze* sharply upended, with what remained of the bow projecting some 100 feet into the air, and slid under the water stern first. Captain Burke radioed that he was going to look for survivors, but Admiral Merrill told him not to. There was no time. Unidentified aircraft were starting to appear on radar, and they still had to take care of the disabled *Foote*, whose location was the site of Task Force 39's rendezvous for withdrawal. Burke left the *Hatsukaze*'s crew to their fate.[257]

As if to emphasize the necessity of leaving immediately, just before 6:00am an unidentified plane was detected on radar coming in low on the port side of the cruiser formation. The twilight attack on the *Chicago* that led to her sinking had been a warning to take these kinds of radar contacts seriously. Admiral Merrill had the cruisers immediately turn 90 degrees to starboard – away from the contact. This seems to have been the Judy commanded by Lieutenant Baba Sakuhiko of the *Zuikaku*, sent from Vunakanau on a search vector of 138 degrees out to 200 miles, hoping to find Merrill's ships and succeeding in so doing, reporting the contact at 6:11am. About five minutes later, Merrill had the cruisers turn back 90 degrees to port and their original course.[258]

The destroyers *Converse* and *Thatcher* joined Admiral Merrill's cruisers at the site of the disabled *Foote*. By now, it was close enough to dawn that visibility had improved and Captain Burke's destroyers were in sight. Not in sight was Admiral Ijuin's light cruiser *Sendai*. She seems to have lingered for anywhere from 30 to 90 minutes after Burke's drive-by and her abandonment, but sank no later than 5:30am.[259]

After Captain Burke's destroyers had finally joined up, Admiral Merrill ordered the *Claxton* to tow the *Foote*, while the *Charles Ausburne* and *Thatcher* were to escort them. As it was, the *Claxton* was unable to tow the *Foote*, but only because the *Thatcher* was already towing the disabled destroyer. By 7:00am, the busy little tug *Sioux* was in sight and would soon take over the tow, so Admiral Merrill's cruisers and four remaining destroyers headed due south toward the returning transports. As Merrill put it, "[t]he question of the moment was, 'How do you want your eggs?'"

The answer was, of course, scrambled. Because at 7:42, when the cruisers were about 40 miles southwest of Empress Augusta Bay, the *Montpelier*'s radar detected a large group of unidentified aircraft, bearing 320 degrees True, distance 59 miles. The bearing was roughly northwest – toward Rabaul. The other cruisers and destroyers picked up the contact as well. Friendly aircraft would not be coming from the direction of Rabaul in large numbers. Admiral Merrill immediately ordered battle stations. The ships shifted into a "circular" antiaircraft formation, increased speed from 18 to 25 knots, which was the *Denver's* maximum speed, and turned to course 140 degrees True – roughly southeast – from which their fighter protection would come. Hopefully. Soon.

But sooner, at 7:45am, a second large contact was detected by the *Denver's* radar bearing 340 degrees True, distance 43 miles. Five minutes later it merged with the first group. The *Montpelier* estimated it was a group of 50–100 aircraft. And it was headed for Admiral Merrill's cruisers like an arrow. Merrill requested Lieutenant Dupuy's team, for the time being still directing the fighter coverage from the destroyer *Conway* who was with the cargo ships at Empress Augusta Bay, to send all available fighters to intercept the attackers and protect the ships assisting the *Foote*. At that point the *Foote's* group was 10 miles north of the cruisers, visible but hull down.[260] Just before 8:00am, four P-40s, apparently Kiwi, were sighted over the cruisers. The admiral was not entirely impressed. The four fighters were, Merrill later wrote, "a small group for the work ahead."[261]

At about the same time, a large group of aircraft appeared over the *Foote* and her escorts. Occupied as Captain Burke was with the *Foote*, he had not been able to keep up with the aerial events over the radio. Additionally, friendly aircraft were coming into radar and visual range from the south. All the approaching aircraft were believed to be friendly aircover amalgamating over the *Foote*. In reality, due to bad weather at Vella Lavella, the air cover was late in arriving and only 16 of the aircraft overhead were friendly – eight Hellcats from US Navy's Fighting 33 and possibly Fighting 38; one Marine Corsair (probably from Marine Fighting 221); and three Army Air Force Lightnings in addition to the Kiwis. Eight Corsairs from Marine Fighting 212 out of Barakoma tried to find the enemy but communications difficulties short-circuited that effort. The sailors quickly realized the lopsided numbers overhead. Because of the reinforcements Admiral Koga had sent in as part of *Ro-Go*, the Japanese badly outnumbered the AirSols defenders with this large air attack, albeit not nearly as large as it had been in times past: 89 Zeros, including 65 from *Kido Butai* (24 from *Shokaku*, 25 from *Zuikaku*, and 16 from *Zuiho*)and 18 dive bombers, all Aichi D3A Vals (nine from the *Shokaku* and nine from the *Zuikaku*), all led by Lieutenant Notomi Kenjiro, commander of the *Zuikaku's* air group. Notomi was a character and something of a legend throughout the Combined Fleet. Notomi had been based on the light carrier *Shoho* when she was sunk at Coral Sea, compelling him to ditch his Zero off Deboyne Island. He was then transferred to the light carrier *Ryujo*, which was promptly sunk at Eastern Solomons, forcing Notomi to ditch again, Now commanding the *Zuikaku's* air group, Notomi had little reason to fear a carrier being sunk out from under him. Because the *Zuikaku* had been left at Truk. With any such fears put aside for now, Notomi had worked with Baba to set up the reconnaissance mission with the best chance of finding the American ships the most quickly, and launched his strike even before Baba reported sighting the Americans at 6:11am.[262]

The *Charles Ausburne, Claxton, Thatcher*, and the *Foote* herself opened up with their 5-inch guns. The sight of the antiaircraft bursts caused Admiral Merrill's heart to sink again; he thought he might be seeing the end for the crippled destroyer and maybe a few of the ships with her. But, no. To his surprise, the Japanese passed up the *Foote* and her friends and headed for the cruisers.

Admiral Merrill did say, "Emergency 9 turn!," a 90-degree turn to port to unmask the 5-inch secondary batteries, at 8:03am, when the Japanese planes came within eight miles of the cruisers. A minute or so later, the Japanese shifted into attack formation and the cruisers started an emergency 360-degree turn to starboard, apparently intended to throw off the aim of the bombers. At 8:05, when the Japanese had closed to 14,000 yards at a bearing of 110 degrees True, the cruisers' 5-inch batteries opened fire "like overgrown machine guns," according to the admiral. The 40mm Bofors and 20mm Oerlikon guns soon joined in. To Merrill, "The scene was one of an organized 'hell' in which it was impossible to speak, hear, or even think."[263]

The AirSols fighters overhead had mixed in with the Japanese and did not much appreciate what they thought was the US Navy ships shooting at them, but the Japanese liked it even less. "[I]t was soon evident," Admiral Merrill reported, "that this particular attack group did not equal the usual high standard expected of the Japs." The Office of Naval Intelligence phrased the assessment a bit more diplomatically: "A very general impression aboard our ships was that the attacking aviators were not the best the Japanese had to offer."[264] Actually, they probably were.

Nevertheless, these Japanese were not the aviators who had screamed in near vertical dives, determined to get a bomb or, if it came to that, their own planes into the *Hornet* at Santa Cruz. Instead of attacking out of the rising sun, thereby using its glare to help hide them from the enemy, they attacked some 30 degrees left of the sun's bearing, which actually made the Vals easier to see. They operated in groups of three, diving at a shallow 45-degree angle, considered not a dive bombing attack per se but a less effective "glide bombing" attack. Each group of three attacked with a wide time interval between its attack and that of the others, allowing the ships' batteries time to train on each individual group. As Admiral Merrill kept his ships turning tightly to starboard, a tactic called "turn, turn and turn again at high speed," the Vals had to corkscrew downward trying to keep the cruisers in their sights, but the corkscrewing was just about the extent of their determination. According to Captain Robert P. Briscoe of the *Denver*, "It is the consensus of the officers of the air defense battery that the Japs were anything but determined to push home aggressively. In fact, they appeared to be imbued with a wholesome respect for our AA fire."[265] For the next year or so, anyway.

The dive bombers soon reached the denouement of their endeavors. The 18 dive bombers. The 18 dive bombers escorted by 89 fighters. Fighters outnumbering their own strike aircraft by just short of five to one. And, in the Questions No One Was Asking Department: *where were the torpedo planes?* The torpedo-carrying Bettys that had been so devastating to the *Prince of Wales, Repulse*, and *Chicago?* Their presence was reported fairly frequently, far more instances of their presence than Japanese records admit. The deadly Kates that had sunk the *Lexington*, *Yorktown*, and *Hornet*? The Kates had largely disappeared.

With no help from their torpedo-carrying sisters, the Vals screamed downward. Sometimes straight into the water without releasing their bombs or any other munitions, without making any attempt to pull up or turn. Most times releasing their bombs that started whistling down. Five bombs were dropped above the *Cleveland*, but though one detonated close to port, throwing water and fragments onto the deck, she was not hit and was not seriously damaged. One bomb fell in the wake of the *Columbia*, rattling the men below decks but causing no damage. The only hits the D3As achieved were two on the *Montpelier* that "completely disable[ed]" the starboard catapult and wounded eight men, one seriously. Another Val, damaged, tried to crash into the *Montpelier*'s bridge but missed. Except for the aforementioned catapult, the performance of Admiral Merrill's flagship was largely unaffected.[266]

By 8:12am, the Japanese attack was over. About 15 miles to the west, the remaining Japanese carrier bombers from the airstrike reformed for the journey back to Rabaul. The Zeros stayed for a bit to strafe the invasion beaches. They were chased off by AirSols fighters, especially eight Kiwi P-40s, joined ten minutes later by eight 339th Fighter Squadron P-38s and Marine Fighting 221 Corsairs; somehow, eight Corsairs from Marine Fighting 215 and four from Navy Fighting 17, also performing fighter protection, managed to miss the action altogether. Admiral Merrill's ships turned toward the southeast to resume their retirement. By 8:35am the radar screen was entirely clear of enemy aircraft.[267]

With their part in current operations at an end – for the moment – Admiral Merrill took the opportunity to send a message to Captain Burke: "Thanks for a job better than well done!"

"That's high praise indeed, Brute," said Burke, "and from a mighty courageous commander."

"You deserve it, boss," replied Reynolds.

"We may deserve it, Brute," Burke corrected him. "It's not me; it's the Squadron, and always will be."[268]

The Japanese were less impressed. They recorded no Zeros lost but six bombers failed to return; two from the *Shokaku* (flown by Flight Petty Officers 1st Class Izuchi Natsuo and Koizumi Shirou) and four from the *Zuikaku* (flown by Flight Petty Officers 1st Class Shimokawa Haruo, Inada Uemi, and Yamaki Tsutomu; and Warrant Officer Tanaka Kichiki). Nevertheless, according to the Japanese, in a demonstration of their aviators' "outstanding agility," their attack had sunk one destroyer, set fire to one cruiser and two transports, and shot down six fighters.[269]

As successful as the Sea Eagles Base Air Force and *Kido Butai* might have been – but really were not – they would not make any more large air attacks that day.

They had more urgent matters to attend to.

CHAPTER 4
BLOODY TUESDAY

It was late morning or so on November 2 when Admiral Omori's Combined Assault Force lumbered into Simpson Harbor.[1] It was not a happy occasion. Sullen and sulking was the theme for pretty much everyone, especially Captain Hara.[2]

The Japanese commodore had to put his anger over the outcome of the Battle of Empress Augusta Bay aside, however. He had to deal with more immediate concerns. The *Shigure's* old engines were "acting up," which Hara attributed to running at full speed for nearly an hour during the engagement. He had to cut the destroyer's speed to 18 knots. He informed Admiral Omori of his predicament, adding a request for the rescue of the *Sendai's* survivors.

Omori quickly responded: "We are slowing to 12 knots so that you may catch up. I have already asked Rabaul for a submarine to pick up crews of *Sendai* and *Hatsukaze*."[3] Indeed, two submarines had gone looking for survivors.

Once the *Shigure* had caught up, the Combined Assault Force was limited to the *Shigure's* top speed of 18 knots. As they entered the anchorage, Captain Hara was happy to see the *Samidare* and *Shiratsuyu* were there. "All things considered, *Shiratsuyu* was in fair shape," Hara recalled, "but *Samidare* was badly beaten up." The *Samidare* signaled her report of the engagement and, after expressing regret for the collision, so did the *Shiratsuyu*, who closed with the remark, "Our withdrawal was easy. Enemy gunfire simply failed to catch up with us!"[4]

The crew of the *Shigure* found that comment humorous, but the message that came in shortly thereafter from the *Myoko* was anything but: "Submarine *I-104* reports the rescue of Admiral Ijuin and 37 others from *Sendai*, but none from *Hatsukaze*."[5] Unfortunately, there was no *I-104*. There was a *Ro-104* under Lieutenant Commander Shoda Keiji that managed to fish the baron and 74 other survivors of the *Sendai* out of the water. Another 236 survivors were rescued by "destroyers" – presumably the *Samidare* and *Shiratsuyu*. The busy *Ro-105* had gone in as well, but found only dead bodies in the water. The *Sendai's* Captain Shoji Kiichiro and 184 officers and men were lost with the light cruiser. None of the 240 officers and enlisted men of the *Hatsukaze* was ever recovered.[6]

Once the ships were at their mooring stations in the anchorage, their bows pointed southeast into the prevailing wind and tide, the *Shigure's* hard-pressed skipper Commander Yamagami suggested a visit to the *Myoko* to deliver a full report in person to Admiral Omori. It was perhaps an odd suggestion under the circumstances, perhaps trying to make a recommendation his superior would find agreeable, as opposed to his borderline insubordination from the night before. But he was rejected again.

"We can do that later, Yamagami. It would not be wise to leave our ship right now," Hara explained. "Rabaul is no longer a safe place. The enemy will probably send a heavy air attack today and we must be ready for them. Prepare *Shigure* for an all-out aerial attack." The commodore gave similar orders to the *Samidare* and *Shiratsuyu*. They worked feverishly – literally in many cases, given the pestilence of Rabaul – to prepare themselves.[7]

Captain Hara was not the only one suspecting an air attack was imminent, nor were his ships the only ones preparing for one. Skipper Uozumi Jisaku of the *Haguro* had just been promoted to rear admiral on November 1. He was quickly living up to that promotion, having the *Haguro's* engines on emergency standby.[8]

Base Air Force thought it was prepared with all the reinforcements from *Kido Butai*. Admirals Kusaka and Ozawa were in "joint command" of the combined air forces. Not normally a good situation, but as one Japanese history happily explained, "since there was a perfect mutual understanding between the two, tactical command functioned smoothly."[9]

Not always. Based at Lakunai were the Zeros of the 201 and 204 Air Groups; the designated night fighters of the 251 Air Group, and the D4Ys and the twin-engine Nakajima J1N1-C *Gekko* ("Moonlight") Type 2 Land Reconnaissance Aircraft (called "Irving" by the Allies) of the small 151 Air Group. But when the fighters from the *Zuikaku* and *Zuiho* joined them, the base was more than stuffed. There were not enough revetments for all the Zeros, so many from the *Zuikaku* and *Zuiho* were lined up along the runway. Like the P-40s had been at Hickam Field on December 7, 1941. Lieutenant Ikuta Makoto, pilot of a Mitsubishi Ki-46 Type 100 Command Reconnaissance Aircraft (the Allies called this "Dinah") as part a detachment of the Japanese Army Air Force's 10th Flying Regiment at Lakunai, was aghast. "Dangerous!" Ikuta thought. "What if the enemy attacks now?"[10]

Already prepared was a Sea Eagle-eyed lookout, a petty officer named Kikawa, in the wooden control tower at Lakunai. He had been given the most important direction to watch, the south, with his 20-power telescope, but when the Allied scout planes did not appear on their normal runs near Cape St George, he got suspicious. Kikawa rarely looked to the east, but on a hunch he did so today, getting a peek between the volcanoes – and saw a large flight of B-25 Mitchells. He immediately went to his high-tech, state-of-the-art procedure for warning the air crews: he banged a metal container. Rabaul historian Bruce Gamble called it "a warning as ancient as the castles of the samurai warlords."[11] The leader of the *Zuiho's* fighter contingent understood what he was hearing: bang a gong, get it on. He burst from the action shack and ran down the crew areas, shouting for his gentlemen to start their engines. The other fighter contingents at Lakunai – the 201 and 204 Air Groups, as well as those from the *Zuikaku* and *Zuiho* – had to get it on. According to

Japanese aviation historian and author Tagaya Osamu, but for that lookout, all these fighters "would have gotten hammered on the ground [...]." Kikawa was cited by the commander of the combined 201–204 Air Groups, Commander Shibata Takeo. As it was, as the Zeros were taking off from Lakunai, P-38s were streaking over the runway.[12]

Why Lakunai had almost been taken by surprise is unknown. The incoming air attack was large and loud and could not have gotten from New Guinea to the Rabaul area without attracting attention. And it had attracted the attention of Flight Petty Officer 2nd Class Kawashima Yoshimi, flying his second reconnaissance patrol of the day in a Yokosuka D4Y of the 501 Air Group flying out of Vunakanau. Kawashima estimated the incoming strike had 50 B-25s flying at low level; he had his observer transmit this information to Rabaul. The report was confirmed by a lookout operating at the top of the tallest volcano in the Rabaul caldera, known to locals as "Kombiu" and to foreigners as "Mother." Two of the other air bases around Rabaul were already getting it on: Lieutenant Satao Masao, the second-most senior carrier fighter pilot after Lieutenant Notomi, led 25 Zeros from the *Shokaku* up from Vunakanau. Lieutenant Commander Okamoto Harutoshi of the 253 Air Group at Tobera had received a warning phone call from Vunakanau that lookouts on New Ireland had spotted a large airstrike inbound and scrambled 19 Zeros of the 253 Air Group, including Flying Seaman 1st Class Kawato and Warrant Officer Tanimizu Takeo, a *Shokaku* pilot attached to the 253 on his first combat mission. How Lakunai managed to miss all this is almost as good a question as how the *Hatsukaze* had not seen the *Myoko* and vice versa. But thanks to Petty Officer Kikawa, the 201 Air Group sent up 21 Zeros, the 204 17, the *Zuikaku* 21, and the *Zuiho* 12, so no harm, no foul.[13]

No harm to the Japanese, at least. There would be harm to the US 5th Air Force. What Kikawa had seen was the vanguard of an air attack. Douglas MacArthur had promised he would do everything "humanly possible" to support the Bougainville operation. Today was supposed to be part of it. Of course, so was yesterday, and the day before that, and the day before that. In fact, they had hoped to launch a low-level attack against shipping in Simpson Harbor on October 27 or so, but the weather had exercised its veto. The crews had been alerted on October 30, only to have the weather veto it again. Same thing on October 31. And on November 1. And on November 2.[14]

Then the photographic and photogenic F-5 Lightnings of the 8th Photo Squadron went out on a later mission that November 2 and decided to override the veto, reporting "clearing skies and good flying weather," along with seven destroyers, one tender, and 20 merchant vessels in Simpson Harbor and a total of 237 planes on the airfields.[15] Well, all right. Time to slap together an air attack ... wait... 237 enemy planes? Seriously? As perverse as it sounds, it represented an improvement from the 300 reported the previous day.

The perversity had begun this day at 4:00am, when 5th Air Force aviators were roused and, according to the 8th Bombardment Squadron's Operations Officer Lieutenant William H. Webster, treated to "a meager breakfast of canned grapefruit juice with its galvanized tin taste, French toast made with dehydrated eggs and powdered milk, a little peanut butter and cheese and a cup of scalding black tea for me (coffee for most)."[16] After that breakfast, bombing Rabaul probably did not sound so bad.

Even so, as pilot Lieutenant Dick Walker of the 13th Bombardment Squadron, 3rd Bombardment Group recalled:

The morning briefing conducted prior to takeoff was a very somber affair. Hearing the latest word on the extent of the Japanese defenses was pretty much a prediction that all of us would not be coming home. The twelve crews that were assigned to fly the mission sat grey faced and quiet during the briefing. The attack was to be carried out by waves of bombers attacking by Squadrons in file with twelve airplanes per squadron flying in a line abreast sweeping across Simpson Harbor. My Squadron was the second Squadron scheduled in. Our approach was "up the chute" between New Britain and New Ireland.[17]

To make matters worse, "The Japanese were now using the newfangled radar and a network of observation lookouts that would warn of our coming," according to Major "Jock" Henebry, who was commanding this mission. "The target was too well protected to sneak up on it."[18]

They didn't intend to sneak up on it; they would instead use the terrain to their advantage, or so they thought. The plan of approach was a rather unique affair necessitated in part by the low-level nature of the mission. Instead of flying straight to Rabaul, the strike aircraft would first pass Rabaul to the south. The idea was to loop around the Crater Peninsula, using Rabaul's resident volcanoes for protection against antiaircraft fire and interception. They would first pass east of the southernmost volcano on the peninsula, often referred to as simply "South Daughter."[19] It would stay on the opposite side of South Daughter from the very active volcano Tavurvur, located to the immediate west of South Daughter at her foot.[20] Continuing northward and turning northwest, the strike would pass the largest of the Crater Peninsula's volcanoes, called "Mother."[21] Going around Mother, the strike would pass between Mother and the northernmost of Rabaul's major volcanoes, called colloquially "North Daughter." This gap, called the Nodup Gap, and the saddle, called "Namanula Hill," was close to downtown Rabaul (if Rabaul can be said to have a downtown) and the Lakunai air base, which was at the foot of Rabalanakaia, the mistaken target of the March 1943 effort to cause an eruption, itself at the foot of Mother.[22] Flying between members of this veritable family of volcanoes was necessary because the B-25s could not fly over them and then dive down low enough for the planned low-level bombing and strafing attack, which would take place after the Americans had gone through the Nodup Gap at a course of 225 degrees True, to catch the ships in the harbor facing southeast and thus presenting their broadsides to the attackers.[23]

The plan for the attack itself was what might be called a complementary affair. First up would be two squadrons of P-38s – the 39th and 80th – who were to make a fighter sweep of the Rabaul airfields, especially Lakunai, to suppress the fighter protection. Behind them in the attack, though leading in the formation for now and the apples of the Lakunai lookout's eye, were the four squadrons (498th, 499th, 500th, and 501st Bombardment) of the 345th Bombardment Group, led by the 345th's deputy commander Major Benjamin W. Fridge. They were escorted by P-38 Lightnings from 431st and 432nd Fighter Squadrons.[24] The 345th was carrying both parafrags and 100lb bombs in which the explosive charge was replaced with white phosphorus, an invention called "Kenney's Cocktail." Its job was to neutralize the antiaircraft batteries with the fiery phosphorus and, in particular, its blinding smoke. With the fighter and antiaircraft opposition thus suppressed, five squadrons of Mitchells – 71st and 405th from the 38th Bombardment Group; and 8th, 13th, and 90th from the 3rd Bombardment Group – were to pass through the Nodup Gap in a line of squadrons in one-minute intervals, and then each of them would hit the ships in Simpson Harbor with 1,000lb bombs in low-level attacks. The B-25s of the 38th would be escorted by the P-38s of the 433rd Fighter Squadron while the 3rd Group bombers would be covered by the P-38s of the 9th Fighter Squadron, whose commander Captain Gerald Johnson commanded the fighters overall in this attack, with fighter ace Captain Dick Bong as his deputy.[25]

It was a decent plan, as far as plans go. The 5th Air Force's Advanced Echelon staff believed it had the potential to be a "knockout punch." But, well, no plan is perfect, and this one certainly was not. One issue was that the point of ingress was, as described, between the Mother and the North Daughter. Leaving aside the fact that it's generally a bad idea to come between a mother and her child, the pass between the two volcanoes was somewhat narrow. The Mitchells would have to go through the pass single-file. In other words, it was a choke point. It meant that as each exited the pass it would be the target of every antiaircraft gun in range, which would just have to aim at the same point in the sky to hit every bomber passing through it.

Second, the plan did not take into account the arrival of several warships in Simpson Harbor, especially the heavy cruisers *Myoko* and *Haguro* and the light cruiser *Agano*. That was partly understandable because the last photoreconnaissance of Simpson Harbor had been conducted before the return of Admiral Omori's Combined Assault Force, though the 5th Cruiser Division had been in Rabaul since at least October 21, so the 5th Air Force should have been aware of the possibility that one or both of the heavy cruisers could be present. In terms of antiaircraft weaponry, the *Myoko* and *Haguro* each carried eight 5-inch dual-purpose guns in four twin high-angle mounts and 14 25mm cannons.[26] The *Agano* was badly underarmed for surface combat, but she could hold her own in an air attack with four 3.15-inch antiaircraft guns in two twin high-angle mounts, 16 25mm cannons in two twin mounts and four triple mounts; and four 13mm guns in two twin mounts.[27] All of which would now be added to Rabaul's already formidable antiaircraft defenses. The now-normal method of gunships suppressing antiaircraft fire by blazing away at the main deck and bridge with those eight .50-cal. guns would have little effect on the *Myoko*, *Haguro*, and *Agano*.

Third, the last photo reconnaissance of the Rabaul area had been on October 29. Those photos indicated that in the area of Rabaul, Kavieng, and Bougainville the Japanese had only 50 fighters and 25 bombers. Late on November 1, an F-5 Lightning had managed to penetrate the storm fronts and get a look-see at Rabaul – and was shocked to find some 300 aircraft at the airfields, more than three times the number reported on October 29. What had happened in the interim was that the aircraft of *Kido Butai* had staged into Rabaul. General Kenney would later plead ignorance of the presence of these reinforcements. However, ever since October 31 Allied intelligence had been aware of the movement of Japanese air units into Rabaul, including the "possible" movement of *Kido Butai*'s air groups. Admiral Halsey was aware of it. General MacArthur had to be aware of it as well.[28]

General Kenney may simply have been trying to hide the source of that information: *Magic*. Covering up *Magic* was usually done in cases like this with photographic reconnaissance missions that could both confirm what *Magic* revealed and provide a plausible source for that information, but with the weather blocking reconnaissance flights between October 29 and November 1, there was no such cover. Nevertheless, the F-5 Lightnings' report of 300 aircraft at Rabaul should have gotten Kenney's attention and prompted a revision of the attack plan. It did neither. Maybe Kenney was concerned that not attacking could possibly reveal to the Japanese that their communications codes had been broken. Or, maybe after the inaction of the previous days, there was a lot of pressure, both actual and perceived, to "get the hell to Rabaul" to "occupy the Jap Air Force" as a diversion to the landings on Bougainville.[29]

One of these aforementioned issues was a calculated risk; the other two arguably fall under the rubric of "The enemy gets a vote as to whether your plan of attack succeeds." But there was a fourth issue, one that might be called a structural problem with the plan of attack. No one expected to take the Japanese by surprise.[30] But if the Japanese would not be taken by surprise, that means their fighters would be in the air. If their fighters are in the air, you're not going to catch them on the ground. Catching the fighters on the ground – suppressing the fighters – was the entire point of the low-level sweep over Lakunai. So why have a low-level fighter sweep over Lakunai? Especially since it required P-38 fighter squadrons to fly at low altitude, where the P-38 Lightning did not perform as well as it did at high altitude. Granted, the Japanese at Lakunai were almost taken by surprise and scrambled late, but they ultimately were not taken by surprise.

Oh, well. They were only attacking the most strongly defended Japanese base in the South Pacific, a base that was even stronger than they had projected, with a flawed plan of attack and inaccurate intelligence. What could go wrong? Well, not so much wrong but a product of the war of attrition was the simple numbers. On October 12, eight squadrons had managed to put 115 gunships into the air; today, eight squadrons managed to scrape together maybe 80. On October 12, the P-38 fighter squadrons had managed to field 125 fighters. Today it was about 80.[31] This was where Admiral Nimitz would remind everyone, "The enemy is hurting, too."

Everything went downhill from there. The Mitchells took off from Dobodura at 11:00am, had organized themselves by 11:20, and headed toward Rabaul; the only events en route were the P-38s taking off from Kiriwina and joining the gunships and a few aircraft turning back because of mechanical issues. The egress from the Nodup Gap was at around 1:30pm, after which both fighter squadrons apparently flew into Simpson Harbor and clipped the western edge of Lakunai, then looped around Tavurvur and shot the gap between Tavurvur and the South Daughter to hit the Matupit seaplane base and Lakunai from the south. The 39th Fighter Squadron was in the lead and higher up; it was apparently the Lightnings of the 39th that were overhead when the Zeros were taking off from Lakunai. The 39th reported little in the way of fighter opposition. On the heels of the 39th came the 80th, which at low level quickly found itself in a fight for its life over Lakunai. According to the 80th's commander Major Edward Cragg, who was personally leading his squadron that day, "The Japs sent up the largest number of planes ever encountered by this squadron. A conservative estimate placed the number at 60 Zeros, but many pilots claimed there were over 100 enemy fighters in the air." Lieutenant John Stanifer of the 80th, in his first air combat, had a slightly higher estimate at 2,000. The "many pilots" were right. Base Air Force had scrambled 57 Zeros from the 201, 204, and 253 Air Groups, while *Kido Butai* had scrambled 58, for a total of 115 fighters, with a few Judys acting as fighters to boot.[32] The 5th Air Force was outnumbered.

As the 80th found out the hard way. Lieutenant Stanifer described it, "As we entered St George's Channel radio silence was abruptly ended with the signal for the fighters to drop tanks and scream for altitude. Shortly afterward someone called out, 'Bandits 12 o'clock high,' then all hell broke loose."[33] He glimpsed his first Zero zooming by and immediately asked himself, "What am I doing here? I could be in training or transports!"[34]

Not having such career regrets was the Japanese Army Air Force's Lieutenant Ikuta, even though he was still on the ground at Lakunai, stuck in the cockpit of his Ki-46 Command Reconnaissance Aircraft, his engines idling. Ikuta was trying to take off so he could ride out the attack and preserve his aircraft, but the Zeros had priority on the runways of Lakunai and were all scrambling. Ikuta finally gave up and went to a shelter. He watched a P-38 roaring across Lakunai hit by antiaircraft fire, roll, crash into the mountain slopes, and explode.[35]

The 80th's attempt at suppressing the Zeros turned into a running battle with the Zeros that extended into the outer Blanche Bay. The Lightnings of 2nd Lieutenant Norman Shea and Flight Officer Willis F. Evers did not make it back to Kiriwina. The body of Evers, who was credited with one victory on this mission, was eventually recovered; his P-38 hit the ground near Raluana Point west of Blanche Bay at such high speed that the engine nacelles and cockpit pod dug 12–15 feet into the ground. No one saw what happened to Shea.[36]

So much for suppressing the fighter protection. Maybe suppressing the antiaircraft guns would go better. The four squadrons of the 345th Bombardment Group separated into individual squadrons, then forced their way through the Nodup Gap. In the lead heading due west were the eight gunships of the 498th who blasted through the gap, then dove down, following the contours of Namanula Hill until the eastern edge of Rabaul's "Chinatown" came into range, at which point they opened fire. Guns blazing, they dropped their parafrags over the business district and wharf on the northern shores of Simpson Harbor, possibly taking out a giant Emily flying boat before zooming off almost untouched.[37]

Not as untouched would be the squadron about a minute behind the 498th, the 500th. While the 498th may have surprised the Japanese defenders, the 500th faced Japanese defenders who were now fully awake, alerted, and at their guns. Nevertheless, the ten gunships of the 500th bravely flew in the wake of the 498th and into the teeth of the Japanese defenses, raking them with the eight .50-cals and dropping dozens of Kenney's Cocktails with the white phosphorus in the hopes of blinding the antiaircraft gunners with its smoke.[38]

Or at least they say that was the intent. There was probably more to it. White phosphorus is often used to create smokescreens, true, but it can be a nasty weapon. It is an incendiary chemical that ignites on contact with air and burns very, very hot, so hot that it can set on fire almost anything it touches, including clothing and skin. Additionally, it can stick to skin, on which it continues to burn and cause hideous injuries. It is not readily extinguished by water; instead, either its supply of oxygen or combustible material must be cut off. When the bomb detonates, it releases white phosphorus flakes that fall like streamers "resemble[ing] a multitentacled monster." Like a solid, modern version of the famously mysterious "Greek Fire." These Kenney's Cocktails were sensitive, almost finicky weapons that were prone to accidents and were thus little loved by the ground crews who had to handle and load them or the air crews who had to carry and deploy them. They could be highly destructive when detonated, whether under the aircraft or in it.[39]

While downtown Rabaul was now enveloped in poisonous smoke and riddled with dozens of fires, antiaircraft fire would be a problem for the 5th Bomber Command. The Japanese gunners hit two adjacent gunships of the 500th, possibly with the same burst of fire, in their vulnerable bomb bays. The B-25 of Captain Max Mortensen had dropped eight of its dozen bombs when one of the four remaining bombs was ignited, sending smoke through the crew compartment and even into the right engine. Mortensen tried jettisoning the bombs, but one remained stuck in the racks. The bomb burned itself out and Mortensen was able to keep flying. The other gunship was not so lucky. Second Lieutenant Alfred R. Krasnickas had his bomb bay doors open but had not yet released his bombs when shrapnel detonated at least one of them inside the fuselage. Smoke filled the crew compartment, then engulfed the entire aircraft, which gained altitude for a moment before it inverted, dove into the ground, and exploded at Vuvu Plantation some three miles west of Rabaul.[40]

Nine B-25s of the 501st Squadron were the next to literally shoot the gap between Mother and North Daughter. Heading into very intense antiaircraft fire, they turned south and dove to 100 feet to begin strafing, but as they did so, the right engine of Lieutenant Orbry H. Moore's gunship was hit – Captain John Manders, leading the 501st on this attack, believed it came from "a cruiser" – and caught fire. Moore deployed the carbon dioxide extinguishing system and put the fire out, then held on long enough to complete the attack run. The .50-cals of the 501st blazed away while it scattered 480 parafrags over antiaircraft emplacements, shore facilities, a floatplane base, and the eastern end of Lakunai.[41]

Then Lieutenant Moore's right engine flared up again and flames started engulfing the wing. Three Zeros started focusing on the dying Mitchell, but Lieutenant Marion Kirby, operations officer of the 431st Fighter Squadron, quickly shot down the Zero of the *Zuiho*'s Ensign Fukui Yoshio, who parachuted into the water and was rescued. Kirby shot down a second, while the third, who had switched to targeting Kirby, was shot down by Lieutenant Fredric F. Champlin. Kirby had been having a bad day. He was supposed to lead his fighter mission, but he had trouble starting his engine and joined late. Then he accidentally disabled his airspeed indicator. But shooting down two Zeros made up for a lot of it. It bought Moore and his crew only a little time. Moore had to ditch in St George's Channel off Rapopo about three miles east of the eponymous airfield. Some of the 501st's Mitchells circled over the crash site hoping to give the crew protection so they could escape, but Moore and his co-pilot were already dead. The circling turned into a running battle with some 50 Zeros. The Japanese gave up the chase south of the Warangoi River without adding to their score. The 501st's effort to protect the three survivors of Moore's B-25 was noble but futile; the three enlisted crew were captured, then murdered four months later.[42]

After all that, the experience of the ten gunships of the 499th led by Captain Glenn W. Taylor was almost boring. They blanketed the reported 83 antiaircraft gun positions near Sulphur Creek with Kenney's Cocktails, then released a few over Lakunai. They were chased by Zeros but suffered no losses.[43]

Part of the reason for the lack of losses may have been the fierce dogfights going on overhead between the escorting P-38s and the defending Zeros. The 9th Fighter Squadron's Lieutenant Carl G. Planck watched his squadron commander Captain Johnson shoot one Zero down in flames. Planck himself flamed one Zero chasing Lightnings below him, then turned into a head-on game of chicken with another Zero. Planck got hits on its motor, but in passing the Zero clipped him at the left engine and left tail boom, knocking out the oil coolers and propeller and damaging the left vertical stabilizer. Improvising, Planck turned on his right side and used the elevator as a rudder in a diving turn for Kiriwina and escape. His wingmen thought he was crashing and had to dodge the falling P-38 as they flew out of the area. One that apparently did not fly out of the area was the P-38 of Lieutenant Francis S. Love. None of the Americans seem to have seen what happened to him, but Lieutenant Ikuta at Lakunai had seen a P-38 roar over the airfield and crash into a hill. There is some belief that this was Love, though it could have been Flight Officer Evers. Decades later, some wreckage from his Lightning was found on Clifton Plantation southeast of Tobera. Like that of Evers, Love's P-38 had hit the ground at high speed, but almost vertically. There was very little left of it on the surface.[44]

The fighter combat on this day was savage, the dogfights involving chomping down and holding. Veteran Captain Grover Gholson was leading the 432nd Fighter Squadron with the B-25s over the entrance to Simpson Harbor when he saw Zeros above. He quickly climbed and got above the Japanese, fired and missed one Zero, then shot down two more. Gholson saw Lieutenant Howard Hedrick flame one more, but Hedrick had to dodge an attempt to ram his fighter. Then Hedrick saw Lieutenant Leo Mayo shoot up a "Tony" – probably a Judy dive bomber – causing it to explode, but in exploding it sheared off his right wing at the engine. Mayo had to bail out, landing in the water off the beach. Members of the squadron moved in to protect him, leaving Hedrick to cover them. In so doing, Hedrick had to hold off five Zeros, one of whom shot out his left engine. But Hedrick proceeded to put on what the others described as "a superb display on one engine" that included shooting down one of the Zeros. The other four escaped. Mayo was never seen again.[45]

The 431st was not having any better luck. The self-inflicted damage to Lieutenant Kirby's aircraft compelled him to turn over command to Lieutenant Lowell Lutton. Somehow, the Japanese seem to have developed an intense hatred for Lutton and made repeated attempts to shoot down the acting mission leader of the squadron. Lieutenant Arthur Edward Wenige saw about 60 Japanese Zeros swarm the 431st. Lieutenant Lutton flamed one Zero, only to attract the attention of another, which Wenige sent into the water. Then a third Zero made for Lutton, but Wenige took care of it in a head-on pass. Then a fourth Zero made for Lutton, who at this point had to be wondering if he had kicked Base Air Force's dog or something. Wenige was out of ammunition, so 2nd Lieutenant Franklin H. Monk shot it down.[46]

Lieutenant Lutton was hardly the only member of the 431st Squadron having issues. Lieutenant Owen Giertsen of the 431st flew across Simpson Harbor from the northeast, only to take an antiaircraft burst below the left engine. He shut down the damaged engine and feathered the propeller, but his radio was out.[47] As the squadron moved to exit the harbor, about a half dozen Zeros were seen making for the Mitchells. Once they were driven off, seven or eight more appeared. Three chased Lieutenant Francis J. Lent over New Britain. When Lent turned to look back, he saw the remainder chasing the P-38 of 2nd Lieutenant Kenneth Richardson over Simpson Harbor. That was the last anyone saw of Richardson.[48]

With the fighter suppression and the antiaircraft suppression completed or at least as completed as they were going to be this day, the time for the main event was at hand: Major "Jock" Henebry with his own 3rd and the 38th Bombardment Groups was going ahead with the low-level bombing of the ships in Simpson Harbor. But the ships in Simpson Harbor were not just sitting there. Admiral Uozumi, for instance, had had the *Haguro* ready; at the first warning of the attack, he raised anchor and got his cruiser moving. Captain Hara had had a few hours to get his destroyers ready, and as the Americans came in at low level, Hara was able to get his *Shigure* under way. The *Samidare* and *Shiratsuyu* were able to get moving as well, and all headed for the open water of Blanche Bay. Their antiaircraft guns were manned, ready, and trained up at the sky. "The ensuing battle," Hara later wrote, "was the most spectacular action of my life."[49]

Superfluous superlatives aside, Captain Hara and his men were determined to make their presence known. "[T]he gun crews worked like fury," he recalled. "They fired everything without pause, seeming to vent the general anger pent up after our unhappy return from Empress Augusta Bay." Hara's plan likely did not include sailing into the path of the bombers, but that's exactly what his destroyers did. "Gunfire from surface ships is usually of little effect against fast airplanes. But it was different that day," he commented. "The enemy planes practically flew right into our gunfire." Saying the Americans "were shredded as they passed us," the commodore "saw at least five planes knocked down by *Shigure*."[50]

Not exactly. More than six decades later, Marion Kirby, who had experienced his own danger and excitement on this mission, "remember[ed] seeing three destroyers at the entrance to Simpson harbor." He added, "Naturally they fired at us, but they didn't hit anything."[51]

They did not have to, however. As war correspondent Lee Van Atta, who was in Captain Richard H. Ellis's bomber *Seabiscuit*, remembered:

> We were running parallel to the coastline near Rapopo, and there was anti-aircraft all over the skies. Most of it was being thrown up by a Jap destroyer flotilla we encountered in a staggered line about fifteen miles from the entrance to Keravia Bay. They were running directly at us and I could see the pungent flashes of their heavy guns. They were coming too damned close for my happiness, but the spectacle of destroyers at 30 knots chasing Mitchells at 200mph was ludicrous enough to make even a tense Ellis and a shaking war correspondent join with [co-pilot Lieutenant John] Dean in a hearty, if slightly forced, laugh.[52]

The official Army Air Force history dispensed with the entertainment value of Hara's destroyers and went straight to the problems they created: "Two [sic] destroyers off the mouth of the Warangoi River, directly in the path of the approaching planes, caused some confusion as their fire, together with that of intercepting fighters, forced the B-25s to break formation and attack in two-plane or individual bombing and strafing runs."[53]

The attack had been carefully timed so each squadron would fly through the saddle at intervals of about one minute between squadrons. Moreover, the attack had been planned to approach the ships in Simpson Harbor from their broadside; the ships' bows would be anchored to face the tide, and the attack would come from the ships' beams. This can present the largest possible target for torpedo planes, but not normally for bombers. A bomb is more likely to overshoot or undershoot a target than it is to miss to either side. That was one reason why the so-called "Battle of the Bismarck Sea" had been so devastating to the Japanese: they had assumed the low-flying attack planes were aiming aerial torpedoes, so they turned to present the narrow bow or stern profile and thus the smallest possible target. In so doing, they had actually presented the biggest possible targets to the low-flying bombers. A beam target is not as bad for low-level bombers as it would be for high-altitude or dive bombers because even if the bomb misses the deck, it could still hit the side of the hull or the superstructure, so it can still work. An additional consideration for this attack seems to have been visibility. The gunship pilots would have to dive down Namanula Hill to keep following the terrain without hitting the ground, then look up and have only seconds to find a target. It's a lot easier to find a target if that target is presenting its largest visible profile.

As a result of Captain Hara's actions, some squadrons turned away from the planned course to Rabaul by veering right while others pressed on as planned. This meant that the squadrons that turned away had to adjust their course to arrive over the harbor at the correct time to maintain the disruptive effect of the leading squadrons and in the correct direction to attack the ships.[54] Hara had pulled the threads, and the fabric of the most important of the attacks, that on the ships in Simpson Harbor, started to fray.

It started with the 71st Squadron of the 38th Bombardment Group. When Captain Hara's destroyers opened up with both their antiaircraft and main batteries, Lieutenant Frank M. Cecil, leading the 71st in this attack, led his Mitchells closer to New Ireland to avoid a fight with the destroyers. It was an understandable and in retrospect a good decision, but it did throw them off schedule and out of sync with the attack plan. Maybe having an attack plan that was so dependent on precise timing was not such a good idea.

Anyway, Lieutenant Cecil tried to do what he had been assigned. He raked some buildings on the Namanula Hill saddle with his .50-cal. and directed his gunships to shoot the gap between the Mother and the North Daughter. Then he saw the gap shooting back. A lot. He didn't like that. So he turned to the right, did not go through the Nodup Gap, and instead led his Mitchells around the North Daughter. Then he turned back to the left, over Rabaul, and plunged through the clouds of white phosphorus heading north to south into the infinite crossfires of Simpson Harbor.

Because they could not see the ships in the harbor until they had cleared the shore with its white phosphorus smoke rising to 400 feet, they had mere seconds to just pick out a target – a target that likely had a much smaller profile than they had anticipated. While constantly doing evasive maneuvers, Lieutenant Cecil kept firing the eight .50-cal. machine guns of his B-25, then released his bombs on a "7,000 to 10,000 ton merchant vessel anchored about 800 yards off the old wharf. This vessel was hit, causing it to explode and was left in a sinking condition." The ship was apparently the *Yamabiko Maru*, a repair ship of roughly 6,800 tons. "[A]nchored close to shore," it was "hit squarely amidships by one or two 1,000lb bombs." She caught fire and took on a list, and was apparently beached to prevent sinking. One crewman was killed and 23 wounded.[55]

It took maybe 60 seconds to completely cross Simpson Harbor. In war, a lot can happen in 60 seconds, as Flight Officer Richard H. Hastings soon learned. Flying right behind Lieutenant Cecil, Hastings dropped his bombs on one of the storeships, maybe the *Arasaki* or *Hayasaki*. He then headed toward Cape Gazelle, only to be hit by a heavy antiaircraft burst that blew off the gun turret, badly injuring the gunner, and ruptured one of the main gas lines. To complicate matters, three Zeros showed up to make firing passes. The navigator tried to tape up the ruptured fuel line, but the break was too big. Not surprisingly, one of the engines went out and its propellers were feathered – feathering, which is changing the pitch of the disabled propellers so that they parallel the incoming airflow and thus are not as big a drag on the aircraft, was a big issue this day – and the Mitchell had to fly on one engine for 180 miles or so until that began to sputter. Hastings radioed their position, some 50 miles northeast of Kiriwina, and ditched. Hastings, his navigator, and the badly injured gunner survived to be rescued by an Australian Catalina and taken to Port Moresby.[56]

Yes, a lot can happen in 60 seconds. Especially in the atmosphere as detailed by the 38th Bombardment Group's history:

> [D]uring this time the entire area was a mass of devastation and murder. One B-25 was seen to go down in flames – many enemy fighters were seen to leave a trail of flame behind them, then splashed with a sickening thud into the water – a parachute with a chard [sic] but limp body of a flier was seen to float past one plane as he was making his run.[57]

The B-25 that "was seen to go down in flames" was flown by Lieutenant James A. Hungerpiller, Jr. He made a run on what was described as a "destroyer" and reportedly scored a direct hit. It was actually the minesweeper *W-26*, which was definitely damaged, but not as much as Hungerpiller's Mitchell. His left engine was hit and set on fire, which soon spread to the fuselage. Hungerpiller reportedly attempted "a final effort to drop his last bomb and make it count" by attacking one of the heavy cruisers. But the bomb fell short, and Hungerpiller's B-25 flew over the cruiser like a comet before plowing into the ground off Blanche Bay with no survivors.[58]

Behind the 71st was the 405th. In theory. In reality, the 405th had fallen apart. Its eight gunships had fallen back during a rain squall. Then they swerved to avoid the gunfire of Captain Hara's destroyers. Before they could get back on the path, the first flight of four was caught by Zeros coming in from the northwest. Flight leader Captain Anthony T. Deptula turned into the attack, but that took his group over Blanche Bay well out of the planned flight path. Three of the gunships reportedly "salvoed their bombs when no suitable targets were sighted." There is no mention of what the fourth did. One of Hara's destroyers, the *Shiratsuyu*, was "slightly" damaged by either a near miss, strafing, or both that killed four and wounded two. It's not clear who was responsible for it, as it seems no one claimed to have attacked Hara's destroyers. The *Shiratsuyu* was probably the last in Hara's column of destroyers, well behind the *Samidare*. If that was the case, these gunships of the 405th were in a good position to have made the reported attack on the *Shiratsuyu*.[59]

That left only the second flight of the 405th under Lieutenant Edward J. Maurer, Jr still in the game. It followed the same course as the 71st around the North Daughter, and attacked Simpson Harbor north to south like the 71st had. But with only four aircraft, each B-25 got that personalized attention from the antiaircraft batteries that the B-25s of the 71st had not. The gunship flown by Lieutenant Robert K. Fox got too much of that personalized attention and was hit in the left engine, which started to smoke. Then it was swarmed by three Zeros who had risen up from Matupit Island. Just above them, Captain Daniel T. "Danny" Roberts kept the escorting fighters of 433rd Squadron low, maybe too low, as Zeros came at his fighters from above and both flanks. Lieutenant Donald D. Revenaugh found two Zeros on his tail, but 2nd Lieutenant Donald Y. King moved in to shoo them off. Apparently, that effort failed, and Revenaugh was left to shake them off. After he did so, he took on the Zeros attacking Fox's B-25, flaming one. But it was not enough, and Fox's Mitchell went into the water, bounced three times and nosed over to disappear into the depths with no survivors. The other three Mitchells were as evasive as they could be and claimed near misses on two large freighters and a direct hit that sank a small coastal vessel of 300 tons. By the time the B-25s cleared the harbor, all three had received moderate damage with one crewman wounded. King was never seen again.[60]

Finally came the heavy hitters: the three squadrons of the 3rd Bombardment Group. In the front was Major Henebry in his *Notre Dame de Victoire* leading the 90th Squadron. Leading the 90th Squadron too much, actually. The 90th had moved so far ahead that Henebry's B-25s were barely visible to the 8th Squadron, flying at the back of the 3rd Group's formation, at a distance of what was later estimated to be four or five miles. Major Raymond H. Wilkins, commander of the 8th in his B-25 with the seriously cool name of *Fifi*, had to increase his speed to keep up, and the entire 8th Squadron had gone to maximum cruise power.[61]

As far as Jock Henebry could tell, it was going according to plan; he does not seem to have seen the disintegration of the 38th Bombardment Group in front of him. He was not even distracted by Captain Hara's destroyers shooting at him at the entrance to Simpson Harbor. As planned, he went around the Crater Peninsula, turned left, and shot the Nodup Gap. As he hit the deck give or take 50 feet and looked into Simpson Harbor, "what a sight. A hunter's dream. The harbor was alive with ships, tenders, and boats. Forewarned, they were armed, ready for our bombardment."[62]

Lee Van Atta, in Captain Ellis's *Seabiscuit* flying beside *Notre Dame de Victoire*, had a darker view: "[A]mid skies which seemed as if they must suddenly be aflame, Simpson Harbour was before us – a bathtub-shaped anchorage barely two miles wide and with an unparalleled defensive machine surrounding its deep water-filled tub."[63]

Major Henebry had two 1,000lb bombs and had talked his ground crew into adding one 500lb bomb aboard, so he had three bombs instead of the usual two. Coincidentally, he had three ships in line ahead of him, at what he estimated were good distances for three broadside attacks. The last of the three ships was the *Haguro*.[64]

But Major Henebry's *Notre Dame de Victoire* had some hurdles before it could attack the *Haguro*. Literally. The first was a small freighter, later identified as the 4,216-ton *Hokuyo Maru*. He raked the deck with his eight .50-cal. machine guns, then pulled up at the last second, barely clearing the mast, and released one of the 1,000lb bombs. It dug into the stern and exploded. Henebry was still lined up on the second ship, a larger one later identified as the transport *Hakusan Maru*, still suffering the effects of the bomb hit on October 17. Henebry shoved the nose over and was still lined up with the beam of the second ship. In what was becoming a standard, perhaps ideal low-level attack, Henebry strafed the ship's superstructure, setting it on fire, then pulled up and released his second 1,000lb bomb. It detonated amidships on the port side, damaging the area at the base of the stack.[65]

Now came the most important target, the *Haguro*. It was also the most difficult, because it was the biggest, fastest, and most heavily armed of Henebry's three targets. And, naturally, it was where things went wrong for Henebry. While he was still lined up on the *Haguro*'s broadside, the cruiser was too close to his second target and he could not get the bomber down to low altitude to strafe the cruiser or even release his 500lb bomb. Worse, while he could not shoot at the *Haguro*, the *Haguro* could shoot at him. And did, hitting the *Notre Dame de Victoire*'s tail, disabling the aft defensive turret guns and causing Henebry problems controlling the plane's rudder. He was able to loop around Vulcan and start heading back, but not before he attracted a Zero who disabled his left engine with 20mm rounds. The Zero broke off before he could finish off the Mitchell, probably because he was out of ammunition. Henebry shut down the engine, but the propeller would not feather and was thus a drag on the plane that had to rely on one engine. Forget hitting the *Haguro*. Henebry now had to worry about just getting home.[66]

Major Henebry's run had crowded out Captain Ellis from his own chosen target, so Ellis switched targets to a "6,600-ton destroyer tender," an awfully specific description for – assuming the description as a "tender" is correct – what may actually have been the 5,150-ton submarine tender *Chogei*.[67] As Lee Van Atta saw it:

We were low on the water and all guns were firing with a monotonous rhythm. Dick was throwing all the lead he could as fast as he could get it out.

The first bomb was away when we were perhaps 50 feet from the tender. One minute it loomed before us and the next was gone. Dick started to put us back on the water and open an attack on an 8,500-ton transport he had already picked out. But between us and the transport lay a 10,000-ton cruiser of the *Nachi* class, Japan's most formidable.[68]

The cruisers. "[T]hose damned cruisers," as the official Army Air Force history calls them. The location of the *Agano* is unknown, but the *Myoko* and *Haguro* dominated Simpson Harbor. American aviators were all aware of the unexpected targets, now targets of opportunity, but very deadly ones. As passenger in *Seabiscuit*, in which Captain Ellis was leading another element of the 90th, Lee Van Atta noticed the *Haguro*:

The cruiser, speeding at full speed out of the harbour, was ablaze with belching anti-aircraft guns. The eight-inch turrets, four in all, were pointed dead at the incoming flights. We held to 50 feet, our Mitchell swaying and bouncing crazily with each concussion. We knifed across the bow of the cruiser a bare ten feet above the forward turrets. The figures of the warship commander and his staff were clearly visible. That cruiser was big, terribly big, and it looked like a floating fortress.[69]

A blast from the *Haguro*'s 8-inch guns splashed under *Seabiscuit*, driving her nose down until Captain Ellis and Lieutenant Dean could regain control – a cool 10 feet above the water. He dropped both of his bombs on a transport, then skedaddled out.[70] Captain Charles W. Howe's element swerved to the left to take on a 2,000-ton transport. Running at 230mph, when he got to within 800 yards of his target Howe began raking it with his eight .50-cals – even one .50-cal. machine gun could sink a thin-skinned freighter or transport. One of his 1000lb bombs dropped early and allegedly skipped into the side of the ship; the other thunked off her decks. In reality, the bomb that had dropped early was a near miss, but it split her stern open and she quickly sank with her bow in the air. The target was later identified as the 1,500-ton storeship *Manko Maru*, who lost eight killed. Howe's element made it out of Simpson Harbor as well. But almost every one of the gunships had sustained damage of some sort from the crossfires in the harbor.[71]

Behind Henebry's section, the attack plan fell apart completely, with what many believe were consequences that were undeniably tragic. It started with the 13th Bombardment Squadron.[72]

The designated leader for the 13th Squadron, squadron commander Major Arthur Small, had gotten sick early in the morning and could not fly. Captain Walter J. Hearn took over the squadron lead. The problem was that Hearn was "a less experienced flight leader." That's not always a bad thing; everyone has to start somewhere and in theory senior officers are supposed to have the most experience, so Hearn's "less experience" should have been no surprise. However, there was a second issue: Hearn had not attended the two group-level briefings on the plan of attack – it's not clear if he was supposed to – and was not thoroughly familiar with it. He was not familiar with why it was so important to fly through the Nodup Gap over the Namanula Hill saddle in those one-minute intervals between squadrons at a course of 225 degrees.[73] This was the nightmare of taking your final exam without having studied or attended class all semester, except if you fail, you die. Or, worse, your men die.

On the inside of the line abreast of the 13th Squadron was Lieutenant Walker. Because making a tight turn while staying in line with a heavy bomb load was tricky, as soon as Walker reached the designated turning point, he just turned. He went through, entered Simpson Harbor, and started his bombing run. "I looked for the rest of my squadron," Walker recalled, "and the only thing I saw was my wing man going down." He saw the Mitchell piloted by Lieutenant John Cunningham – his wingman – with its left engine on fire and losing altitude, but seemingly under control. It crashed between Vunakanau and Kokopo with no survivors.[74]

"I was out in the harbor alone," Walker remembered:

Prior to this, my heart was in my mouth. To say I was scared would be an understatement, but for some reason, at this point I was now more calm. Maybe it was because I was resigned to my fate or because I was fully occupied concentrating on my bomb run, I don't know, but I quickly reasoned that my best chance to survive was to stay low where I was a difficult target while flying between ships rather than above them. I maneuvered among the ships flying as low as I could concentrating on staying between the ships and then lined up on a merchant vessel. That ship's superstructure looked like the Empire State Building towering in front of me, but I drove in, released my bombs and hauled back on the yoke, the plane zoomed up in a steep climb and barely cleared the ship's superstructure. We made a good hit [...] I immediately got back down on the deck and after a minute or two I was out of the harbor and on my way home.[75]

Lieutenant Walker's target may have been the *Hakusan Maru*, which had become more popular than her crewmen would have preferred.[76]

Not popular today was Captain Hearn, who did not follow the course set by Lieutenant Walker. Like Lieutenant Cecil and the 71st Squadron before him, Captain Hearn aimed to shoot the Nodup Gap. And, like Lieutenant Cecil before him, the gap shot back. And like Lieutenant Cecil before him, he didn't like that. "Unfortunately at this point," Webster later recalled, "the combined efforts of thousands of ground personnel and possibly 400 combat crew men literally went down the tubes." Without identifying just what tubes those efforts were literally going down, Webster described what happened next: like Lieutenant Cecil before him, "Hearn opted to not turn the 13th behind the 90th but to continue to fly to the Northwest around the North side of the North Daughter volcano."[77]

This was a bad thing. When Lieutenant Cecil had done it before him, Cecil had already been knocked off the timetable by Captain Hara's destroyers. And Cecil had tried to get back on schedule and course as much as possible by turning in toward Simpson Harbor as soon as he had cleared the North Daughter. Captain Hearn's 13th and, behind him, Major Wilkins' 8th had been on schedule. And it left Wilkins with a major problem.

While many use the phrase "The Man, The Myth, The Legend" sarcastically, it could be used in a very real sense to describe the career of Raymond Wilkins. Wilkins, who was considered one of the Army Air Force's leading attack pilots at the tender age of 26, had taken command of the 8th Bombardment Squadron only in September. It was a well-earned posting. Wilkins had been at Port Moresby since April 1942 when the 8th was originally deployed. He had flown in the very first US attack mission in the Southwest Pacific Area, against Lae, in April 1942, in Douglas A-24 Banshees, the Army Air Force version of the Navy's famous and famously effective Douglas SBD Dauntless dive bomber. But while the Navy and the Dauntless went together like chocolate and peanut butter, the Army Air Force and the Banshee went together like chocolate and sauerkraut. The Army Air Force never mastered this whole dive bombing thing like the Navy and Marines did. Maybe because it did not like dive bombing, maybe because it found dive bombing too difficult, maybe because it found dive bombing too dangerous – within four months of its deployment, the 8th had lost 11 Banshees. The worst was on July 29, 1942, when an attack on Japanese supply ships unloading at Buna turned into disaster when five of the seven Banshees were shot down by Japanese Zeros, with a sixth so badly damaged that it had to land at Milne Bay with a mortally wounded gunner. Wilkins was the only pilot to return to Port Moresby.

Wilkins interpreted his escape from the valley of death over the Owen Stanley Mountains to mean he was destined to survive the war. When the Banshee was scrapped in favor of the A-20 Havoc, Wilkins took to the new aircraft, and, after Pappy Gunn's modifications, which had seen the seasoned aviator adding .50-caliber machine guns to the A-20, and new tactics, Wilkins flew dozens of low-level missions in A-20s, in which he was credited with several ships sunk and precise bombing results against a variety of ground targets. Ironically, he had missed the "Battle of the Bismarck Sea" because he had been on leave, a situation he regretted. Wilkins had turned down two opportunities to conclude his combat career and return home because he believed that he "could personally influence the outcome of the war by his own commitment and example." By November 1943, Wilkins had flown 86 combat sorties and had developed a reputation for taking the most difficult missions himself, never asking his men to do anything that he himself was not willing to do. In fact, Wilkins had cut short his leave in Australia with his fiancée, whom he was to marry in December, to take part in this attack. Historian Lex McAulay called him, "A dedicated officer, who led by example, known to be hard but fair, and respected by all who knew him, regardless of their rank, Ray Wilkins perhaps represented the ideal combat pilot."[78]

And Ray Wilkins could tell when a mission was becoming less than ideal. Major Wilkins, leading the 8th in a right echelon formation preparing to turn into the Nodup Gap, as Webster recalled, "kept waiting for the 13th to turn to [course] 225 [degrees True] as planned, but by the time he realized what Captain Hearn was doing, it was too late for the 8th to get into the right angle of attack." In essence, Wilkins was dependent on the 13th passing through the Nodup Gap one minute ahead of him. When the 13th did not do that, Wilkins felt obligated to follow them. Wilkins broke radio silence "to try to get the 13th leader to realize his error." That's probably too polite a term. Wilkins was reportedly "yelling" at Hearn, and even that is probably too polite a description.[79]

Worse, Captain Hearn did not completely follow Lieutenant Cecil's example and turn toward Simpson Harbor to make his attack as soon as he was around the North Daughter. Instead, Hearn kept going, leading the 13th around the northern periphery of Simpson Harbor and the Rabaul caldera. And Hearn kept going, until he was over the western part of Rabaul, then he turned left and led his squadron to the west of Vulcan. It was later claimed that three of the 13th Squadron Mitchells did break away from Hearn and attack small shipping, probably in Keravia Bay, but that was not the intended target of the mission.

By that time, an exasperated Major Wilkins had led the eight gunships of his coincidentally designated 8th Squadron in breaking away. Wilkins had followed Captain Hearn in the left turn around the North Daughter, but slightly inside. While Hearn kept going over Rabaul, Wilkins continued his left turn almost 180 degrees until he was heading almost due east on the north side of Simpson Harbor over downtown Rabaul.

He appears to have been looking for a break in the phosphorus smoke that was hiding the harbor. When he finally found one and was able to see the ships in the harbor beyond, Wilkins immediately turned right to dash through the opening and get back onto something like the planned course of 225 degrees True to make his attack run. The problem was that when he made that right turn, his squadron was still in the right echelon formation, so when Wilkins turned right, he turned right into the path of his wingman, flown by Flight Officer Woody H. Keyes, Jr and commanded by Flight Officer Daniel Lee Trout. "I don't know how his wing man [Trout] avoided hitting him," Webster observed. "Each pilot had to do a similar vertical right turn to miss the plane on his left and hoped the plane on his right was alert enough to do likewise." Only by the observation and quick reaction times of the pilots was a trainwreck in the sky avoided.[80]

Yet, for some, the benefit was only temporary. Major Wilkins went over the approximate center of Simpson Harbor on the left end of the 8th's formation, with the other seven Mitchells "more or less in an echelon formation to his right, possibly 50 yards between each plane." But the one-minute interval between each squadron had lengthened to five minutes since the 90th had attacked. "The defenders definitely were waiting for us," Webster later admitted. As the 3rd Bombardment Group's history put it, "Antiaircraft gunners on the vessels stood ready, and Simpson Harbor was ringed with living steel through which the Mitchells flew."[81]

Like Alexander at Gaugamela – or the Light Brigade at Balaclava – the gunships charged into the enemy's teeth, hoping to knock out a few. In their path was a "destroyer" – pretty much any warship smaller than a cruiser was described as a "destroyer" – which was likely the already-damaged minesweeper W-26. Major Wilkins dropped his first bomb and reportedly scored a direct hit. It was not, but it was enough. The minesweeper later reported, "Damage sustained. Hull damage from near misses. Flooding engine rooms, etc. and I am unable to move. Was towed to beach to keep from sinking." She was grounded north of Sulphur Creek.[82]

According to the original attack plan, Major Wilkins' Mitchells were to leave Simpson Harbor near Vulcan, just as Henebry's Mitchells squadron had done. But Henebry had gone in the way they were supposed to go in: northeast to southwest. Wilkins had gone in north to south. He could have his squadron turn toward the southwest, but that would bunch up the gunships at the back of his formation and, because they were only dozens of feet above the water, threaten to send them into the water. As Lieutenant Webster later explained, "At wide open throttle and maybe 50 feet off the water, you don't have much maneuverability to make major heading changes." So Wilkins held course heading south.[83]

Except there was a catch. The flight path took the squadron close to at least two destroyers anchored off Lakunai – and the heavy cruiser Haguro. Admiral Uozumi Jisaku was quite happy to play the role of the villain this day as his ship continued to gain speed on her run out of Simpson Harbor into the roomier Blanche Bay. Somewhere around here – no one knows where – was the Agano, and where the Myoko was is anyone's guess.[84]

But the *Haguro* and the destroyers were bad enough, sending up a deadly crossfire of antiaircraft lead. Lieutenant Webster continued his streak south across Simpson Harbor, struggling to acquire a target amidst all the flying tracers, the evasive action, and his squadron mates around him. That is how, "About half way across the Harbor, [Webster] became aware that there were no B-25s to [his] left where there had been three just a few moments earlier."[85]

Lieutenant Webster had no time to worry about that. He had more pressing matters:

We were past a number of possible targets before I had a chance to get properly set up for a good bomb run. Columns of water shot up in our path as the Japs depressed their guns to purposely cause an added hazard. Our plane got a near miss on a large freighter and then tried to "throw" a 1,000 pounder sideways into a corvette. 1000 pounders don't throw well or skip far. We continued strafing at vessels crossing in front of our view as they skittered like water bugs trying to get out of the confines of Simpson Harbor anchorage into the larger Blanche Bay.[86]

Lieutenant Webster continued scurrying toward the planned exit, with one interesting tidbit that illustrated just how low low-level bombing got. As he explained, "I dodged the Beehive rock formations in the middle of the Harbor and was looking up at them as we passed – we were that low." The remaining four 8th Squadron gunships formed up on Webster's B-25 and then hauled out to southwest over the jungles of the Gazelle Peninsula and then open water, fighting off a few half-hearted attacks by Zeros. They had escaped. They had survived.[87]

But it did not feel like much of a victory. "The flight back to New Guinea was like a trance," Webster later recalled. "We took off our helmets, but felt no elation at still being alive. My only conversation was to keep asking the turret gunner if he could see any B-25s trying to catch up, like Wilkins, Mackey or Trout." Lieutenant Webster and his charges passed several P-38s trying to limp back on one engine. He and his men gave them encouragement with gestures. It was all they could do. "Gradually the physical and emotional [strain] of the mission set in. The last thirty minutes of the flight took forever."[88]

But forever finally came to an end as Lieutenant Webster and the other four remaining B-25s of the 8th landed at Dobodura. Then a battle of a different type began:

At my plane's revetment Col. [Jimmy] Downs, the 3rd Group CO and a close personal friend, and Capt. [Rignal] Rig Baldwin [Squadron Intelligence Officer] waited with visible glee. They had heard at Group Operations the en route preliminary strike report that the 90th Squadron had sent in, and they were anxious to find about what the 8th had done. The fact that I had only five ships taxi in didn't sink in on them at the moment. Jimmy was giving me the old two hands over the headvictorious boxer sign and Rig gave me a gleeful "thumbs up" as I swung the plane around and cut the switches. It was after 4:30 o'clock and we had been in that damn coffin for almost 10 hours on a 6:00 hour flight to hell and back with little hope for any good results and, as yet, uncertain losses of our own. […] I was so stiff and wrung out emotionally, that I could barely get out of the plane. During debriefing Captain Baldwin was astonished at how the 13th Squadron had gotten so mixed up on the approach and at how none of us saw what happened to Wilkins' and Mackey's planes. We turned in unenthusiastic damage claims for our bombing and strafing runs, and the tail cameras later verified our poor results.[89]

This disconnect would not only continue, but would get worse. In Lieutenant Webster's view, the only good news would come in about 15 minutes later, when the battered B-25 commanded by Lee Trout and piloted by Flight Officer Woody Keyes landed safely. But in what seemed symbolic of the entire mission, after Trout and Keyes had landed, medics pulled one dead crewman from their plane and treated another for wounds. They had been on Major Wilkins' right wing. The news they brought was not encouraging.[90]

After hitting the "destroyer" *W-26*, Wilkins had continued south, with damage on his right wing taken during that first attack. His next target was a large merchant vessel, which he strafed and bombed, though whether his bomb hit could not be confirmed.

Then Major Wilkins led his entire three-plane lead element on a straight shot at the *Haguro* – even though he himself had no bombs left. The .50-cals' strafing had little effect on the *Haguro*, but the cruiser's return fire did, hitting Wilkins' left vertical stabilizer. But Wilkins kept going all the same, continuing to blaze away with his eight .50-cals. As historian Bruce Gamble speculated, "Perhaps, as the only pilot from the original 8th Squadron to have survived so much aerial combat, Wilkins believed he was invincible."[91]

Admiral Uozumi and his *Haguro* would debate that belief with their own eight 5-inch dual-purpose high-angle guns, 14 25mm cannons, and even the ten 8-inch guns of their main battery. In a maelstrom of missiles, Major Wilkins' left stabilizer tore away. This caused the plane to veer to the right and yet another possible chain reaction train wreck with his squadron mates on his right – or it would have if Wilkins had not apparently made the superhuman effort to instead turn the plane to the left. As Keyes put it, Wilkins "threw his plane into a turn to the left in order to avoid cutting us off or forcing us to make a violent turn right over the cruiser." Makes sense, except, according to Keyes, "This caused his belly and full wing surfaces to be exposed to the direct fire of the cruiser and, as a result, antiaircraft fire caught his left wing, causing one third of it to fold up. The plane then rolled over on its back and split-'S' into the water."[92]

Major Wilkins had been poisoned by his own fairy tale in which he was the hero who would beat the Japanese, get the girl, and fly off into the sunset. It's what anyone in his place would have wanted to believe. It's what had made Ray Wilkins such an exceptional and beloved officer. But war cares not for heroes, villains, fairy tales, or happy endings. War is random, arbitrary, capricious, and cruel. There was no wind in Wilkins' sails or beneath his wings, not enough to keep his *Fifi* airborne with a chance of escaping. The fairy tale of Ray Wilkins, who had survived flying an astounding 86 combat missions in theater for an astounding 23 months, and his crew ended in bubbling white foam at the entrance to Simpson Harbor. William Webster wistfully admitted, "I often wonder to what heights Ray Wilkins could have climbed had our November 2, 1943, Simpson Harbor mission gone as planned."[93]

Sadly, Ray Wilkins was far from the only fairy tale to end that way. The fairy tale – every bit as important – of Wilkins' wingman Lieutenant William C. Mackey and the crew of the B-25 Mitchell *Tugboat Annie* was another, apparently going down after Wilkins' *Fifi*. Eyewitnesses' accounts – as always, the least reliable form of evidence – do not agree on what happened exactly, but they do agree that Mackey's right engine was trailing fire and that his plane rode extremely low over the water. By some accounts, the gunship started to gain a little bit of altitude before the right wing dipped and went into the water, causing the aircraft to cartwheel and break apart off Kokopo to the northwest of Rapopo air base.[94]

It was a cavalcade of damaged aircraft and wet aviators that arrived at Dobodura and Kiriwina. Lieutenant Stanifer had taken a hit in his left engine's junction box, which caused the propeller to "run away" and, evidently, sort of burn itself out. The propeller would not feather and its windmilling – uncontrolled spinning – was a drag on Stanifer's fighter running on only its right engine. As he was leaving the combat zone, Stanifer saw a single B-25 heading out toward Kiriwina. He tucked his damaged P-38 under the Mitchell's wing to get the protection of the gunship's turret and waist guns. Stanifer could not establish radio contact with the plane, but he slowly realized that he did not want to be under this particular B-25 because it was slowly losing altitude. He saw the crew jettisoning all loose equipment including the protective waist guns.[95]

This B-25 seems to have been Major Henebry's *Notre Dame de Victoire*. Henebry tried to make Kiriwina, with what Henebry called its "couple [of] airstrips of sorts," but he and his crew had to sweat out the *Notre Dame de Victoire* slowly but surely losing altitude and speed on the one functional engine. Captain Howe in the *Here's Howe* was keeping pace with his commander riding his wounded steed.[96] Finally, the disabled left engine caught fire due to the friction of the air rubbing against the windmilling propeller that had refused to feather. Henebry was compelled to a water landing within sight of Kiriwina. Howe was ready to report the location of the ditching, which Stanifer actually did report before he himself landed at Kiriwina, but there was no need – a PT boat had seen Henebry's B-25 go down and quickly went out and rescued the entire crew and took them to Kiriwina, from where Howe quickly whisked them back to Dobodura.[97]

Where a major fight was brewing. The enraged aviators of the 3rd Bombardment Group in general and the 8th Bombardment Squadron in particular were out for blood. Not just any blood; the blood of Captain Walter J. Hearn. Many were in shock, distraught over the apparent loss of Ray Wilkins. And they, not unreasonably, blamed Hearn. His inability or unwillingness to follow the 90th Squadron through the Nodup Gap had thrown off the attack of Ray Wilkins' 8th and led to the deaths of him and his men. The calls to court martial Hearn were loud.[98]

What is rather interesting here is the seeming double standard between the treatment of Captain Hearn and that of Lieutenant Cecil. Like Hearn, Cecil had veered away from the chokepoint of the Nodup Gap and gone around the North Daughter. There do not seem to have been any calls to court martial Cecil like there were Hearn. There were some significant differences between the two cases, however. Cecil's 71st Squadron had already been knocked off schedule by the antiaircraft fire of Captain Hara's destroyers, so the timing of his group was already off. Even if it wasn't, the 405th had already fallen apart and was itself off schedule. No one was counting on Cecil to carry out his part of the mission. Major Wilkins had been counting on Captain Hearn to carry out his part of the mission. Additionally, while Cecil had gone around North Daughter, as soon as he had done so, he turned into Simpson Harbor to get as close to the proper attack position as he could. Behind the 71st, the remaining four Mitchells of the 405th did likewise. But after Hearn had gone around the North Daughter, he had not gone over Simpson Harbor at the first opportunity, but continued to head west at the periphery of the harbor and the caldera. He turned to the south when he was almost at Vulcan, away from the heaviest of the combat. Finally, and worst of all, while one could argue that two B-25s were shot down as a result of Cecil's actions – no one has argued that, it would seem, but they could – Hearn's actions had a much closer connection to the loss of more B-25s, including a very popular and respected 23-month combat veteran. The aviators had done the math and did not like the sum.

The calls to court martial Captain Hearn were calmed down by Captain Baldwin and others when it was revealed that Major Wilkins would be recommended for the Medal of Honor. Indeed, Wilkins would later be awarded the Medal of Honor – posthumously, of course. It seems a poor consolation prize for losing your life as a result of an, at best, extremely questionable tactical decision. Whatever Captain Hearn's side of the story was has not been revealed, and Hearn himself became scarce afterwards.[99]

The parade of damaged aircraft and wounded men arriving at Dobodura and Kiriwina was bad enough. Far worse was those that didn't, especially with no clue as to what happened. Such was the case with Lieutenant Lutton. As they were leaving, some of the 431st had formed up on Lieutenant Wenige. Lutton, who apparently made a strafing run over Tobera, was doing so when Wenige had to drive off a pursuing Zero. Once that was done, Wenige saw Lutton at the tail end of his flight, so he radioed, "Let's go home." A moment later, just south of Wide Bay, Wenige looked back and Lutton was gone. A search revealed no trace of Lutton or his P-38. It was "presumed that he ran out of gasoline while circling a bad weather front."[100]

Forty-five pilots and crew members were listed as killed or missing. Eight bombers and nine P-38s were lost. Of the fighter squadrons, the 80th had lost two (Evers and Shea), the 431st four (Richardson, Planck, Giertsen, and Lutton); the 432nd one (Mayo); the 433rd one (King); and the 9th one (Love). Of the bomb squadrons, the 500th lost the crew of one B-25 (that flown by Krasnickas); the 501st one (Moore); the 71st two (Hastings and Hungerpiller); the 405th one (Fox); the 90th one (Henebry); the 13th one (Cunningham);

BLOODY TUESDAY

and the 8th two (Wilkins and Mackey). The entire crew of Henebry's aircraft was rescued almost immediately, as was Hastings and two of his crew. Planck and Giertsen were found by friendly locals on New Britain who had already found Gordon Manuel and Edward Czarnecki. They and others were picked up by the US submarine *Gato* on February 5, 1944, and others. Everyone else was gone. The material losses were not complete, as one B-25 and three P-38s cracked up on landing after the operation.[101]

An operation that was brutal. General Kenney admitted as much when he called it "the toughest, hardest-fought engagement of the war." He would single out the fighting fliers of *Kido Butai*. "These were no amateurs, either," Kenney wrote. "They put up the toughest fight the Fifth Air Force encountered in the whole war."[102] The fighter pilots reported that the caliber of the Japanese pilots was considerably better than anything they had recently encountered.[103] The November 2, 1943 attack on Rabaul would earn the moniker "Bloody Tuesday."

Bloody as it was, the attack on Simpson Harbor was a rousing success. General Kenney sure thought so. As he explained:

> In the space of twelve minutes we had destroyed or damaged 114,000 tons of Japanese shipping, shot down or destroyed on the ground eighty-five Nip airplanes, and burned out half the town of Rabaul, with a loss of supplies to the enemy estimated at 300,000 tons. Never in the long history of warfare had so much destruction been wrought upon the forces of a belligerent nation so swiftly and at such little cost to the victor.[104]

If you say so, General. The Japanese did not. They could not be expected to, but for once at least some of their claims had a ring of truth. The Japanese consistently asserted that about 100 B-25s and 100 P-38s attacked Rabaul.[105] As to how many of these attacking planes were shot down, one leading Japanese history admits, "Claims were quite incredible."[106] The Japanese said they had shot down 85 to 95 P-38s and 24 to 48 B-25s – and a B-26. Even that was not enough for the Japanese, who raised the claimed total to 200, and even that number kept climbing. Not that the more perceptive Japanese brass like Admiral Kusaka actually believed it.[107]

Japanese losses were ... well, it's complicated. After the war, investigators were initially only able to confirm the sinking of the minesweeper *W-26*, the *Manko Maru*, the 3,119-ton *Shinko Maru*, and the 5,000-ton *Shinko Maru No. 2*, which seemed both underwhelming and confusing.[108] The number of damaged ships looked somewhat impressive, with 30 of the reported 40 ships in Simpson Harbor suffering damage of some sort. They included the aforementioned *Hakusan*, *Hokuyo*, and *Yamabiko Marus*. The submarine tender *Chogei* apparently evaded Captain Ellis's bomb and reported only light damage from strafing. Suffering unspecified damage was the 6,667-ton ammunition ship *Onoe Maru*, the 10,000-ton tanker *Kunikawa Maru*, the 2,726-ton water tanker *Wayo Maru*, the *Wakatsuki Maru*; storeships *Hayasaki* and *Arasaki*; and the veteran repair tug *Nagaura*.[109]

157

Even more complicated was the damage to the men-of-war. The destroyer *Shiratsuyu* was lightly damaged by a near miss. The *Myoko*, which had fired 27 8-inch shells, 77 5-inch shells, and 3,200 25mm and 13mm rounds, and *Haguro*, which had fired 18 8-inch shells, 158 5-inch shells, and more than 3,000 25mm and 13mm rounds, allegedly suffered no damage. Or not: the Japanese also reported *Myoko* suffered "light damage" from a near miss that cracked the cradle of a low-pressure turbine, which does not exactly sound "light." Total Japanese aircraft losses are unclear. One Japanese source admitted 18 fighters "lost or failed to return." An analysis by air historian Michael Claringbould says 20 fighters were lost, including six that had "takeoff accidents." The *Shokaku* lost to combat two Zeros, including division officer Lieutenant (jg) Miyabe Kazunori, who died at Rabaul's hospital the next morning from combat wounds, and Chief Petty Officer Kawamura Masatsugu. Three others failed to return, including Petty Officers 1st Class Sato Genshichi and Yamamoto Takeo. The *Zuikaku* lost Chief Petty Officer Ohkura Shigeru, Petty Officers 1st Class Yoshida Saburo and Komaba Kazuo, and Flight Petty Officer 2nd Class Miyakawa Masayoshi. One *Zuiho* Zero failed to return. The 201 Air Group lost two Zeros in combat, while a third was a writeoff. The 204 Air Group lost Chief Petty Officer Shimamoto Katsumi and Petty Officer 1st Class Kaneko Fusa-ichi, while the 253 Air Group lost one to combat.[110]

That was not quite enough for 5th Air Force tastes. General Whitehead called it "one of the major victories of the Pacific War," but, in perhaps a tacit admission of the true nature of the engagement, admitted that because Japanese air power had not been destroyed, the "attack will continue."[111] The 5th's public relations people – General MacArthur always had the best public relations people – produced a coffee-table book titled *Rabaul: 2 November 1943*. It had dozens of dramatic photos from the cameras on the B-25s. It opened with a foreword by General Kenney that should sound a bit familiar:

> In the space of twelve minutes a formidable Japanese sea and air armada, in the powerful, well-organized, well-defended stronghold of Rabaul, was attacked and decisively defeated. Never in the long history of warfare has so much destruction been wrought upon the forces of a belligerent nation so swiftly and at such little cost to the victor.[112]

If you say so, General. The numbers make it look more like a defeat, at least a tactical one. The Japanese later pointed out, "After this attack, large-scale attacks on Rabaul by enemy planes ceased for several days." In fairness, Kenney, always a loud, bombastic figure who loved hyperbole, probably knew he was putting lipstick on the proverbial pig.

Maybe … Recall that the pressure was on to "get the hell to Rabaul" to "occupy the Jap Air Force" and distract them from the ongoing landings on Bougainville. Base Air Force and *Kido Butai* had already launched one attack on November 2. What was to stop them from launching a second? Turns out, 5th Air Force did. That, itself, makes this tactical defeat a strategic victory.

Why?

At 9:05am, guarded by the destroyers *Fullam*, *Guest*, *Hudson*, *Bennett*, and *Braine* of Destroyer Squadron 45, the *Hunter Liggett*, *American Legion*, *Crescent City*, and *Alchiba* returned to Torokina to resume unloading. Admiral Merrill and his exhausted men and depleted ships, with the exception of those with the *Foote*, were denied any relief when Admiral Halsey informed them he was sending up the light cruiser *Nashville* and the destroyer *Pringle* as reinforcements – and ordered them to guard the unloading ships. Like protective zombies, Merrill and his ships turned around and moved in to cover the transports (and one cargo ship), but this understandable precaution turned out to be unnecessary. While numerous unidentified aircraft appeared on radar throughout the day, there was no air attack. By 3:00pm, the *Hunter Liggett*, *American Legion*, *Crescent City*, and *Alchiba* were completely unloaded and headed for Tulagi, where they arrived at 12:45am on November 4. Purvis Bay welcomed Admiral Merrill's cruisers at 4:30pm on November 3 with the conventional signal, "What do you require?" The *Denver*'s Captain Briscoe answered, "Sleep."[113] It was the brutal sacrifice of the 5th Air Force that made this unloading possible.[114] The Marines on Bougainville had everything they needed. For now.

Also returning were Captain Hara's destroyers, albeit to Simpson Harbor. Despite the damaged ships and the smoke from the remaining fires, as the ships pulled in at around noon, "[t]he depressed mood of the morning was completely gone. Officers and men alike were able to joke and laugh again." Hara was able to look at the Empress Augusta Bay action more dispassionately, sort of:

> Ijuin was responsible for the debacle that befell his column. He was a tired, weary, and exhausted man. And, with the loss of cruiser [sic] *Yugumo* a month earlier, he had lost confidence in his own ability. An aristocrat often breaks down quickly in the face of adversity.
>
> Still greater responsibility rests with Admiral Omori. His turnabout in the face of the enemy served to tie Ijuin's hands, severely limiting his possible courses of action.[115]

One Julius Caesar might want a word about that whole aristocrats "break[ing] down quickly in the face of adversity" thing. But Hara's analysis was not unreasonable. In the late afternoon, Hara went to the *Myoko* to report to Admiral Omori on Empress Augusta Bay. What Omori had been doing all day is unclear; in postwar interrogations, Omori said that at "1500 Rabaul [was] attacked by about 200 B-25s. Attack directed at airfields and installation. No ships reported lost or damaged."[116] How Omori could have missed the *Myoko*'s maneuvers or cracking the cradle of that low-pressure turbine if he was on board is anyone's guess.

Anyway, Admiral Omori "greeted [Captain Hara] warmly as usual." The admiral believed he had reason to be in a good mood. Because he had just won a major battle. Off Bougainville in Empress Augusta Bay, he had stared down an enemy force of "at least" seven heavy cruisers and 12 destroyers. He believed he had sunk at least one and as many as five of the heavy cruisers, along with two or three destroyers. Sure, Japan was losing the war, but he had won a battle, and that's what was important.[117]

Patiently, Admiral Omori listened to Hara's description of the activities of Admiral Ijuin's 3rd Destroyer Flotilla. Hara was concerned he would be reprimanded for refusing to follow the baron's order to come to his aid or for simply not doing so regardless of orders. But Omori was supportive. "I think you did the right thing. You were correct in moving away from *Sendai* while she was under concentrated attack." But the admiral was not finished. "On another score, I wish to thank you for the radio message of [2:24am], reporting your discovery of the enemy ships. No one else had then seen the ships. Without your sighting report our whole group would have had a much worse time of it." He was right. When Hara asked permission to leave and turned toward the door, Omori called him back. "Here's 30 yen [$15]," he smiled. "It isn't much, but take it along as my token toward buying drinks for your men."[118] He was right. It wasn't much.

Also not much were the nocturnal attacks by the Japanese, including the first "official" attack of *Ro-Go*. Taking a page from their successful if extremely costly nighttime torpedo attack at Rennell Island that ultimately sank the USS *Chicago*, the Japanese prepared a nighttime air attack by torpedo planes, in this case six of the still-deadly Nakajima B5N carrier attack planes, all from the *Shokaku*. For reasons known only to the Japanese (and maybe not even them), they then threw that page away and armed each of these torpedo planes, legendary for their performance at Pearl Harbor, Coral Sea, Midway, and Santa Cruz, not with the deadly Type 91 torpedo but instead with four 60kg (132lb) bombs, which were ineffective against ships, especially warships. All the same, Lieutenant Ono Hiroji led these six of the dwindling number of veteran aircrews from *Kido Butai* skyward from Vunakanau around dusk toward Torokina on a dangerous nighttime mission armed with weapons they knew to be ineffective. It was just the principle of the thing. But the weather had worsened considerably, and they were unable to find any sea targets, so they just bombed the landing beach and headed back. But on the way back, Ono's wingman vanished in the gloom, and only five of these precious *Kido Butai* crews returned to Vunakanau after a fruitless but frightful five hours of flight. Evidently not as frightful but just as fruitless was the flight of some Type 0 reconnaissance seaplanes from the 938 and 958 Air Groups, who went to Mono Island, dropped two 60kg (132lb) bombs each, and headed back.[119]

The Allies were able to match the fruitlessness and fright with a nocturnal raid by the Beauforts of Nos. 6, 8, and 100 Squadrons on Tobera. Six Beauforts from No. 8 Squadron attacked at around 10:00pm. All their bombs fell south and southwest of the airfield, which does not speak well of the accuracy of nighttime bombing, the preferred method of Royal and Dominion air forces. The other two squadrons attacked the target in the wee hours of the next morning, mostly just as ineffectively. At 3:00am, one Beaufort was wandering trying to find Tobera and, typically, unwilling to ask for directions when a flare path to Tobera appeared and a green light flashed from the base. As a thank you to the Japanese who had mistaken him for a friendly night fighter, the pilot then dove and strafed the south end of the airfield, releasing his bomb load as he went. One of those friendly night fighters, an Irving from the 251 Air Group, attacked the Beaufort of Flying Officer

Clem W. B. Renouf over Wide Bay. Renouf had to jettison his bombs and return to Vivigani.[120]

The next day, November 3, saw the beached *Yamabiko Maru* still burning. The odds of the repair ship needing a repair ship and the irony it would represent seemed to be increasing. Additionally, the submarine *I-104* arrived in Rabaul with the survivors of the *Sendai*. Captain Hara went to the dock to receive them. Among them was the baron. Admiral Ijuin, Hara thought, "was a pitiful sight as he staggered onto the pier." Most survivors fished out of the water after their ships sank probably look that way, but with Ijuin it apparently went further than that. Hara approached him with apologies for failing to come to the *Sendai*'s aid, but the baron would have none of it. "Don't say that, Hara. I am ashamed of my behavior," Ijuin replied. "Never mention an apology for that again. I was a coward. You did the right thing. I must have been out of my mind."[121]

The next day, November 4, Admiral Omori and the 5th Cruiser Division left Simpson Harbor to head back to Japan. Admiral Koga's reaction to the Empress Augusta Bay action seems to have been schizoid. Omori was relieved of command and returned to the Torpedo School like a beaten-up library book. In fact, all of the Japanese flag officers involved in Empress Augusta Bay were sacked, suggesting Admiral Koga did not view the battle as as much of a victory as Omori did. Admiral Osugi had followed up his disastrous escort of the *Nisshin* with an even worse performance, one the Japanese considered "deplorable" – at least the *Nisshin* was sunk by the enemy, unlike Osugi's *Hatsukaze*, mostly – and was bounced around a bit until he was given command of the naval base at Makassar on Celebes (Sulawesi). The worst fate was reserved for Admiral Ijuin. After a short stint on the general staff, he was assigned to duty protecting convoys from submarines. How exciting. Too exciting, actually. He was killed in 1944 after his corvette was torpedoed off Borneo.[122]

The *Myoko* and *Haguro* were being put on the shelf, too. However "light" their damage was, they needed to go back to Japan and a full overhaul. These injured men-of-war would not be needed in Rabaul.[123]

Because the proverbial cavalry was coming.

While the 5th Air Force was taking one for the team at Rabaul, their aerial allies to the southeast were attacking targets not nearly as well defended as Simpson Harbor, simply to keep them that way.

Just before dawn on November 2, Admiral Sherman's carriers renewed their attacks on the Buka and Bonis airfield complex with 16 Hellcats (eight from the *Saratoga* and eight from the *Princeton*) escorting 19 Dauntlesses (all from the *Saratoga*) and ten Avengers (one from the *Saratoga* and nine from the *Princeton*). Only one plane plopped into the water on takeoff, this time because its engine was not running properly, but the entire crew was rescued. With no aerial opposition, the airstrike pretty much had its way with Bonis. Two

2,000lb bombs were planted in the middle of the runway while a third landed in the revetment area. Six 500lb bombs also detonated in the revetment area. Two cargo ships were attacked off the coast as well. The entire airstrike returned, but may have attracted an extra, as a Japanese snooper was intercepted and shot down about 30 miles out a little before 9:00am as the strike was returning. It is unclear if the scout saw and reported the carriers.[124]

The aerial activity in the Solomons ratcheted up a notch. An early morning attempt by AirSols to catch Admiral Omori's Combined Assault Force with 20 Avengers and 18 Dauntlesses escorted by 44 fighters went awry when they found nothing but a big oil slick and a bunch of Japanese Zeros headed to the attack on Admiral Merrill's retreating ships. Other Allied aerial efforts were a bit more successful. A little before 10:00am, 20 B-24s paid a visit to Kahili and dropped 80 tons of explosives on its runway. At the same time, 44 Avengers and 24 Dauntlesses paid a visit to Kara and left 45 tons of housewarming presents along the length of the new base's runway as well as gun positions and bivouac areas. Though neither airstrike had fighter escort, there were no losses, and antiaircraft fire of only light intensity was reported at Kara.[125]

It was only a little more than half an hour after these attacks that Admiral Sherman's carriers struck Bonis again. Now it was a dozen Hellcats (four from the *Saratoga* and eight from the *Princeton*), 20 Dauntlesses (all from the *Saratoga*) and nine Avengers (one from the *Saratoga* and eight from the *Princeton*). The TBFs maneuvered to approach the Bonis runway from the northwest and drop their 13 500lb bombs along the length of the runway, northeast to southwest. Two Avengers dropped incendiaries in dispersal areas and the runway was strafed. Two landing barges and several antiaircraft positions were hit as well. Even though there was no aerial opposition, there were casualties. The *Princeton*'s Ensign Leonard C. Keener was last seen on a strafing run in his Hellcat. The TBF flown by Lieutenant (jg) Charles C. Dyer of the *Princeton* was hit by what was believed to be a 5-inch shell and burst into flames. As Dyer's TBF was plunging toward the ground, where it would explode with no survivors, the Avenger flown by Lieutenant (jg) G. W. Spear of the *Princeton* collided with it from behind. Spear had to ditch near the destroyer *Fullam* in Empress Augusta Bay, from where he and one of his two radiomen were rescued.[126]

With that, Admiral Sherman called it a day and had his task force head back down the Solomons for a badly needed date with the fleet oiler *Kankakee* near Rennell Island, the very name of which could hardly be comforting to US Navy officers and men hoping to avoid air attack from Betty bombers based at Rabaul. In the four strikes on the Buka-Bonis airfield complex, Sherman's aviators had dropped a total of about 93 tons of bombs. It was believed the target area was "well covered," with "both of the landing strips ... made temporarily unserviceable for a considerable time." The aviators of the *Saratoga* and *Princeton* reported that 14 Bettys, two floatplanes, two Zeros, and three unidentified planes were destroyed on the ground; six Bettys, three fighters, and three unidentified planes damaged. Additionally, three freighters, five barges, and one cutter were destroyed, and six freighters, three barges, and two small ships were damaged. Considerable damage was also done to adjacent buildings, supply areas, antiaircraft defenses, and revetments. The human losses were three pilots and four crew members killed or missing. Three Hellcats and two Avengers were lost in combat, and two F6Fs, three TBFs, and one SBD were "operational" losses, in these cases from launching. One F6F from the *Princeton* suffered major damage when it crashed into a barrier on landing; 16 other aircraft received minor damage. Sherman considered the mission a success.[127]

The Japanese countered with another "official" attack of *Ro-Go*. An airstrike was sent up from Rabaul led by Lieutenant Notomi consisting of eight carrier bombers from the *Zuikaku* armed with the more powerful 250kg (550lb) bombs and one Yokusuka D4Y from the *Shokaku* escorted by either 35, 39, or 45 Zeros (in which case they consisted of 16 from the *Shokaku*, 17 from the *Zuikaku*, and 12 from the *Zuiho*). They supposedly took off looking for an enemy convoy near the Treasury Islands, but they found none, so they took some shots at the Torokina landing beaches. At 20,000 feet over Empress Augusta Bay the Zeros met seven Corsairs of Marine Fighting 211 (an eighth had to turn back to Barakoma with engine trouble); eight Warhawks of the 44th Fighter Squadron were present but too far south to engage the intruders. The Vals, at 15,000 feet, were able to break away and attack the Torokina beaches; one Japanese history claims that this attack achieved "some results," which gives some hint as to the decline of standards in *Kido Butai*, though it remained the best the Japanese Naval Air Force had left to offer. The Zeros claimed to have engaged ten or "about 20" defending fighters, shooting down five, while losing Zero pilot Flight Petty Officer 1st Class Aomi Hisashi and the carrier bomber flown by Flight Petty Officer 1st Class Ogura Shinichi, both from the *Zuikaku*. The Marines claimed to have shot down three Zeros. But Marine Major George Moffat was last seen with three Zeros going for high shots on his side, while Lieutenant Robert V. Hatfield simply did not return to base; he appears to have been responsible for shooting down Ogura.[128]

These aerial battles were rapidly overshadowed by a much more disconcerting development. Admiral Halsey and Admiral Nimitz had suspected that an aerial reaction would not be the end of the Japanese response to the Torokina invasion. On November 3, *Magic*, the intelligence gift that kept on giving, indicated that a large Japanese naval force consisting of eight heavy cruisers and the 2nd Destroyer Flotilla had left Truk through its south channel at 9:00am that day and was heading south from Truk. This force was under Vice Admiral Kurita Takeo, who in August had replaced Admiral Kondo as commander of the Japanese 2nd Fleet, the surface battle force.[129]

This had the potential to be a major problem. As Admiral Halsey explained it:

The situation for the South Pacific Command, with respect to surface forces at this time, was becoming desperate; other than Admiral Merrill's task force, consisting of 4 cruisers and their destroyer screen, only the *Saratoga* and *Princeton* were under operational command of the Commander South Pacific. No other heavy forces were available or located near enough. The Japs had superior naval forces in Rabaul.[130]

Halsey elaborated in his memoirs:

> On the fourth, our scouts reported that another enemy force was standing in to Rabaul from Truk – eight heavy cruisers, two light cruisers, and eight destroyers. Presumably they would fuel, then run down to Torokina the following night and sink our transports and bombard our precarious positions. This was the most desperate emergency that confronted me in my entire term as COMSOPAC. Even if Tip Merrill had been within reach, and fresh, he would not have had a prayer of stopping such an armada, yet *Cherryblossom*'s success – perhaps the success of the South Pacific War – hung upon its being stopped.[131]

Admiral Halsey was being a drama queen. Asked about Halsey's claim that this was the most desperate emergency he had encountered as Commander South Pacific, Admirals Callaghan and Scott were unavailable for comment. But once you strip away the melodrama and the cover for *Magic* being the real source of the intelligence (though scout planes did find Admiral Kurita's force on November 4, those planes had been sent up as a result of *Magic*), Halsey was right. The options for countering Kurita's cruisers were extremely limited. This had the potential to be very, very bad.

So Allied reconnaissance planes were out all over the place. And one, apparently a US Navy Liberator, found something. No, not Admiral Kurita's cruisers, but convoy "Tei No. 4" (T4-GO Transportation Strategy). The second echelon of said convoy had left Shanghai on October 21, 1943, carrying elements of the Imperial Army's 17th Okayama Division. Part of Tei No. 4 was a veteran of a few of these operations, the *Gokoku Maru*, carrying 1,759 troops. It also included the auxiliary cruiser *Kiyosumi Maru*, carrying 1,342 troops, the Japanese 14th Cruiser Division under Rear Admiral Ito Kenzo with the light cruisers *Isuzu* (carrying 479 troops) and *Naka* (485 troops); and, last but never least, the destroyer *Yamagumo* (0 troops).[132]

The convoy had barely left Shanghai when the monotony of convoy operations was broken. In the wee hours of October 22, the ships of Tei No. 4 managed to avoid ten torpedoes fired by Lieutenant Commander Edgar J. MacGregor's submarine USS *Shad*. It sure seemed like the Imperial Navy could not lift a finger without a submarine or air attack showing up. The *Shad* had to dive to avoid a depth charge counterattack by an angry *Yamagumo*. Nevertheless, McGregor heard multiple explosions that he believed coincided with the time his first four torpedoes were supposed to hit. When the *Shad* surfaced later that morning, McGregor found a "large, noticeable" two-square-mile oil slick. He claimed four hits on two Japanese battleships, heavy cruisers, or light cruisers. In fact, he had hit nothing. The convoy moved on, arriving at Truk on October 28.[133]

Four days later, in the afternoon of November 1, Tei No. 4 resumed its journey to Rabaul, having picked up as escorts the destroyers *Isokaze* and *Urakaze*. Though everyone knew they were entering dangerous territory, everything seems to have been hunky-dory until about 11:30am on November 3. Then, 60 miles north of Kavieng, 19 B-24s from the 5th Bombardment Group of the 13th Air Force operating from Guadalcanal showed up after having fought through scattered rain squalls and a ceiling of only 1,000 feet to give the convoy a workover. The Army Air Force aviators claimed hits on three ships, but at the cost of the Liberator piloted by 2nd Lieutenant James R. Wilson of the 72nd Bombardment Squadron. Wilson's B-24 took an antiaircraft shell between the engines on the left wing, sending shrapnel into the cockpit that injured Wilson and two others and damaged the instrument panel, the hydraulics, and the oil pressure. Somehow, Wilson and co-pilot 2nd Lieutenant Charles M. Eagan, who was also wounded, kept the Liberator in the air just long enough to get away from Kavieng and Rabaul and ditch north of Bougainville at 4:04pm. On impact, the B-24 broke apart, as B-24s usually did, killing Wilson, Eagan, and both gunners. Two more crew drowned, but four survived to the next day, when they were rescued by a PBY Catalina commanded by Lieutenant (jg) E. E. Perkey from Patrol 71, with a healthy escort of Kiwi Kittyhawks.[134]

The Japanese radioed, "As a result of bombing by 19 large-type enemy planes, *Kiyosumi's* engine room is flooded and she is unable to navigate." A few hours later came a second: *Isuzu* commenced towing *Kiyosumi Maru* at 1500 escorted by *Naka* and *Isokaze* …"[135]

Another of those scout planes sent out to confirm *Magic's* information was another US Navy Liberator, this one piloted by Lieutenant Commander Harry E. Sears, commander of Bombing 104. At 5:30am or so, Sears found something very interesting, maybe 180 miles north of Kavieng. No, not Admiral Kurita's cruisers, but a pair of Japanese tankers, the *Nissho* and *Nichiei Maru*s, heading for Rabaul. They were escorted by Captain Hara's former destroyer *Amatsukaze*, on a mission of her own to Rabaul, and the destroyer *Shimakaze*.[136]

If you've never heard of the *Shimakaze*, don't worry; almost no one else has, either. But you're in for a treat. As Imperial Navy historian and editor of the excellent *Imperial Japanese Navy Page* Jonathan Parshall commented, "One word sums up this magnificent vessel: power." The *Shimakaze* had a main gun battery consisting of six 5-inch dual-purpose guns in three twin mounts, a torpedo battery of 15(!) torpedo tubes – the most of any Japanese destroyer – in three quintuple mounts; and a top speed of 40.9 knots. "She was, in my opinion, the most powerful destroyer of the war," Parshall has opined. The *Shimakaze* had one weakness: cost. She was considered an experimental destroyer, and her engines and power plant were very expensive. Destroyers are supposed to be cheap and almost expendable, and the *Shimakaze* was neither, so the Japanese built only one of her. She was literally one of a kind.[137]

On this day, for reasons known only to the Japanese, that big, experimental destroyer with a top speed of 40.9 knots was escorting two slow tankers to Rabaul. Lieutenant Commander Sears was focused on the tankers, however. After radioing in a contact report, he dove down to masthead height and came in at one of the tankers, apparently the *Nissho Maru*, strafing her deck with .50-cals Pappy Gunn style, and then releasing two 300lb bombs. Both bombs were near misses, but the strafing started fires on the *Nissho Maru's* deck.[138] As they were supposed to. It's one reason why .50-cals were capable of sinking thin-skinned supply ships like freighters and tankers.

And a fire of any type on an oil-carrying vehicle of any kind is, well, a bad thing. While Lieutenant Commander Sears sped off heading for the *Nichiei Maru*, a second Bombing 104 Liberator, this flown by Lieutenant Anderson, arrived to pick up the work on the *Nissho Maru* from where Sears had left off. Roaring in at an altitude of all of 35 feet – no need for special oxygen supplies at that height – Anderson dropped five 300lb bombs and later reported three direct hits. That's not likely, but of whatever bombs did hit home, one apparently detonated in the *Nissho Maru*'s engine room. Sears made his attack on the *Nichiei Maru* and reported two hits on the stern that sent black smoke billowing. Both PB4Ys returned to base, where Anderson would find a 10ft piece of cable his radio antenna had snagged. One of the Japanese ships, probably the *Shimakaze*, signaled, "Two B-24s attacked. *Nissho Maru* suffered hit in upper section of engine room and is unable to navigate."[139]

If the Japanese did not like that attack, there would be others. One more, at least. Lieutenant Commander Gordon Fowler, now the commanding officer of Bombing 102, showed up in another PB4Y. Though this was reportedly 20 miles from the first attack, this attack seems to have been on the *Nissho Maru* as well. Fowler may have interrupted an attempt to tow the oiler; in any event, the tankers had split up, the *Shimakaze* presumably staying with the *Nissho Maru* and the *Amatsukaze* with the *Nichiei Maru*. Fowler dove in at masthead height from the ship's starboard beam and dropped six 300lb bombs. He reported one direct hit amidships and one near miss that produced a large underwater explosion. Fowler saw no evidence that the ship was sinking, listing, burning, or even inconvenienced, so he called it a day and headed back. The *Shimakaze* signaled again, "*Nissho Maru* received a second bombing attack. Fuel oil gushing out." A little more than an hour later came another signal: "Attempted towing *Nissho Maru*, but because of enemy air attack released towline and discontinued towing. Considering extent of damage and repeated enemy air attacks am taking crew aboard temporarily. *Nissho Maru* has 9 dead and 14 wounded."[140]

They were not the stars of the show, so to speak. Admiral Kurita's 2nd Fleet was, and Allied scouts were keeping a close eye on it. As they did so, AirSols conducted a veritable blitz of Bougainville. At 11:00am, 37 Dauntlesses (nine from Marine Scout Bombing 244, the rest from Marine Scout Bombing 234) and 19 Avengers (including 13 from Marine Torpedo Bombing 143) escorted by 28 Corsairs from Fighting 17 dumped 54 tons of bombs on the runway of and gun positions around the Kahili air base. The TBF of Marine Torpedo Bombing 143's Lieutenant John Welch Tunnell was hit, and though three people were seen to bail out and open their parachutes before the plane plunged into the sea some three miles southwest of Kahili, neither Tunnell nor his two crewmen were ever seen again. Four other planes were damaged. After that attack was complete and the remaining strike aircraft safely on their way back, seven of the Corsairs split off to strafe the Cape Mabiri area on the northeast coast of Bougainville, while another eight went to strafe the Bonis area. Which was a bit of a coincidence because 23 B-24 Liberators of the 307th Bombardment Group escorted by eight Corsairs of Marine Fighting 212 and another eight of Marine Fighting 215 were at Buka dropping 46 tons of bombs on the airfield. In the opinion of the crews, "It was not a perfect job, but would disrupt flying activity for a time." Several vessels were damaged by strafing .50-cal. machine guns off Cape Mabiri and Bonis, and while no aerial opposition was encountered, antiaircraft fire was heavy, giving Fighting 17 skipper Lieutenant Commander John Thomas "Tom" Blackburn's Corsair a 20mm shell in the left wing, but he was able to get back to base.[141]

At around noon on November 4, a Liberator, flown by Lieutenant Robert J. Sylvernale of the 400th Bombardment Squadron of the 90th Bombardment Group, found the cruisers near the Admiralties. He managed to shadow Kurita's ships for two hours, radioing regular position reports, despite intense antiaircraft fire and even floatplanes launched by the cruisers to shoot him down. At 3:30pm, an AirSols reconnaissance plane found the same force on a straight line to St George's Channel and Rabaul.[142] So Admiral Halsey had that most important of elements for any military operation: information. He also had that other most important of elements for any military operation: communications, at least if you count Halsey begging Nimitz for help as "communications." Halsey requested fast battleships as a result of "information that a force of cruisers and destroyers left Truk headed south."[143] Halsey pointed out that Admiral Merrill's task force needed rearming. He might have also pointed out that Merrill's task force consisted of five (with the addition of the *Nashville*) light cruisers armed with 6-inch guns – rapid-fire 6-inch guns, but still 6-inch guns – whose effectiveness against a force of eight heavy cruisers armed with 8-inch guns and 24-inch Type 93 torpedoes would be very questionable at best.

Admiral Nimitz sent some additional cruisers and destroyers to the South Pacific but warned he would have to call them back very quickly to the Central Pacific. Nimitz also promised a carrier group, but it was still en route. General MacArthur had ordered the Australian 8-inch-armed heavy cruisers *Australia* and *Shropshire* and four destroyers to Milne Bay to provide support to Halsey, but there was no way they could get to Bougainville in time.[144]

This was ... not exactly the way they had planned *Cherryblossom*. Admiral Nimitz was cautiously optimistic: "In circumstances believe reinforcements being furnished coupled with heavy air superiority held by ComSoPac [Halsey] and CinCSoWesPac [MacArthur] will meet your requirements." In response, Halsey objected that combat with Admiral Kurita's cruisers would undoubtedly be fought at night, when air superiority could not be applied. Additionally, that the Japanese could provide naval reinforcements from Truk much more quickly than he could from the New Hebrides. Halsey also noted that fighting on many fronts "usually" prevented "consistent attacks on Rabaul." Halsey's dispatch to Nimitz finished: "As in the past we will hurt Japs and attack them with everything we have but hate to give them an even break."[145]

Help was coming, but it would not get there in time. For now, Admiral Halsey and the men of the South Pacific Force – the 3rd Fleet, which even Admiral Nimitz seems to have been reluctant to call them – were on their own.

They were outnumbered and outgunned. For now, at least. They would not be later, but they were now and now was when the Japanese were coming.

The Japanese had to be stopped. The Marines on Bougainville, like the Marines on Guadalcanal a year earlier, depended on it. The Japanese had to be stopped.

But how?

CHAPTER 5

A SECOND PEARL HARBOR IN REVERSE

A disgusted Captain Hara "gaped" as he watched Admiral Kurita's flagship *Atago* drop her anchor "nonchalantly" in Simpson Harbor. With the *Atago* was the rest of Kurita's force that had sortied from Truk. Well, most of it. "These new arrivals," Hara recalled, "made me apprehensive and uneasy."[1]

Captain Hara was hardly the only one with a sense of foreboding. Admiral Kusaka had opposed the idea of sending the 2nd Fleet's elements to Rabaul from the outset, and he reiterated his opposition. While Admiral Koga would relieve Admiral Omori of command for his inept performance at Empress Augusta Bay in short order, he still believed Omori's claims of damage inflicted on the Americans. Kusaka did not, but could not convince Koga to be more guarded in his acceptance of those claims, nor could he convince Koga that the big November 2 air attack, despite its relative ineffectiveness, was another indication of Rabaul's vulnerability as a navy base. But Koga believed he was sending Admiral Kurita's cruisers on a mopping-up operation, and there was no convincing him otherwise.[2]

Even now, that operation was starting to fray, as Admiral Kusaka knew. There was the issue with the second echelon of convoy Tei No. 4, intended to bring more elements of the Imperial Army's 17th Kumamoto Division to Rabaul. Except on November 3, Tei No. 4 had gotten hit by Liberators north of Kavieng. Not very well; the best they managed was two near misses and – maybe – one hit.

They got a near miss on the *Naka* that killed seven and wounded 20. Japanese sources do not agree on whether the *Gokoku Maru* took a near miss, but if she did it did not impact her operation. It's also not clear if the *Kiyosumi Maru* took a near miss or was actually hit. What is clear is that she was badly damaged.[3]

The *Gokoku Maru* was ordered to continue on ahead to Rabaul, escorted by the *Urakaze*. The Japanese radioed, "As a result of bombing by 19 large-type enemy planes,

Kiyosumi's engine room is flooded and she is unable to navigate." A few hours later came a second: "*Isuzu* commenced towing *Kiyosumi Maru* at 1500 escorted by *Naka* and *Isokaze* ...."[4]

The *Kiyosumi Maru* and her entourage were diverted to Kavieng. At some point either that night or early the next morning, November 4, the light cruiser *Yubari* and the destroyer *Minazuki* were sent to assist, apparently from Rabaul. Once the rendezvous was made, the Imperial Navy escorts proceeded to remove as many Imperial Army troops and as much equipment, ammunition, and other supplies as possible from the *Kiyosumi Maru*. The *Naka* took off 166 men and four antitank guns; the *Yubari* took another 196 troops and three field guns; the *Isuzu* removed another 196 troops and four "regimental" guns; the *Minazuki* removed 267 troops; and the *Isokaze* took off 236 troops and two mountain guns.[5]

It's not entirely clear what happened next, but this is where it starts getting darkly comical. What seems to have happened is the *Isuzu* then resumed the tow and took the *Kiyosumi Maru* to Kavieng, where they, apparently along with the *Isokaze*, arrived at about 6:00pm on November 4. The *Isuzu* cast off the tow, she and the *Isokaze* disembarked their troops, turned around, and left – and each promptly struck a mine, compliments of the PBY Catalinas of the Royal Australian Air Force's No. 11 Squadron. The *Isuzu* suffered hull damage forward and her Number 1 and Number 3 main guns jammed in train, but she was able to make it to Rabaul. The *Isokaze* was struck in the port quarter, sustained "[m]edium damage" and left "unable to operate in a combat state," with 26 sailors and 24 soldiers slightly wounded. She was compelled to crawl at 16 knots to Truk, where she arrived on November 6 and underwent emergency repairs.[6]

What the other ships did is less clear. The *Gokoku Maru* and *Urakaze* definitely arrived safely at Rabaul. The *Yamagumo* definitely did not, because she was recalled due to the air attacks around Rabaul, so that recall was probably ordered around this time. That left the *Naka*, *Yubari*, and *Minazuki*. By 6:00am on November 5, *Yubari* was in Kavieng, where she was designated the new flagship of the 3rd Destroyer Flotilla, replacing the sunken *Sendai*. Whether *Yubari* stopped in Rabaul first to disembark her troops or just let them off at Kavieng is not clear, but it is known that she was in Rabaul later that day. Conversely, on November 5, the *Naka* and *Minazuki* were in Rabaul. Whether they stopped in Kavieng first to disembark their troops or just let them off at Rabaul is not clear. On November 5, the *Yubari* and *Kiyosumi Maru* were in Kavieng, *Yamagumo* and *Isokaze* were on their way to Truk, and the *Naka*, *Isuzu*, *Urakaze*, *Minazuki*, and *Gokoku Maru* were in Rabaul.[7] Got all that?

While that was going on, the cargo ship *Ryuosan Maru*, escorted by the armed hydrographic survey ship *Tsukushi*, left Rabaul headed for Kavieng.[8] The *Ryuosan Maru*'s job was to get the remaining cargo from *Kiyosumi Maru* and bring it to Rabaul. This must have been very important cargo. The two ships were off Edmago Island, just short of Kavieng, when at 10:10pm, the *Tsukushi* struck a mine and sank. Five minutes later, the *Ryuosan Maru* also hit a mine. The explosion killed or mortally wounded 20 of her crew while injuring 16 more. The *Ryuosan Maru* tried to beach herself on Edmago Island, but before she could do so she succumbed to her own wounds at 7:00pm on November 5.[9]

Not as confusing was whatever was happening to the tankers *Nissho* and *Nichiei Maru*s and their escorting destroyers *Shimakaze* and *Amatsukaze*. When last we left Admiral Kurita's friendly tankers, the *Nissho Maru* was disabled and "[f]uel oil [was] gushing out." The *Nichiei Maru* was also damaged, though exactly how badly is, once again, unclear. Kurita was concerned enough about the situation that he detached one of his heavy cruisers, the luxurious *Chokai*, and the destroyer *Suzunami* to assist. The *Chokai*, *Suzunami*, and, it appears, the *Amatsukaze* shepherded the two damaged tankers back to Truk, where they arrived on November 6. The *Shimakaze* continued onward, toward Rabaul.[10]

Also moseying toward Rabaul was something else. At 8:00am a reconnaissance plane, apparently a D4Y Comet from the *Shokaku* commanded by observer Lieutenant Kibayashi Satoshi, reported an enemy force of "five heavy cruisers, seven destroyers, and two large transports" 150 miles away on a bearing of 140 degrees True from Cape St George. Many of the staff officers of Southeast Area Fleet, 8th Fleet, and Base Air Force concluded that these ships meant an amphibious landing. Or, more accurately, another amphibious landing. In the last six months the Americans had landed in the Trobriand Islands, the New Georgia islands, Lae, Finschhafen, Vella Lavella, the Treasury Islands, Choiseul, and Bougainville. Now they were landing some troops, albeit probably not that many, somewhere else. Big deal. An enemy landing operation was not, to be sure, a good thing, but they had bigger concerns at the moment than a few transports, no matter how big they were. Admiral Kusaka was not so quick to dismiss the reported transports, however. He ordered more scout planes sent up to shadow this enemy force. They took off in short order, but it would take some time to find the enemy.[11]

Meanwhile, Admiral Kurita's force had arrived in Rabaul for the quintessential pit stop: gas up, change the tires, check the oil, clean the windshield. Even though his force had already been reduced by detaching the *Chokai* and *Suzunami* to help those troubled tankers, it was still more powerful than anything the Americans could put into the field – or the sea – in the South Pacific. Kurita had brought with him three members of the 4th Cruiser Division: his flagship *Atago*, her sister ship *Takao*, and her other sister ship *Maya*; two members of the 7th Cruiser Division: the *Suzuya* and her … former sister ship, now the heavy cruiser-seaplane carrier hybrid *Mogami* and one member of the 8th Cruiser Division: the veteran heavy cruiser-seaplane carrier hybrid *Chikuma*. With them was the 2nd Destroyer Flotilla under the veteran Rear Admiral Takama Tamotsu in his flagship, the new light cruiser *Noshiro* (a sister ship to the *Agano* but with a much cooler name) and destroyers *Hayanami*, *Fujinami*, and *Tamanami*.

This was indeed a powerful force, and a necessary force because this attack was important, albeit not important enough for Admiral Koga to risk his precious battleships like the *Yamato*, his flagship *Musashi*, *Nagato*, *Kongo*, and *Haruna*, which spent most of their time sitting around Truk Harbor sunning themselves. Then again, maybe the Japanese were starting to notice that their supply of battleships was starting to run low, what with them being sunk in battle (*Hiei* and *Kirishima*), converted to useless hybrid battleship-seaplane carrier things (*Ise* and *Hyuga*), or blowing up for no apparent reason (*Mutsu*). The battleships had to be saved for that Decisive Battle. This battle would be important, arguably the future of Japan and the entire war effort depended on it, but it was not Decisive Battle-important. Admiral Koga did not know exactly what the Decisive Battle looked like, but this wasn't it. He was sure of it.

Even the most powerful fleets need fuel, however, and after that long trip from Truk, Admiral Kurita's ships were hungry critters. Within 15 minutes of entering Simpson Harbor, the first ships, the *Chikuma* and *Noshiro*, were feeding at the trough that was the tanker *Kokuyo Maru*. At 11:16am, the *Atago* and *Maya* took their places, while the *Suzuya* slurped up fuel from the *Naruto*. It was a scene of domestic naval bliss, as part of Kurita's plan to be ready to leave tonight to hit those Bougainville beaches and any supply ships near them ...[12]

The first warning came at ... well, no one is quite sure. Lieutenant Kibayashi had returned to Vunakanau in his D4Y Comet to report in person at 10:55am. Shortly thereafter at 11:00 am, another D4Y, this from the *Zuikaku*, reported a force similar to that Kibayashi had reported – except instead of two large transports, it had two aircraft carriers. That ... changed things. Base Air Force issued a full alert and started preparing both a fighter defense for the Rabaul caldera and an attack to deal with the carriers.[13]

Those preparations had hardly begun when Base Air Force received warning from one of its aircraft – either a squadron leader for the dozen or so Zeros patrolling over the Rabaul caldera, a Yokosuka D4Y (probably the one from the *Zuikaku*); or one of the scout planes it had just launched to follow the enemy surface force that had just been sighted (again, probably the one from the *Zuikaku*) – that a large flight of aircraft was inbound. Lookouts atop the volcano known as Mother reported sighting that large flight. Morison says Rabaul issued a short warning at 11:10am based on what it heard from the 70 aircraft the Japanese had in the air, except the Japanese do not seem to have had 70 aircraft in the air at this time; it might simply be a garbling of the alert issued by Base Air Force, and this alert does not seem to have reached the ships in Simpson Harbor. The Japanese themselves say warning of an imminent air attack was issued at 11:15am, but even this warning seems to have reached the ships erratically. The *Suzuya* has the first sighting of aircraft at 11:15, notes verification of identity, and has an alert issued by 8th Base Force at 11:18. The *Chikuma* also has the first sighting at 11:15, while the *Mogami* has it at 11:16. But the *Maya* has it significantly later at 11:20, the *Noshiro* at 11:21, and *Yubari* at 11:23, suggesting the word was not passed around evenly. There is no information as to when or if Petty Officer Kikawa in his control tower at Lakunai started banging on his metal drum.[14]

Because word of the imminent attack was not passed around evenly, many of the ships did not quite grasp what was going on. Admiral Kurita's ships had just arrived. They were fueling, anchored, doing some maintenance, catching their breath. They were taken completely by surprise. The ships in the tightly packed Simpson Harbor would struggle to build up steam, to build up speed, to maneuver.

Base Air Force immediately scrambled fighters, but because of the relative lack of warning – and the usual lack of radios – the response was disjointed and uncoordinated. While Rabaul or Simpson Harbor were certainly the target of the incoming aircraft, they were not heading straight to their target. Rather, they were heading up St George's Channel, like the last attack from New Guinea had. This gave the Japanese more time to get additional fighters in the air. What seems to have happened is 15 Zeros from the *Zuikaku* scrambled from Tobera, followed shortly thereafter by 15 Zeros from the 253 Air Group. At the same time, another 15 Zeros, these from the *Zuiho*, took off, apparently from Vunakanau, as did 17 from the *Shokaku*. Once again, Lakunai air base seems to have been sluggish in responding. It was not until 11:30, 15 minutes after the air raid warning, that the 201 Air Group sent up 13 fighters, soon joined by 11 from the 204 Air Group. Nominally, the interception mission was directed by Lieutenant Sato Masao, division officer from the *Zuiho*. The total number of Zeros that got off the ground was 86, though how many of those actually made contact with the enemy is another matter entirely.[15] Flying with the defenders were five Yokosuka D4Ys from the 501 Air Group out of Vunakanau with the Type 3 phosphorus aerial burst bombs, those bombs that did not actually work, but looked cool when they exploded, and, let's face it, that does count for something.[16]

The Zeros moved to position themselves over Lakunai, circling at about 16,000 feet, outside the range of their own antiaircraft guns. They did not pursue. They had a plan. The American fighters would always charge at the Zeros, trying to keep the Japanese as far from the American bombers as possible. But once they did so, they broke formation and left openings for the Japanese to reach those bombers. The Japanese would hold position over Lakunai and wait until the American fighters charged at them.[17]

The American air formation, an unusually compact formation, continued northward in the distance. They did not follow the same route the 5th Air Force had three days earlier. Instead, they went all the way to Tavui Point at the northern edge of the Crater Peninsula. Then they wheeled to the left in an almost 180-degree turn. They were going to sweep Simpson Harbor from the north.

The Zeros over Lakunai waited patiently, ready to ambush the attackers. They had been taken by surprise three days ago, yet had still recovered enough to give the 5th Air Force a bloody nose. They would do so again.

Still they waited. Waited for the fighters to break off from their charges. These strange, boxy-looking fighters ...

These were not the hostile but familiar multi-engine bombers and fighters of Douglas MacArthur's 5th Air Force.

These were carrier planes.

"We looked up with utter astonishment," recalled fighter pilot Lieutenant Marvin D. Harper of the *Saratoga*'s Fighting 12.

"Way above us – it was just mind-boggling. With the number of airplanes and the altitude advantage they had, they should have decimated us."[18]

The Americans knew they were flying into a hornet's nest, knew they were going to be outnumbered, though perhaps not as badly as they actually were. But there were not a whole lot of good options. And the men of the *Saratoga* especially were bursting to take a bite out of the Japanese.

To say this air strike was slapped together is putting it mildly. The intelligence from *Magic* that Admiral Kurita was coming down with eight heavy cruisers (actually seven, which became six when the *Chokai* was detached), two light cruisers (actually one), and eight destroyers (actually four, which became three when the *Suzunami* was detached, unless you count the destroyers escorting convoys down) was two days old. The confirmation of it by scout planes was one day old. And Admiral Halsey was just looking old as he wracked his brain trying to figure out what to do.

Things were not quite as bad as Halsey made them out to be. For one thing, if Kurita's cruisers showed up off Cape Torokina, there was little for them to attack except the Marine beachhead. That would be bad, but it would not be the same as when Kurita showed up with the battleships *Kongo* and *Haruna* off Guadalcanal and almost singlehandedly nearly won the campaign for the Japanese in a space of a few hours. What the cruisers could do was limited. They could not destroy the beachhead, only damage it. And that damage would have little bearing on the land campaign simply because the Imperial Army would be in no position to attack the beachhead for months. Any setback would be temporary.

What Kurita's cruisers could do was cause a lot of casualties, a lot more casualties than was necessary. And thus lead to uncomfortable questions as to why the Bougainville offensive was launched when Admiral Nimitz was about to run with his offensive in the central Pacific, when the Allies did not yet have the forces to run two offensives at the same time. There were logical answers to these questions. Nimitz wanted two offensives to keep the Japanese guessing as to which one would hit next, and thus misallocate their combat assets as well as gain a psychological advantage. Furthermore, and this point is inarguable, the central Pacific, with the Marshall and Gilbert and eventually the Caroline Islands, was literally healthier than the Solomon Islands, with their constant rain, wetness, mold, mud, filth, mosquitos, and pestilence. US Marines were much less likely to be stricken with malaria in the Marshalls and Gilberts than they were in the Solomons. But a logical answer can still be an uncomfortable, even embarrassing answer.

Plus, things really were not as bad as Admiral Halsey made them out to be. As his operations officer, Captain Harry R. "Ray" Thurber, pointed out, Halsey still had two aircraft carriers (well, one and a half). Except Halsey had sent them to refuel near Rennell Island so that they would be far away from the Bettys and Kates in Rabaul, though the

Chicago suggested it was not far enough, but close enough that he could call on them if necessary.[19]

And it would be necessary. Captain Thurber and the staff got to work. Described as "energetic, sleepless, but always urbane," Thurber was responsible for developing many of the plans used during the New Georgia campaign, including those plans that actually worked. Halsey was a fan of Thurber's "brilliant solution of operations problems."[20]

Some on the staff argued for a defensive stance, but a defensive stance was simply not Bill Halsey, and Captain Thurber knew it. If Admiral Sherman's carriers could get into range of Rabaul, they might be able to surprise Admiral Kurita's cruisers as they refueled. Could the carriers get from Rennell Island to striking range of Rabaul? Literally every ship in Sherman's carrier force, including the old *Saratoga* herself, was built for speed. Thurber ran some time and distance calculations with Halsey's aide, Lieutenant H. Douglas Moulton, and checked their numbers – twice. They drafted orders that would send Sherman speeding into range of Rabaul the next morning. They even assigned priority of targets: cruisers first, then destroyers.[21]

They then ran the orders to the chief of staff, Rear Admiral Robert B. "Mick" Carney, who had moved over to that position after completing his stint as skipper of the *Denver* the previous July. With Carney's approval, the three of them walked over to Admiral Halsey's Quonset hut. Without looking at the draft orders, Halsey asked a question. "You're not going to send Merrill to Rabaul, are you?"

"No, sir. This is Ted Sherman again."

Admiral Halsey paused for a moment. "Every one of us knew what was going through the Admiral's mind," Admiral Carney recalled. "It showed in his face, which suddenly looked 150 years old. He studied the dispatch for a few seconds, then handed it back. All he said was, 'Let 'er go!'"[22]

As Halsey later explained it:

I sincerely expected both air groups to be cut to pieces and both carriers to be stricken, if not lost (I tried not to remember that my son Bill was aboard one of them); but we could not let the men at Torokina be wiped out while we stood by and wrung our hands.[23]

"This was Halsey at his best," opined historian Bruce Gamble, "making a difficult decision without waffling."[24] For all of Halsey's faults, some of which were yet to manifest themselves, these are the times when he truly shone. He was decisive. Not always right – Santa Cruz comes to mind – but decisive.

Admiral Sherman's ships had just finished refueling when the new orders arrived: move at all possible speed to a position south of Bougainville, where at first light *Saratoga* and *Princeton* were to launch a maximum-effort strike against Rabaul. Sherman informed the *Saratoga*'s skipper Captain John H. Cassady, then passed word to the other ships.

To get within range of Rabaul in the allotted time, they had to steam 500 miles in 15 hours. Sherman ordered a northwesterly course at flank speed. The task force worked up to its "maximum formation speed" of 27 knots. They would keep this speed throughout the night.[25] It was a strain on their engines and boilers, but it had to be done. That was the easy part.

Now the tough part: getting the air crews ready. Admiral Sherman called this mission "one of the most important and dangerous assignments ever handed to the *Saratoga*." Captain Cassady called the air group commander, Commander Henry Howard Caldwell, and his squadron commanders to his cabin near the bridge. He was blunt and to the point.

"Boys," Cassady said, "we are hitting Rabaul tomorrow morning. This is a hell of a tough assignment." He explained the threat the Japanese cruisers posed to the marines at Bougainville and why they had to be stopped. He also promised the *Saratoga* would be there when they returned from the attack. Cassady concluded with, "You have damn little time. God bless you, boys."[26]

On that cheerful note, the staffs of *Saratoga*'s Air Group 12 and *Princeton*'s Air Group 23 were almost at a loss to find information about Rabaul; there was no time to get that information from the 5th Air Force. The only man in the fleet who was even remotely familiar with Rabaul was Admiral Sherman, who still had never actually been there. As captain of the *Lexington* in 1942, he had gotten within 400 miles of Rabaul. On second thought, Sherman was not even remotely familiar with Rabaul. No one was.

And no one was getting sleep on this night. The operations and intelligence officers spent the entire night working out the strike plan with the little information they had about Rabaul. So they largely had to wing it, no pun intended. With no aerial photographs or charts, they spent the night packing as much pertinent information as they had into the aviators' briefing packets.

Because they expected to be outnumbered by Japanese fighters, Admiral Halsey had ordered what is called a "maximum strike." That meant using every single flyable aircraft the task force had for this air strike, which, in turn, meant not keeping any fighters to defend the carriers if and when the Japanese mounted a counterattack. But Halsey had a solution: AirSols. AirSols was not in range of Rabaul – for now – but it would be in range of the *Saratoga* and *Princeton*, so the Navy fighters of AirSols would protect the carriers. Fighting 17, equipped with F4U Corsairs, and Fighting 33, equipped with F6F Hellcats, to be precise. These pilots were trained for carrier operations. For this mission, Fighting 17, normally based at Ondonga, and Fighting 33, normally based at Munda, would be based on the carriers so they could refuel and rearm, which meant the "Jolly Rogers" of Fighting 17 had to reinstall their fighters' tail hooks.[27]

It was no news to Howard Caldwell that he would lead the combined *Saratoga* and *Princeton* air groups in the attack. The fighters would be led by Commander Joseph C. Clifton, another one of the true characters of the US Navy. After a stint at the University of Kentucky, he went to the Naval Academy, where he was a member of the varsity football team for three seasons. His senior year he was nationally recognized and named All-Eastern and honorable mention All-American.[28]

On board the *Saratoga*, however, Commander Clifton was known as "Jumpin' Joe." It was not a holdover from his football days or a comment on his intensity. Rather, "He couldn't sit still to save his soul," recalled Lieutenant Harper. "He just couldn't do it."[29]

Commander Clifton had other quirks as well. Lieutenant (jg) John D. "Mickey" Gavan, remembered Clifton's addiction to ice cream. "He'd get a gallon of ice cream, and sit there and eat it," said Gavan. What else would you do with a gallon of ice cream?[30]

Every commander – even the good ones, especially the good ones – has his quirks. Commander Clifton, well … no one considered him a great aviator. What he was, was a great leader of men. "He was the only charismatic man I ever met," recalled Harper. "He was truly charismatic. His whole secret was that he could control people."[31]

Commander Clifton had other talents as well. Commander Caldwell rigorously trained his aviators on the *Saratoga* and turned them into a top-flight outfit – no pun intended – in part because of Commander Clifton. Clifton had trained his fighter pilots to fly on top of the dive bombers and torpedo planes to cover them from diving Zero interceptors. Clifton repeated his theory to his fighter jockeys: "It is our job to escort the bomber and torpedo planes and to get them in there, get them out and get them home; no dogfighting. It's our problem to escort."[32]

Also escorting the strike planes would be the *Princeton*'s Fighting 23 under Lieutenant Commander Henry L. "Hank" Miller, who had a colorful episode in his past as well. As a lieutenant in early 1942, he was a flight instructor at Ellyson Field in Pensacola. But he was suddenly sent to Eglin Field on a temporary assignment: he was to teach carrier takeoff techniques to a certain Lieutenant Colonel Jimmy Doolittle and the other B-25 pilots who would fly the raid on Tokyo in April 1942. Miller did not teach them landing techniques, however. That's always suspicious.[33]

It was just before daylight on November 5 when Admiral Sherman's carriers arrived at their launch position, 60 miles southwest of Cape Torokina. "[W]e found the weather to the westward ideal for air operations," Sherman said, "with a number of nearby rain squalls to give us some protection" from snoopers, "but at the same time not sufficient to hamper our flight operations."[34]

At around 8:00am, the fighter protection from AirSols arrived. In the final moments before the attack, Petty Officer Paul T. Barnett, a photographer's mate with Bombing 12, asked Commander Caldwell if he could photograph the attack. Caldwell approved and told Barnett, who rarely got the chance to use his photography skills in his squadron's two-seat Dauntlesses, that he could fly as a fourth man in his command TBF Avenger, which would orbit high above Rabaul during the strike to give tactical commands. Meanwhile, Commander Clifton sat on a couch in Fighting 12's ready room, pulled a pocket-sized Bible from his flight suit, leading anyone of his aviators who cared to join in a prayer from the 23rd Psalm.[35]

With that, it was time to go. The task force turned into the 5-to-7-knot wind coming, oddly, from the southwest. It was just before 9:00am when Commander Clifton took off from the *Saratoga*. He was immediately followed by 15 more F6F Hellcats, launching one at a time. Then 16 TBF Avengers of Torpedo 12, followed by 22 SBD Dauntlesses. At the tail end of the *Saratoga*'s launch were 16 more Hellcats, then one more as a close escort for Commander Caldwell's command TBF. On the *Princeton* – no slouches in terms of aerial expertise – Lieutenant Commander Miller led 19 Hellcats into the air, followed by seven Avengers, and then one more F6F as another close escort for Caldwell. Unlike the Buka and Bonis attacks, neither launch had any aborts, mishaps, or planes plopping into the water. And the 97 planes of the air strike headed off on the two-hour flight to what the aviators knew would be a warm reception at Rabaul.

As they did so, they sorted themselves out. In one of the more bizarre features of this hastily slapped together attack, the group and squadron commanders spent the first half of the flight working out the final details and mechanics of the attack using their radios. Their radios were VHF and were only line-of-sight range, so there was little danger of the Japanese detecting them. Unless, of course, the Japanese had an aircraft of their own in the area. Far greater was the danger of distracted flying. There was not just the risk of colliding with something, but also of plunging thousands of feet to your death, being incinerated by volatile aviation fuel, or blown apart by exploding munitions. Once the group and squadron leaders had slapped together an attack plan, they passed it on to their charges.[36]

The formation was logical, like a layer cake, but without the frosting. In the bottom layer were the torpedo-carrying TBFs. In the middle were the Dauntlesses, each carrying a 1,000lb bomb. Commander Clifton's 16 Hellcats separated into four-plane divisions, each of which covered a corner of the formation. About 2,000 feet above them were 16 more *Saratoga* Hellcats, then another 2,000 up were Lieutenant Commander Miller's Hellcats from the *Princeton*. Above it all were two Hellcats providing close escort for Commander Caldwell. It was in keeping with Clifton's theory of fighter escort.[37]

The weather cooperated like never before. The clouds and occasional squalls at launch surrendered to clear skies as the air strike closed in. Approaching Rabaul, visibility was estimated to be 50 miles. As historian John Prados put it, "It was a brilliant day for a killing." Not something you'll usually see on weather reports, but it was accurate, more accurate than most weather forecasts.[38]

Like a flock of hawks – do such things exist? – the Americans moved into St George's Channel just after 11:00am, right on schedule. As the air strike raced past the volcanoes of the Crater Peninsula, on the other side of those volcanoes, the Japanese were scrambling. For whatever reason, the two Type 1 radar sets the Japanese had positioned at their main observation post at Tomavatur Mission, about two miles southeast of Vunakanau air base, seem to have provided no warning. The first Rabaul learned an attack was imminent was when the air strike flew up St George's Channel.[39]

At 13,000 feet, the attackers headed north in St George's Channel until Tavui Point, then did their 180-degree turn, roared over the North Daughter, and approached Simpson Harbor from the north. As Commander Caldwell and his pilots took in the vignette before them, they were shocked – Captain Thurber's plan had timed this attack perfectly. Simpson Harbor was packed. Six heavy cruisers sat in the anchorage like lazy crocodiles, some refueling, others relaxing at anchor. At least three and maybe five light cruisers, 11 destroyers, freighters, tankers, cargo ships, minesweepers, subchasers, the works. Maybe 50 ships. With the wind now coming from the southeast, they were pointed toward the southeast, almost directly away from the incoming Americans. Admiral Kurita's ships had arrived maybe two hours earlier, just enough time for them to start to stop, refuel, and relax. Captain Hara called them "sitting ducks."[40]

No ducks, sitting or otherwise, would be harmed in this engagement. The Americans and the Japanese would be another story. The shock and joy of Commander Caldwell and the US Navy aviators was tempered by the swarm of Zeros over Lakunai air base, staying above the range of the Japanese antiaircraft artillery. Strangely, the Zeros were holding back. Oh, well. No one said this would be easy.

As the Americans crossed the shoreline into Simpson Harbor, the Avengers and Dauntlesses moved into a tight attack formation and, very quickly, chose their targets. Overhead, Commander Caldwell made "suggestions" as to those targets. Commander Clifton kept his Hellcats in close over the strike planes, just as he had planned. Not planned was the sheer volume of Japanese antiaircraft fire. "The antiaircraft fire over the harbor area was of terrific intensity," reported members of Fighting 12. "The shore batteries and the ships in the harbor put up a barrage from heavy and automatic guns which covered all levels from 10,000 feet on down. The CLs [heavy cruisers] and CAs [light cruisers] fired their largest guns."[41] In desperation. Like those Type 3 burst bombs (or, for that matter, those Type 3 shells), using the main cruiser batteries never worked. But they did look kind of cool.

The first to pay the price for the heavy ack-ack were the Hellcats on the outside of the formation. Lieutenant (jg) Tom G. Atwell, in the lowest layer of fighters, was hit and was last seen heading south at 6,000 feet over the Gazelle Peninsula. The next was the *Princeton*'s Lieutenant J. A. Smith, whose Hellcat was hit and went down, apparently in the water. Other US Navy planes were hit in the gale of gunfire, but the pilots grimly held their courses.[42]

Which was a problem for the defending Japanese fighters. Those boxy, muscular-looking American fighters that the Sea Eagles of *Kido Butai* had never seen before had not broken off to attack the Zeros, but had instead held their position with the strike planes. The Zeros, with their altitude advantage, could pounce, but as long as those fighters held their position, the Zeros could get at only them, and not the dive and torpedo bombers they really wanted. And the Zero pilots from the *Zuikaku* and the *Zuiho* were not sure just what these strange, new US Navy fighters were capable of, but were sure what their own antiaircraft guns could do if the Zeros mixed it up too much. Frustrated by this American intransigence, the Japanese fighters held their position over Lakunai.

While the Zeros waited, the Dauntlesses had descended to 10,000 feet. They reached their pushover points and promptly pushed over into their dives on their targets. Plunging from almost two miles up at angles from 60 to even 90 degrees, though normally in the area of 75 degrees.[43] Interestingly, among the first targets was a ship who had spent most of her career as a fleet flagship and, indeed, was now Admiral Kurita's fleet flagship, the heavy cruiser *Atago*. She had been fueling from the *Kokuyo Maru* when the Americans arrived. Captain Nakaoka Nobuyoshi ordered antiaircraft action to port and cast off from the tanker, but the *Atago* struggled to build up speed. At 11:28am three *Saratoga* Dauntlesses released their 1,000lb bombs over the cruiser. All missed, but all were near misses to port just forward of the beam. Several compartments near Number 1 engine room and boiler rooms Numbers 3–9 were flooded. Shrapnel opened steam lines and set fire to torpedo oxygen flasks; more shrapnel flew across the bridge and ripped away half of Captain Nakaoka's face. The *Atago* listed to port. Nakaoka was taken from the bridge on a stretcher, managing a weak, "Banzai!" as he passed a stunned Admiral Kurita. Seven Avengers turned to make torpedo attacks on the cruiser without success. On his way to the *Atago* in a little boat to deliver a message from Admiral Kusaka to Kurita was Commander Ohmae Toshikazu, who missed the shrapnel on the *Atago*'s bridge, but did get strafed by one of the Hellcats.[44]

Also fueling from the *Kokuyo Maru* had been the *Atago*'s sister ship *Maya*. But the *Maya*'s skipper, Captain Kato Yoshiro, had only been in command for less than a month and was, as historian John Prados put it, "not so familiar with his vessel as he could have been." The cruiser had been late to recognize the air attack, struggled to cast off from the tanker, and could not build up speed before Lieutenant Commander James Newell, leader of the *Saratoga*'s Bombing 12, led a flock of SBDs down on her. One 1,000lb bomb, possibly from Newell himself, pierced the aircraft deck on the port side above the *Maya*'s Number 3 engine room, where it detonated. The explosion wrecked the aircraft deck, twisted the hull, and turned the Number 3 engine room into an inferno.[45]

The namesake third member of the *Takao* class in Rabaul on this day started out better than her two sisters. Not tied to the umbilical cord of a tanker, skipper Captain Hayashi Shigetaka was able to get her moving quickly toward Blanche Bay and, by 11:25, the *Takao*'s guns were firing. But as she was closing in on the exit from Simpson Harbor into Blanche Bay, the destroyer *Wakatsuki*, apparently having not learned her lesson at Empress Augusta Bay, cut in front of her. Hayashi ordered hard right rudder, and the *Takao* turned into the trajectory of at least one 1,000lb bomb. The bomb penetrated the main deck on the starboard side, apparently between the Number 1 and Number 2 8-inch turrets, and exploded. The Number 1 turret was perforated; the barbette of turret Number 2 turret was damaged. The *Takao* also sustained damage to her steering and a ruptured hull below the waterline. Hayashi's crew suffered 22 killed and 22 wounded.[46]

The pounding the Japanese seemed to be taking was not being inflicted without a bitter price. After the *Saratoga*'s Lieutenant (jg) John V. Lucas pushed over, his rear gunner, Aviation Radioman First Class Myles C. James, like all the SBD rear gunners, was almost on his back, and in the backwards rollercoaster from Hell, diving almost straight down, unable to see where they were going, unsure when or even if they would pull out of the dive, but able to see people shooting at them. A lot. Once they have pushed over, dive bombers are extremely difficult for antiaircraft artillery to hit – until they come out of their dives.

Probably at least in part to handle the fear that any of us would feel in his situation, over the intercom James called for Lucas an excellent and entertaining play-by-play of the antiaircraft fire. He reported that most of the shell bursts were behind them, but the Japanese gunners adjusted.

"They are hitting on our left now!" James called out. Moments later, "They are hitting on our right ..."

"I give up; they are all around us."[47]

Lieutenant (jg) Lucas released his bomb over a "*Tone*-class cruiser." Then he pulled out of the dive, but as he did so, the Dauntless was jolted by a direct hit in the center of the rear compartment on the starboard side. Lucas tried to raise James on the intercom, but there was no response, nor would there be.[48]

Lieutenant (jg) Lucas' bomb had missed. It splashed just off the starboard catapult of the Allied nemesis heavy cruiser-seaplane carrier hybrid *Chikuma*. Skipper Captain Shigenaga Kazue had been faster on the uptake than other Japanese captains, quickly ordering his guns into action. It was probably the *Chikuma*'s guns that killed Myles James, thus continuing her role as an Allied nemesis. The near miss caused a little flooding and disabled the Number 3 torpedo mount, which, since the *Chikuma*'s main battery was all forward, was a significant impairment to her combat capability. Three crewmen were wounded.[49]

Lieutenant (jg) Lucas would not be the only one to attack the *Chikuma*. Also diving on the mutated heavy cruiser was Lieutenant Commander Vincent W. Hathorn, executive officer of the *Saratoga*'s Bombing 12. After releasing his bomb over *Chikuma* – it missed – Hathorn pulled out of his dive and found himself "face-to-face with the eight-inch guns of a Jap cruiser." The warship seemed to be firing everything it had at Hathorn at point-blank range.[50] This was ... awkward. Later, Hathorn said:

> The only thing I could think of doing was to pull my gun switch and give him return fire with my two fixed .50-caliber guns. I thought, "This is pretty silly, me dueling with this joker." And then I got past him, and there were two destroyers, about twenty-four hundred tons each, doing the same thing to me. That made the battle a little more even.[51]

Lieutenant Commander Hathorn might have felt more guilty for his obviously unfair advantage had he known he was, most likely, not facing 8-inch guns – he was facing 6-inch guns. These particular 6-inch guns belonged to the light cruiser *Noshiro*. Captain Tawara Yoshiaki would report that a strafing run had punched holes in the light cruiser's hull, which, if true, does not speak well of Japanese ship design. Then again, the holes might have been caused by the Mark 13 aerial torpedo that hit the *Noshiro*'s hull with a loud THUNK, leaving at least an unsightly dent.[52]

Hoping to get away without so much as an unsightly dent was Captain Aitoku Ichiro and his heavy cruiser-seaplane carrier hybrid *Mogami*. Aitoku was quick to start moving and quicker to start shooting. She glided through Simpson Harbor and reached Blanche

Bay – almost. At 11:32, the SBDs of the *Saratoga* dove on the *Mogami* and, one minute later, released their 1,000lb bombs. Aitoku ordered hard to port, and the *Mogami* had started turning when a bomb hit between the Numbers 1 and 2 8-inch turrets, leaving more than an unsightly dent. The explosion started a large fire and blew out a section of the starboard bow just above the waterline, limiting the *Mogami*'s top speed to just 12 knots. Aitoku kept the cruiser going, and though she suffered a few near misses, the *Mogami* fought off a torpedo attack and made it to Blanche Bay at her reduced speed.[53]

Torpedo attacks were not going the Americans' way today. Near Sulphur Creek, the TBFs had spiraled down to 250 feet, then roared parallel to the Japanese ships, turning toward their targets and aiming near the bow before releasing, hoping flying among the Japanese would help limit the antiaircraft fire. The Avengers claimed five hits; in reality, they got two. One was the aforementioned dud on the *Noshiro*. The other hit the destroyer *Fujinami* – and also did not explode, although it did leave more than an unsightly dent. It punched a hole in one of the destroyer's fuel tanks, killed one, and injured nine. Surely, you didn't think all the US Navy torpedo problems had been fixed yet, did you?[54]

Despite the US Navy starting to phase in the Curtiss SB2C Helldiver, the true star of the Pacific Fleet's strike aircraft remained the good ol' Douglas SBD Dauntless. Tough, reliable, comfortable as an old shoe, though perhaps not as effective on this day as was expected or hoped. The light cruiser *Agano* had survived Empress Augusta Bay without a scratch, largely because when danger reared its ugly head, she bravely turned her tail and fled. As she bravely ran away away, a 1,000lb bomb splashed close by, damaging a high-angle antiaircraft gun and killing one.[55] Veteran pest *Amagiri* suffered a near miss that caused minor flooding.[56] Big new antiaircraft destroyer *Wakatsuki* was also damaged by a near miss.[57]

Because of Commander Crawford's plotting, even before they attacked, the US Navy fliers were pointed toward the exits to the south. They had made one pass, now they would take their leave. If they could. One catch: there were still some 70 vengeful Zeros hanging out over Lakunai. They had numbers, they had the high ground, so to speak, and now they didn't care if they hit fighters or bombers.

For the American pilots, this was the precursor to the Death Star trench: wedged within the family of volcanoes around Simpson Harbor, flying as fast as the laws of plot armor would allow; weaving between and sometimes above warships, tracers crossing every which way but loose, enemy fighters swarming on top. At least there was no Darth Vader.

Not for lack of trying. The Zeros from the *Zuikaku* and *Zuiho* pounced. Commander Clifton's Hellcats held their position, however. Zeros that tried to break through were themselves jumped, but only momentarily. For the US Navy fliers, it was open the throttles, must go faster, must go faster, go go go! The Dauntless of the *Saratoga*'s Lieutenant (jg) Arthur L. Teall did not go fast enough and was shot down in Simpson Harbor. What happened to his gunner is unknown, but it's known that Teall was fished out by the Japanese, only to disappear in one of the Kempeitai's hellholes.[58]

Commander Clifton's tactics had largely worked. Teall's and Atwell's were the only two *Saratoga* aircraft shot down. The *Princeton* did not get off so lucky. Two of the seven Avengers from Composite 23 were shot down outright, and a third lost all hydraulics; it was able to reach the *Princeton* and ditch alongside, three crew being recovered. Three Hellcats of Fighting 23 and three Avengers of Composite 23 were lost, five pilots and four crew killed or missing in action. Almost all of the aircraft for both carriers suffered some sort of damage.[59]

There were still some American aircraft in the area, however. As the US Navy fliers were leaving, they saw eight US Army Air Force planes inbound.[60] One Hellcat, apparently piloted by Lieutenant (jg) Earl B. Crawford, roared over Rapopo air base while trying to escape and saw a Mitsubishi Ki-21 Type 97 Heavy Bomber – this is why the Allies gave Japanese aircraft reporting names, in this case "Sally" – from the Japanese Army Air Force's 14th Air Division was taking off. An appropriate amount of ammunition shot into the Sally's right engine rudely aborted that attempt. What the US Navy aviators did not see were six Kates from the *Zuiho* returning from a visit to Kavieng who, warned by radio – the B5Ns had radios – that an attack was in progress, prudently held off on landing until the attack was over. Nor did the US Navy aviators apparently see their own chief well behind them.[61]

During the attack, Commander Caldwell had been up in his command Avenger at 10,000 feet with a close escort of two Hellcats. Behind him, Photographer's Mate Paul Barnett was happily clicking away with his camera. All the guys up top were amazed at the confusion the attack caused among the Japanese.[62]

From up on high it was, presumably, *Thank God I'm only watching the game, controlling it.*[63] Or was he?

Because Commander Caldwell watched the Japanese warships sluggishly mill about in confusion. Some of those warships suffered explosions. Soon, all of those warships were scurrying toward the exit from Simpson Harbor into Blanche Bay. And the American strike aircraft were flying away.

But Commander Caldwell and his companions had overstayed their welcome. They were alone high over Simpson Harbor.

Now they headed back toward home, but in their egress, they had flown over Rapopo air base. Eight Zeros showed up, hoping to convince them to stay awhile. A single TBF Avenger with two of those new boxy fighters for escorts? Must be important.

The eight Zeros swarmed the three US Navy planes. One of the escorting Hellcats, that piloted by Ensign Carlton W. Roberts, had its battery cable severed, causing Roberts to lose his instruments. He sheered off into a cloud to lose his attackers. Which he did, but he lost his commander and his other fighter, too. And without instruments, he was unable to find the *Saratoga*. He ended up making an emergency landing at Barakoma.

The other Hellcat was flown by Lieutenant (jg) Stanley K. Crockett of the *Princeton*. Crockett's fighter took a beating, with one Zero closing to about 150 feet and mercilessly blasting it, but he resolutely weaved back and forth to protect the air strike commander.

The gunfire broke Crockett's inner cooler and sprung the cowl flaps open, but he still managed to whip his F6F around to flame one of the Zeros and damage another. Yet more Japanese bullets lashed at Crockett's instrument panel, destroying almost everything except the magnetic compass, shooting the throttle handle out of his hand, and wounding him in the head, shoulder, and arm. The armored seat back ensured that his injuries were not worse. The Japanese fighters riddled Crockett's tub with more than 268 holes, including 54 in the cockpit alone, and 180 in the port fuselage and wing. Despite the damage, his injuries, and nearby clouds that seemed to beckon him with their cover, Crockett resolutely stuck with Commander Caldwell until they were safely back at the carriers. Though his injuries were not life-threatening, Crockett did not remember landing on the *Princeton;* he collapsed upon landing and had to be carried to sick bay.[64]

Lieutenant (jg) Crockett did everything he could short of ramming the pursuing Zeros to protect Commander Caldwell, but there were too many Zeros and not enough Lieutenant (jg) Crocketts. So Caldwell's command Avenger was in for its share of Japanese shooting at it. On board the command Avenger, Aviation Ordnanceman 2nd Class Kenneth Bratton, Chief Radioman Robert W. Morey, and Photographer's Mate Paul Barnett were all shooting back – Bratton with his single .50-cal. 12.7mm machine gun in the rear turret, Morey with his the single .30-cal. 7.62mm ventral machine gun; and Barnett with his camera. Together, Bratton and Morey shot down one Zero, after which Bratton damaged two more.[65]

But there were still too many Zeros. First, Japanese machine guns shattered the Plexiglass rear turret and wounded Bratton. Another machine-gun barrage wounded Morey. That left Barnett, who was fearless in shooting back at the Japanese with his camera. It was smashed by a bullet. Barnett grabbed another camera and kept shooting. Tough kid. A Zero came straight at him, its black engine cowling almost filling his viewfinder, and still Barnett kept shooting. So did the Zero. According to the *Saturday Evening Post*'s Eugene Burns, Barnett "had barely finished snapping the shutter when a 7.7mm bullet – about the size of his fiancée's little finger – tore the back of his head off. He fell forward over his camera, and his warm blood carried forward and covered the group commander, so that he had to remove his goggles and wipe off the blood smears."[66]

After putting 109 holes in the TBF's fuselage, wings, and tail, the Zeros gave up and broke off. They had used up their ammunition. Their 7.7mm ammunition. All 109 holes in Commander Caldwell's plane and 268 holes in Lieutenant (jg) Crockett's tub were from 7.7mm bullets. The Zeros had apparently exhausted their supply of 20mm cannon shells beforehand. As for Caldwell, unable to see what was going on behind him and after feeling and hearing the punishment from the Zeros, he thought he was alone with three dead crewmen. Then Morey handed him a deliberately optimistic note: "Bratton and Barnett are out of commission. Everything else O.K."[67]

Well, not quite. The command Avenger had no radio, no hydraulics, no flaps, no ailerons, and, it turned out, only one main wheel of the landing gear would extend. No problem for Commander Caldwell. He landed on the *Saratoga* on his first attempt almost perfectly.[68] The film from Barnett's cameras was taken to be developed and analyzed. Barnett had been as heroic as any photojournalist, capturing the truth of the Rabaul attack, the truth of war, for the American military, for the American people, and for history.

The deaths of heroes like Paul Barnett and the others over Rabaul would be recognized by the crews of the *Saratoga* and *Princeton*, but the losses were relatively mild, far less than Admiral Halsey had been expecting.

The day was hardly done, especially in Rabaul. Those eight Army Air Force planes the retiring US Navy aviators had seen were part of an attack by 5th Air Force. The three squadrons (64th, 65th, and 403rd) of the 43rd Bombardment Group each sent nine Liberators to Rabaul with an escort of 58 Lightnings (including 11 from the 9th Fighter Squadron, 49th Fighter Group; and 14 from the 39th Fighter Squadron, 35th Fighter Group; also some from the 475th Fighter Group). This air attack seems to have been timed to hit Rabaul while many of the Japanese fighters were away chasing the US Navy planes back toward their carriers. For that reason, General Kenney later said, he decided to attack the warehouse district on the northwest side of Simpson Harbor, technically in Rabaul Township and not Rabaul City, because the warehouses were probably loaded with supplies. As they were arriving over the target, the escorting P-38s saw single-engine fighters in the distance and released their drop tanks to prepare for combat, only to later realize those fighters were US Navy "Corsairs" (actually Hellcats) from the carrier airstrike. The Lightnings did report a rather perfunctory but nevertheless deadly intercept by 13 Zeros. The 43rd dropped a total of 54 1,000lb bombs on the warehouse district, including oil and coal wharfs, starting fires whose black smoke was visible 100 miles away. Ace P-38 pilot Captain Richard Bong was credited with shooting down two Zeros, but as the Army Air Force planes were heading out, his wingman, 2nd Lieutenant George C. Haniotis, disappeared. Haniotis radioed his position to rescue teams at Kiriwina and is believed to have bailed out near Arawe, but his fate and the cause of the damage to his plane are unknown. Casualties among the Japanese were reportedly in the hundreds, though the Japanese did not consider the damage to the facilities particularly bad.[69]

For his part, Admiral Halsey did not consider General Kenney's attack to have been particularly helpful:

> General Kenney had promised a simultaneous attack in strength by his heavy bombers and had assured us that they could lay Rabaul flat. The last thing our pilots saw as they ducked back into the clouds – the same clouds that hid our carriers – was Kenney's bombers, eight of them. I have always resented the feebleness of his support at this critical time, and I told General MacArthur as much the next time I saw him.[70]

It was not exactly a fair criticism. Admiral Halsey took as gospel the sighting of eight aircraft in the distance meaning there were only eight in the entire attack. He should have known better. Moreover, according to General Kenney:

I told the General that my maximum effort would be pretty low until I got some replacements and repaired all the shot-up airplanes which had gotten way ahead of the repair and maintenance crews during the past couple of weeks.

The strafers came out of the November 2nd attack pretty well shot up so that I could not count on any of them. I said I thought I could promise about twenty-five B-24s and fifty P-38s for an attack on Rabaul on the 5th, arriving over the town about twelve-thirty.[71]

Kenney was exactly right. The 5th Air Force had been pretty badly beaten up just three days earlier. To have expected it to be at full strength for Admiral Halsey's attack was unreasonable.

Interservice rivalries aside, for now, there was reason to celebrate. With only 22 1,000lb bombs (we won't talk about the torpedoes), the Dauntlesses had damaged five of the six heavy cruisers Admiral Kurita had on hand, along with two light cruisers, and two destroyers. The damage to the five cruisers was bad enough to cripple Kurita's force, reducing the threat it posed to the Torokina beachhead. Admiral Sherman went so far as to call it "a glorious victory, a second Pearl Harbor in reverse."[72]

Not quite. Not one enemy ship had been sunk. But that had not been the objective. Just like Admiral Merrill at Empress Augusta Bay, Admiral Sherman's objective had not been to destroy the Japanese, but to merely repulse them. That, the Americans knew they had.

"I took a deep breath," Admiral Halsey wrote. "So did the men at Torokina; so did Ted Sherman."[73]

Halsey sent Admiral Sherman's carriers a special message:

Report of attack is real music to me. When the *Saratoga* is given a chance she is deadly. *Princeton* too takes a deep initial bow in the South Pacific. May the Jap cripples permanently be buried in Davy Jones locker. A funeral dirge has been sounded for Tojo's strongest South Pacific base.[74]

It was indeed a funeral dirge, but for what exactly had yet to be determined.

In Rabaul, the reaction was … not as positive.

The ordinarily mild-mannered Admiral Kusaka was livid. "He bellowed imprecations at everyone," according to the not-ordinarily mild-mannered Captain Hara, whose own opinion was short and to the point: "What a disgrace!"[75]

There is just no pleasing some people. Admiral Kurita's six heavy cruisers had fired 1,421 5-inch antiaircraft rounds and nearly 24,000 light cannon and machine-gun bullets. They had even fired more than 356 8-inch shells from their main batteries. For their part, the light cruisers chipped in with at least 95 6-inch shells.[76]

But the Japanese had not gotten bang for their yen. The burning *Mogami* had managed to reach Blanche Bay, but with the fires still blazing out of control near the Numbers 1 and 2 main turrets, at 11:45am Captain Aitoku had to stop engines and flood the forward magazines to prevent a potentially catastrophic explosion, which left her with only seven feet of freeboard at the bow. By 1:00pm, however, the fires were out. The *Mogami* had 19 dead and 37 wounded. And with two magazines flooded and a hole in her bow, she was lost to any potential move against the Torokina beachhead.[77]

In somewhat similar straits (no pun intended) was the *Takao*. She, too, had made it to Blanche Bay, but she, too, had her two forward main turrets disabled. She, too, had damage below the water line. She, too, was in no shape for combat operations. But the *Takao* was in much better shape than her sister *Maya*, whose Number 3 engine room was still blazing. She had lost 70 killed and 60 wounded.[78]

Fleet flagship *Atago* had used counterflooding to eliminate her port list by 12:11pm, but having filled voids to keep an even keel is no way to go into battle. Her skipper Captain Nakaoka was dead. Admiral Kurita was shocked, as were Nakaoka's classmates at Etajima, Rear Admiral Komura Keizo, Admiral Ozawa's chief of staff; and newly promoted rear admiral, the Baron Tomioka Sadatoshi, who was Admiral Kusaka's chief of staff at Southeast Area Fleet. The *Atago* had 21 other dead and 64 wounded.[79] Speaking of Ozawa, wasn't the staging of *Kido Butai* fliers into Rabaul supposed to prevent stuff like this?

There was always the heavy cruiser-seaplane carrier hybrid *Chikuma*. She had only lost a torpedo mount. She was still kind of in fighting shape. There was also the *Suzuya*. The *Suzuya* had lost ... nothing. She was not hit, not damaged, not even scratched. She was ready for any combat operation. Arguably, so was *Chikuma*. Two heavy cruisers ... well, one and a half. Two heavy cruisers had not been enough at Empress Augusta Bay. How could one and half be expected to do better?

Base Air Force and *Kido Butai* survived a bit better than might be expected. Three pilots were killed: Flight Petty Officers 1st Class Nishimura Hiroshi and Miyamoto Yoshio from the *Zuikaku* and 201 Air Group, respectively, and the *Zuiho*'s Flight Chief Petty Officer Minato Kosaku, and FPO1c Miyamoto Yoshio from the 201 Air Group. Also lost was a D4Y Comet from the 501 Air Group, with Flight Chief Petty Officer Hamoto Ichirou and his observer killed. One fighter from the 204 Air Group crash-landed at Lakunai, badly injuring the pilot.[80] Even so, for the aviators of *Kido Butai*, the attitude of Admiral Kusaka and Admiral Ozawa was: *You better earn your pay.*

Just after the attack had concluded, Admiral Kusaka sent out D4Y reconnaissance planes to find the reported enemy carriers that had, rather obviously, launched the first part of the attack. Maybe an hour later, at 1:55pm (Solomon Islands time) Warrant Officer I'ida Uetada of the *Zuikaku* reported two aircraft carriers surrounded by nine more substantive ships offshore Bougainville's southeastern coast, bearing 145 degrees True (roughly southeast) distance 235 nautical miles from Rabaul. Wisely, I'ida kept his distance from the enemy while transmitting regular reports of its movements until low fuel forced him to return to Vunakanau.[81]

With the news from I'ida, *Kido Butai* could finally counterattack. Another *Zuikaku* Comet, this flown by Warrant Officer Yoshikawa Takeshi, departed Vunakanau to take over shadowing the Americans from I'ida and to guide in the subsequent air strike. At 4:20pm, Yoshikawa reported a group of three ships. He returned to Vunakanau at 5:00pm, a good 90 minutes before the fuel-starved I'ida.

Well, now what? They had two potentially conflicting sighting reports. Tasked with dealing with the US Navy carriers was a division officer from the *Zuikaku*, Lieutenant Kiyomiya Tsuyoshi.[82] Kiyomiya sent up two pairs of Nakajima B5N Type 97 carrier attack planes – one pair from the *Zuikaku* and one from the *Zuiho* – on a "search and contact" mission; that is, find the enemy and hopefully keep the enemy in sight to direct an airstrike against them.

Maybe an hour after the scouts had left, Lieutenant Kiyomiya assembled a strike made up of B5N carrier attack planes: four from the *Shokaku*, seven from the *Zuikaku*, and four from the *Zuiho* who had been among the six *Zuiho* planes that had returned to Vunakanau from Kavieng just after the American attack. All were armed with aerial torpedoes. For reasons known only to Kiyomiya, he divided the attack force into two groups. Four B5Ns from the *Zuiho* left at 5:15pm, those from the *Shokaku* and *Zuikaku* took off 15 minutes later. The two groups formed up and headed into the growing darkness.[83]

In the meantime, the pair of scouts from the *Zuikaku* had split up. Leading Aircraftsman Itokawa Morio reported three ships 175 miles from Rabaul, while Flight Petty Officer 2nd Class Yamazaki Saburo reported four cruisers, five destroyers, and "two transports resembling carriers" 300 statute miles from Rabaul, bearing 130 degrees. The other pair of Type 97s reported finding three ships, then returned to Vunakanau.[84]

He had them, Kiyomiya thought. He maneuvered them into attack position, though it seems that one was forced to turn back for some reason.[85]

With the complete lack of fighter escort, the idea here seems to have been to make a torpedo attack on the US Navy carriers at dusk. In other words, a repeat of the January air attack that sank the heavy cruiser USS *Chicago*, but with carrier attack planes. Lieutenant Kiyomiya led his air strike on a heading of 138 degrees from Rabaul until 6:02pm, when one of the pathfinder B5Ns, apparently Itokawa, reportedly started transmitting a homing signal. Kiyomiya turned his force left to a heading of 120 degrees. Eight minutes later, about midway between the Treasury and Woodlark Islands south of Bougainville, Kiyomiya and his air crews finally found their targets.[86]

Which reportedly comprised two aircraft carriers (one slightly smaller than the other), four cruisers, and five destroyers. And no aerial opposition. Lieutenant Kiyomiya led his attack planes in torpedo runs. Several reportedly struck the bigger of the carriers, causing "a violent explosion" amidships that sank the carrier in two minutes. The other carrier was quickly hit, which caused a large fire that doomed her as well. The 14 Sea Eagles also sank two large cruisers and two destroyers.[87]

As described, this attack was an incredible victory for the Japanese. As described. And the description of the attack was completely accurate. Except the Japanese had not found a task force of two aircraft carriers, four cruisers, and five destroyers, but instead a convoy of two landing craft (gunboat infantry landing craft *LCI(G)-70* and tank landing craft *LCT-68*) and a PT boat (*PT-167*) 28 miles southwest of Cape Torokina heading toward the Treasuries. The largest of these targets was 158 feet long. It's easy to call these Japanese pilots "incompetent" for mistaking what were basically transports for aircraft carriers and motor torpedo boats for cruisers, but let he who is without sin cast the first stone. Who among us can truly say they have not mistaken a passenger ship for an aircraft carrier? Well, maybe the Imperial Japanese Army, but having mistaken an empty field for an air base on Guadalcanal, they don't exactly have much room to cast stones, either. Even by the normal Japanese standards of reconnaissance incompetence (the *Chikuma* excepted), the disparity here between report and reality was far more incredible than the reported results of the attack.[88]

The other exception to the Japanese description of their attack is that instead of sinking two aircraft carriers, two large cruisers, and two cruisers or destroyers out of nine ships, they sank, roughly, nothing. As the 14 Kates bore in at an altitude of 200 feet from the western twilight – ignoring the tactic of coming out of the darkened east that had made the attack on the *Chicago* so successful – *PT-167*'s Ensign Theodore Berlin, commanding this convoy, had all of it open fire. The lead attack plane, flown by Lieutenant Kiyomiya, went all the way down to about 20 feet over the water and released its torpedo, but as it continued onward over the boat, a wing clipped *PT-167*'s antenna, causing the Nakajima to spin into the water, killing Kiyomiya and his crew. As it did so, Berlin and his men felt a major jarring of their boat.[89]

The Japanese reformed to try again from the west. This time, the 20mm gunners on the *PT-167*'s fantail brought down another Kate, that of the *Zuikaku*'s Flight Petty Officer 1st Class Nishiyama Hisao, which exploded, killing everyone on board, and splashed so close to the port quarter that Ensign Berlin's crewmen were drenched. A torpedo was seen passing under the stern of the boat.[90]

The remaining Kates decided to swarm the *LCI(G)-70*, so the *PT-167* positioned herself to help fend them off. Four torpedoes were launched at the gunboat landing craft, but they were set too deep for her shallow draft and three of them passed under her. The fourth porpoised upward and introduced itself to the *LCI(G)-70*'s engine room – without exploding, but still killing one sailor. Two more Kates went down, one flown by Leading Airman Taguchi Goro, the other commanded by Leading Airman Kobayashi Kiyoto, both of the *Zuiho*. The only aviator to survive was Taguchi, who was picked up the next afternoon by a US Navy destroyer and spent the rest of the war as a prisoner.[91]

When the attack was over, Ensign Berlin discovered what had jarred his *PT-167*: a torpedo had passed completely through the bow without exploding, leaving pieces of its fins and one of its rudders. Miraculously, the holes were well above the waterline, so the boat was in no danger of sinking. Ensign Berlin went to the *LCI(G)-70*, now disabled by that torpedo hit, and took off all of the gunboat landing craft's crew, including two injured men. He then went to the *LCT-68*, which the Japanese had ignored. A volunteer crew went to the gunboat so the tank landing craft could take it in tow.[92]

While Lieutenant Kiyomiya's remaining attack planes were returning from their mission of misfortune, the Royal Australian Air Force was trying to follow up on the daytime attacks with a night attack of its own. Air Commodore Joseph Eric "Joe" Hewitt, commanding No. 9 Operational Group, planned a two-prong air attack. Four Beauforts from No. 8 Squadron would make a torpedo attack on a tanker and other enemy shipping found in Keravia Bay by the earlier attack. While that was going on, four Beauforts from No. 100 Squadron would attack nearby Vunakanau. The torpedo attack was a difficult mission with considerable stakes. The Bristol Beaufort torpedo bomber was considered obsolete. It was limited in range, uncomfortable for the crew, and overloaded when carrying a torpedo, which does not speak well for the design of this supposed torpedo bomber. There was a lot of criticism of the use of the Beaufort as a torpedo bomber; if it was discontinued, it would moot the need for the expensive torpedo bomber training base at Nowra on the coast of New South Wales south of Sydney. Hewitt seems to have wanted to put the Beaufort in the best possible light. Four Beauforts from No. 8 Squadron under the command of Flight Lieutenant Noel Quinn took off from Kiriwina, or tried to, as one was unable to take off because of mechanical issues. They got to Keravia Bay all right, and at 10:40pm, Quinn made a torpedo run at an altitude of 150 feet at one of the ships. A Japanese searchlight snapped on and pinned his Beaufort. Blinded by the searchlight – Japanese searchlights were usually brighter than their western counterparts – the flight lieutenant bore on and released his torpedo, then pulled away, but he was unable to see if his torpedo hit the target. Well played, Imperial Japanese Navy. A second Beaufort ran at a different target and released its torpedo, only to watch helplessly as the torpedo veered to the left. The third Beaufort took aim at a "cruiser" and dropped its torpedo; the pilot believed he "probably" hit it. Japanese records do not confirm any hits. No. 8 Squadron headed back to Kiriwina as the four Beauforts from No. 100 Squadron bombed Vunakanau without much effect. All seven aircraft returned to base, but otherwise it was not a good night for the Bristol Beaufort.[93]

The Japanese seem to have taken little notice of the Australian attack. Back in Rabaul – indeed, in Japan – there was considerable celebration over sinking two aircraft carriers, two cruisers, and two destroyers. The celebration was not tempered by the flames from the still-burning *Maya* in Simpson Harbor or the fact that four of the B5Ns, including that of Lieutenant Kiyomiya, failed to return. At the Imperial Palace, Admiral Nagano Osami reported the same claims for American carriers sunk. The emperor believed the news and greeted it with joy. Imperial General Headquarters, referring to this engagement as the "First Air Battle off Bougainville," specifically commended the outstanding work performed single-handedly by the air forces.[94] They were so happy.

But Admiral Kusaka had his doubts as to the accuracy of these fantastic claims of damage inflicted on the enemy:

> I was skeptical of these claims, as of Japanese claims generally at this time, knowing full well the marked drop in the skill of our pilots during the past year. But to question the claims, or request verifications, would simply have frustrated the men, who were doing the best they could.[95]

In other words, Admiral Kusaka did not want to damage their self-esteem. So fantasy was called reality, then another fantasy the Japanese again called reality was built on top of that, then another fantasy they called reality was built on top of that, and so on, and so on, and so forth. The problem was that these fantasies the Japanese insisted were reality were getting more and more men killed, especially the skilled fliers of the Japanese Naval Air Force.

This "First Air Battle off Bougainville" was but another example. This was a poorly conceived attack that was even more poorly executed. Mistaking transports for aircraft carriers. And vice versa. Attacking out of the setting sun – twice – so the enemy can see you. Losing a B5N, its entire aircrew, and, indeed, the mission leader, because you clipped the antenna of a PT boat.

There were more immediate problems to consider, however: what to do with Admiral Kurita's damaged cruisers. Both the *Mogami* and *Takao* had lost the services of their two forward turrets. Both cruisers as well as the *Atago* had hull damage; the *Atago* had also lost her skipper. As for the *Maya*, according to Captain Hara, "[h]er vitals were destroyed."[96] None of these ships were capable of combat operations.

Admiral Kurita still had two serviceable heavy cruisers: the *Suzuya* and *Chikuma*, though the latter was nicked up and had lost a torpedo battery. With the lightly damaged *Noshiro* and *Agano* and whatever destroyers they could scrounge up, Kurita could still mount a dangerous counterattack.

Yet in contrast to the overconfidence of the air crews, Admiral Koga, Admiral Kurita, and brass of the Imperial Navy had been broken by the attack of November 5. Thus, according to one Japanese history:

> It was decided that the entire strength of the 2 Fleet except the *Maya*, which required emergency repairs, and the 2 Destroyer Squadron, which was to participate in the counterlanding operation, would retire to Truk. They departed immediately, passing outside the range of enemy air raids on the 6th and arriving in Truk on the 8th.[97]

And so it was done, though not exactly in the manner described. The *Atago* and *Takao*, together as usual, left the night of November 5. Also leaving that night was the *Chikuma*, escorted by destroyer *Wakatsuki*. The next day, November 6, the *Mogami*, after some emergency repairs, left Simpson Harbor escorted by her one-time sister ship *Suzuya*, and destroyers *Shimakaze*, which had arrived after the attack, and *Tamanami*. For the time being, the *Maya* was going nowhere.[98]

Captain Hara was beside himself:

> It was sickening to watch the departure of these five cruisers, when one considered that their sortie probably was the most fruitless of the entire war. [...] The futility of our losses and the stupidity of our high command struck me forcibly, and I cursed aloud while wondering what Japan could do.[99]

None of those cruisers would ever return to Rabaul. That was the funeral dirge for Rabaul.

CHAPTER 6

A CLOSE MARGIN BETWEEN VICTORY AND DISASTER

Between all these sea battles, air attacks, convoys, and the like, it's easy to forget that there was also a land battle going on.

By sunset on November 5, the I Marine Amphibious Corps beachhead extended about 10,000 yards along the beach around Cape Torokina and about 5,000 yards inland. General Turnage had been compelled to bring the flanks in for the purpose of developing some form of reserve. He had also had to shuffle his units for some semblance of unit integrity, so that after three days, the 3rd and 9th Marine Regiments had traded positions on the perimeter and had exchanged one battalion. From the left to the right, the Allied line consisted now of the 3rd Battalion of the 9th Marine Regiment; the 3rd and 2nd Battalions of the 3rd Marine Regiment; and the 2nd and 1st Battalions of the 9th. The 1st Battalion of the 3rd Marines was in reserve. The 2nd Marine Raider Battalion had left one company blocking Mission Trail that went toward the village of Piva and the Piva River and was believed to be the main route of travel by the Japanese. Backing this up were the guns of the 12th Marine Regiment and the 3rd Defense Battalion.[1]

On the other side, displaying that same strategic acumen that had proven so successful on Guadalcanal, General Hyakutake continued to insist that the American landings at Cape Torokina were a feint and that the real landings would come elsewhere. Hyakutake seemed to have finally dropped the idea that the real landing would be at Buin or something, but Buka was something else. So, naturally, it had to be reinforced.

At noon on November 6, Captain Hara was summoned to 8th Fleet headquarters, where Admiral Samejima was gloomy. As Hara related the conversation, Samejima said,

"I want you to take *Shigure* and *Yubari*, which is the only operable cruiser we have, on a mission tonight." The baron continued, "The situation is bad. We may be forced to give up Bougainville, but we must hang on to the nearby base of Buka. It has been decided to reinforce the defenses at Buka."[2]

As the commodore saluted and turned to go, Admiral Samejima stopped him. "I must also tell you, Hara, that this will be your last assignment in my command," the baron said. "I hate the idea of having you go, especially at this time, but *Shigure* is badly in need of dry-dock repairs, and you are entitled to a rest." It was not an overly difficult operation – for now. The *Shigure* and *Yubari* went to Buka that night, landed 700 troops of the 17th Okayama Division and 25 tons of supplies, and scurried on back.[3]

Captain Hara reported to Admiral Samejima at 8th Fleet headquarters. "Our assignment turned out to be very easy," Hara said, "But the next one like it will not be easy. Repeated tactics always seem to backfire." Samejima nodded and said, "I appreciate your warning and will pass it on to other ships making the same mission." For all the good that would do. Hara had voiced the same warning just before Vella Gulf, and you see how that turned out. Be that as it may, the commodore and the admiral bid their farewells. "I am really going to miss you, Hara. We have lost so many experienced officers and men. I certainly want you to come back."[4]

It was early the next morning when Captain Hara had his *Shigure* lead transports *Mitakesan* and *Tokyo Maru*s out of the Simpson Harbor anchorage. Even leaving for the last time, Hara had been stuck with escorting the transports to Kavieng to drop off some supplies and then Truk because 8th Fleet was now so short of ships. The mission appeared much easier than any Hara had had in recent months, and so he accepted it graciously. As the *Shigure* pulled out with the rising sun, Hara Tameichi turned and took one last look:

> I gazed at the towering volcanoes behind the port. Rabaul was a drab and dreary place. But having been based there since July, I had developed a deep feeling for the place without realizing it. There was nothing attractive about Rabaul, but, when we sortied, we always hoped desperately to return. Now we were leaving for home and would probably never see Rabaul again.
>
> In three brief months we had lost island after island in the Solomons group, until only Buka remained in Japanese hands. Buka might fall any day and then Rabaul would fall too. We did not talk of this possibility but everyone was aware of it.
>
> I thought of many friends who had perished in the savage battles in this area, and also of the many others who were staying behind, and tears came to my eyes. Looking around I saw that my feelings were shared by others in Shigure. Men on deck waved frantically at the few standing watch in ships we passed on our way out. From somewhere came the lilting tune, "Saraba Rabauru-yo, mata kuru made wa ..." (Farewell, Rabaul, see you soon again ...). This sad song had become a hit all over the Pacific in a very short time, though no one knew just where it had started.[5]

Not exactly Lot's wife turning to take one last look at doomed Sodom as the Lord sent down fire and brimstone on the cities of the plain. Then again, Tavurvur and Vulcan could, and would, make a fairly decent approximation. After standing on the deck like a pillar of salt for some time staring at receding Rabaul, Hara turned to his latest assignment.

Captain Hara likely misremembered Admiral Samejima's comments about the *Yubari* being the only operable cruiser they had. They did have the *Agano* and *Noshiro*, though they were nicked up a little, but they were spoken for. While General Hyakutake was convinced the Torokina landing was a feint, General Inamura and Admiral Kusaka were not. So Hyakutake was ordered to crush the wide but shallow American beachhead at Torokina. To do so, the Japanese were going to try – again – that favorite Japanese tactic against enemy landings: the counterlanding.

That is, largely the same counterlanding they had tried the night of November 1–2, but aborted because of what became the Battle of Empress Augusta Bay. Then they wanted to try it the night of November 5–6, but aborted it again after Admiral Sherman's attack on Simpson Harbor. Tonight, they would go through with it.

But that was tonight. As for today, November 6, dawn brought full alert to the Rabaul caldera. Enemy carriers were lurking out there, waiting to pounce on Rabaul again, and it was essential that the Japanese find them and attack as soon as humanly possible, preferably even sooner. Patrols were sent out north of Bougainville and south of Bougainville all the way to Kiriwina. The first patrols were a G4M Type 1 medium land attack plane sent to scout New Ireland, a second G4M sent to scout Bougainville, and a mixed flight of four B5N carrier attack planes from the *Shokaku*, *Zuikaku*, and *Zuiho* led by division officer Lieutenant Matsukawa Mutsuro from the *Zuikaku*. Hoping to do better than the last division officer from the *Zuikaku* to lead an air mission, Matsukawa split the scouts into two pairs, who both flew into a sky cloudy with scattered showers. Matsukawa radioed Rabaul at 6:35am that he had found four enemy ships east of Bougainville. The other pair confirmed the sighting a little more than an hour later, but did not see Matsukawa's B5N. Neither he nor his crew were ever heard from again. Allied records show no engagement that could have claimed Matsukawa's Kate; it seems those scattered showers swallowed it whole.[6]

Finding and neutralizing the enemy carriers that had done so much damage the previous day was only part of it. Once they found the carriers, they had to get fighters up to defend Rabaul, or at least better defend it than the previous day. Just after 7:00am, 11 Zeros from the *Zuiho* scrambled from Vunakanau. They were recalled about a half hour later – false alarm. At 12:30pm, 28 Zeros from the 201 and 204 Air Groups led by 201 pilot Lieutenant (jg) O'oba Yoshio, scrambled from Lakunai. They were recalled only 40 minutes later – false alarm. So it continued through the rest of the day. The last was an extended three-hour patrol led by 201 Air Group pilot Warrant Officer Kibayashi Itsuo that returned around dusk at 5:50 pm.[7]

After a day of many air missions by *Kido Butai* and Base Air Force, none of which were productive, it was time for that counterlanding that all the Japanese had dreamed of.

As usual for the Imperial Japanese Navy, this was an overly complicated operation. There was the 1st Cover Force under the 10th Destroyer Flotilla's Admiral Osugi, with his flagship light cruiser *Agano* and destroyers *Wakatsuki*, *Kazagumo*, and *Urakaze*. If you didn't like that cover force, well, the Japanese had others. Such as the 2nd Cover Force, this one under the 2nd Destroyer Flotilla's veteran Admiral Takama, with his light cruiser flagship *Noshiro*, and destroyers *Hayanami* and *Naganami*. And if you didn't like that cover force, well, the Japanese had others. Like the Transport Unit Cover Force, with the new-ish destroyers *Onami* and *Makinami* under Captain Kagawa Kiyoto, the commander of Destroyer Division 31, who was also commanding the four destroyers doing the actual transporting: *Amagiri*, *Fumizuki*, *Uzuki*, and *Yunagi*.[8] If you're scoring at home, that's three covering forces – not covering ships, covering forces, each with multiple ships – for four transport destroyers.

Those four transport destroyers were to transport a "provisional battalion," which was basically a hodgepodge of units from the 17th Okayama Division slapped together and, allegedly, specially trained for a counterlanding. How training for a counterlanding is different from training for a landing is perhaps one of those deep unknowable philosophical questions of life. Specifically, this "provisional battalion" included the 6th Company from the 53rd Infantry Regiment; and the 5th Company, one platoon from the 7th Company, and a machine gun company from the 54th Infantry Regiment, for a total of some 850 troops.[9]

As one US Marine history put it:

> The counterlanding fulfilled an ambition long cherished by the Japanese. At Rendova, an attempted landing against the Allied invasion forces fizzled out during a downpour that prevented the rendezvous of the Japanese assault force; and at New Georgia, the enemy considered – then rejected – an idea to land behind the 43rd Division on Zanana Beach. The Cape Torokina operation, however, gave the Japanese a chance to try this favored counterstroke.[10]

If anything, the US Marine history understated it. The Japanese had tried a counterlanding of sorts way back in August 1942 on Guadalcanal when they had Imperial Army Colonel Ichiki Kiyonao land with 916 troops – slightly less than 12 days after the Americans had landed. So maybe it was not technically a counterlanding; the principle was still the same. Ichiki had taken all but about 100 of those soldiers and launched a nighttime surprise frontal attack on Allied positions manned by, according to some Japanese estimates at that time, some 10,000 US Marines. The actual number was significantly higher. And it wasn't a surprise. The attack turned out just about the way you'd expect a 1-to-12.5 frontal attack to turn out. But while most military organizations who try something and find that it does not work go on to try something else and something else again until they find something that does, when the Imperial Japanese military tried something and found that it did not work, they would try it again and again until it did.

So the Japanese had dreamed of trying the counterlanding again, only to have those dreams shattered at Rendova and New Georgia. Now, they would finally realize those dreams of a counterlanding.

And they would not even be attacking at 1-to-12.5 odds like Colonel Ichiki had. Instead, they planned to have 850 troops facing 14,000 US Marines – 1-to-16.5 or so odds – but that was not entirely the truth of the matter. First, there were not 14,000 US Marines on Bougainville; there were closer to 18,000 – 1-to-21 or so. Six US Navy destroyers (*Waller, Phillip, Saufley, Pringle, Conway,* and *Eaton*) had escorted eight of those incredibly useful fast destroyer transports (*McKean, Stringham, Talbot, Waters, Dent, Kilty, Ward,* and *Crosby*), eight tank landing ships (which in the South Pacific almost never carried tanks) and the busy tug *Sioux.* The transports were carrying 3,548 Marines, mostly from the 21st Marine Regiment, and 6,080 tons of cargo. After a night of ineffectual harassment by Japanese planes, these reinforcements landed near Cape Torokina on the morning of November 6. The destroyer transports skedaddled back down The Slot, but the tank landing ships were sluggish in unloading and took much longer than planned. Captain Grayson B. Carter, in charge of this landing force, advised Admiral Wilkinson that he would have his tank landing ships work through the entire night to offload their troops and cargo.[11]

The Japanese had seen the Allied reinforcements land, but the Japanese were never ones to let a change in the enemy dispositions change their tactical or operational plans. Plus, the Japanese did not believe there were 18,000 US Marines at the Torokina beachhead, but, instead, only 5,000.[12] So, instead of 1-to-21 or so, it would be about 1-to-6. That made it so much better. Could turn any battle into a real nailbiter.

Yet perhaps that is not quite fair. The counterlanding was to be on the left flank of the American beachhead. There was supposed to be action on the American right as well. General Hyakutake would send the two battalions of the 23rd Infantry Regiment under Major General Iwasa Shun, infantry group commander of the 6th Kumamoto Division, from the Buin area to attack that right flank, preferably slightly after the time that "provisional battalion" attacked the American left or even the rear.

Instead, because of the delay in the counterlanding caused by Empress Augusta Bay, the attack on the right flank started slightly before the provisional battalion had even landed. The attack was not unexpected, however. One of the objectives of the initial *Cherryblossom* landing was for the 2nd Marine Raider Battalion to set up a road block on the Buretoni Mission–Piva Trail, which led from the invasion beaches toward the east, where it intersected with the more important Numa Numa Trail; the combination was projected to be the main avenue of any predicted Japanese attack. Though the Marines killed "several stray Japanese," they met no organized resistance and were able to establish the road block about 300 yards west of the junction between the Piva and Numa Numa trails. Behind the roadblock, the 2nd Marine Raiders had pushed the main line of resistance some 1,200 yards inland from the beach.[13]

Then things started to happen. Shortly before midnight on November 6, the 2nd Marine Raiders were attacked twice by an "undetermined number of Japanese." Not that much of a surprise because it was expected the Japanese would attack from this sector, but it was noted that these Japanese "were larger men, in better physical condition and better equipped than enemy previously seen." Worse, some of these larger men were able to slip around the roadblock through the jungle.[14] The next day passed uneventfully for the Marine Raiders, like a lull before the storm.

Though who was providing the storm was unclear, the drizzle had started in other sectors. That morning, six Mitchells from the 42nd Bombardment Group's 75th Bombardment Squadron, led by Lieutenant Rudolph Matlock, were ordered to find two ammunition barges just west of Buka. Instead, they found two cargo ships and a gunboat. Starting at 7:30am, they made six attack runs, reportedly scoring seven direct hits and six near misses. Sunk were the submarine chaser *Ch-11*, auxiliary submarine chaser *No. 9 Asahi Maru*, and water tanker *Asayama Maru*.[15] Two other vessels, described as an auxiliary submarine chaser called the *Cha 30* and the small cargo vessel *No. 3 Nissen Maru*, were reported sunk in this area and may also have been targets of this attack.[16] Though the air strike had as an escort 16 Corsairs from Fighting 17, on the return trip the six were ambushed by eight Zeros and, though no B-25s were shot down, four crewmen were wounded. In return, one Zero was reportedly damaged. At least four of the escorting Corsairs, led by Lieutenant Merl W. "Butch" Davenport, were drawn off by a Betty that had just attacked the Torokina beachhead. This G4M, operated by pilot Flight Petty Officer 1st Class O'ota Kazuyoshi and a crew of five from the 751 Air Group, had been sent up from Vunakanau for an extended reconnaissance of Bougainville. After ten runs and 4,200 rounds of .50-cal. ammunition in what squadron commander Lieutenant Commander Blackburn called "crummy marksmanship" that caused the Japanese air crew "prolonged agony," the Betty was shot down.[17]

At noon, the airfield at Kara got a visit from 54 SBDs (including 29 from Marine Scout Bombing 244; 19 from Marine Scout Bombing 234; and six from "Compositing" 38); 20 TBFs (all from newly arrived Marine Torpedo Bombing 233), and 32 escorting fighters. Around 15 minutes later came 24 B-25s from the 42nd Bombardment Group (18 from the 70th Bombardment Squadron and six from 75th) led by 2nd Lieutenant William T. Morrison, with an escort that included four F4Us from Marine Fighting 212. As a result of this meeting of the malevolent, the Kara air base was almost completely hammered, and not in a good way. Pilots reported "little or no anti-aircraft fire" and said the base "looked deserted." The B-25s reported seeing two Zeros at 12,000 feet who were bounced by escorting Corsairs, but they were alone in seeing any Japanese fighters. Nevertheless, one SBD from Marine Scout Bombing 234 disappeared after its engine cut out en route to the target; it returned to Munda the next day, having made an emergency landing at Barakoma in the interim.[18]

Though the Kara air base suffered severe damage, there was little of value there, so the effect on Japanese operations was negligible. A noontime attack by 17 unescorted AirSols Army Air Force Liberators on Bonis also had no immediate effects. The shipping losses off Buka, while significant, also did not affect current plans to any significant degree. But the same could be said about Japanese operations on this day. Four D4Y reconnaissance planes from *Kido Butai* went out at 11:00am. One from the *Shokaku* had to dodge an annoying P-38 to find a force of two cruisers and seven destroyers about 25 miles southwest of Mutupina Point, but, as was typical for the D4Y when it found a significant enemy force, and unbeknownst to the aviators, their radio report did not reach Rabaul and they had to report the sighting after they landed. At 5:00pm, two pairs of carrier attack planes from the *Zuiho* took off from Vunakanau. They found enemy ships off Cape St George, bearing 138 degrees True, but they lost the contact when the weather turned foul and returned to Vunakanau around 11:00pm.[19]

Determined to attack enemy ships – any enemy ships – at 7:40pm, ten carrier bombers from the *Shokaku* and four from the *Zuikaku* took off from Vunakanau to find the reported enemy ships. They were led by *Zuikaku* division officer Lieutenant Hira Kunikiyo, who hoped to do better than the last two division officers from the *Zuikaku* who led these missions. Having heard nothing from Hira, just before 8:00pm Base Air Force sent up 21 B5N carrier attack planes (14 from the *Shokaku*, four from the *Zuikaku*, and three from the *Zuiho*) under Lieutenant Ono Hiroji, observer from the *Shokaku*. While that was going on, Hira's Aichis returned to Vunakanau, turned back by inclement weather. That same weather scattered Ono's Nakajima B5Ns, who were lucky to return to Vunakanau around 1:00am. At the same time, about a dozen Type 0 reconnaissance seaplanes from the 958 Air Group had departed Rabaul's Malaguna anchorage at various times and fanned out to search individually for the enemy ships, but found nothing in the murky darkness. Four Type 0 reconnaissance seaplanes of the 938 Air Group found a convoy near Torokina and bombed it, but without obvious effect. A dozen G4Ms bombed Finschhafen in the night. Allegedly, 17 G4Ms took off to make night attacks in the Munda, Biloa, and Torokina areas, but Allied reports make no mention of them.[20]

That settled, shortly after midnight on November 7, the group of Japanese destroyer transports entered their landing area, but bravely turned about and fled when "five or six enemy cruisers or destroyers" were sighted blocking the way. This appears to have been Captain Carter's tank landing ships, still unloading at the Torokina beachhead, and their six escorting destroyers. It might have been an opportunity for the Japanese to strike a significant blow against the Bougainville beachhead, but the Japanese had overestimated the enemy strength and were hoping their counterlanding would go unnoticed.[21]

The Japanese transports tried again, this time stopping some two miles from the beaches to unload the troops. The provisional battalion demanded a shore bombardment from the destroyers, which would defeat the idea of going unnoticed. The demand was thus ignored, but the fact that the Imperial Army officers on site made the demand in the first place is yet more evidence of the shocking lack of common sense in the Imperial Army. Not that the Imperial Navy had a surplus of it. The convoy commander reported happily, "We met no surface opposition. The enemy fleet was obviously mending the wounds it had received from the Omori force."[22]

The troops loaded in 21 barges (always a Japanese favorite), little boats, and landing craft and headed for shore, roughly between the Laruma River in the west and Koromokina River in the east. By 6:00am, all were landed safely, though not quite where they were supposed to. Ten had landed just outside the western limits of the Marine perimeter, which given the thinness of the area they held was more like a cloud with small groups of Marines holding the flank. Unfortunately for the Marines, the Americans had slipped back into Savo Island levels of vigilance. Since November 3, eight US Navy PT boats had been operating from a new base on Puruata Island patrolling the area within ten miles of Cape Torokina, but they were not on station this night and thus missed the Japanese destroyers completely, while a Marine antitank platoon on shore saw the landing craft but thought they were American. Multiple Marine patrols were cut off by the Japanese intruders; one outpost had to creep to the coast where it was taken back to the perimeter by two tank lighters.[23]

With the Japanese both inside and outside the Torokina defense perimeter and the mistaken identification of the Japanese barges as American – the Marines who witnessed the landings said that the Japanese ramp boats looked almost identical to American boats, including numbers in white paint on the bow – the initial Marine response to the counterlanding was a bit confused. Then again, so was the counterlanding itself. Just as the Americans had struggled with the surf, the Japanese had struggled with the surf as well, and also with the dark and not landing quite where they had planned. As a result, the Japanese landing was scattered across a large area, on both sides of the Laruma, and unable to amalgamate quickly. Faced with the decision of whether to wait to gather more troops together or attack with less than 100 soldiers, the Imperial Army officers, of course, chose to attack.

On the American left, the 3rd Battalion of the 9th Marines Regiment under Lieutenant Colonel Walter Asmuth, Jr was ordered to stop the Japanese attack. With artillery support, the Marines stepped off at 8:20am and advanced maybe 150 yards in front of the perimeter before they ran into a hastily arranged Japanese line based on entrenchments the Americans had abandoned when General Turnage initially pulled the flanks in. As more and more Japanese found their way to this line of entrenchments, the Marines' attack bogged down. At 1:15pm, the 1st Battalion of the 3rd Marine Regiment took over for the 9th, but fared little better. Some M3 "Stuart" tanks were brought in, those tanks that had been an annoyance to Rommel in North Africa were something more to the Japanese. The 37mm guns of the Stuart were more than enough to wipe out foxholes, strip camouflage, and knock snipers out of trees. The newly arrived 1st Battalion of the 21st Marine Regiment was supposed to launch an attack at 5:00pm following an artillery bombardment. The artillery bombardment took place, but the approaching darkness caused the ground assault to be rescheduled to the following morning.

Base Air Force tried to support the counterlanding in the only way it knew how: by attacking enemy ships. Because attacking the Torokina beachhead and the Marines and supply caches packed therein was evidently just too complicated. On this day, attacking enemy shipping was also just too complicated; for that matter, so was just finding enemy shipping. At 8:00am, Shortland sent a report to 8th Fleet to the effect of "a powerful enemy surface force totaling 23 vessels, including two aircraft carriers, had been sighted." A response was delayed by bad weather until 1:23pm, when a D4Y reconnaissance plane flown by Warrant Officer Yoshikawa Takeshi from the *Zuikaku* was sent up to locate that force, but its two-hour search of the Treasury Islands area in ongoing unfavorable weather turned up nothing. There was another search by 13 D3As and 13 B5Ns, this out to 300 miles from Rabaul. According to one Japanese history, they "started to attack enemy force west of Mutupina, but gave it up." According to another Japanese history, "due to the failure of part of the planes to return" – whatever that means, as no aerial losses were reported from this mission – "the overall picture of the enemy situation could not be obtained."[24] That failed mission may have enabled the strike planes to avoid an ignominious fate on the ground.

Because General Kenney threw another attack at Rabaul. This time it was the Consolidated B-24 Liberators of the 90th Bombardment Group. The "Jolly Rogers," as the 90th was nicknamed, had a famous logo: a skull and crossed bombs. The skull was always missing a few teeth, as was the 90th on this day. The 90th's four squadrons could only scrape together 26 Liberators (including eight from the 319th Bombardment Squadron and six each from the 400th, 320th, and 321st Bombardment Squadrons) with an escort of 64 P-38s from the 8th (including nine from the 80th Fighter Squadron), 35th, 49th (including seven "tattered" P-38s from the 9th Fighter Squadron), and 475th (including 12 from the 431st Fighter Squadron) Fighter Groups. They resolved to bomb the Rapopo air base from high altitude, but with the fighters of *Kido Butai* still at Rabaul, the mission was a potentially expensive proposition. Exactly how many Zeros met the attackers is unclear, with reported numbers ranging from 58 to 78 (22 from Base Air Force and 56 from *Kido Butai*) to 88 (50 from Base Air Force and 11 from *Kido Butai*). The latest scholarship has 38 Zeros from *Kido Butai* under the *Zuikaku*'s veteran Lieutenant Notomi, who had been extremely busy during *Ro-Go* planning and sometimes conducting combat missions. They were joined 20 minutes later by 27 Zeros of the 201 Air Group under Lieutenant (jg) O'oba Yoshio.[25] In short, no one knows how many Japanese fighters rose up in defense of Rabaul, but it was a lot.

The Americans had apparently hoped to mount a fighter sweep while the bombing run was taking place. If so, the large number of defending fighters complicated the sweep. The 9th Fighter Squadron reported that some 50 aerial burst bombs were dropped on the Liberators. The phosphorus aerial bombs did not do any actual damage, but their explosions looked cool, and, really, isn't that what counts?[26] The Liberators released about 90 tons of bombs over Rapopo, then headed back little the worse for wear. The P-38s were not so lucky, with five of their number not returning. At least one, that of the 80th Fighter Squadron's Flight Officer Robert M. Gentile, was an operational casualty and at least one was shot down, the pilot, 2nd Lieutenant Alphonse D. "Al" Quinones, surviving to be captured by the Kempeitai and spending the rest of the war in the Rabaul POW camp.

The circumstances under which the other three were lost, including Lieutenant Howard H. Round and Lieutenant Stanley Johnson, Captain Bong's wingman, remain unclear. About Johnson's loss all that is known is that he was last seen being chased by four fighters and he did not return, leaving Bong "devastated" and refusing to fly with anyone else; good wingmen are hard to find.[27] General Kenney claimed 23 Japanese fighters were shot down and 13 were destroyed on the ground.[28] The Japanese claimed to have shot down three Liberators and 13 Lightnings while taking no losses of their own.[29] A more neutral assessment said, "[i]t appears six Japanese planes were burned on the ground and four shot down in combat."[30] The Japanese maintained no fighters were lost in combat, only that four were "hit."[31] Lieutenant (jg) O'oba celebrated the apparent Japanese victory by leading four Zeros of the 201 Air Group in patrolling over Rabaul for an hour.[32]

Even though the attack was cheaper than the Bloody Tuesday of November 2, losing five P-38s is still an expensive proposition. It made the strike more of a wash, though the Americans could afford a wash at this point much more than the Japanese could. But the attack on Rapopo was hardly the only 5th Air Force operation that went sideways on this November 7.

The dominoes started with a new campaign by the Japanese Army Air Force's 4th Air Army, based in the Wewak area, to neutralize the American air base complex at Nadzab in the Markham Valley. To that end, the previous day, November 6, 15 Mitsubishi Ki-21 Type 97 heavy bombers escorted by 16 Nakajima Ki-43 Army Type 1 ("Oscar") fighters from the 13th, 59th, 78th, and 248th Air Regiments had bombed Nadzab. After the bombing was complete, four fighters returned to strafe Nadzab; another three raked a new airstrip at Gusap with gunfire. They managed to destroy two P-39s and damage 23 other aircraft at Nadzab, and destroy a C-47 and damage two others. All without encountering fighter opposition. That was embarrassing for the 5th Air Force, albeit not as embarrassing as the Japanese return to their airfield at Alexishafen. The runway had been "inadequately repaired," which caused several landing accidents among the 248th. The commander of the 248th 3rd *chutai* (squadron), Lieutenant Ota Hideo, was killed and 2nd Lieutenant Mayekawa Yoshihari was injured.[33]

The morning of November 7, nine Mitsubishi Ki-21 Type 97 heavy bombers from the Japanese Army Air Force's 14th Air Regiment took off from Wewak. They made a side trip to Alexishafen to hook up with their fighter escorts, about 20 Nakajima Ki-43 Army Type 1 fighters from the 13th, 59th, and 248th Air Regiments. The rendezvous was delayed by mechanical issues with some of the 248th's fighters. The delay would prove costly when at around 7:20am the rendezvous attracted the attention of veteran Captain Clyde H. Barnett, Jr and his four P-40 Warhawks of the 49th Fighter Group's 8th Fighter Squadron, who were on a fighter sweep to stop Japanese air attacks that were delaying the construction of new runways at the recently constructed Gusap air base. Barnett had the Warhawks attack directly out of the morning sun, taking the Oscars of the 248th, who were flying top cover led by the 248th's commanding officer, Major Muraoka Shin-ichi, completely by surprise. After shooting down two Oscars, those flown by Sergeant Major

Suzuki Sosaku and Sergeant Toda Shiro, in the rear of the formation, three of the outnumbered Warhawks skedaddled away before the Japanese could even fire a shot; the fourth, flown by Lieutenant Nelson Flack, mixed it up for a bit then departed himself, with a bullet hole in his fuel tank for his trouble. Barnett would later call this attack "damned near perfection."[34]

At this point, Major Muraoka decided to call it a day for the 248th, whose mechanical issues seem to have cropped up again. He may have wanted to talk it over with his maintenance people, but the vast majority of those maintenance people – 201 – had been lost when their transport ship *Delagoa Maru* was sunk by the submarine USS *Trigger* on November 2. Anyway, the Japanese reformed their attack group, now with just the 13th and 59th Flying Regiments' fighters for protection. They all climbed over Finisterre Range, and arrived over the Markham Valley between 19,700 and 21,000 feet. There they found seven P-39 Airacobras from the 40th Fighter Squadron (an eighth had to abort). The Oscars kept the Airacobras at bay while the Sallys completed their bombing run at Nadzab and started heading back to their base at Wewak. The Airacobras moved in but found that four P-47 Thunderbolts from the 36th and four more from the 352nd Fighter Squadrons had moved in for the kill. The result was a rumble that was brutal for the Sallys. The damage only started when the Americans shot down two, one of whom put some drama into it by spectacularly exploding in midair. Four more Ki-21s had to ditch off the coast, while another three landed at Madang with heavy damage. Three Ki-43s, including those of Lieutenant Sakata Koichi of the 13th and Sergeant Shimanto Kikuo of the 59th, also failed to return to base; a fourth force-landed at Alexishafen, but two pilots of the 40th were killed when their Airacobras were shot down. On the ground at Nadzab, four more Airacobras were destroyed and 12 transports were "slightly damaged."[35]

Additionally, this attack on Nadzab seems to have had the effect of kneecapping a planned attack on Wewak by 45 B-25 gunships (36 from all four squadrons of the 38th Bombardment Group and nine from the 13th Squadron of the 3rd Bombardment Group). The fighter escorts for the attack were diverted to handling the Japanese attack on Nadzab, which convinced the 13th, 71st, 405th, and, apparently, the 823rd squadrons to abort their attack. The 822nd was actually tied up by Zeros over Nadzab but suffered no losses.[36]

The 5th Air Force was about to exit stage left in the Guadalcanal-Solomons Campaign, with AirSols and the 13th Air Force taking over as they finally got bases closer to Rabaul. But the Torokina area of Bougainville had to be secured in order to get the newest and so far most important of those bases built. So AirSols gave what help it could to the Marines. Shortly after 11:00am, 21 B-24 Liberators dropped 655 fragmentation clusters on the Buka air base's north and south revetment areas. Seven more, reportedly unable to make it through adverse weather to Buka, chose to dump 17½ tons of bombs on Kara instead. Shortly thereafter, six B-25s returning from a fruitless search for enemy shipping chose to take out their frustrations on Kieta. At 1:30pm, 18 SBDs and 14 TBFs (five from Marine Torpedo Bombing 233, five from Compositing 40) escorted by 14 F4Us (four from

Marine Fighting 212, the rest from Marine Fighting 215) headed for the west coast of Bougainville and the village of Jaba, the huts, gun positions, and supply dumps marking Japanese occupation targets for bombing and strafing. The air crews reported there was no antiaircraft fire or enemy fighters visible.[37]

About 20 minutes later, 16 Corsairs from Fighting 17 showed up escorting three Venturas to bomb and strafe the area around where Laruma River empties into Atsinima Bay, which was where the Japanese "counterlanding" force had … counterlanded. Maybe 10 minutes later, eight B-25s from the 42nd Bombardment Group added their two cents to the same area. The result was a bunch of barges destroyed.[38]

It was in midafternoon when the storm on the American right finally broke. Well, at least the squall on the American right. At 2:30pm, at least roughly in conjunction with the counterlanding, the Japanese attacked the roadblock, now held by one company of Marine Raiders. After a second Marine Raider company was funneled in and the 9th Marine Regiment provided supporting mortar fire, the Japanese were beaten back after 80 minutes of fighting. But the Japanese were seen digging in and preparing to resume the attack later.[39]

That was pretty much how daylight on November 7 ended. The night would be confusing, at least on land. A few Marine patrols had been cut off by the Japanese landing, or, more accurately, intermingled with Japanese patrols. The Marines mostly had to get to the coast, where they were picked up, or fight their way back to the expanding defense perimeter. One platoon from Company K, 3rd Battalion, 9th Marine Regiment, was scouting the upper Laruma River region when the Japanese landed. The Japanese moved in on the platoon, but the Marines turned the tables on their Japanese pursuers, ambushing the Japanese multiple times before escaping into the jungle. This platoon returned to the Torokina perimeter about 30 hours later with one man wounded and one man missing.[40]

The early morning of November 8 saw the squall on the American right break once again. At 7:30am, the Japanese – now identified as elements of the 1st and 3rd Battalions of the 23rd Infantry Regiment – attacked the roadblock following a four-hour preparatory mortar barrage. The defending Marines Raiders held until 2:00pm, when two companies were sent forward to counterattack, driving the Imperial Army troops back somewhat. There the counterattack stalled at about 4:00pm, with even the addition of a weapons company and two tanks not enough to keep it going.[41]

The morning of November 8 also saw the short-delayed ground assault on the Japanese counterlanders finally take place. After a 20-minute preparation by five batteries of artillery along with machine guns, mortars, and antitank guns – the Marines had landed a *lot* of stuff – Stuart tanks protected by the men of the 1st Battalion of the 21st Marine Regiment moved off to lead the attack. It was overkill, quite literally. Only a few dazed survivors of two artillery bombardments and multiple air attack remained, and they were quickly overcome. The Marines counted more than 250 dead Japanese. The 1st Battalion from the 21st Marines moved about 1,500 yards through the jungle along the coast without resistance. That afternoon the battalion established a defensive line behind a lagoon and sent out patrols to deal with any remaining Japanese, but none were encountered. The remaining Japanese on the Marines' left had all scattered. The threat from that direction was eliminated.[42] Unless the Japanese landed … counterlanded more troops.

That was the concern of General Turnage. He was not happy with the PT boats who were supposed to be patrolling the coast. The Japanese counterlanding force had landed on the night of November 6–7 and the PT boats had missed them completely. Had not even been on patrol. But that was by design. The PT boats were under orders that they were authorized to leave their base only if they had received instructions from the commander of the amphibious force – Admiral Wilkinson – at Guadalcanal.[43] This was probably to keep them on a tight leash given the precocious PTs' propensity for putting torpedoes into the water aimed at friendly ships, especially flagships.

And for the first two days of their deployment to Bougainville, this had worked out fine. They had received such instructions from Admiral Wilkinson's headquarters and had dutifully patrolled. But they had received no such instructions since then, so they were restricted to their base at Puruata Island. It was during these three days that the Japanese had landed.[44]

General Turnage was most displeased with this situation, so much so that he gave a direct order to the commander of the PTs, Commander Henry Farrow, that the boats were to maintain continuous 24-hour patrols whether orders were received from Guadalcanal or not. Fully understanding the reason for the orders from Admiral Wilkinson, Farrow asked if friendly ships might be in the area, but Turnage's headquarters had no information.[45]

So, out the PTs went into Empress Augusta Bay, two patrols of three boats each. One patrol, headed by *PT-170* skipper Lieutenant Edward Macauley III, had one PT boat poking around in the dark while two others were stopped off the Magine Islands, all just hoping nothing bad would happen. Those hopes were pretty much dashed at 3:15am on November 8 when illumination rounds were fired over them. Someone was trying to see who they were. Shortly thereafter came the shell splashes. A pair of destroyers had appeared and started shooting at the PTs. Macauley radioed that he was being attacked by a pair of enemy destroyers and ordered evasive action.[46]

The US Navy PTs were in a bad position. They had apparently been taken by surprise by enemy destroyers who outgunned them. They were divided. And two of them had to get moving from a literal stop. Worse still, the destroyers were working their way between the boats and the beach.

The Second Battle of Empress Augusta Bay was under way. For 45 minutes, the PTs had to dance around the shell splashes from the two destroyers. Or was it three destroyers? Lieutenant Macauley may have been too busy turning his boat this way and that to get a good count. Macauley was trying to set up a mass torpedo attack, but the destroyers' pursuit was complicating it. Instead, he invited a friend to try to take out the destroyers or at least distract them. Macauley radioed *PT-163* announcing he was leading "three Nip cans" his way and "wouldn't he like to take a whack at them?" He would. *PT-163* fired one torpedo. It missed. The destroyers don't seem to have even noticed it.[47]

Suddenly, at about 3:00am, the destroyers ceased firing and turned away, heading back out to sea. Why would they do that? It was strange, but Macauley wasn't about to look a gift horse in the mouth. He tried to organize his boats for a mass torpedo attack. And then Macauley saw what might have been the reason the destroyers turned away.

A new contact had appeared on the *PT-170*'s radar, a big one, about 10,000 yards ahead. Then the sailors started seeing projectiles that "looked like large ashcans" flying over them.[48] That wasn't good.

Lieutenant Macauley was still trying to make sense of these developments and formulate a coherent response when the *PT-170*'s voice radio started to crackle.

"Humblest apologies, we are friendly vessels."

The voice was that of Commander Edmund B. Taylor, commodore of Destroyer Division 90, on board the destroyer USS *Anthony*.

The PTs had done it again. Fired on friendly ships. Though, to be sure, this time, it was not the fault of the PTs. The destroyers *Anthony* and *Hudson* had fired first.

Both destroyers were the vanguard of the convoy carrying the next wave of reinforcements to the Torokina beachhead. The 148th Infantry Regiment of the US Army's 37th Infantry Division and a battery of antiaircraft guns were coming in a convoy under the overall command of Captain Anderson that consisted of the "attack transports" *President Jackson*, *President Adams*, *President Hayes*, and *Fuller*; and the cargo ships *Titania* and *Libra*; who were escorted by destroyers *Guest*, *Bennett*, *Wadsworth*, *Warrington*, and the aforementioned *Anthony* and *Hudson*.[49]

These last two were ordered by Admiral Wilkinson to speed on ahead to Empress Augusta Bay and sweep the area around the beachhead for Japanese barges trying to land reinforcements. The destroyers had been told that the PT boats would remain at their base, and Guadalcanal had sent a message to the PTs at Torokina warning them that friendly destroyers were due to arrive that night and specifically ordering them not to go out. Except the orders were muddled with inclusion of a directive to "be prepared to counter any enemy surface forces threatening that area." Even worse, and of much more relevance, this message arrived on November 9. Slightly late. In fact, communications between the Puruata Island Navy base and Guadalcanal had completely broken down. Since that second day on Bougainville, the PT boats had received nothing from Guadalcanal. For their part, the destroyers had believed the PT boats were Japanese barges they had been ordered to wipe out. Only when the PTs had accelerated to speeds beyond those of which the Japanese *daihatsu* was capable did the destroyers realize their error, a realization that was confirmed when they picked up the voice radio communications of the PTs organizing a torpedo attack, at which point they moved to clear the area. Communications and information, those two pillars of any military operation, were missing here. But no harm, no foul, and everyone had an amusing story. Except for one nagging little thing.[50]

What about that radar contact Lieutenant Macauley's *PT-170* had picked up? What was that? And what were those "large ashcans" the sailors saw flying overhead? What was the deal with that? What that radar contact was and who fired those projectiles over the PTs has never been determined.[51]

With this Second Battle of Empress Augusta Bay having reached a harmless if somewhat mystifying conclusion, attention turned to more pressing matters. In the predawn darkness, a dozen Corsairs of the US Navy's Fighting 17 took off from Ondonga, northwest of Munda on New Georgia, to escort six B-25 gunships from the 42nd Bombardment Group in skip-bombing some ships in Matchin Harbor near Bonis. The mission went wrong from the beginning. A driving rainstorm struck just before takeoff. The weather remained so bad that seven of the Corsairs turned back. Five, including Lieutenant Commander Blackburn, continued onward, but the weather also prevented rendezvous with the Mitchells. Even so, Blackburn and his remaining "Jolly Rogers" – a common name for air squadrons, it would seem – continued toward Matchin Bay. Halfway there, the sky cleared and it turned into a sunny day, which was no longer good because they were so few and going so close to two major enemy air bases. When they arrived, no one was in Matchin Harbor, so Blackburn and two other Corsairs strafed practically empty Buka while the other two strafed equally practically empty Bonis. Blackburn and Lieutenant Harry A. "Dirty Eddie" March opened fire on an aircraft turning into final approach that they identified as a "Ruth," a Fiat I-Type (BR.20) medium bomber. It was actually a Mitsubishi G3M Type 96 land attack plane, a "Nell," delivering supplies from Rabaul, at least until Blackburn and March shot it down in flames. Then the fighter groups got back together and headed back to base, strafing Ballale en route. For their part, though they had missed the rendezvous because of the weather, the B-25s also tried to make the most of it and swooped in on Kieta airfield, bombing and strafing it before heading back themselves.[52]

That would not be Fighting 17's only mission this day. The "attack" transports and cargo ships bringing in the regiment of the 37th Infantry Division arrived at around 8:00am and began unloading. An old hand of the South Pacific, Laurance T. DuBose, returned as commander of Cruiser Division 13, with the light cruisers *Santa Fe*, DuBose's flagship, *Birmingham*, and *Nashville*; screened by destroyers *John Rodgers*, *Harrison*, *McKee*, and *Murray*. Rear Admiral DuBose was ordered to come in and guard the transport force to seaward as they unloaded and cleared the area.[53]

At 11:40am, the fighter director, who was on board the destroyer *Wadsworth*, reported a large bogey 56 miles away bearing 267 degrees True. Captain Anderson ordered his little flotilla to halt all offloading, get under way, and get out of the harbor. The escorting destroyers, all from Destroyer Squadron 45 under the command of Commander Ralph Earle, Jr were to assume screening positions to repel air attack. The fighter director on the *Wadsworth* reported vectoring in a dozen Corsairs and 16 Hellcats, with another dozen fighters on station if needed.[54]

They would be. It had been a struggle for AirSols to put up its normal patrol over the landing zone because of bad weather between Munda and the Treasury Islands. The first shift of the AirSols fighter patrol over the beachhead had trouble getting into position because the storm blocked their route from Vella Lavella and Munda; those that did passed some of the time by strafing suspected Japanese positions on the Laruma River. Nevertheless, the second shift was able to get on station and when the Japanese arrived, they found a welcoming committee that included six Corsairs from Fighting 17 (two others had to abort), eight Corsairs from Marine Fighting 212, eight Lightnings from the US Army Air Force's 339th Fighter Squadron, and several Hellcats from Fighting 33.[55]

The bogey was the latest swipe by Base Air Force and *Kido Butai* at the Bougainville invasion force. At 7:45am, Rabaul had received a message from Shortland reporting 16 enemy transports escorted by cruisers and destroyers had anchored off Mutupina Point and were sending reinforcements ashore into the Torokina beachhead. The Japanese considered this to be a bad thing. Admirals Ozawa and Kusaka had the indefatigable Lieutenant Notomi organize a major strike, a rather complicated assignment because it involved sending up both carrier and land air units from multiple bases. The final tally for fighters was seven from the 201 Air Group under Lieutenant (jg) O'oba, 27 from the 204 Air Group under Lieutenant (jg) Morita Heitaro, 15 from *Shokaku*, ten from *Zuikaku*, and 15 from the *Zuiho*, for a total of 74 fighters, though it seems three, all from Base Air Force, had to abort for unknown reasons. With the Zeros were 26 Aichi D3A carrier bombers, 16 from the *Shokaku* and ten from the *Zuikaku*, under the command of Lieutenant Matsumara Katsuhisa, a division officer from the *Shokaku*, sitting as an observer in the lead bomber. Because the ground crews had finally switched out the ordnance pylons, these dive bombers carried the more effective 250kg (550lb) bomb. Strangely, no torpedo bombers, what the Japanese called "attack planes." At 9:10am (local time), the first of Base Air Force's Zeros took off from Lakunai air base. Five minutes later, the carrier bombers took off from Vunakanau. Then at 9:30, *Kido Butai*'s fighters took off. The *Shokaku*'s Zeros stuck with the Aichis. The other Zeros formed two different groups, one ahead, the other above, the carrier bombers. Learning, Lieutenant Notomi seemed to be doing. The Japanese Naval Air Force had a history of keeping their Zeros behind their strike or other very important aircraft, such as that of Admiral Yamamoto, a tactic that had a history of getting those strike or other very important aircraft shot down, such as that of the aforementioned Admiral Yamamoto. Notomi would not make that mistake. In all probability, Admiral Ozawa also had a hand in this tactical adjustment. Be that as it may, the Japanese arrived over Torokina at around noon (local time).[56]

It added up to a frightful flying fracas over Empress Augusta Bay, one in which AirSols was outnumbered. The first to make contact with the imperial intruders were eight Lightnings of the 339th Fighter Squadron under Major Henry Lawrence. Strangely, even though they were attacking and had the numerical advantage, the Japanese Zeros broke into two big Lufbery Circles, inherently defensive formations in which the fighters fly around in a circle so that getting one in your crosshairs puts you in the crosshairs of the plane behind it. It was typically used only by pilots who are badly outnumbered or inexperienced. Neither would apply to the cocky fliers of *Kido Butai*, but Base Air Force's fliers probably fit the latter.[57] The *Wadsworth* vectored Lawrence toward the formation with the Vals. Around this time, eight Corsairs from Marine Fighting 212 and six Corsairs from Fighting 17 arrived. The Jolly Rogers, mystified as to why the Japanese were using a Lufbery Circle here, decided they were probably decoys to get the defenders' attention while a second group of Zeros snuck in behind them. Marine Fighting 212 started making vertical passes at the Lufbery Circle without getting into the enemy sights. Two such passes broke up one of the circles. The air battle got messy, and the fighter director on board the destroyer *Wadsworth* had to commit the P-40 Warhawks of the 44th and 70th Fighter Squadrons, who were being held back at intermediate altitude because of their performance limitations. The 44th's Captain John D. Voss led six Warhawks from the two Army Air Force squadrons into the fray; they were already down one, as the P-40 of the 70th's Lieutenant Herbert Schafer disappeared in those clouds between Munda and the Treasury Islands. As they did so, the Corsairs moved toward the Vals' formation. Marine Fighting 212's Captain Wilbur A. Free lined up one of the Vals in his sights, only to have five of his six .50-cal. machine guns jam. Typical. Free claimed to have killed the dive bomber's gunner and said the Val was "last seen scooting west at an altitude of about 25ft."[58]

But it was not enough. The Zeros bounced AirSols' interception and several Aichi D3As got through to Captain Anderson's transport force. At 12:12pm, three Vals dove on the transport *President Jackson* from astern. The got two near misses, while a third bomb bounced off the Number 4 hatch cover, flattening the bomb's nose but not convincing it to detonate. Five sailors were required to roll the bomb over the side. As they did so, they saw rust on the bomb.[59]

The cargo ship *Fuller* was not so lucky. "[A] group of six or eight enemy planes" was reported off the port quarter. "[S]ingly and in pairs," those on the port side began to peel off in a shallow glide attack from the port beam and quarter. The attack transport was at the rear of the formation, and it was speculated that this position caused the Japanese to focus on her.[60] Like the bomb that hit the *President Jackson*, one bomb bounced, this one off the Number 4 3-inch gun, and went on through the gun platform and main deck, into the Number 7 hold. Unlike the bomb that hit the *President Jackson*, this bomb exploded. The blast killed six, wounded several, left a 12-foot hole in the main deck, severed electrical, communications, sanitary, and fresh water lines to the stern area; and caused a number of small fires in the crew quarters. Another 15 minutes of bombing by the Japanese netted only two near misses off the Number 1 and 2 holds, sending shrapnel into each and causing more small fires.[61]

That was it for the air strike. It was an expensive day for AirSols. Captain Voss was credited with shooting down one Val, but his Warhawk was badly hit. He announced he was going to try to ditch in the Treasury Islands, but he was never heard from again. Shortly thereafter, a plane was seen plunging out of control into the Treasuries' Blanche Harbor, where it exploded.[62] Voss' Warhawk was one of two P-40s from the 44th Fighter Squadron shot down; the other was that of Lieutenant John Dollen, who was rescued. Marine Fighting 212's Lieutenant Edward T. Brown vanished after the initial engagement; what was believed to be his Corsair was seen in shallow water off the Torokina River with what was believed to be Brown standing on the wing, but he was never seen again.[63] That "Corsair" may have actually been the Hellcat of Fighting 33's Lieutenant (jg) James Joseph Kinsella, who had an eerily similar scenario, except he was quickly rescued. Also lost under mysterious circumstances was the 339th's Lieutenant Carl Squires, who after the initial engagement was also never seen again.[64] Topping it off, one more Hellcat, that of Fighting 33's Ensign M. E. Patterson, vanished during the action.[65]

The Japanese fared even worse. The *Zuiho* lost one fighter pilot, Flight Petty Officer 1st Class Muraoka Nobuyuki.[66] The *Shokaku* lost one fighter pilot who, in the words of aviation historian Michael Claringbould, "cannot be identified due to the eccentric handwriting of the *Shokaku* operations clerk." The 201 Air Group lost Leading Airman Hida Ebisu, while the 204 Air Group lost no fighter pilots. The *Zuikaku* lost one fighter pilot, and he was the big one: Lieutenant Notomi Kenjiro himself. The commander of the *Zuikaku*'s air group and leader of this attack was reportedly "bounced by F4Us from above, and was killed," but precisely where, when, and by whom are unknown. His was a disastrous loss: yet another one of *Kido Butai*'s few remaining veteran fighter leaders, the operational head of *Ro-Go* who planned and, as here, sometimes even conducted air combat missions. Additionally, of the 26 Aichi D3A carrier bombers in the attack, ten or 11 (seven from the *Shokaku* and four from the *Zuikaku*) failed to return. The Japanese claimed to have sunk two transports and three destroyers; severely damaged a heavy cruiser and transport; and shot down a dozen aircraft; all against an alleged 60 fighters.[67]

While counting trees – no small feat in Empress Augusta Bay – is important, even more important is looking at the whole forest and just what this air attack meant in the overall scheme of the Pacific War. The Japanese had planned this attack well and set it up almost perfectly, a testimony to the talent of Lieutenant Notomi. It was a generally well-executed attack, the only major quibble being the glide bombing by the Aichis, which is less demanding but also less effective than dive bombing. There was an almost 3-to-1 ratio of escorting fighters to strike aircraft. The Zeros had the advantage of numbers and bounced the intercepting Americans. Yet, the carrier bombers hit their targets with only two of their bombs, and one of those was a dud. Neither target was seriously damaged.

The Sea Eagles had done almost everything right, and had still not sunk anything, had not even seriously damaged anything, had not delayed or otherwise impacted the landings on Bougainville. And had lost four fighters, including one irreplaceable veteran fighter leader, and ten or 11 of 26 carrier bombers. Was this how it was going to be? Was this the new normal? Do everything right and still have it amount to nothing except more losses? If that's all that's possible at the Sea Eagles' best – not the best in the Pacific War, but the best they could now achieve – what will happen when the Sea Eagles are not at their best?

It would be a chilling thought, but it had to wait. At 1:30pm, the *Zuikaku*'s Warrant Officer Yoshikawa was sent up in his Comet reconnaissance plane again to search the Torokina area. He reported three battleships and three or four destroyers in the vicinity of Mono Island in the Treasuries. Admiral Kusaka wondered how he could turn it into another Battle of Rennell Island. At 4:00pm, two Nakajima B5N carrier attack planes from the *Shokaku* and two from the *Zuikaku* took off, followed 15 minutes later by two Mitsubishi G4Ms of the 702 Air Group. Their job was to find this force, shadow it, and radio its position to a following air strike.[68]

Or following air strikes. Because at 4:30, nine more B5N attack planes (five from the *Shokaku*, four *Zuikaku*) launched under the leadership of the *Shokaku*'s Lieutenant Ono followed 15 minutes later by six more G4M land attack planes of the 751 Air Group led by pilot Lieutenant Nozaka Michio, followed another 15 minutes later by yet another six G4Ms, these from the 702 Air Group under Lieutenant (jg) Sato Yutaka. All were armed with torpedoes.[69] Admiral Kusaka was indeed trying to repeat the success of Rennell Island and the sinking of the USS *Chicago*. Hopefully with a battleship or three.

On that, the Japanese were to be disappointed. There were no battleships or even heavy cruisers like the *Chicago* near Bougainville, but there was Admiral DuBose's force of light cruisers. This was a bit of a problem for Admiral Halsey. DuBose's force was only on loan to Halsey from Admiral Nimitz's Central Pacific force to temporarily cover for Admiral Merrill's overused and battered force of light cruisers – DuBose's force did not even have a task group numerical designation – and Nimitz would soon want this force back in just as good a shape as Halsey had found it.

While he had served in the South Pacific, most importantly a year earlier when he had commanded the heavy cruiser *Portland* during the Friday the 13th Battle, Admiral DuBose was not familiar with the latest developments in the South and Southwest Pacific areas. So he had borrowed Admiral Merrill's operations officer and taken him aboard DuBose's flagship *Santa Fe*. He had also borrowed Merrill's communications officer so the unnumbered task force would be able to handle South Pacific communications protocols. Also lent to DuBose's group was Merrill's fighter director, though he was stationed on the *Mobile*. That last one was a bit of a sore point with Admiral DuBose. The air search radar on the *Santa Fe* went out on the way to Bougainville. "[I]t may be mentioned that radar work as done by Pearl Harbor for ships of this division has not been satisfactory[…]." Never one to mince words, Laurance DuBose. That's why he had been an excellent and popular skipper of the *Portland*.[70]

Admiral DuBose's force had spent the day patrolling north and northwest of the Treasury Islands, in position to block the movement of any surface ships toward the "attack" transports and cargo ships. Indeed, at 5:00pm a fighter pilot reported three large ships to the west of the transports. So, there were three large ships west of the transports, and Admiral DuBose's group was west of the transports. That seemed like more than a coincidence to the admiral, but just in case, he moved into a blocking position. Better safe than sorry. Remember Savo Island. The offloading operations were completed without further incident.[71]

At 6:15pm, radar – albeit not on the *Santa Fe*, but on the *Mobile* – detected unidentified aircraft between 30 and 50 miles away. Admiral DuBose tried to keep his ships between Captain Anderson's ships and Rabaul. He had been warned there might be snoopers after dark. Just in case, though, he shifted into an antiaircraft disposition. Better safe than sorry. Remember Rennell Island.[72]

Most likely, the *Mobile*'s air search radar had detected the Japanese scout planes, who had pinpointed Admiral DuBose's location at 6:20.[73] They would keep tabs on his group as the air strikes got into position.

Sunset was at 6:31. Six minutes later, Captain Anderson's group left the Torokina beachhead during a downpour that had hidden them from the Japanese. Shortly thereafter, based on the reports he was getting from the *Mobile*, Admiral DuBose determined the unidentified aircraft were forming up for an attack. They were all at a low attitude – this would be a torpedo attack. A twin-engine aircraft became visible off the starboard bow. The *Santa Fe* and *Mobile* fired at it and drove it off. For now. As DuBose later pointedly pointed out, "This engagement is an excellent example of one which might well have been warded off or minimized by the use of night fighters, had they been available."[74] They were available, actually. But Lieutenant Jack M. Plunkett of Marine Night Fighting 531 operating out of Barakoma had been vectored to northern Choiseul to investigate an unidentified radar contact in his night fighter, a modified Ventura. He would be a while.[75]

What to do? Admiral DuBose had his ships increase speed to 29 knots and make for a squall that had appeared to the northwest about 15 miles away. But the Japanese beat him to it. Around 7:00pm, those staples of the Imperial Navy's night warfare started appearing – flares to illuminate the US Navy ships, floatlights to mark their course, all in pretty colors of green, red, and white.[76] Like Christmas in the South Pacific. Or the Solomon Islands' Annual Italian Festival, if they were to have one.

But as much as the Americans might wish it, this would be no pizza party, Neapolitan, Sicilian, or otherwise. And as much as the Japanese might wish it, this would be no Rennell Island. Admiral DuBose was an aggressive veteran of the South Pacific. Instead of speeding in a straight line or zigzagging in a decipherable pattern, DuBose had his ships maneuver "rapidly and frequently [...] in the hope of throwing off at least part of the (torpedo) attack."[77] In other words, just like Admiral Merrill had at Empress Augusta Bay, but in a more random fashion. And it worked.

For a while. With no American night fighters to worry about, the force was able to open fire using full radar control on any aircraft that came into range starting at 7:11 or so. The Japanese helped by attacking from the west, thus revealing themselves in the fading twilight; at Rennell Island, attack leader Lieutenant Commander Higai Joji had looped around the Americans so he could attack from the darkened east. These Japanese did not have Higai Joji. No one had Higai Joji. He was dead.[78]

Even so, at night, "the planes were rarely seen before they were set afire by hits [...]." The *Birmingham* fired a 6-inch salvo at the attackers, then shifted to her 5-inch dual-purpose guns. Except the 6-inch salvo had jarred the fire control radar out of tune and thus the 5-inch shells missed badly until the radar issue was corrected.[79] There would be a price.

At 7:17, a plane identified as a "'Val' with retractable landing gear" came in very low off the starboard quarter. Just before passing over the stern, it released a bomb, then continued onward, at which point it was shot down. It crashed about 500–1,000 yards off the port beam, burning fiercely on the water and backlighting the cruiser just like Higai Joji's G3M did at Rennell Island. The plane's bomb detonated just above the waterline at about frame 149.[80]

Japanese records indicate there were no Aichi D3A "Val" Type 99 carrier bombers in this attack, only Nakajima B5N "Kate" Type 97 carrier attack planes and Mitsubishi G4M "Betty" Type 1 land attack planes, and there were no Aichi D3A Vals with retractable landing gear in any case. Japanese records also explicitly state that all the aircraft in the designated airstrikes carried aerial torpedoes, but there is no such proviso for the four B5Ns and two G4Ms who had launched ahead of the air strike on "search and contact" missions to pin the targets for them. Thus, the most logical explanation here is that the four Kates took part in this attack, one of whom was the "'Val' with retractable landing gear" responsible for this bomb hit. While the detonation killed one and was jarring to the *Birmingham* as a whole, the damage report says "there was negligible damage except in the immediate vicinity of the hit."[81]

The next hit would not be so negligible. At the same time as the bomb hit, an unknown party had warned over the voice radio "Torpedo course 270."[82] The *Birmingham* had been having issues keeping in touch with Admiral DuBose using the "Talk Between Ships" voice radio, and the message would have been lost in the momentary chaos of the bomb hit in any case. Missing the warning may have contributed to what followed.

About a minute later, heading northwest with the other cruisers, the *Birmingham* suffered an underwater explosion on her port side at frame 20 about 10 feet below the waterline, sending up a towering plume of water that came down onto the bridge. The blast left an irregular-shaped hole, roughly 28 by 32 feet, near the port bow.[83] Maybe three minutes later, Admiral DuBose ordered an emergency 40-degree turn to starboard.[84] Closing barn doors and all that. He would not repeat the same mistake. At 7:24pm came another voice radio warning from an unidentified party, "Torpedo coming on course 090." DuBose immediately ordered an emergency turn to head due west to comb it.[85]

At the time, there was some question as to what caused the explosion.[86] It was later determined to have been caused by a Type 91 aerial torpedo, released by an aircraft the *Birmingham*'s gunners had neither seen nor heard, so whether a Kate or a Betty was responsible for the torpedo remains unclear.[87] Several compartments were flooded, but, even considering some minor flooding near the stern caused by the bomb hit, "[s]tructural damage at both bow and stern was sharply localized, and was relatively light when compared with that sustained by other vessels from torpedo attack." The *Birmingham* "was able to make 29 knots with little difficulty." "I first thought that we must be badly crippled," skipper Captain Thomas B. Inglis recalled, "but to my astonishment the hits did not interfere with the *Birmingham*'s fighting efficiency. She could still float, move and shoot."[88]

The *Birmingham* would have to float, move, and shoot some more, and she did them all very well. Perhaps too well. At 7:42, her gunners opened fire on a plane approaching low from the port beam silhouetted against the twilight. The plane was hit and exploded over the ship, crashing into the water less than 100 yards from the starboard beam. But a bomb from the aircraft, either dropped just before it was hit or released as the plane disintegrated, detonated on the faceplate of the Number 4 6-inch turret. The faceplate, guns, and deck were gouged by shrapnel, and the guns were jammed in elevation, but fears that the magazines had been hit as well proved unfounded. Captain Inglis remembered this moment "particularly vividly, for at one time there were two Jap planes burning in the air off the port quarter, and four more on the starboard side." Interestingly, no one could find the bomb's point of impact or any impact damage. This led to the conclusion that the bomb was a general-purpose bomb fused to explode about 18 inches above the target, not an armor-piercing bomb intended for warships. [89]

This bomb hit is revealing on a number of levels. It was later theorized that the bomb was originally intended for use against ground troops on Bougainville, but was diverted to the *Birmingham* instead. That may be true on its face, but, again, all the strike aircraft, which were only Kates and Bettys, were armed with torpedoes. So this bomb had to have come from one of the Kates that was sent on the "search and contact" mission to find the enemy ships for the following air strike. Furthermore, when combined with the bomb hit on the stern later determined to have come from a 550lb armor-piercing bomb, it's easy to infer that the Japanese were launching what they had available at that time as soon as possible just to re-establish and maintain contact with the enemy force.[90]

Also revealing was the altitude of the attack: very low, almost like torpedo attacks. Like at Bismarck Sea. Admiral DuBose certainly noticed. "All planes approached at low altitude, and the bombing was definitely masthead bombing," Dubose wrote. Captain Inglis used a different term: "skip bombing." That is, masthead bombing which is also called skip-bombing or low-level bombing, the same thing the Allies had done to the Japanese at Bismarck Sea. The admiral added, "It is believed that this is the first instance of Japanese use of this type of bombing."[91]

And the Japanese did it mixed in with what was predominantly a torpedo attack. And they did it at night. Give the Imperial Japanese Navy points for creativity and degree of difficulty.

If not for effectiveness. According to her damage report, "(The) *Birmingham* suffered surprisingly little reduction in fighting efficiency for such widespread damage. While this was partly because of the favorable location of the hits, it was also due to prompt and effective damage control measures."[92]

That was it for this attack. Admiral DuBose's ships reached the squall at 7:45pm and invited themselves inside. This, then, concluded what the Japanese called "The Second Air Battle off Bougainville." Normally, an air battle consists entirely, or at least mostly, of aircraft of one side attacking aircraft of the other side, and vice versa. Thus, the Japanese morning attack on the transports off Torokina could credibly be called an air battle, because Japanese fighters were fighting Allied fighters, with some Japanese bombing thrown in. But "The Second Air Battle off Bougainville" consisted entirely of the aircraft of one side attacking the ships of the other side. It was no more an air battle than the sinking of the *Prince of Wales* and the *Repulse*, which the Japanese call "The Naval Battle of Malaya," though that was not really a naval battle, either. Now, if the ships had been in the air, then it might make sense to call it an air battle. But the ships were not in the air, as putting warships in the air has proven to be rather difficult. Only the Imperial Japanese Navy would call an engagement in which only one side had aircraft an air battle. That's what they were going with.

The Imperial Japanese Navy was also sticking to its assessment of the damage its Sea Eagles inflicted on the Allies in this "Second Air Battle off Bougainville." Not "Americans," but "Allies." You'll see.

In this version of events, here is what the Nakajima B5N carrier attacks planes of *Kido Butai*, who reportedly attacked from 7:12 to 7:20pm, accomplished:

- One battleship – sunk.
- Two cruisers – sunk. And not just "sunk," but "blown up and sunk," which, of course, is so much better, so much more strategically advantageous than just "sunk."
- One cruiser – set afire.
- Three cruisers or destroyers – set afire.

And here is what the Mitsubishi G4M land attack planes of Base Air Force, who reportedly attacked from 7:25 until 8:00pm, accomplished:

- One battleship ("*King George* class") – sunk
- Two battleships ("*Renown* class") – sunk. And not just sunk, but "each hit by two or three torpedoes," which, again, is so much better. It's like the more torpedo hits they got, the more points they got. If only those two *Renown*-class battleships could have stayed afloat for just a little bit longer.
- One destroyer – set afire; "Sinking virtually certain."
- One cruiser – set afire.[93]

Perhaps the Japanese needed the belief in both the claims of incredible damage caused and the apparent denudation of the Royal Navy's Home Fleet – with the German battleship *Tirpitz* still afloat out there – to distract itself from the seemingly small but still disastrous losses from this "air battle": four B5N torpedo bombers from the *Shokaku* (out of 13 launched overall), and seven G4M land attack planes (out of a total of 14 launched), comprising four from the 702, including that of Lieutenant (jg) Sato, another by Warrant Officer Miho Kunimi, and a third by Warrant Officer Ogawa Harakyo; and three from the 751 Air Group, including that of Lieutenant Nozaka.[94] Even if the Japanese claims of damage inflicted on the enemy were taken as true, the margin of aircrew losses was beyond unsustainable.

It wasn't over. Oh, the "Second Air Battle off Bougainville" was over, but the Japanese attacks of this night – and their losses therefrom – were not. While Admiral DuBose's ships were enjoying themselves in the spring shower, the Japanese strike planes returned to Rabaul. A pair of Type 0 reconnaissance seaplanes from the 938 Air Group at Buka remained to keep tabs on the "battleships" and cruisers and drop the occasional bomb on the Torokina beachhead as best they could considering the storm, which forced one to divert to Shortland and return to Buka after dawn.[95]

But all good things must come to an end, including this squall. There were others around, but Admiral DuBose was now more focused on protecting the departing convoy. At around 10:30pm, he put the cruisers in a column, with the slightly slowed *Birmingham* bringing up the rear. The admiral maneuvered to position his force about ten miles behind the convoy, between it and Rabaul.

Good thing, because at 1:10am on November 9, Base Air Force returned. Admiral DuBose saw the Japanese forming up for an attack and shifted from a column to an antiaircraft formation. According to DuBose, there "seemed to be some 10 to 15 planes." He called this "a most peculiar attack" in that the Japanese repeatedly simulated a torpedo approach, only to pull away out of gunnery range. Thus, "[their]] attack was not pressed home." Japanese records disagree inasmuch as the attack definitively involved only four G4M Type 1 land attack planes from the 751 Air Group and a separate reconnaissance mission by two Type 0 reconnaissance seaplanes from the 958 Air Group out of Buka, though it may have also involved two B5N carrier attack planes, one or two "reconnaissance seaplanes," and a "seaplane fighter" (probably a float Zero, or "Rufe"). This dance of death in the dark continued until about 3:00am, at which point the Japanese attackers withdrew, minus two more land attack planes and crews they could not afford to lose. On this day, the 751 had lost not just Lieutenant Nozaka and his crew, but Lieutenant (jg) Kaneda Yoshikazu, Flight Chief Petty Officer Takeda Akeo, and Warrant Officers Arae Toshio and Marugo Shigeru, and their crews. Base Air Force later determined that the 751's efforts at this time caused "Considerable Losses" to the Americans. The two floatplanes basically just hung around the task force but do not seem to have actually attacked the US Navy ships.[96]

It was about that time that the night fighter finally entered stage right, courtesy of Captain Anderson's fighter director on the *Wadsworth*.[97] Of course, there were no more attackers at this point. It was just the principle of the thing. This was apparently Marine Night Fighting 531's commander, Lieutenant Colonel Frank H. Schwable. Lieutenant Plunkett, who seems to have arrived just after the first Japanese attack but been unable to find any Japanese before he was relieved by Schwable. All Schwable could do was chase but not catch a few snoopers, probably including the two floatplanes from the 958 Air Group, before a particularly bad squall developed that forced him from the scene.[98] Night aerial battles were still in their infancy, especially in the Pacific.

The night was not just for Japanese aviators anymore, however. At least that's what Australian Air Commodore Hewitt was hoping. He was still determined to prove the viability of the Bristol Beaufort as a torpedo bomber, this despite the fact that this aircraft designed and designated as a torpedo bomber was overloaded when actually armed with a torpedo. Hewitt had saved up all of his Beauforts for a big strike against the ships left at Rabaul on the night of November 8. While the Japanese were attacking Admiral DuBose's ships, a cool dozen Beauforts from No. 8 Squadron armed with torpedoes would descend on Simpson Harbor in formation of two flights of six. They were to be aided by diversionary bombing attacks on Vunakanau and Rapopo by No. 6 Squadron.[99]

To his credit, Air Commodore Hewitt wanted the latest intelligence on Rabaul, including the weather and dispositions of ships in Simpson Harbor. To that end, late in the afternoon of November 8, he sent up one Beaufort to check it out ahead of the main attack. The Beaufort got to Rabaul all right, but ran away when confronted by three of those Type 0 reconnaissance seaplanes. Nevertheless, the naval observer on board, Lieutenant Lloyd Russell Greentree, got a look into the Rabaul caldera. When they returned to Kiriwina, Greentree reported his observations to Wing Commander Geoffrey Dimmock Nicoll, commanding officer of No 8. Squadron, who was to lead this attack.[100]

Lieutenant Greentree was not encouraging. He reported that heavy rain was falling in St George's Channel. Worse, he also said the Japanese had arranged their ships defensively in groups to maximize the effectiveness of their antiaircraft guns, especially those of the cruisers, against low-flying aircraft.[101]

The crews of the torpedo-carrying Beauforts were privy to this report and insisted the attack could not succeed. Wing Commander Nicoll went up to Air Commodore Hewitt and loudly declared the "show was off."[102]

Well, wasn't that special? The guy supposed to lead the attack was now saying there'd be no attack. Hewitt went to this impromptu tactical conference held outside the operations room of Kiriwana air base in the moonlight with a map of the Rabaul caldera opened on the hood of a Jeep. The senior officers crowded around the map, with the torpedo crews anxiously waiting in the background for the decision. Lieutenant Greentree was adamant that the Japanese ships were in defensive formations. Tempers were short. Nicoll shouting his opposition to the mission didn't help dial things down. This was an extremely important mission, Hewitt knew. Lives hung in the balance, but so did the future of the Bristol Beaufort. He had been husbanding his Beauforts for just this mission, and the window for launching this mission was rapidly closing. Yet, again to his credit, Hewitt was reluctant to overrule the mission commander.[103] It's always dangerous to have a military operation commanded by someone who opposes it; remember Ghormley and Fletcher.

And to his credit, Wing Commander Nicoll tried to suggest a compromise: have the Beauforts assigned to bomb the airfields bomb the ships instead, which would cause the ships to maneuver to avoid the bombs, thus breaking up their formation and opening them up to the torpedo attack. Air Commodore Hewitt approved, and called up Wing Commander Colin Thomas Hannah of No. 6 Squadron. No can do, Hannah replied; his bombs were no good for attacks on ships. Not that that ever stopped the Japanese … Anyway, back to the drawing board with time running out, Hewitt suggested this dozen-bomber attack be pared down to three. He asked for volunteers. Who wants to be among the three lucky crews who get to make a dangerous torpedo attack in an overloaded bomber on ships in Japan's most heavily defended base in the South Pacific? Hewitt thought that all 12 crews would find this offer irresistible. They resisted. So Nicoll and the two flight commanders, Squadron Leader Owen Price and Flight Lieutenant Noel Thomas Quinn, volunteered to go. They took off together at 12:30am on November 9, arranged themselves in a "V" formation, then headed toward Rabaul.[104]

They would need that formation, as they went through a heavy thunderstorm with frequent lightning. But the weather cleared as they approached the caldera. They continued onward until they reached Talili Bay, in the Bismarck Sea on the opposite side of the Gazelle Peninsula from Rabaul. Then they went to an altitude of less than 100 feet, arranged themselves in a column with Wing Commander Nicoll leading, and headed over the strip of land into the northwest portion of Simpson Harbor. It was 2:40am.[105]

If they were hoping for a surprise by attacking from this rather unusual direction, they would be disappointed. It seemed that every antiaircraft gun in the caldera opened up at them. But as they flew through the fusillade, they could see the ships in the harbor – which were not anchored in defensive groups as Lieutenant Greentree had so adamantly insisted they were, but were instead anchored in their usual positions per Imperial Japanese Navy doctrine. All the angst back at Kiriwina had been for nothing; the mission could have proceeded as planned. The reaction of Greentree, who was in Lieutenant Quinn's Beaufort, is not recorded.[106]

Oh, well. Wing Commander Nicoll aimed his torpedo at a tanker, released, and skedaddled out. It was reported as a hit, though Nicoll did not see it. Behind Nicoll, Squadron Leader Price bravely turned his Beaufort toward the middle of a reported line of cruisers from which the heaviest antiaircraft fire was coming. Behind Price, Lieutenant Quinn saw the barrage lift as Price's bomber neared the cruisers, but in the midst of Quinn's violent evasive maneuvers, Lieutenant Greentree pointed out a light cruiser off Keravia Bay. Quinn headed there, released his torpedo, and promptly turned the wrong way to escape, flying through the heaviest of the gunfire. But fly through it he did, joining Nicoll and landing at Kiriwina at about dawn. The Japanese recorded no hits from this torpedo attack. Price and his crew never returned.[107]

The loss of Squadron Leader Price and his crew and the apparent failure of the mission caused the tension at Kiriwina, as evinced by the overly heated conference and the obvious reluctance of the Beaufort crews to take part in any torpedo attack, to snap. Two days later, however, Air Commodore Hewitt directed that Wing Commander Nicoll be transferred from No. 8 Squadron at Kiriwina and thus the front line to the command of No. 7 Squadron at Townsville on the Australian mainland. Hewitt then appointed Lieutenant

Quinn to the command of No. 8 in Nicoll's place. However, he had been beaten to the punch. A report had been sent by a senior officer of the No. 9 Operations Group to Royal Australian Air Force headquarters in Melbourne concerning Hewitt's command. As explained in a later memo to Australian Prime Minister Curtin, it already "was quite apparent that morale and discipline of senior officers in No. 9 (Operational) Group were suffering as the result of Air Commodore Hewitt's administration. Now, the situation as between [Hewitt] and his senior officers is deteriorating." Headquarters canceled Nicoll's transfer and Hewitt himself was transferred back to his earlier position of Director of Intelligence at Allied Air Forces Headquarters in Brisbane. Air Commodore Francis William Fellowes Lukis would replace Hewitt.[108]

The sacking of Hewitt represented a vindication for General MacArthur, who had opposed Hewitt's appointment in the first place, declaring him not an "adequate replacement" for his predecessor, Air Vice Marshal William Dowling Bostock, with whom MacArthur supposedly had a good relationship. However, General Kenney and General Whitehead seem to have thought highly of Hewitt, not so much Lukis.[109]

Be that as it may, it is fair to wonder if something unspoken was going on here. Lieutenant Greentree was a trained naval observer. He gave a report that could be used to justify canceling the torpedo attack. His report turned out to be very, very wrong, something one would not expect from a trained naval observer. Yet Wing Commander Nicoll immediately seized on that report to justify canceling the mission, as did the rest of No. 8 Squadron, even though they were well aware of the importance Air Commodore Hewitt placed on this mission. Hewitt tried to find a way out, and resorted to reducing the attack and seeking volunteers, but the senior officers of No. 8 ended up volunteering, which suggests that none of the other, lower-ranking pilots volunteered. Put bluntly, this could have been a conspiracy by No. 8 and Greentree to get the mission canceled because they considered any torpedo attack by the Beaufort to be too dangerous, but especially a torpedo attack made solely for the purpose of showing the Beaufort could execute an effective torpedo attack. Put simply, it was a mutiny couched in terms that did not look like mutiny. This is just speculation, however.

In the interim, the sun had come up on Admiral DuBose's force. "Thanks for taking on those bastards that were laying (in wait) for us."[110] Those were the words of Captain Anderson and his sailors to DuBose and his sailors. Laurance DuBose was the consummate professional and a well-respected commander. However, though it's nothing you can put your finger on, DuBose's after-action report on his cruiser division's South Pacific diversion seems to have a cold, sullen tone to it, especially in comparison to the reports penned by such frontline South Pacific commanders as Tip Merrill and Arleigh Burke. It makes for some jarring reading given the colorful reputation DuBose had earned as skipper of the *Portland* both during and after the Friday the 13th Battle. Maybe DuBose was just upset at losing the *Birmingham* to a shipyard as a result of the torpedo hit. Maybe DuBose was upset at being diverted at all. Maybe DuBose was both. In that light, Anderson's note of thanks was probably appreciated more than usual.

The *Birmingham* would indeed have to head back to Pearl Harbor for repairs, which is not the easiest thing with a hole in your bow. When you move, the water coming in would put pressure on the interior bulkheads not designed for that level of pressure, and, unless properly controlled, could cause the bulkheads to collapse in a cascade, which could sink the ship. Rough seas complicates the problem, and the *Birmingham* was stuck with rough seas on her way back. Every time her bow plunged into a wave, air was caught and compressed and threatened to collapse the bulkheads. A vent in the main deck near the forecastle was opened to allow the air to escape. That relieved the pressure, but in a way that became comical – now when her bow plunged into a wave, sea water would squirt from the vent, shooting almost mast-high. "We became the only ship ever to boast a geyser," Captain Inglis later wrote. The crew named it "Old Faithful."[111]

The fliers of *Kido Butai* and Base Air Force seem to have taken the remainder of November 9 off. They conducted no air attacks and it's not clear how much, if any, scouting missions they undertook. It was a missed opportunity. The *Birmingham* was headed back to Pearl Harbor for repairs, which, again, is not the easiest thing with a hole in your bow. It is even more not the easiest thing when a submarine is stalking you.[112] Admiral Kusaka understood that well enough, and vectored the submarine *Ro-104* to catch the *Birmingham*. But *Ro-104* could not find the damaged light cruiser.[113] Maybe with some aerial scouting reports the submarine could have found her.

Just because *Kido Butai* and Base Air Force took the day off does not mean AirSols did the same. The airfield at Kara was visited by 17 TBF Avengers of Marine Torpedo Bombing 233, 39 SBD Dauntlesses (33 from Marine Scout Bombing 244, a 34th had aborted, and five from Compositing 40), and 16 P-39 Airacobras. After the bombing was completed, the Airacobras split off to strafe the Shortlands area; Airacobras were really good at ground attacks. Not wanting Ballale to feel left out, another 35 SBDs (including five from Marine Scout Bombing 244) and 13 TBFs of Marine Torpedo Bombing 143, escorted by eight P-38 Lightnings, visited it.[114] Most importantly, on this day, the Seabees started construction of a runway within the Torokina perimeter. It was estimated it would be finished in 30 days.[115]

After their relaxing day off in Rabaul, *Kido Butai* and Base Air Force decided to sleep in on the morning of November 10. AirSols did not, however, and got an early start with a morning strike on Buka and Bonis by 57 Dauntlesses (39 from Compositing 24, seven from Marine Scout Bombing 244, and 14 from Compositing 40; nine had to abort but there were six spares) and 33 Avengers (five from Marine Torpedo Bombing 233, 11 from Compositing 38, nine from Compositing 40, and eight from Marine Torpedo Bombing 143) escorted by 72 fighters (24 Corsairs from Fighting 17; four Corsairs from Marine Fighting 212, eight Corsairs from 221, four Hellcats from Fighting 33, four Hellcats from Fighting 38, four Hellcats from Fighting 40; and 24 Kiwi Kittyhawks; as many as 18 fighters had to abort).[116] They reportedly put seven craters in the runway at Buka and ten at Bonis, but the SBD Dauntless of Compositing 24's Lieutenant Francis B. McIntire and his gunner Aviation Radioman 2nd Class William L. Russell disappeared during this mission. It was thought that a bomb hit on an ammunition cache at Buka may have inadvertently taken out McIntire's Dauntless, which was flying at low altitude.[117]

AirSols was just getting started. The previous night, the 3rd Marine Division requested close air support for an attack in the morning to try to unclog the trail on the right of the Torokina perimeter. The Marines had followed up the action of November 8 with an artillery preparation early in the morning of November 9, followed by an assault by elements of the 2nd Marine Raider Regiment supported by a few Stuart tanks and a weapons company.

But this is the Solomon Islands, so, naturally, the attack did not go according to plan. The US Marines had a roadblock on the trail, therefore the Imperial Japanese Army troops had to have a roadblock, too. It was only fair. The Japanese set theirs up in front of the Marines and anchored on both flanks by "impassable" swamp and jungle. Japanese troops had also closed in on the Marine roadblock during the night, so the Marine artillery bombardment went literally over the heads of the Japanese. The Americans had hardly begun their assault before they were met by an unexpected typhoon of hot lead from the famous Japanese "knee mortars" and the Nambu machine guns that had made life hell at Gifu on Guadalcanal and on New Georgia.

Because of the "impassable" swamp on either side of the trail, the Marine Raiders were stuck making a frontal attack on the Japanese roadblock. After some 90 minutes, the Marine Raiders had advanced only some 50 yards. The swamp was not so impassable to the Japanese, however, and an effort to outflank the Marines on the American right was stopped only by the deployment of the weapons company to the right rear of the American attack. The fighting continued, the Marines making a slow, grinding advance, punctuated, as fighting often is, by taunting and insults shouted from both sides. The threat was implicit: *Now go away or I shall taunt you a second time.*

The implicit threat seemed to work on the Imperial Army troops. As one Marine history put it, "quite suddenly at [12:30pm], for reasons still obscure, enemy resistance collapsed."[118] The American advance picked up steam and encountered only stragglers and snipers, and maybe some straggling snipers. By 3:00pm, the Marines had reached the junction of the Piva and Numa Numa trails. There, they dug in and sent out patrols, which found an empty Japanese bivouac area some 300 feet ahead. This action cost the Marines 12 killed and 30 wounded; the bodies of more than 100 Japanese were counted on the field.[119]

The advance was in the hands of Colonel Edward A. Craig, commanding the 9th Marine Regiment. Craig's goal was to push the Japanese outward and gain breathing room for the new airfield. To that end, he decided to dial up some close air support. There were probably some audible groans from the Marines when they found out about it.

You see, close support, whether in the form of artillery (especially naval artillery) or air attacks, had a spotty record in the Pacific War. The materiel superiority of the Allies in general and the United States in particular did not count for much if the Allied gunners and pilots could not get the Allied munitions on the target, but all too often, that is what happened with close support. Worse, also all too often, those Allied munitions landed on Allied troops.[120]

The Marines decided to do something about this problem. Based on extensive testing, they developed a matrix showing how close various munitions could land to friendly troops without hitting them. Three months before the Torokina landing, nine members of the 1st Marine Air Wing (three officers who were bomber pilots and six enlisted radiomen) reported to the 3rd Marine Division's Air Officer, Lieutenant Colonel John T. L. D. Gabbert. Gabbert organized special training for air liaisons to embed with ground units and keep in contact with air units. They practiced constantly with communications equipment. They also made sure the artillery had shells that released colored smoke. If the Japanese could have colored flares, the Americans could have colored smoke. It was only fair.

At 9:15am on November 10, a dozen TBF Avengers (six each from Marine Torpedo Bombing 143 and 233) arrived on station over the Piva River area of the Torokina beachhead in preparation for the attack. Colonel Craig had requested 18 Avengers, but AirSols was of the opinion that he would get 12 and like it.[121] This would be a historic mission for the Pacific War.

The artillery was a big part of this close air support, but it was delayed while a scouting party from the 2nd Marine Raiders returned to the Allied lines. Then the artillery started firing those smoke shells: white smoke to mark the Allied lines, colored smoke to mark the target areas.[122] Or colored smoke to mark the Allied lines and white smoke to mark the target areas.[123] The Marine histories can't seem to keep straight which was which. Fortunately, the aviators of Marine Torpedo Bombing 143 and 233 could. And did.

The friendly lines were marked and the targets were marked. With the air liaison on the ground to guide them via radio, each of the dozen TBF Avengers dropped 12 100lb bombs and strafed a 50-yard strip on both sides of the Numa Numa Trail. The bombs landed within 120 yards of friendly lines.[124]

The bombing attack was quickly followed by two battalions of the 9th Marine Regiment. They encountered no opposition, finding 30–40 Japanese dead and a lot of Japanese equipment, ammunition, and even guns, suggesting the Japanese had not only fled, but had broken. Piva village was taken by 11:00am.[125] Marine historians Henry I. Shaw, Jr and Major Douglas T. Kane explained just what the Americans had accomplished:

In the space of three days, the threat to the beachhead from either flank had been wiped out by the immediate offensive reactions of the 3d Marine Division. The attempted mouse-trap play by the Japanese to draw the Marine forces off balance towards the Koromokina flank, to set the stage for a strike from the Piva River area, had been erased by well conducted and aggressive attacks supported by artillery and air. The landing force of nearly 475 Japanese on the left flank had been almost annihilated, and at least 411 Japanese died in the attacks on the right flank.[126]

One Japanese naval history gives a slightly different take: "[T]he counterattacks of our land forces were so extremely feeble that the enemy easily occupied the areas which he desired to take."[127] But he's not bitter.

Part of that outcome was due to the close air support mission, which had been a rousing success. It was, in the words of Marine aviation historian Robert Sherrod, "the beginning of such tactics in the 'modern' sense of the term."[128]

Other missions were less historically significant but no less important to the war effort. A dozen B-25s from the 42nd Bombardment Group attacked Ballale, 11 more attacked Kara, and, that evening, still three more headed to Matchin Bay to attack a reported freighter. Captain L. J. Davidson led the B-25s of Flight Officers William A. Snyder and Jack B. Routh in a low-level left echelon run at a freighter anchored just off shore from Tarlena village in Matchin Bay. Heavy antiaircraft fire from shore complicated the run, and Davidson was only able to get two near misses as his bombs overshot the ship. Snyder "probably saved [Davidson's] plane from destruction" when instead of going after the freighter he went after the shore batteries and was able to silence them. This left an opening for Routh to drop his bomb "perfectly amidships," causing the freighter to sink immediately. This may have been the 877-ton *Giyu Maru*, which was reportedly damaged in a US Navy air attack on November 4 (probably the strafing attack by Fighting 17's Corsairs) in Matchin Bay and appears to have sunk this day. All three bombers returned to base safely.[129]

By this time, *Kido Butai* and Base Air Force had managed to drag themselves out of bed and get a brunch in. At 1:30pm, one D4Y Comet reconnaissance plane from *Kido Butai* was sent up to do some reconnoitering. Two hours later, it found two "large" transports and three destroyers 20 miles northwest of the Treasuries. But – stop if you've heard this one before – the transmitter on the D4Y was unable to raise Rabaul, so the report had to wait until it landed.[130] As much as had changed during the almost two years of the Pacific War, it's nice to know that some things stayed the same, that some traditions were maintained. And the Japanese seemed determined to maintain that tradition of the D4Y Comet making an important discovery and being unable to share it in a timely manner with headquarters because of radio issues.

Yet the Japanese were not done. Lieutenant Miyao Usuru, yet another division officer from the *Zuikaku*, was tasked with organizing a strike. At 6:00pm, they sent up three B5N carrier attack planes as scouts with no ordnance but with extra fuel tanks. At 6:50, Miyao led up eight more carrier attack planes, these from *Kido Butai* and armed with those 60kg (132lb) bombs that were useless against ships. Twenty minutes later came six more, armed with torpedoes. One of the scouts reported that at 7:45, two transports had been spotted two miles south of Mutupina. So the torpedo-carrying planes went there, where they found nothing. The enemy was actually south of Torokina.[131]

Oh, well. Details. Five carrier attack planes did sight "the enemy" and attack. Or so the Japanese say. The Americans don't actually record an air attack on this night, just some snoopers harassing Admiral Merrill's ships. Three of the Japanese were caught in searchlight beams at 9:15pm and decided to attack … something. Maybe the searchlights, which were either on shore or on a ship. The Japanese figured they had a 50-50 chance, so they aimed for the searchlights and dropped their torpedoes, which all ran up onto the beach; the searchlights had been on shore.[132]

Several attack planes chose to target the Puruata Island boat pool, killing two and wounding 13. One Kate aimed its torpedo at *PT-61*, but a tight turn by the devil boat evaded the torpedo, while a vengeful *PT-319* put a stream of bullets into the belly of another Kate as it passed overhead, causing it to crash about a mile inland from the beach. The Japanese lost five B5Ns to antiaircraft fire, including mission leader Lieutenant Miyao and the *Shokaku*'s Flight Petty Officer Sato Yasuhiko, who was captured. Two more were forced to ditch.[133]

A while later at 11:50pm, Lieutenant (jg) Masaki Yukio, a veteran naval observer in a Type 0 reconnaissance seaplane from the 938 Air Group out of Buka, reported seeing a transport on fire. He may have seen the flaming wreckage of two Japanese planes, which was reported by a Black Cat. From this report, the Japanese concluded they had sunk a transport and a destroyer. They hadn't, but believing they had made them happy.[134]

Yet Lieutenant Masaki was not done for the night. At around midnight, he reported two aircraft carriers bearing 203 degrees 26 miles from Mono Island. Not just two aircraft carriers, but ten more ships surrounding them in a circular formation. Carriers? Again? The circular formation helped confirm that it was indeed aircraft carriers and not, say, transports or motor torpedo boats. The Japanese looked for corroboration.[135]

The next day, November 11, was abnormally busy for the Japanese. It started off before dawn with a breakfast air attack by the 5th Air Force. The 43rd Bombardment Group had sent 23 Liberators (including a dozen from the 64th Bombardment Squadron) up from Dobodura at midnight to make individual attacks at Lakunai with 100lb demolition bombs and parafrag cluster bombs. They dropped their bombs, enduring antiaircraft fire and, reportedly, one Japanese night fighter, then headed back. It was a preliminary to a bigger attack to be launched later that morning, but between the time the Liberators had returned from their nocturnal attack on Lakunai and 7:00am, when a far larger strike was supposed to take off, a storm front had settled in between Dobodura and Rabaul all the way up to 35,000 feet. The attack took off on schedule, but General Whitehead recalled the planes a little before 9:00am.[136]

This aborted air strike was the last attempted attack on Rabaul by the 5th Air Force. From now on, General Kenney's fliers could focus on New Guinea, especially the Japanese base complex at Wewak. However, there were a few other errands to attend to as well.

After General Kenney's nocturnal attack, the Japanese got down to business. At 5:45am, a "reconnaissance seaplane" of the 958 Air Group, this piloted by Leading Airman Sugiki Yoshikazu, found one large aircraft carrier, one medium aircraft carrier, and approximately ten other ships in a ring formation bearing 320 degrees, distance 30 miles from Mono Island in the Treasuries. Rabaul being the city that never sleeps, Admirals Kusaka and Ozawa tabbed Pearl Harbor veteran Lieutenant Sato Masao, division officer from the *Zuiho*, as the best replacement for the deceased Lieutenant Notomi as strike commander. Sato, the admirals, and their staffs immediately got to work preparing an air strike set for dawn.[137]

While that was going on, at 7:05 a reconnaissance plane of the 151 Air Group spotted three cruisers and five destroyers heading due east 15 miles due south of Mono Island. Then at 8:45, four battleships, three destroyers, and two transports were seen between Shortland and "the right tip of Mono Island." It was apparently during this time that the dawn air strike was canceled due to thick clouds over Rabaul. The attack order was issued again, and then canceled again.[138]

Before Admirals Kusaka and Ozawa could change their minds yet again, at 9:00am, they were paid a visit by Admiral Sherman's aviators. With Marine Fighting 215's Corsairs providing air cover for the *Saratoga* and *Princeton*, the latter seems to have launched 22 Hellcats and nine Avengers and the former 36 Hellcats, 23 Dauntlesses, and 15 Avengers, but did so fashionably late, as much as an hour behind schedule due to mechanical issues with aircraft handling. Even so, they all attacked Rabaul's Simpson Harbor. Or tried to. Simpson Harbor was almost completely obscured by the thick rainstorm that was also impeding Japanese operations – the *Saratoga*'s report describes the weather over the target as "unfavorable" – so Admiral Sherman's aviators contented themselves with attacking a reported light cruiser and one "destroyer leader" followed by three destroyers just outside the harbor running at high speed toward another squall, this one over Praed Point. The Americans' opposition depends on whom you ask, with figures running from 68 Zeros to 78 (35 from *Kido Butai*, 19 from 201 Air Group, and 24 from 204) to 107 (15 *Shokaku*, 12 *Zuikaku*, 12 *Zuiho*, 19 from 201 Air Group, 24 from 204, and 25 from 253).[139] Ultimately, 107 fighters were put into the air, but not all at once. You can't just snap your fingers and make 107 planes airborne at once.

Whatever the number of Zeros, only an estimated 30–40 Japanese aircraft moved to intervene, but Commander Caldwell, head of the *Saratoga*'s air group once again directing the attack from his Avenger, later commented, "It is not known whether enemy fighters were airborne in large numbers or not but in any event it is known that our Group formation was not heavily attacked." The logistics of getting aircraft off the ground, the standard poor Japanese fighter communications and the weather likely were factors. Supposedly, the SBDs and TBFs got one "certain" bomb hit, one probable bomb hit and one probable torpedo hit on a light cruiser or destroyer leader; two "probable torpedo hits" on "a DD of *Terutsuki* Class"; and two "possible" torpedo hits on two other destroyers. Also claimed was shooting down one Zero and one "Kate." All of the *Princeton*'s aircraft returned, but the *Saratoga* lost the TBF of Lieutenant (jg) Stefan A. Nyarady, which was shot down by antiaircraft fire. Nyarady's radioman was killed, but Nyarady and his gunner, Aviation Ordnanceman 2nd Class Harlan J. Burrus, survived to be taken prisoner, only for Burrus to be beheaded November 24. The *Saratoga* lost one F6F, that of Lieutenant (jg) W. W. Culver, crashed off the carrier's starboard bow, but he was picked up by the destroyer *Grayson*.[140]

Today would be a marathon for Admiral Halsey's South Pacific command and Base Air Force. Halsey had a plan for this day: "Five air groups, we figured, ought to change the name of Rabaul to Rubble."[141] Two of those air groups, from the *Saratoga* and *Princeton*, had already attacked. You might count the night bombing of Lakunai by the 5th Air Force as a third, but neither Halsey nor General Kenney did, and the big air raid by the 5th Air Force that Halsey had requested had been washed out. Where were those other three air groups going to come from?

The answer came at 9:35am, when three more air groups, these from a second carrier task force, arrived to attack Rabaul. This was Task Group 50.3 under Rear Admiral Alfred E. Montgomery. He had the new fast fleet carriers *Essex* and *Bunker Hill* and the new light carrier *Independence*. Admiral Nimitz had assembled 11 fast carriers and a dozen battleships, together with supporting cruisers and destroyers, for his Central Pacific offensive.[142] The Bougainville offensive was still being hamstrung by what one historian called "Nimitz's over-preparation" for that Central Pacific offensive.[143] Nimitz himself was coming to realize that, so he loaned Admiral Halsey Montgomery's carrier task force, complete with its screening ships. Those screening ships consisted of Admiral DuBose's cruisers and destroyers but they had already been detached and used for possible surface action off Cape Torokina, so Admiral Halsey's staff had to scramble to find enough ships for something resembling a proper screen for three aircraft carriers. As it was, the screen they slapped together consisted entirely of destroyers, specifically the *Sterett*, *Bullard*, *Murray*, *McKee*, *Stack*, *Edwards*, *Wilson*, *Kidd*, and *Chauncey*.[144] It violated Halsey's new maxim about not throwing ships who have not worked together into combat together, but here we are.

At least the carriers' air groups had worked together, and, by a quirk of fate, had worked with some of their land-based air support as well. Similar to the November 5 air strike on Rabaul, the carriers would be able to send their entire fighter complement as escort for the strike planes because land-based fighters would protect the carriers. Specifically, Fighting 17 and 33 with 24 Corsairs and 12 Hellcats, respectively. Well, 23 Corsairs, because one had to abort. Fighting 17 had trained on the *Bunker Hill*, so it was like coming back to their home away from home away from home.[145] The carrier's combat information center even printed out a message for them: "Welcome home, Fighting-17!" And while Fighting 17 and 33 were being welcomed – and refueled – they were getting air cover of their own in the form of 16 Corsairs from Marine Fighting 212 and 221. So the air cover was getting air cover. Which was important, as the air cover being covered by the air cover would have three more Fighting 17 Corsairs forced to head back because of various mechanical issues.[146]

Under Fighting 17's and 33's aegis, Admiral Montgomery's carriers reached a point 226 miles southeast of Rabaul and south of Bougainville, where they launched 72 F6Fs (29 from the *Essex*, 27 from the *Bunker Hill*, and 16 from the *Independence*) who escorted 46 TBFs (18 from the *Essex*, 19 from *Bunker Hill*, and nine from *Independence*, plus one command TBF for *Essex*'s acting air group commander, Commander Paul E. Emrick) and

51 dive bombers, of which 28 were the standard SBD Dauntlesses (all from the *Essex*) but 23 were the new Curtiss SB2C Helldivers, all from the *Bunker Hill*. Because having single-handedly kept the US Navy in the Pacific War when literally everything else was going wrong, the Douglas SBD Dauntless dive bomber was obviously not good enough. One Helldiver pilot later explained the feelings about the Helldiver: "We knew this aircraft was meant as a replacement for the SBD Dauntless, which won glory at Midway ... Some of the men thought the Dauntless performed better over all [sic], even though the Helldiver was bigger and more powerful."[147]

So the US Navy started phasing in the Helldiver, a bigger, faster aircraft its crews nicknamed "the Beast." It proved to be a beast for pilot Lieutenant (jg) Ralph L. Gunville, who does not seem to have had complete confidence in the Helldiver. While most aircraft taking off from a carrier would fly off the bow end of the flight deck and climb away, the overweight, underpowered Helldivers would typically reach the bow end of the deck and simply drop out of sight beneath it. They would usually reappear a few seconds later, fighting to gain altitude, but all too often they did not. Gunville's did not; it had simply plopped into the water. Engine failure, something else that was common with the Helldivers. Worse, while Gunville survived the ditching, he drowned before he could be rescued, reportedly because his pockets were stuffed with extra rations for the plane's life raft. His gunner, Aviation Radioman 3rd Class E. S. Burrow, was rescued by the destroyer *Wilson*. Not a good start for the Helldiver, but then little about the Helldiver's entry into service had been good. "Early production models of the Helldiver had a lot of defects," one Helldiver pilot later explained. "It was rushed into production at a new factory in Columbus while engineering specifications were constantly being revised." The nickname "The Beast" was not meant as a compliment, and aviators quickly decided that the Helldiver's SB2C designation stood for "Son-of-a-Bitch, 2nd Class."[148]

"Son of a bitch" was probably uttered more than a few times when the Americans approaching Rabaul saw that, once again, stormy weather took over Simpson Harbor. The US Navy fliers persisted; so did a force of Japanese Zeros, who found the strike group some 40 miles from Rabaul, but instead of attacking was content to shadow the Americans.[149] And while Admiral Sherman's fliers had gotten off as much as an hour late, Admiral Montgomery's fliers got off a half hour early.[150] As a result, instead of the planned interval between attacks, Montgomery's strike arrived near the end of Sherman's attack. Once again, pilots estimated that thy encountered only 30–40 Zeros, suggesting that the Japanese fighter defense was split between the two attacks from two directions and had issues with the weather just like the Americans did.[151] The strike's escort of Hellcats reportedly repeated the tactic of the November 5 attack by sticking tightly with their charges.[152] A tactic not used on November 5 was downing a Zero by dropping an appropriately named drop tank onto it, but that reportedly happened this day. With the Japanese dropping their fuel bombs into formations of enemy aircraft, and as often as Allied aircraft had to dodge falling drop tanks from their own fighters, it seemed like an obvious thing to try, at least if one was out of ammunition. If it was intentional at all.

At any rate, there were multiple witnesses to an incident in which a falling drop tank struck a Zero, which proceeded to spin out of control into the ground and explode.[153] Spectacular and effective, or at least more effective than the fuel bombs, which is not saying much.

At least one of the bombing results was spectacular as well. *Bunker Hill* Helldiver pilot Lieutenant R. P. Friesz dove on a destroyer near the eastern end of Keravia Bay and claimed he got a hit on the target's fantail and, according to Bombing 17 commanding officer Lieutenant Commander James E. "Moe" Vose, who helped put the *Shokaku* out of action at Santa Cruz, "apparently [set] off its depth charges." The circumstances of this attack, if not its location, suggest the target was the destroyer *Suzunami*. The *Suzunami* was new, completed only the previous July with a flock of sister ships of the *Yugumo* class. When the Americans arrived, the *Suzunami* was reportedly near the mouth of the harbor loading torpedoes. During an enemy air attack is a time peculiarly suited for not loading torpedoes. One bomb, either on the torpedoes or the depth charges, resulted in an earth-shattering kaboom, and the *Suzunami*'s brief wartime career was ended. Ending with her were skipper Commander Kamiyama Masao and 147 officers and men.[154]

The Helldivers would claim to have sunk one cruiser (heavy or light) with three bomb hits, one "three-stack" light cruiser with three bomb hits, and yet another light cruiser with two bomb hits. They claimed to have damaged one destroyer with one bomb hit.[155] Though Lieutenant Commander Vose had been an early supporter of the SB2C Helldiver, calling it "a damn good airplane," he was much less so after losing seven of the Beasts to operational accidents during Bombing 17's training on the aircraft; this mission did nothing to harness that decline in opinion. Vose would say that, except for folding wings, which the Dauntless lacked – a critical consideration for the cramped hangar decks of US Navy carriers – "the SB2C offered little improvement on the SBD … the SBD would be my choice."[156] Alas, it was not his choice, nor the choice of most bomber pilots in the Navy and Marines.[157] Those who still flew the Dauntless claimed one hit on a heavy cruiser, and one hit on each of two light cruisers.[158]

Less successful were the aerial torpedo attacks by the Avengers. The issue was not just the weather, but also the performance of the Mark 13 aerial torpedo, which recalled the bad ol' days of perfectly aimed torpedoes somehow still missing the *Hornet* or thunking off the side of the battleship *Hiei*. The *Independence* reported that one of her TBF's torpedoes ran at right angles to the direction in which it was launched. One or two more "failed to run" and just sank into the depths.[159] The *Bunker Hill*'s Avenger crews reported two or three torpedoes that hit "a heavy cruiser" but failed to explode, while two more ran under it. Three more were believed to have "run on erratic courses."[160] Overall, Admiral Montgomery's fliers claimed one light cruiser and two destroyers sunk with a further two heavy cruisers, one light cruiser, five "destroyer leaders," and three destroyers damaged.[161] The overestimation of damage inflicted was almost Japanese in its scope. Almost.

Attacking Rabaul is always a very dangerous proposition, as the losses bore out. They lost to combat four Hellcats. Two were from the *Independence*, one that of Ensign Bascom

Eugene Gates, Jr, last seen with a Zero on its tail, the other of Lieutenant Earl Willis Marsh, last seen parachuting into the mouth of St George's Channel. One was that of the *Essex*'s Ensign Robert E. Kapp, which on the way out took a 20mm shell from a Zero under the cowling and caught fire, requiring Kapp to ditch just north of Ralavana Point; he was never seen again. The *Bunker Hill*'s Ensign C. J. Husted, Jr, disappeared when his division was involved in a particularly vicious dogfight with about a dozen Zeros. The *Bunker Hill* also lost the TBF of Lieutenant R. H. Higley, who was delayed in taking off, never rendezvoused with his unit, and was never seen again. Two more *Bunker Hill* Avengers suffered severe damage from enemy fire. One, that of Lieutenant (jg) Henry Clayton Carby, Jr, already plagued by a faulty drop mechanism that would not release his torpedo, made it back to the carrier, but on landing plowed into three of the crash barriers, probably a consequence of the 207 bullet holes in his TBF. Lieutenant William F. "Red" Krantz was not so lucky. While maneuvering to get away after releasing his torpedo, Krantz took a hit that nearly inverted his Avenger and cut the oil line. The tough TBF managed to stay aloft for about 150 miles, but the engine seized up some 40 miles northwest of Buka, compelling Krantz to ditch; he and his two crew were rescued from the bush of New Britain the following March. The Dauntless of the *Essex*'s Lieutenant James (jg) Winfred Walker and gunner Aviation Radioman 3rd Class John Thomas, which on its way out took a 20mm shell from a Zero, burst into flames, and crashed in the channel just north of Cape Gazelle.[162]

To top off the morning of mayhem, 42 B-24 Liberators from AirSols (12 from the 372nd and 12 from the 424th Bombardment Squadrons of the 307th Bombardment Group, the rest from the 23rd and 31st Bombardment Squadrons of the 5th Bombardment Group) who had staged in to Munda, each armed with six 1,000lb bombs, showed up five minutes later. They, too, were flummoxed by the stormy weather, but also by adhering to the Army Air Force's standard operating procedure in bombing from the high altitudes of 16,000–20,000 feet. The 307th ended up bombing moving targets at sea, which even the 307th's history admits was "not one of the strong points of the B-24." Colonel Marion D. Unruh, commander of the 5th, led his "Bomber Barons" down to a more reasonable 8,500 feet through heavy fighter opposition and "a veritable wall of AA fire" to bomb a "cruiser," but they were unable to see the results. Dropping to a similar altitude were the Liberators of 424th Squadron Lieutenants James Jelley and Emilio Ratti so they could make a second run over Simpson Harbor after their bombs hung up in the racks on the first. Zeros made a head-on approach at both bothersome B-24s, succeeding in shredding Jelley's Liberator, even sending a 20mm shell into his instrument panel. Jelley was wounded, his co-pilot knocked unconscious, and four others were wounded, two mortally. With Ratti escorting him, Jelley's B-24 was able to stagger away from Rabaul, get over water, and even find a US Navy destroyer; actually, Admiral Merrill's task force, which was hanging out off the Treasuries. Expecting to have to ditch – also not one of the strong points of the B-24 – Jelley ordered everyone who could to bail out. Five did so; all were picked up by Merrill's ships. Jelley indeed ditched the Liberator; a quick rescue by a Dumbo ensured he and his co-pilot would live to fight another day. Despite these efforts, Admiral Halsey wrote that the AirSols attack achieved "unsuccessful results."[163] This air attack seems ineffective and mediocre in almost every way, except for one thing: this was the first attack on Rabaul by AirSols and the first attack on Rabaul by the 13th Air Force. They would take over for the 5th Air Force in bombing Rabaul.

Even with the overestimation of damage inflicted that was almost Japanese in its scope, Admiral Halsey was not happy with the reported haul from these air strikes. "Due to unfortunate weather conditions," he later wrote, "the strike was not coordinated as planned and was not overly successful."[164] And that was just the reported results, not the actual results, which were not then known. Morison admits that no one "could tell who hit what during the attack," though the *Suzunami* seems pretty clear.[165] She was the only ship actually sunk, but the Japanese did admit damage to several other ships. One was the light cruiser *Agano*, Admiral Osugi's flagship. The *Agano* was the recipient of a Mark 13 aerial torpedo in her stern, blowing off the very end of the stern and damaging her propeller shafts and after engine room, but leaving her rudder unscathed; losing your stern but keeping your propellers is a pretty neat trick, and keeping your rudder at all, let alone undamaged, is an even neater trick. Also receiving a Mark 13 aerial torpedo in the stern was the destroyer *Naganami*, another survivor of Empress Augusta Bay. Unlike the *Agano*, however, this hit seems to have blown off her entire stern aft of the Number 3 5-inch mount. There was no buffing that right out. Unnavigable, she had to be towed back into Rabaul by the destroyer *Makinami*. Light cruisers *Noshiro* and *Yubari* and destroyers *Urakaze* and *Umikaze* were slightly damaged by strafing.[166]

It certainly was not Halsey's hoped-for haul, though one Japanese history said, "Huge damage was sustained by our surface craft."[167] You can't attack what ain't there. The November 5 attack by the *Saratoga* and *Princeton* had worked too well in that regard. The Japanese were too scared to base anything larger than a light cruiser at Rabaul now. Perhaps Halsey's ire was really over the inability of the attacks to finish off the monster heavy cruiser *Maya*, immobilized since the November 5 attack. But the *Maya* was hidden by the squall that had protected Simpson Harbor.

The purported ineffectiveness of the air attack did nothing to lessen the apprehension of the Japanese concerning the safety of their ships at Rabaul. Later that day, Admiral Kusaka ordered the *Maya*, along with the *Noshiro*, destroyers *Kazagumo*, *Samidare*, *Wakatsuki*, *Hayanami*, and *Fujinami*, and the submarine tender *Chogei* to form up and leave for Truk.[168]

Implicit in that order was yet another loss in confidence in the Sea Eagles, a loss in confidence not limited to Combined Fleet. According to the *Essex*'s Commander Emrick, "The enemy once again showed that he is unwilling to press home attacks on a good compact group of planes."[169] He also noted "their failure to press home their attacks against any but single planes."[170] However many Zeros Admirals Kusaka and Ozawa put up, they would claim 35 enemy aircraft destroyed and 11 probables for the loss of nine fighter pilots killed. The 201 Air Group lost two; the 204 one, with one more hospitalized with serious injuries; and the 253 two, including Leading Airman Shibayama Sekizen. But, once again, those deaths included a damaging command loss: Lieutenant Araki Shigeru, a junior fighter division leader from the *Zuikaku*. Another officer lost was from the *Zuiho*: Reserve Ensign Yamada Shoichiro. Lost from the *Shokaku* were Petty Officers 1st Class Tachizumi Kazuo and Isobe Ryuzo.[171] And the day was not done yet.

The Japanese had seen these carrier planes attacking Rabaul and had jumped to the conclusion they had come from a carrier. At 10:45am, two Yokosuka D4Y Comets from *Kido Butai* took off on a so-called "search and contact" mission to find the carriers and pin them for the follow-up air strike. Which indeed followed up 15 minutes later. The commander of the *Zuiho*'s air group, Pearl Harbor veteran Lieutenant Sato Masao, would lead 80 Zeros (32 from the 204 Air Group under Lieutenant (jg) Morita Heitaro; a composite flight of 12 from the 201 Air Group and three from the 204 under an Ensign Katayama from the 204 Air Group; 15 from the *Shokaku*, nine from the *Zuikaku*, and nine from the *Zuiho*), 23 Aichi Type 99 carrier bombers (16 from the *Shokaku* and seven from the *Zuikaku*); four Yokosuka D4Y Comets from the 501 Air Group under observer Flight Chief Petty Officer Morita Itsuo, and 14 Nakajima B5N carrier attack planes (five from the *Shokaku*, five *Zuikaku*, and four *Zuiho*) in what the Japanese called a "pursuit attack." The Zeros from Base Air Force were to tie up the defending American fighters for the following strike from *Kido Butai* to break through and get the carriers.[172]

But just as the Americans had been plagued by bad luck, at least in terms of the weather, the Japanese were also plagued by bad luck. Seven of the carrier bombers (three from the *Shokaku*, three from the *Zuikaku*, one not recorded) had to abort because of "inadequate maintenance." At 11:22 the search Comet from the *Shokaku* reported "operations normal" some 70 miles from Rabaul, but was never heard from again. A half hour later, the search D4Y from the *Zuikaku* reported a powerful enemy force "300 degrees and 120 nautical miles from Mono Island, course 230 degrees, speed 24 knots, weather ..." The message was cut off, but given the record of the D4Y in finding enemy carrier forces and then suffering radio failures that prevented getting that information to the people who could use it until it was too late, getting any kind of report out at all must qualify as a victory. The strike aircraft themselves receiving the message is just gravy, considering. But, this being a D4Y Comet, not everyone who needed this information received it. The air strike turned toward the reported location of the enemy, but it seems Lieutenant (jg) Morita, who has been called "a young officer with little combat experience," did not receive this report and, unable to find the target, had his 32 Zeros from the 204 Air Group turn back to Lakunai after being in the air for two hours with no particular place to go. Ensign Katayama also did not receive the updated contact reports and had his 15 Zeros turn back as well. The Japanese termed this "poor communications."[173] This left only 33 fighters from *Kido Butai* to escort the strike planes. Granted, the scout planes were from *Kido Butai*, so they may have had better communications with the other aircraft of *Kido Butai* than they did the Zeros of Base Air Force. Having all of Base Air Force's fighters turn back because they were unable to receive the reports from the scout planes suggests that maybe someone did not give the correct radio frequencies to Morita and Katayama. Maybe if more Zeros had radios, they could have found the enemy, but that extra four knots of speed gained by not carrying a radio was helpful in fleeing the enemy.

One Yokosuka Comet circled Admiral Montgomery's carrier force "at tremendous altitude – where [American] radars could not track or guns shoot," which was apparently 20,000 feet, or 8,000 feet above the level of the carriers' protective fighters. Recovery of the air strike on Rabaul was completed at 11:45, and Montgomery started preparing to launch a second strike.[174] But there were indications that the Japanese were not going to take these latest attacks lying down, or even sitting down. At 12:25pm radar on the *Independence* detected an unidentified aircraft approaching from the northwest at a distance of 97 miles. She vectored four fighters of the combat air patrol to intercept. At 12:53 the bogey was seen on radar turning northeast. The fighters reported that at 1:09 they had shot down a "Zero" 38 miles northeast of the *Independence*, noting that when they first encountered the aircraft it had been above 25,000 feet. Oddly, at 12:26pm radar on the *Independence* detected an unidentified aircraft approaching from the northwest at a distance of 81 miles. The *Essex* vectored fighters in to attack this intruder; these fighters reported shooting down one Japanese plane, but did not specify the type. One or both of these contacts may have been the same aircraft as the "dive bomber" the *Bunker Hill* recorded fighters encountering at 12:53, which in turn may have been the *Zuikaku* D4Y that had reported finding the carriers before its message was cut off.[175]

At 1:20, the *Essex*'s radar showed "many bogeys" 104 miles away. By this time, however, most of the aircraft from the first strike had been rearmed and refueled. With carriers now almost full of fully armed and fueled aircraft, there really was not much choice as to what to do next, and at 1:28, the carriers started launching their aircraft. Montgomery was obviously hoping to get everyone launched before the Japanese arrived, but just in case he could not, he tried to time everything so that the most dog-fight capable aircraft were in the air. The *Essex* launched 16 Avengers and 31 of her 34 Hellcats.[176] The launch did not go smoothly, however. Upon takeoff, the TBF piloted by Lieutenant (jg) Charles Denby-Wilkes, Jr spun into the sea. The destroyer *Kidd* was detached to drop back and fish the aviators out of the water. Her skipper Commander Allan Roby did not appreciate being ordered to perform rescue work when an air attack was imminent.[177] In fact, it was actually worse than Roby believed. When Denby-Wilkes' Avenger crashed, its torpedo was released and ran hot, compelling evasive action by the *Kidd* and even the *Essex*.[178] That was just … insulting. The *Kidd* was able to rescue Denby-Wilkes and gunner Aviation Machinist's Mate 2nd Class R. H. Garwood, but Aviation Radioman 3rd Class Ray Donald Bright was declared dead on board the *Kidd* from shock and drowning.[179]

Meanwhile, the *Bunker Hill* sent up 21 Hellcats, one of Fighting 17's Corsairs, and five Avengers.[180] The *Independence* sent up 12 Hellcats and two Avengers.[181] But the launching of the second strike came to a screeching halt when the Japanese air strike arrived. Though the fact that his aircraft were refueled and rearmed made the choice fairly obvious, Admiral Montgomery had gambled that he could get his second air strike into the air before the

Japanese arrived – and lost. For losing that bet, his carrier task force would be facing an air attack by *Kido Butai* with fully armed and fueled Avengers and, especially, dive bombers spotted for launch on the flight decks of the *Essex* (19 SBDs, each armed with a 1,000lb bomb) and *Bunker Hill*.[182] The *Essex*'s air officer Commander C. D. Griffin would later write, "From the Air department vulnerability point of view the attack came at exactly the wrong time, i.e., while launching."[183]

By that same token, it seems the Japanese had tried to time their attack to catch the US Navy carriers with decks full of fully armed and fueled aircraft, indicating it was developed by *Kido Butai*'s Admiral Ozawa and his staff.[184] They had not quite timed it perfectly, but they were close. One bomb landing among fully armed and fueled aircraft had been enough to turn the Japanese carrier *Akagi*, then flagship of *Kido Butai*, into a raging inferno that forced her scuttling at Midway. Now the roles were reversed. The *Essex* and *Bunker Hill* were depending on their fighters to prevent them from suffering a similar fate.

And something went wrong with those fighters. It's not entirely clear what. First contact between the Japanese and the defending American combat air patrol was made 40 miles out. The fighter director, the *Essex*'s Lieutenant Commander F. G. Marshall, Jr, asked, "How many?" An unidentified pilot blurted out over the voice radio, "Jesus Christ! There are millions of them! Let's go to work!"[185] Which, to be fair, did answer the question, though Marshall did not have complete confidence in the reported figure. And, as was pointed out later, he still had no confirmation of altitude and no information concerning the composition of the attack or the formation it was using.

Fighting 17's Lieutenant Commander Blackburn, whose voice radio transmitter had gone out, forcing him to transfer command to Lieutenant Charles A. "Chuck" Pillsbury, said that his Jolly Rogers got warning of the incoming attack when the Japanese were only 30 miles out – too close for the Corsairs to get into proper interception position.[186] Commander Marshall complained afterwards that the land-based fighters of Fighting 17 and 33 did not have radios with VHF capability (though, unlike Japanese Zeros, they did have radios), which limited the communications from the fighter director.[187]

The result was that, according to the *Independence*, "There were over 100 fighters in this Task Force and not over 20 intercepted the raid at 35 miles from the Task Force."[188] It's the thought that counts.

And the Americans thought they were about to be swamped. The description of "millions" of incoming Japanese aircraft was only a slight exaggeration of what the US Navy believed was happening; according to the *Bunker Hill*, "a less exaggerated, less colorful estimate would place the number (of enemy aircraft) at about 160 consisting of about 75 dive bombers, 50 fighters, and 35 torpedo planes."[189] Admiral Montgomery estimated "55–60 Vals, 15–20 Tonys, Haps, and Zekes, 45–50 Kates, and 5–8 Bettys."[190] The reporting name "Tony" is a reference to the Japanese Army Air Force Kawasaki Ki-61 *Hien* Army Type 3 Fighter. "Hien" means "flying swallow," but one would be more likely to find an African or European swallow in a Japanese Naval Air Force formation than a Japanese Army Air Force fighter. There is no indication of any panic whatsoever among the US Navy officers, sailors, or aviators, so the massive overestimation of the size of the Japanese attack is most likely reflective of this being the first time *Essex*-class carriers had faced a large and determined enemy air attack.[191] These impressions remained hard to shake even after the war; James C. Shaw, who as lieutenant commander was the assistant gunnery officer on the *Bunker Hill*, went so far as to call the Japanese attack "one of the largest anti-carrier strikes since the start of the war."[192]

Now firmly ensconced as "one of the largest anti-carrier strikes since the start of the war," the formation of 35 Zeros, 20 Aichi D3A Type 99 carrier bombers, and 14 Nakajima B5N Type 97 carrier attack planes, all from *Kido Butai*, split up, apparently in order to attack the carriers from different directions.[193] This was not exactly playing chess while the Americans played checkers, but it was superior in terms of tactics to what the Japanese had been using lately. Even so, it did not go according to plan. Admiral Montgomery himself called the attack "a poorly coordinated affair"; the *Essex*'s Commander Emrick said, "There was no sign of coordination between the enemy [dive bombers] and [torpedo bombers]." The skipper of the *Bunker Hill*, Captain J. J. Ballentine, would not go quite that far and instead called the attack "almost coordinated."[194] Generally, though not from ideal positions, especially altitude, the US Navy fighters were able to engage the Japanese strike planes. Generally, but there was an exception: the first wave of Vals got through completely untouched: "a beautiful flat V unopposed by fighters."[195]

This was a bad thing. Midway was now reversed. Japanese carrier dive bombers attacking American carriers with fully armed and fueled aircraft on their flight decks. A very dangerous scenario for the Americans. There were significant differences from Midway, however. With their radar, the Americans were aware the Japanese were coming. The task force was in an antiaircraft formation, with the destroyers forming a protective ring around the carriers, who were themselves arranged in a triangle, the *Essex* at the point with the *Independence* and *Bunker Hill* on her starboard and port quarters, respectively.[196] And with 5-inch dual-purpose guns, 40mm Bofors, and 20mm Oerlikons, the American *Essex*-class carriers had much better antiaircraft weaponry than *Kido Butai*.

Eight Vals came in at the *Essex* from the starboard bow. As the Aichis reached their pushover point, Admiral Montgomery bellowed to the fleet, "Get your guns ready and let's blast these bastards right out of the sky!"[197] The carrier bombers approached in columns, with each Type 99 pushing over from the same point, one after the other. As Montgomery put it, "Groups of single planes dribbled in one at a time."[198] How one could have a group of a single plane he left to the imagination. Only after the Vals in front had started their dives did a pair of US Navy fighters start to hack away at the Vals in the back. The heavy volume of antiaircraft fire, especially from the *Essex*, convinced several of the carrier bombers to take evasive action, which did nothing to help their aim.[199] Nor did their technique help their aim; Montgomery observed, "With the possible exception of three Vals who dove on the *Essex* using fairly steep dives, the remainder of the dive bombing attacks were only of fair caliber."[200] It was apparently during this attack that a Val pulled out of its dive on the *Essex* right in front of the Hellcat of Ensign Charles E. Watts, who had literally just cleared the flight deck of the *Bunker Hill* as the last fighter launched. Watts rather nonchalantly shot down the carrier bomber and then started to gain altitude as he usually would.[201]

It was also apparently during this attack that a bomb detonated in the water about 75 feet off the *Essex*'s port quarter. Hot fragments peppered the carrier's hull above the waterline up to the gallery just below the flight deck – and the fully fueled SBD Dauntlesses, each carrying a 1,000lb bomb still spotted for launch. That pretty much spiked the remainder of the launch of the second attack. The SBDs engines were stopped and the aviators and deck crews were ordered below. Shortly thereafter, flight operations were halted and orders issued to remove all bombs and torpedoes from the strike planes and move them back to the magazines.[202] That was as close as the Japanese got to the *Essex*.

For now. Maybe 11 other carrier bombers dove on the *Independence*. They threatened to overwhelm the light carrier, who targeted only five with her guns. Ensign J. B. Thomas had just taken off in his TBF and did a 180 to pass down the light carrier's port side when his top gunner, Aviation Ordnanceman 3rd Class V. C. Thomas, found a Val pulling out of its dive on the *Independence* and exposing its belly. The gunner rubbed it with machine-gun fire all over the Val's fuselage and engine, sending it flaming into the drink. But the bombs were still falling toward the *Independence*. One exploded only 30 feet from the *Independence*'s island superstructure, reportedly because it was hit by a 40mm antiaircraft shell from the Number 3 mount. That may not have counted as a near miss, but the bomb that struck the water and exploded 75 feet from the stern did. The after gun tubs were showered with fragments. Another bomb splashed even closer – 20 yards – but did not detonate, nor did another bomb that splashed 2,000 yards off the port quarter, but one did explode 50 yards from that same port quarter. Zeros strafed the *Independence*'s flight deck with 7.7mm machine-gun fire, causing slight damage. Considering she also had fully loaded aircraft on the flight deck, the *Independence* got off very lucky.[203]

For now. The attack was not over. Another wave of maybe nine bombers dove on the *Bunker Hill*. But they had not gotten through without resistance, and instead of an organized and coordinated attack on the carrier, they all "straggled in one by one from all directions."[204] The *Bunker Hill* responded with her formidable array of 5-inch, 40mm Bofors, and 20mm Oerlikons, though the Oerlikons tended to hit the bombers only after they had completed their dives. The most the Japanese could manage on the carrier was four near misses. Two bombs splashed about 50 yards off the port quarter at about frame 170. It seems to have been one of these bombs that sent shrapnel on deck, piercing a fuel tank on one of the planes spotted there, causing it to spew flammable (and inflammable) aviation fuel on the Number 6 40mm Bofors quad mount and its crew, but there was no diminution of fire or, for that matter, actual fire. Another two bombs splashed about 50 yards off the starboard bow at about frame 80. Further away, one bomb hit the water about 150 yards off the starboard quarter, another dropped late by a struggling Val detonated 1,000 yards off the starboard beam.[205]

By now the defending US Navy fighters had fully engaged the Japanese, which created problems for just about everyone. There were US Navy Hellcats and Corsairs and a few Avengers duking it out with *Kido Butai* aircraft well within the range of US Navy antiaircraft guns, who were firing as fast as they could. Lieutenant Commander Blackburn called it "Technicolor bedlam, and then some"; you probably had to be there. The Technicolor bedlam caused issues for Lieutenant Commander Marshall trying to direct the fighters and tell friend from foe on the radar, and the antiaircraft gunners who struggled to identify fast-moving aircraft at low altitude that passed in the blink of an eye or aircraft taking what looked like an aggressive posture toward the ship when that posture was actually directed at a Japanese plane.[206] At one point Admiral Montgomery had to admonish his antiaircraft gunners, "Knock off firing at our own planes."[207] There were also the problems of how antiaircraft gunners were to handle dogfights, as the *Bunker Hill* experienced when her gunners took under fire a Val who was being pursued by a Corsair who was being pursued by a Zero.[208]

Not yet making their formal appearance were the deadly Nakajima B5Ns, the Kates, which had been the bane of Allied navies since Pearl Harbor, where they had been devastating. They were also devastating in the Indian Ocean, and they contributed to the sinkings of the US Navy carriers *Lexington*, *Yorktown*, and *Hornet*.

Part of the Kates' infamy came from one Lieutenant Commander Murata Shigeharu. Murata had been a veteran of the "Manchuria incident" in China and had led the carrier attack planes of the *Akagi* at Pearl Harbor. After the *Akagi*'s loss at Midway, he was transferred to the *Shokaku*, whose Nakajima B5Ns he would command. Murata could credibly claim to be the best torpedo attack pilot in the world.

Except for Pearl Harbor, perhaps Lieutenant Commander Murata's brightest moment came at Santa Cruz. He led a well-coordinated attack on the *Hornet* that turned into a chess match between Murata and the *Hornet*'s skipper Captain Charles Mason. The carrier's maneuvering had put Murata's attack planes approaching from the stern, the worst place from which to launch torpedoes at a ship. Mason kept trying to keep his stern facing Murata and Murata kept trying to catch up to a good angle from which to launch. Finally, he found his angle, released his torpedo and turned away. His torpedo, one of two to hit the *Hornet* in this attack, lanced into her engine room, depriving her of power and mobility and ultimately leading to her loss. But the *Hornet* had gotten a measure of revenge, plunging her stinger into Murata, by shooting down his plane in flames.

When the Japanese airstrike split off into its groups to attack from different directions, the Type 97s appear to have split into two such groups, probably to attempt a hammer-and-anvil attack that occurs from two different directions such that the target cannot turn to avoid torpedoes from one direction without exposing its beam and therefore biggest target to those from the other. If this was the plan, it failed. The *Essex*'s skipper Captain Ralph Andrew Ofstie described the Kates' attacks as "not well executed" because they all approached from astern and did not take advantage of available cloud cover.[209]

A stern chase is the most difficult angle from which to launch a torpedo attack. Captain Ofstie seemed to blame the Japanese aviators for attacking from astern, and indeed it might have been that they botched it. However, when the attack started, Admiral Montgomery's task force had been heading northwest. It immediately turned to head roughly south or just east of south and basically zigzagged on a course roughly south, then late in the attack made a sharp turn to the northwest.[210] If the two groups of Type 97 carrier attack planes had worked themselves ahead of Montgomery's carriers to attack off both bows in the classic anvil strike, it is entirely possible that Montgomery's turn threw them off and left the Nakajimas behind the task force and having to play catch up. Lieutenant Commander Murata could attack successfully from astern and did, in the case of the *Hornet*. But Murata was dead. So was the *Hornet*, but a new *Hornet* of the *Essex* class would be commissioned by the end of the month, while there were no new Murata Shigeharus coming out of Japanese flight academies.

Regardless of the cause, the Japanese torpedo planes were left in two separate groups making a long stern chase just to launch their torpedoes. The first torpedo attack came between 2:04 and 2:20pm from what was described as "21 Kates and a few Bettys"; if the hypothesis that the Type 97s had split into two groups for an anvil attack is taken as true, there were probably just seven Kates.[211] The long chase left the Nakajimas vulnerable to the defending US Navy fighters and even several Avengers, who, though ordered to hide in a cloud during the attack, found themselves in a perfect position to take down their opposite numbers. As Torpedo 9 explained, "It is not Squadron doctrine to act as fighters in attempting to drive off attacking dive-bombers and torpedo planes. However under certain conditions it may be necessary." They did complain, "Enemy much faster than TBF aircraft. Torpedo load on TBFs cut down maneuverability. Armament inadequate for fighter work."[212]

Nevertheless, the Japanese of *Kido Butai* would not be dissuaded by gunfire from the ships or their aerial defenders and held their course to aim their torpedoes, evasive maneuvers be damned. Commander Emrick called their technique "daring, persistent, and suicidal" and went on to say, "Steady straight and level flight was held despite heavy [antiaircraft fire] from our forces and even when under fire by our [fighters]."[213] The head of Torpedo 9, Lieutenant Commander D. M. White, noted that the Japanese torpedo planes "used no evasive tactics whatever, holding course and altitude under both aircraft and [antiaircraft] attack."[214] Even so, the Kates "failed to press [their] attack home" in the opinion of Montgomery.[215] According to the *Bunker Hill*, the Kates' "only objectives were apparently to get rid of the torpedoes and head for home."[216] They got rid of at least three torpedoes, which were seen to penetrate the circle of destroyers protecting the carriers; one passed no closer than 200 yards astern of the *Bunker Hill*.[217] But there were no hits. And the cost to the Japanese was disastrous – all of the Kates were shot down.[218] One was credited to Fighting 33's Lieutenant Johnny Kleinman, who, right after shooting down the Kate, took a 20mm round from one of the *Bunker Hill*'s Oerlikons in his windshield. His face was cut up, but his flight goggles saved his eyes, and Kleinman made it back to Ondonga air base and healed in full.[219]

It's unclear when the second wave of Nakajima B5Ns attacked, or tried to attack, but it was probably several minutes. The *Independence* had used the slight lull before the first torpedo attack to launch six more F6Fs. A swarm of US Navy fighters overwhelmed the Kates more than 20 miles from the carriers. The Kates never got into range to launch their torpedoes. Again, all of them were shot down.[220]

The remaining Japanese Zeros and carrier bombers turned back toward Rabaul, but the US Navy pilots, embarrassed by having so many fighters in the air and barely even making contact with the Japanese before the strike planes made their attacks, would vengefully slash at the retiring Japanese aircraft, mostly at the dive bombers. So ended what the Japanese would call the Third Air Battle off Bougainville, which the Japanese would later describe as "a furious and heroic 20-minute battle."[221] According to one Japanese Naval Air Force history, "excellent results were obtained, but the losses on our side were also heavy."[222] The "excellent results" included "2 aircraft carriers hit by one or two bombs." How two aircraft carriers could be hit by one bomb is not addressed; presumably in the case of one bomb hit they would cut the bomb in half. Additionally, they claimed one cruiser or destroyer "[b]lown up and sunk," which is so much better than being just plain sunk. Also, "3 cruisers or destroyers set afire," and two enemy planes shot down.[223] Officially, anyway. *Kido Butai*'s Zero pilots claimed five shot down and one probable.[224] For once, Japanese claims were not comical and were actually closer to the truth than Allied estimates, though they still overstated the damage inflicted, but more along the lines of the normal overstatement, which suggests maybe Admiral Ozawa took a hard look at the battle damage assessments and imposed some sanity on them.

On the other hand, the Japanese may simply have had no one to claim damaging enemy ships. As aviation historian Michael Claringbould put it, this attack was the "biggest air power calamity the Japanese had suffered in the theater to date."[225] The cost of this attack was simply catastrophic: of the 20 carrier bombers that attacked Admiral Montgomery's carriers, only three returned; of the 14 carrier attack planes that tried to attack the US Navy carriers, none returned; on top of that, two Zeros and two "reconnaissance planes" – Yokosuka D4Y Comets – were shot down.[226] What's especially curious about these statistics is the lack of losses among the Zeros, even though they were badly outnumbered by the defending US Navy fighters, at least once the majority of those fighters were fully engaged. Montgomery noticed, "[F]ighter cover for the enemy's attack group was almost entirely lacking (or were [sic] very little in evidence)."[227] Then again, one of those two Zero pilots killed was Lieutenant Sato, the leader of the *Zuiho*'s air group who had taken part in the Pearl Harbor attack and also served with the 12th, *Zuikaku*, and *Kaga* air groups. The other was Warrant Officer Sato Hitoshi of the *Shokaku*.[228] It's fair to wonder if Lieutenant Sato, leading this attack, was shot down early, thus contributing to the attack losing cohesion and the seeming hesitancy of the Zeros to engage their opposite numbers.

Whatever sanity was imposed on the battle damage assessments by Admiral Ozawa, the "excellent results" were enough for the Imperial Information Bureau to put out a statement to the Japanese news media:

The Imperial Navy air arm sighted a powerful enemy mobile unit comprised of aircraft carriers and warships in the waters to the west of Mono Island. Without losing any momentum, the Imperial Navy Wild Eagles carried out devastating attacks, blitz-sinking one cruiser, inflicting slight damage on two aircraft carriers, and setting three cruisers, possibly large destroyers, ablaze. In addition, two enemy planes were shot down. The number of Imperial Navy planes that crashed onto the enemy or have yet to return totaled 30. This is indeed regrettable.[229]

Regrettable, indeed, for Admiral Ozawa. And for others. One grizzled US Navy veteran commented, "Ships fightin' ships is right and so's planes fightin' planes, but ships fightin' planes just ain't natural."[230] Hell, yeah! The *Essex*'s Captain Ofstie was all too aware of how close a call this attack had been for the Americans:

These operations by carrier based [sic] aircraft, against and in the vicinity of the strongest enemy position in the South Pacific, resulted in serious material damage to enemy ships and the destruction of a large number of his aircraft and his flying personnel. On our side, damage to ships was negligible, and losses incurred by our air forces were very small comparatively. It must be remembered, however, that enemy dive bombers and torpedo planes <u>did</u> reach attack positions, and that all carrier decks – spotted with numerous bomb-loaded planes – were only narrowly missed. There is a rather close margin, in these affairs, between victory and disaster. [Emphasis in original.][231]

There is a lot of wisdom in these words from Captain Ofstie. One learns more from defeat than from victory, but Ofstie wanted everyone to understand just how close to a defeat this was. A bomb released a second earlier or a second later, a bomb dropped at a slightly different angle, and the bomb lands among the fully loaded and spotted aircraft on the flight deck, and this attack becomes the fast carriers' version of Tassafaronga. Ofstie did not have to explain it to the veterans of Guadalcanal. The *Bunker Hill*'s Lieutenant Commander Shaw noticed that they "*really* took fright now that [the attack] was over, imagining from experience what those bombs might have done." (Emphasis in original.)[232]

Just when you thought Rabaul was down and close to being out, it inflicts a damaging bloody nose on the US Navy. Perhaps not a strategic defeat for the US Navy, but a strategic delay and a major embarrassment. All that, if only a bomb had been released a second earlier or a second later, or dropped at a slightly different angle. This "Third Air Battle of Bougainville" was a far closer battle than has generally been recognized. It is not a criticism of the US Navy to point this out, except to the extent that something did go wrong with the direction of the defending fighters. The preparations by Admirals Halsey and

Montgomery for this operation were excellent, but it must be remembered that, in the success or failure of any operation, the enemy gets a vote, too.

For the moment, however, the enemy was voting for retreating back to Rabaul to lick their wounds. And the US Navy fliers were voting to go back to base. The vast majority of the shore-based fighters just disappeared, heading back to their own bases, low on fuel. A few were too low in fuel, like Fighting 17's Ensign Ira C. "Ike" Kepford. Kepford noticed his fuel gauge was on empty. It's a guy thing to see a fuel gauge on "empty" not as a warning, but as a challenge, a challenge to continue running the engine to get as close to actually empty as possible without actually emptying the fuel tank.[233] But Kepford was a little more mature, and calculated that he was 150 miles from the nearest runway. So he asked to land on one of the carriers so he could refuel. That carrier ended up being the *Bunker Hill*. Kepford landed with five gallons left in his tank. Kepford just wanted a quickie pit stop and off he would go back to Ondonga. The crew of the *Bunker Hill* had other ideas.[234]

As Ensign Kepford got out of his Corsair, he was mobbed by crewmen, who were determined to give him the red carpet treatment, at least as much red carpet treatment as is possible in a place with no carpeting because it's a fire hazard. Kepford was led to the bridge, where Captain Ballentine happily greeted him. "Welcome home, Ike! *Bunker Hill* thanks you and the rest of Fighting Seventeen. I doubt that we'd have made it without your help." It was a sentiment shared by all the officers and men of the *Bunker Hill*. They wanted to appropriately thank the entire squadron, but since Kepford was the only squadron member present, he would have to do. Ballentine continued, "Anything we have is yours. What would you like?"

Ensign Kepford was left speechless. He was only an ensign, and here he was being treated as a rock star by one of the most respected skippers in the fleet. It took Kepford a moment to regain his composure. "Er, I could use some coffee, sir."

Within seconds, the master of a brand-new, complete-with-new-ship-smell fast fleet carrier handed the ensign a cup of hot coffee. Because after a day of fighting in the insufferably hot and humid South Pacific, what could be more refreshing than a cup of steaming coffee?

Probably still in some shock from the skipper playing waiter, Ensign Kepford then requested to take off to rejoin his squadron. Captain Ballentine agreed, and after a half-hour break during which his Corsair was refueled, rearmed, and checked out, Kepford was catapulted back into the air for a happy return to Ondonga.

It was late in the day. All the aircraft that had been launched for the second strike at Rabaul were now low on fuel. They would have to land and refuel. By the time that was done, it would be close to dark. Too late for an air attack – at least a US Navy air attack. Consequently, at 5:20pm, Admiral Montgomery decided to call it a day and turned back toward Espiritu Santo. He kept his ships at 25 knots until dark, then slowed to 20. Fuel was becoming an issue, but Montgomery wanted to put as much distance between his force and Rabaul as possible.[235] He probably knew the old adage, "No matter where you go, there you are."

And Base Air Force was trying to find where he was. At around 8:30, the *Essex*'s radar picked up multiple unidentified aircraft, bearing 35 degrees True (roughly north northeast) at a distance of 90 miles. About eight minutes later came more unidentified aircraft, bearing 335 degrees True (roughly north northwest) at a distance of 90 miles. At 8:49 it was more unidentified aircraft, bearing 355 degrees True (just west of due north) 35 miles away at low altitude. These contacts closed to within 25 miles of the American carriers, then pulled away. Two minutes later it was even more unidentified aircraft, bearing 50 degrees True (just south of northeast) 39 miles away. They started circling that area at low altitude. One more aircraft appeared, bearing 290 degrees True (roughly west northwest) distance 33 miles. This one also closed to within 25 miles of Admiral Montgomery's ships, then pulled away. The aircraft that had been circling headed away to the east northeast.[236]

The *Essex*'s Executive Officer, Commander Fitzhugh Lee III, and Fighter Director Lieutenant Commander Marshall thought Japanese torpedo planes were combing the area of their afternoon attack hoping to find Admiral Montgomery's carriers for a literal moonlight torpedo attack.[237] They were.

Not happy with the "failure of the daylight air raid," Admiral Kusaka decided on nightdark air raids. Two G4M land attack planes were sent out on search and contact missions at 4:55pm.[238] Kusaka sent out 16 G4M land attack planes (for reasons known only to the admiral, he divided them into flights of five and 11) to search for the carriers on what was probably another search and contact mission. As they combed the waters south of Bougainville, to the extent waters can be combed, Kusaka tabbed Lieutenant Hada Kiyoshi of the 702 Air Group to "[organize] an attack unit composed of members of Base Air Force medium attack plane units with ample night action experience" – whether it was good experience or not is not specified – followed at 5:00pm by six more from the 751 Air Group.[239]

Search and contact succeeded again, sort of. Although struggling with scattered showers, at 6:00pm one of the scouting Mitsubishis reported three battleships, two heavy cruisers, and four destroyers 35 miles southwest of Mutupina. Aircraft were left to shadow the Allied ships while other scouts continued southward to look for the carriers. An hour later, six G4M Type 1 land attack planes of the 702 Air Group started taking off, albeit not all at once. And one of them, Flight Chief Petty Officer Miyahara Masakazu, aborted and returned to Vunakanau after becoming lost. Meanwhile, at 8:10pm, another scout G4M reported an "aircraft carrier (or possibly a transport)" – the Japanese did have difficulty telling the two apart – escorted by "ten-odd" cruisers or destroyers in a triple column formation 20 miles west southwest of Mutupina.[240]

The former force of "battleships" was actually Admiral Merrill's Task Force 39. His force was somewhat reduced from the Battle of Empress Augusta Bay, but still had his flagship light cruiser *Montpelier* and her fellow 6-inch-armed cruisers *Columbia* and

Denver, screened by Captain Burke's Little Beavers, with the commodore riding in the destroyer *Charles Ausburne*, with the *Claxton*, *Stanly*, *Spence*, and *Converse*. Merrill's assignment was to protect the latest convoy of reinforcements for the Torokina beachhead. This involved tank landing ships *LST-334, -390, -398, -397, -446, -447,* and *-472*; the fast destroyer transports *Stringham, Waters, Dent, Talbot, Kilty, Crosby, Ward,* and *McKean*; and, acting as escorts, destroyers *Saufley, Philip, Renshaw, Eaton, Sigourney,* and *Waller,* the last named carrying the convoy's commander, Destroyer Squadron 22 skipper Captain J. E. Hurff.[241]

This convoy arrived at Torokina at around 7:00am and started unloading. In an hour, the fast destroyer transports had unloaded all their passengers; they proceeded to take on board some 200 casualties. They left at around noon, heading southwest from Bougainville with the destroyers *Conway* and *Philip* as escorts. The fast destroyer transports made their way to the Treasuries, where the *Conway* and *Philip* bid them farewell and headed back to screen the tank landing ships still at Torokina.[242] The rest of the transports completed their offloading at 7:30pm and began heading back.

Admiral Merrill's cruiser force was continuing to cover Captain Hurff's tank landing ships, and at 6:37pm went to general quarters. On Admiral Halsey's order, the destroyer *Eaton* had been detached from the convoy to join Captain Burke's destroyers in relief of the *Spence*, who was crippled by dirty boilers that had not been cleaned in four months. But that relief would not come quite just yet because Merrill expected a nocturnal Japanese attack. "The moon was practically full. The sky was clear in patches but generally studded with thunderheads and occasional rain squalls. It was an ideal night for enemy plane operations."[243]

Maybe the admiral meant that ironically, or that from the American standpoint it was an ideal night for enemy plane operations, because the Japanese would not agree. It was 6:50pm when unidentified aircraft began to appear on Admiral Merrill's radar. He arranged his cruisers in an antiaircraft formation with the cruisers forming a triangle in the center of a tight circle of destroyers. The aircraft approached the US Navy flotilla from the port quarter. More Japanese aircraft joined in, and soon there were four or five Bettys some 8,000 yards away, dropping red flares to mark the American force and warn that the force included cruisers.[244]

The attackers were five G4Ms from the 702 Air Group. They appear to have split into two groups, probably in another effort at an anvil attack. Admiral Merrill headed for the nearest rain squall at a heightened speed of 25 knots. But not speedy enough. At 7:54 the destroyer *Claxton* raised the alarm that she had just seen a torpedo to starboard headed for the flagship *Montpelier*. That was guaranteed to get the admiral's attention. Merrill ordered an emergency 90-degree turn to port. The torpedo (or at least a torpedo) was seen passing to starboard on a parallel course.[245]

As the malicious Mitsubishis of the 702 Air Group tried to close in on the American ships, Admiral Merrill ordered another emergency turn, this one 90 degrees to starboard, at 7:57:30. It would mess up a few torpedo firing solutions. At 8:00pm, the task force opened fire on their tormentors, a task complicated by the presence of a friendly night fighter, who had already been mistaken for enemy. The ships turned 90 degrees to port again.[246] The admiral seems to have had a thing for 90-degree turns, which, to be fair, were both sharp turns that would mess up firing solutions and easy to keep track of. Keep it simple, stupid. Merrill understood the principle well, as did Captain Burke, so that's what they were going with.

The alleged squall was getting closer and closer, now off the starboard bow. Admiral Merrill ordered a 60-degree turn to starboard to get to it more quickly. The Bettys appeared hesitant to press their attack, like the Kates against the carriers that afternoon, perhaps even more so. While the Kates at least held their course through a torrent of gunfire before releasing their torpedoes at the first opportunity, the mere sight of gunfire aimed at them would cause the Bettys to turn away.[247] Slightly after 8:00pm, the night fighter reported seeing a Betty go down in flames; seeing one of their own go down may have spooked the Japanese aviators.[248] Not "daring, persistent, and suicidal," these guys. Well, not daring or suicidal. They were persistent. For a while, anyway.

At 8:06, Admiral Merrill's ships reached the squall, or what they had thought was a squall. There was a lot of clouds and lightning, but no rain. How disappointing. But it was still effective. Night with clouds is not a good formula for locating enemy ships when you don't have airborne radar. The Japanese started heading away.

According to the Japanese, the 702 Air Group attacked the "battleship force" between 7:45 and 8:15pm Solomon Islands time, but at 8:30 visual contact with the enemy "was broken." The Japanese reported hitting a battleship, a cruiser, and a destroyer with torpedoes, but lost two G4Ms in the process. They had feared contact with this group of enemy ships "would be lost on account of the poor weather"; it can be inferred that the poor weather caused the loss of contact at 8:30, especially since that was shortly after Admiral Merrill's ships entered the strangely rainless rain squall.[249]

But not a complete loss of contact. The Japanese seemed to be lurking in the dark maybe nine miles away. Maybe it had something to do with the unidentified surface contact the *Montpelier* and *Denver* picked up at 8:12, 24,000 yards away on a bearing of 345 degrees True. The radar return looked fairly large, and the *Claxton* was sent out to determine what it was. It turned out to be the *Saufley*, returning to Captain Hurff's convoy after recovering Fighting 33's Ensign Frank Stalfa, who had ditched in his F6F.[250]

After about a half hour of steaming in the rain watching the Japanese aircraft poke around – one came to within two miles of Admiral Merrill's ships, drawing aircraft fire that drove it off but also compelling an emergency turn – the US Navy ships left their sanctuarious squall and headed due south. The radar showed one friendly plane and four enemy. Though the Japanese appeared on radar, the idea that they were skulking out there in the dark – one in particular liked to "hang around" about four miles to the southwest – and could not physically be seen proved understandably disconcerting for the American sailors, who undoubtedly knew the *Chicago* was sunk in similar circumstances and likely knew the *Birmingham* was hit as well.[251] They started seeing things and shooting at things that may or may not have been there.

At 8:42, the *Converse* opened fire at "something" on her starboard side. The *Columbia* also started firing at what she described as a "bogey" on her starboard – or port – side. The *Saufley* from Captain Hurff's convoy reported sighting a Rufe. The *Pringle*, also from Hurff's convoy, reported that she shot down a Rufe. A floatlight was reported to the east southeast. A minute later, the floatlight was confirmed to be the planet Venus.[252] At least they did not try to shoot it down. That we know of.

After about an hour of watching the Japanese aircraft on radar creeping in and out, but not necessarily attacking, Admiral Merrill's ships entered another squall, this one with actual rain. And a lot of it. He would keep playing. He did not think the heavy stuff was going to come down for quite a while. But the Japanese had other ideas. They melted away in all their beautiful wickedness, the last plane loitering at range of 11 miles, before Merrill determined the attack was over at 10:15pm.[253]

The attack was indeed over, to the extent it was an attack at all. The Japanese would later claim to have hit one battleship with one torpedo, one cruiser with one torpedo, and one destroyer with one torpedo; that last "was confirmed" to have sunk. Admiral Merrill's ships reported sighting only one torpedo and that one missed. Merrill was mystified as to why the Japanese had ended their attack when they had not even pressed it particularly seriously and had not gotten one hit. And had lost at least three Bettys to boot. Well, two, actually, confirmed by Base Air Force, though, given that it had "confirmed" sinking an enemy destroyer when no ships at all were sunk, that is of dubious value.[254]

The six G4Ms of the 751 Air Group under Lieutenant Commander Adachi Jiro were still out there. Their job had been to find and attack the reported "aircraft carrier (or possibly a transport)" escorted by "ten-odd" cruisers or destroyers in a triple column formation 20 miles west southwest of Mutupina.[255] They seem to have split up to poke blindly in the gloom for the enemy until shortly after 10:00pm, then headed back to Vunakanau in frustration.[256]

The carriers were out there, to be sure, but Admiral Merrill had acted as bait, unwittingly. According to the report from the carrier *Essex*:

> The enemy was combing the area in which we were attacked in order to launch a night torpedo attack. It is believed possible that these bogeys failed to detect TF50.3 because other bogeys to the north contacted TF39 and reported their contact to the night torpedo planes. This appears to be the only logical explanation since the torpedo attack did not materialize on Task Force 50.3, but did actually attack Task Force 39.[257]

Not one to be dissuaded so easily, Admiral Kusaka got Admiral Ozawa to order up four Nakajima B5N carrier attack planes (two from the *Shokaku*, two from the *Zuikaku*), armed with actual torpedoes this time, led by the *Shokaku*'s Lieutenant Ono. Scraping up four B5Ns was no small feat since by this time *Kido Butai* was seriously running out of torpedo planes. But five hours of night flight netted nothing and they returned to Vunakanau around midnight-ish.[258]

The Japanese latest nighttime efforts to find the US Navy carriers had been sent up in driblets and either attacked the wrong target or none at all. As the *Essex*'s report put it, "That the enemy failed to attempt an all-out night torpedo attack against so lucrative a target which he knew was in the area, and under ideal conditions prevailing (full moon and excellent visibility), can only be satisfactorily explained by his physical inability to do so."[259]

That was it for the Japanese air attacks for the day (well, day and night). That was it for a lot of things. During these attacks, Admiral Sherman's Task Force 38 with the carriers *Saratoga* and *Princeton* and Admiral Montgomery's Task Group 50.3 with the *Essex*, *Bunker Hill*, and *Independence* was dissolved. All five carriers were ordered to the central Pacific to join Admiral Nimitz's new offensive.

They would not be the only ones leaving the South Pacific.

CHAPTER 7

"GUADALCANAL – MINUS MOST OF THE ERRORS"

While the Sea Eagles of *Kido Butai* were taking their shot at Admiral Montgomery's carriers, Captain Hara Tameichi and his destroyer *Shigure* were entering the anchorage at Truk. His welcome was not what he expected.[1]

When last we left everyone's favorite combustible cavalier commodore, the *Shigure* was leading transports *Mitakesan* and *Tokyo Maru*s out of the Simpson Harbor anchorage, bound for Kavieng. It was the first leg of the return of the overworked *Shigure* and her mercurial commodore to Japan for some rest, recuperation, repair, and refit.

"We reached the open sea quickly," Hara would recall. "The day was bright and sunny, the water calm. Everything was as pleasant as a holiday cruise. Enjoying the fresh breeze on the bridge, my thoughts turned to my many missions and sorties while based at Rabaul."[2]

As they crept along the southwestern coast of New Ireland, Captain Hara pondered his experience in the South Pacific since his arrival the previous spring. Two of the biggest problems the Imperial Navy had faced in the South Pacific were the enemy's radar-controlled gunfire and skip-bombing. Hara was satisfied with himself, as he frequently was, at having "whipped" the problem of radar-controlled gunfire. He actually had not, just been one of the fortunate beneficiaries when the opening round of that gunfire landed like an avalanche on the first, hapless ship the enemy targeted, because while that ship was usually overwhelmed and sunk (see, e.g., the *Niizuki*, *Jintsu*, and *Sendai*), the enemy had a tough time hitting much else after that. But that false satisfaction led him to a thought that was truly a reason to be very, very proud: he had led the *Shigure* through this entire period without losing a single man.[3]

The little convoy appears to have gone around New Hanover to approach Kavieng from the west, instead of going in the straits between New Ireland and New Hanover to approach Kavieng from the south. Maybe a few too many bad experiences with enemy mines or submarines in or around the straits. So, instead, according to Captain Hara, the convoy went through the Ysabel Strait off the western tip of New Hanover. It was a clear night sky full of stars as the convoy rounded New Hanover and turned east to head to Kavieng. That was when the *Shigure*'s radio started squawking with messages the Japanese could not understand. The messages were in code and not a Japanese code. Worse, the signal was strong; that meant it was nearby. Enemy aircraft.[4]

So much for the holiday cruise, Captain Hara thought. He ordered the *Shigure* to battle stations, and raised her speed to 18 knots so she could cruise around and in between the *Mitakesan* and *Tokyo Maru*s while laying down a smokescreen. A smokescreen is kind of silly to use against aircraft when you're at sea, because the aircraft can just fly over it; it's much more effective in a place like Simpson Harbor, where attacking aircraft have less room to maneuver, or Kavieng, so close, yet so far away. The transports strained their engines to work up to 16 knots in a desperate effort to reach that increasingly dubious haven.

One of the *Shigure*'s lookouts reported two planes, 50 degrees to starboard. Captain Hara saw them heading directly for his ship and decided they were "[d]efinitely bombers." They swung parallel to the *Shigure* on an opposite course and were swallowed up in the dark far astern. After a few moments, a lookout shouted, "Planes returning on port quarter!"

Well, that wasn't good. Even worse, Captain Hara thought, they were coming in at low altitude. They were going to skip-bomb the *Shigure*, he figured. That was the one problem Hara had not solved. Until he did.

"All guns prepare for antiaircraft fire 150 degrees to port!" Then the commodore turned to the *Shigure*'s navigation officer, Lieutenant (jg) Tsukihara Yoshio, who was apparently serving as helmsman, and bellowed, "No zigzagging. We will follow a straight course!"

Tsukihara was dumbfounded. He followed Captain Hara's order, but during this tense time he repeatedly questioned it, a distraction the commodore did not need. The *Shigure* built up her speed to maybe 30 knots.

When the aircraft were "a few hundred feet away," Hara gave the order to open fire. "Guns and machine guns responded instantly," he later wrote. "With shrieking, spine-quivering sounds" – and with the helmsman still asking if they should still go straight – "the bombers flew past our masts from port to starboard and two bombs fell. They skipped all right, but over the ship, missing their target by seven or eight meters."

The attackers headed away to the south into the night. An uneasy five minutes passed in which there was no sign of the planes. Then word came from the radio room: "Enemy pilots are transmitting in plain language." The *Shigure*'s resident English expert, Ensign Chosa Hiroshi Chosa, answered, "OK boys, I'm coming to hear what they have to say." And he left the bridge.

A minute or two later the ensign announced, "One enemy plane reporting its controls are damaged, is giving its position in code. Another plane says its left wing is damaged and it is going to ditch." The *Shigure*'s bridge crew cheered. Chosa continued, "The enemy base replies that a flying boat is rushing to the rescue. The locations, unfortunately, are given in unreadable ciphers. Wait … The planes say, 'Thank you,' and they are now ditching!"

Or not. Ensign Chosa's translation may not have been completely accurate. Exactly who attacked the convoy is unclear, but if Captain Hara or the US 5th Air Force was fuzzy on the date, the attacker was probably a single radar-equipped B-24 Liberator, *Art's Cart*, from the 63rd Bombardment Squadron of the 43rd Bombardment Group. The Liberator crew reported finding a 7,000-ton tanker, a light cruiser, and a destroyer just off the western tip of New Hanover on the night of November 8. The *Art's Cart* braved heavy antiaircraft fire that destroyed one of its wing flaps and slashed an aileron control cable to drop three 1,000lb bombs from 1,500 feet. Reportedly, the result was one direct hit and two near misses that sent the tanker under in six minutes.[5]

Or not. Obviously, no ships were sunk or even damaged; Japanese records do not confirm a sinking in this area at this time. By that same token, the B-24 *Art's Cart* was not shot down or forced to ditch, though its damage probably convinced it to warn Dobodura that it might have to. It returned to base safely.

Hara would later explain that he kept the *Shigure* on a straight course because: 1. Turning as part of evasive maneuvers would slow the destroyer down; and 2. Enemy bomber pilots anticipate the target taking evasive action, so if the target takes no evasive action, that would throw off the bombers' aim. Well, OK, then.

The *Shigure* slowed down and rejoined the transports. In Captain Hara's words, "We resumed our 'holiday cruise' toward Kavieng." A holiday cruise that involved stopping at a tiny, remote, malaria-infested South Pacific port, unloading cargo, and then leaving, which they did the morning of November 8.

So, back to the holiday cruise. All the way until midmorning. Then Captain Hara was informed that the *Shigure*'s sonar was disabled. All efforts to repair it had failed. That was, well, a bad thing, especially on the route to Truk that was a known hunting ground for enemy submarines.

The commodore quickly came up with the best solution under the circumstances. He ordered the depth charge racks manned at all times. He also ordered the two transports to spread out in column, keeping a distance of 1,500 meters between them. The *Shigure* took position between them, but to starboard.[6]

They got through the rest of the day and night all right, and also the next day and night. But by the morning of the third day, November 10, the depth charge crews were exhausted. The commodore responded by ordering intense antisubmarine exercises. He did sympathize with his sailors, but he had a duty to protect the largely defenseless transports. If the men could hold out for one more day, everyone would be safe at Truk.[7]

At around noon, Captain Hara ordered a break from the exercises. The sailors spread out on the deck to unwind. The commodore took a bit of a breather himself, hardly noticing the wake of a torpedo cutting through the whitecaps ahead of the *Shigure* moving from starboard to port. He was shaken free of his stupor only by the underwater explosion amidships of the *Tokyo Maru* some 700 meters off the port bow.

Hara ordered "fighting speed" – 24 knots – and charged down the track of the torpedo wake, depth charges ready. The *Shigure* dropped a dozen depth charges. No results.

Then another five. Nothing.

Three more. Nothing.

One more. Still nothing.[8]

"The submarine had gotten away," Hara later wrote. "Not surprising, I thought, with a skipper clever enough to score with just one torpedo. I stood stunned and angry on the bridge. My sluggish reaction had let the submarine escape."[9]

The *Shigure* headed back to her wounded charge. The *Tokyo Maru*'s engine room and Number 4 hold were flooding; she lost power and drifted to a stop.[10] The destroyer circled the transports while keeping an eye on where her enraged commodore thought was the location of the submarine.

Which was the USS *Scamp* under the direction of Lieutenant Commander Walter Gale Ebert – the same submarine with the same skipper who had sunk the *Kamikawa Maru* in the same area. Ebert had actually fired four torpedoes from her stern tubes at the *Tokyo Maru* at a range of 1,000 yards. One hit, while a second had what is called a "sympathetic detonation," which was a premature detonation caused by the shock wave of the first torpedo hitting. The other two missed. Evidently, the problems of US Navy torpedoes still had not been fixed.

Now, as Lieutenant Commander Ebert later explained:

For the fourth time in our career we were faced with the problem of finishing off a stopped ship. It is the general opinion among those that haven't tried it that it is a push over. On the other hand it is one of the toughest assignments a submarine can have, and compares with penetrating a patrolled harbor. It should not be forgotten that the escorts know we are there, and pretty accurately where.[11]

Pretty accurately despite not having sonar. The *Shigure*'s first attack, which Lieutenant Commander Ebert described as "close," forced the *Scamp* to go deep to 350 feet. The second attack was "[v]ery accurate" and the third "[s]till close." The fourth was maybe 200 yards away. Not bad for a destroyer without sonar. Captain Hara could have bragged (and don't think he would not have) had he known Ebert had given his depth charge attacks a thumbs-up. Even so, however accurate these attacks were, Ebert did not report any damage resulting from them.

So, Lieutenant Commander Ebert approached the *Tokyo Maru*. After two hours of making certain everything was in order, the *Scamp* fired three torpedoes from her bow tubes at a range of 5,500 yards. The first torpedo ran for 25 seconds, then exploded. Unfortunately, the Mark 14 had neglected to hit the target first, or even reach the target.

According to Ebert, the *Shigure* "was on us in a flash." The destroyer dropped two depth charges that were "close" and passed directly over the *Scamp*. The *Shigure* made another pass but did not drop any depth charges. At 4:22pm, more than an hour later, the *Scamp* returned to periscope depth to see the *Mitakesan Maru* had started towing the *Tokyo Maru*, unnavigable and listing to starboard.

At that point, the two opposing commanders decided to call it a day. Captain Hara was frustrated with his nonfunctioning sonar and his own perceived lethargy. Lieutenant Commander Ebert was frustrated with his malfunctioning torpedoes – it was at least the 13th (maybe the 15th) torpedo from the *Scamp* to detonate prematurely; out of 17 torpedo salvoes launched by the *Scamp*, at least 11 and as many as 13 involved a premature detonation, which on nine occasions was the first torpedo launched. Rear Admiral Ralph W. Christie, in charge of all Southwest Pacific submarines, had helped design the Mark 6 exploder with the now-infamous magnetic influence feature and refused to accept that the magnetic influence feature simply did not work because of those pesky laws of physics. Christie had threatened to court martial anyone who disabled the magnetic influence feature. But Ebert would rather risk a court martial than his boat. He would not make another attack until the magnetic influence feature had been disabled on all the Mark 14 torpedoes remaining on board.[12]

Captain Hara went on with his "little convoy," as he put it, now inching toward Truk. But the *Tokyo Maru* continued to take on water, her starboard list continued to increase. That evening, some eight hours after the transport had been torpedoed, her skipper ordered her abandoned. The tow was cut, and Captain Hara had the *Shigure* move in to take the *Tokyo Maru*'s 70 officers and sailors. They were recovered just before the *Tokyo Maru* took her final plunge.[13]

Captain Hara was not happy. This was the first ship under his command, the first ship under his escort, he had ever lost. Hara consoled himself with the knowledge that the ship's entire crew had been rescued and her cargo had already been delivered. Plus, after he had a long time for reflection:

> I would like to salute that submarine and her skipper for the skill of the approach, torpedo firing, and evasion in the attack on *Tokyo Maru*. I do not know if more than one torpedo was fired, but that was all I saw. The sub did a very good job.[14]

Hara had no idea. The *Scamp*, her skipper Lieutenant Commander Ebert, and her crew had sent some prominent Japanese vessels to the depths, including the veteran seaplane tender *Kamikawa Maru* and the submarine *I-168*, executioner of the original carrier *Yorktown*. And they were not done yet.

But Captain Hara and his *Shigure* were. That was the situation when they arrived at Truk with the *Mitakesan Maru* around 1pm-ish on November 11. He went to the heavy cruiser *Atago*, Admiral Kurita's flagship, to make his report to Admiral Kurita and his chief of staff Admiral Koyanagi.[15]

Except no one seemed interested in hearing his report. "Everything on board was in a turmoil," Hara recalled. And not just from having the workers from the repair ship *Akashi* still trying to repair the *Atago*'s damage from the November 5 carrier air attack on Rabaul. "Staff officers were running around and would not even listen to my report," Hara later wrote. "Kurita, they said, was 'tied up,' and Koyanagi was with him."

Captain Hara was finally able to snag Admiral Koyanagi while the chief of staff was on his way to the restroom. Koyanagi stopped and shook hands with the commodore, saying, "I'm glad to see you again, Hara."

Captain Hara went on to describe his return trip from Rabaul, including the loss of the *Tokyo Maru*, for which he blamed himself. Admiral Koyanagi waved his hand and said, "That's all right, perfectly all right. You did a wonderful job. No one else could have done better. I am glad you had no casualties."

Hara tried to go into more detail, but the chief of staff seemed dazed, like he was not listening to him. Hara paused his report. The silence shook Admiral Koyanagi out of his trance. "Oh, I beg your pardon," he stammered, embarrassed. "My apologies ... well, Hara, let me explain my rudeness. The enemy struck Rabaul again, this very morning, and mauled it badly. That's why we've all been tied up, and ... well ... indeed, upset."

Admiral Koyanagi described the carrier attack on Rabaul. He finished with, "Excuse me, Hara, I must get back to the strategy conference. Oh, say, Admiral Kurita wants you to escort cruisers *Myoko* and *Haguro* when they leave tomorrow morning for Sasebo. Good luck. See you again." And Koyanagi literally ran away.

Hara, stunned at the news about Rabaul, was in a hurry to leave too. The repair crews at Truk were unable to get the *Shigure*'s sonar working again, so when the destroyer left at 9:00 the next morning, she was depending on the *Myoko* and *Haguro* to provide the antisubmarine capability. Heavy 8-inch-armed cruisers are not exactly known for antisubmarine prowess, but their floatplanes could spot submarines at periscope depth. If they still had their floatplanes, that is. What they did not have was Admiral Omori. A few days after the Battle of Empress Augusta Bay, Omori, in the words of one historian, "was relieved of his command for displaying little skill and less resolution."[16]

While Captain Hara was schmoozing at Truk, his rival Lieutenant Commander Ebert was furiously (in more ways than one) deactivating the magnetic influence features of the Mark 6 exploder in all his remaining torpedoes. Once that was done, the *Scamp* surfaced just before dawn on November 12 and boldly sailed on the surface in broad daylight.[17]

Four distant explosions were heard a little before 9:00am, so Lieutenant Commander Ebert went to investigate. Just after 9:00am, he saw "tops of heavy cruiser," so he had the *Scamp* submerge and start to approach. The sea was "the glassiest ever seen," which could put the *Scamp* in danger as the periscope would show. Ebert now saw a large destroyer well ahead of the cruiser, which was keeping a straight course but effecting radical changes to its speed.

With that complication in mind, Lieutenant Commander Ebert launched six torpedoes. One hit "under stack" with an explosion that lasted seven seconds. The escort charged at the *Scamp*, so he went deep.

Lieutenant Commander Ebert was satisfied that the damage caused by the seven-second explosion would not just buff right out. He began to consider the cruiser. It "resembled none of the silhouettes supplied," and Ebert wondered if it was a new class of ship.

But before he could consider it much further, the *Scamp* had to avoid the cruiser's angry escorts. Ebert reported hearing four explosions; he wondered if they came from the cruiser. The first counterattack consisted of eight depth charges "well laid astern," according to Ebert. The second was six depth charges, also "well laid astern." Throughout the day, the escorts would drop depth charges intermittently; they were apparently all "well laid astern," whatever that means.

It was 11:30am before Lieutenant Commander Ebert could get back to periscope depth. When he finally took a look, well, his frustrations come through in his patrol report: "Another stopped ship! Why don't they sink or keep going?" The cruiser was dead in the water and down by the bow, with her escorting destroyers between her and the *Scamp*.

Lieutenant Commander Ebert surfaced after dark and began making a night approach on the disabled cruiser. Patrolling aircraft forced the *Scamp* to submerge again. After about an hour, he surfaced again at 11:23pm and continued his approach. And then he saw another submarine.

Not to worry. The submarine was the USS *Albacore* under skipper Commander Oscar Emil Hagberg. Hagberg had something of a dilemma. At 12:25am on November 10, the *Albacore* was running on the surface when she sighted a four-engine bomber dead ahead, two miles away, at an altitude of 200 feet. That was not a good thing. Hagberg sounded the diving alarm, but about 20 seconds later, the aircraft dropped a stick of bombs, which near missed the *Albacore*'s bow.

The bombs "knock[ed] out all auxiliary power, and ma[de] a shambles out of the ship. Everything movable changed location, other objects broke their moorings, and the ship was plunged in darkness." Worst of all, the submarine had dived before the main induction could be closed, and as a result it was filled, very nearly causing the boat to sink right then and there. As it was, for the next 2½ hours, the *Albacore* bounced between depths of 30 feet and 400 feet, at one point having an up angle of 25 degrees. "This was a terrific blasting," Commander Hagberg reported, "and we really started to fight to save the boat."[18]

They were able to surface again at 3:16am, and Commander Hagberg was able to take stock of the *Albacore*'s situation. Most of the damage consisted of loose gauges, air leaks, an oil leak that could not be located, grounded electrical gear, and a lost suite of radio antennas. The crew fashioned one so they could signal Brisbane of their damage situation. Then Hagberg had the *Albacore* submerge again so they could make repairs.

This was just the latest of what one pair of submarine historians called "a nightmare patrol."[19] It was worse than Commander Hagberg knew. The *Albacore*'s attacker had not been Japanese, but a B-24 from the 5th Air Force. Even worse, it was the second attack by a B-24 from the 5th Air Force within the last 48 hours. The first one was while the

Albacore was stalking a convoy, when B-24s showed up over the convoy, but ignored it and attacked the *Albacore* instead. The submarine never saw her attacker. That first bombing caused no damage. It was probably just one of those things.

Considering his boat "hors de combat," which sounds like a snack to be eaten while shooting someone, Commander Hagberg had the *Albacore* stay submerged making repairs until about 7:30 that night. Brisbane had responded to his report by ordering the *Albacore* to patrol to the north, if able to do so. No self-respecting submarine skipper would turn that down, so Hagberg had the *Albacore* head north while making more repairs, figuring that by the time she found a target, she would be able to attack.

The *Albacore* spent all day on November 11 finishing what repairs she could while she made her way northward. Finally, she surfaced around 7:30pm on November 12 in her assigned patrol area. Just before 11:00pm, she sighted a "dim shape" due north. Commander Hagberg approached to investigate. The *Albacore* found two destroyers circling around a "large ship" that was stopped. Unfortunately, one of the destroyers turned her searchlight on to the *Albacore*'s bridge. She charged at the submarine, and Hagberg ordered another dive.

More than four hours later, the destroyers were still dropping depth charges on the submerged *Albacore*. It seemed like the depth charges were dropped in such a pattern that indicated the Japanese were more interested in showing Commander Hagberg they knew where he was and in keeping the submarine down than they were in sinking it. But the *Albacore* could not stay submerged long in the shape she was in. She managed to escape, but so did the Japanese.

The ship the *Albacore* had said was similar to a *Yubari*-class light cruiser was the same ship the *Scamp* had torpedoed and afterward wondered if it was a new class of ship. It was, or at least it was one the Allies had not really seen before. It was the light cruiser *Agano*.

The *Agano* had taken a Mark 13 aerial torpedo in her stern area during the November 11 attack on Rabaul. The damage was very serious; the very end of the stern was blown off, and her engines and some of her propeller shafts were damaged. Strangely, the rudder, normally damaged almost any time the stern is hit, was not damaged at all. The *Agano*s had little in the way of armor but were heavily compartmentalized, which limited the flooding from the loss of her stern. Her crew managed some emergency repairs to get her navigable, though she would still be slowed by the damaged propeller shafts, and early on November 12 she left Rabaul in the company of the destroyers *Urakaze*, *Hayanami*, and *Fujinami*.[20]

Already struggling along while her stern area was practically held together with duct tape, the *Agano* could not take much more damage. But she did that very morning, some 250 miles north northwest of Kavieng, when one of the *Scamp*'s Mark 14 torpedoes plowed into her starboard side underneath the bridge. The explosion killed 85 of the *Agano*'s officers and men and wounded 79. All five of the cruiser's boiler rooms were flooded, depriving her of power. On the bridge, Admiral Osugi was injured and could not stay on an unnavigable ship in any case; he was taken off by the *Urakaze*, which seems to have taken the lead in depth charging and holding down the *Albacore*.[21]

The *Agano*'s sister ship *Noshiro* and the destroyers *Fujinami* and *Hayanami*, already involved in trying to shepherd the badly damaged *Maya* from Rabaul to Truk, were now diverted from that assignment to help the disabled *Agano*. Veteran light cruiser *Nagara* was also ordered out from Truk to assist. The *Noshiro* and her friends rendezvoused with the *Agano* and her friends on November 13, and the *Noshiro* began towing her sister to Truk, escorted by the *Nagara* and the destroyer *Urakaze* with Admiral Osugi on board.[22]

The next day, the tow line snapped, and the *Nagara* took over the tow. The *Noshiro* took off for Truk, arriving on November 15, and the *Agano* was left with just the *Nagara* towing her and the *Urakaze* with Admiral Osugi on board escorting her.[23]

Perhaps leaving Admiral Osugi with his now-useless flagship was a sign of what Combined Fleet thought of him. The *Nagara*, *Agano*, and *Urakaze* arrived at Truk on November 16. The *Agano* was taken directly to the repair ship *Akashi* because she was reportedly in "sinking condition," a term that could be used to describe Osugi Morikazu's career. Disgusted with his performance at Empress Augusta Bay, Combined Fleet sacked Osugi.[24]

If, while they were making their way back to Truk, the officers and men on the *Agano*, *Noshiro*, *Nagara*, and *Urakaze* had looked up, they might have seen a momentous event: the aircraft of *Kido Butai* making their way back to Truk to be reunited with their carriers. Sort of.

The emperor issued an Imperial Rescript celebrating the achievements of *Ro-Go*. Everyone was so happy; at least everyone who was left. As one Japanese history explained, "The cumulative losses suffered in successive battles, however, had put the carrier air force in a position where further combat would rob it of even a skeleton force around which to rebuild; heavy losses among vitally essential crew members, in particular, had drastically reduced combat strength."[25] For that reason, Admiral Koga decided to pull the aviators of *Kido Butai* out of *Ro-Go*. Orders to that effect were issued on November 12, and the Sea Eagles returned to Truk the next day.[26]

As the eminent historian John Prados put it, "The proud legions of the 'sea eagles' were heavily thinned."[27] A better description might be to say the proud legions of Sea Eagles were now more like proud cohorts. Admiral Koga had sent 173 aircraft of *Kido Butai* to Rabaul; only 53 returned to Truk. *Kido Butai* had lost 69 percent of its aircraft during *Ro-Go*.[28]

A breakdown of the numbers did not improve the visual. Of the Zeros, 82 had gone to Rabaul; only 43 returned, a loss rate of 52 percent. Among the strike aircraft, the numbers were even worse. In terms of "carrier bombers" – the Imperial Navy's term for dive bombers, in this case the Aichi D3A Type 99 – 45 were sent to Rabaul, only seven returned, a loss rate of 84 percent. For the "carrier attack planes" – the Imperial Navy's term for torpedo bombers, in this case the Nakajima B5N Type 97 – 40 went to Rabaul, and only six returned, a loss rate of 85 percent. Of the "reconnaissance planes" – the Imperial Navy's placeholder term and role for the Yokosuka D4Y Type 2 Comet until the aircraft's structural problems were resolved and it could go into full production as a carrier bomber – six had gone to Rabaul and none had returned, a loss rate of 100 percent.[29]

Among the aircrews, the losses were not quite as bad – some of the downed aviators were rescued, and many of the planes written off as losses had managed to make it back to base with their crews – but were bad enough. Of the 80 Zero pilots sent to Rabaul, 56 returned, a loss rate of 30 percent. Of the 59 carrier attack crews sent to Rabaul, 35 returned, a loss rate of 41 percent. Three of the six reconnaissance plane crews returned, for a loss rate of 50 percent. For the carrier bombers, however, 47 crews had been sent to Rabaul and only 12 came back for an incredible loss rate of 74 percent. Basically, three out of every four D3A crews were lost.[30] This despite the fact that dive bombing is considered safer than trying to launch aerial torpedoes. The disparity in losses is more the result of using the carrier bombers more often than the carrier attack planes.

It bears repeating that these losses were catastrophic. Admiral Ozawa had to be content just to salvage what he could of *Kido Butai*'s aviators before they were all wiped out, except for the reconnaissance planes, which were already wiped out. But he was certainly not happy about it. Upon the aviators' return, Ozawa gave them the "commander's speech of instruction that customarily followed an operation." According to witnesses, "Ozawa had climbed the platform to address them and, being overcome with dismay at how few of his men had survived, was unable to utter a word. He stood there on the platform in silence for a very long time, weeping bitterly."[31]

For his part, Admiral Kusaka does not seem to have been too broken up about losing the fliers of *Kido Butai* to Truk, but it did mean that he and Base Air Force were on their own for the moment. Kusaka was determined to make the best of what he had left.

While the *Scamp* was stalking the *Agano* on the morning of November 12, Admiral Kusaka had launched two reconnaissance planes in the hope they would find the US Navy carriers who had attacked Rabaul the previous day. That afternoon, two reconnaissance seaplanes took off from Rabaul. An enemy task force was sighted southwest of Simbo Island, which is itself south of Ganongga Island, which is south of Vella Lavella.[32]

At 8:50pm, a "reconnaissance seaplane" (probably an Aichi E13A Type 0 Reconnaissance Seaplane) of the 938 Air Group reported two groups of enemy ships, each with a nucleus of two battleships and two carriers, some 50 miles southwest of Mutupina Point. This was a weird report, with a hint that the enemy force filled the crew's eyes with that double vision.[33]

Uncertainty over the quality of the sighting report might explain why it took Admiral Kusaka almost 3½ hours to respond to it. At 12:15am, he sent two G4M land attack planes on missions to find the enemy force and keep it pinned for the follow-up air strike. That air strike was launched from Vunakanau 45 minutes later, with six G4Ms from the 702 Air Group and a night fighter from the Official Night Fighter Squadron of Base Air Force, the 251 Air Group.[34] The night fighter was a Nakajima J1N1 *Gekko* ("Moonlight") Navy Type 2 Reconnaissance Plane modified to serve as a night fighter with a pair of

20mm Type 99 Model 1 cannons firing upward at a 30-degree angle and a second pair firing downward at a 30-degree angle.[35] Then at 1:20am, another five G4Ms, these from the 751 Air Group, took off from Vunakanau.[36]

Just as planned, at 1:58am one of the two advance land attack planes reported an enemy task force, bearing 228 degrees, distance 50 miles from Mutupina. This was another weird report, suggesting the enemy naval force had not moved in more than five hours.[37]

It hadn't. That enemy task force was Admiral Merrill's cruiser force once again. The flagship light cruiser *Montpelier* was leading the *Columbia* and *Denver*, while Captain Burke in his trusty *Charles Ausburne* was leading the destroyers *Claxton*, *Stanly*, *Converse*, and *Eaton*. Their job on this night was to cover the arrival of the so-called "Fourth Echelon" of reinforcements – in this case the 129th Infantry Regiment – to the Torokina beachhead. Commodore Reifsnider lead this convoy from the "attack" transport *George Clymer* with the fellow "attack" transports *American Legion*, *Hunter Liggett*, and *Crescent City*; and the "attack" cargo ships *Alhena* and *Alchiba*; with an escort of destroyers led by Commander Earle in the *Guest* with the *Wadsworth*, *Bennett*, *Anthony*, *Terry*, and *Braine*; destroyer minesweepers *Dorsey* and *Trever*; and, joining the convoy fashionably late, the tug *Sioux*. They were all still making their way from Guadalcanal and due to arrive at 8:00am on November 13. They weren't there yet.[38]

Admiral Merrill's cruisers and destroyers were. The Mitsubishi G4M had orders to shadow the enemy ships and report their position for the coming air strike, but at 2:50am, Base Air Force lost radio contact with the scout plane.[39]

Sick and tired of intrusions by Japanese warships (see, e.g., Battle of Empress Augusta Bay) and aircraft (see, e.g., the air attack of the previous night), Admiral Merrill had retained the services of a Black Cat to deal with the former and night fighters to deal with the latter. This night was a problem with the latter. According to the *Columbia's* Captain Beatty, "During the entire night after [9:30pm], the formation was annoyed by Japanese snooper planes who remained at almost all times just out of gun range. The sky was cloudless with a full moon affording the snooper an excellent view of the formation."[40] The night fighters, which consisted of a few PV-1 Venturas of Marine Night Fighting 531 on a rotation, at various times had included Lieutenant Colonel Schwable and Lieutenant Plunkett. Even so, they had little success chasing the various bogeys because the radar on the light cruiser *Columbia*, which was handling fighter direction, had trouble determining the target's altitude.[41]

And then Captain Duane R. Jenkins arrived on the scene at 3:35am. "Exasperated by the persistence of the snooper," Admiral Merrill gave the order, "to attempt interception on a particular snooper that had been with us for several hours." The *Columbia's* fighter director Lieutenant Robert N. Conn vectored Jenkins to the intruder. It was about 23 miles to the southwest headed due east. Jenkins' turret gunner Sergeant Thomas J. Glennon reported seeing six "large planes" to starboard, or tried to report it; Conn was directing the fighter over the radio at the time, so Jenkins never got Glennon's heads-up.[42]

Vice Admiral Baron Samejima Tomoshige, who was tabbed to head the IJN's 8th Fleet in the aftermath of the catastrophic Battle of the Bismarck Sea. (NHHC)

Vice Admiral Kusaka Jinichi, commander of the IJN's Southeast Area Fleet as well as the 11th Air Fleet (Base Air Force). (NHHC)

Japanese heavy cruiser *Haguro* under air attack by 5th Air Force bombers in Simpson Harbor, November 2, 1942. (USAF/NHHC)

Rabaul's Simpson Harbor under attack by aircraft from the *Saratoga* and *Princeton*, November 5, 1943. This photo was taken from one of the gunner's positions on the Command TBF Avenger of the *Saratoga*'s air group commander, Commander Henry Howard Caldwell, by Petty Officer Paul T. Barnett, who was killed during this attack. (NARA)

The Japanese destroyer *Amagiri* before the Pacific War. (NHHC)

The Japanese cruiser *Noshiro* under attack by aircraft from the USS *Bunker Hill* (CV-17) off Kavieng, New Ireland on January 1, 1944. (NARA)

Captain Arleigh Burke (third from left) and senior officers of of Destroyer Squadron 23 at Cloob Des-Slot, Purvis Bay, Solomon Islands, May 24, 1944. (Naval Historical Foundation/ Collection of Admiral Arleigh A. Burke, USN/NHHC)

Destroyer USS *Spence* in San Francisco Bay, July 24, 1943. (NHHC)

Destroyer USS *Charles Ausburne* off Boston, Massachusetts, on March 6, 1943.
(Bureau of Ships Collection, NARA)

VMF-214 (Marine Fighting 214 or Marine Fighter Squadron 214) pilots run to their Vought
F4U-1 Corsair aircraft, September 11, 1943, at Turtle Bay air base, Espiritu Santo. (NARA)

Douglas SBD Dauntless dive bombers take off from Munda airfield, October 28, 1943. (NARA)

Rear Admiral Frederick C. Sherman (center, in cap), Task Force 38 commander, gets good news from Commander Joseph C. Clifton (far right), *Saratoga's* fighter group commander, concerning the air attack on Rabaul's Simpson Harbor, on board flagship USS *Saratoga*. (NARA)

Admiral William F. Halsey (left), Commander, South Pacific Force/3rd Fleet and Commander Clifton celebrate the successful November 1943 attacks on Rabaul at a party at Espiritu Santo, New Hebrides. (US Navy/NARA)

Rear Admiral A. Stanton Merrill, Commander, Task Force 39, on board flagship *Montpelier* in December 1943. (US Navy/NARA)

Japanese heavy cruiser/seaplane carrier thing *Chikuma* under attack by US Navy carrier planes in Simpson Harbor during the November 5, 1943 raid on Rabaul. (US Navy/NARA)

USS *Saratoga* arrives at Pearl Harbor from the US West Coast, June 6, 1942. (US Navy/NARA)

Curtiss SB2C Helldivers flying in formation off Norfolk, VA, December 1943.
(Lieutenant Horace Bristol/NARA)

At Yokosuka, September 6, 1945. These appear to be largely experimental models of standard Japanese combat aircraft types, including two G4Ms (Betty); one J1N (Irving); and two D4Ys (Judy).(NARA)

The highly respected Vice Admiral Ozawa Jisaburo took over command of a reduced and renamed *Kido Butai* in November 1943 after Admiral Yamamoto sacked Admiral Nagumo. (NHHC)

Admiral Koga Mineichi became commander-in-chief of the Combined Fleet of the IJN following the death of Admiral Yamamoto. (NHHC)

The light carrier USS *Princeton* during her shakedown cruise. (NARA)

By 4:05am, Captain Jenkins was eight miles from the target. The Japanese plane may have seen what was coming, because it turned around and bravely ran away. Or tried to. Jenkins had Lieutenant Conn manning the *Columbia*'s air search radar and telling Jenkins where to go. The Japanese plane was on its own. Finally, in the bright moonlight, Jenkins saw the unidentified aircraft and recognized it as a Betty. He turned to port to attack it.[43]

On the *Columbia*, lookouts reported seeing tracer fire high in the air, then a small burst of flames that got larger and larger as it descended "comet like" until striking the water and exploding at 4:20am. It was a visually impressive show in the dark, except for one thing: they had no way of knowing which plane had gone down.[44]

Lieutenant Conn waited a few moments, but heard nothing over the radio. In the words of Captain Beatty, Conn "screwed up his nerve to ask the question." The question no one really wanted to ask but had to: "Are you all right? Are you all right? Over."

"Hell, yes! We just got a Betty!" came the jubilant response of Captain Jenkins. "Where are the rest of them?"[45] Since the entire task force was watching these proceedings, Jenkins also saw fit to announce to everyone, "That's one Betty that will not annoy you any more."[46] It was more than that – it was the first ever night air combat victory by the US Marine Corps, as well as the PV-1 Ventura.[47]

But the annoyance had done its job before it was shot down, leaving the radio room at Base Air Force hanging. It had vectored in the six land attack planes of the 702 Air Group, who meant to do much more than annoy Admiral Merrill's ships. They were – again – trying for a repeat of Rennell Island and the sinking of the *Chicago*.

Finally, at 4:46am, the *Denver* reported an enemy plane three miles to the southwest. Admiral Merrill immediately ordered an emergency 60-degree turn to starboard, followed one minute later by a 30-degree turn to port. At 4:51 came news that multiple Japanese aircraft were six miles to the southeast. In response, Merrill ordered an emergency 40-degree turn to port. A second group of attacking Japanese was detected four miles to the northeast.[48]

One would think radar would have picked them up further away, and normally it would. But the cunning Japanese were flying their G4M Type 1 land attack planes at almost wavetop height, maybe 50 feet. That made it extremely difficult for radar to detect them or for them to be seen visually until they were already in range to launch their deadly torpedoes.

The US Navy ships opened fire, but, nevertheless, at 4:54, the *Stanly* reported a torpedo passing to starboard on a course of 310 degrees True; the other shoe dropped when *Converse* reported a torpedo on the same course. Admiral Merrill immediately ordered speed increased to 25 knot and an emergency 90-degree turn to starboard.

The *Denver* blasted a Betty to pieces with her 5-inch antiaircraft guns, but only after the Betty had released her torpedo. Two more dropped their torpedoes and turned away to the east. Lookouts on the *Denver* saw two torpedoes astern on her starboard quarter. Captain Briscoe turned the cruiser to comb the torpedoes on a course of about 300 degrees True, and both torpedoes were seen on parallel courses to the *Denver* on either quarter;

that is, the *Denver* was between and moving on the same vector as the torpedoes.[49] That's an almost perfect comb. She just had to hold that course and not turn at all until the torpedoes completed their runs. A bit unnerving, but otherwise easy peasy.

Unless another attacker comes in from a different direction. Sure enough, one more Betty was seen off the starboard beam, very low and very close. The land attack plane released its torpedo at a range of only about 700 yards and turned away. The forward 20mm Oerlikons lashed out furiously, reportedly cutting the plane in two before it crashed off the port bow.[50]

Hemmed in by torpedoes, the *Denver* could take no evasive action whatsoever. At 4:55, the last torpedo introduced itself to the cruiser's starboard side at about frame 100 – the after engine room. There was no flash or fire, but a plume of water was thrown what seemed to be a mile high before crashing down on the after area like the Red Sea swamping the chariots of Pharaoh Ramesses II. The forward part of the *Denver* bucked like a bronco with dangerously large flexing of the hull, so much so that Captain Briscoe and the bridge crew were thrown about.[51]

While the *Birmingham* had shrugged off her torpedo hit – barely noticed it, even – the *Denver's* was unusually nasty. Hit in the after engine room, the *Denver* lost power and started to coast. With a giant 48-by-24-foot bite taken out of her hull and bilge keel, she quickly took a seven-degree list to starboard. That was a bad sign. A worse sign was that the list slowly increased. She was down three-and-a-half feet by the stern. The veteran Captain Briscoe ordered all starboard tanks, most of which were contaminated by seawater as a result of the explosion, emptied, which checked the list just short of 12 degrees. Damage control quickly and quietly got to work. By 5:23, the list was back at seven degrees; an hour later the list was down to maybe one degree.[52]

Power was restored to the forward part of the *Denver*. The after boiler room was completely flooded. Three of the four propeller shafts were disabled. Damage control managed to get the Number 4 propeller shaft going and the *Denver* started moving slowly to the southeast at 4.5 knots.[53]

Of course, 4.5 knots was not going to get you away from Rabaul. The Japanese air attacks had stopped for the moment, but Admiral Merrill and Captain Briscoe were certain the dawn would be rocky for the *Denver* as Japanese air attacks would resume to put the *Denver* under. Briscoe focused on getting all the ship's guns ready and operable. By a jury-rigged system involving welding cables, electricity was restored to the aft 5-inch guns, and casualty power was used for the aft 40mm Bofors, steering, and one of the radios.[54]

There was still the problem of that 4.5 knots. Commodore Reifsnider, commanding the convoy, ordered the tug *Sioux* to help the *Denver*. Admiral Merrill ordered the *Stanly* and *Eaton* to stand by the limping cruiser. Merrill also requested fighter coverage for the *Denver*. The first of the special patrols from Fighting 17 and Marine Fighting 211, 212, and 221 showed up at 6:02am, "a gorgeous sight to see" in the words of Captain Briscoe. The *Sioux* showed up shortly after 8:00am and by 8:20 the tow line was rigged; between the busy tug and the *Denver's* one functional propeller, they managed to work up to 7 knots. The fighter cover eventually reached 24 Corsairs; this was in addition to the normal AirSols fighter patrols over Empress Augusta Bay. It would be difficult for any Japanese attack to get through all that, especially if the Japanese only sent five aircraft, a mix of carrier bombers and attack planes. It would be impossible if they did not get through the big storm that had positioned itself between Rabaul and Bougainville. And they didn't, so they didn't. That little nugget of information might have been useful to the *Denver* and her companions, but better safe than sorry. The men of the *Denver* were certainly happy to have the aerial company as they headed for Tulagi, which they reached without further incident at 9:00am on November 14.[55]

The Japanese seemed happy with what they were told were the results of this nocturnal attack. The 702 Air Group claimed to have put one torpedo into a "medium" aircraft carrier and another torpedo into a battleship, "blown up" and sunk two cruisers, and set afire one destroyer whose "sinking [was] virtually assured." Two G4Ms failed to return; presumably this included the snooper shot down by Captain Jenkins.[56] It did not include the one reportedly shot down by the *Denver* after dropping the torpedo that would go on to hit the light cruiser, because that report was wrong. The G4M was piloted by the 702 Air Group's Lieutenant (jg) Maruyama Hidezumi, who not only accomplished his mission admirably, but made it back to Vunakanau with at least 380 more holes in the land attack plane's wing and fuselage than it had when it came from the Mitsubishi factory. The G4M was written off.[57]

But the Japanese could not have been happy with the 751 Air Group. Its five land attack planes loitered south of Bougainville until dawn but could find no one to attack and returned to Vunakanau. So ended what the Japanese called the "Fourth Air Battle off Bougainville."[58] And, for once, it included an actual air battle, but only Captain Jenkins versus that snooper, and Jenkins won that particular matchup. The rest was just an air attack.

Air attacks were on the minds of the US Navy commanders. The waters south of Bougainville were rapidly becoming "Torpedo Junction II," but where the original Torpedo Junction – the route between Espiritu Santo and Guadalcanal, especially east of Malaita – involved repeated torpedo attacks from submarines, Torpedo Junction II involved repeated night torpedo attacks by aircraft. And the American officers were sick of the apparent lack of defense against it.

The *Columbia's* Captain Beatty commented:

During the nights that this task force had operated off Empress Augusta Bay, it has been under constant scrutiny by snooper planes who have shown an extraordinary ability to avoid our projectiles, and at the same time, remain within good observation distance. An improvement in our ability to destroy these planes either by more effective bombing of their daylight hideouts or by bettering our gunnery and night fighter technique would stop at the beginning the torpedo and bombing attacks, and seems to be essential if we are to continue operations in such areas.[59]

Later in that same report, Captain Beatty expressed appreciation for the work and efforts of the night fighter pilots, indicating his comments were not to be taken as a criticism of them, but of how they were used.[60]

Nevertheless, Captain Beatty was hardly alone in his frustration. Admiral Merrill wrote, "[T]he Task Force Commander is gravely concerned over our present lack of defense against enemy night attacks by torpedo planes."[61] Commodore Reifsnider added, "The lack of adequate night fighters was again felt during the night of 12–13 November when this force and its covering force (Task Force 39) were surrounded and attacked by enemy planes."[62] However, the *Eaton*'s Lieutenant Commander Edward Frank Jackson took a different angle. "A friendly plane at night with doubtful or variable IFF [Identification Friend or Foe] is a thorough nuisance which required search radar attention that can ill afford to be spared."[63]

Speaking of nuisances, since the Battle of the Roadblock, the Imperial Japanese Army troops facing the 3rd Marine Division on the American left had been reduced to a nuisance, but they were about to be upgraded to a thorough nuisance. Expansion of the Torokina perimeter had been slow thanks to the surrounding swamps. To supply the troops at the front, you needed roads through those swamps. And building a road in a swamp is not easy, especially when building that road is competing for scarce supplies, tools, skilled workers, and earth movers with things like building that airfield.

A site for another airfield had been found about midway between the Koromokina and Piva Rivers about 5,500 yards inland – and about 1,500 yards in front of the lines of the 3rd Marine Division. Though the Japanese had not regularly challenged Marine scouts, there had been firefights between patrols in the area. Because the advance was moving too slowly for government work, General Turnage decided to set up a "combat outpost," which he defined as an improved position capable of sustaining itself for short periods and, more importantly, defending the selected area, at the junction of the Numa Numa and East-West Trails until the Torokina perimeter could be expanded to include it. The 2nd Battalion of the 21st Marine Regiment was ordered to seize the crossroads ... well, crosstrails ... before the Japanese got wind of it.[64]

The morning of November 13, the day when General Geiger, who had arrived to take over the Bougainville land operations on November 9 from General Vandegrift, would take over the operation from Admiral Wilkinson and report directly to Admiral Halsey, did not start off well. At least in part because of the aforementioned lack of roads, the 2nd Battalion was sluggish supplying up and getting into position, as was its artillery forward observers, so that at 7:30am one compay was ordered to begin the advance with the rest of the battalion to follow. So that one company, Company E, began the advance all by its lonesome, and with no proper reconnaissance made of the objective or its approaches. And just after 11:00am, it was ambushed by a strong force of Japanese with machine guns and mortars in an "overgrown" grove of coconut palms some 200 yards south of their objective. By what is believed to have been coincidence, elements of the Japanese 23rd Infantry Regiment had seized the junction and had dug in defensively.[65]

Company E deployed for battle with the unexpected interlopers and sent back a message reporting its situation to the battalion commander, Lieutenant Commander Eustace R. Smoak, which Bougainville historian Harry Gailey described as "the first of many messages on the situation in the grove that Smoak would receive, most of them inaccurate and some tinged with panic."[66]

In large part because of those messages, and also because of combat inexperience – this was the 2nd Battalion's first combat – and the density of the jungle, what followed was a very confused action, at least from the American standpoint, which as of this writing has apparently not been completely settled. Short story long, Lieutenant Colonel Smoak was given the impression – mistakenly – that Company E was being annihilated. He ordered Company G, on Company E's left, to close up with and support Company E and sent Company F up to relieve Company E. Company E tried to disengage by shifting to its right, opening a gap between it and Company G. Company F missed Company E completely by moving even further to the right, blundered into and through the Japanese left flank, suffering heavy casualties and becoming disorganized. By 4:30pm, Smoak had no idea where Company F was and had lost communications with the 21st Marines and the artillery, so he decided to dig in for the night. Company F was led back around the battalion's right flank and rejoined the Marine line at 5:45. By 6:30, communications with regiment and artillery were re-established, and the guns of the 12th Marine Regiment fired harassing rounds into the grove outside the 2nd Battalion's perimeter.[67]

After a tense but uneventful night, the Marines were ready to try again the next morning, November 14. This time they would be reinforced with the 1st Battalion of the 21st Marine Regiment, the very busy 2nd Marine Raider Battalion, five of those Stuart light tanks, and more of that new-fangled ground support, this time 20 TBF Avengers (12 from Compositing 38 and eight from Compositing 40) complete with a ground liaison team. Once again, artillery placed smoke shells to mark friendly lines and the target area, hopefully with no overlap. At 9:05am, the air attack began. Fortunately, the Avengers placed 95 percent of their bombs within the target area, much of which was as close as 100 yards from the Marine lines. Unfortunately, the benefit of the air attack was lost because the ground attack was delayed while the Marines got water. Then a break in communications caused another delay, so the attack did not begin until just before noon after a 20-minute artillery barrage.[68]

The attack stepped off just fine, then fell apart completely. The Japanese had abandoned their positions before the artillery barrage, then reoccupied them and poured withering rifle and machine-gun fire into the Marines. Between the enemy fire, the noise of the tanks, and the smoke from the barrage, the Marines became confused. The tanks, who were depending on the Marines for vision, became really confused, at one point firing on the Marines on the left flank, and in frantic maneuvering even ran over several men.[69]

An exasperated Lieutenant Colonel Smoak, leader of the attack, personally moved to the front and ordered the Marines to cease fire and halt in place. Japanese fire had stopped, probably bemused as to what they were watching, and Marine officers "were soon able to make the troops realize how foolish they had been." After that embarrassing false start, Smoak called a "do-over" and this time the assault went much more according to plan. By 3:30pm, the junction was in American hands with proper defenses being set up. Marine losses amounted to 20 killed (including five officers) and 39 wounded. With the capture of the Numa Numa and East-West Trail junction, the so-called "Battle of the Coconut Grove" was over and the Torokina beachhead advanced some 1,000–1,500 yards.[70]

It was advances like that and the air base(s) that such advances permitted that worried Admiral Kusaka, but he had more immediate concerns: replacing the 53 aircraft of *Kido Butai* that had withdrawn to Truk. Combined Fleet was not completely unmindful of his plight. On that same November 14, Lieutenant (jg) Haruta Torajiro led 16 Zeros of the 281 Air Group from Chishima into Lakunai air base, where eight were transferred to the 201 Air Group and eight to the 204 Air Group.[71] The next day, reportedly 29 "carrier bombers" arrived from the Marshall Islands. Of these, 26 were brand-new Aichi D3A2 Model 22 carrier bombers (two dozen plus two spares) from the 552 Air Group led by Captain Tanaka Yoshio. If they were indeed 29 carrier bombers, the other three would have been Yokosuka D4Y Comets for the 501 Air Group. Initially, the Aichis of the 552 were crammed into Vunakanau with the 582, but on December 18 were sent to the Kerevat air base, on the opposite side of Blanche Bay from Rabaul, where they had had severe drainage issues due to the rainforest location.[72] It was a boost to Base Air Force's strike capability, as degraded as it had become, and Admiral Kusaka decided to make use of it.

On the night of November 16, Imperial Army intelligence on Bougainville informed 8th Fleet that there was an enemy task force south of Bougainville. 8th Fleet relayed it to Base Air Force – no mean feat considering how many times contradictory orders had come out of the two – who sent up two G4Ms and a "reconnaissance seaplane" to find the enemy. The seaplane found the enemy task force and was soon joined by the two land attack planes, who reported three enemy aircraft carriers and 20 cruisers and destroyers 65 miles west northwest of Mutupina Point.[73]

Aircraft carriers? Then again, the Japanese had shown a striking inability to distinguish an aircraft carrier from a transport – in daylight. At night, who knows what they saw? But, better safe than sorry, a saying used frequently in these pages which could have applied to the war in the Solomons in general.

So Admiral Kusaka ordered up from Vunakanau six G4M land attack planes of the 751 Air Group; one had to turn back because of mechanical issues. Ten minutes later came three more land attack planes, these from the 702 Air Group, plus five Nakajima B5N carrier attack planes of the 582 Air Group.[74] It would be interesting to see if the 582 was rusty, and, given how poorly the Japanese had maintained their air units, that should be taken literally as well as figuratively. Additionally, the 582 had been a composite fighter and dive bomber unit, then it was just a dive bomber unit, and now it was a composite dive and torpedo bomber unit.[75] How would the 582 handle its new torpedo attack function?

The Japanese scout planes had apparently found the Fifth Echelon of reinforcements to the Torokina beachhead. Captain Carter, in charge of this convoy on the destroyer *Renshaw*, had the tank landing ships *LST-353*, *-341*, *-70*, *-207*, *-339*, *-488*, *-354*, and *-395*; and, joining fashionably late, the fast destroyer transports *Stringham*, *McKean*, *Talbot*, *Waters*, *Dent*, *Kilty*, *Crosby*, and *Ward*, all carrying elements of the 21st Marine Regiment. Escorting were a bunch of destroyers led by Captain Hurff in the *Waller* with the *Pringle*, *Conway*, *Sigourney*, *Saufley*, and the aforementioned *Renshaw*, with another tug joining late, the *Pawnee*.[76]

Everything was hunky-dory until the wee hours of November 17. The convoy was moving at about 12 knots in a formation of concentric circles, the *Pawnee* in the center; the tank landing ships in a circle outside her (or in three columns with the *Pawnee* the second ship in the middle column), the destroyer transports in a circle outside the landing ships, and the destroyers in a circle outside the destroyer transports. They were headed northeast into Empress Augusta Bay when at around 3:00am unidentified aircraft were reported on radar from the northwest and north northeast by, apparently, pretty much everyone in the force. Within five minutes, unidentified aircraft were seen passing over the convoy.[77]

Though visibility was described in American accounts as excellent, with the moon more than half full and clear skies, what followed was very confused. According to the Japanese, "[p]oor visibility forced the planes to strike singly," which certainly contributed to that confusion, although it is curious that the Japanese complained of poor visibility when the Americans had the same weather conditions and thought visibility was excellent. The three land attack planes of the 702 Air Group attacked first for about an hour. A half hour into the 702's attack, the five B5N carrier attack planes of the 582 Air Group started their attack and continued for about an hour. Some 20 minutes into the 582's attack, the five remaining G4Ms of the 751 Air Group's strike put in their appearance and continued for almost two hours.[78] Aside from this rundown of the attacking units, the Japanese appear to have loitered outside gun range with individual planes making torpedo attacks at random times, but only one at a time.

For the recipients, this would be a marathon night attack. Captain Carter had expected a night air attack and had experimented on some tactical theories to see if they might work. Laying smoke screens sounded good in principle but when he tested it, the smoke was "not satisfactory" and so Carter did not use it. Because visibility was reportedly excellent during this attack, the landing ships and destroyer transports were ordered to rely on their guns combined with that of the escorting destroyers to deal with the attackers. Nonetheless, Carter did have a unique twist: barrage balloons. He instructed the landing ships to raise their barrage balloons overhead, which may have discouraged the Japanese from approaching the landing ships.

But while the barrage balloons might have helped the center of the formation, they did little for the ships closer to the edge. It certainly did nothing for the destroyer *Pringle*, which at 3:20am was the recipient of what was apparently the first single-plane attack, if you can call it that. A Betty had circled the formation and disappeared to starboard. The *Pringle*, on the right side of the formation, turned toward last position of the bomber. They heard the hum of the plane's engines from dead ahead. Then the Betty itself appeared out of the dark at an altitude of about 50 feet and a distance of ... well, it was close. Too close – for the G4M's pilot, at least, who apparently had no interest in becoming an early kamikaze. He dipped the G4M's left wing to clear the *Pringle*. It cleared the *Pringle* but not the water. As the left wing dipped, the land attack plane lost altitude and the tip of the wing caught the water, which tore the wing clean off. The rest of the Betty spun into the sea off the destroyer's port bow and exploded – without releasing its torpedo, without the *Pringle* even opening fire.[79]

The Japanese continued lurking outside of gun range. They dropped floatlights to mark the convoy's course, and every now and then one would make a feint at the ships or pass over the formation. The *Stringham*, at the head of the destroyer transports, saw a Betty go through the formation from astern and pass her to port. As the bomber pulled on ahead, the gunners opened fire on it, "probably driving it away," in the words of Commander John D. Sweeney, head of Transport Division 12, who was on the *Stringham*.[80]

As Commander Sweeney explained, "[T]here was plenty of evidence that the convoy was being attacked."[81] That this needed to be clarified suggests maybe too much imagination. A white flare appearing over the convoy at 3:35 convinced Captain Hurff to end consideration of this burning question and order his Destroyer Squadron 22 into antiaircraft disposition.[82]

One aircraft was seen to crash into the water and explode, leaving a brightly burning wreck for a few minutes. Another plane, a Betty, was seen passing through the convoy heading astern. A few moments later, the night was suddenly lit up by a cataclysmic explosion. It was in the back of the formation.[83] The *Talbot* radioed, "Believe that last one got *McKean*."[84]

It had. The *McKean* was at the very back of the destroyer-transport circle, off the port quarter of the *Talbot*. The Betty that had just passed through the convoy headed astern looked like it was making a torpedo run at the *Talbot*. Instead, he passed the *Talbot*, made a loop to the right, and took aim at the *McKean*.[85]

The destroyer transport was handcuffed. The Betty was close. Too close – certainly for the *McKean*. Skipper Lieutenant Commander Ralph Lester Ramey ordered a hard left to try to turn the *McKean*'s stern toward her attacker, but there was no room and no time. *Talbot* was in her line of fire, so she could not use her 3-inch guns, only her 20mm automatics. The Betty released her torpedo at a range of about 300 yards and turned to the right to parallel the destroyer transport before speeding away. At that point, the 20mms reportedly got the bomber, and it crashed off the starboard bow. Miraculously, its torpedo appeared to be passing astern of the *McKean*. Ramsey ordered the rudder to "full right" ...[86]

The torpedo was not passing astern. Instead, at 3:50am it plowed into the *McKean*'s starboard side at about frame 140 with an explosion that was almost volcanic, sending up a fireball 300 feet high. The after magazine and depth charge stowage detonated. Three fuel oil tanks were ruptured by the blast, spewing flaming fuel all over the after part of the ship and even the fire control platform on top of the bridge. Flames burst from the hatches to the after engine room, indicating the fires had overwhelmed it. The four landing boats caught fire. Electrical power and communications were lost almost immediately. To add insult to injury, flying debris caused the ship's siren to blast continuously.[87]

Damage control went into action quickly, but, according to Lieutenant Commander Ramey, "[t]he entire ship aft of #1 stack was a complete mass of flames." The area of the Number 1 stack was such a raging inferno that it was impossible to cross it from either forward or aft, so no one could get to the after part of the ship to try to fight the fire or find survivors. There was little point in either. With no power, there was no water pressure to even attempt to douse the intense flames, which were already spreading forward, and thus little damage control could do. Worse, while some sailors stationed aft were blown off the ship, only three survivors were identified from the area aft of the Number 1 stack. Everyone else was apparently killed by the concussion of the torpedo's detonation, the flames and the heat, or the smoke and other gases.[88]

There was nothing that could be done to save the *McKean*. Burning, flooding, and no power. She was doomed.

About ten minutes after the hit, the *McKean* drifted to a stop. Explosions rocked the after part of the ship, including a particularly large blast at about 4:00am that was witnessed by the other ships of the force, and the destroyer transport started settling by the stern. Lieutenant Commander Ramey prepared to abandon ship. In contravention of orders to stay on the ship while it was moving until the order to evacuate was given, several of the Marine passengers, all of whom were from the headquarters company of the 3rd Battalion, 21st Marine Regiment, had gotten a head start on abandoning ship a few minutes after the hit. This was a bad idea. Still moving at the time, the *McKean* was trailing burning oil, and those who jumped overboard without orders were dragged by the ship's momentum into the burning oil slick, where they were incinerated.[89]

Though the inferno was spreading forward, there was no panic or confusion in the crew or the Marine passengers as they made their preparations to evacuate and made sure the injured got first dibs on the life rafts. Finally, at 4:10, Lieutenant Commander Ramey ordered the men over the side. He spent about two minutes making certain the *McKean* was clear of living crewmen, then he himself went over the port side of the well deck.[90]

Not a moment too soon. At 4:15, just after everyone had evacuated, a massive explosion shattered the heretofore little damaged forward section of the *McKean*. The fires had detonated the forward magazine and oil tanks at the same time. Lieutenant Commander Ramey said the forward part of the ship just "disintegrat[ed]." He said the smokestacks were "the last part of the ship afloat" and then for only a few minutes, disappearing at 4:18.[91]

At 3:55, Captain Hurff had ordered the *Sigourney*, "Stop in vicinity (of the *McKean*) to make rescue if possible."[92] Commander Sweeney had ordered the *Talbot* to assist the men of the stricken destroyer transport. The *Talbot's* skipper Lieutenant Commander Charles

Cushman Morgan protested to no avail that recovering survivors was the job of screening destroyers.[93] Charming. The families of the dead from the *McKean* would surely have been comforted to know that the *Talbot* might have saved them, but, dammit, that wasn't her job. Bureaucratically justified or not, it's a horrible look. Then again, to be fair, Morgan likely had a few concerns on his mind. His *Talbot* still had her Marine passengers to disembark. There was also one other slight complication: the Japanese were still attacking.

Yes, the *Sigourney* and *Talbot* were moving to help the *McKean* and her survivors while Japanese aircraft were still loitering in the dark trying to aim more torpedoes at Captain Carter's surviving ships. In terms of combat, the area was still hot. This was perhaps the most complicated sea rescue scenario imaginable.

The *Talbot* reported "two planes making alternate runs on (the) rear of (the) screen." She opened fire as she circled the sinking *McKean*.[94] She reported in, "The *McKean* was torpedoed. Believe she shot down plane but got torpedo. There are no survivors as yet."[95] The *Sigourney* weaved around debris windward of the wreck, which she noted was burning fiercely and illuminating a large area, but saw no survivors. As she moved leeward, she finally saw men in the water and reported, "There are survivors all around us." She requested the *Talbot* send landing boats to help pick them up. The *Sigourney* started taking on survivors by means of cargo nets and launched a whaleboat of her own.[96]

Of course, any ship that stops in the middle of an air attack might as well put up a big flashing neon sign that says, "Torpedo me!" The *Talbot*, rather smartly, lowered four landing craft with orders to look for survivors, then she took off, trying to gain speed to avoid the next attack. As for the *Sigourney*, after about ten minutes of fishing the *McKean*'s crew and Marine passengers out of the water, at 4:45 skipper Commander Walter Leo Dyer ordered the *Sigourney* to go to emergency flank speed. Japanese planes were coming in from astern, like they had the *McKean*. The destroyer fired all her guns that would bear as she started radical evasive maneuvers – in the midst of the survivors of the *McKean*.

The destroyer *Waller*, with Captain Hurff on board, fired briefly at aircraft she thought she saw. The *Pringle* chipped in by radioing Captain Carter, "Send for aircover to be here prior to dawn, I think we will be in for it."[97] *LST-354* warned that two torpedoes were passing just astern of the *Renshaw*, but the *Renshaw* does not appear to have seen them.[98] The rest of the formation fired intermittently, both because the Japanese were attacking only intermittently and because in most cases the range was fouled by other friendly ships.

The attention seemed to be almost exclusively on the *Sigourney* and the *Talbot*, however. Commander Dyer reported that at 4:50 a plane who had taken a 5-inch shell from the *Sigourney* just disintegrated, but there were plenty more showing on radar. She fired at a plane crossing in front of her bow, then fired at a group of planes off the starboard quarter, where she saw a torpedo pass 75 yards astern. Multiple aircraft came in from the starboard bow, one looping around to come in from the still-dark west and release her torpedo, which the *Sigourney* avoided. For the *Sigourney*, the next few hours were about shooting at attacking Japanese aircraft.[99]

For the *Talbot*, the next few hours were a pattern of stopping to pick up survivors, then powering up to full speed when an air attack seemed imminent. Repeat *ad infinitum*. But at 6:00am the Japanese were finally gone and both the *Talbot* and the *Sigourney*, joined by the *Waller*, were finally able to stop to fish the *McKean's* crew and passengers out of the water. Of the *McKean's* crew of 153, 64 died as a result of injuries suffered during this attack. Of the 185 Marines she was carrying, 52 were killed.[100] Considering the circumstances, it could have been a lot worse.

Even so, Lieutenant Commander Ramey made one rather pointed comment in his report:

> Rescue ships should not attempt to enter water where survivors are if danger of attack is imminent as there is a great possibility that some men will be run down if the rescue ship is forced by circumstances to speed up. Boats with medical personnel could be dropped and sent to the rescue while rescue ships steam clear.[101]

While not saying so specifically, Ramey's comment seems directed at the *Sigourney*. The *Talbot* appears to have done something close to Ramey's recommendation: just dropped boats and steered clear until pauses in the attack allowed the destroyer transport to stop and receive survivors from the boats. The *Waller* came in after the attack. The *Sigourney* did drop boats, but seems to have weaved through the vicinity of the sinking where survivors were in the water.

Beyond the mechanics of rescue, this engagement bothered many of the US Navy commanders. Admiral Wilkinson explained, "The Task Group was confronted with the as yet unsolved problem of defeating a determined and persistent night aerial torpedo attack."[102] Believed to be part of the solution were night fighters of Night Fighting 75 and Marine Night Fighting 531. In his endorsement to Lieutenant Commander Ramey's report, Admiral Halsey's Chief of Staff, Rear Admiral James B. Carney, was more to the point: "This action serves to emphasize the urgent need for night fighters."[103] Captain Carney's force had a Black Cat, but the lumbering PBY Catalina was not much use against blazing fast Bettys and Kates.

At least one night fighter was indeed up that night, because Admirals Halsey and Wilkinson were determined to protect this convoy. Wilkinson had scheduled Captain Carter's convoy to arrive in the early morning and finish before dark "[i]n recognition of the greater danger of night air attack while in port."[104] Halsey had arranged daytime air cover, nighttime air cover, daytime air attacks, nighttime air attacks, shore bombardments – the whole shebang, whatever a shebang is.

The night fighter was a Ventura from Marine Night Fighting 531. It was not guarding Captain Carter's convoy per se, though that was one intended effect of its mission. It was guarding Captain Burke's Destroyer Squadron 23, with the commodore in his usual *Charles Ausburne* leading the *Claxton* and *Dyson* of his own Destroyer Division 45 and the

Converse and *Stanly* of Commander Austin's Destroyer Division 46.[105] It was their job to provide surface protection to Captain Carter's transports.

Captain Burke was to hold a blocking position northwest of Captain Carter's transports to intercept any surface ships attempting to interfere. There were no surface ships, but there was, according to Burke, a Japanese submarine on the surface, detected by the radar on the *Converse* at 9:43pm. Commander Austin's destroyers were ordered to confirm the target and sink it with gunfire or ramming if necessary. Austin reported hitting the submarine with gunfire and believing it was sunk. It's not known what they were firing at. Japanese submarines *Ro-104* and *-109* were in the area, but do not seem to have reported any damage and eventually returned to Rabaul.[106]

AirSols had scheduled a nocturnal air attack of its own: eight B-25 Mitchells of the 42nd Bombardment Group would be over Buka and Bonis between 2:45 and 3:30am, clearing out by 3:45. Eight bombed Buka and Bonis. This was to cover eight Venturas of Bombing 104 who were deploying mines in the eastern end of Buka Passage. It was the second night in a row of mining the Buka Passage; the previous night, 39 TBF Avengers, including 11 from Marine Torpedo 143 and 17 from Marine Torpedo Bombing 233, mined the western end. When this mining was done, another eight B-25s bombed Buka and Bonis.[107]

After that, Burke was busy bombarding Buka while being bothered by bombers. The aerial protection afforded by the night fighter was nullified by its inability to approach the task force because it was firing its antiaircraft guns at the snoopers, who frequently seemed to be heading east and southeast – many were headed toward Captain Carter's transports. The fighter director destroyer *Claxton* would vector the Ventura to find them, but they outran the Ventura every time. "Nevertheless," as Burke put it, "it was a comforting thought to have him there."[108]

When the bombardment was completed, Burke again found his brood bothered by bombers, but this time coming from the west. They were driven off within 20 minutes with relatively little effort.[109] Japanese records do not indicate other aircraft up that night except for the air strike on Captain Carter's transports and the strike's advance planes. In all likelihood, the bogeys that bothered the Little Beavers were advance and strike planes from that attack on their ingress and egress; the Japanese seem to have tangled a bit with the Venturas of Bombing 140 on their own egress.[110] From that point forward, Burke's destroyers maintained a blocking position to the northwest of the transports. The efforts to suppress Buka continued through the morning. Three more B-25s bombed and strafed Buka, then on their route back bombed and strafed Kieta. Later that morning, Buka's runway was hit by two squadrons of Liberators from AirSols.[111] There was indeed a night fighter up, but it was assigned to cover another unit. In so doing, it was hoped it would protect the transports as well. That didn't happen. There were not enough night fighters to go around. All of the efforts to suppress Buka and Bonis were not enough to protect the transports from attack.

There were other complaints about the action in which the *McKean* was sunk. Commander Sweeney criticized the destroyer transports. Not their performance, but the ships themselves. He pointed out that the *McKean* was the fourth destroyer transport his division had lost in the war. Sweeney explained, "All gave a good accounting of themselves, performing much good work." And then the inevitable *but*, "[T]hese old type destroyers are weak, old, and brittle. There is no strength left in the metal of the hulls. An explosion causes the nearby parts to fold up like an old shoe box."[112] It's unclear as to what type of old shoe box he was referring; a better analogy might be folding like a cheap lawn chair or, given this was a military organization, folding like a cheap tent.

Imperfect analogies aside, even a modern destroyer would struggle to survive just one torpedo hit. The survival of the *Foote* after having her stern blown off by a torpedo is the exception. The *Strong* and the *Gwin*, each sunk by a single torpedo in separate engagements in Kula Gulf, is much more the norm.

Furthermore, most ships – not most destroyers, most ships – do not survive a magazine detonation. It does not matter if the magazine is set off by a torpedo or a lit cigarette. Size matters not. The most famous example in the US Navy is, of course, the battleship *Arizona* during the Pearl Harbor attack. The Royal Navy, also rather famously, had the battlecruiser *Hood* in its clash with the German battleship *Bismarck*. Both the *Arizona* and the *Hood* were so badly damaged that the precise cause of the magazine explosions could not be conclusively determined. Now the Imperial Japanese Navy had one of its own, one not well known in the West: the battleship *Mutsu*.[113]

On June 8, 1943, the *Mutsu* was sitting in Hashirajima anchorage, minding her own business, waiting for that whole Decisive Battle thing when, shortly after noon, the magazine for her Number 3 16-inch turret just blew up in a red and brown fireball. The battleship was broken in two, the larger forepart capsizing and sinking immediately, the much smaller stern section capsizing but continuing to float for some 14 more hours. The death toll was catastrophic: of the *Mutsu*'s crew of 1,474 officers and men, only 353 survived. Even worse, assuming that's possible, 113 flight cadets and 40 instructors of the Tsuchiura Naval Air Group had been touring the battleship; only 13 survived.[114]

These are about the only facts known definitively about the *Mutsu*'s explosion and loss. To date, exactly why the magazine exploded has not been conclusively determined. The most accepted theory is that it was, in the words of an Imperial Navy investigation, "most likely caused by human interference"; that is, sabotage. The perpetrator is believed to have been a gunner's mate from the Number 3 turret who was supposed to be tried that day by a naval court for petty theft. The theory goes that he created a fire in the Number 3 magazine as a diversion so he could escape from the ship. Why did the Japanese give a sailor facing legal proceedings access to such large amounts of explosives? Don't know. But he apparently did not even escape from the magazine. His body was never recovered.[115]

If the *Mutsu*, the *Hood*, and the *Arizona* could not survive a magazine explosion, it's a bit unfair to expect an old, converted destroyer to do so. These fast destroyer transports were not intended for serious combat. They were a case of, as Admiral King would say,

"Mak[ing] the best of what you have." Their job was only to get troops and supplies in and out quickly. An American version of the Tokyo Express; maybe a "Washington Express" or something.

And the Japanese believed they had derailed the Washington Express, which, admittedly, didn't have that ring to it. Base Air Force was ecstatic with the results achieved in what the Japanese called "The Fifth Air Battle off Bougainville," or at least the results reported achieved in what the Japanese called "The Fifth Air Battle off Bougainville": one large carrier "blown up and sunk"; two "medium" carriers sunk; three cruisers sunk; and one "unidentified type" sunk. Well, the Japanese did have issues telling an aircraft carrier from a transport and vice versa. Of the five 582 Air Group's Nakajima B5N carrier attack planes committed to the attack, one did not return. Of the nine G4M land attack planes, four did not return, while a fifth returned "heavily damaged." That fifth was likely the plane of the 702 Air Group's Senior Flight Petty Officer Kobayashi Gintaro. As he started his torpedo run, his starboard engine caught fire, but he blew out the flames "with an adroit side-slipping manoeuvre" and released his torpedo – which hit the *McKean*. He returned to Vunakanau on one engine.[116]

While the "The Fifth Air Battle off Bougainville" – which involved no air-to-air combat, just a long air attack – was over, the combat was not. The remaining transports moved to the Torokina beachhead to offload their Marines and supplies. Captain Hurff's destroyers moved into protective positions, the necessity of which was proved at around 7:30am when radar detected a large formation of unidentified aircraft approaching from the northwest.[117] It was assumed they were not friendly.

They weren't. Rabaul had been informed that eight transports and ten destroyers were off Torokina. That Admiral Kusaka and his staff did not make the connection with the force of "aircraft carriers" they had just sunk in roughly the same place as these 18 ships is rather curious. Anyway, at 5:25pm, 55 Zeros took off to escort a strike by … ten carrier bombers. These were apparently not Aichi D3As but Yokosuka D4Y Comets from the 501 Air Group.[118] Once again, the number of strike aircraft was pitiful.

But the number of fighters was a problem for AirSols and its new northern Solomons subcommand, AirNorSols. Over Empress Augusta Bay was a defense that included eight Corsairs of Fighting 17, seven Corsairs of Marine Fighting 215 (an eighth was unable to take off), and six Corsairs of Marine Fighting 221.[119] In theory, anyway. Due to various issues, the American fighters were unable to rendezvous before the Japanese arrived.

The result was that the alleged Allied air superiority was certainly not superior when the Japanese arrived. The eight Corsairs of Fighting 17 were present and took on the Zeros.[120] When Marine Fighting 221 arrived on scene, however, it was vectored to pursue "scattered, fleeing Jap[anese], so that when an attack came in, only Major [Nathan] Post and [Lieutenant Harold] Segal were there to make contact." Marine Fighting 215 arrived, the Judys (misidentified as "Vals") were completing their dives, having made their attacks almost completely unopposed.[121]

Fortunately for the Americans, the Judys' attack was almost completely ineffective, not only not getting any hits, but not even a near miss. Captain Carter thought the carrier bombers "seemed not to attack with much determination." He attributed it to the heavy antiaircraft fire and his barrage balloons.[122] Barrage balloons. Is there nothing they can't do?

The American fighter pilots tried to make up for their ineffectual interception by hacking away at the Japanese as they headed back to Rabaul. It certainly made an impression on the Japanese, who claimed they "engaged in combat with approximately 110 enemy fighters and bombers on the return trip."[123] Then again, maybe they really did engage in combat with approximately 110 enemy fighters and bombers on the return trip. Because while the Japanese were attacking the transports, the Americans were bombing Bonis with 48 Dauntlesses and 30 Avengers (all from Marine Torpedo Bombing 233) escorted by 26 fighters (including 14 from Marine Fighting 212, four others had to abort; and four from Marine Fighting 221). And bombing Buka with a dozen more Mitchells of the 42nd Bombardment Group with an escort of eight Corsairs from Fighting 17. Some of the US Navy and Marine Corsairs reported skirmishing with Japanese fighters off Buka, which could only have been escorts from the airstrike. The Americans dropped 53 tons of bombs on Bonis, but Marine Lieutenant Louie P. Harris and his Avenger crewmates were killed when they bailed out of their damaged TBF over Empress Augusta Bay, but, curiously, none of their parachutes opened.[124]

The Japanese would go on to claim three transports sunk, one transport "run aground by a near miss," one destroyer set afire, and two "carrier fighters" shot down.[125] On that last one, the Japanese were accurate. The Corsair of Fighting 17's Lieutenant (jg) Robert S. Anderson was set afire and he had to bail out – inverted – breaking an ankle and a rib and injuring his back in the process; he was rescued by a PT boat the next morning. At some point during the engagement, Anderson's squadron mate Ensign Bradford W. Baker was apparently shot down. No one saw what happened to him; Baker was never seen again.[126]

For their part, the Americans would claim 16 Japanese aircraft shot down: two Tonys, six Zekes, one Val, one Kate, and six "unidentified." The reference to "Tonys" and other aircraft that were not present is a reflection of the confusion over the Judy, whose existence was rumored but had not been seen by most Allied fighter pilots. Marine Fighting 221's Major Post and Lieutenant Segal were each credited with three "dive bombers." The Japanese admitted four carrier bombers and six carrier fighters failed to return. Among the fighter pilots lost were veterans Ensign Aiso Yukio and Petty Officer 1st Class Yoshino Jisuke, both of the 201 Air Group.[127]

The debarkation and offloading proceeded on schedule, the only hiccup coming when the *LST-339* was stuck on the beach and unable to depart with the rest of the convoy at around 6:00pm. The *Pawnee* tried to pull the tank landing ship off the beach without luck. It was 2:00 the next afternoon before the *LST-339* was able to pull herself off the Torokina beach and head back.[128]

By that time, Base Air Force had tried another one of its nocturnal air attacks. A reconnaissance seaplane had conducted a search. Not clear what it found, if anything. Four G4Ms took off and bombed the "landing beach at Torokina," claiming to have seen three fires afterward. Another attack by one or more reconnaissance seaplanes (Japanese records can't agree which) also attacked the Torokina beachhead, with Allied losses "unknown."[129] The former seems to have been the attack that left five Americans dead, a dozen wounded, an antiaircraft gun destroyed, and a radar rectifier van wrecked. The latter seems to have been the attack on Puruata Island, that killed two and wounded six.[130]

AirSols countered with a working lunch. Over the noon hour, one B-24 bombed Porporang Island, two dropped five tons of bombs on Ballale; another 16 dropped 43 tons of bombs on Kara, and 18 more dropped 72 tons of bombs on Buka. Also during the noon hour, 18 B-25s dropped 82 fragmentation clusters at "enemy concentrations" at Chabai, Matchin Bay and destroyed two buildings by strafing. No aerial opposition was encountered, and all aircraft returned safely. Later that afternoon, three B-25s returning from an unsuccessful antishipping strike bombed and strafed the Kieta area.[131]

Similar results seemed to follow the next day. Four G4M land attack planes "attacked Torokina," but the Japanese did not report the results. Maybe because there weren't any. Maybe because they did not exactly attack.[132]

The only air action on the night of November 18–19 centered around the so-called 6th Echelon of reinforcements to Torokina. Attack transports *President Jackson*, *President Adams*, *President Hayes*, and *Fuller*, and attack cargo ships *Libra* and *Titania* were escorted by destroyers *Guest*, *Fullam*, *Hudson*, *Anthony*, *Terry*, and *Braine*, and minesweepers *Southard* and *Hovey*. They were covered by a PV-1 night fighter piloted by Major John D. Harshberger from Marine Night Fighting 531. The convoy encountered some unidentified aircraft, but reported "they seemed indisposed" to come within 20 miles of the formation, "making no attempt to close or launch an attack." Then they left. Harshberger tried to intercept, but the fighter director on the *Terry* instructed him to remain within 15 miles of the task force, so his pursuit options were limited. The convoy arrived at Torokina on time without incident, offloaded its troops and cargo, and headed back.[133]

Nevertheless, AirSols was doing what it could to cover it. In addition to the normal fighter patrols over Torokina, AirSols sent an air strike to bomb Kahili over the noon hour. This one comprised 62 SBD Dauntlesses (including 22 from Marine Scout Bombing 244 and 20 from Composite 24) and 25 TBF Avengers from Marine Torpedo Bombing 233, escorted by 15 Corsairs from Marine Fighting 222.[134] AirSols was developing a thing for bombing at lunchtime for some reason. And it had not visited Kahili for a while, spending a lot of time on Buka and Bonis. That focus may have had some interesting, if unforeseen, consequences.

Be that as it may or may not, there was still some important ground combat on the agenda. By November 14, the first four echelons had landed 33,861 members of the 3rd Marine Division and the US Army's 37th Infantry Division, and 23,137 tons of supplies at the Torokina beachhead.[135] After the Battle of the Coconut Grove, contact with the bulk of the Japanese forces was broken as the Imperial Army troops withdrew and went inert for a while, albeit not completely broken and not completely inert. The priorities for the Allied troops became completing roads inside the perimeter and to the front lines, which could then be pushed forward to give more room to build runway facilities inside the Torokina perimeter and reduce possible interference from Japanese snipers and artillery but not beyond the edges of the mountain range, which would expose the defenders to flanking attacks.

In the sector of the US Army's 37th Infantry Division, which was being slid in to replace the Marines on the Allied left, there was literally no Japanese activity. Between that and the relatively favorable terrain, the soldiers of the division's 129th and 148th Infantry Regiments were able to cautiously expand the perimeter of the Torokina beachhead rather easily. The Japanese would do nothing in this sector until March of the following year.

In the sector of the 3rd Marine Division on the Allied right, it was much more difficult. The Marines had to deal with the results of the frequent rainstorms – it was a *rain* forest, after all – which was extremely wet terrain, including mud, swamps, and even lagoons. You wouldn't think water would be a problem for fighting men known as "marines," but it wasn't so much a problem as a major discomfort. The water was usually at least knee deep, was often waist deep, and sometimes was up to the arm pits. The defensive perimeter in the Marine sector actually consisted of a number of isolated strongpoints, sort of like the German concept of "hedgehogs," located in what was known locally as "dry swamps" – dry inasmuch as the water went only up to the tops of shoes. Digging foxholes or gun emplacements in such terrain only served to dig new ponds; guns had to be lashed to trees to keep them out of the water.

The bayou-like landscape complicated supply and communications. Construction crews had to hold off working on the new air base runways so they could drain the swamp and build some roads or at least reasonable approximations thereof. By November 16, a lateral road – in the loosest sense of the word – along the front of the perimeter had been completed, running from the Koromokina River to the Numa Numa Trail. The progress on the road allowed the Marines to use aggressive patrolling to push forward by about 1,000 yards, seizing control of the junction of the Numa Numa and Piva trails and starting the process of bringing them within the nascent road network.[136]

It was right after that momentous accomplishment that unpleasant things started happening in the Marine sector. Increasing exchanges of fire with Japanese outposts. Increasing skirmishes with Japanese patrols. The 3rd Battalion of the 3rd Marine Regiment found one unoccupied roadblock and, in true aggressive patrolling fashion, occupied it. When Japanese from the 23rd Infantry Regiment tried to reoccupy the roadblock, the Marines ambushed them, killing eight soldiers and one officer – who had in his possession a sketch of Japanese defenses. Document security had never been a strongpoint of the Japanese military. Between that and other intelligence, the Japanese were preparing strong defenses along both the Numa Numa and East-West trails east of the Torokina perimeter.

A patrol from the aforementioned 3rd Battalion confirmed the roadblock on the Numa Numa Trail, while a patrol from the 1st Battalion of the 21st Marine Regiment confirmed the roadblock on the East-West Trail.[137]

Well, that just wouldn't do. If the Marines hurried, they could disrupt the Japanese before their defenses were fully prepared. The 3rd Battalion of the 3rd Marine Regiment was the hot hand, though it was a dry heat, so, on November 19, it was given some Stuart tanks and, after an artillery bombardment, it attacked the Numa Numa position from the right flank and swept the Japanese away, killing 16, which was only a small fraction of the Japanese troops. Which was emphasized the next morning when the Japanese counterattacked, but they were driven back again. The 3rd Battalion advanced. Late in the afternoon of that same day, a patrol of the 2nd Battalion of the 3rd Marines found a ridge that was maybe 400 feet high just north of the East-West Trail. One Marine history described it as "the first high ground to be discovered near our front lines." Though it was, in fact, in front of the front lines, this ridge, called Cibik's Ridge, would be occupied by the platoon of Lieutenant Steve Cibik in either an amazing coincidence or an impetus for later changing the ridge's name in honor for Cibik's defense of the ridge in the face of three banzai charges on November 21 and repeated banzai charges for the following two days, all by the problematic 23rd Infantry Regiment.[138] In fact, the 3rd Marines in general would be locked in combat with the 23rd for the next three days, the most intense combat the Marines would face on Bougainville.

Lieutenant Cibik's platoon was relieved on November 23, as the remainder of the 3rd Marine Regiment advanced to Cibik's Ridge. The next morning, seven battalions of artillery – four Marine and three Army – spent some 20 minutes lobbing more than 5,600 75mm and 105mm howitzer shells into an area of 800 square yards before the 3rd Marine Regiment stepped off on its own attack, intended to push forward to a line that would basically leave the planned airfields free to operate with little Japanese interference. The initial Japanese positions had been destroyed by the bombardment, but as the supporting artillery had to deal with some counterbattery fire situations directed by forwarded observers on Cibik's Ridge against bothersome Japanese 90mm mortars and 75mm field guns, the advance went on two different tracks, both subject to Japanese mortars and artillery that ranged from a nuisance to a major problem. To the right of the East-West Trail, the 2nd Battalion faced a Gifu-like network of camouflaged pillboxes that had stymied initial attacks, but after another artillery bombardment, it didn't so much hold up the advance as cause significant casualties to the assault engineers tasked with reducing them. To the left of the East-West Trail, the 3rd Battalion had an easier time advancing, moving 500 yards before facing a Japanese flanking counterattack that they pushed through, but with vicious hand-to-hand and even tree-to-tree combat. By noon, the initial objectives had been achieved. Casualties during what would be called the Battle of Piva Forks (because it was around forks in the Piva River) belied the relatively small area of combat. The Imperial Army's 23rd Infantry Regiment was "almost completely destroyed," with at least 1,071 Japanese dead, including its commander, while the

3rd Marine Regiment's casualties were 115 casualties.[139] The fighting continued the next day, with the 3rd Marines' place in the fighting being taken by the 1st Battalion of the 9th Marine Regiment and the 2nd Marine Raider Battalion struggling to take the position known as "Grenade Hill" overlooking the East-West Road. They were able to occupy it on November 26 after the Japanese defenders withdrew. Why did they withdraw?

As Samuel Eliot Morison put it, "This Battle of Piva Forks, as the Marines named it, was the last serious ground resistance (on Bougainville) for a long time."[140] With the 23rd Infantry Regiment effectively wiped out, there were simply not enough Japanese troops to do much, certainly not with entry into the Torokina beachhead limited to passages between the mountains and Empress Augusta Bay. It was part of the brilliance of Admiral Halsey's plan.

General Vandegrift had spent just one day on Bougainville and then withdrew to Guadalcanal to move the later echelons forward.[141] He had reported the *Cherryblossom* landings and the initial operations on Bougainville to Marine Commandant Lieutenant General Thomas Holcomb:

[T]he Bougainville operation [...] went off beautifully and was one of the best examples of co-ordinated amphibious effort that I have seen so far. The timing was perfect. The air, both fighter and bombardment, was superior ... the landing went off smoothly, the air, surface and ground co-ordinating as a well-running team. The Third Marine Division that made the assault landing were green troops in their first engagement. Their morale was high; they did not flinch under the spattering of machine gun fire on the approach to the beach, pushed in rapidly, and accomplished their mission in a very expeditious and excellent manner ...[142]

In his memoirs, Vandegrift would add:

I cannot overstate my satisfaction with the initial phases of this operation which demonstrated how much we had progressed in both means and techniques since the Guadalcanal landing fifteen months earlier. Obviously, our training programs were sound and were paying off. On Bougainville, besides providing excellent cover and prelanding bombardment, our airmen exercised the first of the real close air support tactics that were to become such an integral part of Fleet Marine Force doctrine.[143]

Although, as was typical of Vandegrift, he had left out a very significant factor in the success of *Cherryblossom* – himself. One later analysis credited Vandegrift's "experience and keen sense of tactical judgment" should get "most of the credit for the success of the Bougainville undertaking." Put simply, "With Vandegrift in charge, and working on a parallel echelon with a cooperative naval attack force commander, it is hardly accidental that the Bougainville operation resembled that of Guadalcanal – minus most of the errors."[144]

But why put it simply when you can put it more complicatedly? That same analysis did so:

Aside from similarity of terrain, the strongest resemblance to Guadalcanal is that from the outset the plan, by design rather than by reaction of the enemy, called for a perimeter around an airfield. This time the marines were evacuated once the perimeter had been expanded to its strongest terrain features. The major landings were removed from the known center of enemy strength, and land communications on Bougainville were such that an estimated three months would elapse before the Japanese could move the bulk of their strength into positions needed before attacking the perimeter.

Also, the plans made provision for moving in an army division on the eighth day of the operation. Thus the Third Marine Division seized and held the beachhead against attacks from the air and against counterlandings by sea, both of which were anticipated and both developed. Then, as the marines fanned out to secure the perimeter, their units were displaced laterally, turning over to the army the relatively quiet sectors. The marines devoted their full attention to occupying the difficult but commanding terrain and to enlarging the perimeter so as to prevent the enemy from eventually registering artillery on the airstrips. [...]

Further army assistance in the Bougainville operation was fundamental to the plan. Once the airstrips were operational and marine fighters were ready to clear the enemy's combat air patrol from Rabaul, marine ground troops, save for the highly trained antiaircraft and coast defense battalion, were evacuated altogether. This was economical employment of well-trained amphibious personnel. A corps of army troops, backed by artillery, moved into a prepared perimeter and waited for the Japanese to attack. Since the seas remained under American control, the heavy fighting came just as had been anticipated. It took the enemy three months to deploy two divisions from southern Bougainville and adjacent positions for an all-out assault on the perimeter. Once the Japanese had spent themselves struggling with heavy equipment over mountains and jungle trails and ramming into the stone wall of a prepared defense, the army troops in turn were moved out to fight in the Philippines, and the perimeter was turned over to raw Australian militia. The Bougainville perimeter stands as an example of the manner in which the entire Solomons fighting should have been waged, if the means and the time had been available.[145]

The entire Solomons fighting.

For some 15 months, since August 1942, the main stage of the Pacific War had been in the South Pacific – the Solomon Islands, the Bismarck Archipelago, and Papua New Guinea. Brutal combat, even more brutal climate. A long, hot, sticky, muddy slog.

But the spotlights for this particular stage were about to be turned off, and those of another stage switched on.

Because of something called "Galvanic."

CHAPTER 8

AN ALMOST PERFECT ACTION

Amidst all this stuff about echelons, transports, and "[Insert ordinal here] Air Battle[s] off Bougainville," it is easy to forget that a Combined Fleet operation was still in progress, *Ro-Go*. In theory.

In practice, *Ro-Go* had coincided almost perfectly – or, from the Japanese standpoint, perfectly imperfectly – with *Cherryblossom* and the Torokina landing. What had started out as more or less an operation to temporarily regain air superiority had run into an Allied effort to seize and hold air superiority over Bougainville. *Ro-go* had never been intended to go into the teeth of Allied air power, but after *Cherryblossom* that's exactly what it was doing. Bombing attacks and fighter sweeps over Allied airfields on Vella Lavella and New Georgia never took place because the fliers of *Kido Butai* and Base Air Force were either defending their own bases around Rabaul or attacking the Torokina area. The exceptions, and really the only times when *Ro-go* even attempted to carry out its original objective, such as it was, were the attempted attack on the *Saratoga* and *Princeton*, which missed the carriers altogether, and the attack on the *Essex*, *Bunker Hill*, and *Independence*, which ultimately left the carriers only slightly damaged at a frightful cost that included all of the Nakajima B5N Type 97 carrier attack planes from *Kido Butai* committed to the attack.

By this time, construction activities within the Torokina beachhead were becoming apparent. But what did it mean? And what to do about it?

This was where the usual disagreements between the Imperial Army and the Imperial Navy, mostly absent since the arrival of the laid-back General Inamura, who had developed a good working relationship with Admiral Kusaka, manifested themselves once again. Kusaka and the staff of the Southeast Area Fleet guessed the Americans were building an air base at Torokina. This would be a bad thing because, Kusaka believed, such an air base would render Japanese operations on Bougainville impractical and sea movements between Bougainville and Rabaul, or even just around Bougainville, almost impossible.

General Hyakutake, commanding the 17th Army at Buin, in the words of one history, "chose to take a lighter, more optimistic view of the situation than the Navy." Although "lighter" is not a term one would associate with the Imperial Japanese Army normally, Hyakutake's view was certainly more optimistic. Showing that same acumen that had been so successful on Guadalcanal, Hyakutake had modified his assessment of Allied intentions on Bougainville somewhat. He no longer believed the Torokina landing was a diversion, but instead believed the Allies would create a base of operations inside the beachhead. From there, the Allies, as Hyakutake had always believed, would send the bulk of the ground troops to move in on Buin while sending a smaller force to seize the Buka sector. In that case, it was better to make the enemy come attack the Japanese in defensive fortifications in the Buin and Buka areas than to abandon these already-prepared positions to counterattack the Torokina beachhead.[1] In short, Hyakutake was applying the ancient maxim used by such diverse figures as Leonidas, Hannibal Barca (especially), Publius Cornelius Scipio Africanus Major, Salah al-Din, and George Gordon Meade: make the enemy come to you, fight you on your terms.

But what if the enemy does not come? Or has no reason to come? What reason did the Allies have to come to General Hyakutake? He never answered these questions.

Even in the intellectual sludge that generally passed for operational analysis in the Imperial Japanese Army, General Hyakutake's belief was beyond delusional – "This may have been wishful thinking," one US Marine history opined – and simply idiotic. Granted, hindsight is 20-20, especially sitting at a computer some eight decades removed from the events described herein. But if the Allies were playing chess, Hyakutake was – again – playing Tic-Tac-Toe. And losing.

Despite all the efforts of Combined Fleet and the Imperial Army to fortify Bougainville and pack it with defending troops, the Allies had managed to land in the one spot on the island that was almost undefended. Worse, that one spot was about as far from the main Japanese troop concentrations at Buin and Buka as was possible on the island, and thus difficult for the 17th Army to reach because of the lack of roads across the Bougainville jungle. Worse yet, that one spot only had two major points of entry, both of which were on the flanks of the Torokina perimeter, both of which were choke points that could be almost impenetrable if properly defended (a qualification that almost always gets forgotten).

The Americans had already seized both choke points. The Japanese had tried to capture both points, but the counterlanding force sent to the American left had been almost completely wiped out, while on the American right, General Iwasa's force had come up from Buin only to be repulsed with heavy losses. The Allies now controlled both land routes into the beachhead.

Why would the Allies throw away such a beautiful defensive position and all of its benefits to attack the Japanese at the two places where the Japanese were the strongest in both numbers of troops and fortifications? It made no sense.

In fairness, General Hyakutake based his opinion in part (but only in part) on the Guadalcanal and New Georgia campaigns, in which the Allies had refused to share an island with the Japanese like Carthage and the Greeks did in ancient Sicily and instead spared no effort in driving the Japanese from both islands. However, in neither case did the Allies hold such a magnificent defensive position. In neither case had the Japanese had such fortified bases so far from the Allied beachhead. And as Admiral Kusaka had explained, all the Allies needed to do was build an air base within the Torokina beachhead and Bougainville was effectively cut off. The Allies did not need to take the whole island, not as long as they had enough room for the air base.

As the Imperial Army had done so many times on Guadalcanal and as the Imperial Navy had done at Midway, General Hyakutake believed the enemy would do exactly what the Japanese wanted them to do. Admiral Kusaka had only rarely fallen into that trap, but he did not control the troops on Bougainville. Hyakutake did, backed up by Hyakutake's superior with the 8th Area Army, General Inamura. And Hyakutake largely just sat there.

Over all of this proactivity was the head of the Combined Fleet, Admiral Koga. Koga was old school, meaning he believed in the concept of the single "Decisive Battle" winning the Pacific War. Koga was hoping to fight that Decisive Battle when and if the Allies launched their attack on the Marshall and/or Gilbert Islands.

Admiral Koga also seemed to firmly believe that if he kept predicting something would happen, it would eventually happen. On two earlier occasions, there had been ominous rumblings of Allied activity in the Marshalls and Gilberts area. Koga determined the long-awaited Allied central Pacific offensive was imminent. He responded by leading the Combined Fleet out of Truk toward the enemy. That rumbling turned into grumbling by the Japanese when the purported Allied offensive failed to materialize and Koga was compelled to return to Truk. But Koga was sure that no matter how many times it had not happened, if he kept predicting it would happen, it would happen.

The third week of November saw more of those ominous rumblings. Specifically, there were larger and more damaging air attacks on places like Tarawa, Nauru, Millie, and Makin by both US Navy and Army Air Force planes. Among these larger and more damaging attacks was one small but significant attack. On November 18, the extremely veteran light cruiser *Yubari* was making a troop transport run to Garove Island off New Britain when she was found by B-24 Liberators, whose bombs "repeatedly straddled" her. The *Yubari* kept going but later that same November 18, she was found by PBY Catalina flying boats, which caused damage of an unspecified nature. This apparently included damage to her hull and weapons, and was enough to cause the *Yubari* to abort her mission and return to Rabaul for temporary repairs before heading back to Japan on December 3.[2]

That tiny little matter was overshadowed a bit when, that same day, a series of major air attacks swept over the Gilberts, Marshalls, and Nauru. The aircraft carriers of Admiral Sherman (Frederick, not Forrest) hit Nauru heavily. Admiral Koga was ready to make another declaration that the Allies were about to begin their big central Pacific offensive, so it seemed that big Decisive Battle was on the cards, but Koga seems to have been especially spooked by the events of November 19. On that particular day, 19 B-24s of the 7th Bomber Command operating out of Nanumea bombed Mille; two more hit Tarawa. Tarawa was also hit by Admiral Montgomery's carriers *Essex*, *Bunker Hill*, and *Independence*. Meanwhile, Admiral Sherman's *Saratoga* and *Princeton* bombed Nauru – again. The Japanese ordered the land attack planes of the 755 Air Group and fighters of the 252 Air Group to stage into Roi, where they would join fighters of the 281 Air Group.[3]

But it was not the bombing attacks that most bothered Admiral Koga, although they did bother him. What was evidently the most disconcerting was the presence of US Navy carriers. Scout planes had reported one task force that included three carriers; a second force had one. Worse, a third force had invasion transports.[4]

The very afternoon of that November 19, Admiral Koga canceled a planned reinforcement of Admiral Kusaka's Base Air Force. A single "medium attack plane unit" of 36 or 37, oddly enough, medium land attack planes had been scheduled for transfer from the Northeast Area to the Southeast Area – that is, Southeast Area Fleet. The "medium attack plane unit" in question appears to have been the 752 Air Group, equipped with Mitsubishi G4M Type 1 land attack planes.[5] Now, the 752 was going to be sent to the Marshalls-Gilberts area instead. But could they get there in time?

Because early on November 20 came another ominous sighting report: two US Navy carriers 100 miles south of Tarawa heading north. US Navy carrier planes and US Army Air Force B-24s mounted heavy air strikes on Tarawa, Millie, Makin, and Nauru. A force of three US Navy heavy cruisers (*Chester*, *Salt Lake City*, and *Pensacola*) and two destroyers (*Erben* and *Hale*) bombarded Tarawa. Another enemy force that included one battleship and two cruisers was found 130 miles northeast of Tarawa. Four G4Ms of the 755 Air Group were sent up on another one of those "search and contact" missions to find the enemy fleet and shadow them for the following air strike, which in this case consisted of 15 G4Ms from the same 755 Air Group. The Japanese never determined exactly how that attack turned out, but ten of the land attack planes failed to return. The Sea Eagles were picking up where they had left off in the Solomons.[6]

The Solomons were hardly getting better for the Japanese. The runway at Bonis was bombed by 30 B-25 and PV bombers (including six US Navy Venturas of Bombing 138) escorted by 15 P-38s. Meanwhile, 36 TBFs (15 from Marine Torpedo Bombing 143; eight from Marine Torpedo Bombing 233, and 13 from Composite 38) and 57 SBDs (including six from Composite 24) escorted by eight Corsairs from Fighting 17 bombed Japanese positions on the west coast of Bougainville between Mawaraka and the Mibo River, including the village of Mosigetta. The airfields on Bougainville remained unusable, the Japanese ones, at any rate.[7]

The big event of November 20 in the South Pacific for the Allies was the continuation of the American tradition of changing commanding officers just before a major operation. General Twining was being rewarded for his exemplary service as commander of AirSols with a transfer to Italy to command the 15th Air Force. His replacement as commander of AirSols was Marine Major General Ralph J. Mitchell.

Later that night, following the pomp and circumstance of the change in command, a convoy of three Japanese ships escorted by two subchasers had been found following the south coast of New Ireland by a Black Cat PBY of the 5th Air Force's Patrol 101. A few bombs spelled the end of the cargo ship *Naples Maru*, which had been carrying 517 troops making up a section each of the Imperial Japanese Army's 4 Air Group and 51st Division. The subchasers *Ch-17* and *Ch-18* rescued survivors, but 121 of these troops and five of the crew were killed.[8]

The next day, November 21 (November 20 at Pearl Harbor), proved the third time was the charm for Admiral Koga's prediction of an Allied offensive in the Central Pacific.[9] Following bombardment by US Navy warships and bombing by carrier aircraft, elements of the US Army's veteran 27th Infantry Division landed at Butaritari Island in Makin Atoll and the 2nd Marine Division waded at Betio Island in Tarawa Atoll as part of Operation *Galvanic*, among the cooler names for military operations during the war.[10]

Admiral Koga promptly activated his contingency plan for this invasion, code-named *Hei*. As part of *Hei*, he ordered the Sea Eagles of *Kido Butai* to stage into the Marshall Islands and … ohhhh …[11]

At the moment, *Kido Butai* had no Sea Eagles because most of them were lost during *Ro-Go*, and because aircraft carriers are not particularly useful without aircraft – a proposition Combined Fleet would test a year later – *Kido Butai* was back in the Home Islands training a new group of Sea Eagles, who were not yet even out of the nest. "The almost complete loss of carrier planes was a mortal blow to the fleet since it would require six months for replacement," recalled Vice Admiral Fukudome Shigeru, Admiral Koga's chief of staff. "[I]t was felt that it would take until May or June of 1944 to complete that replacement. In the interim, any fighting with (the) carrier force was rendered impossible."[12]

The catastrophe of the losses incurred during *Ro-Go* now intersected with the catastrophe that was the Japanese system of training aviators to form, as Admiral Halsey or Frederick Lanchester might have said, a catastrophe squared. The Imperial Japanese Navy's most powerful weapon by far was going to be down for *six months* as it trained new air crews.

A catastrophe squared is a decent way to describe what now faced Admiral Koga. The losses suffered by *Kido Butai*'s air groups during *Ro-Go* compelled their withdrawal. Admiral Kusaka and his Base Air Force needed replacements for them, so Koga had sent 29 "carrier bombers" from … the Marshall Islands. Exactly the area now threatened by the Allies. Koga had robbed proverbial Peter to pay proverbial Paul. Now he had to rob proverbial Paul to pay back proverbial Peter by sending the 752 Air Group to the Marshalls-Gilberts instead of Base Air Force, as had originally been intended.

"Admiral Koga's idea was to save up his full strength for one decisive engagement," Admiral Fukudome later explained. "That was the reason why he disregarded the constant request for air reinforcement from Rabaul, because the only planes that could be sent were carrier planes."[13]

Admiral Fukudome went into detail:

[A]fter the failure of the decisive surface engagement planned from Brown, Admiral Koga finally decided to send a small number of carrier-based planes to be used for a short time at Rabaul. The actual strength that was sent to Rabaul was most of the planes of [Admiral] Ozawa's Air Fleet [*Kido Butai*]. They were to be used for a very short time, about a ten[-]day period, and then returned to the fleet so as to maintain the strength of the fleet as a whole. Looking back on it now, this was a bad mistake because having sent the carrier planes to Rabaul for a period of about ten days, on about the very day they were supposed to return, the occupation of Bougainville and Shortland took place; and in spite of the fact they didn't intend to use these planes for such operations, they just couldn't stand by and not employ them. They were finally employed against these US landing operations and the majority were lost. With the loss of these planes, the fleet as a whole lost considerable efficiency.[14]

The effect on the defense of the Marshalls and Gilberts was, again, catastrophe squared: "[A]lthough the Gilbert fight appeared to be the last chance for a decisive fight, the fact that the fleet's air strength had been so badly depleted enabled us to send only very small air support to Tarawa and Makin."[15] Part of that "very small air support" was the aforementioned 752 Air Group.

Captain Ohmae Toshikazu, who was on Admiral Kusaka's staff during this time, went further and was even more blunt:

The specific plan to counter an American invasion of the Gilberts was as follows: Long-range aircraft from the Bismarks [sic] would attack the US invasion forces and then land at fields in the Marshalls-Gilberts. Short range aircraft would start from or stage through Truk and proceed to Marshalls-Gilberts fields and from there attack the US forces. It was expected to require four days for the short range aircraft to reach the attack position from the Bismarks [sic]. Warships at Truk would sortie and move to the Gilbert Islands where they would attack American surface and invasion forces. Six or seven submarines, which were employed in supply service in the Bismarks [sic], also would be ordered to assist in repelling the invasion.

Two factors radically changed these plans. The first was the serious damage received by several Second Fleet cruisers at Rabaul by carrier air attack on 5 November 1943. These ships and other units had just arrived from Truk to assist in the serious situation at Bougainville. The second factor was the intensified air war in the Solomons related to further landings at Munda which absorbed our air forces already in the Western Solomons and also required employment of the short range planes which were being held at Truk for defense of the Marshalls-Gilberts. Consequently the original plans for defense of those islands could not be carried out when American forces invaded in November, because there was insufficient surface and air strength available to make effective resistance.[16]

But the catastrophe squared reached well beyond the immediate problem of how to support the defense of the Gilberts without *Kido Butai*. *Kido Butai* would be back. Once the new air group was trained, *Kido Butai* would be back in the thick of the fight as it usually was, in some form, anyway. It had always come back, but every time it came back, it did so weaker than before. That was not entirely unexpected; there was simply no way to replicate the regimen of training and combat against an inferior opponent – and combat against even an inferior opponent is better than all the training in the world – that had made the Sea Eagles the best in the world. But the trend line was now unmistakable. Midway had masked it a bit, as many of the surviving aviators were packed aboard the *Shokaku*, *Zuikaku*, and *Zuiho*, giving those three carriers excellent air groups. But those air groups had taken heavy losses at Eastern Solomons and severe losses at Santa Cruz. Almost six months of training enabled them to return for *I-Go*, in which they showed they were not as good as the air crews they had replaced. Heavy losses during *I-Go* meant training new air groups, which were committed the previous August, in which they showed they were not as good as the air crews they had replaced, and then suffered heavy losses again. Lather, rinse, repeat. Now the losses for *Ro-Go* had been beyond severe. Admiral Ozawa and *Kido Butai* had to train another new air group. Could they stop the drop-off? Hide the decline? If not, how much would it be this time? How much longer could *Kido Butai* keep repeating this pattern without its aviators losing effectiveness altogether?

Those were questions for the very shaken Admiral Ozawa. At least Ozawa would not have to send *Kido Butai*'s few remaining aviators back to the front lines; Admiral Koga canceled their deployment order later that afternoon.[17] By that time, contact with the Makin garrison had been lost. Japanese scout planes had found an enemy force of two carriers and two battleships approaching Tarawa from the southeast and another force of three carriers southeast of Makin. There were heavy air attacks reported on Mille and Nauru (including one by 30 B-24 Liberators from AirSols' 23rd and 31st Bombardment Squadrons from the 5th Bombardment Group and the 372nd and 424th Bombardment Squadrons from the 307th Bombardment Group, though bad weather forced the 372nd to turn back and the 424th's bombs ended up in the water); a smaller one on Jaluit, and a tiny one on Ocean Island.[18]

In response to these discouraging developments, Admiral Koga announced to the entire Combined Fleet that the 2nd Base Air Force (also known as the 12th Air Fleet) – the inferior production-line model to the original Base Air Force (11th Air Fleet) – would stage into Truk on November 22 to "clarify the enemy situation by search and patrol." Then, on November 23, the Combined Fleet would depart Truk "to contact and annihilate the enemy at an opportune time."[19] Presumably, this did not include all the ships of the Combined Fleet that were still under repair from the Solomons campaign. Without those damaged ships, Koga's battle fleet would sortie from Truk to face the largest fleet ever assembled for a single operation during the Pacific War: one that included six fleet carriers, five light carriers, six new battleships, six old battleships, eight heavy cruisers, three light antiaircraft cruisers, three ordinary light cruisers, and 56 destroyers.

Admiral Koga did get off to a good start, sort of. Late that afternoon, two of those land attack planes took off on another "search and contact" mission to pin the enemy for the air attack that was launched about 45 minutes later. An enemy carrier force was found near Tarawa just before sunset and 14 G4M land attack planes of the 755 Air Group were vectored to attack it with torpedoes. They looped around to attack from the dark side, like Higai Joji had at Rennell Island what seemed like years ago.[20]

Their targets were Admiral Montgomery's carriers who had escaped the wrath of Base Air Force off Rabaul. This time, Montgomery's light carrier *Independence* was not so lucky, taking a torpedo in her starboard side, albeit during a hard port turn that resulted in the hit being much higher than it normally would have been. The after engine room was flooded, three of the four propeller shafts were disabled, and a 12-degree list to starboard quickly developed. But the list was reduced to seven degrees within minutes. According to the Bureau of Ships, "The stability of *Independence* was never critical, although the Commanding Officer [Captain Rudolf Lincoln Johnson] reported some anxiety until progressive flooding was eliminated." The light carrier made it back on one shaft for repairs.[21] For this result, better than Base Air Force had achieved of late against aircraft carriers but still not particularly good under the circumstances, the 755 Air Group was decimated by a late-afternoon combat air patrol and heavy antiaircraft fire. Nine of the G4Ms failed to return to base.[22]

So, 2nd Base Air Force was holding up the high-casualty tradition of Base Air Force, a tradition of which Admiral Kusaka was all too aware. If the redirection of the 752 Air Group was not enough of a message to him, then the Allied invasion of Tarawa and Makin and the activation of the *Hei* plan in response was hard to miss: there would be no more reinforcements for the Southeast Area Fleet. Kusaka would have to win with what he had, and maybe not even that.

All of which meant that *Ro-Go* was, well, technically continuing. No orders terminating it were ever issued. But the attack that sank the *McKean* was the last of *Ro-Go*. After that, the Japanese adopted the attitude of *Never mind*. Which was easier said than done for the 70 air crews Base Air Force had lost, or the 86 air crews *Kido Butai* had lost.[23]

Be that as it may, Base Air Force was continuing to lash out at the Torokina beachhead, but mostly with nuisance strikes. Four Corsairs from the Fighting 17 "Jolly Rogers" started the morning of November 21 just after 5:30am when they reportedly intercepted six Zeros and shot down all six Zeros and one "Tony." When you engage six planes and shoot down seven of them, you are having a good day. The "Tony" appears to have actually fallen foul to Lieutenant William Haymes of the 67th Fighter Squadron, who had a flight of P-39 Airacobras up at around this time. The Japanese admitted only that two carrier attack planes and one dive bomber attacked Torokina, with the dive bomber failing to return. The reference to the one "Tony" suggests the dive bomber was a D4Y Judy from the 501 Air Group. Curiously, though the Japanese say they sent no fighters to Torokina, three prominent fighter pilots, all from the 253 Air Group, Warrant Officer Tomoishi Masateru and Petty Officers 1st Class Matsumura Hidemichi and Fukuda Isao, were killed over Torokina this day.[24]

That was just breakfast for AirSols. After lunch, eight Corsairs from Marine Fighting 212 and another eight from Marine Fighting 215 escorted 59 Dauntlesses (including 39 from Marine Scout Bombing 244, with one aborting because of engine trouble; eight from Marine Scout Bombing 243 in its first action of the campaign; and 12 from Composite 38) and 35 Avengers from Marine Torpedo 233 in an attack on the Kara air base, with some saved for the Kahili (Buin) air base as well.[25] AirSols was determined to hold all the Japanese bases on Bougainville and Buka down, but you know the rule about air strips made of dirt.

AirSols was also determined to do what it could to help the ground troops inside the Torokina perimeter, but in so doing it prematurely ended what had been a jolly day for the Jolly Rogers. After completing their patrol over Empress Augusta Bay, six Corsairs from Fighting 17 went to strafe targets of opportunity on the Monoitu-Kahili Trail, which the Japanese were using to supply their troops in the Torokina sector. Veteran Lieutenant Charles A. "Chuck" Pillsbury led his wingman Ensign Robert R. Hogan in machine-gunning five trucks on the trail into flaming wreckage. They looped around Kangu Hill short of Kahili and that was the last Hogan saw of Pillsbury or his plane. Four Jolly Rogers spent two hours searching for Pillsbury and found nothing. Only in 1968 was the wreck of a Corsair believed to be Pillsbury's found in the jungle west of Kangu Hill. All that was left of the young Navy veteran, as far as investigators could tell, were two vertebrae and one lieutenant's bar. The cause of the crash or Pillsbury's death were never determined.[26]

Admiral Kusaka continued trying to strike back, but Base Air Force's efforts became increasingly feeble. During the early hours of November 22, five land attack planes bombed the Torokina beachhead. The Japanese reported starting a fire within the perimeter, but the Americans reported no damage.[27] This was followed by another attack by one "bomber" and two carrier attack planes, who seem to have accomplished nothing but lost nothing. At 8:15am, four P-40s of the Royal New Zealand Air Force's No. 18 Squadron patrolling the beachhead were startled to encounter 48 Japanese Zeros on what seems to have been a fighter sweep. The encounter apparently turned into a running battle from maybe ten miles northeast of Mutupina to Torokina itself. The Kiwis reported shooting down five Zeros with no losses, while the Japanese reported shooting down four Kittyhawks with no losses. In actuality, the Kiwis took no losses, though one P-40 was badly damaged, but at least two Zero pilots, Petty Officers 1st Class Yamaguchi Shotoku and Kobayashi Yorihisa, were killed in this engagement. Four other Kiwi Kittyhawks did not make contact with the Zeros.[28]

As the day went on, even with its new commander General Mitchell, AirSols settled more firmly and comfortably into its daily game of Air Raid Roulette. Which air base(s) will we attack today? Buka? Bonis? Both? Kahili/Buin? Kara? Both? Kieta? Ballale? Today, during the lunch hour, five Venturas of Bombing 138 joined some two dozen B-25 Mitchells of the 42nd Bombardment Group, escorted by eight Corsairs of Marine Fighting 211 and eight Army Air Force P-38s in bombing Buka.[29] After that came a midafternoon bombing of Kahili by 52 SBDs (including 19 from Composite 24, three more aborted because of engine trouble) and 24 TBFs (14 from Marine Torpedo Bombing 143 and 10 from Composite 38) with 16 Corsairs from Fighting 17.[30]

The next day, November 23, was more Air Raid Roulette. The wheel landed on Bonis and Buka. The day's festivities started at 9:15am, with a bombing and strafing attack on Japanese positions at Chabai, on Bougainville inland of Bonis. The 23 B-25 Mitchells of the Army Air Force's 42nd Bombardment Group (including 12 from the 75th Bombardment Squadron, four from the 70th, and an unknown number from the 69th) and six Venturas from Navy Bombing 138, with an escort of 24 Corsairs (including 15 from Fighting 17 and eight from Marine Fighting 222) were to use parafrags and fragmentation clusters to ruin any festive moods the Japanese ground troops may have had. In this the Americans succeeded, but the Japanese returned the favor with intense antiaircraft fire, damaging three planes. The worst was the B-25 of the 75th Bombardment Squadron's Flight Officer Richard Schaffner. With a smoking left engine, Schaffner tried to make a water landing in Matchin Bay, but just before he hit the water, the left engine exploded, causing the Mitchell to crash hard and disintegrate. Flight Officer Schaffner and crew, the worst hit, went into the water and were lost. Co-pilot 2nd Lieutenant John A. Bailey survived, only to be captured and taken to Rabaul. He would not survive his captivity.[31]

AirSols would get some measure of revenge when, less than three hours later, two B-24s bombed Chabai, though they could not see the results. At the same time, 16 Liberators bombed the runway and revetments at Bonis. Three more Liberators hit Buka. All were from the 5th Bombardment Group.[32]

The vengeance continued on November 24 as the Chabai area was simply plastered. It started at 10:00am when 57 Dauntlesses (from Marine Scout Bombing 244 and 243, and Composite 38; two more aborted with engine trouble and a third aborted for unknown reasons) and 37 Avengers (15 from Marine Torpedo Bombing 143, eight from Marine Torpedo Bombing 233, and 14 from Composite 38) escorted by 48 fighters (including 24 Corsairs from Fighting 17) unloaded 50 tons of bombs on the bothersome base before strafing it for good measure. Numerous buildings believed to hold supplies were destroyed and the damaging antiaircraft guns at least appeared to be suppressed by the attack.[33]

A half hour later came 14 Liberators of the 5th Bombardment Group who dropped 23 tons of bombs while another nine of the 5th bombed Buka. At the same time, 20 Mitchells of the 42nd Bombardment Group dropped 30 tons of bombs on the runway at Kahili, but again could not escape unscathed as a B-25 piloted by the 70th Squadron's Lieutenant James H. Dickinson took a direct hit that caused the left engine to burst into flames, which quickly spread to the bomb bay and the navigator's compartment.[34] Dickinson had to ditch off Maifu Island, one of the Shortlands. The entire crew was able to escape and get into a life raft, but they were stuck in the second-biggest Japanese fortress in the South Pacific.[35]

No problem, said Milton Cheverton of Patrol Squadron 23. With about a dozen Kiwi Kittyhawks for cover, Cheverton swooped in with a Dumbo PBY Catalina – maybe "swooped in" is not quite the right term to use with a PBY – and plucked the crewmen from off Ballale and took off again, with every Japanese gun in sight shooting at the fat, slow PBY and still not hitting it.[36]

Lieutenant Dickinson told Cheverton, "I've always thought the PBY was the ugliest airplane I had ever seen until I saw you coming in to pick us up – then I decided it was the most beautiful craft in the world!"[37]

Beauty is indeed in the eye of the beholder. As the night ahead would show.

Nine of those wild and wacky PT boats, these under Commander Henry Farrow, had been deployed in the Buka Passage, that narrow strait between Buka and Bougainville, to await this reported Tokyo Express.[38] One never knew what the PT boats were going to do, and neither did they. They had a record of attacking enemy ships and attacking friendly ships. The identity of the target did not matter to them.

Usually. It was after midnight on November 25 when two sections of the boats detected two large surface targets on radar. The ships appeared to be patrolling off the western entrance to Buka's anchorage.[39] They were undoubtedly warships. It was time to go to work.

Or was it? Some US Navy destroyers were reportedly in the area. In the past, that had not mattered much to the PTs, but some "'unhappy' incidents with [American] surface and aircraft" had made some of these arguably overaggressive boats gun shy. On this night, they thought they might actually be facing US Navy destroyers. As a result, they did not attack, except for one torpedo launched by *PT-64* because of a misunderstanding of orders.[40]

Even so, they watched the two targets carefully, looking for any confirmation one way or the other. The two dark shapes suspended their patrolling and turned toward the southernmost section of PT boats. Could be to investigate, the US Navy sailors wondered. Neither the ships nor the boats made an attempt at visual communication. OK, maybe they wanted to continue to investigate. They were indeed destroyers, but were they American?

The two men-of-war kept coming …

And increased their speed …

And aimed directly at the PT boats.

Maybe they were American destroyers who really, *really* wanted to investigate the PTs. That had to be the thinking when one of the destroyers headed straight for *PT-318*. Friends or enemies, a repeat of John F. Kennedy's (in)famous *PT-109* incident was in the offing. Or not, as the boat's skipper Lieutenant (jg) Charles A. Bernier, Jr was able to avoid the tender caresses of the warships' slicing bows.

Maybe they were American destroyers who had not even seen the PTs. The night is dark, after all. Though it lit up a bit with gunflashes when the destroyers opened fire on the PTs with their main guns at 12:24am.[41] The PTs boats did not return fire or attempt to launch torpedoes but instead zigzagged away under cover of smokescreens.[42]

The PT boats had almost attacked friendly ships. Again. These PT boats were determined to not make that mistake. Again.

Instead, they made a completely different mistake. The two destroyers they had encountered were the *Onami* and *Makinami* under the command of Captain Kagawa Kiyoto of the Imperial Japanese Navy.[43]

Captain Kagawa, the *Onami*, and the *Makinami* were indeed there to run troops to Buka. Because the Imperial Japanese Army believed that Buka was the true objective of the Allied advance. Because that's what the Japanese themselves would do if they were in the Allies' shoes. The Japanese had often made their tactical, operational, and even strategic plans based on the assumption that the Allies would do what the Japanese would do. Of course, the Allies rarely, if ever, did what the Japanese would do, so those Japanese plans usually failed as a result, but the Japanese were not so much oblivious as they were determined to ignore this catch in their thinking.

Be that as it may:

> Not only was it feared that the hasty relinquishment of Buka, the last remaining outpost of Rabaul in the Solomons' area, would result in the sudden deterioration of the strategic situation at Rabaul, but also Buka itself was badly needed as a supply base to enable the Buin sector to hold out for an extended period of time.[44]

The Army demanded the Imperial Navy rush troops from the 27th Division to Buka.[45] And what better way to run these troops to Buka than good old fashioned rat transportation?

This time, there would be no neat organization by destroyer flotillas or even destroyer divisions, but just whatever destroyers the Japanese had lying around the house, grouped into units with pretty names like "Transport Group." The tiny destroyer *Uzuki* from Destroyer Division 30 would follow *Yugiri*, who in turn would follow veteran and sister ship *Amagiri* under Destroyer Division 11's Captain Yamashiro Katsumori, a veteran of a few of these runs. The Transportation Group would be screened by, oddly enough, the "Screening Group" consisting of the very new-ish *Onami* and *Makinami* of Destroyer Division 31 under the command of Captain Kiyoto, who was also in command of this entire mission.[46] While Yamashiro was a veteran of a few rat runs, Kagawa had no night battle experience whatsoever.[47] But a night battle was just like a day battle, except it was fought at night. How hard could it be? Admiral Tanaka had done it and he ended up banished to Burma, so if he could do it, anyone could do it.

Captain Kagawa's little squadron arrived off Buka around 11:00pm on November 24. Kagawa had his own *Onami* and sister ship *Makinami* wait offshore for Captain Yamashiro's *Amagiri*, *Yugiri*, and *Uzuki* to land their 920 troops and 35 tons of supplies on Buka while embarking some 700 troops to return to Rabaul. Hara called these troops "sick and ailing" while the Americans called them "aviation personnel."[48] Maybe they were sick and ailing aviation personnel.

Of course, Hara also says "[n]o opposition was encountered on the way in" and that Captain Yamashiro's Transport Group landed their troops and supplies "without incident."[49] Which is not entirely accurate. Because of the aforementioned encounter with those American devil boats in which the Japanese believed each of the screening destroyers had sunk one boat.[50]

As that was going on, Captain Yamashiro had completed landing the Imperial Army troops at 12:10am, loaded the *Amagiri*, *Yugiri*, and *Uzuki* with the sick and ailing aviation personnel, and headed out at 12:45am. When Captain Kagawa's Screening Group saw Yamashiro's Transport Group heading out of the anchorage, they moved into position eight miles ahead of Yamashiro's group, and headed for the now-dubious safety of Rabaul as fast as they could.[51]

Though the *Onami* and *Makinami* were equipped with the Type 22 General Purpose Radar, they do not seem to have used it.[52] Because not even 15 minutes later, lookouts on the *Onami* reported "three hostile cruisers" off the port bow west of Buka.[53] That wasn't good. What to do about it …?

Any chance at answering that question was rudely cut off by an alarming jolt, followed by a veritable freight train of fiery gases rapidly expanding outward, sending slicing debris in every direction as Captain Kagawa's ship disintegrated from under him.

Kagawa Kiyoto would never finish that thought, or any other.

———————————————⊙———————————————

With grim satisfaction – for the moment – Captain Arleigh Burke watched as the stricken *Onami* "completely disintegrated in a ball of fire approximately 300 feet high, illuminating the falling debris […]."[54] After just short of two years of war, the US Navy was finally getting the hang of this night surface combat thing. And all it had involved was combining Japanese tactics with American technological superiority, plus a generous helping of the craziness that comes packaged with the genius that people like Arleigh Albert Burke possess.

Thanks to *Magic*, the gift that kept on giving, Admiral Halsey's headquarters had (given Burke) 24 hours' advance warning of the Tokyo Express run to Buka, albeit not 24 hours' advance warning that Burke's squadron would be on any mission.[55] Since November 22, the Little Beavers had been spending their nights loitering off Bougainville and their days in Hathorn Sound slurping up fuel so they could continue to spend their nights loitering off Bougainville. But on November 24, Captain Burke received orders to finish taking on oil as soon as possible and head for a place called "Point Uncle." No other information, like where exactly Point Uncle was or what they were supposed to do when they got there. Further instructions and information would follow. "Proceed … you know what to do," headquarters added.[56]

So the commodore had to scramble to get his destroyers moving. Flags were hoisted on the yardarms of the *Charles Ausburne* ordering everyone to get ready to leave ASAP. The departure was a hard deadline. If men were ashore and did not get the word that their ships were leaving ASAP, the ships would have to leave without them.[57]

Captain Burke prepared to leave with all the destroyers he could scrounge up – all five of them. They were names familiar from Empress Augusta Bay: *Charles Ausburne*, *Dyson*, and *Claxton* from Burke's own Destroyer Division 45; and the *Converse* and *Spence* from Commander Austin's Destroyer Division 46. Of the other three squadron mates, the damaged *Foote* and *Thatcher* were en route to Pearl Harbor and then the Bremerton Navy Yard, and *Stanly* was undergoing some emergency repairs to her engineering spaces by the teams from the destroyer tender *Whitney*.[58] Five destroyers would have to do.

By 12:30pm, the *Converse* and *Spence* finished fueling and were sent ahead at 20 knots to try to flush out any submarines which might be waiting in ambush. At 2:05 that afternoon, Captain Burke left Hathorn Sound with his own *Charles Ausburne* leading the *Dyson* and *Claxton*. They would catch up with Commander Austin's scouting destroyers before dark.[59]

During the voyage, South Pacific/3rd Fleet operations officer Captain Thurber, acting for Admiral Halsey while the latter was in Brisbane meeting with General MacArthur, filled in the blanks in Captain Burke's orders – orders that, to be honest, were far more blanks than words. "Point Uncle" was defined as latitude 6-47 South; longitude 154-46 East. There was nothing special about Point Uncle on its own; it was just an empty space in the ocean. It was only to be used as a point of reference. Intelligence believed that the Tokyo Express run was intended to evacuate aviation personnel from the now-useless Buka air base complex. Burke's destroyers were "to take care of it."[60]

But nothing comes easy in the Solomon Islands, and merely traveling to Point Uncle was no exception. The destroyer *Spence* was operating with only three of her four boilers, partly because some genius had jammed a tube brush into a boiler tube, which caused the tubes to burn out, necessitating taking the boiler down for repairs. The issues caused Commander Austin to switch his command to the *Converse*. When Admiral Halsey's orders came down, Captain Burke had hoisted the flag ordering four destroyers to get ready to sail – but not the *Spence*.[61]

Upon seeing that order, the *Spence*'s skipper Lieutenant Commander Henry Jacques "Heinie" Armstrong immediately went to the *Charles Ausburne*. He told Captain Burke, "We are lighting off the three boilers we have in commission and we want to go with the rest of you for we know you expect to get in a fight."

The commodore reminded him his ship could not keep up on three boilers. "We can if we can cross-connect," Lieutenant Commander Armstrong replied. "[T]hen we can make 31 knots or more." Both Burke and Armstrong knew that if the ship went into battle cross-connected, one hit destroying any part of her steam lines would bring the ship to a dead stop. For that reason, in the circumstances of expectant combat, a cross-connected plant was a technical violation of US Navy regulations.

For that reason, Captain Burke's answer was, "No." But Armstrong would not take "No" for an answer. And the commodore suspected the *Spence* would be needed.

"Commodore, please let us come for we want to do our share," implored Armstrong. In Burke's words, "[T]hat decided the question."[62]

"Very well," said Burke, "you may come along and our formation speed will be 31 knots."[63]

The *Spence*'s engineering issues seem to have gotten back to Admiral Halsey's headquarters, however. By 5:30pm, the Little Beavers were rounding Vella Lavella, but there was some confusion as to just how many ships Burke had with him. Captain Thurber sent a message to Burke, "Report ships with you, your speed, and ETA 'Point Uncle.'"[64]

In response, Burke reported the five ships in his formation and his ETA at "Point Uncle" as 10:00 that night via a route south of the Treasuries. He added, "Proceeding at 31 knots." Admiral Halsey's headquarters found that top speed amusing. All of the destroyers of Squadron 23 were rated for 38 knots, though in practice their top speed was 34 knots. However, for some time, Burke had been ending his reports with "Proceeding at 30 knots" in protest of the lack of essential maintenance for his destroyers that had, for instance, cost him the services of the *Stanly* for the current mission. Captain Thurber decided to have some fun with that one-knot increase in speed.[65]

The Little Beavers were closing on the Treasury Islands when Lieutenant John H. "Stinky" Davis, communications officer for Destroyer Squadron 23, climbed the ladder to the *Charles Ausburne*'s bridge and handed Captain Burke a message from Admiral Halsey. It was addressed, "For Thirty-one knot Burke."[66]

The commodore roared with laughter, so hard his body shook and he had tears in his eyes. It took Burke a moment to compose himself before he could read the rest of the message: "[G]et athwart the Buka-Rabaul evacuation line about 35 miles west of Buka. If no enemy contact by 0300 Love [3:00am local time] 25th come South to refuel same place. If enemy contact you know what to do."[67]

Thus a nickname was born. So Arleigh Burke had that going for him. Which was nice. Admiral Halsey added a note for AirSols: "Get this word to your B-24s and Black Cats. Add a night fighter for Burke from 0330 [3:30am] to sunrise and give him day air cover."[68] AirSols warned Captain Burke that "a friendly snooper" was in the area "loaded for a kill" and if Burke's destroyers encountered it to make "liberal use of IFF [Identification Friend or Foe]." A night fighter would arrive over the squadron at 3:30am.[69]

The commodore spent the late afternoon slapping together an operational plan:

1. To fuel as quickly as possible (though his ships had already done that.)
2. To proceed at maximum speed (the famous 31 knots) to the Rabaul-Buka route.
3. To arrive athwart the Rabaul-Buka route at 1:45am.
4. To hit the Rabaul-Buka line as far west as possible.
5. After arriving on the Rabaul-Buka line to slow to 23 knots in order to reduce wake.

6. To search the Rabaul-Buka line on the northern side so as to make contact northwest of the enemy, the direction from which the enemy could least expect interception.

7. To conduct any battle in accordance with the Squadron Doctrine. (That is, the Burke Doctrine.)[70]

Even with that unnecessary first step, Captain Burke quickly completed the plan, a task helped immeasurably by the experience these ships had in working with each other and under their commander, a facet that was largely absent from Allied naval operations in the Solomons until, say, early August 1943. By 7:30pm, Burke was ready to announce his battle plans to his skippers. With no way to have an in-person conference when all the ships were speeding at a now-famous 31 knots on a course of 325 degrees True – roughly north northwest – Burke summoned Commander Austin and their skippers and their senior officers to a conference via the Talk Between Ships voice radio circuit.[71]

The commodore first explained what the Japanese were doing, then explained that the squadron's job was to seek out and destroy the enemy. It was fortunate that Captain Burke already had a nickname, albeit a very new one, so no one could call him Captain Obvious. He closed his remarks with the optimistic observation, "Gentlemen, this is lovely work if you can get it – and we've got it!

"Now, fellas," Burke continued after concluding his remarks:

I've got a hunch the farther north and west we go on this deal the better off we'll be when we meet the Jap. We'll drive northwest, then, until we intersect the Buka-Rabaul route about 0130 [1:30] tomorrow morning. If we get there earlier than that and thus have a little extra time we'll use it to get farther west. Then we'll come right a little and patrol athwart that line at 23 knots. By doing it that way, should we meet the enemy as I fervently hope we shall, we'll be coming from the direction of his own home base – the quarter he's least likely to look for us in – and if he does discover us he may confuse us with a formation of his own ships. long enough for us to get in our surprise torpedo attack. Incidentally, you'd better turn on your IFF [Identification Friend or Foe] at 2245 [10:45pm]. I don't think it's likely we'll encounter anything friendly where we're going, but it may help keep us together.

If we meet the enemy we will keep both divisions on the same side of him to avoid such a melee as happened at Empress Augusta Bay, and so the supporting division will be instantly ready to carry on the attack in case there are other enemy forces in the vicinity. We will attack immediately on contact. We will not withdraw while a ship floats and can fight. We will not abandon a cripple. Now, does everybody savvy this thing? Or has anyone any questions or suggestions? I don't want any confusion or misunderstanding this time. How about you, Heinie?

"It sounds like good dope to me, Commodore," replied Lieutenant Commander Armstrong, using 1940s slang that today is used on street corners and in back alleys with a completely different meaning. "*Spence* will come to the party. I have no suggestions."

"Ham …?"

"*Converse* is ready," answered her skipper Commander DeWitt Clinton Ellis "Ham" Hamberger. "As I understand your plan it's straight doctrine once contact is made, and I haven't any suggestions for improving that."

"Heraldo …?"

"Check an' double check!" said Commander Herald "Heraldo" Franklin Stout. "*Claxton* will be there. No questions; no suggestions."

"Roy …?"

"Just a minute, boss," replied the *Dyson*'s Commander Roy Alexander Gano with exaggerated solemnity. "Major Smith is studying it."

"Who in blazes is Major Smith?" snapped Captain Burke. "Don't tell me you've got a stowaway in *Dyson*!"

"No, Commodore. I'm Major Smith. Don't you remember? General Grant used to have his dumbest officer, Major Smith, read all orders before they were issued. If Major Smith could understand an order, it was all right. But if Major Smith couldn't understand an order, it had to be rewritten. Well, now I think I grasp what you have in mind. *Dyson* will be in there pitching." Everyone laughed.

"Very well," said Captain Burke concluding the conference. "We have search planes, a Black Cat, and night fighters. There is nothing to be desired but an enemy contact." The commodore was a man of simple tastes, obviously. And those tastes were increasingly likely to be sated as his Little Beavers with every foot were swimming deeper into enemy territory than any US surface force had dared go since the beginning of the Guadalcanal-Solomons campaign. As Captain Burke later elaborated:

This job was another one which every destroyer sailor likes to have. The Squadron was powerful enough to take care of any surface craft which it might encounter. Our orders were elastic enough to permit us to cruise in those areas in which we would most likely make contact with the enemy. There was sufficient air cover provided so that the Squadron would not be without air support against enemy plane attacks to which it had been repeatedly subjected and which were always expected.[72]

Expected, but not welcomed. Of any variety. After two reports from scout planes of "boats" that the commodore considered unreliable, at around midnight, the *Claxton* reported, "Have many bogies. Am tracking." A minute later Commander Stout was back on the voice radio, "I'm sorry, but my bogies were a flock of seagulls."

The commodore was not one to run so far away from such a *faux pas*. "Heraldo," Captain Burke responded, "were those seagulls enemy or friendly?" "Seemingly trivial," according to historian Ken Jones, but, remember, seagulls are known to be dangerous bombers.[73]

Onward the Little Beavers went. The night was dark, as nights tend to be, only more so, because there was no moon. It was overcast with frequent squalls and a temperature of 85 degrees – and no, it was not a dry heat. Visibility was about 3,000 yards. According to Captain Burke, "It was an ideal night for a nice quiet torpedo attack."[74]

The ability to concoct such romantic imagery was part of what made Arleigh Burke the best destroyer commander in the US Navy. At 1:30am, the Little Beavers slowed to 23 knots, just as planned. At 1:40am, slightly ahead of schedule, the entire squadron turned to course due north, with Commander Austin's two destroyers in a column bearing 225 degrees' distance 5,000 yards from Destroyer Division 45's column of three destroyers led by the *Charles Ausburne*.[75]

Good thing they were slightly ahead of schedule. At 1:41, the *Dyson*'s Commander Gano radioed, "Please check bearing zero-eight-five, distance 22,000. We have two apple gadgets at zero-seven-five, distance 22,000." Within seconds, the *Spence*'s Lieutenant Commander Armstrong reported, "We have two applegadgets at zero-seven-five, distance 22,000." After a few seconds more came the *Claxton*'s Commander Stout: "We have course 280, 20 knots for applegadgets." Captain Burke could not help himself, nor did he need to: "Hello, DesRon-23! Hang on to your hats, boys, here we go!"[76]

It was time to make that traditional American applegadget pie using almost the same recipe Commander Frederick Moosbrugger had used at Vella Gulf – a recipe developed by one Arleigh Burke. Burke had been robbed of the chance to try it at Vella Gulf, but now he would get his chance to try it himself. It's better to do it yourself. Then you know it's done right.

The commodore had two targets on his radar, but he knew there were more. Burke ordered the three destroyers of Destroyer Division 45 to perform a column turn to 85 degrees True, almost a collision course with the enemy. He admonished Commander Austin, "Hold your Division back until you get your proper bearing, which is 225 degrees. Commander Division 46 acknowledge."[77]

"Wilco," answered Austin, with all the enthusiasm of a 3-year-old just told to eat his broccoli. It was a hint that not everything in Destroyer Squadron 23 was roses and chocolates.

Bernard "Count" Austin was the consummate professional who would go on to have a very long and illustrious career in the US Navy. But while Captain Burke was unapologetically aggressive, Commander Austin would spend much of this operation being more passive-aggressive. Under Squadron Doctrine – Burke Doctrine, the same doctrine that had worked so well at Vella Gulf – one group of destroyers would attack with torpedoes while a second group of destroyers covered them. It was Burke's answer to the many ambush jobs Japanese destroyers had pulled on Allied ships, though it only addressed one facet of those ambuscades, not the better Japanese situational awareness or, most important of all, the exceptional range of the Long Lance torpedo.

Be that as it may, the Burke Doctrine had succeeded and Captain Burke wanted to use it again. He had his group of destroyers and Commander Austin's destroyers. Burke had direct control over his group, who had trained together for this, and it was his theory – that he knew better than anyone else – that was being used. So, Burke's Destroyer Division 45 would launch the torpedo attack while Austin's Destroyer Division 46 would cover them. It was like a stage production: there were the stars and there were the supporting cast members. The stars cannot shine without the supporting cast, and the supporting cast cannot all be the stars or else the production falls apart. Put in military terms, you could have two squads working together to take a hill. One squad moves to the top of the hill while the second squad covers them. Thus, the first squad gets the "glory" – if you could call it that – of capturing the hill. But if both squads moved to capture the hill, they could both be slaughtered by the hidden enemy machine gun that the second squad's covering fire was supposed to suppress.

Count Austin, whose nickname was bestowed as a result of his regal bearing, understood his group was the supporting cast, the covering squad, and he did not like it. For a commander who complained about destroyers being tied to the apron strings of the cruisers, Captain Burke was tying Austin's destroyers to himself, keeping close control of them. Which was understandable inasmuch as while the Americans had won the Battle of Empress Augusta Bay, there was still room for improvement. Except for the hits on the *Sendai*, the marksmanship of Admiral Merrill's cruisers was stormtrooper-esque. Captain Burke's own Destroyer Division 45 had spent an hour chasing its tail. But the worst performance for the Americans was from Commander Austin's Destroyer Division 46. The *Foote* had (understandably) misunderstood an order and turned too early, putting her out of position for the operation but in position to have her stern blown off by a Japanese torpedo. Then the *Thatcher* and Austin's own *Spence* sideswiped each other. Austin then led his destroyers too close to the *Myoko* and the *Spence* got whacked on the starboard quarter by a shattered 6-inch shell that most likely came from Merrill's cruisers. To add insult to injury, Austin was told that the *Myoko* right in front of him was a friendly ship, so he did not attack her, instead attacking the already-disabled *Sendai*. To top it off, the *Thatcher* and *Converse* were sent off chasing the Japanese but not catching them, while Burke's division spent much of the last hours of the battle playing the game "Where in the world is the *Spence*?" while the *Spence* herself stumbled across half a Japanese destroyer – the severely damaged *Hatsukaze* – and could not finish her off.

While the Japanese performance was so inept it crossed the border into slapstick, Division 46's performance was, at best, star-crossed. That Captain Burke wanted Division 46 to cover him and intended to keep tight control over Austin and his ships is understandable in that light. Then again, Burke had issues of his own to clean up from Empress Augusta Bay, of which he was undoubtedly aware. The aforementioned chasing of his own tail occurred because he had lost track of two of his destroyers and was not sure if they were friendly or enemy. In that light, Burke intending to keep tight control of all his destroyers and not letting any of them run off is understandable. Burke later acknowledged "the disappointment of the Commander Destroyer Division 46" in being kept on a tight leash, but, as he explained it:

> [I]t was necessary that one Division be assigned the important but non-spectacular duty of supporting the attack of the other Division. It had been decided to keep both Divisions on the same side of the enemy to avoid a melee such as this Squadron had previously experienced

and to keep the supporting division instantly ready to carry on the attack in the event that other enemy forces were in the vicinity. It was particularly desirable for the Divisions to so maneuver that there would be no possibility of one Division getting into the torpedo water of the other Division.[78]

Reasonable and understandable. Nevertheless, some hints of tension would seep in over the next few hours.

As Captain Burke's three destroyers made their turn, Burke messaged headquarters, "Enemy vessels, strength unknown, at lat. 05-16; long. 153-44. I am attacking. This is my first report this force. Time 0145 Love [1:45am local time]."[79] With the *Charles Ausburne*, *Claxton*, and *Dyson* moving into attack position, at 1:48, Burke radioed his ships, "We think he is on course 290, speed 20. If anybody thinks differently, pipe up." Two minutes later, he added, "We will fire on his port bow. We will fire to port I hope." It was a warning to Commander Austin to stay on Burke's disengaged side. Now the other destroyers started piping up on the targets' course and speed. The *Claxton* piped up with, "I get course 280, 25 knots" while the *Dyson* said, "I get course 285 speed 30 knots." Burke revised his solution, "I get course 280, speed 25."[80] Seeking input from your subordinates is a good thing. But when none of them agree …

That thought would have to wait. The targets were changing course. Allegedly. "Target coming right to 295," Captain Burke announced. Then, "Target coming left to 290." The commodore finally settled on the Japanese on course 290 – west northwest. He adjusted his course to 100 degrees – roughly east southeast – to unmask his torpedo tubes. There was still no indication the Japanese had seen him.

Commander Austin piped up. "I suggest," he radioed Burke, "that I cross under your stern and cover your other side." He was hoping to pass behind Burke's division and unmask his own torpedo batteries while staying out of Burke's line of fire.

"Stay where you are," Burke snapped.[81]

"OK, but that will keep me out of the show," Austin lamented. That figured. It was pretty predictable, really. It was an act of purest optimism to pose the question in the first place. Burke didn't care. He had bigger fish to fry. And fire.

"We will fire half-salvos," Burke ordered at 1:54. One minute later he said, "Stand by to execute William."

There would be no explanation as to why William was about to be executed – again – when Lieutenant Davis chose this time to charge onto the bridge waving a piece of paper like Neville Chamberlain. In the midst of a torpedo attack.

"What in hell is that?" barked Captain Burke.

"It's a message from a B-24 about enemy ships in our immediate vicinity, sir," Davis answered.

"To hell with it!" Burke snarled. He would not look at it until after the battle.[82]

It was a rude response to people just doing their jobs, but Burke was in the middle of a job himself and very much did not appreciate the interruption. Captain Burke had determined that under the current atmospheric and sea conditions, his ships would be detected if they got closer than 4,500 yards to the enemy. By 1:56, Burke's destroyers were right at that 4,500 mark. The angle on the bow was 50 degrees …

"Execute William!"

The order for the execution of William were barely out of the commodore's mouth when he added, "Standby to execute turn 9." The torpedoes were swooshing out of the tubes …

"Execute turn 9." One minute later he elaborated, "190 should be the new course; increase speed to 30 knots." Just in case the Japanese had launched torpedoes. It would be just like them to play unawares while launching their Long Lances, and he wanted to be clear. And he would be. Unlike other US Navy commanders, Burke understood what to expect from the Japanese.

They started counting down the seconds until the torpedoes were supposed to hit. Well, Burke was not. "Stay on the port bow of enemy," he ordered Commander Austin.

"I am on port bow of enemy and opposite from you," the Count responded.

Even more awkward was what the radar showed while the torpedoes were still 90 seconds away from their targets. "I have surface radar target bearing 090," Captain Burke announced. "Anybody else get it?"

No response from the squadron was recorded, but the commodore had made his decision. His first torpedoes were already committed. He would go after these new targets. At 1:59 he radioed Commander Austin, "We have second target bearing east from us. Polish off first targets fired on. Watch yourself now; don't get separated from one another, and don't get too far away. We're going after new targets."

"Wilco," answered the Count. This order from Captain Burke is a very interesting, and suggests he was indeed taking the lessons of Empress Augusta Bay to heart. Two of Burke's own destroyers had gotten separated from him and he spent an hour trying to determine if their returns on radar were enemy. Then there was the saga of the *Spence*, when she was being fired upon, yet no one could figure out where she was. And vice versa. This order may have come off as patronizing to an already frustrated Commander Austin, but it was meant to avoid a similar situation.

The order was also a case of counting the proverbial chickens before they proverbially hatch, but the hatchings were only a few seconds away. As Captain Burke's division headed southeast and Commander Austin's destroyers moved into position, the Americans counted three large detonations. At least two massive explosions marked the spot where one of the targets, the Japanese destroyer *Onami*, had been. In a scene whose descriptions sound reminiscent of the sinking of the *Juneau* barely one year before, the *Onami*, which did not exist when the *Juneau* was sunk, was just obliterated. With a fireball some 300 feet high, the destroyer which was not even one year old just disappeared; Burke said she "completely disintegrated." Disappearing with her was her entire crew, including Captain Kagawa and her skipper, a Pacific War veteran, Commander Kikkawa Kiyoshi, who had commanded the destroyer *Oshio* to victory off Bali in February 1942 and then led the *Yudachi* with distinction in the Friday the 13th Battle. Kikkawa would later be posthumously promoted two ranks, the only Imperial Japanese Navy destroyer skipper so honored.[83]

The third explosion, well separated from the small volcanic eruption that engulfed the *Onami*, was one torpedo hitting the *Makinami*, leaving her disabled. Beyond that, it's not entirely clear what damage the Mark 15 caused, in part because Captain Burke and his men, rather curiously, thought there were three Japanese ships in this first group, not two. Several secondary explosions seem to have occurred near the *Makinami*'s bow and stern in the areas of the main guns. The bow and stern themselves appeared to be raised, suggesting that the *Makinami* had broken in two, but she had not. Not yet, anyway, but her hull appeared to have buckled and it's reasonable to presume that her keel snapped. Nevertheless, she did not sink.[84]

Well, well, well. Captain Burke's starring performance was not entirely perfect. The *Makinami* was still afloat. And Commander Austin was not going to let that one slip by: "I'm coming to north to finish off what you didn't finish."

"Keep your transmissions short, please," snapped Captain Burke.[85] In other words, *you got me.*

But the commodore had bigger fish to fry. And launch. At 2:01am, Captain Burke announced to his divisional destroyers, "We're coming left 120 to fire other half salvo."[86] It was an unnecessary explanation because his *Charles Ausburne* was leading his destroyers in column, so they would just follow him. But it did make for smoother maneuvering, and Burke took some pride in letting his men know what was going on. For the next few minutes, Burke ordered several minor course changes, trying to close the distance to the three radar contacts to the east, hoping to get into position to launch torpedoes.

Those contacts to the east were Captain Yamashiro's three destroyers – his command ship *Amagiri* in the lead followed by the *Yugiri* and then the *Uzuki*. Yamashiro was commodore of Destroyer Division 11 and a veteran of a few of these operations. And he realized enemy ships – three cruisers, he determined – waited in ambush ahead of him, though it did not take any special talent to see two large explosions in the night and reach the obvious deduction.[87]

And Captain Yamashiro chose the obvious solution: with his decks packed with a total of some 700 sick and ailing aviation personnel, bravely he turned about and gallantly he chickened out. With an immediate line turn to slightly east of due north. The *Amagiri*, *Yugiri*, and *Uzuki* went from being in a column at intervals of about 1,000 yards to line abreast at intervals of about 1,000 yards. And then Yamashiro poured on as much speed as the old engines – reduced in the case of the *Uzuki*, poorly maintained in the case of the *Amagiri* – in his destroyers could produce.[88]

This was not what Captain Burke had planned or anticipated. "Boy, we got something here!" shouted the commodore. The *Charles Ausburne* led the *Claxton* and *Dyson* in a turn to the north northeast. Captain Yamashiro's destroyers had a head start of about 11,000 yards – about seven miles. Burke called for "all the turns the engineers could make."[89] The chase was on.

At this time Captain Burke sent an update to Admiral Halsey, which meant to Captain Thurber: "Have made contact with two groups of enemy ships. The first group consisted of two ships destroyed by torpedo; the second group of three ships. I am attacking second group." He closed it with, "Making 31 knots to intercept enemy."

Ignoring the role he himself had played in making 31 knots an issue, Captain Thurber replied, "31-Knot Burke, you've got to get up off your ass and make 33 if you're going to catch those boys."[90] He was right. In response, 31-Knot Burke added a knot of speed to 32 knots. He also made several small course changes, ultimately settling on course 25 degrees True at 2:12am.[91]

Meanwhile, Commander Austin had his own mission, albeit unglamorous grunt work. He was to finish off what Captain Burke didn't finish – the destroyer *Makinami*. She was disabled, burning, probably had a cracked keel, and was not firing any of her guns. How hard could it be?

"Don't get too far away," Burke directed the Count, explaining, "We may need you for the other half salvo of torpedoes, for these fellows."

"I won't. I want to close in enough on this to make my torpedoes good," Austin replied.

"If you can, stay on same side of target I am, and still not lose us," Burke added. It was probably an unnecessary coda. Commander Austin knew what he was doing.

But as the range ever so slowly closed and individual destroyers started standing out from the dark blob that was the Japanese column, this pursuit was about to get more complicated. The last surface battle of the Guadalcanal Campaign had been Tassafaronga, in which Japanese destroyers had been on a supply run. Allied cruisers showed up to contest it. The Japanese destroyers launched torpedoes and fled. The Allied ships chased them. And blundered into the torpedoes. The first surface battle of the New Georgia Campaign had been in the Kula Gulf off Rice Anchorage, in which Japanese destroyers had been on a supply run. Allied cruisers showed up to contest it. The Japanese destroyers launched torpedoes and fled. The Allied ships blundered into the torpedoes. The second part of the first surface battle of the New Georgia Campaign had been at the northern entrance to Kula Gulf, in which Japanese destroyers had been on a supply run. Allied cruisers showed up to contest it. The Japanese destroyers launched torpedoes and fled. The Allied ships chased them. And blundered into the torpedoes. The second battle of the New Georgia Campaign had been at Kolombangara, in which Japanese destroyers had been on a supply run. Allied cruisers showed up to contest it. The Japanese destroyers launched torpedoes and fled. The Allied ships chased them ...

At 2:15, out of the proverbial blue, Captain Burke said, "Coming right. Steady up on [course] 060.[92] It was a 35-degree change of course to starboard. He was sacrificing closing speed. That did not make sense. After one minute on this new course, Burke had his destroyers swing back to port on a course of 015 degrees True. He did not explain this action. He didn't need to.

Because at 2:16, Captain Burke and everyone in Destroyer Division 45 were badly shaken by an underwater explosion, followed by a second, then a third. All in the wake of the *Charles Ausburne*. "The explosions were so heavy the ships were badly jarred and the Squadron Commander could not resist the temptation to look at the bow to see whether or not it was still there." Or resist the temptation to ask his skipper, "Is our bow still there, Brute?"[93]

It was, but Captain Burke wondered if the *Claxton* or the *Dyson* behind him had been hit by torpedoes. The feeling was mutual, and each of the divisional destroyers had to look around believing one of the other ships had been hit.[94] No one had, but they almost were. The explosions were from Long Lance torpedoes, whose oh-so-sensitive detonators had been triggered by merely passing through the thick wake of the *Charles Ausburne*, between her and the *Claxton*. It was a trait the Type 93 had shown since, at the latest, the Battle of the Java Sea, and it was not going to change now. The Long Lances had come compliments of the destroyer *Yugiri*, which had pulled up to allow the *Amagiri* to clear her line of fire before releasing her Type 93s.[95]

And the *Yugiri* was succeeding, as were the *Amagiri* and *Uzuki*. Captain Burke's division had not closed the range all that much. He was not happy about that. The *Yugiri*'s torpedo attack was a dramatic illustration of the danger they were in the longer this chase lasted. The attack was avoided only by that 35-degree turn to starboard Burke had ordered out of the blue, based, he later wrote, "on a hunch" that torpedoes might be inbound.[96] He was probably not giving himself enough credit; the tactic used in the Battle of Empress Augusta Bay of not staying on the same course for long enough for the Japanese torpedoes with a solution based on that course to reach them had probably been instinctivized by now. That said, Burke was not happy about that torpedo attack, either.

"This is remarkable," he observed, probably thinking out loud. "Here we are all lighted up and silhouetted by that blazing ship behind us, yet that monkey up ahead doesn't fire with guns."

"Maybe he has his decks crowded with personnel, sir," suggested Lieutenant Hank Ereckson, the *Charles Ausburne*'s executive officer.

"Well," pondered the commodore, "it doesn't look as though we're going to catch him unless we slow him down. We'll never reach him with torpedoes now, so let's see if we still know how to shoot."[97]

At 2:16, Captain Burke ordered the *Claxton* and *Dyson*, "Take station left echelon. Cannot catch these sons of bitches so we will open up with gun fire as soon as you are open." The hope was to use the gunfire to get the Japanese ships to slow down by getting a hit in the engine spaces or steering compartment or on the rudder or propeller shafts, or even just forcing them into evasive action. Five minutes later, the *Claxton* and *Dyson* responded, "On echelon and ready."[98]

"Standby to execute dog with guns."[99] Before he could order the execution, Burke radioed Commander Austin an acknowledgment of how complicated the chase had become. "Please finish your target and come on to help us. We may need you."[100]

But Commander Austin's mission had become more complicated as well. He did not want to use any more ammunition on it than absolutely necessary, so he had directed the

Spence to take position behind the *Converse* and not fire unless specifically directed to do so. The *Converse* then led the *Spence* around the *Makinami* until he was northeast of the disabled destroyer. In short, he was between the *Makinami* and Captain Burke's destroyers, so he could fire his torpedoes without worrying about any of them would miss the target and go on to hit any of Burke's destroyers.

The threat of his own torpedoes hitting Burke's destroyers was quickly overshadowed, however. At 2:19, the *Converse* felt a "heavy thud … as though the ship had been struck by a dud torpedo." Maybe the *Makinami* was not as helpless as she seemed. The *Converse* quickly released a half salvo of Mark 15s at a range of 4,600 yards, then the *Converse* and *Spence* turned away just in case there were more such surprises.[101]

There were none, so at 2:21 the *Converse* and *Spence* headed back toward the *Makinami*. "[T]wo pronounced explosions were noted," the results of the *Converse*'s torpedoes.[102] Surely, the *Makinami* was doomed … but she did not sink. "Think we have finished him, but may have to use gunfire," Austin responded to Captain Burke.[103]

The *Charles Ausburne*, with the *Claxton* on her port quarter, and the *Dyson* on the *Claxton*'s port quarter opened fire with the two forward guns of each destroyer at a range of 8,000 yards. Hits were observed almost immediately, Burke later wrote, but they seemed to have no effect. The Japanese destroyers took evasive action and returned the gunfire. They also made smoke, but Burke was uncertain if it was intentional. They appear to have shuffled themselves as well, probably in the course of the *Yugiri* making her torpedo attack.[104]

Three or four minutes later, Captain Burke added, "Start fishtailing. Not too much, just enough to confuse the range."[105] "Fishtailing" is just like what it sounds: the stern of the ship swinging without changing the heading too much. Burke wanted it within 30 degrees of the base course, so, basically, it was zigzagging, intended as both an evasive maneuver and a way to occasionally unmask the aft guns. The prudence of this action was demonstrated moments later when everyone on the port bridge wing of the *Claxton* was drenched by the towering splash of a near miss. While those crew on the wing got a shower, those inside the bridge got a bath as the water from the near miss ended up sloshing back and forth on the bridge.[106]

As the US Navy had come to expect, the Japanese salvos were well grouped and the patterns small. And they were close, but "for some unaccountable reason," as Captain Burke put it, there were no direct hits. Fortunate, but also frustrating. "There were no fires in the beginning, the targets did not slow," he reported, "and in spite of the magnificent efforts of the gunners of the 45th Division, we seemed to be conducting a futile gun practice."[107]

That would change, though not necessarily for the better. On the bridge of the *Charles Ausburne*, Captain Burke was keeping a close watch for his greatest fear: an enemy mass torpedo attack. While the *Amagiri*, *Yugiri*, and *Uzuki* were showing their sterns, their torpedo batteries were masked. But if they turned, they could both cap his T, which would, at the very least, lead US Navy officers to question Burke's manhood, but would also open him up to a mass torpedo attack, and one of the worst sort – a "down the throat" shot. It's normally difficult for a torpedo to hit a ship in a narrow bow or stern profile, which is why when facing torpedo attack, many ships relied on turning on a course parallel to that of the torpedoes, called "combing the torpedoes" or "combing the wakes." However, there was a major exception: if the target was already showing a bow profile and the enemy launched torpedoes aimed with the correct solution at that bow profile, the target would have a difficult time avoiding it. And if a "down the throat" shot hits, it can blow off the entire bow.

And Captain Burke was completely mystified as to why the Japanese did not turn and launch torpedoes, why the Japanese did not turn to fight:

> Even with troops aboard, when it became obvious to him after we had opened gunfire and were keeping at a constant range that somebody was going to get sunk, he had but one proper action to take. The enemy should have turned towards us and slugged it out. The ranges were short. It would have been a point blank battle and the advantages of our radars would have been lessened. This, the Squadron Commander expected the enemy to do and was the reason for keeping the torpedo battery ready for immediate use.[108]

That was Captain Burke's playbook, and he was sticking to it. But Captain Yamashiro was not only not using the same book, he didn't even have a library card. As brilliant and as much good as Burke had done and would later do for the US Navy, his determination of the "proper (Japanese) action to take" in this engagement is highly questionable.

For starters, Captain Yamashiro thought he was facing a division of cruisers, not destroyers, so he did not believe both forces were equal. Rather, he believed he was badly outgunned. Additionally, all three of his destroyers were designed so that the majority of their main guns were aft, not forward: remember that a destroyer's main armament is usually considered its torpedo tubes, not its guns. The *Amagiri* and *Yugiri* were of the relatively elderly *Fubuki* class and thus had six 5-inch guns in three twin mounts, one mount forward and two aft. The *Uzuki* was a member of the almost prehistoric *Mutsuki* class, somewhat akin to the US Navy's "four-piper" destroyers. She had started her life with four 4.7-inch guns in single open mounts, one forward, one midships, and two aft. Also like the US Navy's four pipers, the *Mutsuki*s were considered obsolete, so some were being converted to other uses, in the *Uzuki*'s case a fast destroyer transport, though that conversion as of yet was not complete. Her stern had been pared down toward the waterline to facilitate launching and recovery of landing barges; the Japanese did love their barges. Additionally, her midships and furthest aft main guns, the aft torpedo mount, and the Number 4 boiler were removed. It meant that the *Uzuki* could no longer shoot directly behind her and her rated speed for 37 knots was a distant memory, if it ever existed at all.[109] Nevertheless, it meant that Yamashiro's destroyers had a total of eight 5-inch guns facing directly behind them.

Meanwhile, the *Fletcher*-class destroyers that comprised Destroyer Squadron 23 each had five 5-inch dual-purpose guns in five single-gun mounts, two forward, two aft, and one amidships with an extremely limited field of fire behind the stacks, but closer to aft.[110] So Captain Burke had six 5-inch guns facing forward against Captain Yamashiro's eight 5-inch guns facing aft. While Burke's destroyers had better fire control, it still meant that Yamashiro had a gunnery advantage.

Finally, Captain Yamashiro was a veteran of a few of these operations, some of which involved combat, specifically Kula Gulf and running over the future President of the United States. He had learned a few things, especially about running convoys. And he indeed had one "proper action to take" that Burke had not considered.

The Japanese formation had started to fray and split at around 2:10am. This was about the time that the *Yugiri* had slowed down to launch her torpedoes. This action appears to have prompted a reshuffling of the Japanese formation, which necessitated an opening of the range between the destroyers so they would not collide. Captain Burke said the space between the Japanese ships had opened up to "at least" 1,000 yards.[111] The *Claxton*'s skipper, Commander Stout, described it as not line abreast but an "apparent spear-head formation," which complicated radar tracking of the two ships that formed the base of the spearhead.[112] It appears that after making her torpedo attack, the *Yugiri* moved to the starboard side of the base of the spearhead. The *Uzuki* shifted to the port side, and the *Amagiri* moved to the middle and took position ahead of both.[113] With Burke's divisional destroyers in a left echelon formation, the commodore matched his destroyers with the Japanese one-on-one. The *Dyson*, on the left side and back of the echelon, was to take under fire the left-hand Japanese destroyer, the *Uzuki*, reportedly hitting the ancient destroyer and setting her on fire. The *Claxton*, in the middle of the left echelon, was given the duty of firing at the middle Japanese destroyer, Captain Yamashiro's *Amagiri*, while Burke's own *Charles Ausburne*, on the right, targeted the right-hand Japanese destroyer, the *Yugiri*.[114]

Starting at 2:25am, the Japanese force split up altogether. Because of the aforementioned difficulties in tracking the two rear destroyers, it is not entirely clear who went where or even who started where. The *Uzuki* and the *Yugiri* both split off from the *Amagiri* in opposite directions from each other. The *Uzuki* initially turned due north with the *Amagiri* continuing to head northeast and the *Yugiri* turning to east northeast. The *Amagiri* quickly turned to 350 degrees True – just west of due north. The *Yugiri* quickly turned to parallel the *Amagiri*'s course. The *Uzuki* also quickly turned, but away from the *Amagiri*, heading just north of due west for maybe two or three miles.[115] The technical term for what this little convoy had done was "scattered."[116]

This was not a good thing. For either side. In theory, anyway. For convoys, it was a tactic of desperation. In reference to the destruction of most of Convoy PQ-17 by German aircraft and U-boats after a very questionable order for the convoy to scatter left the individual ships defenseless, Winston Churchill himself said, "The order to scatter was only used under immediate threat of surface attack."[117] Commander Jack Broome, who headed the close escort of that convoy (and was as outraged by the controversial order to scatter as anyone) said, "An order to scatter [...] is in my impression, given when the threat is imminent, from surface forces more powerful than the escort. By imminent I mean that surface forces are in sight."[118] In such a case, the ships of the convoy are to disperse and maneuver on their own. It trades the collective defense of the mass of ships of the convoy – which, theoretically, would be overwhelmed by the enemy surface forces anyway – for mobility and independence. All the convoy ships would not be in one place. After they scattered, the enemy would have to hunt each of them down independently. It virtually guaranteed the loss of some ships because the loss of the convoy's collective defense would leave each individual ship practically defenseless, but the hope would be that, if scattered, *some* of the ships would get through.

While that was the general principle, in Captain Yamashiro's case, it was slightly different. If his little convoy scattered, it did increase the possibility that, again, some of his ships would get through. But even by themselves, the *Amagiri*, *Yugiri*, and *Uzuki* were hardly defenseless.

It put Captain Burke on the horns of a dilemma, which had to be painful and brought up the question of how a dilemma could grow horns. Should he chase all three Japanese destroyers, paring up one chaser with one shot? Or should he have all three of his destroyers chase one Japanese destroyer? And if so which one?

The answer to that question would be affected by some difficulties the commodore's own *Charles Ausburne* was experiencing. In front of the bridge was the Number 2 5-inch mount, which looked like a turret with a single gun barrel, but it was a mount. The Number 2 mount was "superfiring"; that means it was positioned higher than the Number 1 5-inch mount, which was immediately in front of it, and thus could fire over the Number 1 mount. With the *Charles Ausburne* chasing the Japanese, both the Number 1 and 2 5-inch mounts were firing more or less directly forward, which meant the barrel for the Number 2 mount was firing right over the enclosure for the Number 1 mount – and right over the access hatch on the roof of the Number 1 mount. In so doing, the Number 2 5-inch gun had managed to blow the hatch off. So, every time the Number 2 5-inch gun fired, the crew inside the Number 1 mount had to deal with the literally deafening, earth-shattering ka-BOOM! along with smoke, cordite fumes, particulates, and hot gases entering the mount. When members of the gun crew were overcome by the fumes or the heat, they were dragged out and replacements sent in. The gun continued firing, albeit at a reduced rate. Interestingly, Commander Stout reported that the same thing happened on the *Claxton*, with the added complication of the lights shattering inside the mount.[119] The technical term for these two events is "design flaw."

Captain Burke made his decision. He would keep his Little Beavers together, especially since they were close to Rabaul and dawn was only a few hours away, which promised Japanese air attacks. Those attacks could pick off a destroyer all by itself, but five destroyers operating together for mutual defense would have a good chance. At 2:29, the commodore directed the *Dyson* to keep shooting at the *Uzuki* on the far left "and finish him off." The *Charles Ausburne* and *Claxton* would fire on the target on the right, which was generating the biggest radar return, the *Yugiri*.[120]

As that was going on, Captain Burke signaled Admiral Halsey. "Have made contact with two groups of enemy ships. The first group consisted of two ships destroyed by torpedoes. 2nd group of three ships. Am attacking 2nd group."[121]

As the *Dyson* took shots at the *Uzuki*, the prehistoric destroyer turned to starboard to roughly parallel the course of the *Amagiri*. The *Uzuki* continued north northeast for maybe five minutes, in the process paralleling the course of Captain Burke's destroyers. Then the *Uzuki* swerved to port to a base course of almost due west, but zigzagging slightly. Burke reported that the *Dyson* was "pounding him unmercifully with 5 guns."[122]

It was not all fun and games for the good commodore. First, he was getting a bit impatient with Commander Austin. At 2:36 Captain Burke requested, "Report whether first three targets sank." After not getting an answer for three minutes, he asked, "Have you finished your job and are you closing?"[123]

But Commander Austin and his men were witnessing an incredible demonstration of naval durability. In the Japanese Naval Air Force, the aircraft were so fragile you could just look at one of them wrong and it would burst into flames. But the Imperial Navy's surface ships were a different matter, if the *Makinami* was any indication. One torpedo is normally fatal to a destroyer, but the *Makinami* had supposedly been hit by three torpedoes, yet she was still afloat. Not in the best shape, true, but still afloat.

At 2:28, the *Converse* and *Spence* opened fire on the recalcitrant destroyer at a range of 5,200 yards. "Fires immediately broke out over the length of the enemy ship until it was completely outlined," Commander Hamberger later reported. Commander Austin reported two major explosions occurred at 2:34, which in turn led to more explosions and more fires. But the *Makinami* … would … not … sink.[124]

"Many explosions on target but he's still afloat," Austin admitted.

"Sink him!" roared Burke, adding, "On your way you will encounter two or three cripples. Hope none of them are [sic] us!"[125]

And in trying to avoid becoming one of those cripples, Captain Burke went out on to the port wing of the *Charles Ausburne*'s bridge wing, where he took a long look astern, and found himself staring down the barrels of the 5-inch guns of the *Claxton*. "Brute," he said upon returning to the pilot house, "I was just out there looking right down the nozzles of *Claxton*'s guns. Heraldo's astern of us. He's shooting right over us, and he's paying us no mind whatever! It's a funny sort of feeling … just suppose …"

"Well, you want him to shoot, don't you, boss?" asked Commander Reynolds.

"I sure as hell do!" snickered Burke, "and he's doing it in style! I just hope he doesn't blow us out of the water! But then, he's such an insouciant chap, even if he did sink us he'd manage to make a joke out of it!"[126]

Obviously, Captain Burke had a rich and varied vocabulary. After the *Uzuki* turned to the west, the *Claxton* shifted some of her gunfire to the ancient auxiliary, which, Burke reported, "was some relief to [the] *Charles Ausburne* because the combination of the enemy maneuvers ahead and *Charles Ausburne*'s fishtailing must have given the Captain of [the] *Claxton* considerable concern about firing over us." Burke continued his cheeky report by noting that he "was very pleased to note that the *Claxton*'s fire was not held up because of this minor obstruction."[127]

Not that minor obstruction, but the *Claxton*'s fire was held up by a different obstruction in the form of a dented shell that jammed the Number 1 5-inch gun. The gunners had to work in the dark to clear it, but by 2:42 the gun was operational again. The *Claxton* witnessed "several hits and fires occurring" on the *Uzuki*, who was herself speeding westward, at 2:39am as a result of the gunfire of herself and the *Dyson*. Captain Burke reported that at about 2:40 the *Uzuki* was "on fire, slowing down, and headed west." At around 2:45, the Americans passed her latitude, but the *Dyson* and *Claxton* continued targeting her. The *Dyson* reported that the *Uzuki*'s speed had been determined to be 32–33 knots but was slowing down as a result of the American gunfire before the *Uzuki* exited stage left off the radar screens at 2:50. Despite all these reports of damage to and fires on the Neolithic destroyer, in actuality, the *Uzuki* was hit by exactly one 5-inch shell, and that 5-inch shell failed to explode.[128] She made Simpson Harbor easily.

The inability to sink the ancient destroyer did not sit well with Captain Burke. His mood would not be improved by the next message he got from Commander Austin. "We get a number of explosions and five fires on him," the Count reported at 2:47. "Shall we continue, or join you?"

"Sink him!" Burke thundered.

"If you do not yell so loud [sic] I can hear you better," Commander Austin deadpanned.[129] He was enjoying this.

Captain Burke was not. He sensed that the rate of fire of his ships had fallen off. He got on the voice radio to the *Claxton* and *Dyson* and implored them, "Please for Christ's sake continue to fire."

Commander Gano responded immediately, "Target out of range. We will close yours."

"Get another target!"[130] That's exactly what Gano said he was doing, but Burke was in a mood.

A mood that would not be improved by the two remaining prey in this chase, the *Amagiri* and *Yugiri*. As they continued northward, more space opened up between the two destroyers. At maybe 2:40, the *Amagiri* turned to the north northwest, opening up the range to the *Yugiri* even more, and by 2:50 Captain Yamashiro's destroyer was heading northwest. The *Claxton* continued firing at her, and as the *Amagiri* pulled away to the northwest, opening the range to 15,000 yards, all of the *Claxton*'s guns were unmasked. Commander Stout reported getting several hits on the *Amagiri* at 2:58, which caused her to slow down to 26 knots. Or not; the *Amagiri* likely slowed down because of the poor condition of her engines. She exited stage left off the radar screens at 3:06. Otherwise, she got off without a scratch.[131]

As she was doing so, Captain Burke updated Admiral Halsey. "The gun battle continues. The enemy has scattered. Some may get away. These are tough babies to sink!"[132]

Now came the catch in the tactic of scattering. Sure, it increases the possibility of someone making it to safety, but if the enemy decides to keep his ships together and focus on one target, that one target is basically screwed. On this night, that one target was the

Yugiri – which was now being chased by three US Navy destroyers, with two more en route. What the *Yugiri*'s skipper Lieutenant Commander Otsuji Shuuichi thought about this catch in the tactic of scattering is not recorded.[133] Maybe he was too busy zigzagging trying to avoid the shells that were splashing all around his ship. The Americans were slashing away at the *Yugiri*, trying to chop her speed down by damaging her engine spaces or even her steering, but despite her appearing to take numerous hits, she was still zigzagging at high speed northward, seemingly unaffected.

"I don't understand why you're not firing to the north! He's getting away!" barked the commodore.

"We're firing with all the guns that will bear," replied Commander Stout.

Captain Burke was cursing. "Someone ought to be able to slow down this target."[134]

His frustration at the long stern chase devolving into a scattered convoy was palpable. Burke turned to Commander Reynolds. "That guy up ahead just can't take much more of the kind of punishment we're giving him, Brute."

"Well, don't look now, Boss, but I think he's slowing down," Reynolds answered.[135]

The thought was cut short by a report from Commander Austin. "One more rising sun has set. Joining you now." It had been a stubborn but spectacular end for the *Makinami*. Five major fires were burning when, Commander Hamberger later wrote, "At [2:54am] after a series of four major explosions, apparently of individual magazines, the target sank quickly."[136] That description might not do it justice; according to some Japanese sources, the buckled midships finally gave way and the *Makinami* broke into two before sinking.[137] The destroyer's toughness perhaps inspired Hamberger to guess that the target was "a *Yubari* class [sic] cruiser."[138] With his services badly needed elsewhere, Austin did not stay to look for survivors, and only 28 of the *Makinami*'s crew, none of which was Commander Hitomi, managed to reach shore, all in the same boat.[139] Either way, that long national nightmare was over.

And Captain Burke was trying to end other long national nightmares as well. "Close up if you can," he ordered Commander Austin. "Our targets have spread out in two groups. One target is on port beam 15,600 yards bearing 310 degrees True from us is target for you."[140] This was Captain Yamashiro's *Amagiri*, which had yet to be even scratched. But Austin never received this order. Burke and Austin would spend much of the rest of the battle asking if the other was there or could hear him, like a case of bad cell phone reception.

While he was unintentionally ghosting Commander Austin and vice versa, Captain Burke was finally starting to see some success in his long, long, long chase of the *Yugiri*. Starting at 2:53am, the *Yugiri*'s speed was cut from 32 knots to 15 within the space of four minutes. But Lieutenant Commander Otsuji still had a trick or two up his sleeve, and by 3:00am, the *Yugiri* was back up to 31 knots.[141]

Captain Burke was having none of it. He and his men believed the *Yugiri* was just "pumping his last resources of energy into his failing system" for "only a few extra minutes [of] existence." "That's just his dying gasp," Burke exclaimed. "That guy's number definitely has been posted!" Whatever you say, commodore.[142]

But if "[t]hat guy's number" had not "been posted" – whatever that means – at 3:00am, it was at 3:05 and 30 seconds. That was when a 5-inch shell exploded in the *Yugiri*'s engine spaces. Still 7,800 yards behind the Japanese destroyer, the *Charles Ausburne* noted a large explosion on the *Yugiri*. "Target obviously hit. All ships noted big explosions and target afire," Burke reported. Of course, they had said the same thing about the *Uzuki* and all those big "explosions" turned out to be one dud shell. Except this time, those reports were accompanied by a precipitous drop in speed. At 3:05:30, the *Yugiri* had been making 22 knots. At 3:06, that speed was 10 knots, another 30 seconds it was down to five knots, and at 3:07 the *Yugiri* "went dead in the water."[143]

Of course, because this was still the Solomon Islands, nothing could be that straightforward. Within another minute, the *Yugiri* was moving again, but at only 2–5 knots, slowly circling to starboard. At least Captain Burke and his three Little Beavers could finally overtake the now-burning destroyer. Burke's divisional destroyers steadied on a course of 000 degrees True – due north – and moved toward the *Yugiri*, keeping the Japanese destroyer on their starboard hand at a range of 4,000 to 5,000 yards. Now able to fire full broadsides, the *Charles Ausburne*, *Claxton*, and *Dyson* unloaded on the unfortunate *Yugiri*, each "pounding him unmercifully with 5 guns," to recycle the commodore's phrase from earlier. They passed her at 3:10 …[144]

And found that despite each pounding him unmercifully with five guns, despite the numerous fires and explosions on board, the *Yugiri* was still not sinking. "I guess you'll have to put a fish into her, Brute," Captain Burke told Commander Reynolds.[145] The commodore went on to announce the *Charles Ausburne* would fire her (remaining) half-salvo of torpedoes to put the Japanese destroyer out of her misery. Of course, because this was still the Solomon Islands, nothing could be that straightforward. The same concussions that had jarred loose the hatch on top of her Number 1 5-inch mount had also damaged the powertrain for the torpedo tubes. So, *Claxton*, you fire torpedoes …[146]

Or not. While Captain Burke was giving this order, the *Yugiri* heeled way over to starboard, exposing part of her bottom. "Belay last word. Torpedoes not needed now." The Japanese destroyer was about to capsize …

Or not. Having heeled way over to starboard, exposing part of her bottom, the *Yugiri* just hung there, almost on her side, which is a pretty decent trick if you can manage it. Captain Burke was not amused, however; more like exasperated. He ordered a line turn to 30 degrees True, a course he held for four minutes, apparently to close the range on the *Yugiri*. Then he reformed the column, which the *Charles Ausburne* then led in a reversal of course to starboard. The commodore also ordered his ships to cease firing; firing would just complicate things.[147]

With all that taken care of, at 3:21, Captain Burke gave the order, "Execute Dog again," a phrase not normally heard in any context. "Sink him this time!" How hard could it be? The *Yugiri* was already on her side and down by the bow. The *Charles Ausburne* led the *Claxton* and *Dyson* to a new course of 210 degrees True – roughly south southwest – as they unloaded their guns once again. "Fire at maximum rate of fire," Burke urged, "Get them out and sink this bastard!"[148]

Captain Burke's three divisional destroyers poured more and more 5-inch shells into the *Yugiri* for another five minutes. But the *Yugiri* still … would … not … sink.

Finally, at 3:27, a fully exasperated commodore ordered the *Dyson*'s Commander Gano to "Put five fish into that God damned thing – she won't sink any other way."[149] As Gano later wrote, "In a final effort to sink the tenacious enemy, the *Dyson* passing the burning ship about 2,800 yards to port launched its second half-salvo of torpedoes; but before the torpedoes had reached their destination, the [*Yugiri*] sank beneath the surface of the water."[150] Doesn't that just figure? You pound her and pound her with shells hoping to sink her without using scarce torpedoes, but she won't sink. So you give in and fire the torpedoes, but she sinks before they can hit, so you just wasted those scarce torpedoes. That's life in the Solomon Islands.

Reportedly, Captain Burke got on the voice radio and joked to Commander Gano, "Roy, you must have fired those torpedoes at too much altitude!"[151] Or not. The alleged joke does not show up in the voice radio logs, but Gano was very careful to put the complete torpedo solution he used in his report, so maybe he did not take it as a joke.[152] Or maybe Gano understood what most US Navy officers and sailors had not: in the Solomon Islands, nothing is as it seems.

And if it seemed the battle was over, well, Captain Burke had other ideas. He still wanted to chase down the *Amagiri* and the *Uzuki*. Of course, they had separated from each other, so the Little Beavers would have to chase each of them down separately. And the *Amagiri* and the *Uzuki* were now so far away they no longer showed on radar screens.

No matter. Captain Burke ordered Commander Austin to have his *Converse* and *Spence* turn to course 330 degrees True – roughly northwest – "and see if you can find some enemy there." It was the first of the commodore's orders to look for the two fugitive Japanese destroyers that had actually reached Austin after three previous iterations of it had gone unanswered because the *Converse* was apparently having some issues connecting with the *Charles Ausburne* and vice versa. Speaking of the *Charles Ausburne*, she, *Claxton*, and *Dyson* turned to course 265 degrees True – just south of west – on orders from Burke. He signaled Admiral Halsey again: "Have just sunk one enemy ship in Lat. 04-47-30 South, Long. 153-55-30 East. Am pursuing others to West. Will need a hell of a lot of air cover."[153] Which presumably meant more fighters than Admiral Yamamoto had escorting him at Bougainville.

Captain Burke got together with his people and compared the courses of the ships that had escaped him. They were headed for – duh! – Rabaul, via St George's Channel. This wasn't exactly rocket science. Nevertheless, once again following his own (very good) policy of letting his subordinates know what he was doing, at 3:34 Captain Burke radioed Commander Austin, "Two ships that escaped appeared to be on (course) 265. Course to St George's Channel is 265 – that is our course from now on."[154] Acknowledging his new nickname, Burke also let his superior Admiral Halsey know, "One, perhaps two, enemy ships have escaped toward St Georges Channel. Am headed for St Georges Channel on course 265 degrees T[rue], usual speed 31 knots. Hope to overtake damaged ships. No damage to us. Repeat, no damage to us."[155]

And now the relaxed banter often held in the aftermath of a successful battle took over the "Talk Between Ships" voice radio circuit. By 3:45, Commander Austin's divisional destroyers had closed to within three miles of Captain Burke's divisional destroyers.[156] "How many did you polish off while I was back doing the chores?" Austin asked.

"Just one up here. Two got away to West toward Rabaul – that's where we're going," the commodore explained.

"We saw three big explosions ahead when we were closing you," Austin added.

"Yes, we did it to light the way for you," Burke joked.

"As usual, you're most considerate," Austin played along.

Talking seriously just for a moment, the commodore announced, "We'll stay on this course till [4:15am] then we turn toward Treasury Island. Unless, of course, we get a pip before then."

Austin did not object, but had some concerns. "I don't think we can go much longer than that because of our limitation in speed."

"Unless we can get fuel in Rabaul," Burke suggested.

Lieutenant Commander Armstrong warned, "The only trouble with that is we might have trouble with the (fuel line) connections."

Because he was the officer in tactical command, it fell to Captain Burke to ask the obvious question, which he did at 3:56: "Does anybody think we can catch these babies?"

"It's getting to look like they got away, unless we go right into Rabaul after them," answered Austin.

"Does your outfit have enough ammunition to go in after them?"

"Affirmative," deadpanned Austin.

"I would like to go back and get the one I left circling," Commander Stout interjected.

"That's the one we're after," Burke responded, "He got away to [the] West." Referring to the *Uzuki*, whom Stout believed had been badly damaged.

But the *Spence*, always having issues, was low on fresh water for her boilers, as skipper Lieutenant Commander Armstrong reminded the commodore, "I guess I'll have to put beer in my boilers."

"Don't put that beer in boilers," Burke told him. "We'll need that later – put it on ice." Which is, truth be told, a good suggestion for any beer.

"I think I see the southern tip of [New Ireland] over there on our SG [radar]," the *Dyson*'s Commander Gano advised.[157]

"That's right, boys! It's over there!" Burke agreed.[158] The tip of southern New Ireland was Cape St George. Cape St George meant St George's Channel. St George's Channel meant Rabaul. Some decisions had to be made soon. Real soon.

"Happy Thanksgiving to you and yours," Commander Gano announced.

"Thank you – we appreciate the sentiment and return the same in kind."

"DesDiv 46 appreciates your kind sentiments and hopes you will have many *more* successful ones like this," added Commander Austin

"I get it," Burke responded, probably with a sigh. "Stand by to execute 150 corpen."

And one minute later, at 4:05 am, the commodore ordered, "Execute," and the *Charles Ausburne* led the column in a 150-degree left turn and headed back to base.

"For a Thanksgiving present, we'll give you a half-knot more (speed)," Lieutenant Commander Armstrong announced.

"That won't take the beer, will it?" Captain Burke asked.

"We'll worry about that later," Armstrong answered.

And with that, what would be called the Battle of Cape St George – the last surface engagement of the Guadalcanal-Solomons Campaign that had started on August 7, 1942 – had ended. Though that was not known at the time.

At 4:35am, Burke messaged Admiral Halsey: "On this Thanksgiving Day we are to be thankful to ComAirSols for cover. At 0410 Love [4:10am Local Time], in Lat. 04-55'; Long.153-38' have come to course 150, speed 31, our maximum. Low on ammunition. Few torpedoes. Have enough fuel. Some ships getting low on feed water. Four enemy ships sunk, seen visually. One damaged, one undamaged escaped west."[159]

Halsey replied, "31-Knot-Burke: Return to refuel at Purvis. Your Thanksgiving rendezvous with the enemy was a very excellent one, conceived by the Creator, and directed by Commander, Destroyer Squadron 23!"[160]

Very excellent, indeed. As Captain Burke commented in his report:

The navy stresses devotion to duty, aggressiveness, boldness, determination, courage. The full realization of exactly what these traits of character mean was brought out by the officers and crews during this engagement. The universal desire of all hands to do damage to the enemy regardless of consequences is the greates [sic] exhilaration that any Commander can possibly have. This desire was exemplified by the plea of the torpedoman of the *Charles Ausburne* to [sic] "Please can't we get more speed so that we can close him to torpedo range." [sic] The complete loyalty, understanding coupled with and [sic] wholehearted desire to mutually support the operation, the courage and valiant determination to do it, were the outstanding characteristics of these ships. There was no person who did not know that we were far away from any air or surface support and there was no one who did not believe some of our ships would be damaged in the battle. Yet every ship threw itself into battle with a cheerful willingness that I hope is an American trait. Few men can be outstanding among such outstanding men. Ships take on the character of their Captains. These Captains had the qualities to produce Men Of War.[161]

The commodore was less effusive in his praise of the Japanese:

There is one thing to be said for the Japanese. When they make up their minds to run, they let nothing interfere with the carrying out of their decision. Considering the reported Japanese traits, this lack of willingness to fight an equal force is not understood.[162]

As his incredible career would show, Captain Burke was much smarter and possessed much more imagination than this comment would indicate. His opposite number at the end of the engagement, Captain Yamashiro, had orders to bring what were more than likely skilled aviation mechanics and technicians back to Rabaul. The decks of his ships were packed with them, which inhibited combat operations. The best chance of getting those scarce technicians back to Rabaul was to run from combat and, when it was clear that would not be entirely successful, to have his ships scatter. Maybe it's not what Burke would have done, and maybe it's not what Burke expected from the same people who would later give the world the Kamikaze Corps. But it got two of Yamashiro's three ships with all their passengers back to Rabaul. Of the third, the *Yugiri*, she was able to radio Rabaul, and two submarines were dispatched to search for survivors. At least 278 of the *Yugiri*'s passengers and crew were rescued by the submarine *I-177*; 11 more were rescued by the submarine *I-181*. None of those rescued was her skipper Lieutenant Commander Otsuji. For her trouble, *I-177* was attacked by Ventura from US Navy Patrol Squadron 138 off Cape St George on November 26, but the submarine was still able to make Rabaul and offload the survivors.[163]

This Battle of Cape St George, though small, was a momentous occasion nonetheless. As historian William Tuohy explained:

The Battle of Cape St George on Thanksgiving Day was a jewel of an action: three enemy ships sunk with nary a nick to the US destroyers. Tip Merrill awarded Arleigh Burke the Navy Cross for the battle. Admiral Pye, president of the Naval War College, called it "an almost perfect action, that may be considered a classic."[164]

Historian Vincent P. O'Hara gave a slightly different take:

Although Burke did not prevent the Japanese from landing their reinforcements, or from evacuating the bulk of the aviation personnel, the Americans did sink three enemy destroyers at no loss to themselves and did it in the ideal fashion – with a surprise torpedo attack. On the other hand, Burke underutilized Austin's division. If he had released them to head northwest as Austin had requested and much like Moosbrugger had done with Simpson's division at Vella Gulf, the *Amagiri* and *Uzuki* would, at the very least, have had their best escape route cut off. Two Japanese torpedo attacks that might have turned the results into a draw or even an American defeat failed by a narrow margin. Nonetheless, Burke won an outstanding victory that made a fitting end to a long, arduous naval surface warfare campaign that began so horrifically at Savo Island.[165]

Nitpicky, perhaps, especially when one can argue there is no such thing as a "perfect action." But it is no less of a standard than that to which Burke would hold himself. Which he and every officer in the US Navy had to hold themselves, had had to hold themselves ever since that disaster at Savo Island.

But as Burke himself pointed out eloquently if not entirely politically correct for a modern audience:

> If this battle brings out no other points, it should clearly demonstrate that fortune of war is a fickle wench and that results hang by a narrow thread. There are many things which would have prevented this battle from being fought, and the Squadron Commander would much prefer to say that these matters were foreseen and steps taken to insure doing the proper thing. But they were not foreseen. The time of [1:45am] for reaching the Rabaul-Buka line was chosen merely at random. The desire to reach as far westward as possible was not based on abstruse reasoning. A fifteen-minute delay in time of fueling, the run north at anything less than maximum speed, an investigation of false surface contacts, an attack by bogies which would have required maneuvering, the reporting of our force by bogies which would have alerted Japanese vessels, all or any would have prevented the battle from being fought. We reached the enemy by the narrowest of margins. The Squadron as a whole was so spontaneously grateful for being assigned this mission, for being so fortunate in making contact, and for attacking a larger enemy force with considerable damage to the enemy and no damage received in spite of fairly heavy fire from the enemy that Thanksgiving services were held upon its return to port. The Squadron is proud of its accomplishments, but it is also humbly aware that these accomplishments were made possible by a Force beyond its control.[166]

One can argue that Captain Burke's pushing of his ships so hard was what enabled the US Navy sailors to take advantage of the fortune of war just as assuming the best, a prewar mentality, and just plain laziness had made the US and Royal Australian Navy ships vulnerable at Savo Island.

Savo Island. What a long way the US Navy had traveled. Figuratively and literally.

CHAPTER 9

RING AROUND RABAUL

By the time Captain Burke and his Little Beavers were headed back to base, *Galvanic* was largely complete. At 10:30am on November 23, Major General Ralph Smith, commander of the US Army's 27th Infantry Division and one of three general officers at the top of *Galvanic* with the surname "Smith," signaled victory and started a slew of jokes and, eventually, internet memes when he reported to Admiral Turner, "Makin taken."[1]

It was, and at a seemingly cheap cost for the US Army: 66 killed or mortally wounded in action, 150 wounded non-fatally in action, and 35 injured, but not in combat. The defenders of the Gilbert Islands had been Special Naval Landing Force troops, those naval infantrymen with a reputation for never surrendering, a reputation they had preserved by simply running away when it looked like they were about to lose. In this case, they had been the 6th Yokosuka Special Naval Landing Force, who had been sent to the Gilberts after the American raid on Makin in August 1942. Ultimately, about three platoons of the 6th Yokosuka ended up on Makin; the rest were sent to Tarawa. Both were heavily reinforced by artillery. Presumably because they had already fulfilled the "landing" part of their mission, they were redesignated the 3rd Special Base Force in February 1943.[2]

The Japanese had about 800 men on Makin, but fewer than 300 of them were the trained combat troops of the 3rd Special Base Force's "Makin Detachment." The atoll was commanded by Lieutenant (jg) Ishikawa Seizo, which is indicative of the importance the Japanese apparently attached to Makin.[3] Nevertheless, with no place to run, the Special Naval Landing Force troops were compelled to fight tenaciously just to hope to preserve their reputation for never surrendering. For the most part, they did. Only 104 prisoners were taken; all but three were Korean laborers. The rest were annihilated.[4] Nevertheless, one US Army history has pointed out, "[F]or every three Japanese fighters killed, two

Americans were either killed or wounded. Thus the cost of taking Makin was not quite so low as it had first seemed."[5]

Even so, it was the US Navy that suffered disproportionately at Makin: 752 killed or mortally wounded, 291 wounded non-fatally or injured. It was the result of what might be considered some freakish occurrences. During the bombardment on D-Day, the battleship *Mississippi* suffered a "flareback" in her Number 2 main turret from unexpelled gases from a previous round that ignited the powder bags as they were being loaded, starting a fire in the turret that killed 43 men.[6]

Far worse would come. Just before dawn on November 24, the little escort carriers, operating southwest of Makin, were getting ready to initiate flight operations. As the escort carrier *Liscome Bay* did so, an officer stationed at one of her 40mm Bofors on the starboard side yelled into his telephone, "Christ, here comes a torpedo!" That was the only warning the little escort carrier had, and it was far too late.[7]

Because mere seconds later the torpedo bulled its way into the *Liscome Bay*'s starboard side near the after engine room with a deafening explosion. Which, in turn, set off a second, absolutely cataclysmic explosion by detonating the carrier's bomb magazine. With a mushroom cloud that rose several hundred feet into the air, the after half of the *Liscome Bay* was literally blown off, completely shattered with such force that debris fell almost three miles away. What remained of the *Liscome Bay* was simply wrecked, with no power or water, burning with the heat and intensity of a blast furnace that quickly cooked off munitions.

It was quickly apparent there was no way to save the *Liscome Bay*. Even so, the stricken escort carrier held on for 23 minutes, before, hissing, she surrendered to the depths. Surrendering with her were 644 officers and men, most of whom were likely killed in the magazine blast. The dead included master Captain Irving D. Wiltsie, who died trying to personally pass the word to abandon ship; and Rear Admiral Henry M. Mullinix, the popular and respected commander of Carrier Division 24 and the first flag officer lost since Admirals Callaghan and Scott were killed in the Friday the 13th Action just over a year before. Among the 272 survivors was Admiral Mullinix's very capable chief of staff, Captain John Crommelin, who as air officer of the carrier *Enterprise* at Santa Cruz had been responsible for saving so many US Navy aviators and thus so much Allied air power in the South Pacific during that disaster.

The abrupt, ghastly end of the *Liscome Bay* came courtesy of Lieutenant Commander Tabata Sunao and the Japanese submarine *I-175*, who endured a six-hour depth charging to escape with an impressive victory that did not change the course of the war, *Galvanic*, or even the Makin campaign by as much as a millimeter.

Tarawa would match the *Liscome Bay* in ghastliness if not abruptness. Once again, the defenders were Special Naval Landing Force troops of the 3rd Special Base Force, though this time augmented by the 7th Sasebo Special Naval Landing Force, for a total of some 2,600 naval infantry along with some 2,300 laborers and 14 light tanks. For a long time the atoll was commanded by Rear Admiral Tomonari Saichiro, who was an engineer by training and built excellent defensive fortifications, almost all of which were on or overlooking the beaches of the major island in Tarawa and location of its air base, Betio, mostly on the south, west, and east sides because the north side was covered by a coral reef. In July, Tomonari was replaced by the charismatic Rear Admiral Shibasaki Keiji, who continued the defensive preparations, but with the fortifications largely complete, he focused on training instead, which had often been lacking in the Special Naval Landing Forces. Shibasaki was ready for an attack, expected it, even welcomed it, telling his troops, "[O]ne million Americans couldn't take Tarawa in a hundred years." He would be killed in the first hours of the Allied attack.[8]

Once again, with no place to run, the Special Naval Landing Force troops put up fierce resistance against the invading 2nd Marine Division, who had landed in the spot with the fewest fortifications: the north side. The Americans were hamstrung by several issues that they thought had been addressed, but had not. While a gun duel between US Navy battleships and four defending Japanese 8-inch guns (dating from the Russo-Japanese War) resulted in the destruction of three of the latter, the preparatory naval bombardment was largely ineffective at destroying the Japanese fortifications or the defenders inside them. Marine planners had miscalculated the tides, so the landing craft got caught on the reefs, leaving men stranded there some 500 yards from the shore. Other Marines had to wade ashore in chest-high surf into the teeth of Japanese gunfire and ended up pinned against a seawall ashore. Attempts to get tanks ashore literally foundered when Stuart tanks were released into the surf only to fall into underwater shell holes caused by the naval bombardment.

Colonel David Shoup took command of the Marines ashore and, though wounded early on, rallied the first wave of Marines caught at the sea wall and began a methodical advance against the Japanese strongpoints, assisted by some Sherman tanks which had successfully made it ashore.

Badly outnumbered, the Japanese naval troops were crippled by severe command and control issues. The soft sand had prevented Japanese communications lines from being adequately buried, and thus the wires were severed by the naval bombardment. Admiral Shibasaki was apparently killed as he was trying to shift his command post from a concrete blockhouse in order to make the blockhouse available for use as a hospital for the hundreds of wounded in the vicinity. As he and his staff were waiting outside for some cover from Japanese light tanks, a US Navy destroyer's 5-inch shell, probably from the *Dashiell* but possibly from the *Ringgold*, exploded above their heads, killing Shibasaki and almost his entire staff.

As a result, the Japanese defenders were pretty much isolated and paralyzed. Holding only a thin piece of ground and with little protection, the Marines were seriously concerned about a night counterattack from their thin left flank where about 1,000 Japanese waited that would drive them back into the sea. But there was no counterattack that night. The death of the charismatic Shibasaki completely changed the battle for Tarawa from that point forward. The Japanese largely just sat in their bunkers and pillboxes shooting at the

Americans, extracting a fearful price, but otherwise just waiting for Marine teams to arrive to reduce the fortifications and kill everyone inside. Counterattacks were few, local, and disorganized. And beaten back, sometimes with difficulty.[9]

After a little more than three days of brutal fighting, at 1:30pm, Marine Major General Julian Smith announced the end of organized resistance on Tarawa's Betio Island. Mopping up pockets remaining on Betio and clearing out the remaining islands in the atoll remained, but the bulk of the campaign was over.[10] As it was on Bougainville.

Bougainville was not like Tarawa, would not be like Tarawa. The Americans were not attacking the Japanese on Bougainville. Rather, the Americans had compelled the Japanese to attack them. By seizing that little strip of land at Cape Torokina and then starting to build air bases there. The Torokina beachhead still had to be maintained, and that meant supplies and reinforcements. And that meant continued naval and air combat. The dangers of maintaining these supply lines were long apparent, but they continued to manifest themselves.

On November 19, the Japanese submarine *Ro-100* was in Rabaul taking on food. Way too much food for the boat's crew. It was sealed in rubber containers. (The food, not the submarine or the crew.) Loading was eventually completed, and at 6:00am on November 23, skipper Lieutenant Okane Hisao directed his *Ro-100* out of Simpson Harbor and on her mission: an emergency supply run to Buin.

She almost made it.

The *Ro-100* had steered to the north side of Bougainville and by 7:00pm on November 25, she was maybe two miles west of Oema Island. The boat was now running on the surface to enter the north channel to Buin.

At 7:10, the submarine suffered an underwater explosion, port side amidships. There had been no attack of which anyone was aware. The blast was caused by a mine. It's not clear whose. The anchorage was protected by minefields, but US Navy submarines and AirSols had also run mining missions in the area in the past.

When a submarine meets a mine, usually neither survive. The explosion threw Lieutenant Okane and everyone on the bridge into the water. The engineering officer gave the order to abandon ship – technically, "abandon boat" – but the *Ro-100* sank very quickly. Worse, survivors in the water were attacked by sharks as they tried to swim to shore. Of 50 crew members, only 12 made it to Buin. Lieutenant Okane was not one of them.[11]

But the Japanese were hardly the only ones with important convoys. On December 3, an incredible ninth echelon was headed to Cape Torokina, with eight tank landing ships and five infantry landing craft escorted by the destroyers *Fullam*, *Guest*, *Bennett*, *Terry*, *Braine*, and *Renshaw* who were directed by the now-promoted Captain Ralph Earle, Jr, commodore of Destroyer Squadron 45.[12] Escorting the escorts were destroyers *Charles Ausburne*, *Dyson*, *Converse*, and *Claxton* under Captain Burke.[13] Japanese scout planes found this force some 30 miles west of the Treasury Islands and were convinced this echelon actually had four carriers, two battleships, seven cruisers, and 17 destroyers.[14] Why? Don't know.

Anyway, just before 8:00pm that evening, the Japanese showed just how much they wanted to sink this convoy with a rather composite air strike.[15] It consisted of four Mitsubishi G4M land attack planes from the 751 Air Group, which on December 1 became the only remaining land attack plane unit at Rabaul, 11 Nakajima B5N carrier attack planes, and 15 Aichi D3A carrier bombers. Supporting this strike were two carrier bombers who would illuminate the targets with flares and floatlights; one land attack plane for tracking the target; and even one Zero for "radar deception."[16]

They did not attack all at once or even all attack the same force. Radar detected 20–25 unidentified aircraft. Captain Burke's destroyers, about 15 miles away from Captain Earle's echelon, seemed to draw most of the flares and about half the planes. The attacking aircraft followed the typical pattern of Japanese night attacks of hanging out outside the range of antiaircraft guns, feinting attacks, and then one of those feints would become real.[17]

According to the Japanese, "exceptionally fine results were attained in a systematic 30-minute attack."[18] The attacks were probably closer to an hour.[19] Two medium attack planes, six carrier attack planes, and two carrier bombers "failed to return." In exchange, the Japanese reported sinking two carriers, one battleship or cruiser, and one heavy cruiser; and damaging one battleship, one cruiser, and one destroyer.[20] In reality, they had hit nothing.

Nevertheless, they had shaken Captain Burke. He described this attack as "the most persistent, prolonged and confusing attack by well-trained, experienced Japanese pilots we have observed. The Japanese meant business and they wasted no time getting on with it in a most efficient manner."[21] So ended what the Japanese called the "Sixth Air Battle of Bougainville."[22]

But, like a movie franchise that had a few too many sequels the "[Insert ordinal here] Air Battle off Bougainville" had to stop sometime. The Torokina strip, which was literally at water's edge, was finally declared operational on December 10 after just one month of construction by the 71st Construction Battalion.[23] Thus at dawn of that day, Marine Fighting 216 with 17 F4U Corsairs staged into the baby base along with six SBD Dauntlesses and one cargo plane. The following day three Marine TBF Avengers landed, to be joined in short order by the US Army Air Force's 17th Photographic Reconnaissance Squadron of the 4th Photographic Reconnaissance Group. The Piva bomber field received its first planes on December 19, and was fully operational on December 30. The Piva fighter field was delayed by lack of Marston matting, but was still operational on January 9. "With the opening of three Allied airfields on Bougainville," wrote one pair of historians, "the Japanese capability to threaten the Allied position on Cape Torokina from the air was virtually eliminated."[24] That left only attacking on the ground as an option for destroying the Allied air bases. And to do so, the Japanese would have to march from their widely scattered bases across miles and miles of thick jungle. None of this was easy. Or fast.

Not that sometimes the Americans did not come up with some wacky ideas of their own. The Torokina perimeter could be anchored on the Koromokina River to the west and the Piva River and Cibik's Ridge to the east, but due to the requirements of keeping the runways of the air bases clear of Japanese interference, the perimeter was pushed beyond these natural defensive features. And while the perimeter was relatively quiet in the sector of the 37th Infantry Division on the American left, the right flank, closest to the biggest Japanese base at Kahili/Buin, was always a concern. When intelligence determined the Japanese were building up and possibly reinforcing the allegedly destroyed 23rd Infantry Regiment in the area of Koiari, some ten miles southeast of Cape Torokina, the possibility of a Japanese counterattack became much more substantial.

Enter the 1st Marine Parachute Battalion, veterans of Guadalcanal, especially Edson's Ridge, where their performance left something to be desired. Having arrived on Bougainville from Vella Lavella on November 23, they were now commanded by Major Richard Fagan. General Geiger decided to send the newly arrived Marine paratroopers on an extended raid behind Japanese lines in order to ... well, that's not entirely clear, but the stated idea was to disrupt communications, destroy enemy assets, and gather information. Fagan's men were to harass enemy units as far inland as the East-West trail but, at the same time, avoid major engagements with superior Japanese forces. This would be kind of like guerilla warfare, but without the guerillas. Or the warfare.

The operation moved with Clockwork Orange precision. After a scouting party on November 27 found the landing area devoid of Japanese, the landing was scheduled for November 28 to take advantage of destroyers escorting a convoy in to provide naval gunfire support, but it was delayed until the next day, which meant no destroyers, although the Marine paratroopers would have forward observers with radio contact for long range fire support from Torokina. Another scouting mission found no Japanese near the landing beach, so Major Fagan and his paratroopers landed in the wee hours of November 29.

The first indication that things were going wrong was a Japanese officer who approached them, unarmed except for a sword, acting as if he was expecting friendly reinforcements. He was quickly disavowed of that notion permanently.[25] The Marine paratroopers had landed in the midst of a major Japanese supply dump, home to forces twice as large as their own. Both of the earlier scouting parties had managed to miss the intended landing point, which, except for the potentially fatal consequences for the Marines, is actually fairly impressive.

Not as impressive as the means by which the Japanese were trying to bring about those fatal consequences, with 90mm mortars, machine guns and small arms. While the Marines repulsed a Japanese charge at dawn, by 8:00am, it was clear that there were only two ways out of here, and one of them was in a body bag. The other was behind them, back the way they had come, offshore. They would have to be quickly withdrawn. To complicate things further, the 1st Marine Parachute Battalion's radio broke down, able to transmit but not receive.

Major Fagan knew he was facing a considerably stronger Japanese force and that he had become fully engaged. He believed that he was unable to maneuver, and that the enemy had a fair estimate of the size of the Marine force. With the malfunctioning radio,

Fagan "excitedly" requested that his unit be withdrawn. Until that could be accomplished, they had no choice but to dig in and just hold.

Which he ordered, and the Marines turned to erecting hasty defenses under fire. This was not Edson's Ridge redux. According to one history:

> The combat efficiency of the command left little to be desired; the men responded quickly, intelligently and bravely to all orders. Lines never gave ground despite severe casualties and determined enemy assaults. No panic existed at any time, although all hands knew that ammunition was greatly depleted and that the chances of withdrawing in the face of a night or dawn attack (which was considered inevitable) were slim.[26]

Fortunately for the Marines, the forward observers still had communications with the artillery inside the Torokina perimeter, and a generous helping of 155mm shells helped keep the Japanese at bay. Even so, rescue boats were twice driven back by Japanese gunfire. The destroyers *Fullam*, *Lansdowne*, and *Lardner* and an LCI-gunboat arrived about 6:00pm to provide naval gunfire support and air support was also intermittently on hand. Eventually, this combination of fire was able to drive the Japanese to ground and the Marines were able to complete the withdrawal at 8:40pm. Information and communications, those twin pillars of any operation, had both failed this operation, resulting in a dismal – albeit not disastrous – failure. Casualties were reported 15 killed or mortally wounded, 99 wounded, and seven missing.[27]

Already being a casualty does not protect one from being a casualty again. Like a double casualty or a casualty squared or something. But that is what happened to an alleged Japanese hospital ship.[28]

On November 26, the former passenger-cargo liner *Buenos Aires Maru* left Simpson Harbor, allegedly as part of an unidentified convoy bound for Palau. She would not be a part of it for long. Around 8:30 the next morning, when they were in the Steffen Strait between New Ireland and New Hanover, a B-24 Liberator of unknown provenance attacked the ship. Reportedly, a bomb struck on the port side and flooded the engine room. The *Buenos Aires Maru* started listing to port, and between 20 and 50 minutes later, she would sink by the bow off Saint Matthias Island. Probably closer to 50 minutes later, because there were enough survivors to fill 16 lifeboats and two motor launches.

Rather curiously for a convoy, no one seems to have stopped to rescue these survivors. The Liberator certainly would not do it. Reportedly, the B-24 descended to 300 feet and strafed the survivors. It would be December 3 before unidentified subchasers would arrive and rescue about 1,000 survivors, but 158 were dead.

The wrinkle here: the *Buenos Aires Maru* was a hospital ship. Allegedly. Converted in October and November 1942, the *Buenos Aires Maru* had been reported by the Japanese Foreign Ministry to the warring powers as a protected hospital ship on November 21, 1942. On her last mission, she carried 63 nurses and an unknown number of Japanese servicemen repatriating from Rabaul Naval Hospital and 1,129 wounded and sick Imperial Army soldiers.

Or so they say. On April 24, 1943, while she was south of Hong Kong in the South China Sea, the *Buenos Aires Maru* was torpedoed by the submarine USS *Runner*. She suffered hull damage and seven men were injured. She managed to make her way to Hong Kong for temporary repairs and eventually back to Japan. The skipper of the *Runner*, Lieutenant Commander Frank W. Fenno, reported the *Buenos Aires Maru* had been zigzagging. He also reported hearing propellers and believing they were from escorts, though he never saw them. He had seen a plane earlier. Fenno also reported the *Runner* had been attacked with one depth charge.

Article IV of the Hague Convention X of 1907 and the 1929 Geneva Convention treaties stated that hospital ships were to display electrically powered lights to illuminate their red cross signs on the sides of the ship and upon the deck. Hospital ships were to be painted all white with a broad green stripe round the hull and red crosses painted on the sides to make them easily identified by the enemy. Vessels so protected were not to engage in warlike acts and violations could result in the loss of protected status and make the violating vessel a lawful military target. Zigzagging was a violation, as was being escorted by warships and attacking with depth charges, though Fenno's report is equivocal on the last two.

The *Buenos Aires Maru* had also been attacked in the Bismarck Sea by an unidentified American aircraft, possibly a B-25, on August 17. She escaped unharmed, and the next day made Rabaul, where she was photographed in her proper hospital ship livery.

After the *Buenos Aires Maru* was sunk, Brigadier General Dr Percy Carrol, the US Army's Command Surgeon in the Southwest Pacific, recommended an apology be made for the attack. However, General McArthur vetoed the idea and no apology was made. Not surprisingly, since it's not clear it was even one of his 5th Air Force aircraft that attacked. Some have claimed it was the 13th Air Force.

At 4:00am on November 30, a large convoy consisting of the *Awa*, *Himalaya*, *Nikki*, *Shinyu*, *Shoho*, and *Wales Maru*s and escorting *Ch-37* and *Ch-38* departed Rabaul northwest bound and down for Palau. Civilian cargo and passenger ships, even ones requisitioned by the military, don't move that fast, and by midnight on December 1 or so, they had only gotten to the south side of New Hanover.

And, at the same time, so had a PBY Catalina or two. Particular notice was taken of the 5,229-ton passenger-cargo ship *Himalaya Maru*, which was carrying 2,564 passengers and crew, including men of the 14th Field Repair workshop, 16th Signals Regiment, and the 7th Supply Hospital, 645 wounded servicemen, and some of the Korean and Japanese "comfort women" that would become infamous in the book of Imperial Japanese crimes against humanity. Three bombs were dropped on the *Himalaya Maru*. Only one hit, but it was an incendiary and enough to doom the vessel with a large fire. The ship was abandoned and sank six miles south of New Hanover on December 1. Six crew, two comfort women, and 27 soldiers were killed, an incredibly small loss of life considering how many were on the *Himalaya Maru*. The rest of the crew and passengers were rescued by other ships in the convoy, who continued onward.[29]

That same December 1 was important for General Kenney's 5th Air Force. From almost nothing when Douglas MacArthur had arrived in Australia to now, which, though reduced by its campaign to reduce Rabaul, was a behemoth compared to its remaining Japanese aerial opposition in Papua New Guinea. Not that the remaining opposition was not dangerous.

Wewak was starting to recover from the pasting it had taken in August, so General Kenney, whose own air power was starting to recover somewhat, decided Wewak needed a renewal of its uselessness. Time for some B-24s (eight each from the 64th and 65th Bombardment Squadrons; and nine from the 403rd, all from the 43rd Bombardment Group; and six each from the 319th, 320th, 321st, and 400th Bombardment Squadrons of the 90th Bombardment Group.) In theory, they were to be escorted by 22 Republic P-47 Thunderbolts (13 from the 36th Fighter Squadron of the 8th Fighter Group and nine from the 341st Fighter Squadron of the 348th Fighter Group). The goal was to hit the main air base at Wewak, known as "Wewak Central."[30]

Later, it was speculated that a predawn scouting flight by one B-24 of the 321st to check out the weather over Wewak may have tipped off the Japanese that an attack was coming. The attacking bombers took off from Port Moresby, only to find the 36th Fighter Squadron's fighters, intended to fly top cover, flying too top cover. Worse, the strike became strung out, with the 43rd Bombardment Group's Liberators getting well ahead of the 90th's "Jolly Rogers." Arriving around 11:00am on December 1, the 43rd's B-24s seem to have gotten through ok, but the 90th ran into a veritable ambush by Japanese Army Air Force's 59th and 248th Air Groups.[31] Both air groups flew what the Allies called the "Oscar" or, more often, the "Army Zero," the Nakajima Ki-43 Army Type 1 Fighter, nicknamed *Hayabusa* or "Peregrine falcon."[32] The bombing attack was carried out successfully, with "serious damage" reportedly done to the Wewak air base, including planes destroyed on the ground, and ammunition caches and fuel dumps set afire.[33] The 64th Squadron reported the entire area was covered in black smoke from fuel fires, while the 65th noted five explosions and a dozen fires.[34] Additionally, the small cargo vessel *No.16 Yoshitomo Maru* was reported sunk, though that loss was not confirmed postwar.[35] But the 90th incurred painful losses. A "Tony" flying out of the sun fired into the port wing of the Liberator flown by the 321st's Lieutenant Oliver Sheehan. The Number 2 engine caught fire and the plane lost altitude as it broke apart in midair. The B-24 of the 320th's Captain Lawrence N. Smith fell foul of two Oscars, who shot out two of its engines from above. As it was descending, a third Oscar shot out its ball turret, causing the gunner to fall out without a parachute. Most of the crew was seen to bail out, but they were strafed by Japanese fighters. The Liberator of the 319th's Lieutenant Richard A. Adams was badly damaged over Wewak and had to ditch off Finschhafen, at which point it cartwheeled and, as usual, broke apart, killing four of the crew. A Liberator flown by the

319th's Lieutenant Stanley Roebeck had escorted Adams' bomber back from Wewak, and when the plane ditched, Roebeck dropped survival equipment to the aircrew, then circled until fuel levels forced him to land at Dobodura. The next day he returned to the site to direct efforts to rescue Adams and his crew, who were picked up. None of the other men was ever seen again.[36] The Japanese admitted to the aerial loss of eight Army fighters (one from 59th Air Group and seven from 248th Air Group).[37]

The bombings would continue until morale improved. The morning of December 13, bad weather prevented two squadrons from the 380th Bombardment Group, who were trying to make their first attack on New Britain, and two from the 43rd for a total of 34 B-24 Liberators from bombing their primary target of the air base at Cape Hoskins.[38] So they instead hit Lindenhafen, about ten miles from Gasmata, with 1,000lb bombs. Early in the afternoon, 26 B-25 gunships from the 38th Bombardment Group visited the same area and left presents from minimum altitude in the form of bombs and almost 30,000 rounds of .50-cal. ammunition. At around the same time, 26 B-24s of the 90th Bombardment Group and 24 B-25s of the 345th Bombardment Group hit Ring Ring Plantation, again near the small Gasmata air base on the south coast of New Britain, a base that seemingly should have been more important to both sides than it actually was.[39]

But there's always tomorrow to start over again. With Gasmata. On December 14, the little air base was the target of 31 B-25s and nine B-26s from the 22nd Bombardment Group, who, in the words of one US Army Air Force history, "on the whole, made a poor showing." Coming in at altitudes of 8,000 to 10,800 feet (considered "medium" altitude), the Americans got through heavy but inaccurate antiaircraft fire to drop 120 1,000lb bombs, but that same history points out only about 30 percent hit the runway.[40] On the other hand, another history says the attack "plant[ed] more than 80 bombs on the runway and in revetment areas."[41] It's all in the spin. Still, that was nothing compared to the bombing marathon the Cape Merkus area received. The Amalut Plantation, which covers most of the Arawe Peninsula, was the recipient of 204 1,000lb bombs in two separate missions (or 70 sorties) from 35 B-24s of the 43rd Bombardment Group. Pilelo Island, off Cape Merkus, got 208 1,000lb bombs from 28 B-24s of the 90th Bombardment Group. Then it was Amalut Plantation again, on which 37 B-24s from the 380th Bombardment Group dropped 252 1,000lb bombs, again in two separate missions (or 74 sorties). Arawe Island proper was visited by 26 B-25 gunships of the 38th Bombardment Group, who dropped 168 300lb bombs and drilled in almost 32,000 rounds of .50-cal. ammunition. Then it was back to Amalut with 71 A-20 Havocs from the 3rd Bombardment Group who appropriately deposited 87,800lbs of bombs and more than 12,000 .50-cal. rounds on that particular locale, again in two separate missions (or 142 sorties). On the heels of the Havocs came 36 B-25 gunships of the 345th Bombardment Group, who dropped 234 300lb bombs and fired more than 18,000 .30-cal. rounds and almost 60,000 .50-cal. rounds. The Cape Merkus area was under almost continuous attack from 6:45am until 3:48pm, the single biggest attack of the war in the Southwest Pacific Area, an attack that lost not one single aircraft.[42] Impressive.

As impressive as that may have been, the war was going on at other places, too. Like off New Hanover. Lieutenant (jg) Rudolph Lloyd of Patrolling 52 was following the west coast of New Ireland north and west in the dark in his Consolidated Catalina flying boat until he came to the Steffen Strait between Kavieng and New Hanover. There, at 1:10am on December 14, he found what he reported to be a "cruiser." He was wary of the Japanese antiaircraft guns ashore, who could pick him out in the bright moonlight, but not wary enough to be turned away from his prize. Lloyd climbed to 1,500 feet and began a glide attack in the face of intense antiaircraft fire. At 300 feet, he released his bombs, at least two of which, he reported, had detonated aft of midships. Then his Catalina, with one new bullet hole, chugged back to the seaplane tender USS *Half Moon* in Namoai Bay off the eastern tip of the Papua Peninsula. The Japanese reported that the 1,203-ton cargo ship *Tokiwa Maru* was sunk off New Hanover by a US Navy PBY Catalina. While the coordinates for the *Tokiwa Maru*'s sinking don't completely match Lloyd's report, Lloyd's was the only such attack at that time.[43]

The area around New Hanover was rather popular at this time. At noon on December 12, the convoy N-206 left Palau bound southeast and down for Rabaul with the *Alaska*, *Ceylon*, *Kaika*, *Kaito*, *Pacific*, and *Ryua Maru*s escorted by subchasers *Ch-37* and *Ch-38*. All was hunky-dory until the evening of December 19. At 8:10pm, when the convoy was off Kavieng, it was attacked by PBY Catalina flying boats. The Americans scored no hits, but they would be back, At 9:40pm, to be precise, when a second attack by Catalinas set the 2,745-ton cargo ship *Kaito Maru* and its cargo of coal and 420 men of the 212th Naval Construction Unit – mostly the coal – on fire, killing 26 crew and 262 troops. The ship seems to have been abandoned and left behind, but the fire apparently continued, serving as a beacon in the dark for enemy aircraft. Not quite an hour later came one more attack. This time, the Catalinas went after two ships, the *Pacific* and *Alaska Maru*s. The *Pacific Maru* was damaged, but the 7,378-ton *Alaska Maru*, carrying 12,000 cubic meters of food, clothing, weapons, and general goods, had to be abandoned; it had apparently been disabled and possibly also set afire, with one crewman killed. Both the *Kaito* and *Alaska Maru*s sank the next day, the former southwest of Kavieng, the latter 30 miles off the Gazelle Peninsula. The rest of the convoy arrived safely at Rabaul on December 20.[44]

Things were happening much more quickly now. Big air attacks on Cape Merkus, Cape Gloucester, and Gasmata. Every day. A Black Cat sinking a cargo ship one day, a submarine torpedoing an alleged "hospital ship" the next. Even an amphibious landing by the 1st Marine Parachute Battalion. Putting aside the question of why you would have a unit of paratroopers try an amphibious landing, it did seem like the Allies were getting the hang of this amphibious operation thing.[45] Because they started conducting a lot of them in a fashion fast and furious.

Or at least it seemed that way to those who struggled to conduct a "counterlanding."

It had not been the smoothest patrol for the Japanese submarine *Ro-105*.[46] She had left Rabaul on December 6, 1943 to run 11 tons of ammunition, provisions, stores and drugs to Imperial Army and Navy troops at Sarmi, on the north coast of Papua New Guinea west of Hollandia (Jayapura, Indonesia).[47] But a breakdown in communications, which seemed to be occurring more and more, delayed the offloading until 5:30pm on December 10. Then, the submarine went to conduct her war patrol south of Cape Merkus, at the southern tip of New Britain.[48]

The night of December 14–15 was clear and bright, with the moon four days past full. A submarine would have found visibility good, or at least as good as you could expect at night. Around midnight, the *Ro-105* saw five destroyers sailing gently to the north. Merrily, she reported it to Rabaul, but heard nothing back. The submarine did not attack the five destroyers, probably because they were five destroyers. Destroyers were not considered an especially valuable target, even in an Imperial Japanese submarine force obsessed with attacking warships instead of the far more vulnerable supply ships. An attack would prompt a counterattack that could easily be fatal to the boat. Barring orders to the contrary, it was considered high-risk, low-reward. The *Ro-105* continued her patrol.[49]

At 3:00am, a Japanese Type 0 Reconnaissance Seaplane flown by Lieutenant Nishiyama Chohei of the 958 Air Group found five destroyers and five transports six miles southeast of Cape Merkus heading north.[50] That changed the equation. Those ships were heading toward the small Japanese base at Arawe.[51] Not so merrily, she radioed Rabaul. Not so merrily did Rabaul receive the report, although they did characterize Nishiyama's performance as "an act of noteworthy merit." At 5:00am, Rabaul lost communications with Arawe. When Admiral Kusaka combined all this with the previous day's bombing raid on Arawe by the 5th Air Force, he determined that enemy troops were landing at Cape Merkus.[52]

There were no bombings by the 5th Air Force on this day, but there was a bombardment by Allied ships that started at 5:20am that December 15 heralding the start – "Z-Day," it was called, probably because of some copyright issue with the owners of "D-Day" – of Operation *Director*. It was Task Force 76, consisting of the destroyer *Conyngham*, flagship of General MacArthur's amphibious commander Rear Admiral Daniel E. Barbey, and fellow destroyer veterans *Shaw*, *Drayton*, *Bagley*, *Reid*, *Smith*, *Lamson*, *Flusser*, and *Mahan*; fast destroyer transports *Humphreys* and *Sands*; Australian auxiliary cruiser HMAS *Westralia*, landing dock ship USS *Carter Hall*, two patrol craft, and two submarine chasers. After ten minutes of lobbing 5-inch shells, the landing itself began: 1,600 troops directed by US Army Brigadier General Julian W. Cunningham centered around Colonel Alexander M. Miller's 112th Cavalry Regiment (with no horses, who were not especially oceangoing), reinforced with artillery, combat engineers, and the 26th Quartermaster War Dog Platoon. Mark Antony did say, "Cry 'Havoc!' and let slip the dogs of war."[53] He didn't mean that literally – or maybe he did; the Roman legions did use war dogs.

Hanging around offshore in case there was trouble was a covering force with some old friends. Royal Navy Rear Admiral Victor Alexander Charles Crutchley, in his flagship heavy cruiser *Australia*, directed sister ship *Shropshire*, Royal Australian Navy destroyers *Arunta* and *Warramunga*, and US Navy destroyers *Ralph Talbot* and *Helm*. All but the Australian destroyers had some connection to the disastrous August 1942 Battle of Savo Island that had started the Guadalcanal-Solomons Campaign off on not just the wrong foot but on no foot. The *Ralph Talbot* and *Helm* had actually taken part in the battle, more or less, the former more, the latter less. Crutchley was nominally in command of the force that was beaten so badly at Savo Island, but he had left in the *Australia* for a ludicrously mistimed conference, while the Royal Navy had sent the *Shropshire* to replace the Australian cruiser (perhaps unnecessarily) sunk at Savo Island, *Canberra*. Through little (albeit not no) fault of his own, Crutchley was smeared with the Savo Island disaster without even having a chance to fight. Extremely unfortunate, because Crutchley, a veteran of World War I's Battle of Jutland and recipient of the Victoria Cross, was a brave and honorable officer who could have been very valuable in the engagement.

That engagement was long over, but another one was imminent because the Japanese were responding to the landing with unusual alacrity. For them. At 6:00am, Lieutenant Nishiyama reported that the Japanese garrison at Arawe, consisting of two companies of the Imperial Army's 51st Division, was fighting enemy landing craft.[54] While this confirmation caused extreme consternation in Rabaul, it was hardly unexpected, as Allied control of Papua New Guinea's Huon Peninsula and its tiny port of Finschhafen, not to mention the bigger port of Lae, suggested a jump to New Britain in the near future, so Admiral Kusaka had a plan. Kind of. He initially ordered an interception of the invasion force, but after receiving the report of ground fighting at Arawe, he put forth the idea of a counterlanding operation. The Japanese did love their counterlanding operations. And, really, who doesn't love a counterlanding operation? Well, General Inamura, for starters, who "was not overly enthusiastic about counterlanding operations."[55]

But Inamura was more optimistic about air operations, and did alert the Japanese Army Air Force's 4th Air Army in Wewak. Because they had to bring bombers forward from rear areas like Hollandia that were much safer for Japanese aircraft than the Wewak area, it could be a while before they could send something up. Admiral Kusaka sent up what he had immediately available: eight Aichi D3A carrier bombers from the 582 Air Group escorted by 54 Zeros, all led by the 201 Air Group's Lieutenant (jg) Oba Toshio, who had graduated from pilot training all of ten months earlier. Of the Zeros, 15 commanded by Warrant Officer Yamanaka Tadao of the 204 Air Group were ordered to strafe the US Army invaders. This attack was relatively lucky. That day saw a total of 82 P-38 Lightnings of the US 8th, 49th, and 475th Fighter Groups, 46 P-47 Thunderbolts of the US 348th Fighter Group, and P-40 Kittyhawks of Australia's No. 76 Squadron fly cover for the Arawe landings. Base Air Force arrived only minutes after the Kittyhawks had departed. Over the Vitiaz Strait, a dozen P-38s of the 431st Fighter Squadron of the 475th Fighter Group reported "12 Zekes, 10 Bettys, 20 Oscars" approaching from the west just before 9:00am. No one knows what they saw, only that they were distracted. Maybe a 4th Air Army air strike was approaching from Wewak; if so, it never attacked nor engaged. Not distracted was the destroyer *Reid*, who detected Base Air Force's strike on radar, and the destroyer *Shaw* vectored fighters to intercept. A dozen P-38s were over the beachhead, several other flights of Lightnings were in the area, and en route were 16 Thunderbolts of the 341st Fighter Squadron from Finschhafen and eight Lightnings of the 433rd from Dobodura. Nevertheless, the only defenders to make contact with the Japanese were a dozen P-38s from the 431st that were attacked by a dozen Zeros and beat a hasty retreat with no losses on either side. That was the extent of the Japanese good luck. Facing only antiaircraft fire, the air attack itself was relatively ineffective, destroying one landing craft, damaging several others, getting some near misses on the destroyer *Conyngham* that caused no damage, and causing some casualties, while all of Warrant Officer Yamanaka's strafers were damaged by antiaircraft fire, compelling two to force-land at Rabaul. The Japanese reported that two Zeros and two carrier bombers failed to return, but believed they had sunk one transport and three sea trucks while damaging one cruiser and one cruiser or destroyer, and "destroying about half the small craft." An official US Army Air Force analysis says, "The Japanese were fortunate in their Z-day bombing attack which, while ineffective, succeeded in avoiding most of our patrolling fighters." A second Base Air Force attack was attempted that afternoon, "but because of bad weather conditions, with great regret, it was suspended."[56]

The "small craft" may have been rubber boats, which are not necessarily the best things to use for a contested amphibious landing, but the Americans did it anyway. Anyway, "A" Troop of the 112th tried to land at Umtingalu on the coast just east of the base of the Arawe Peninsula, but after the defenders sank all but three of the rubber boats, the destroyer *Shaw* made a successful if belated effort to silence the defenders, effectively covering the swimming, rescue, and withdrawal of the cavalry troopers.

Elsewhere, the landing went more according to plan, in part because they used landing craft stronger than rubber boats. "B" Troop successfully took Pilelo Island, where Royal Australian Air Force's No. 335 Radar Station personnel quickly set up, oddly enough, a radar station. The main landing was by the 2nd Squadron of the 112th Cavalry at House Fireman Beach. While destroyers bombarded the beach with 1,800 rounds of 5-inch ammunition between 6:10am and 6:25, quickly followed by strafing runs by B-25 gunships, the landing troops struggled with inconvenient currents and were not able to hit the beach itself until 7:28, almost an hour behind schedule. This enabled the Japanese defenders to recover and fire on the landing boats, only to be silenced by those new-fangled rockets. Silenced enough that the first wave of cavalry troopers faced little opposition. Which was good because subsequent landing waves were delayed again. Four follow-up waves were scheduled to land at five-minute intervals, but the second landed 25 minutes after the first, and the next three waves all landed at the same time 15 minutes after the second. But such meticulously timed landings – meticulously timed military operations in general – rarely work as scheduled, so this just let everyone know *Director* was going OK.

If the landings had been on schedule, then you would have had to worry. Within two hours of the landing, all the large Allied ships other than Barbey's flagship *Conyngham* had left the area. The *Conyngham* stayed only long enough to rescue the survivors of "A" Troop's failed landing at Umtingalu; she took her leave later that day.[57]

Also later that day was a curious reconnaissance mission by the 4th Air Army. At 6:10pm, the Tuluvu air base signaled Rabaul, "Report from army reconnaissance plane at this base to the effect that the enemy was in the process of landing Cape Merkus [4:35pm]. Force consisted of 5 destroyers, 4 transports, and some 20 large landing barges." This "army reconnaissance plane" was a Kawasaki Ki-48 Army Type 99 Twin-engined Light Bomber – the Allies called this plane the "Lily" – flown by 2nd Lieutenant Nishida Tsutomu and a Sergeant Major Kobayashi. They had flown from Tuluvu to Arawe over the mountains of New Britain, observed the enemy in rain showers, and returned safely after a 40-minute flight.[58]

The report does not appear to have reached the 4th Air Army in time as it attempted its attack, maybe for the second time. The centerpiece was 11 examples of the Nakajima Ki-49 Army Type 100 Heavy Bomber – the Japanese nicknamed this heavily armed bomber the *Donryu* ("Storm Dragon") but the Allies called it the "Helen," which was not nearly as cool as "Storm Dragon," which was probably the point – from the 9th Air Brigade. Escorting the bombers were 22 Type 1 Peregrine Falcon fighters from the 59th and 248th Air Groups, while the 68th and 78th Air Groups contributed 22 of what the Allies called the "Tony," the Kawasaki Ki-61 "Army Type 3 Fighter," nicknamed *Hien* or "flying swallow."[59] They tried to attack the Cape Merkus area but between efforts to redirect their missions already planned for that day, the worsening weather, and their own general incompetence, they never made it there. So they bombed boats in Langemack Bay near Finschhafen instead. They were found by two P-38s from the 432nd Fighter Squadron under Lieutenant William Ritter at 5:30pm, but the Lightnings were at an altitude 8,000 feet lower altitude than their adversaries and at a much lower altitude than that needed for their optimal performance, so they balked at attacking a force whose fighters outnumbered them 11-to-1 while the Japanese by this point had concerns about fuel, so after the 432nd made two or three passes everybody broke off and headed back to base.[60]

Back at Arawe, the landing at the curiously named House Fireman Beach was completed successfully, if somewhat late, and by dusk the cavalry troopers controlled the entirety of the Arawe Peninsula. Supplies were built up to sustain the 1,600 troops that had landed, including new ones to re-equip "A" Troop, all of whose equipment was at the bottom of the sea, and construction of a base started.

The Japanese could not stop General MacArthur at Arawe. They could only hope to contain him. And attempt to contain him they did. The 1st Battalion of the Imperial Army's 81st Infantry Regiment under Major Komori Masamitsu had been assigned to defend Arawe, but it wasn't there because it was having issues. Part of the 17th Okayama Division, its trip from China to Rabaul was interrupted when its ship was sunk. It had to be reorganized in Rabaul, where it was stripped of half its infantry, all its heavy weapons, and almost all its machine guns, leaving it with only its headquarters, two rifle companies, and a machine gun platoon. It left in December headed for Arawe, but was still four days away when the Allies landed.

While the battalion was en route from Rabaul, Rabaul decided to keep up the air attacks. Indeed, Combined Fleet decided to keep up the air attacks. Admiral Koga decided to forward to Rabaul 20 Zeros and 36 carrier bombers who were loitering around Truk doing little – and carrier planes with little to do could always get into trouble.[61] Like PT boats. One never knew what the PT boats were going to do and, usually, neither did they. Late in the evening of December 15, *PTs-131* and *-133* operating out of Morobe, near Lae, were poking around off Gasmata when they spotted two white flares in the distance, source unknown. Shortly before midnight on December 16, *PT-133* spotted an unidentified plane maybe two miles away. Looked like a Kawanishi H6K "Type 97 Large Flying Boat" ("Mavis"). Then at 1:45am, a "large unidentified seaplane" flew low over the *PT-133*. Again, it looked like a Mavis. And it looked like a Mavis that was starting its bombing run. The PT boats opened fire. The thing about the Mavis was, you could practically just look at one of those things and it would blow up. And this one did. As it flew overhead, it jerked to starboard and the US sailors could see that it was on fire. Flying erratically, the plane seems to have tried to reach Gasmata, but crashed into the jungle short of the air base and exploded. The PTs reported they had shot down a Mavis.[62]

Curiously enough, at around the same time during the wee hours of December 16, Port Moresby received a radio message from US Army Air Force Lieutenant James J. Harris, Jr of the 43rd Bombardment Group's 63rd Bombardment Squadron reporting several enemy aircraft were following his B-24 Liberator. Several enemy aircraft were following him? At night? At 2:00am Harris reported his position off Gasmata. At 3:00am Port Moresby radio was listening and reading as the B-24 transmitted, "065 ..." and then stopped. The message was never completed, and Harris and his nine crew were never heard from again.[63]

Even more curiously, there were some Consolidated Catalina flying boats from Patrolling 52 in the area that night. Lieutenant (jg) Robert Vincent DeGuzman had taken off from Namoai Bay at 6:01pm to prowl the Dampier Strait but at some point he was ordered to scout the south coast of New Britain. Not that difficult an assignment, even at night, but at maybe 2:15am on December 16 when he was ten miles west of Gasmata, two boats opened fire on him, causing slight damage to the port wing and elevator.[64] DeGuzman made no other sighting and made it back to base, landing at 8:45am. Another Patrolling 52 Catalina flown by Lieutenant (jg) William James Pattison had taken off at 6:04pm to patrol the south coast of New Britain from Arawe to Wide Bay. In both cases, the Catalinas were probably assigned to look for movement of Japanese troops along the coast in their beloved barges. In any event, at 2:30am, Pattison came across two friendly motor torpedo boats some 18 miles southwest of Gasmata. At the same time, a twin-engine Helen came out of the dark and made a pass at him without firing. A few minutes later, as Pattison was passing over the PT boats again, the Helen started to make another pass, but was "shot down in flames" by the PT boats before it could open fire.[65] Pattison landed back at base at 7:25am.[66]

Adding all these together gives not a perfect storm of misunderstanding, but at least a drizzle. The PT boats said of the aircraft they shot down, "Plane was seen by various personnel aboard having the following characteristics: four engines, high parasol wing, rounded wing tips, heavy hull, twin tails, prominent struts, from hull outboard and upward to wing. These specifications fit the Japanese long range patrol bomber seaplane, MAVIS." They do. And, except for the four engines and the twin tail, they also fit the Consolidated PBY Catalina flying boat. But there was an aircraft over the PT boats that night with four engines and a twin tail: Lieutenant Harris's Consolidated B-24 Liberator. The PTs did not report seeing any other aircraft except the Mavis. In the fleeting glimpses they got of the aircraft in the moonlight, they saw four engines at one point, wing struts at another, twin tails at a third and so on, and came to the conclusion they were all one aircraft. They apparently did not realize they were dealing with not one but at least two and possibly three different aircraft, all friendly. They never opened fire on Lieutenant (jg) Pattison. More than likely, they did open fire on Lieutenant (jg) DeGuzman, driving him away. And they did open fire on Lieutenant Harris. Harris, seeing the tracers zipping past his cockpit and possibly glimpsing Pattison's PBY, thought enemy aircraft were targeting him and so reported. Flying low to take advantage of the PTs' antiaircraft fire in driving off his pursuers, Harris instead seemed to the PTs and Pattison to be making an attack run.[67] It was a tragic but understandable misunderstanding.

Later that morning, December 16, the second day of the invasion, at 8:00am to be precise, Arawe was visited by seven Aichi D3A carrier bombers from the 582 Air Group escorted by 56 Zeros, of which 28 were from the 204 Air Group (of which eight, who were led by Chief Petty Officer Ogiya Nobuo of the 204, were armed with bombs and were ordered to strafe the American positions), 17 from the 253, and 11 from the 201 air groups. There was no interception by defending fighters, but antiaircraft fire did take a toll. Two Aichis and one Zero failed to return, but the Zero pilot from the 204 Air Group survived and apparently was recovered.[68]

In the early afternoon, between 1:00 and 3:00pm, 19 B-25s from the 33rd and 408th Bombardment Squadrons of the 22nd Bombardment Group, and one B-17 dropped 10 tons of fresh supplies to the American troops, still trying to make up for "A" Troop's lost supplies. All of the ordnance and almost all of the clothing and equipment reached the "A" Troop, which was ready for combat the next day, several days sooner than if aerial supply was not available.[69] At around the same time, the 4th Air Army in Wewak made its second attempt to get at Arawe. Seven Nakajima Storm Dragon bombers from the 7th and 61st Air Groups of the 9th Air Brigade commanded by the 7th's Captain Fukuda Shigeo took to the air from Wewak's Dagua air base with 16 Ki-43 Peregrine Falcons of which nine were from the 248th Air Group, all led by 248th commanding officer Major Muraoka Shinich, charged with protecting the left flank of the bomber formation, and the rest presumably from the 59th Air Group to fly close escort; and 18 Ki-61 Flying Swallows from the 68th and 78th Air Groups to fly top cover.[70] One of the bombers apparently had to abort, so they were down to six by the time they reached the coast of New Britain. While they were within sight of Japan's Tuluvu air base, they bumped into four P-38s from the US Army Air Force's 432nd Fighter Squadron. The Lightnings had been flying escort B-24 Liberators who were about to bomb the Cape Gloucester area when, at 1:45pm, the new radar at Arawe radioed 431st Captain Thomas McGuire to check out unidentified aircraft that had appeared on radar over Baker Island. Beginning a somewhat confused action, McGuire seems to have delegated that task to four P-38s from the 432nd, who had been delayed by poor weather in taking off to escort the Liberators and so were behind the main strike. These Lightnings introduced themselves to the Japanese east of Rook Island.[71] The Lightnings made diving passes at the escorting Oscars, starting a sprawling affair over western New Britain that drew in a total of 25 Lightnings from the 431st as well as the 432nd. It turned into a disaster for the 4th Air Army. The Storm Dragons never reached Cape Merkus. Five of the Helens were shot down, and the sixth Storm Dragon force-landed at Tuluvu, where it took up residence. Lamenting the inability of his unit to protect the Storm Dragons, Captain Nango Shigeo, leading the fighters of the 59th, admitted in his diary that it was no longer the day of the Peregrine Falcon. Even worse, three Oscars of the 248th Air Group went down as well. Lieutenants Ejiri Hisomatsu and Fueki Shoji of the 248th Air Group disappeared and were never found, but Sergeant Major Saito Yasuo was able to land at Gavuvu (what the Allies called Cape Hoskins) east of Tuluvu. He returned to Wewak two days later flying his fighter. The Americans apparently suffered no losses in this exchange.[72]

The day over Arawe was not over yet. At 4:00 that afternoon 54 Zeros returned to the area, 15 to strafe, the others to escort one lousy Aichi D3A carrier bomber from the 582 Air Group. This time they faced significant opposition: 15 P-47s of the 342nd Fighter Squadron reported intercepting 12–15 Zeros at 7,000 feet and claimed four "Zekes" and a "Kate" without loss of their own.[73] The Japanese claimed four aerial victories, including two by the aforementioned Chief Petty Officer Ogiya, and one probable, but two Zeros failed to return, including that of Petty Officer 1st Class Tagami Ten-ichi of the 201 Air Group.[74]

And while this description of events may not sound particularly productive from the Japanese standpoint, it was enough for Combined Fleet to award a citation to Lieutenant (jg) Oba's 201 Air Group. Accordingly to the Imperial Navy:

> Citation was awarded to the 201 Naval Air Unit Fighter Plane Unit which was under the command of Lt (jg) OBA, for the setting ablaze of one enemy cruiser, the sinking of three transports and approximately 50 landing barges and the shooting down of five interceptor planes at Merkus Cape on 15–16 Dec 1943.[75]

Others were less impressed. Lieutenant (jg) Oba had graduated flight school only the previous February, yet he was the only surviving flight *buntaicho* (division commander), so here he was commanding large air strikes. The 201 Air Group's most successful pilot was Warrant Officer Iwamoto Tetsuzo, but Japanese protocol would not allow him to command an air strike if a unit commander was available because Iwamoto was neither an officer nor a unit commander. More importantly, Iwamoto was ill with fever from malaria as well as dengue fever and unable to fly, so Oba it was. For now. Iwamoto, who was in short order transferred to the 204 Air Group, later assessed Oba's ability as "trivial." Oba was shot down and killed in air combat over Rabaul a week later.[76]

If daytime air attacks during the day didn't work, Rabaul thought, how about nighttime air attacks? Beginning the night of December 16–17, Base Air Force's 5th Air Attack Force began a series of night raids targeting the Cape Merkus area. They were generally mounted by carrier attack planes of the 582 Air Group, not just the now-famous Nakajima B5N Type 97 Carrier Attack Plane, but now the B5N Type 97's replacement: the Nakajima B6N Navy Carrier Attack Bomber *Tenzan*. "Tenzan" means "Heavenly Mountain," which seems a rather immobile name for an aircraft. But it was part of the official Navy designation of the B6N instead of the usual "Type" designation, which was normally the last two digits of the Japanese year. So not having it was kind of an insult to Japan. Some attacks included more *Tenzan*s detached from the *Zuikaku* temporarily.[77] Still others of these raids included Type 1 land attack planes from the 751 Air Group, now the only *Rikko* unit left in the South Pacific after the incorporation of the G4Ms from the 702 Air Group, which had been disbanded on December 1. These attacks did no damage to shipping and, though they caused minor damage and casualties on shore, were almost totally ineffective.[78]

More effective was a morning attack by Base Air Force on December 17. This one consisted of 55 Zeros escorting a dozen dive bombers. Waiting for them were supposed to be eight Thunderbolts from the 341st Fighter Squadron of the 348th Fighter Group and two from the 69th Fighter Squadron of the 58th Fighter Group. Except one of the 341st's Thunderbolts developed engine problems and a second escorted him back to base. So it was 8-on-67, which were not encouraging odds. But radar vectored the Americans into an ambush position, sort of. The P-47s went after the Vals, but antiaircraft fire from below discouraged them from following for too long, so they focused on attacking the Vals after they completed their attacks. Perhaps as a result, this was the most successful Japanese attack on the Cape Merkus beachhead to date, not that that was saying a whole lot. The 100-ton coastal transport *APc-21* took a direct hit that ultimately blew her in half. A near miss on her was academic and she sank. The 207-ton minesweeper *YMS-50* was damaged by a near miss, and four tank landing craft were seriously damaged, and the Americans suffered 40 casualties. The Americans claimed to have shot down eight Vals and two Oscars; actually, three dive bombers and a Zero failed to return.[79]

There would be no afternoon follow-up attack from Rabaul. AirSols decided to make use of its new Torokina air base to send fighters to Rabaul. Fighter sweeps. This would be a big 'un, in more ways than one. This would be the first fighter sweep over the Rabaul caldera, which required AirSols fighters to stage into Torokina, top off the fuel tanks, then make for Rabaul. And it would be a big sweep.

Marine Fighting 214's commander Major Gregory "Pappy" Boyington (no relation to Pappy Gunn) was chosen to lead the fighter sweeps.[80] On December 17, Boyington sent up 76 fighters: 22 US Navy F6F Hellcats, including 16 from Fighting 33 (apparently two aborted) and eight from Fighting 40; 31 US Marine F4U Corsairs, including eight from Marine Fighting 214 with one aborted, eight from 216, eight from 222, and eight from 223, and 24 Kiwi P-40 Kittyhawks from Nos. 14 and 16 Squadrons (two aborted).[81]

It kind of went according to plan. But makee learnee. Getting all these fighters formed up in the air took such a long time that Royal New Zealand Air Force Wing Commander Trevor O. Freeman led his Kittyhawks on ahead. After Major Boyington got his American charges organized, he led them to Rabaul, where they found the Kiwis already duking it out with a dozen Zeros from the 204 Air Group. For now. These Japanese fighters, led by Ensign Ito Suzuo, would be joined by 20 more of their squadron mates, plus 15 from the 201 and 25 from the 253 air groups. The Kiwis with their obsolete fighters gave a good accounting of themselves, but they lost two of their own. Flight Officer John O. McFarlane, of No. 16 Squadron, collided in midair with the Zero of the indefatigable Petty Flight Seaman 1st Class Kawato of the 253 Air Group. Both pilots were rescued, if, in the case of McFarlane, you can call being fished out of the water to be thrown into the hell that was the 6th Field Kempeitai's prison "rescued." Wing Commander Freeman is believed to have downed one, yelling, "Tojo eats Spam!" into his microphone. After this obviously unforgivable insult, the other Zeros swarmed his P-40. Freeman was last seen circling a valley over New Ireland with smoke coming out of his P-40, looking for a place to bail out. His squadron mates came to his aid, but were driven off by Zeros, and Freeman was never seen again.[82] He was a major loss. "He was one of the RNZAF's most able and inspiring leaders," says the official New Zealand history.[83] The Kiwis did not lack courage.

The original plan called for the New Zealanders to approach the enemy at 10,000 to 15,000 feet, with the Navy Hellcats 5,000 feet above them and the Marine Corsairs above them at 26,000 feet. The Kiwis had done their job taking on the Zeros at the lower altitudes. Then the rest of Major Boyington's posse showed up. Looking at Lakunai air base, they could see 30–40 Zeros just loafing on the ground. Boyington waited for the Zeros to come up and engage him … and waited … and waited …

What Zeros were in the air were staying at lower altitudes, where they had an advantage in maneuverability. And the longer Major Boyington waited, the more fuel would become an issue. So he allegedly tried a tactic he had used a few times before: taunting. Boyington had known for some time that the Japanese were monitoring the Allied tactical frequencies with English-language specialists. He had learned this last fall after a bombing attack on Kahili when an unknown voice broke in over his radio.

"Major Boyington, what is your position?" Boyington later said it "came in as clear as a bell without the slightest trace of an accent."[84] It sounded like one of the strike craft he had been escorting had gotten lost and was trying to find him. Except Boyington had already escorted the bombers to safety, then had his squadron turn back toward Kahili, and he knew the radios in those bombers did not have the range to reach him. In fact, he doubted he would have recognized it as Japanese if the caller had not used such perfect English; his own men would have asked, "Hey, Pappy, where the hell are you?"[85]

Knowing Japanese Zeros were in the air looking for the Allied strike planes, Major Boyington played along. The question was repeated: "Major Boyington, what is your position?"

"Over Treasury Island," answered Boyington. Technically, Treasury Islands because there are two of them, neither of which is called "Treasury," but who's counting?

"What are your angels, Major Boyington?" "Angels" was a reference to thousands of feet in altitude.

"Twenty angels, repeating, twenty angels," replied the major.

"I receive you five by five," which meant and means loud and clear, then broke off. Boyington had lied about his altitude – he was at 25,000 and climbing – and his position.[86]

Then Major Boyington saw about 30 Zeros appearing from beneath a white cloud, ascending, heading toward the east – the wrong direction. Boyington and his pilots were set up behind them, and coming out of the midday sun, to boot. Marine Fighting 214 got several kills before the Japanese retreated back into the clouds.[87]

When did this happen? Don't know. Boyington never said in his memoirs.[88] But now Boyington expected the Japanese to break into his radio comms, and he would be ready.

The story more or less goes that during one fighter sweep of Kahili, probably October 18, 1943 involving 16 Corsairs from Marine Fighting 214 and eight from 221, most of the Japanese Zeros did not take to the skies and instead stayed parked at their airfield.[89] That wasn't good for a fighter sweep. The Zeros attacking at Pearl Harbor and Clark Field were devastating in strafing the US Army P-40s on the ground because the Warhawks were all lined up in nice rows wingtip to wingtip. The Zeros were not so lined up at Kahili. They were dispersed, hard to destroy en masse with even 20mm cannons, let alone machine guns. Boyington expected another Japanese break into his comms chatter. He decided to respond by trash-talking, hoping to anger them into coming up.

Sure enough, an accented voice broke into his tactical frequency with the same question, "Major Boyington, what is your position, please?"

"Right over your lousy airfield, you yellow bellies," the major answered. "Come on up and fight."[90] For this attack, he expected a reply to his taunt. He got it.

"Why don't you come down, Major Boyington?" said the person on the ground at Kahili.

Instructing his remaining Corsairs to stay at altitude, Boyington and his wingman Lieutenant William "Casey" Case pushed over and went down in a screaming dive, spraying the field with their .50-cal. guns apiece. Antiaircraft fire burst all around him, but the Corsairs zoomed up, up, and away, Boyington's Corsair untouched while Case was scalped from behind by a 7.7mm round that lodged in his gunsight but otherwise did not prevent him from continuing the mission. Rejoining his flight, Boyington taunted the Japanese once more: "Now, come up and fight, you dirty yellow bastards!"[91]

A few of the some 60 Zeros seen on the ground at Kahili started taking off. In total some 20–40 Zeros took off and wrestled with Boyington's charges. The result was the loss of five Zeros, including Petty Officer 2nd Class Koyama Isamu of the 204 Air Group, with only Flight Seaman Kawato surviving, while the US Marines lost Lieutenant Milton E. Schneider of Marine Fighting 221.[92]

But that was then. This was now. That was southern Bougainville and the Shortlands. This was New Britain. That was Kahili, or, as the Japanese called it, Buin. This was Rabaul: The Show, the Major Leagues, the Premier League. Could it work again?

"Come on up and fight!" Boyington snarled on the radio.

"Come on down, sucker!" came the response. In perfect English.

Trying to get him to come down. And they succeeded. For a while.

From 10,000 feet, Major Boyington strafed two antiaircraft gun positions near Lakunai air base.[93] They were too dangerous for the Americans to stay at low altitude. Machine-gunning parked aircraft might have destroyed some aircraft, but it would have been fatal.

So the story goes. There are multiple versions of this conversation, if the exchange took place at all. Major Boyington and Lieutenant Walton did not include it in their report, or any of these exchanges for that matter. Some find it suspicious. Bruce Gamble opined:

> Neither of these exchanges was mentioned in the otherwise highly detailed mission reports compiled by Frank Walton, a notable omission. Information that the enemy was not only listening to tactical frequencies but actually broadcasting to an individual by name should have been significant news from an intelligence officer's point of view.[94]

Maybe, but most of these types of stories don't make official reports. Captain Joe Foss flipping off the Japanese as he pirouetted his F4F Wildcat in front of the bridge tower of the battleship *Hiei* did not. And the Japanese had long been listening in in Allied tactical frequencies, since at least the Battle of the Bismarck Sea in March 1943, when a Japanese voice taunted the crew of a burning B-17.

But there was no response to Major Boyington's strafing run that December 17, either from the Zeros on the ground or from the voice on the radio, which more than likely was 32-year-old Edward Chikaki Honda. Honda was a former Japanese baseball star raised in Hawaii, and as a result not only spoke English fluently, but also knew American slang.[95]

Marine Fighting 214's Lieutenant Robert M. Bragdon, a 1939 Princeton graduate, had gotten off late, but managed to join up with another plane and arrived over Rabaul at 11:00am.[96] As the other Allied planes left Rabaul, a seemingly frustrated Bragdon dove and strafed ... something. He then climbed back to 8,000 feet, turned to head back, and then saw tracers shooting past him. He had been jumped by six "Tonys." He described his pursuers:

> They were a vivid California blue, shiny with white tails. They had white diagonals on the wings and white ... longitudinal stripes on the fuselage extending from the rear of the

cockpit to the tail assembly. The meat balls were indistinct; it was difficult to make them out against their blue background. Roundels were definitely on the fuselage and possibly on the upper wing surfaces.[97]

These fighters started to chase him. Bragdon dove into a cloud, checked his bearings, and turned for home, his engine roaring, his Corsair screaming at almost 400 knots. Even so, he only pulled away from his dogged shadows slowly, only losing them after 65 miles or so. It's unclear if anyone ever told him his pursuers were actually Kiwi P-40 Kittyhawk IIIs. As stated earlier, the "Tony" was the Allied reporting name for the Kawasaki Ki-61 "Army Type 3 Fighter," nicknamed *Hien* or "flying swallow." This fighter was unique to the Imperial Army Air Force, who had no units in the Rabaul caldera at this time. Oddly, the Kiwis painted their P-40s with bold markings, including white slashes on the wings and vertical stabilizer – but not the famous shark mouth – to prevent confusion with the Tony, though perhaps what would have been more effective in preventing such confusion was not opening fire on the Americans in (yet) another case of mistaken identity, as the Kiwis seem to have done here.[98] And while the US Army Air Force didn't like flying over water and only did it as a necessary evil, they were practically sharks compared to the Japanese Army Air Force, who struggled to navigate over water, which explained their relative lack of presence covering the now-infamous Lae convoy the previous March.

Major Boyington found the December 17 fighter sweep less than satisfactory:

Major Boyington is of the opinion that far too many fighter planes were sent on the sweep. He thinks 24 sufficient. He is also strongly of the opinion that all planes should be the same type – thus eliminating the necessity for continually checking on other planes in the sky.[99]

Some of these recommendations seem like best practices, such as all attacking aircraft being of the same type, at least on a fighter sweep. Boyington also believed that the large size of this fighter sweep was too unwieldy to manage, hence the limit to 24 fighters on such sweeps. The only problem with that is if the Japanese did, in fact, respond by scrambling 72 fighters, Boyington would be attacking at a 1-to-3 disadvantage. That makes no sense. The large number of fighters on this sweep was due to the large number of fighters the Japanese had based in the Rabaul caldera, especially at Lakunai air base. While the Allied fighters had better armor protection for the pilots and self-sealing fuel tanks, 1-to-3 is still 1-to-3. That protection won't last forever if three Zeros are shooting at one Allied fighter. Just ask Wing Commander Freeman. It might have been better to recommend 24 fighters per group, not per sweep. For example, if the December 17 sweep had been so divided, there would have been three groups of 24 each. Indeed, Boyington himself later amended his recommendation to 36 to 48 planes per sweep.[100] And the next sweep six days later had 48 fighters.

In Major Boyington's assessment, "All in all the sweep was not too successful since the Japs failed to accept the challenge – perhaps this was partially due to the landing which had been made at Arawe."[101] The Japanese "failed to accept the challenge." Or did they?

Accounts of this air attack that give the numbers of defending Japanese fighters consistently report 72 Zeros having scrambled to intercept the Allied strike, which one report says consisted of 35 aircraft.[102] Again, these 72 fighters consisted of 32 from the 204 Air Group, 15 from the 201, and 25 from the 253 air groups. So far, so good. Additionally, Major Boyington reported 30–40 Zeros lined up at Lakunai air base, which would have been with the 204 Air Group, for a total of 102–112 Zeros in the air and on the ground, including 62–72 for the 204 Air Group. The New Zealand P-40s of Nos. 14 and 16 Squadrons engaged the Japanese Zeros, losing two of their own, including the popular and respected Wing Commander Freeman, while actually shooting down three, from which only one pilot survived.[103] Yet according to Marine Fighting 214's report, the Americans saw *none* of these 72 Zeros? Really? If all of these reports are taken as true (a sizable "if"), then it may have been that the Zeros were at low altitude where they had a performance advantage with the P-40s on a day with broken clouds, in which several pilots, including Lieutenant Bragdon, hid. Major Boyington and his American pilots may not have seen the Zeros in the air below the broken clouds – and the Japanese, in turn, may not have seen the Americans. One Japanese report gives the number of attacking Allied fighters as 35, which is consistent with seeing only the two squadrons of Kiwis.[104]

Nevertheless, this attack by Major Pappy Boyington and his Black Sheep marked a new phase in the war in the South Pacific. Almost every day thereafter, Rabaul would be attacked in some way, whether with bombing or fighter sweeps. It would turn into the reckoning of Admiral Kusaka's Base Air Force.

Because Base Air Force was tied up defending Rabaul on this December 17, it was left to the 4th Air Army to mount the afternoon attack. Sort of. It had no heavy bombers available, and for some reason its commanding officer Lieutenant General Teramoto Kumaichi was evidently disinclined to acquiesce to requests to send his Kawasaki Ki-48 Army Type 99 twin-engine light bombers against Cape Merkus with its serious air defenses both in the air and on the ground.[105] So, he decided to try a fighter sweep. Why would you try a fighter sweep against a target with no airfield? Don't know. Maybe it was to escort the Mitsubishi Ki-46 Type 100 Command Reconnaissance Aircraft. If so, it didn't work. The Ki-46 disappeared over Cape Merkus. Eight American Thunderbolts of the 342nd Fighter Squadron, 348th Fighter Group arrived over Arawe at 2:30pm and encountered a Dinah near the shore. Captain Edward Roddy, leader of the second flight, peeled off from 15,000 feet and shot the Dinah down. But the Thunderbolts and the 4th Air Army fighters missed each other. The Japanese briefly strafed Arawe, then headed toward their assembly point over Tuluvu for the trip back. Some of the fighters took the opportunity to land at Tuluvu. Meanwhile, 16 P-38 Lightnings of the 80th Fighter Squadron, 8th Fighter Group had been patrolling over Arawe from 3:00 to 4:40pm. After their patrol ended and before heading back to base, 80th squadron commander Major Edward "Porky" Cragg led them on a sweep toward Cape Gloucester. When they were 10,000 feet over Tuluvu, Cragg saw two fighters taxiing for takeoff. Cragg and his wingman dove to take them out, but the P-38s had built up too much speed in the dive and overshot the targets. The Japanese managed to get off the ground. Captain Kenneth G. Ladd and his wingman 2nd Lieutenant C. B. Ray dropped their fuel tanks and went after the enemy fighters, identified as a Tony and a Zeke; in actuality, the Zeke was an Oscar, which was often mistaken for a Zero and even called an "Army Zero." In this case, the Oscar got up to about 500 feet and poured on the speed, heading, oddly enough, for Rabaul. On a 90-degree full deflection shot, Ladd managed to hit the cockpit of the Oscar, which started a fire. Ladd's second pass sent the Type 1 Peregrine Falcon fighter crashing in flames, killing its pilot 2nd Lieutenant Masuzawa Masanao of 59th Air Group.[106] What happened to the other fighter is unknown.

When Lieutenant General Sakai Yasushi, commander of the 17th Division, heard about the *Director* landings, he went fishing around Cape Gloucester for some reinforcements. The 1st Battalion of the 141st Infantry Regiment moved from its base at Cape Bushing on the south coast of New Britain some 40 miles east of Arawe by the Imperial Army's beloved barges. According to Japanese records, this, called the "Tobuse Battalion," tried a counterlanding, but landed at the wrong place. They ended up at Omoi in the early hours of December 19, then struggled through the jungle to join up with Major Komori's troops at Didmop.[107] Komori gathered the survivors of the landing at Arawe and decided to launch a counterattack to retake the Arawe Peninsula.

So began a lengthy stalemate between the US Army and the Imperial Japanese Army in the area around Cape Merkus. The cavalry troopers had fortified the base of the Arawe Peninsula and were able to relatively easily if uncomfortably repulse repeated Japanese attacks, which were initially by air and later by land. This was not the outcome the Japanese wanted, but if they did not like this Allied landing, well, there would be others. Believe that.

It was in part to clear the way for those others that the next day, December 18, B-24 Liberators from the 90th Bombardment Group visited Tuluvu bearing gifts. Seeing fighters take off from the Tuluvu's Number 2 runway the previous day and seeing some aircraft at Tuluvu on this day – reportedly, five twin-engine bombers, two "silver" bombers, three green aircraft all near the runway, with six or more unidentified fighters spotted in a wooded area north of the runway – suggested that the air base could, well, be an inconvenience to future operations. So the 90th dropped on the runways 198 1,000lb bombs. Or 80 2,000lb bombs. Or both. The 5th Air Force preferred its history to be multiple choice. Either way, they turned Tuluvu into a moonscape. The 4th Air Army's 26th Air Group reported suffering no damage to its aircraft, but the damage to the runway would prevent any air operations for the time being.[108] The same could be said of the Gavuvu air base at Cape Hoskins after some 40 Liberators from the 43rd and 380th Bombardment Groups plastered it with 1,000lb bombs.[109]

Meanwhile, the 4th Air Army tried another fighter sweep over Cape Merkus with four Ki-43 Type 1 Peregrine Falcons of the 248th Air Group joining Ki-61 Type 3 Flying Swallows of the 59th Air Group. These guys apparently amalgamated with Ki-61 Type 3 fighters of the 68th Air Group, who all seem to have operated out of Madang for this mission.[110] They ran headlong into 16 P-38s of the 433rd Fighter Squadron, 475th Fighter Group. The Lightnings positioned themselves to jump one of the Japanese fighter formations, believed to be 59 Air Group. The Lightnings, in turn, were jumped by fighters from the 68th and 248th and ended fighting for their lives. One US Army Air Force official history described the combat:

> [E]nemy pilots displayed considerable skill and aggressiveness. This was especially true on 18 December when 16 P-38s, 433rd Fighter Sq., jumped 10 to 15 ZEKES (sic), OSCARS, and TONYS at midday. The P-38s dove through the enemy fighters and were in turn jumped by about 15 fighters, which had been hiding in cumulous clouds. Definitely on the defensive and outmaneuvered, the P-38s destroyed only three of the enemy while losing two P-38s…[111]

It was a curious engagement. The erudite Lieutenant William Glen "Jake" Jeakle, flying the P-38 "*Regina Coeli*," which means "Queen of Heaven" in Latin, was preparing to attack a Japanese fighter when the Lightning of Lieutenant Austin K. Neely collided with him "like a Mac [sic] Truck." Neely's plane sustained propeller and wing damage but managed to return to Dobodura. Jeakle, on the other hand, suffered damage to the right boom and lost all control of the fighter. "This is Jeakle, going in!" was all he managed to blurt on the radio. Jeakle was last seen spiraling at 9,000 feet near the Pulie River roughly 15 miles north of Arawe. No one saw a parachute.[112]

Nevertheless, considering their proverbial backs were against the proverbial wall, the 433rd Fighter Squadron got off light and gave as good as they got. Lieutenant Robert Tomberg was given credit for shooting down the Tony of Sergeant Major Yamazaki Tamisaku of the already decimated 68th Air Group – by the beginning of December, there were only three officer pilots left in the air group.[113]

The Arawe beachhead got some protection from inclement weather for the next few days, but the air war came back with a vengeance on December 21. It started out small. The Royal Australian Air Force's No. 79 Squadron had been sitting on standby at Kiriwina and had seen little action, much to their disgust. On November 28, Flying Officer A. W. Moore was flying a Supermarine Spitfire on a test flight when he got a scramble order from Kiriwina, indicating enemy aircraft were approaching. Kiriwina vectored him to an area some five miles south of Kitava Island in the Trobriands where he found the aircraft, a Dinah reconnaissance plane, uncomfortably close to Kiriwina. Moore then had managed the neat trick of shooting down the Dinah despite both of his cannons failing. Nevertheless, through no fault of their own, the men of No. 79 Squadron had done little since. On this day, they would do more than a little. They seem to have been called upon for a long-range interception. Flying Officer James Richards and one Pilot Officer Barrie, flying Supermarine Spitfires, claimed to have shot down a Tony off the south coast of New Britain.[114] Curiously, the Tony in question had been tracked from the general direction of Rabaul. For that reason, it has been speculated that this plan was actually a Base Air Force reconnaissance plane. Although the 501 Air Group was based in Kavieng, it was probably a Judy from the 501 that had staged into Rabaul.[115]

It was the first air combat of the day, but it was ... nothing compared to what happened next. Around 11:00am came 64 Zeros and 29 dive bombers from Rabaul targeting the ships off Cape Merkus. Loitering over Arawe to meet them were 18 P-38s under Lieutenant Colonel Charles MacDonald of the 432nd Fighter Squadron, 475th Fighter Group. They reported contact with only about ten Vals and 15 Zeros and Oscars, so they missed most of the attacking aircraft, unsurprising when they were outnumbered by enemy fighters more than three to one. The Japanese were just here for the ratio. The ships sent up heavy antiaircraft fire that disrupted the bombing attacks by the Vals, who managed to damage the 100-ton US Coast Guard-operated coastal transport *APc-2*.[116] The Lightnings claimed eight Vals, one Zero, and one Oscar. The Japanese reported attacking "two large transports, seven to nine medium transports, five or six cruisers and destroyers, and a great number of landing craft, sinking two large and four or five medium transports and two cruisers or destroyers and damaging and setting fire to one destroyer and a large number of small boats," but lost four bombers and one Zero. Or four Zeros. Or both. Base Air Force preferred its history to be multiple choice.[117]

And given multiple choice, Base Air Force chose violence. And the most violence Admiral Kusaka could come up with was 16 dive bombers escorted by 64 Zeros, who, after a significant lull, arrived over Cape Merkus at 4:30pm. Again, they were targeting the ships, barges (always a Japanese favorite) and boats offshore. Defending Arawe were seven Thunderbolts (one had aborted) of the 342nd Fighter Squadron, who reported encountering about 20–30 Vals, which, obviously, was more than the Japanese had sent, strangely scattered about 500 feet over the water. Eight of the Zeros strafed the landing craft, and claimed to have sunk two landing craft and set fire to about 30 small vessels. The tank landing craft *LCT-171* was damaged by bomb shrapnel, but there was little other damage and only a few casualties. The Americans claimed eight Vals shot down and others probably destroyed or damaged. In actuality, they had shot down five Aichis, which, despite the reinforcements from Truk, was a price Base Air Force and especially the 582 Air Group could not sustain. Considering the Japanese fighters outnumbered the defending Americans 9-to-1, the Zeros turned in an abysmal performance, neither effectively protecting the carrier bombers nor extracting a price from the Americans, and are hardly mentioned in American accounts of the engagement. A single Thunderbolt was reportedly shot down, but US Army Air Force records do not confirm it.[118]

It did seem as if there were not enough fighters to protect the Arawe beachhead this day, but there may have been an explanation. Aviation historian Richard L. Dunn would later say, "Fighter direction at Arawe was less than perfect on this day as on other occasions. There were American fighters that were misdirected and failed to engage or engaged only after the Japanese had dropped their bombs." Fighter direction is something of an art form, and, as was the case at Santa Cruz, the fighter director here was not exactly Leonardo or Michaelangelo. Then again, according to Dunn, "[I]t seems clear that the Japanese went to some effort to disguise their approach routes utilizing terrain, sending part of the escort as a diversionary force and probably also using metal coated paper strips ('window') as a radar counter-measure."[119] Maybe, but except for the use of radar countermeasures such as "window," which is now called "chaff," the Japanese had used such tactics ever since Admiral Kusaka had taken over Base Air Force during the Guadalcanal Campaign. They had generally not been successful over Guadalcanal, but they did have some notable successes over New Georgia. These tactics seem to have been more successful against the 5th Fighter Command than they were against AirSols.

It seems to have been as Base Air Force was leaving that the 4th Air Army arrived with its attack at 5:20pm. This consisted of eight Ki-48 Type 99 twin-engine light bombers from 208th Air Group. The escort was a dozen Peregrine Falcons from the 59th and 248th Air Groups and eight Flying Swallows from the 68th. Possibly as a result of the aforementioned underwhelming fighter direction, the Americans again got ratioed in this attack, with only four P-47 Thunderbolts of the 340th Fighter Squadron on hand to oppose them, and of these four, only two, Lieutenant Guy Roberts and his wingman 2nd Lieutenant Stanley Souders, actually engaged the Japanese. Later reporting they had faced 20 Tonys and Hamps covering 10–12 Nells, they dove to each make one pass at the Japanese, and each claimed to have shot down a Hamp before making a discreet exit. There were no Hamps here (or Nells, for that matter), only Oscars and Tonys (and Lilys). But three of the Flying Swallows, all from the already hard hit 68th Air Group, would fly no more. Two, those of Sergeant Ikeda Hideo and Sergeant Major Nagashima Hideshi, went down over Cape Merkus. The third was longer and more tragic. Captain Takeuchi Shogo had served with the 64 Air Group in the China-Burma-India theater, reportedly shooting down no less than 30 enemy planes, before he was transferred to Papua New Guinea and the newly formed 68th Air Group in April 1942. Here, Takeuchi had flown about 90 missions and was given credit for shooting down another 16 enemy aircraft. The total score probably made the popular Takeuchi the leading Japanese Army Air Force ace in-theater. Hit and wounded during an interception in October 1943, he returned 15 days later, covered in bandages, drawing cheers from his men. On December 21, Takeuchi reportedly shot down one "Grumman fighter" that had been chasing the 68th Air Group commander, Major Kimura Kiyoshi.[120] While Takeuchi's efforts were successful, his Type 3 Flying Swallow was damaged and he may have been wounded. All alone, he limped across the straits toward New Guinea, making it to an apparently designated emergency air field inland of Hansa Bay called Nubia.[121] But as Takeuchi approached for landing, his engine died. His Ki-61 crashed into some trees and inverted. He would not be walking this one off. Gravely injured, Takeuchi died three hours later. To add insult to literal injury, Takeuchi in his final mission had not shot down a Grumman fighter or any other fighter, just damaged a P-47 that made it back to base. Takeuchi's career efforts did earn him a posthumous promotion to major.[122]

5th Air Force was hardly taking the Japanese air attacks lying down, but though the Allies' tormentors here were both Base Air Force (11th Air Fleet) and the 4th Air Army, the 5th Air Force focused almost exclusively on the 4th Air Army. On December 18, more than 70 Consolidated B-24 Liberators, North American B-25 Mitchells, and even Martin B-26 Marauders hammered the Tuluvu air base at Cape Gloucester. Then again, dirt airfields and all that. More than 20 gunships attacked the Borgen Bay area east of Cape Gloucester, and almost 40 Liberators hit the Gavuvu air base. For good measure, 33 A-20s bombed and strafed dumps and troop concentrations north of Finschhafen. The next day, December 19, more than 140 Consolidated B-24 Liberators, North American B-25 Mitchells, and Martin B-26 Marauders hammered the Tuluvu air base at Cape Gloucester. Then again, dirt airfields and all that. Gasmata was visited by 37 P-40s. With General Kenney suspicious that some of the attacks were coming from Madang, 30 Mitchells and Marauders bombed that particular air base, while about 30 B-25s, A-20s, and P-39s hit barges, bivouac areas, and gun positions north and west of Finschhafen. On December 20, 35 Mitchells of the 38th Bombardment Group (including nine from the 71st Bombardment Squadron, seven from the 405th, nine from the 822nd, eight from the 823rd; two apparently aborted) bombed Alexishafen, north of Madang. The next day, December 21, while Arawe was enduring an entire day of air attacks, more than 100 B-24s, B-25s, and A-20s plastered the Cape Gloucester area, while seven Australian A-20s from No. 22 Squadron under Wing Commander J. G. Emerton operating out of Kiriwina joined a bunch of Australian Kittyhawks (who had been irritated by their lack of action) in an attack on the Gavuvu air base.[123]

And so on, and so on. The morning of December 22, Cape Gloucester again had to deal with aerial tourists in the form of at least 30 B-24s, B-25s, and A-20s; and the messes they left behind. As that was going on, B-25s and P-39s attacked Madang and Alexishafen. Again.[124] That night, the Japanese did try a counterattack out of Rabaul with ten Mitsubishi G4M Type 1 land attack planes of the 751 Air Group escorted by two fighters which were probably Nakajima J1N Navy Type 2 reconnaissance planes moonlighting as night fighters from the 251 Air Group, Base Air Force's night fighter unit, but only "minor damage" was reported.[125] The next day, 61 Liberators bombed Cape Gloucester during the day, while at night Liberators came back to keep the Japanese awake by dropping small bombs, hand grenades, and even beer bottles, which hopefully were empty; otherwise it would be a great waste of beer.[126] That same night, Base Air Force counterattacked again, with six carrier attack planes hitting the Arawe Peninsula and two hitting Arawe Island itself. Again, these were probably Nakajima B5Ns, possibly with some B6Ns mixed in, and probably from the 582 Air Group out of Kavieng, though a detachment from the *Zuikaku* was now operating out of Vunakanau. P-39s strafed from Borgen Bay to Rein Bay. Gasmata, Gavuvu, Alexishafen, and Wewak were hit again. And in case that was not enough, on December 24, 190 B-24s, B-25s, and A-20s spent the entire day pummeling the Cape Gloucester area. Christmas Day was celebrated with more than 180 B-24s, B-25s, B-26s, and A-20s providing large fireworks of a sort at Cape Gloucester.[127]

Where was Rabaul and Base Air Force during all this? As one Japanese history tried to explain, "Since the beginning of December, with the exception of Rabaul as our main air base and Kavieng as our auxiliary air base, we were without a practical base."[128] It continued, "Moreover, the mobility of our air operation was almost nil. Consequently enemy air raids on Rabaul obstructed our operations and in addition the lack of advance air bases which increased our attacking distance did in [sic] great damage."[129] While this explanation might be word salad, the gist is clear: Base Air Force could not move, so it had to defend itself against repeated attacks instead of staging outside the range of the Allies and instead of mounting operations of its own, in part because the enemy was too far away.

Nevertheless, all of that did not mean Base Air Force was not still extremely dangerous. On December 23, 18 B-24 Liberators from the 5th Bombardment Group, escorted by 48 fighters, including eight Corsairs from each of Marine Fighting 214, 216, and 222; 16 Hellcats from Fighting 33, and eight Hellcats from Fighting 40, were to attack Lakunai and Vunakanau air bases. After they left was to come a fighter sweep consisting of four dozen fighters – just what Major Pappy Boyington had recommended – including 28 P-38 Lightnings from the 44th Fighter Squadron on Guadalcanal, eight Corsairs from Marine Fighting 214 led by Boyington himself, and a dozen more Corsairs from Marine Fighting 223. Major Marion Carl, commander of Marine Fighting 223, led this attack. Once the bombers were done and safely away, the fighters would perform a, um, fighter sweep, which they were perfectly suited for doing, being fighters and all.[130]

Slight problem: Base Air Force was not going down like this. Admiral Kusaka scrambled a lot of fighters: 30 Zeros from the 201 Air Group, 38 from the 204, and 31 from the 253. One seems to have aborted, because 98 Zeros were reported to have swarmed over the Allied intruders, divided as they were in two groups. Lakunai and Vunakanau were bombed, but at a perilous price. Marine Fighting 214's Major Pierre Carnagey and Lieutenant James Brubaker, and Fighting 33's Ensign James A. Warren all vanished in the melee during this attack; Warren is known to have survived, but died in a Japanese prisoner of war camp. The fighter sweep, which was engaged over St George's Channel, was little better. Marine Fighting 214's Lieutenant Bruce Ffoulkes disappeared into another melee over St George's Channel and was never seen again. However, six pilots were lost including Reserve Ensign Matsuo Kagemitsu Matsuo of the 253 Air Group, one of the rare college graduate pilots of the Imperial Japanese Navy, along with Lieutenant (jg) Ohba Yoshio and Petty Officer 1st Class Kijiya Masanobu of the 201 Air Group; and Chief Petty Officer Fujii Takeshi and Petty Officer 1st Class Uchida Jiro of the 204.[131]

Major Boyington had some aerial victories on this day, and on his way out had even strafed a surfaced Japanese submarine two miles east of Sperber Point.[132] Nevertheless, he found himself troubled. For a very peculiar reason:

I shot down my twenty-fifth plane on December 27. And if I thought that I ever had any troubles previously, they were a drop in the bucket to what followed. There was nothing at all spectacular in this single victory, but it so happened that this left me just one short of the record jointly held by Eddie Rickenbacker of World War I and Joe Foss of World War II. Then everybody, it seemed to me, clamored for me to break the two-way tie. The reason for all the anxiety was caused by my having only ten more days to accomplish it; 214 was very near completion of its third tour, and everyone knew I would never have another chance. My combat-pilot days would close in ten days, win, lose, or draw.[133]

Win, lose, or draw, Base Air Force could not help the 4th Air Army if it could barely defend its own bases, so General Teramoto's charges had to face General Kenney's attacks alone for now. If the repeated 5th Air Force attacks were numbing – and it should be noted that these were hardly the only air attacks, as for instance, US Army Air Force A-20s attacked suspected Japanese positions around Arawe, where the Americans were struggling to keep the Japanese outside their defense perimeter – the US Navy would add a twist. While in those dark days of late 1941 and early 1942, the Japanese had been the octopus using all eight legs to reach down southeast Asia and into the East Indies, west toward India, east toward the Philippines, Guam, and beyond, now the Allies were not so much the octopus as the kraken, snarling, reaching everywhere, squeezing its prey.

On Christmas Day, 1943, Admiral Frederick Sherman played Santa Claus, with his flying creatures delivering gifts to the Japanese at Kavieng courtesy of the fleet sleigh *Bunker Hill* and the light sleigh *Monterey*. The Imperial Navy had tried moving ships from Rabaul to Kavieng to protect them from the increasingly frequent air attacks at the former. It was not entirely effective. The 4,861-ton transport *Tenryu Maru* was sunk, killing five. Damaged were the armed merchant cruiser *Kiyosumi Maru* and minesweepers *W-21* and *W-22*. Though she did not sink, the *W-21* seems to have been especially hard hit, losing nine of her crew and being forced to stay in Kavieng for the next month getting repairs.[134]

Also on Christmas Day, at 8:00am, to be precise, an Imperial Army Air Force reconnaissance plane found a significant Allied convoy in eastern New Guinea. And it was a big one: four cruisers, 14 destroyers, 38 transports, and 20 sea trucks 80 kilometers northwest of Buna, all heading north. Also found were four destroyers, 15 transports, and three subchasers 50 kilometers northwest of Buna, also headed north. At anchor in Buna's Oro Bay were 25 transports, ten sea trucks, 20 tank landing ships, and "numerous small craft." In the Finschhafen area were 34 transports, ten sea trucks, and five tank landing ships.[135]

This was a remarkably successful reconnaissance mission. It gathered a lot of information, one of the twin pillars of any operation. The other pillar is communications. They are intertwined. Information is worthless if you can't get it to the people who can use it. Communications are worthless if you have nothing to say. Once this information was gathered for a mission at 8:00am on December 25, all that was left was to get it to Rabaul. So that report reached Rabaul … the night of December 25–26. "If the report had been received before noon an attack on the convoy would have been possible," one Japanese history explained, "but the opportunity was lost through faulty operational functioning."[136]

Admiral Kusaka didn't care. He figured all these transports meant something big, either a reinforcement of Arawe or a landing somewhere in the Dampier Strait. He ordered the submarine *I-177*, at that time off Cape Merkus, to head south into the strait. Kusaka also put Base Air Force on alert for an attack early on December 26.

So, early that morning, Admiral Kusaka and his staff, having determined that this big convoy was meant to reinforce Arawe, sent up 63 Zeros and 25 carrier bombers to bomb the Cape Merkus area. When they arrived over Arawe around 9:00am, they found relatively few worthwhile targets, but they attacked all the same and returned to Rabaul. Only to find out that Kusaka had been trying to radio them to change targets. Kusaka had guessed wrong. At 7:00am, Allied troops had landed at Tuluvu, Cape Gloucester, at the far western tip of New Britain. He tried to radio the strike to head to Tuluvu instead, but "because of a delay in transmission the change was not accomplished."[137] That's what they were going with. It couldn't possibly have had anything to do with taking the radios out of the Zeros.

Up again went Base Air Force, whose pilots could not have been happy at being sent on a mistake, and an early morning one to boot. What they found off Cape Gloucester was Operation *Backhander*, the invasion of Cape Gloucester, itself the second part of the three-part Operation *Dexterity*, the first part of which was *Director*, the landing at Arawe. That was meant to be something of a diversion, with the hope being that the Japanese would overreact to it and divert forces that would be needed to defend Cape Gloucester and its air bases. That did not happen, in part because General Sakai suspected *Director* was a diversion. It's kind of a dumb idea to try a diversion against a military organization that uses diversions as if they were a religion and thus suspects everything the enemy does is a diversion.

Be that as it may, this *Backhander* would be tricky. Cape Gloucester itself and its settlement of Tuluvu, with its resident air base, was on something of a peninsula, facing the Bismarck Sea. On one side of the peninsula was Borgen Bay, an extension of the Bismarck Sea. On the other the Dampier Strait, not the Bismarck Sea. Inland was the rugged Mount Talawe, the eastern shoulder of which was the smoking volcano Mount Langla. Between Mount Talawe and the coast were very narrow beaches and lots and lots of swamp. As historian Eric Hammel described it:

> Cape Gloucester is among the rainiest regions on Earth, and the landings were to take place at the height of the northwestern monsoon season. Moreover, as was the case at Cape Torokina on Bougainville, the landing area was filled with largely unmapped swampy lowlands, high ridges, and rugged rain forests with few trails and waterways to aid in movement through the region. On a typical day, temperatures stood at an extremely humid and strength-sapping 90 degrees, and 72 degrees at night.[138]

Defending this rainiest region on Earth was, in the words of one US Marine monograph, "something designated the 65th Brigade."[139] In the words of another history, "The 65th Brigade [was] apparently so called because there were not sixty-four others like it, nor even one."[140] There is inherent value in uniqueness, however, or so its commander, Major General Matsuda Iwao, whose area of expertise was in transportation rather than combat because his job was to keep the supply lines to New Guinea open, had to have believed as he struggled to manage the table of organization and equipment for this matchless unit. Again, as a Marine history put it, "To set up a detailed order of battle for the 65th Brigade would be confusing and futile. In a strength report to 17th Division, dated 1 December 1943, [citation omitted] General Matsuda listed 41 separate components, ranging in numbers from four men to 3,365, of which in many cases only elements – sometimes very small elements – were actually present."[141] Well, he did have the 53rd and 141st Infantry Regiments and the 51st Reconnaissance Regiment. Anyway, in this report, Matsuda listed the 65th Brigade's present strength as 15,018, but its effective strength as 12,078. To put it in perspective, that's about the size of a division, which is supposed to be larger than a brigade. Yet, like Matsuda himself, most of these men were transportation and logistics specialists, not fighters; most of those that were fighters had no combat experience. And these men were scattered around western New Britain; a total of only 3,883 were in the immediate target area of the *Dexterity* landings. Like the Imperial Navy flag officers who were skillful in navigation, Matsuda could get you there, but once there, could he do anything else? Then again, in this case, he was already there, so he probably had a good way to get out.

It would be needed, because this transportation specialist was about to face the entire 1st Marine Division, now recovered from its bruising experience on Guadalcanal, and now commanded by Major General William H. Rupertus, himself a veteran of the Tulagi and Gavutu and Tanambogo operations. Under the umbrella of the so-called "Alamo Force" (the US 6th Army) commanded by Lieutenant General Walter Krueger, as *Director* had been, they would be backed up by General Kenney's 5th Air Force and almost the entirety of General MacArthur's navy, the 7th Fleet, now under the command of Santa Cruz and Guadalcanal veteran Vice Admiral Thomas C. Kinkaid. Anyway, today's force was again Task Force 76 under the command of Admiral Barbey in his faithful destroyer *Conyngham*. To deliver elements of the 1st Marine Division, Barbey had 33 landing ships; 45 landing craft of various types, and, the tip of this particular spear, ten of the now-famous fast destroyer transports, most of them veterans (*Stringham, Crosby, Kilty, Dent, Ward, Brooks, Gilmer, Sands, Humphreys,* and *Noa*), escorted by destroyers *Shaw, Flusser, Mahan, Reid, Smith, Hutchins, Beale, Daly, Brownson, Drayton, Lamson, Mugford,* and *Bagley* in addition to Barbey's own *Conyngham*. Admiral Crutchley was back with an enlarged cruiser force, now divided into two to bombard separate areas. Australian heavy cruisers *Australia* and *Shropshire* were joined by destroyers HMAS *Warramunga*, HMAS *Arunta*, USS *Helm*, and USS *Ralph Talbot* in bombarding the Tuluvu air base while US Navy light cruisers *Nashville* and *Phoenix* and destroyers *Bush, Ammen, Bache,* and *Mullany* were to handle one of the invasion beaches.[142]

Because there were two. One, the small beach of Tauali on the Dampier Strait side of the peninsula, was quickly seized by a reinforced battalion from the 2nd Marine Regiment as a diversion. Again, using a diversion to divert people who already use diversions as a religion and consider everything the enemy does as a diversion could have only limited effectiveness. General MacArthur's people got too cute here. But there were no Japanese in the area and the landing was successful.

The other landing beach was much larger, on the Bismarck Sea side of the peninsula in the area of Silimati Point and Borgen Bay, about 5 miles southeast of the Tuluvu air base. This would be taken by the 7th Marine Regiment, with the 1st Marine Regiment coming in behind it to take point once the 7th had taken the beach.

It was hoped that resistance would be limited after a short period of intense air attacks like the ones just described. Three days after the Arawe landing, the bombing campaign against Cape Gloucester had been increased and intensified, especially against the air bases at Tuluvu and Gavuvu, where General Sakai was located. To put these attacks just described into some context, on December 19, two squadrons of the 380th flew two missions from Dobodura, while the 43rd flew double missions every day from December 21 through December 25 inclusive. Every target of importance was hit.[143] So intense was this campaign that within the 5th Air Force it birthed a term for the complete obliteration of a target – "Gloucesterizing."[144]

Whether these targets were obliterated or Gloucesterized enough is somewhat of an open question. That December 26, more than 270 B-25s, B-24s, and A-20s bludgeoned the area between Cape Gloucester and Borgen Bay for nine hours starting a little after 7:00am. Leading this armada was Colonel Bill Miller of the 380th Bombardment Group commanding five squadrons of B-24 Liberators, each B-24 carrying eight 1,000lb bombs, which was not a comforting thought to Lieutenant Harold S. Mulhollen of the 530th Bombardment Squadron, 380th Bombardment Group. These huge formations of bombers can get kind of tight. Approaching Cape Gloucester, Mulhollen saw that his B-24 was about to collide with another bomber. Mulhollen instinctively pulled up his right wing to avoid the collision, but instead of the wing going up a bit until the danger was over, Mulhollen's Liberator snapped over inverted and then dropped off in a left hand spin heading straight down. No, those four tons of explosives were not comforting right about now, nor were the nearly full fuel tanks. After plunging 6,000 feet, Mulhollen and co-pilot Lieutenant Russell Fleming had to brace their feet against the control panel to get leverage to pull back on the control yokes, which succeeded in pulling them out of the dive at 3,500 feet. It was the only documented time a B-24 was ever brought out of a spin. They made it back to base – with the bomb load – but the stresses of the dive left the plane trashed. Anyway, after the Liberators came the B-25 gunships, including all four squadrons of the 345th Bombardment Group, under the command of the 345th's Lieutenant Colonel Clinton U. True, and all four squadrons of the 38th Bombardment Group; and A-20s. The B-25s and A-20s bombed the landing zones, then strafed them with their numerous (thanks to Pappy Gunn) .50-cal. machine guns, then headed away. After all that, the 7th Marine Regiment landed successfully, in part because General Matsuda had left the beach undefended. Because right behind the very narrow beach was a very large swamp. Matsuda didn't think anyone would try to land there because of that swamp. But the Americans outsmarted him – they had in fact no idea the swamp was there.[145]

Anyway, the 1st Marine Regiment landed and passed through the 7th Marines to take point, the drawbacks of which quickly became apparent. The 1st ran into an area of Gifu-style fortifications and the only major combat this day, as a company commander was killed by fire from a well-positioned bunker until an amphibious tractor literally ran over it. The Marines started digging in and consolidating the beachhead. Around 13,000 Marines and about 7,600 tons of supplies were landed by the end of the day.[146]

But the end of the day did not come soon enough. At 2:30pm, Admiral Kusaka's air strike finally arrived: 25 dive bombers and 51 Zeros. The destroyer *Shaw*, which had the fighter director on board, first plotted the incoming strike at 2:20pm, when the Japanese were 65 miles to the northeast.[147] There were 49 P-38s, 16 P-47s, and 16 P-40s over the landing area, and the *Shaw* first sent elements of the 80th Fighter Squadron to meet the Japanese. Five minutes later, the *Shaw* vectored Captain Thomas McGuire, who was leading 16 Lightnings of the 431st Fighter Squadron on this day, toward unidentified aircraft 50 miles away to the east northeast. When McGuire had closed to 30 miles, the *Shaw* lost the plot. Everyone was now blind, electronically speaking. The two squadrons sent for interception were out of position. A dozen Lightnings of Major Cragg's 80th Fighter Squadron had to use the Mark 1 eyeball to spot incoming Zeros through a hole in the clouds 5,000 feet above them. The 80th, 431st, and 475th Fighter Squadrons climbed to get their shot at the 30–40 Zeros they counted. The problem was that because the fighters had been out of position, the Vals got through to the convoy and planted two bombs on the destroyer *Brownson*. Reportedly, the bombs struck to the starboard of her centerline, near the Number 2 funnel. A very large explosion pretty much eliminated her entire superstructure above her main deck, as well as her deck plating. The *Brownson* immediately listed 10 to 15 degrees to starboard and settled rapidly amidships with the bow and stern pointed upward. Skipper Lieutenant Commander Joseph B. Maher ordered abandon ship, but the *Brownson* sank so fast the loss of life was heavy: 108 killed. The destroyers *Lamson*, *Shaw*, and *Mugford* were damaged by near misses, as were two tank landing ships.[148]

Major Cragg, Captain McGuire, and their men had tried to get at the Vals before they dove, or, more likely, glided at not nearly the usual near-perpendicular angle for dive bombing. The best the Americans could do was lash at the Vals after they had come out of their dives, which were more like the less effective glide technique. Cragg and his wingman Lieutenant Burnell W. Adams took the first pass at the Vals. It was ineffective, and Adams moved off to tackle one on his left, and reportedly shot it down. He chased another over the coast and shot it down as well. Adams had lost track of Cragg, however. He saw one P-38 nearby attacking a Val, but it was not Cragg. In the distance to his left, Adams saw what he identified as a "Tojo" fighter being chased – and ultimately shot down – by a P-38, who in turn was being chased by another "Tojo" – a "Nakajima Ki-44 Shoki ("Devil Queller") Army Type 2 Single-Seat Fighter." Adams tried to intervene, but was unable to affect the outcome, and he watched the "Tojo" – actually a Zero – shoot up the P-38's engine. The Lightning went straight up into the clouds smoking, and the Zero attacked Adams head on before Adams went into a cloud himself. After he came out, Adams waited at the base of the clouds, and so he saw the tragic ending. "The P-38 came out of the clouds, a ball of fire and spinning badly," Adams reported. "It went in just like that and exploded when it hit. It landed about fifty yards inland on the western shore of Borgen Bay." Adams went on. "Thinking that the pilot might have bailed out while in the clouds I stayed in this area for approximately five minutes but observed no parachute ... I decided against going down to view the wreckage." When he got back, he heard Cragg was the only one from his squadron missing. This day, Porky Cragg had gotten his 15th aerial victory – over an "Oscar" – highlighting his exceptional flying skills, but Adams saw him become someone else's victory. Such is the caprice of war.[149]

But caprice is indifferent to suffering, to side, to cause. When the leader of the 36th Fighter Squadron, 8th Fighter Group saw Japanese fighters descending behind him, he had his P-47 Thunderbolts pull a 180. As Lieutenant Thomas R. Huff completed the turn, he saw his wingman 2nd Lieutenant Devin H. Gilchrist behind him but losing altitude, then puffs of black smoke coming from his exhaust indicated his engine had cut out. The cause was unclear because there were no enemy aircraft around Gilchrist's plane at the time. The good news was that Gilchrist was able to bail out of his Thunderbolt before the plane hit the water and exploded. Gilchrist parachuted into the water about four miles northwest of Silimati Point, east of Cape Gloucester and west of Borgen Bay, inflated his life vest, and started swimming. The bad news was that Huff saw a boat heading toward Gilchrist – the coast was held by the Japanese. Gilchrist was never seen again.[150]

Caprice. Fortune. Could they be the same? Chief Petty Officer Kanamaru Takeo, newly transferred to the 204 Air Group, claimed four enemy aircraft destroyed; he may have been the one who shot down Cragg. The Japanese believed they had sunk two cruisers and two transports, damaged three more transports, and shot down 20 "night fighters." But even if this figure was true, the cost was ruinous. Four Zeros and three pilots were lost, including Petty Officer 1st Class Kitaguchi Chihara of the 253 Air Group. Additionally, 13 of the 25 Aichi D3A Type 99 carrier bombers failed to return.[151]

As Base Air Force was finishing up, the 4th Air Army's 6th Air Division came in from the northwest at about 5:00pm at an altitude of 16,000 feet to attempt a feeble attack on the beachhead. After several aircraft turned back, the strike was left with all of five Type 100 Storm Dragon heavy bombers escorted by ten Flying Swallows from the 59th and 78th Air Groups and 18 Peregrine Falcons from the 248th. With the 5th Air Force and AirSols in the midst of a stretch of air missions that went sideways, it was about time that the Japanese had a similar stretch. And, as aviation historian James Dunn opined, "This raid was poorly executed. The bombers failed to rendezvous on time and part of the escort never joined the main force."[152] Oh, well, details. The Japanese ran into an afternoon air strike requested by the Marines on the Cape Gloucester positions by the 315th Bombardment Group escorted by 20 Thunderbolts from the 342nd Fighter Squadron, 348th Fighter Group.[153] Not surprisingly, with a Base Air Force strike leaving, a 4th Air Army strike arriving, a 5th Bomber Command strike arriving, and 5th Fighter Command interceptors still defending the landing craft and Cape Gloucester beachhead, this became a very strange engagement that does not seem to have gone well for either side. Perhaps unsurprisingly, all of the bombers were shot down. Major Muraoka Shinichi, commander of the 248th Air Group, was not impressed with the Thunderbolts. He later wrote lessons learned from this battle including a description of the combat:

> When we met some P-47s on the way, we were immediately surrounded and separated from the bomber formation … They attacked us from above with three or four times our number, however … we suffered no losses … All in all, we were not losers (even the fighter which failed to drop one of its fuel tanks survived). I am of the firm opinion that even P-47s can be shot down if advantage is taken of their mistakes. Four enemy P-47s really only amount to one or two planes.[154]

It never occurred to Major Muraoka that maybe his fighters suffered no losses because the Americans were focused on something else, like shooting down the Japanese bombers or protecting their own. And maybe the 248th Air Group suffered no losses, but the 78th Air Group lost two fighters, including Sergeant Matsumoto Makoto, to go alongside those five bombers. Hubris. Typical of the Imperial Japanese Army.[155]

But while Major Muraoka might have been dismissive of Japanese losses, the Americans were not. Near Sakar Island to the west of Cape Gloucester, the 342nd's Lieutenant Wynans E. Frankfort, one of the escorts for the Allied air strike, watched squadron mate Lieutenant James Pratt peel off from formation to go into a long dive after a fighter and disappear into a cloud at 6,000 feet. Pratt may have been shot down by "friendly" antiaircraft fire from the ships and landing craft. It seems that some of the Vals tried to escape the vengeful fighters of the 5th Air Force by flying low over the flotilla offshore. The cost for the Americans was Pratt and two B-25 Mitchells from the 345th Bombardment Group. One was that of Lieutenant Colonel Clinton U. True of the 498th Bombardment Squadron, who managed to ditch his wounded plane six miles from Silimati Point into Borgen Bay. With almost everyone injured in the crash, True risked going ashore and managed to find some US Marines at about 2:00am. The next morning, True and his crew were evacuated. Not as lucky was Lieutenant William T. Kyser and his crew from the 500th Bombardment Squadron, 345th Bombardment Group. Flying low over the New Gloucester beachhead, his B-25 was hit by antiaircraft fire from the landing craft that set fire to his right engine. The gunship flipped over to the left, crashed into Borgen Bay, and exploded with no survivors. It should be mentioned that until 5:00pm, only the Allies had twin-engine aircraft over New Gloucester, and even after 5:00pm, there were only five twin-engine Japanese planes. It seems that maybe a warning to not shoot at aircraft with more than one engine might have been beneficial here.[156]

The sacrifice by pilots like Major Cragg, Lieutenant Pratt, 2nd Lieutenant Gilchrist, Lieutenant Kyser, and his crew, and by vessels like the *Brownson*, helped ensure the success of the mission, but another enemy arrived that afternoon: rain. And lots of it. With the trade winds headed toward the southeast, which famously impaired US Navy carrier air operations during the Guadalcanal Campaign, here they blew across the Bismarck Sea and slam into the first point it reaches on New Britain: Cape Gloucester. The result was a monsoon. Torrential rains akin to the Canadian side of Niagara Falls combined with hurricane velocity winds for three months.[157] Fighting a war in the constant rain and the black, foul, stinking mud recalled, again, Dante's *Inferno*, specifically the fifth circle of hell in which the actively wrathful eternally fight each other in the poisonous swamp of the River Styx, while the passively wrathful are completely submerged in the morass, choking and gurgling. The 1st Marine Division after-action report described it:

> Rains continued for the next five days causing the ground to become a sea of mud. Water backed up in the swamps in the rear of the shore-line making them impassible for wheeled and tracked vehicles. Amphibian tractors were the only vehicles able to transport ammunition and food to troops in the forward areas. The many streams that emptied into the sea in the beachhead area and along the route of the advance toward the airfield became raging torrents and increased the difficulties of transportation. Troops were soaked to the skin and their clothes never dried out during the entire operation.[158]

"Every veteran in the 1st Division swore that Cape Gloucester was worse than Guadalcanal, for the rain never let up," wrote Morison. "This was the operation in which nature proved to be a worse enemy than the Japanese."[159]

Surviving that enemy while avoiding the other enemy was the mission of the 433rd Fighter Squadron's Lieutenant Jeakle. Recall that on December 18, Jeakle had been flying a P-38 in defense of Arawe when his fighter collided with that of Lieutenant Neely. Neely was able to hobble back to base, but Jeakle lost all control of his fighter. He was last seen spiraling at 9,000 feet near the Pulie River roughly 15 miles north of Arawe. No one saw a parachute. Nevertheless, holding his chute to avoid Japanese fighters looking to finish him off, Jeakle got his chute open when he was almost at the trees. He got to the ground alive, but he had wrenched his knee. Stuck behind enemy lines, limping, most of his survival supplies caught in the trees with his chute, Jeakle, in his own words, "was in bad, bad shape." He recalled his survival training: "If shot down, form a group and head for the hills." Sounds simple enough, except with whom and what hills? So that was out. He was also told if you get shot down on New Britain, head toward Rabaul, because possibly Australian scouts or Melanesian natives would help him. Except heading toward Japan's biggest, most heavily defended base in the South Pacific seemed, well, stupid. Jeakle had been told the Marines would land at Cape Gloucester on Christmas Day. So Jeakle staggered toward Cape Gloucester. Sure, it had a Japanese base, but that base was not nearly as big as Rabaul. And that base might be gone before he arrived. Indeed, Jeakle reached the coast and on December 27 was able to signal a PBY Catalina serving as a Dumbo to rescue downed pilots. The Dumbo picked him up. Jeakle was returned to his unit the next day. After treatment of his injuries and rest, Jeakle returned to duty on January 6, 1944.[160]

The Marines had landed successfully on either side of Cape Gloucester and could go after the Tuluvu air base in a pincer movement. They encountered few Japanese until they were almost at the runways, and, once the 5th Marine Regiment was brought in, they swept aside the outnumbered and outgunned defenders. On December 31 the American flag was raised over the Tuluvu air base and General Rupertus radioed General Krueger, "First Marine Division presents to you an early New Year's gift of the complete airdrome of Cape Gloucester."[161]

But the Marines were stunned to see just how extensive the Japanese base was, as the ground installations had been hidden by foliage, so well camouflaged as to escape detection from the air and resultant bombing and gunfire. These facilities included a number of well-constructed lumber and thatch buildings which served as living quarters, kitchens, mess halls, offices for brigade staff personnel, a field hospital, and supply storage.[162]

Eventually, the Marines captured General Matsuda's own humble abode, which:

[...] includes a bedroom, complete with double-width mattress and four-poster bed; kitchen and fancy toilet facilities; and a deep air raid shelter reached by ladder from the kitchen, containing candles, canned heat and rice bowls ... [The residence] is constructed about ten feet off the damp soil and is both dry and cool. The walls are made of bamboo and saplings; the roof is galvanized iron; the floors of inlaid wood. The furniture was for the most part imported, featured by a wicker easy chair ... Not only did General Matsuda have plenty of saki on hand, as witnessed by the empty bottles, but he had an ample supply of Pilsen, bottled in Manila, according to the labels. We even found one Coca-Cola bottle cap ... Among the abandoned effects and supplies are all kinds of goods – toilet articles, stationery, canned foods, clothing – manufactured in America, Australia and England ... Prize booty for the occupying Marines is a Jap phonograph with records.[163]

This description closed with the following: "The living quarters also included a small prayer room with altar window where the eminent warrior might sit cross-legged in leisurely contemplation of his navel when he could think of nothing better to do, which might have been quite often to judge by some aspects of the subsequent operation."[164]

General Matsuda had been promoted for his skills in transportation, not combat. Or intelligence. "From a study of captured Japanese documents and prisoner of war interrogations," one Marine study opined, "[Matsuda] emerges as an officer capable of making sound plans, then bungling them egregiously in the execution."[165] Matsuda had looked at the report of the giant convoy headed to Cape Gloucester and determined that it carried 2,500 enemy troops.[166] So he began a series of counterattacks against the Americans superior in numbers and firepower that accomplished only the decimation of his unit. On January 21, 1944, General Sakai, Matsuda's superior, ordered him to retreat from his headquarters and regroup a dozen miles to the northeast. Matsuda did as ordered. Then he retreated another 158 miles to Cape Hoskins, where Sakai was located, just to be safe.

Meanwhile, the Americans got to work on repairing the air base, which was easier said than done. All the rain created drainage problems, and the Japanese had never been good at drainage.

Nevertheless, *Backhander* had been a smashing success – quite literally if you count the amtrac running over the bunker. As Morison put it, "[T]he Cape Gloucester operation was well planned, well led and superbly executed by the VII Amphibious Force (Rear Admiral Barbey) and the 1st Marine Division (Major General Rupertus)." An official Marine history says, "At the tactical level, the 1st Marine Division achieved a degree of perfection probably never equaled in jungle operations; from the surprise achieved in selecting the landing beaches, to the adaptation of amphibious techniques [...]."[167]

The *Dexterity/Backhander* landing had not turned out well for the Japanese. But if they did not like that landing, well, there would be others.

And to prepare for those others, the Allies continued the pattern of air attacks, and the thousand cuts that had plagued the Japanese for at least the past year continued to get worse. December 30 saw the Japanese transport Operation *Bo-3*. The light cruiser *Noshiro*, the flagship of Rear Admiral Hayakawa Mikio, led light cruiser *Oyodo*, big antiaircraft destroyer *Akizuki*, and normal boring destroyer *Yamagumo* from Truk on a transport run to Kavieng. *Oyodo* carried 1,000 tons of cargo including several artillery pieces and 500 troops, while the *Noshiro* carried 1,500 tons of equipment and supplies and 600 men of the 51st Infantry Division and the 1st Mixed Independent Regiment, about whom more will be heard later.[168]

At 5:45am On New Year's Day 1944, this little convoy arrived in Kavieng. The *Noshiro* commenced unloading, which was complete by 7:30. Kavieng was not a large port, so the *Oyodo* had to wait until the *Noshiro* was done to begin her own unloading. At 9:27, warning of an air attack was issued, and Admiral Hayakawa's convoy got under way to gain maneuvering room, heading northwest in a modified right echelon formation, the two cruisers in column, with one destroyer off the port bow and the second off the starboard quarter.[169]

The maneuvering room was not enough. The fleet carrier *Bunker Hill* and light carrier *Monterey* of Admiral (Frederick, not Forrest) Sherman were sending their strike aircraft to see the sights of Kavieng. And one of those sights was the light cruiser *Noshiro*. She took a bomb hit on her starboard side that knocked out her Number 2 turret. A near miss off the starboard bow flooded the forward powder magazine. Ten men were killed. Later that day, the *Noshiro* left Kavieng headed for Truk with the *Oyodo* and *Yamagumo*.[170]

It would not be a good day for either side. The US Navy carrier fliers could not sink the *Noshiro*, but US Navy PBYs from New Guinea gave a consolation prize by sinking the 543-ton cargo ship *Kanaiyama Maru* off Lorengau in the Admiralty Islands, which were getting more attention of late. Or it would have been a consolation prize if Admiral Kinkaid's destroyers *Smith* and *Hutchins* had not collided off eastern New Guinea. Both destroyers were damaged, but stayed in operation. Because they had big plans for the next day, January 2.[171]

That was when a bunch of Admiral Barbey's landing craft and transports, escorted by Barbey's flagship destroyer *Conyngham* with fellow destroyers *Beale*, *Mahan*, *Drayton*, *Lamson*, *Flusser*, and *Reid*, along with the collision brothers *Smith* and *Hutchins*, just showed up uninvited and unannounced off the tiny village of Gumbi.[172] For some reason, the Japanese stretched to identify this operation with Gumbi, but the actual objective of this Operation *Michaelmas* and its landing by 2,400 troops of the US Army's reinforced 126th Infantry Regiment of the 32nd Infantry Division was the nearby village of Saidor, which also had an air base.[173] This is starting to sound vaguely familiar.

There were literally no Japanese combat units in the area of Saidor or Gumbi. They learned of the Saidor landing only when a morning reconnaissance flight spotted the invasion fleet offshore. The 4th Air Army tried to mount an immediate counterattack, but bad weather pushed it to midafternoon, when it sent up a rather feeble strike of 34 Flying Swallow and Peregrine Falcon fighters from the 68th, 78th, and 248th Air Groups and nine Storm Dragon bombers, probably from the 7th Air Group out of Dagua. Over Astrolabe Bay, they ran into a patrol of 11 P-40 Warhawks from the 7th Fighter Squadron led by Captain Duncan C. Myers. Either ignoring or not seeing the Tonys who were flying top cover, Myers went after the Oscars flying close escort with the Helen bombers. A burst into the cockpit of one Oscar apparently killed the pilot, as the Peregrine Falcon showed no damage but dove into the ground. This was the Ki-43 Type 1 Peregrine Falcon of Major Muraoka Shinichi, commanding officer of the 248th Fighter Group. The man who was so dismissive of the P-47 fell to a "lowly" P-40. Hubris. The Storm Dragons turned back toward Wewak; as they did so, the Flying Swallows got involved. The Warhawks gained some altitude then dove on their attackers. Lieutenant Robert DeHaven intervened in a circular dogfight, unsuccessfully until he got a four-or-five-second burst into the right wing of a Tony, causing it to break off. The pilot, who was from the 78th Air Group, was seen bailing out. Three Storm Dragons were shot down as well, but Captain William Lown, who was from the 49th Fighter Group's headquarters, disappeared during the fight and was never seen again.[174]

Yet, with no ground forces in the area, the Japanese could not defend Saidor, so the air base was taken in a day. That was the strategic objective completed: yet another air base switching hands from the Japanese to the Allies, yet another air base able to house aircraft that could attack Rabaul. But there was an operational component to *Michaelmas* as well. The Japanese 18th Army had not given up on recapturing Finschhafen, but its repeated attacks had led to severe losses among its 20th and 51st Divisions. In the four months between the landings at Finschhafen and the Allied seizure of Sio on the north coast, an estimated 7,800 of the 12,600 Japanese troops in the area were killed or wounded, and about 4,500 escaped westward. By comparison, casualties in the Australian 9th Division during their three and a half months in combat were 284 killed and missing and 744 wounded.[175]

Anyway, the Japanese were trying to retreat through the jungle to Madang. By landing at Saidor, General MacArthur hoped to trap these Imperial Army troops between what would be the new Allied base at Saidor and Australian troops moving up from the Finschhafen area. But though they took the Saidor air base quickly enough, General Krueger was concerned about overextending his troops by having them march into the jungle to try to stop the Japanese from escaping, so, indeed, the remnants of the 20th and 51st Divisions made their way from Sio to Madang. Krueger, who was developing a reputation for caution, later reported that the "*Michaelmas* Task Force tried hard to block these escape routes. But the torrential rain, the ruggedness of the country with its impenetrable rain forests and jungles and impassable rivers, and the resistance of enemy troops pushed forward from Madang to guard the trails leading eastward, made this effort fall short of success."[176] Angry Australian officers felt somewhat differently. Lieutenant General Sir Leslie Morshead reported that the *Michaelmas* Task Force appeared not to have made "any appreciable effort" to cut off the retreating Japanese.[177] Lieutenant General Frank Berryman, commander of the Australian II Corps, who had visited Krueger in an attempt to ensure that the Japanese would not escape, wrote that "about 8,000 semi-starved, ill-equipped and dispirited Japanese bypassed Saidor. It was disappointing that the fruits of victory were not fully reaped, and that once again the remnants of the 51st Division escaped our clutches."[178]

The Japanese were getting good at pulling out the beaten remnants of their armies from under the noses of Allied commanders. The trick they had yet to master was to not be beaten in the first place. The *Dexterity/Michaelmas* landing had not turned out well for the Japanese. But if they did not like that landing, well, there would be others.

Again, to set up those others, the bombings would continue. And so would the fighter sweeps. Black Sheep Major Pappy Boyington had been struggling to get that last aerial victory that would tie the Rickenbacker-Foss record, and Boyington admitted the pressure was getting to him. The chase for the record was attracting media attention, which Boyington did not like. But it wasn't just that. There was the empty bunk where his friend Major Carnagey had slept. "It's sure lonesome here without old Pierre," Boyington told his other tent mates. Stress and fatigue affected all of them, but were proportionately worse for Boyington, the unit commander. He drank. A lot. Over a stretch of three days and four nights, Boyington binged instead of flying, though he had less than two weeks remaining as a squadron commander. No one knew what was torturing him, perhaps including him. Historian Bruce Gamble pointed out that his behavior was suggestive of a manic-depressive. He added that one of Boyington's own relatives, a health-care professional, described him as bipolar.[179]

Even so, everyone was trying to help Major Boyington get the record by giving him as many missions as they could. His way of thanks was to try as hard as he could. On January 3, 1944, Boyington led a tour group to Rabaul consisting of 46 fighters, including eight Corsairs from his own Marine Fighting 214, 12 Corsairs from Marine Fighting 211, seven Corsairs from Marine Fighting 223, and 16 Hellcats from Fighting 33. This mission was cursed from the start. Fully half of Marine Fighting 214's Corsairs had to abort because of mechanical problems.[180] The fighters reached Rabaul, all right, but there would be no need to taunt the Japanese into rising to the challenge. While the 201 Air Group was ordered to Saipan on this day, Base Air Force managed to put up 70 Zeros from the two remaining air groups: 33 from the 204 Air Group, now led by Lieutenant Yamaguchi Sadao, and 37 from the 253, now led by Lieutenant Nakagawa Kenji.[181] These were not necessarily the odds Boyington had contemplated when he suggested using only 48 fighters for sweeps. Even worse, the Japanese later reported engaging only 22 to 30 American fighters, so around half of the American fighters missed the engagement.[182] Boyington was able to tie and then break the record in front of multiple witnesses, but at a steep price. Boyington watched helplessly as his wingman Captain George M. Ashmun was hit and plunged into the waters of St George's Channel. So entranced was he that he did not notice the Zeros coming after him. It was Boyington's turn:

> I could feel the impact of the enemy fire against my armor plate, behind my back, like hail on a tin roof. I could see enemy shots progressing along my wing tips, making patterns. [...] I threw everything in the cockpit all the way forward – this means full speed ahead – and nosed my plane over to pick up extra speed until I was forced by the water to level off. I had gone practically a half mile at a speed of about four hundred knots, when all of a sudden my main gas tank went up in flames in front of my very eyes. The sensation was much the same as opening the door of a furnace and sticking one's head into the thing. Though I was about a hundred feet off the water, I didn't have a chance of trying to gain altitude. I was fully aware that if I tried to gain altitude for a bail-out I would be fried in a few more seconds.[183]

The Devil sure had a lot of furnace rooms in the South Pacific. Boyington later wrote that he pulled his rip cord, and almost instantaneously found himself safely slammed into the water.[184] Nevertheless, according to the Marine Fighting 214 War Diary, "someone was heard to call Dane Base reporting that he was going to have to make a water landing."[185] It has been speculated that this message indicates Boyington actually ditched, but the statement on the radio is not necessarily inconsistent with his story. "I ended up in the water almost abreast of Cape St George, New Ireland," he later recalled, "about five miles from shore. I knew we had a coast watcher at this point, and had high hopes of having him rescue me."[186] Those hopes were dashed when the Japanese submarine *I-181* showed up later that day and fished Boyington out of the water and took him to Rabaul.[187] He would spend the rest of the war as a guest of the Japanese, neither honored nor well treated, but at least he survived. While the combat over St George's Channel was savage, the only recorded losses for the Americans were Boyington and his wingman Captain Ashmun, who was never seen again, while the only Japanese losses recorded were Petty Officers Tanimoto Hideshi and Kitade Yoshige from the 204 Air Group.[188]

Not surprisingly, Major Boyington's disappearance immediately after he had set the new record on January 3 was the 1940s version of the Red Dinner to the Marine Corps, the news media who had been covering Boyington (much to his disgust), and, indeed, the American public, who had taken to the brash, charismatic Boyington. Every country at war needs its heroes. Sometimes, those heroes must be manufactured with the proverbial smoke and mirrors – Douglas MacArthur could be seen as an example of that – and sometimes those heroes just show up. Boyington was the latter. And just as their presence has a disproportionately positive effect on morale, their destruction has a disproportionately negative effect. Captain John Foster of Marine Fighting 222 was blunt. "If the Japs had been able to get Gregory Boyington – the man, above all men, who knew what to expect from a Jap in a fight, who had learned during four long dangerous years how to hate and how to avenge that hate," Foster later wrote, "then what was the chance for the rest of us, who were rank amateurs by comparison?" But they remained hopeful. "None of us believed he was lost for good. He was too tough, too hickory-like."[189] And indeed Boyington was not lost for good, but no one would know that until after the war had ended.

And it had not ended yet. On January 4, 18 P-38 Lightnings of the 44th Fighter Squadron took off to escort 18 B-24s to attack Lakunai air base. The plan was to rendezvous with anywhere from 42 to 56 US Navy and Marine fighters near Torokina. Except the weather would not cooperate; clouds had enveloped the area and the two groups missed each other. The bombing mission was diverted to Buka instead. But the Navy and Marine fighters, including eight Corsairs from Marine Fighting 211, eight Corsairs from 214, eight Corsairs from 223, eight Corsairs from 321, and eight Hellcats from Fighting 40 went ahead with a fighter sweep. Once again, mechanical issues reared their proverbial ugly heads, and two Corsairs from Marine Fighting 214 and five from 223 had to abort. The remainder continued onward, and found that Base Air Force – again – did not need to be taunted to rise to the challenge, as 27 Zeros from the 204 Air Group led by Lieutenant Yamaguchi and another 27 from the 253 formed a welcoming committee for the Americans. The two groups danced over Rabaul, as they were wont to do. The Americans reported downing a dozen Japanese. The 204 claimed to have shot down eight Corsairs and two Hellcats destroyed; their only casualty was Petty Officer Kubota Koichi failing to return. The 253 reported downing eight Corsairs, but lost two of their own in Petty Officers Baba Ryosuke and Kuwahara Hiroshi. In fact, the Japanese had shot down only one fighter, that being the Corsair of Marine Fighting 213's Captain Harvey F. Carter. As far as the Americans knew, Carter had just disappeared over St George's Channel, but there was more to it, giving rise to a curious incident highlighting the brotherhood of even opposing aviators. Petty Officer Tanimizu Takeo, originally transferred to Rabaul the previous November with the pilots from the *Zuikaku* and now assigned to the 253 Air Group, saw a parachute floating down into the sea off Cape St George, leaving the American bobbing in the water. Tanimizu, a veteran carrier pilot – and it should be noted that the aviators and men of *Kido Butai* had much more respect for their adversaries than their land-based brethren did – circled low over the pilot and dropped him a life ring. The man swam to it, and gave Tanimizu a big wave as thanks. Tanimizu circled one more time, then headed back the base. That was the last anyone saw of the man, believed to have been Carter. A Catalina Dumbo sent the next day could not find him. Years later, Tanimizu was saddened to learn that Carter had not been rescued.[190]

Facing the perils of the sea and the perils of the air at the same time are what made and continue to make carrier pilots the best in the world, though still not perfect. That same January 4, Admiral Frederick Sherman's USS *Bunker Hill* made a return visit to Kavieng, which, since his last visit, had been reinforced by 36 Zeros from the carriers *Hiyo* and *Ryuho*.[191] His strike aircraft caught the Japanese destroyers *Fumizuki* and *Satsuki* in the Steffen Strait heading to Kavieng from Rabaul. Both destroyers adroitly maneuvered to avoid the munitions, but both were damaged by near misses and strafing. The *Satsuki* came off a bit worse, however, as her speed was limited to 24 knots. The two destroyers had a total of 40 casualties, but one of the *Satsuki*'s was her skipper of four months, Lieutenant Commander Iino Tadao, who was mortally wounded. *Bunker Hill* F6F pilot Ensign Robert W. Beedle was shot down and killed by Japanese Zeros while trying to protect the strike craft.[192]

While the Pacific Fleet carriers appeared sporadically, the air attacks by AirSols and the 5th Air Force continued. AirSols planned a fighter sweep over Rabaul for January 6. The plan was for 20 P-38s from the 44th Fighter Squadron under squadron commander Major Robert Westbrook to fly at 27,000–28,000 feet, with 32 Corsairs (eight from Marine Fighting 211, 16 from Marine Fighting 214, and eight from Marine Fighting 321) and 24 Hellcats (including eight from Fighting 40) stepped down in 1,000-foot intervals to 20,000 feet. After this sweep, they would perform a second one at 10,000 feet. But, well, nothing was going according to plan for AirSols these days. The fighters rendezvoused over Torokina as planned, but at 17,000 feet because of bad weather ahead in St George's Channel. Then two Lightnings had to turn back because of engine trouble. They each took their wingmen with them, meaning the force just lost four P-38s. The weather deteriorated, convincing all of the Hellcats and all but eight of the Corsairs to turn back. Sort of. The eight F4Us of Marine Fighting 11 kept going. The planned 76-fighter sweep was now down to 24, but 24 was close enough to 76 for Westbrook, so they went on ahead. No one wanted to disappoint Westbrook's wingman for the day, Lieutenant Colonel Leo Dusard, who was the new commander of the 44th's parent unit, the 347th Fighter Group. Base Air Force responded to this intrusion with 38 Zeros, who seem to have formed up over the Rapopo air base. Like aerial cavalry, the two enemy fighter groups charged at each other head-on – and completely missed each other, so they both turned around, and a running battle formed over Cape Gazelle. Dusard was rewarded for seeing what his pilots had to endure with a left engine intake that blew up and significant damage from a Zero, but he bravely did not feather his left propeller so as to convince the Japanese his fighter was undamaged and thus draw their fire. Also drawing their fire was Marine Fighting 214's Lieutenant Harry C. Johnson. When the Corsairs had aborted, a dozen of 214's fighters stayed in the general area to see what trouble they could cause. Johnson ran into 15–20 Zeros. When one turned toward him, he turned toward the Zero, raked the Zero with his .50-cal., and sent it smoking into the water. Then he saw a Zero making a lazy turn. Johnson moved toward it, then he remembered the warning of Major Boyington, "when you have an easy shot and they're in a gentle turn, look for the catch." Johnson looked, and saw two Zeros making a run at him from behind. He redlined his engine and escaped into a cloud. The Americans claimed to have shot down nine Zeros, but the Japanese admitted only two Zeros failed to return. The Japanese in turn claimed eight victories. Two pilots from the 44th, Lieutenant Travis Wells and 2nd Lieutenant Robert Stoll, disappeared during combat and were never seen again.[193]

Rabaul bombed one day, Wewak that same day, then Madang the next. Or some such. Mix and match. Yet other things were happening as well, the continued nicks and cuts that were causing Imperial Japan to exsanguinate, ever so slowly but surely nonetheless. Shortly before midnight on January 12, convoy No. 2112 left Rabaul's Simpson Harbor bound for Truk. It consisted of the 3,352-ton cargo ship *Haguro Maru* and the 2,087-ton auxiliary transport *Kaika Maru*.[194] The escorts were the veteran destroyer *Satsuki*, the practically prehistoric destroyer *Oite*, and the auxiliary gunboat *Choun Maru*, which was little more than a small freighter with some guns and depth charges added on. The convoy plodded on until some time on January 13, when it was some 35 miles west southwest of New Hanover. The convoy was attacked by a 5th Air Force B-24. The *Haguro Maru* was hit and later sank with the loss of ten passengers and eight crew. The little convoy continued onward, but the destroyer *Satsuki* and her new skipper, Lieutenant Commander Sugiyama Tadayoshi, would be detached to go on ahead to Truk, taking her antiaircraft and antisubmarine protection with her. Not to worry, though. With the *Haguro Maru* sunk, the convoy was smaller, so they didn't need as many escorts. Right?[195]

On that same January 13 when the *Haguro Maru* was sunk, the Japanese convoy O-905 left Truk southeast bound. They were going to do what they said couldn't be done: get to Rabaul safely. The convoy consisted of the freighters *Shunko*, *Kosei*, *Hozugawa*, and *Meisho Maru*s escorted by subchaser *Ch-24*, but they had a long way to go and a short time to get there.[196]

Not fast enough. In the early hours of January 16, the long arm of the PBY Catalinas of Patrolling 34 had reached from Milne Bay all the way to the other side of New Hanover, where five of the pesky PBY flying boats under Lieutenant Commander Thomas A. Christopher, the squadron's skipper, appear to have set up an ambush.[197] At 3:30am, the Black Cats swarmed the Japanese some 30 miles northwest of New Hanover with the Pappy Gunn-inspired low-level bombing attacks, made possible by the Black Cats' possession of the radio altimeter that was so crucial to night operations that if it malfunctioned the PBY was to immediately return to base. The masthead-height bombing appears to have scored multiple bomb hits on each of the 1,925-ton *Hozugawa Maru*, the 2,735-ton *Meisho Maru*, and the 4,027-ton *Shunko Maru*.[198] Nevertheless, some eight hours later, a US Army Air Force B-24 flying reconnaissance found all three still afloat. One of them, probably the *Shunko Maru*, was seen to sink. The other two were burning and abandoned. They do not appear to have been seen to sink, but they were never seen again. The *Shunko Maru* sank with 20 crewmen and 30 passengers, while the *Hozugawa Maru* lost three crew and the *Meisho Maru* 12. Continuing onward were the *Ch-24* and the *Kosei Maru*.[199] Patrolling 34 tried to finish them off the next day, but bad weather and even worse torpedoes – one torpedo was released, hit the water, and immediately turned 90 degrees to the left of and perpendicular to its intended course – allowed their prey to escape to Rabaul. *Ch-24* and the *Kosei Maru* were not sunk. Yet.[200]

That same January 13 when Convoy O-905 left Truk, two Japanese submarines, *I-181* and *Ro-104*, apparently as a result of orders issued the previous day, left Rabaul bound for Gali on the north coast of Papua New Guinea. Both were making a "rat run," transporting supplies to outlying bases in danger of being or already cut off. It was not a few of the submariners' favorite things. The *Ro-104* in particular was carrying 11 tons of provisions and ammunition (including five tons of food in rubber containers carried on the deck) and seven passengers. The *I-181* was carrying the commander of Submarine Division 22, Captain Maejima Toshihide and his staff.[201]

The *Ro-104* arrived off Gali on the night of January 16–17, but could not approach the landing area because of the presence of enemy destroyers. This happened an awful lot. Anyway, the *Ro-104* had to wait until January 18 to offload her supplies, then she scampered back to the increasingly dubious safety of Rabaul. The *I-181*, however, was never seen again.

At least in Rabaul. She was possibly seen at Gali, though. The evening of January 16, members of the Japanese garrison witnessed a running battle offshore between a submarine, a US Navy destroyer, and a US Navy motor torpedo boat. The battle ended with the sinking of the submarine, killing Captain Maejima and his staff skipper Lieutenant Commander Taoka Kiyoshi, and all 88 crew. Who were these American vessels? Rather curiously, they have never been identified.[202] If they sank the *I-181* at all. Some American sources insist the *I-181* was sunk in St George's Channel that same January 16.[203]

The US Navy Fleet Radio Unit in Melbourne had decrypted the orders from Japanese Submarine Squadron 7 to the *Ro-104*, including a complete itinerary. As a result, US Navy destroyers were patrolling off Gali for the boat's arrival.[204] The destroyers *Ammen* and *Mullany* were sent to the Gali area with the "primary mission" of locating and destroying the submarine they anticipated would be in the area. If no submarine was found, they were to look for barges, and, after all that, just bombard Gali before leaving. In the event, they found neither submarines nor barges, so they bombarded Gali, then left. The problem is not only did they not find any submarines, they were deployed off Gali the night of January 17–18 – one night after the *I-181* was reportedly sunk. In any event, neither the *I-181* nor her crew were ever seen again.[205]

The same January 16 the *I-181* was allegedly sunk, another submarine would make an appearance. Convoy No. 2112, minus the *Haguro Maru*, which was sunk, and the destroyer *Satsuki*, which apparently had better things to do, continued moseying toward its destination of Truk. Well, the *Kaika Maru*, carrying 102 passengers and a cargo of empty drums, old engines, and scrap metal that were obviously critical to the war effort.[206] The *Oite* was to port, running to and fro. She picked a bad side. Shortly before 5:00pm, the *Kaika Maru* shuddered with a big underwater explosion. Right at the bow, starboard side. Two more large detonations on the starboard side followed in short order. Three of six Mark 14 torpedoes launched had struck, compliments of Lieutenant Commander John F. Davidson and his submarine USS *Blackfish*. There was no saving the *Kaika Maru*, which rolled over to starboard as the flooding touched off her boilers, the explosions ripping her apart as she sank, taking 27 passengers and one crewman with her. Davidson had no time to watch. He tried another attack from his stern tubes directed at the *Choun Maru*. Through the hull, the *Blackfish* heard more explosions, but could not see them because the *Oite* had charged at her with a very professional and very thorough depth charging that kept the submarine pinned down until 7:40pm, when Davidson had her return to periscope depth. With the destroyer still visible, Davidson would not surface until 10:00 that night. He thought the explosions meant they had sunk the *Choun Maru* as well. They had not, but sinking the *Kaika Maru* was pretty remarkable nonetheless. First, a timely maneuver by the convoy had left Davidson with no choice but to try the so-called "down-the-throat" shot, aiming at the narrow bow profile of a ship, in this case the *Kaika Maru*, coming right at him, only about 1,000 yards away. If aimed properly, it's a difficult shot to avoid, but it's difficult to aim properly, not to mention dangerous for the submarine, which could easily be rammed and sunk. Additionally, the *Blackfish* had lost the use of her radar the previous day, so Davidson had managed to find the convoy by feeling his way around and getting lucky. At least luckier than the commanders of the *Oite* and the *Choun Maru*, who had to go on to Truk and explain to Combined Fleet how they had to escort a convoy of two ships and lost them *both*. Awkward.[207]

Albeit not as awkward as the position in which Admiral Kusaka found himself on January 17. That was when 24 P-38 Lightnings from the 44th and 339th Fighter Squadrons led by the 44th's Captain Frank Gaunt escorted 18 TBF Avengers from Marine Torpedo 232, each carrying one 2,000lb bomb; and 49 SBD Dauntlesses, including four from Marine Scouting 236, 29 from Marine Scouting 341, and 13 from Bombing 98 into the Rabaul caldera to strike at shipping in Simpson Harbor.[208]

This was another mission that was cursed from the start. Five P-38s had to abort because of mechanical issues, as did 14 Dauntlesses from Marine Scouting 341 and three from Bombing 98. US Navy F6F Hellcats and Marine F4U Corsairs were supposed to arrive with the strike aircraft and rendezvous with the Lightnings west of Taiof Island. But when the bombers and Captain Gaunt's fighters hooked up, there were no Hellcats or Corsairs to be seen. Where were they? Don't know. The Lightnings reorganized themselves to provide proper escort and continued onward.[209]

When they arrived at Rabaul around 1:00pm, they discovered two layers of clouds over Simpson Harbor, and the formation flew between them like an airplane sandwich. The plan was for the bombers to call in the fighters when they reached the target, and then they would begin their bomb runs. But that was just a little too complicated. The bombers saw a hole in the clouds revealing Simpson Harbor below, so they peeled off and dove through the hole without telling Captain Gaunt. Communications and information, those intertwined twin pillars of any military operation. Soon enough, the bombers called for fighter support. Gaunt had his Lightnings dive at a near 90-degree angle to reach the bombers. He reached them, all right, but the dive had dispersed his fighters. Worse, it left them trapped at a low altitude – not the P-38's forte – with Japanese Zeros above them. Specifically, 36 Zeros from the 253 Air Group, 16 from the 252, who had apparently staged in as reinforcements separated from the bulk of their unit, which was in the Central Pacific, and an unspecified but large number from the 204. They pounced on the Allied aircraft. The P-38s stuck by their charges, but while they performed very well at higher altitudes, at lower altitudes the Lightnings were lumbering lugs compared to the Zeros and thus at a severe disadvantage.[210]

The Lightnings' sacrifice meant the AirSols' bombers would have a good day with the ships in Simpson Harbor. Just before noon, a 1,000lb bomb introduced itself to the engine room of the 5,110-ton repair ship *Hakkai Maru*.[211] The detonation caused the engine room to flood, and she sank by the stern about an hour later with the loss of 23 gunners and two crewmen.[212] Also hit was the 3,126-ton cargo ship *Kenshin Maru*.[213] She may have just arrived, as her port anchor was still retracted. She took a 1,000lb bomb in the starboard side near the stern, causing severe damage that proved fatal to the ship as well as 22 of her crew. The 1,920-ton Imperial Army cargo ship *Kosei Maru*, carrying barges, steel water tanks, and general cargo, including 14 of the barges the Japanese so loved, was also sunk with two of her crew. Reportedly sunk as well was the 1,500-ton freighter *Tenshin Maru*.[214] The aircraft transport *Lyons Maru* suffered damage that left her disabled, but was not sunk. Yet.[215]

It was reportedly as the strike aircraft were leaving the caldera that the US Navy and Marine fighters showed up. They included a dozen Corsairs from Marine Fighting 211, another dozen from 321, and seven Hellcats from Fighting 40.[216] They engaged the pursuing Zeros, creating yet another melee over Cape St George before the Allied aircraft took their leave.

And they needed to take their leave. Because while the strike may have sunk three ships, it came at a generally grievous cost. Eight P-38 Lightnings were shot down. Four pilots from the 44th Fighter Squadron were lost: Lieutenant Earl R. Heckler and 2nd Lieutenants John R. Munson and Theodore Schoettel were last seen over Blanche Bay; and 2nd Lieutenant George W. Snell was last seen over the southwest coast of New Ireland, but no one saw what happened to them and they did not return to Stirling Field.[217] None of these pilots was ever seen again. The 339th Fighter Squadron also lost four P-38s: 2nd Lieutenant Charles E. Black was also last seen over Blanche Bay, the Lightning of 2nd Lieutenant John E. Langen was last seen in flames going down over Blanche Bay, and the Lightning of Lieutenant Gifford G. Brown was seen actually crashing in Blanche Bay. None of these pilots was ever seen again. Lieutenant Glen E. Hart's P-38 was last seen over New Ireland. Hart had parachuted into the water safely a few miles south of Ambitle Island in the Feni Islands off New Ireland. No one saw what happened to the Hellcat of Fighting 40's Ensign Kenneth P. Babkirk, but he never returned to base. The SBD Dauntless flown by Lieutenant Robert E. Bishop of Marine Scouting 341 was last seen crashing into the sea two miles east of Cape Gazelle. Not shot down per se was the TBF

Avenger flown by Marine Torpedo 232's Lieutenant Harold H. Millar, but it might as well have been; as it pulled out of its glide after releasing its bomb, its wings fell off. Not something one would expect from a Grumman. A Boeing, maybe, these days; a Mitsubishi, definitely – in fact, it had already happened at Santa Cruz to a *Zuikaku* Zero – but not a Grumman. The Allied pilots claimed to have shot down 17 or 18 Japanese planes, including six by the 44th Fighter Squadron, but to add insult to injury, the Japanese reported no fighter lost during this combat. The 253 Air Group claimed ten and the 204 claimed an incredible 47 enemy planes destroyed and 20 probables, also without loss. Warrant Officers Iwamoto Tatsuzo and Maeda Hideo of the 204 claimed five apiece and Chief Petty Officer Ogiya Nobuo of the 204 claimed four.[218]

Was this the second wind of Base Air Force or a last gasp? The day after Base Air Force's commendable performance of January 17, the Allies returned to the Rabaul caldera with 34 B-25 Mitchells of the 70th, 75th, and 390th Bombardment Squadrons of the 42nd Bombardment Group escorted by 70 fighters … give or take 56. Once again, the mission went sideways – literally, in the case of Marine Fighting 211's Lieutenant W. R. Culler. The Army Air Force bombers and their 14 escorting P-38 Lightnings from the 44th Fighter Squadron stopped and circled over Torokina waiting for US Marine Corsairs and Navy Hellcats to join them, but as the fighters were taking off from Torokina, Lieutenant Culler's Corsair "cracked up in the middle of the runway," throwing him clear of the plane and leaving a fortunate Culler with only moderate injuries. The "totally damaged" plane blocked the runway, so other fighters were not able to take off in a timely manner. Even though eight Corsairs from Marine Fighting 321 managed to take off before the accident, the US Army Air Force B-25s went on ahead, with an escort of only 14 P-38s led by Captain Cotesworth B. Head, Jr. The mission that day was for the B-25 gunships to perform a low-level strafing and bombing of the Tobera air base. The P-38s were intended to provide top cover, which is by definition at high altitude, with the Corsairs and Hellcats guarding the B-25s at low altitude, but with the P-38s the only escorts available, they had to go down to low altitude, where their performance was impaired. And the target was the air base where the 252 and 253 Air Groups – and sometimes the detachment from the *Zuikaku* – were based. The gunships went down to about 150 feet and raked the runways with .50-cals, reportedly getting a Zero warming up on the taxiways, and left bombs behind. But as they were on their way out over the coast of New Britain, 20–30 Zeros followed them with an altitude advantage of about 4,000 feet. The Zeros did not swarm but attacked singly; gee, wouldn't radios would have been useful here? The P-38s broke into pairs and started Thach weaving, shooting Zeros off each other's tails while maintaining a close umbrella over the B-25s, which worked for a while, but not totally. It was fortunate that around this time came those eight Corsairs from Marine Fighting 321, who had taken off before the accident at Torokina, but had not been able to make radio contact with the strike planes. Nevertheless, they headed toward the rally point near Duke of York Island in St George's Channel at which the air strike was to form up for the return to base.[219] The B-25 of Lieutenant Carter Williamson, Jr was hit by a 20mm round in the left engine that set the nacelle afire. The Mitchell was seen to set down safely in the waters of St George's Channel, but numerous Japanese fighters were circling the stricken gunship like vultures contemplating their imminent next meal. Williamson and his five crew were never seen again. On his proverbial heels, Captain Head was scissoring over the B-25s with the rest of his squadron, in so doing reportedly shooting down a Zero, which was the objective of the Thach scissoring tactic. But as he came out of that victory, two Zeros came after him and put a 20mm shell into his right engine. Several other P-38s managed to chase off the Zeros, with Lieutenant John Roehm going on an extended chase to shoot a particularly tough Zero into the water, then returning to cover Head. Then Head did a 180-degree turn while gaining altitude, a maneuver known as a "chandelle." He passed behind Roehm and the others out of view. One of the B-25s saw Head's Lightning "making water landing 10 miles east of mouth of Warangoi River" off New Britain. The Mitchell radioed the position to PBY Dumbos waiting to come in and rescue downed aviators. But the area was still a combat zone. Captain James Reddington took over for Head, still trying to fight off 8–12 Zeros. As they engaged the Zeros, more reinforcements arrived: eight US Navy F6F Hellcats from Fighting 40, who had taken off after the "totally damaged" Corsair of Lieutenant Culler had been cleared from the Torokina runway. The Marine and Navy fighters tried to cover the retirement of the B-25s and P-38s, and the mass melee continued over Duke of York Island. Reddington personally chased Zeros off the tails of the Mitchells, shooting down three in the process – three Zeros, not three Mitchells. That was the good news; the bad news was that those were his only victories of the war. The 44th Fighter Squadron claimed six Zeros destroyed. Marine Fighting 321 claimed two, with no losses, as did Fighting 40. During the retirement, the tail gunner in the B-25 of Lieutenant Roland C. Shaw also claimed a Zero. Actual Japanese losses were four fighters.[220]

But the talk upon return to base was Captain Head, an ace with 14 victories. The Allies never found him. And there seems to have been considerable anger. According to one history of the 13th Fighter Command, "It was the 13AF's low-level escort orders that contributed to Head's death. Almost two-thirds of the P-38 losses came on SBD/TBF escort missions that were flown between 2,000 and 15,000 feet, far too low for effective P-38 combat operations." The issue with altitude is completely correct, but it's also irrelevant. The fighter escort arrangements had fallen apart because Lieutenant Culler's Corsair had fallen apart, leaving the P-38s as the only escorts for the time being. The low-level orders for the P-38s likely came from Head, who was making the best of what he had. And not to put too fine a point on it, but this was not a SBD/TBF mission; this was a B-25 mission. And, to also be perfectly accurate, while the low-level escort orders contributed to Head's death, they were neither the proximate nor the actual cause of his death.[221]

The middle of January 1944 had been less than satisfactory for Allied air power, both for AirSols and the 5th Air Force. Because though General Kenney's group was regularly attacking places like Madang and Alexishafen, the 4th Air Army was becoming more of a problem. Lieutenant General Itabana Yoshikazu, commanding the 6th Air Division of the

4th Air Army – the Japanese Army Air Force preferred to use the same terminology for its air units that it did for its land units – was not happy about the new Allied air base at Nadzab, which was being expanded, or the even newer Allied fighter base at Gusap, northwest of Nadzab, that had been completed in very late 1943. So he decided to do something about it. Unfortunately, the losses and damage from the New Gloucester campaign meant he had no bombers handy, but he had managed to scrape together some fighters, so he decided to use them to attack the annoying air dromes. On January 15, Lieutenant Koga Keiji was to lead eight Ki-48 Type 1 Peregrine Falcons of the 248th Air Group in an attack on Gusap, then cover a dozen Ki-61 Type 3 Flying Swallows of the 68th and 78th Air Groups in an attack on Nadzab. Sounds simple enough.[222]

At the same time and operating in the same area were 11 Peregrine Falcons of the 59th Air Group led by Captain Nango, a fighter ace with ten victories. Why were two groups of Japanese Army fighter planes operating in the same area independently, thus seriously increasing the risk of confusion and friendly fire? Don't know. In any event, Nango caught sight of a patrol of four US Army P-40 Warhawks, curiously, of the 388th Bombardment Squadron of the 312th Bombardment Group. These Warhawks were to be used as ground attack fighter bombers, but currently they were on a fighter patrol. Nango and two wingmen came out of the clouds and ambushed the Americans, scattering their formation. Captain Glenn H. Cathcart, Jr, the 388th Squadron operations officer, got a quick radio warning that the Japanese were attacking. As he turned to face their tormentors, one of Nango's wingmen sent a burst into Cathcart's cockpit, incapacitating him at the very least. With no one at the yoke, Cathcart's P-40 Warhawk plunged into the ground some five miles northeast of Kaigulan near Dumpu, within sight of the Gusap air base. Cathcart was the 388th's first casualty of the war. The engagement that had lasted only a matter of seconds left the other three Warhawks badly shot up, but they managed to get back to Gusap. The air attacks were executed almost perfectly, and while one of the 248th Air Group's fighters was damaged, the Japanese pilots returned to base. For the day the Japanese claimed four P-40s and two C-47s (both by Warrant Officer Noguchi Takashi of the 68th Air Group) shot down, and 34 planes "damaged or set afire" on the ground. Of this total, the 248th claimed to have destroyed 13 aircraft (seven medium and six small) at Gusap. The actual damage at Gusap included an A-20 and two P-47s totally destroyed. It was a significant embarrassment to the 5th Air Force.[223]

But there's always tomorrow, to start over again. And that tomorrow, January 16, saw General Kenney's 5th Air Force send B-25s, A-20s, and P-40s to hit Madang, Erima, and Bogadjim. The 4th Air Army was not down with this, so the 68th Air Group's Major Kimura Kiyoshi – Kimura is a common Japanese surname – headed toward Nadzab for a fighter sweep. The 248th Air Group's Lieutenant Tozuka Nobuyoshi led the 248th's contingent as part of the 59th Air Group's formation under Captain Nango. The 63rd Air Group also contributed fighters in what would be its first combat.[224]

It did not go well for the Japanese even though they only faced only P-40 Warhawks – 15 from the 35th Fighter Squadron, 8th Fighter Group. The 35th was stacked in four equal sections, and they made the most of their Warhawks, claiming 19 victories, with Lieutenant Lynn Elwood Witt, Jr, by himself claiming three. The Japanese compounded their error by getting themselves into a 25-minute battle with a nearby strike of 21 B-25s from all four squadrons of the 38th Bombardment Group escorted by 16 P-38 Lightnings under Captain Warren Lewis of the 433rd Fighter Squadron, 475th Fighter Group, though this engagement ended with only one aircraft, the B-25 of the 71st Bombardment Squadron's Lieutenant Harry Serser, shot down, with the entire crew killed, though it does appear a second B-25, that of the 822nd Bombardment Squadron's Lieutenant Ralph E. Freek, missed a turn during the air attacks, kept on going, and was never seen again. For the day the Japanese claimed seven bombers, three P-38s, and three P-40s. In actuality, with the lost B-25s mentioned above, three P-40s and three P-38s were damaged. On the Japanese side, Captain Nango's formation came out intact, but the newly arrived 63rd Air Group lost five pilots, including Lieutenant Hasegawa Kiyoshi, Sergeant Majors Iwamitsu Isao and Oishi Tadashi; and Corporal Kono Mitsuhiro. The 68th Air Group came out even worse because of the loss of its veteran leadership. Going down was Major Kimura himself, while Warrant Officer Noguchi, an ace with 14 victories, was shot down and captured.[225]

General Kenney's men had a productive January 17, with B-24s sinking the 1,943-ton freighter *Chiburi Maru* some 80 miles east of Manus, as well as the 617-ton *Fukei Maru No.9*.[226] What they really wanted, however, came the following day, January 18. While the 5th Bomber command was making its usual attacks on Madang and Hansa Bay, 5th Fighter Command sent 55 P-38s on a fighter sweep of Wewak to try to stomp the 4th Air Army down again. The lead would be four P-38s of the 340th Fighter Squadron, 348th Fighter Group; then 18 P-38s under Major Meryl M. Smith of the 431st Fighter Squadron followed by 15 more P-38s under Lieutenant Colonel MacDonald of the 432nd, both of the 475th Fighter Group, then the 80th Fighter Squadron of the 8th Fighter Group. The 4th Air Army was not going to take this lying down, scrambling 56 fighters, with 21 Flying Swallows of the 68th and 78th Air Groups, ten Peregrine Falcons from the 248th Air Group, and another 25 Peregrine Falcons from the 59th and 63rd Air Groups. What followed was a multistage and unusually savage aerial melee that does not seem to have turned out the way anyone wanted. According to Major Smith, the Japanese had an altitude advantage and dove at the Americans. When the P-38s moved to engage, Smith saw Japanese fighters behind them, and had his fighters dive to get out of the trap. The problem was that, except, for 16 P-38s from the 433rd Fighter Squadron who were flying top cover, the Lightnings were pinned to lower altitudes where they lost much of their efficacy. As a practical matter, when you have an aircraft that is phenomenal at higher altitudes and much less effective at lower altitudes, if you're planning a fighter sweep, keeping this fighter at higher altitudes would seem to be a requirement. That did not happen here, but the Americans fought ferociously nonetheless, and were impressed by the tactics of their Japanese opponents. One P-38 pilot wrote, "The enemy pilots apparently were experienced as they would lead our planes to tree-top level and turn sharply ... The enemy consistently dived to the deck and disappeared throughout the entire combat. We could not pursue because of our lesser maneuverability and the extremely low altitude." Another P-38 pilot rated the Japanese as "experienced, determined and aggressive." In this combat the Americans claimed 14 victories and the Japanese claimed 13. In actuality, the Americans lost three. As the strike approached Wewak from the south, the 433rd's P-38s, who were flying top cover, released their drop tanks, one of which hit the right wing of the 431st's 2nd Lieutenant Joseph A. Robertson, and sent him into a spiral that reportedly tore off part of his wing. He was never seen again. Considering how packed these aerial formations sometimes were, it's amazing this did not happen more often. Smith last saw the 431st's 2nd Lieutenant John R. Weldon, Jr at 15,000 feet with a fighter on his tail. The wreckage of Weldon's P-38 was later found south of Wewak, but no sign of Weldon himself was ever found. Lieutenants John E. Michener and William T. Ritter of the 432nd were combining to shoot down a Tony right in front of them, but when Ritter set the Tony on fire, the enemy fighter pulled up and caught Ritter's right wing, setting Ritter's plane on fire and starting it on its plunge to the ground. This Japanese Tony, if that's an accurate description, may have been the Flying Swallow of 78th Air Group's Sergeant Aiko Shinsuku. Aiko was shot down, but bailed out and survived. He later reported that he had shot down his attacker, who also bailed out and landed near him. According to Aiko, they wrestled and Aiko captured the American. In any event, no one knows what happened to Ritter after that. In addition to Aiko, the Japanese lost three fighters, but it wasn't quantity, but quality that made these Japanese losses crippling. The 63rd Air Group's veteran Captain Matsumoto Tomio allegedly shot down three P-38s in his Peregrine Falcon, then rammed a fourth. Ramming does not usually work out well for either party – Ritter is a candidate here, too, for the rammed party – and Matsumoto was killed. The 248th Air Group suffered the heaviest blow, as its acting commander, Captain Kojima Shigeo, was shot down and killed.[227]

The nicks and cuts continued. On January 19, the cargo ship *Kaishu Maru* was reportedly sunk at Manus in the Admiralties by 5th Air Force B-24s, though JANAC (Joint Army–Navy Assessment Committee) records do not confirm this.[228] Not to worry, though. At noon that same day, convoy SO-903 left Palau for Rabaul with subchasers *Ch-17* and *Ch-18* escorting *Takatori Maru No. 2*, *Nipponkai Maru*, and *Neikai Maru*.[229] The *Takatori Maru No. 2* was towing a target barge, which seems to be asking for trouble when sailing under enemy-controlled or even enemy-contested skies. Maybe they were hoping the Allies would target the barge instead of the rest of the convoy. Maybe the Americans were really inaccurate, because on January 28, when the convoy was in the Bismarck Sea some 110km west northwest of Cape Lambert, New Britain, the AirSols showed up with some PBY Catalinas from Patrolling 81 as well as B-24 Liberators and who bombed the 2,827-ton *Neikai Maru*. She sank some 50 miles south of Dyaul Island, taking with her the midget submarine she had been carrying, *Ha-49*. Lieutenant (jg) Mashima Shiro, who was supposed to command the submarine, was rescued and landed at Rabaul. At least that target barge was okay. Maybe the next Allied air attack would target it.[230]

The Japanese had to hope so. It was at around this time that Admiral Kusaka and his staff took stock of just where his 11th Air Fleet – Base Air Force – was and where it was going. It was easy to see it was going downward. The Allied kraken was squeezing harder and harder. Just a little bit harder every day, but so hard the Japanese could not take a breath. As one Japanese history explained:

> Since January, air operations in the Southeast Area, became series of aerial combat, but the increase in the number of enemy air raids and aircraft made it impossible for us to check the enemy air raids with our fighters and ground antiaircraft guns. The damage on the ground increased with every air raid and we were barely able to hold out by coonsentrating [sic] on repairs and maintenance. Consequently, it was difficult for us to carry out, [sic] positive operations by our initiative.[231]

That was kind of the idea. Give the Japanese no rest. No time to catch their breath. It was having an effect.

> The number of our operational aircraft in the Southeast Area on 19 January was 80 fighters, 15 carrier bombers, 11 carrier attack plan[e]s, 32 land attack planes (some of which were training in the Tinian Area)[,] four night fighters, four land reconnaissance planes, and 20 reconnaissance seaplanes, a total of 166. Because of illness, approximately 30 percent of the flight personnel were unable to participate in operations.[232]

It goes without saying that if a land attack plane is training in Tinian, it is not in Rabaul or Kavieng, and its usefulness in conducting attacks on, say, Torokina, or Munda, or Mono, or Woodlark is rather limited.

> Although efforts were made for the construction of dispersed shelters and trenches in order to limit losses, damages gradually increased and maintenance and replacement of aircraft and material did not progress smoothly. Supply from the rear became difficult. Furthermore long periods of continuous operations together with a gradual decline in the battle situation tended to lower the morale of flight personnel.[233]

This was a war of attrition by the book, assuming they have a book for such things. The Japanese and especially Base Air Force now had the advantage of interior lines, but the Allies were using their advantage in numbers ruthlessly, if not profligately, unlike some other countries like the Soviet Union. Imagine one AirSols attack a day. The Japanese lose no fighters but a number of them are damaged. How many of them can be repaired before the next air attack? How many of them will have to take to the air damaged because there's no time to repair them? How does that weaken the defense to the next attack? Which leads to more damaged aircraft. Assuming you can get the supplies to repair them in. Every day. Every single day. Maybe not always at Rabaul. But somewhere. Just enough to continue the deterioration.

The best way the Japanese had to counterattack was night bombing raids, which became fairly common over Torokina. On the night of January 12, eight Mitsubishi G4M Type 1 land attack planes of the 751 Air Group bombed Torokina and Mono, three more attacked Munda, and yet one more bombed Mono again. On the night of January 13, six Aichi D3A Type 99 carrier bombers attacked Mono, one more attacked what the Japanese called Murua Island and what the Allies called Woodlark; four Nakajima B5N Type 97 carrier attack planes bombed Torokina, and five G4M land attack planes Munda. Several night fighters were scrambled at Torokina, who seem to have shot down one plane. On the night of January 14, four of the carrier bombers hit Torokina again. On the night of January 16 it was five G4M Type 1s and four carrier attack planes bombing Torokina.[234] But this held little potential for changing the direction of the war, or even significantly slowing the journey in that direction. One Japanese history called it, "throwing water on a hot rock," admitting "the effect of neutralization on enemy aircraft must have been very small."[235]

Of course, the Allies could attack at night, too. As well as the day. On January 20, a bunch of B-24s headed toward Rabaul. When Base Air Force put up a defense, the Liberators veered off and bombed Kahili instead. Sneaky. The idea was to weaken the fighter defenses of Rabaul by making the Zeros run low on fuel and have to land just as the real strike was coming. This was 18 B-25 gunships of the 70th and 390th Bombardment Squadrons of the 42nd Bombardment Group, escorted by 70 fighters, including a dozen P-38 Lightnings under Major William Lawrence of the 339th Fighter Squadron; eight Hellcats from Fighting 40; a dozen Corsairs from Marine Fighting 211, 17 from Marine Fighting 215, and 11 from Marine Fighting 321; as well as Kiwi Kittyhawks. Now, the Lockheed P-38 Lightning was well-known to be, at high altitude, a very effective fighter. At low altitude, not so much, due to its size and weight. Naturally, on this day, the Lightnings were assigned to be low-altitude escort for the Mitchells, while the Corsairs provided top cover at high altitude. Why? Don't know. It was probably just one of those things. Maybe it was some Navy or Marine guy who was (inexcusably) unaware of the P-38's performance quirks. Maybe it was someone who did not believe those quirks mattered as much as keeping all the US Army Air Force planes together and not mixing and matching them with US Navy, US Marine, or Royal New Zealand aircraft. Most command staffs, regardless of service, could employ a chief of operations, a chief of logistics, a chief of intelligence, and a chief of common sense, a senior officer who could look at a battle plan and say what everyone not planning that plan would say, "This is illogical and stupid. Don't do it." Alas, most command staffs had the first three chiefs, but not that last one.[236]

Not to worry, though. The target was Vunakanau, not the hornet's nest of Lakunai. According to the history of the 42nd Bombardment Group, "The enemy took off from Tobera to meet the 25s as they came in from the water." That would be the 253 Air Group, taking off from Tobera, though the 204 was taking off from Lakunai as well. "Lieut. Paul Nadler's plane was intercepted near Karavia Bay by five Zeros, who closed to about

1000 yards before being dispersed by our fighter cover. Flight Officer Edward J. Brisick was also attacked as he was retiring near Tobera."[237] But the Zeros were not nearly as big a problem for the gunships as the antiaircraft fire:

> From the time landfall was reached until the formation retired over the water, intense automatic, medium, and heavy fire streaked up in sheets. [...] The AA fire came from all around the proverbial clock – from Warangoi River, Tobera's guns, Karavia Bay shoreline and the knolls to the west. Ralabang Plantation even threw in its four-bits, tracking the formation for a mile over water on retirement.[238]

The 42nd said this mission "produced the most intensive and sustained AA fire ever encountered by the Group to that time."[239] It went into detail:

> There is no question about the quality of fighting men the Japanese have in this area. This is definitely their first team and its shooting is accurate. They lead the planes with their AA and they throw up a lot of it. Strafing their positions does not seem to silence them as easily as it did in the Solomons. There was absolutely no element of surprise in our favor, and although the formation flew at treetop all the way into and out of New Britain, we never for a moment escaped drawing AA from the enemy. Our fighter cover unquestionably saved our formation from being subjected to some very rough interception as well.[240]

Nevertheless, the 42nd did what it was supposed to do, bombing and strafing Vunakanau, starting a large fire at the northwest end of the runway – probably a fuel dump – and causing a large explosion south of the runway, though no bombs were seen to hit the runway itself. But before they would get out, that antiaircraft fire would take its proverbial and literal pound of flesh. Lieutenant Earl Swartzfager of the 390th and his crew would not get out. As his B-25 was heading away from Vunakanau, it was hit in the tail and its right rudder was shot away. The plane inverted, then the nose pointed down and the Mitchell did one complete inverted spin before crashing into trees and exploding south southwest of Tobera between the Warangoi and Sigut Rivers, near the bank of the Ibrangoi River. As the 42nd history put it, "It was a severe blow to the 390th to lose Swartzfager, one of its outstanding figures on every count, an exceptional man, and a superb pilot."[241]

The horrific end of Lieutenant Swartzfager and his crew may have been witnessed by the 339th's Captain George Chandler. Chandler had just lost a duel with a Zero who had set his left engine on fire, but he was still alive and in the air. For now. He was going to bail out before the fire reached his main fuel tank, but once he saw enemy antiaircraft gunners on a nearby hilltop, Chandler thought better of it, was able to cut the fuel to the burning engine and was surprised when the fire went out. No fuel, no fire. Seems pretty simple. Chandler feathered the propeller and looked for a B-25 to escort him back to base.

That B-25 seems to have been Swartzfager's, for Chandler watched in horror as the Mitchell destroyed a gun position, then crashed into the jungle in a violent explosion immediately thereafter.

Also hit by antiaircraft fire on the way out was the B-25 of the 70th Bombardment Squadron's Lieutenant John Edward Warner. Upon being hit, the gunship was seen to lurch, then straighten out, but as the 42nd's bombers tried to rally for the trip back, Warner's B-25 was lagging, with a smoking engine, losing airspeed and altitude, and possibly hit by fire from the dogfights that were taking place nearby. Warner made a "good" water landing ten miles south of Cape St George, but then Zeros made two passes to try to blow up the Mitchell on the water. Six Allied fighters drove them off, then stayed overhead for a bit as Warner and his men successfully deployed their life raft. Flight Officer Brisick was instructed to race back to Torokina to have a PBY Dumbo sent to pick up Warner and his crew.

It was not a good day for the Americans, and while some of the difficulties were of their own making – like having the P-38s fly low-altitude escort – some were of a more nebulous cause. Like the weather. The cloud ceiling had been low upon leaving Torokina, and while the clouds had broken up, they were still enough to allow the Zeros to hide in the clouds and ambush unwary enemies. The P-38 pilots knew better than their mission planners that their machines were impaired at low altitude and as soon as they saw the first Zero, they dropped their external tanks and desperately tried to gain altitude. But they still were very off balance dealing with Japanese Zeros who, at low altitude and low speed, were in their element. Captain Chandler's Lightning had lost an engine, as had the P-38 of Lieutenant Charles E. Smith.[242] The Corsairs at high altitude fared somewhat better. Can't imagine why. The Marines got credit for shooting down 15 Zeros, with Marine Fighting 211 and 215 each destroying six and 321 three. Actual Japanese losses were not reported.[243]

US Marine losses were, however, and all were from Marine Fighting 321. The Corsairs flying top cover at 4,000 feet had been attacked by about 40 Japanese Zeros. As the Marines flying were moving to engage the Zeros, Lieutenant Robert B. See reportedly and literally blew a Zero off the tail of Captain Marion R. McCown, Jr, but, all the same, McCown was never seen again. It was later determined that McCown crashed into a stream bank near Viveren village and Mount Varzin and was killed. Marine Fighting 211 Lieutenant C. I. Cobb, Jr and 321's Lieutenant Robert W. Marshall were heading out; the pair flew over Makurapau Plantation, where they were both hit by 20mm gunfire. Cobb could see oil spraying all over the inside of Marshall's canopy. Marshall ditched his damaged F4U in St George's Channel roughly 18 miles south of Cape Gazelle. On impact, Marshall's Corsair split into two pieces. Cobb circled to make sure Marshall exited the plane, but he never did. When the Marines returned to Torokina, Lieutenant Roger Hugh Brindos was not among them and no one saw what happened to him. In fact, Brindos's battle was not quite over yet because he had been shot down, but had bailed out and landed safely. Unfortunately, Brindos was captured two days later and executed in early March.[244]

The US Army Air Force's battle of this day was not quite over yet, either. A few hours later after the B-25 of 70th Bombardment Squadron's Lieutenant Warner had ditched off Cape St George, a Catalina Dumbo of Patrolling 14 flown by a Lieutenant B. Smith picked up Warner and his entire crew unharmed. Not as lucky was the 339th Fighter Squadron's Lieutenant Charles Smith. Coming in to land at Stirling – too slow – Smith saw that he would not clear the cliff at the west end of the runway. He tried to apply power, but it was too little, too late, and Smith crashed into the water and was unable to escape his aircraft as it sank. Coming in behind Smith was Captain Chandler, who was also minus an engine and his hydraulics, and so had to manually crank down the landing gear, which was tiring, but he was able to land safely. Meanwhile the P-38 of 2nd Lieutenant Dwight M. Kelly never returned to base.[245]

But 2nd Lieutenant Dwight Kelly's battle was not over. He had vanished during the engagement in the vicinity of the Warangoi River, but he was still very much alive. For now.[246] As best as can be determined, Kelly had parachuted from his dying P-38 and made his way to shore. Here, he surely remembered his survival training: "If shot down, form a group and head for the hills." Again, with whom and what hills? After a while, Kelly got an answer to that first question. Surprisingly, he ran into Captain Cotesworth Head, his squadron commander, who two days earlier had also been compelled to ditch off the mouth of the Warangoi River. No one had seen Head since, but here he was. Head had seen Kelly's parachute floating down and went looking for him.

But what hills? There are hills in western New Britain near Arawe and New Gloucester. Maybe go there? First, however, Captain Head had seen another parachute floating down. They went to look for it. Bizarrely, in this thick rainforest, they found the pilot, exhausted, his face burned. He was Petty Officer 2nd Class Ishida Teigo of the 204 Air Group. Ishida was unarmed, but he knew judo. In fact, he was a 2nd degree black belt in judo. Head and Kelly also knew judo. Well, they knew of it. More importantly, one of them was pointing a pistol at Ishida. What was Ishida going to do about it? Strangle them with his black belt?

In a word, yes. Ishida smiled and approached the Americans, as if he was going to shake hands. The Americans saw that he was unarmed, smiled, and came toward him. Suddenly, Ishida kicked the gun out of the American's hand. Ishida immediately followed that up with a punch in between the American's eyes – it's not clear whether it was Head or Kelly. Then came a literal hand-to-hand, to-the-death melee. Ishida strangled one of the Americans with a leather belt. He undoubtedly killed the other one as well. Ishida then fled in the direction from which he heard engine sounds. He ran into an Imperial Army patrol who brought Ishida back to civilization, or whatever it is one would call Rabaul, where Ishida was hospitalized until he left for Japan on February 5. The bodies of Captain Head and Lieutenant Kelly were never recovered.[247]

As these two US Army Air Force unfortunately saw firsthand, the Japanese Empire strikes back. As it did on January 22, when the oiler *Cache* was moseying along toward Espiritu Santo in the company of the redoubtable minesweeper *Southard* some 155 miles southeast of San Cristobal when at 11:30am she was hit by one torpedo in her port side, blowing two men over the side, causing her to lose all power, and take on a 12-degree list. Power was restored in about a minute, but two more torpedoes were seen approaching. A depth charge was fired from the port side, but with the *Cache* responding sluggishly to the helm, the torpedoes were sure to hit – if they both had not swerved to parallel the oiler's course. This may have been a consequence of the depth charge's detonation. Both torpedoes paralleled the oiler, with one torpedo staying about 50–75 yards away, slowly catching up to the *Cache* – the torpedo was set at a low speed, indicating it was fired from extreme range. The torpedo kept porpoising, hopping out of the water and slightly changing course each time, sometimes in the direction of the *Cache*, sometimes away from her. The oiler tried to neutralize the torpedoes with gunfire until it was determined that a torpedo detonation at that range would hurt the *Cache*. While the oiler was in this race with death, the *Southard* interposed herself between the *Cache* and the suspected position of the submarine and tried to find their attacker. At no time either before or after the attack did she have a sonar contact – the submarine might have been out of sonar range – and after searching for the enemy boat unsuccessfully, she was only able to rescue one of the two men blown off the ship. The *Cache* eventually outlasted her shadowing torpedoes. She did not sink, however, but did send out a distress call, which was picked up by the destroyer USS *Buchanan*. The *Cache* reported she had everything under control, and suggested the *Buchanan* find her attempted assassin. The destroyer sprinted toward the spot where the *Cache* was stricken. At 8:55pm that evening, the *Buchanan* was still coming to save the day when, 130 miles east southeast of San Cristobal and still 25 miles northwest of where the *Cache* had been hit, the *Buchanan*'s SG radar picked up a "good surface contact" at a range of 12,750 yards. Visibility was "extremely poor," forcing *Buchanan* skipper Commander Floyd B. T. Myhre to rely on his radar. The information he had was ominous. Myhre surmised he was dealing with a hunter-killer vessel, one the radar indicated was "a fair size surface ship," and in a main shipping lane to boot. But Japanese surface ship this far from the front? Myhre was worried this might be a friendly ship, and went the extra mile to identify the contact. He had the *Buchanan* close the range to 2,000yds, at which point he snapped on his 36-inch light on the contact. It revealed the conning tower of a submarine, submerging before Myhre could get a shot off. That was disappointing, but the *Buchanan* quickly got a sound contact at 1,250 yards. Over the next three hours, the *Buchanan* made six separate attacks marked with floatlights with a total of 53 depth charges. Finally, after the last attack at 11:41pm, the *Buchanan* saw oil "which had a distinct kerosene-like smell" welling to the surface. Myhre had the destroyer continue to box the submarine in. By sunrise, the oil slick was observed to cover five square miles. A large amount of wooden and cork debris was also sighted in the attack area, indicative of not just damage but a sinking. So ended the Japanese submarine *Ro-37*, which under the direction of skipper Lieutenant Commander Sato Sakuma had gifted the torpedo to the *Cache*. None of the submarine's 61 crew was ever recovered. For her part, the *Cache* made it to port and was eventually repaired.[248]

While the *Cache* was starting her ordeal on January 22, AirSols did a big raid on the troublesome Lakunai air base with 27 B-25 gunships escorted by an eclectic mix of 91 fighters: eight F6F Hellcats from Fighting 40, 16 Vought F4U Corsairs from Marine Fighting 211, 27 Vought F4U Corsairs from Marine Fighting 215; 11 Vought F4U Corsairs and five Goodyear FG Corsairs from Marine Fighting 321; a dozen P-38s from the 339th Fighter Squadron, and a dozen P-40 Kittyhawks from New Zealand's No. 15 Squadron.[249] The B-25s hammered the runways at Lakunai, but Base Air Force was going to have a say in this rather violent discussion. The 204 Air Group sent up 28 Zeros from the targeted Lakunai, while the 253 sent up 25 from Tobera, and a vicious melee ensued. The 204 would claim to have destroyed 35 enemy planes, including eight B-25s, and five probables. Leading Seaman Hashimoto Isamu claimed three B-25s and an F4U, Leading Seaman Ichioka Matao claimed three aircraft destroyed and two probables, and Warrant Officer Iwamoto four destroyed and two probables. The only B-25 that was shot down was that of the 75th Bombardment Squadron's Lieutenant Thomas O. Thompson, which crashed into Simpson Harbor. Four were seen bailing out, their parachutes opening, but nothing more was heard of them. On the egress over Duke of York Island, 2nd Lieutenant Frederick W. Seaman of the 339th was unfortunate enough to have one of those phosphorus bombs the Japanese liked to drop on enemy planes in the air detonate right in front of his P-38; both of his engines caught fire and he spun into the water between Duke of York Island and New Ireland. The Kittyhawk of No. 15 Squadron's Sergeant Colin B. Grubb disappeared during the engagement; the wreckage of his fighter and his remains were found on the Gazelle Peninsula shortly after the war ended. The P-38 of the 339th's 2nd Lieutenant Edwin M. Studley was hit, but he coaxed enough out of it to get to Buka Passage before he ditched. Patrolling 14's Lieutenant (jg) O. H. Patterson interrupted an unsuccessful search for Sergeant Grubb to pick up Studley, but the PBY's batteries were low, so it could not stop for Studley, and it had to throw him a line and reel him in through the blister like a fish. The Corsairs of Lieutenant Lelen T. Wardle and Lieutenant Eugene V. Smith did not return to base; no one saw what happened to them, though a burning Corsair was seen crashing off Cape St George. Wardle was never found, but Smith deployed his life raft and floated all night until he was picked up the next day by the PBY Dumbo of Patrolling 14's Lieutenant B. Smith. The Allied aviators claimed 18 enemy aircraft destroyed. The 204 lost three aircraft and two pilots, including Superior Seaman Shibagaki Hiroshi, while the 253 lost one pilot. In something of an odd turn of events, AirSols decided to bomb Rabaul proper early that evening with six B-25s and at least 30 B-24s which pounded the town of Rabaul. What they accomplished is anyone's guess, and they saw the runways at Lakunai had been repaired but they lost two more B-25s, those of the 75th Bombardment Squadron's Lieutenants Thomas O. Thompson and William E. Eastwood, Jr.[250]

Whatever they accomplished in Rabaul, General Kenney hoped to do much better in Wewak on January 23. General MacArthur's intelligence section found air power staging into the Wewak air complex. When they saw that, Kenney decided now was the time to bring the pain. Then he decided, no, wait, he needed to get all his bombers and fighters together first. Today, it would be big: 16 P-38 Lightnings under Captain Albon Hailey from the 80th Fighter Squadron, 8th Fighter Group. The 475th Fighter Group sent 16 more Lightnings under the 432nd Fighter Squadron's Lieutenant Colonel MacDonald and 13 under 433rd Fighter Squadron's Captain Richard Kimball. The 49th Fighter Group sent 17 P-40 Warhawks under the 7th Fighter Squadron's Captain Arland Stanton and 14 Warhawks under the 8th Fighter Squadron's head Captain Bernard Makowski. The 9th Fighter Squadron flew top cover in P-47 Thunderbolts. Their mission was to escort 36 B-24 Liberators from the 43rd and 90th Bombardment Groups to Wewak. Of course, there was the usual litany of fighters dropping out for one reason or another. Lieutenant Colonel MacDonald had to abort because one of his external fuel tanks dropped early; hope no one was under that. Four more from the 432nd had to abort because of mechanical issues, as did four from the 433rd. The 4th Air Army scrambled 51 fighters, including eight Peregrine Falcons from the 248th Air Group as well as more Peregrine Falcons from the 59th and Flying Swallows from 68th Air Group. Only about half of these fighters had sufficient altitude to take on the B-24s, and they seem to have waited until the Liberators had completed their bombing runs. Nevertheless, the air battle over Wewak was savage. The 59th Air Group ambushed a flight of the 7th Fighter Squadron from behind. The two Warhawks in front, including the flight leader, Lieutenant Robert M. DeHaven, sensed the danger and pulled up into a climb, but Lieutenant John F. Crowley saw it too late and pulled out of his dive much too close to the water. An Oscar trapped Crowley against the water, denying him maneuvering room, and a burst sent Crowley's P-40 nosing over into the water off Cape Moem, killing him. The Peregrine Falcon got no time to celebrate its victory, as DeHaven had dived again and was now on the distracted Oscar's tail. At point-blank range, an undoubtedly enraged DeHaven sent a burst into the Oscar's cockpit, which filled with fire and went down. It is believed this Nakajima Ki-43 Type 1 Peregrine Falcon was flown by the 59th's Captain Nango, the top Japanese fighter ace in New Guinea. And here the Imperial Army Air Force had planned to transfer him back to Japan at the end of the month for eventual leadership of the Akeno Fighter School. The Japanese had been learning about the American way of training pilots. Too late. While the Americans claim to have destroyed a dozen Japanese fighters, this battle cost the Americans five fighters including Lieutenant Crowley. During a particularly nasty brawl about five miles east of Boram along the coast near Cape Moem, witnesses saw three P-38s going down. One collided with a Tony and the other two were shot down, with one pilot reportedly bailing out, his plane crashing to the east of Cape Moem. One of these Lightnings was likely the 433rd's Lieutenant Donald D. Revenaugh, who was element leader for a three-ship flight led by Kimball. Kimball and his men made two passes on Tonys, then got tied up with about a dozen Oscars and Tonys. Revenaugh radioed Kimball that he was starting home and was on the southern side of the Sepik River. Kimball's wingman had been 2nd Lieutenant Carl A. Danforth, who was with Kimball at the beginning of the engagement, but not seen after that. Slightly west of where Danforth was last seen was where the 80th's Lieutenant Jess E. Gidley's mission went south. Gidley dropped back in formation and radioed his element leader Lieutenant Leland B. Blair that "he was snafu." Blair thought Gidley would head back, but Lieutenant Cyril F. Homer thought he saw Gidley's P-38 smoking and diving into the water at a steep angle with a Japanese fighter on its tail. The Japanese claimed eight P-38s, three P-40s, and a B-24 – Lieutenant Koga Keiji claimed the B-24 and one P-38 – while losing six aircraft, but it might as well have been a dozen, so costly was the loss of ace Nango. The 68th Air Group lost Sergeant Major Kajita Yoshizo, while the already hard-hit 248th lost Captain Tozuka Nobuyoshi and Sergeant Major Saito Akeji.[251]

But the Wewak of New Britain was Rabaul, or maybe Wewak was the Rabaul of New Guinea. That same January 23, AirSols decided to hit Lakunai air base, which they knew was a proverbial hornet's nest. In went 18 TBF Avengers from Marine Torpedo 143 carrying 2,000lb bombs; 48 SBD Dauntlesses, with 36 from Marine Scouting 236, seven from Marine Scouting 341, five from Bombing 98, and a dozen from Compositing 40 – yes, that adds up to 60, which is more than 48, and also more than 54, which is the total number of SBDs ordered for this attack plus six spares also ordered, but every official report on this attack says exactly 48 SBDs attacked. It is a mystery why every official report says exactly 48 SBDs attacked when the math adds up to 60. They were escorted by 80 fighters including 12 Corsairs from Marine Fighting 211, 24 from 212, 13 from 215, and four Vought and four Corsairs from 321; eight Hellcats from Fighting 40, and a dozen P-38s from the 339th Fighter Squadron. Except only nine P-38s were operational, and three of these had to abort. Also aborting was Marine Fighting 321's Lieutenant Richard S. Marsh, who was having engine trouble. All the same, they bombed Lakunai all right, catching ground crews still scampering to cover and Base Air Force still scrambling fighters from the 204 Air Group. The bombers cratered the concrete runway and destroyed some planes on the ground. Once that was done, the Japanese Zeros engaged the Americans. Why did the Japanese wait until after their base had been hit hard to attack the Americans instead of trying to divert or distract them from attacking the air base? This is another mystery. Scrambling were 33 Zeros of 253 Air Group from Tobera and 34 of the 204 from Lakunai. Once again, a vicious aerial brawl was the order of the day. The 339th Fighter Squadron's 2nd Lieutenant Arthur T. Yeilding was shot down in flames and crashed into the water, apparently killing him. After Marine Fighting 212's Major Donald W. Boyle had apparently shot down a Zero, he was last seen low over St George's Channel, where he had to ditch. Boyle made his way to the Duke of York Islands, where he was captured. Marine Torpedo 143's Lieutenant Arthur H. Johnson and his crew were compelled to make a water landing after their TBF was hit. Lieutenant Marsh's engine issues had compelled him to ditch some 30 miles off Cape St George, but he was picked up later that day by Patrolling 14's indefatigable Lieutenant Smith. The 204 Air Group claimed 25 enemy aircraft destroyed and nine probables for the loss of three pilots. The 253 Air Group claimed nine destroyed and six probables for the loss of two pilots. The Americans claimed to have shot down 30 Zeros and one Tony, plus a dozen probables.[252]

That wasn't enough for AirSols, who came back that afternoon with a fighter sweep of a reported 48 fighters featuring 15 Corsairs from Marine Fighting 211, seven Corsairs from Marine Fighting 212, four Vought and four Goodyear Corsairs from Marine Fighting 321. The Americans returned to find the damage to Lakunai already repaired. Base Air Force's 253 Air Group returned to, by its own admission, shoot down one enemy fighter. The Americans claimed to have shot down 16 Zeros on this mission, and while that was overstated a bit, the reality was bad enough. The 253 lost four pilots, while the 204 Air Group, who scrambled 28 Zeros, claimed two enemy fighters destroyed and two probables for the loss of another three pilots. For the day, the 204 Air Group lost six pilots, including Chief Petty Officer Oh-iwa Hiroshi and Petty Officers 1st Class Kanenobu Susumu and Hashimasa Namio.[253]

The night brought Rabaul no relief. AirSols was probably not enjoying being the targets of Base Air Force's nocturnal attacks, another of which took place on this night when six G4M land attack planes from the lonely 751 Air Group hit Torokina again, killing three and wounding six. In turn, seven B-25 gunships hit Tobera with 24 500lb bombs.[254]

The dawn of January 24 brought nothing different, just a shuffle of what had already happened time and again since August 1942, except instead of Rabaul bombing Guadalcanal every day, it was Guadalcanal, staging through Torokina, Munda, and a few other places, bombing Rabaul every day. On this day, AirSols sent 84 fighters (including 16 Corsairs from Marine Fighting 211, 29 from 215, and 12 from 321; eight Hellcats from Fighting 38; and a dozen Kittyhawks from New Zealand's No. 15 Squadron) to escort 18 TBF Avengers (of which a dozen were from Compositing 40 and six from Marine Torpedo 143), each Avenger carrying a 2,000lb bomb. This was a fairly revolting day for the Allied fighters. Of the 29 fighters from Marine Fighting 215 planned to take part in this attack, ten were found disabled, leaving 19 to take off from Torokina, of which six were compelled to turn back by mechanical issues. As expected, the Japanese Zeros rose up from Lakunai and Tobera – 26 from the 204 Air Group led by Ensign Ito, and 18 from the 253 – but the Allied fighters, who arrived about 10–15 minutes ahead of the Avengers, made two circles over the Rabaul caldera (Rabaul, Vunakanau, Tobera, Cape Gazelle) and kept the Japanese at arm's length from the TBFs by making three passes at the Japanese and keeping much of the combat over Duke of York Island. Compositing 40 attacked ships in Simpson Harbor from masthead height with those 2,000lb bombs. And there were some big-ish ships in Simpson Harbor this day. Maybe not the *Yamato*, *Musashi*, or *Shinano*, but big nonetheless. Like the 7,017-ton aircraft transport *Lyons Maru*, rendered unnavigable in the air attack of January 17 and now finished off. The *Koan Maru*, a 3,462-ton water carrier whose mission was to provide potable water to ships and bases, who may have been contemplating the irony of needing a water tanker at a base located in a rainforest, had such contemplations cut short permanently, with the loss of 47 crew and 13 passengers. The 5,028-ton freighter *Yamayuri Maru* was sunk with the loss of three crew, while the 4,815-ton cargo ship *Taisho Maru* was sunk with the loss of four. AirSols' biggest target, the 6,500-ton tanker *Naruto*, apparently suffered heavy damage, but was still functional. In their report, Compositing 40 and Marine Torpedo 143 each took credit for sinking all the ships. The Americans believed they had shot down at least 20 Japanese planes. The 204 Air Group claimed to have shot down ten Allied aircraft, with Chief Petty Officer Ogiya himself claiming three, plus five probables, for no losses, though one Zero was badly damaged and another force-landed. The 253 Air Group claimed one and one probable with no loss of their own. In fact, they had shot down ... no one, though the Corsair of Major Robert G. Owens, Jr, commander of Marine Fighting 215, was so badly shot up that he had to make a water landing 30 miles short of Torokina. Venturas from New Zealand's No. 1 Squadron spotted a raft and directed Patrolling 14's Lieutenant (jg) Patterson to pick him up in a PBY Dumbo. The poor survivor turned out to be US Army Air Force Lieutenant Hart of the 339th Fighter Squadron, who had parachuted from his dying P-38 and floated in his life raft for a week. Then Patterson picked up a message from Owens reporting he was in trouble, so went and picked up Owens. The busy Lieutenant B. Smith saw smoke rising from the water, so he went to it and found a raft carrying Marine Torpedo 143's Lieutenant Arthur H. Johnson and the crew of his Avenger that had been shot up over Rabaul and forced to ditch the previous day, and picked them up [255]

AirSols was not alone in bombing shipping this day. The 5th Air Force paid a visit to Manus in the Admiralties. With two squadrons of protective P-38s performing the longest escort mission in the history of, at least, the 432nd Fighter Squadron, all four squadrons of the 345th Bombardment Group – 501st leading the 498th, 499th, and 500th – in their B-25 gunships hit Salami Plantation before getting to the meat of this attack, which was the ships in the harbor, with 1,000lb bombs, sinking the 5,578-ton transport *Heiwa Maru* and the auxiliary minelayer *Tatsu Maru,* while damaging another auxiliary minelayer, the *Matsu Maru.* At the same time, P-47s escorted more B-25 gunships, these of the 71st, 405th, and 823rd Bombardment Squadrons from the 38th Bombardment Group, in hitting Madang.[256]

The Admiralties were getting more attention of late. On January 25, it was even more B-25s – the 500th Bombardment Squadron, followed by the 501st, 499th, and 498th, in that order, all from the 375th Bombardment Group; and the 71st, 405th, and 823rd Bombardment Squadrons from the 38th Bombardment Group escorted by three squadrons of P-38s. The commerce destroyer formation broke up into nine-abreast squadron formations to bomb Lorengau and the Momote air base on Manus, with the Salami Plantation sandwiched between the two, with five 500lb bombs per B-25. The bombing was called "excellent," but it came with a cost. The 500th's Lieutenant John P. McLean, Jr was hit by antiaircraft fire at the end of Momote's runway. McLean reportedly waved before crashing on Salami Plantation on the eastern shore of Papitalai Harbor and exploding, killing everyone on board.[257]

Yet January 25 was a big day.[258] On or around this day, eight Zeros led by Lieutenant Yamaguchi Sadao left for Truk for some rest, relaxation, retraining, and refit, never to return. This was basically all that remained of the 204 Air Group, whose titles as the 6th Air

Attack Force operationally or the 26th Air Flotilla administratively now seemed laughably overstated; nevertheless, also going to Truk was the 6th's commander, Sakamaki Munetaka, a vice admiral, which was a grandiose rank for a commander of eight airplanes. It was being withdrawn. This was not a popular move within Base Air Force. One Japanese history says it "effected [sic] the morale of the remaining forces to such a degree that some key officers of the flotilla presented strong opposition to this transfer which was for rebuilding purposes."[259] Perhaps in an effort to placate the complainants, some of the 204's remaining pilots, such as ace Warrant Officer Iwamoto, Chief Petty Officer Ogiya and others, were not withdrawn but instead transferred to the 253 Air Group. To replace them in 204, Combined Fleet sent to Lakunai 69 Zeros, 18 carrier bombers, and 18 carrier attack planes under the command of Rear Admiral Jojima Takatsugu.[260] Jojima had commanded the *Shokaku* at Pearl Harbor and the cryptically named R-Area Air Force during the Guadalcanal Campaign. He had also, in vain, warned Admiral Yamamoto not to fly to Bougainville. These days, Jojima was commanding what was called the 2nd Carrier Division or the 2nd Air Flotilla, which were the carrier aviators from the *Junyo*, *Hiyo*, and *Ryuho*. In other words, the "B Team" of *Kido Butai*, whose "A Team" was not exactly the equal of its Pearl Harbor days.[261] As it was, the *Junyo* and *Hiyo*, though veteran carriers, were converted ocean liners whose machinery was not up to the specs of the Pearl Harbor *Kido Butai*, while everything about the *Ryuho* was just wrong, which was to be expected from the only ship significantly damaged by the Doolittle Raid. And these were just the carriers themselves. As for the air crews, as the Japanese history put it, "The personnel of the 2d Carrier Division consisted of a large group of relatively young men who possessed basic technique but lacked sufficient training and acclimatization to properly equip them for operations in this area. After the transfer, they did not produce any remarkable operational achievements but instead sustained considerable losses (including losses resulting from poor weather conditions)."[262] This was not just the proverbial robbing of Peter to pay Paul, but not fully paying Paul. And robbing Peter again, because it was around this time that the aerial contingent from the *Zuikaku* was also withdrawn.[263]

It was as if the Guadalcanal Campaign, in which planes from Rabaul bombed Guadalcanal every day and dropped a few bombs every night, had been flipped. Now, planes from Guadalcanal, albeit staged through Munda, Stirling, or Torokina, were bombing every day and often at night as well. The evening of January 25, three B-24 Liberators acted as guides and dropped illuminating flares for another 19 who bombed Lakunai air base.[264] That same January 25–26, Rear Admiral Russell S. Berkey had the 7th Fleet light cruisers *Phoenix* and *Boise* and destroyers *Bush*, *Mullany*, and *Ammen* add naval bombardment to the list of ills affecting Madang and Alexishafen.[265]

But it was Rabaul and its problematic Lakunai air base that would be on the menu for January 26, with Base Air Force's new toys from the *Junyo*, *Hiyo*, and *Ryuho* in the spotlight, to mix metaphors. AirSols was hitting Lakunai – again – with a mess of Dauntless dive bombers (20 from Bombing 98 and 32 from Marine Scouting 341) and 18 TBF Avengers from Marine Torpedo 143, with escort provided of at least 80 fighters, including

24 Corsairs from Marine Fighting 215, 30 Corsairs from Fighting 17 in their first mission since returning to duty, and 16 P-38s from the 339th Fighter Squadron. Two of 215's Corsairs aborted, as did two of 98's Dauntlesses and six of 341's. The bombing specifically targeted revetments and gun positions around Lakunai, and, sure enough, three fires were seen in the revetment areas. It was after the bombing runs that Base Air Force met the attackers with 38 Zeros from the 253 Air Group and 54 from the 2nd Carrier Division. And the dogfights began. The Allies claimed to have destroyed 22 Zeros and one Tony. Fighting 17's Lieutenant (jg) James W. Farley was shot down, his plane exploding on hitting the ground. Squadron mate Lieutenant (jg) Robert R. Hogan took a freakish hit that sheared off his right wing. Hogan was last seen in his parachute, but was never recovered. The Corsair of squadron mate Ensign Robert H. Hill was battered by 20mm shells that destroyed his left aileron and most of his tail. He spun down to 9,000 feet, recovered, and headed back to base alone. Hill got back all right, but just after he touched down his damaged F4U flipped over, totaling it and giving Hill a severe head gash. No one saw what happened to the Dauntless of Marine Scouting 341's Lieutenant Howard M. Coonley, but he and his gunner, Private 1st Class Jack B. Thomann, were never seen again. For their part, the 204 Air Group claimed ten enemy aircraft destroyed and five probables, but lost three pilots, including veteran Petty Officer 1st Class Shimizu Kiyoshi, a friend of Warrant Officer Iwamoto's. The 2nd Carrier Division, in its first combat, claimed 19 destroyed and ten probables for the loss of four pilots, including Petty Officer 1st Class Yoshioka Sanemori of the *Ryuho*. Losing four pilots is not how these green aviators wanted to survive their first combat, but the more veteran Fighting 17 wasn't much better. "The loss of two comrades on our first day back shook Fighting-17 to its core," wrote squadron skipper Lieutenant Commander Thomas Blackburn. He wondered, "Were we locked in a game of attrition we could not possibly overcome?"[266]

Attrition was the Japanese theme right now, however. January 30 saw the Rabaul caldera honored by being the target of a trifecta of air attacks. First at 11:25am was 26 B-25s escorted by 47 fighters (including eight Corsairs from Marine Fighting 211, but three had to abort; 20 Corsairs from Marine Fighting 215; and eight from Marine Fighting 217 and 17 Corsairs from Fighting 17). The gunships hit Lakunai air base hard, setting a big fire at the northern end of the runway, facing heavy antiaircraft fire that damaged six B-25s, but no interference from Zeros. That was because the American fighters were fighting the Zeros – 28 from the 253 Air Group and 29 from the 2nd Air Flotilla. The 2nd Air Flotilla lost one Zero during this clash, but Marine Fighting 215's Lieutenant John Joseph Fitzgerald never returned to base; he had been shot down, captured, and thrown into a prisoner of war camp, where he died of beri beri and dysentery in August 1944. Marine Fighting 217's Lieutenant Robert M. Ranagan, whose Corsair repeatedly lost power over the Rabaul caldera, lost power one last time on the way back to Torokina and had to ditch about 30 miles from Bougainville. He was seen to get into his raft, but attempts by the squadron to find him after that failed. The very curious part of this attack was that the B-25s reported a "possible CV [aircraft carrier] in

Simpson Harbor opposite Matupi[t]." AirSols was not going to let that one go. Toward the end of the first attack came the second attack, which consisted of 16 P-38s under Major William Lawrence from the 339th Fighter Squadron escorting 18 B-24s who dropped 394 fragmentation clusters on Vunakanau. AirSols had the P-38s flying top cover well over the B-24s, which flummoxed the Japanese who did not want to get caught between the Lightnings above them and the defensive guns of the Liberators below them, so Base Air Force reportedly backed off and all the P-38s and B-24s returned to base safely. In the interim, AirSols slapped together a third air strike with 30 Dauntlesses from Marine Scouting 341 and 18 Avengers from Marine Torpedo 233 covered by 50 fighters (including Corsairs eight from Marine Fighting 211, 15 from Marine Fighting 215, four from Marine Fighting 217, and 15 from Fighting 17) to deal with that reported aircraft carrier. An incredible 15 of the SBDs had to abort with engine trouble and a 16th, Lieutenant Perry Crellin, aborted when he saw a raft and circled it until the destroyer *Guest* could make out its location and pick up the survivor, who turned out to be Lieutenant Ranagan, so six spare Dauntlesses were moved up to make up some of the shortfall. One Corsair from Marine Fighting 217 had to abort when a carbon dioxide bottle exploded in the hands of the pilot. The pilot was uninjured. The US Navy and Marine fliers found no aircraft carrier in Simpson Harbor – indeed, no aircraft carrier had been in Simpson Harbor in the first place – but the *Iwate Maru*, a 2,984-ton water carrier whose mission was to provide potable water to ships and bases, was present. And, technically, the *Iwate Maru* is still present at this point, as she suffered multiple bomb hits and sank. The auxiliary vessel *Juzan Maru* suffered minor damage. This time, the antiaircraft fire was reported to be "the heaviest encountered to date" and the Zeros asserted themselves, with 26 from the 2nd Air Flotilla and 18 from the 253 Air Group led by Warrant Officer Iwamoto. On the approach to Simpson Harbor, the TBF of Marine Captain Paul C. Lamale, leading the second section of Avengers, was hit by antiaircraft fire over the North Daughter and spun into the water with no survivors. Fighting 17's Lieutenant (jg) Thomas F. Kropf never returned to base; the F4U of squadron mate Lieutenant Shelton R. Beacham was so badly damaged that he had to ditch off Torokina, giving him a broken nose and forcing his hospitalization. Fighting 17's Lieutenant (jg) Douglas Hugo Gutenkunst and Marine Fighting 211's Major Robert Lee Hopkins did return to base, only to collide with each other in midair as both were trying to land at Torokina in the gathering darkness in an airspace crowded with damaged aircraft. The Americans claimed to have shot down 18 Zeros, two Tojos, and a Tony. This figure was not even close –there were no Japanese Army Air Force aircraft in Rabaul – but Base Air Force hardly got off easy. The 2nd Air Flotilla claimed 23 victories, but four pilots were killed, and a fifth bailed out and survived. The 253 Air Group claimed ten Corsairs shot down, with one pilot bailing out and injured.[267]

No matter how bad Admiral Kusaka and General Inamura thought things were, they could only get worse. On February 12, 1944, the convoy SO-903 left Palau southeast bound and for Rabaul. Palau had been the base for most of the ships of the Combined

Fleet that had attacked the Philippines and the Netherlands East Indies two years before. The Philippines had been cut off (though Douglas MacArthur would never admit it) by Japanese control of the air. During the Java Sea Campaign, every convoy was that of the collier-turned-aircraft carrier-turned seaplane tender *Langley*, heading into the Javanese port of Tjilatjap with a cargo of desperately needed P-40 fighters, hoping against hope that Japanese bombers would not find them on this bright sunny day, and having those hopes, and ultimately their ship, sunk. Or the fleet oiler *Pecos*, which took the survivors of the *Langley* and headed into the Indian Ocean, only for Japanese bombers, these of *Kido Butai* to find them again. Every move the Allies made was under the threat – almost a guarantee – of air attack. Now ...

The convoy SO-903 consisted of the cargo ships *Tatsukiku Maru*, *Shinto Maru No. 1*, and *Sanko Maru* escorted by subchasers *Ch-22* and *Ch-39* and auxiliary subchaser *Cha-16*. In something of an odd arrangement, the *Sanko Maru* was towing the midget submarine *Ha-52*. The Japanese did love their midget submarines. Near Mussau Island in the St Matthias group northwest of New Hanover, the *Sanko Maru* and *Ch-39* were detached to head for Kavieng.[268]

They had stopped in Three Island Harbor, on the north coast of New Hanover, when they were found the morning of February 16 by nine B-25 gunships led by Captain Max Mortensen of the 500th Bombardment Squadron – the "Rough Raiders" – of the 345th Bombardment Group of General Kenney's 5th Air Force. The *Sanko Maru*, a 5,461-ton tanker, was anchored and had no chance. A rain of 500lb bombs sent her in flames to the bottom very quickly. The *Ch-39* was not anchored and sped and pirouetted all she could, but all she could do was run aground on a reef, sunk by the stern, and abandoned. Lieutenant (jg) Nishi Hitoshi's *Ha-52* was damaged as well, but not sunk.[269]

That afternoon, B-25 gunships of the 499th Bombardment Squadron – nicknamed "Bats Outta Hell" – also of the 345th Bombardment Group visited Three Mile Harbor and found the *Ch-39* sunk by the stern on a reef, but not entirely abandoned. Most of the crew was swimming for shore, but a few were on board fighting a small fire. Not for long. After the 499th dropped 13 500lb bombs on her, the subchaser's magazine exploded, then her boiler exploded, and all that was left was a ruined wreck. The Bats also claimed to have sunk the midget submarine.[270]

Maybe they did and maybe they didn't. The next day, February 17, the 500th returned to the scene and found the *Ha-52* still afloat. They finally put her under. But no one put under her skipper, Lieutenant Nishi. He managed to swim to shore, then he survived a two-month trek by land and by sea to reach Rabaul. Nishi was later promoted to full lieutenant and assigned to the 86th Guard Unit. Whether he would have fought so hard to survive if he knew this would be his reward is not clear.[271]

February 17 was not a good day for the Japanese, especially the Japanese at Truk, for reasons that will soon be apparent. But it was not a good day for Admiral Kusaka's Southeast Area Fleet, either. While General Kenney's 5th Air Force was completing the destruction of the convoy in Three Island Harbor, AirSols was attacking Japanese shipping in Keravia Bay, the bay outside Rabaul's Simpson Harbor, with 47 Dauntlesses (from Marine Scouting 244 and Bombing 98) and Avengers armed with 2,000lb bombs, 1,000lb bombs, 500lb bombs, and rockets; escorted by 74 American Corsairs (including 19 from Fighting 17 and 16 from Marine Fighting 217) and Hellcats and Kiwi Kittyhawks.[272] According to the Marine Fighting 217 war diary:

> [P]lanes from this squadron experienced the most intense opposition from the enemy who appeared eager for combat. Jap aircraft attacked from all angles, singly and in pairs. When one or two had attained a tail position, others would join the attack until eight or ten enemy were in the rear of one of our planes.[273]

As painful as that sounds, Marine Fighting 217 got off light. One of its Corsairs, that of Lieutenant F. J. Lenihan, took two 20mm shells in the fuselage and left wing, piercing the left wing fuel tank and exploding inside. Not to worry, though. Despite this and a bad oil leak, Lenihan managed to return to base safely.[274]

At that point, the Japanese Zero pilots – 40–50, including 28 from the 253 Air Group and the 2nd Carrier Division – had to be wondering, *What do we have to do to shoot down one of these?* Even so, the Japanese did manage to shoot down two Corsairs from Fighting 217 (one by antiaircraft fire) and, reportedly, a Dauntless.[275] But the army cargo ship *Iwate Maru* and guardboat *Fuku Maru No. 2* had been sunk. Most frustratingly for the Japanese, aground in Keravia Bay was the minesweeper *W-26*, damaged and in sinking condition after being hit in the attacks on Rabaul of November 2, 1943. The Japanese had put considerable effort into repairing the minesweeper, including reinforcing her cracked hull and draining her flooded boiler room. All for naught. The *W-26* was finally and fully sunk this day. On the bright side of life, apparently there were no casualties from these sinkings.[276]

On the dark side, things had been happening behind Rabaul's back. At 10:00am on January 31, lookouts on Green Island reported an invasion.[277] Not like amphibious invasions were rare these days, so Admiral Kusaka was ready. He ordered up some reconnaissance planes to check out the general area. First instinct was to get information. Second, he would send up six fighters equipped with bombs. Third, they would use two submarines to stage a counterlanding.[278]

The scout planes flew over the Green Islands, and the only evidence of an enemy landing they found was a single barge. Maybe the Green Island garrison were exaggerating. The response went to a more leisurely pace. That afternoon, six Zeros went to the Green Islands and found six motor torpedo boats there. The Zeros attacked, and sank one and set two more on fire. Or so they reported.[279] No PT boats were sunk or damaged.

That evening of January 31, the garrison on Green Island (12 naval lookouts and about 80 Imperial Army troops) reported they were under attack, they had taken heavy losses, they needed reinforcements, and they were about to cease communications with Rabaul because they were burning their code books.[280] Which made them smarter than the crew of the *I-1.*

Admiral Kusaka then had two submarines – exactly which is anybody's guess – packed with 123 men of a "naval amphibious force" and, at 1:00pm on February 1, sent them to the Green Islands.[281] They arrived at the northeast side of the Green Islands at midnight on February 3, but bad weather cut short their counterlanding and they were only able to counterland 77 men. Nevertheless, they had successfully counterlanded.[282]

The garrison learned on February 5 that the invading troops had left the islands on February 1. Admiral Kusaka, General Inamura, and the powers that be in Rabaul concluded that this had been a reconnaissance operation.[283] And if that was not enough, the submarine *I-171*, which had left Rabaul on January 30 on an emergency supply run to Buka carrying rubber containers on her deck, had disappeared. The Buka garrison reported seeing an enemy destroyer west of the island on February 1.[284]

As there had been. Because it was indeed a reconnaissance operation. On the evening of January 30–31, Captain Earle led four of his destroyers (*Fullam*, *Bennett*, *Hudson*, and *Guest*) in escorting three of those fast destroyer transports (*Dickerson*, *Waters*, and *Talbot*), along with *PTs-176* and *-178*.[285] Those fast destroyer transports were carrying 300 men of the 30th Battalion of the 14th Brigade of the 3rd New Zealand Division, who themselves were guarding US Navy specialists. For this landing, they were under the direction of the 30th's commander, Lieutenant Colonel Frederick Cornwall, a veteran of Gallipoli and the Western Front of World War I.[286]

The landing party – the Kiwis preferred the term "commandos," as the British had given that word a glamorous glaze – landed in the early hours of January 31. Then a Royal New Zealand Air Force Ventura scouting overhead flashed an Aldis lamp at them, but they could not make out the signal. Some thought it was a prank. Then a roll of toilet paper streamed out of the Ventura.[287] The commandos disregarded it – the message tucked inside it that five Japanese barges had been spotted on the south coast had fallen out.[288]

This became a problem when one of the scouting teams ran into those Japanese and a hailstorm of gunfire. The commandos tried to destroy the barges with light mortars. That afternoon, they planned an attack to destroy the Japanese barges, but these preparations were interrupted by the Japanese Zeros' attack. Their target was the commandos' own barges, one of which was filled with ammunition. The bombing and strafing attack was beaten off, but at a cost of one killed and two wounded.[289]

That was enough for Lieutenant Colonel Cornwall, who decided to call it a day. Just after midnight on February 1, Commodore Earle and his ships returned. Re-embarking the landing team was complicated by choppy seas, but was completed successfully, and the ships departed. The cost of this operation was one New Zealander and three Americans killed, with three Americans and two native guides wounded.[290] The Green Islands would come up again.

A little after 4:00am, as Captain Earle's force headed south maybe 15 miles west of Buka, Earle's destroyer *Fullam* picked up an unidentified radar contact to the south southeast at a range of 12,500 yards. The destroyer *Guest* detected this contact as well, determining that it was headed east at 10 knots. At 4:25, Earle ordered the *Guest* and

Hudson to investigate the unknown vessel, but not to remain past 6:00am so as to get within friendly fighter range before Base Air Force out of Rabaul could reach them.

The two destroyers closed the contact, but could not see it. Lieutenant Commander Earle K. McLaren had his *Guest* snap on her 36-inch searchlight, but still could not find it. When the range closed to 3,500 yards, the contact disappeared from radar screens – but the *Guest* then picked up a sonar contact at 4:41am. She lost the contact, but maneuvered and quickly got it back. Just before 5:00am, the *Guest* attacked with depth charges. No results were observed. The two destroyers continued searching. About a half hour later, the *Guest* "made excellent contact" and dropped depth charges once again. Several minutes after the depth charges had all detonated, "two additional and totally dissimilar explosions were heard and felt by both *Guest* and *Hudson*."[291]

There were no more sonar contacts. Two destroyers remained on site until 6:00am, then left as ordered. Captain Burke came in with his destroyers to maintain the vigil. They found no contacts, either, but saw an oil slick in the vicinity of the *Guest*'s second attack.

An oil slick by itself is not conclusive evidence of a sunk submarine, but on February 5 Rabaul reported that the *I-171* had not arrived at Buka at 7:00pm on February 5 as scheduled, and efforts to contact her had failed. Oddly, the commander of submarines at Rabaul reported that the submarine had arrived at Buka on February 1 and completed unloading, and departed to continue her "special transportation duties," but there had been no contact with her since that date. Whatever the truth, Lieutenant Commander Shimada Takeo's submarine *I-171* and the 91 men on board were never seen again.[292]

Meanwhile, on February 3, US Navy PBY Catalinas and 5th Air Force B-25s attacked a convoy west of New Hanover and sank the 5,439-ton cargo ship *Nichiai Maru*.[293] On February 5, more B-25s hit the Wewak area, including Hansa Bay, southeast of Wewak, managing to sink the 850-ton cargo ship *Tatsumi Maru*.[294] The next day, it was A-20s and P-40s hitting the waters off Wewak, reportedly sinking the Japanese ships *Kaiyu* and *Takegiku Maru*s and damaging the *Torihime Maru* off Wewak, though none of it could be confirmed.[295] After a slight lull, on February 10, a PBY Catalina reportedly sank Japanese fishing boat *Inawa Maru* off Wewak, though, again, this could not be confirmed. Three days later, more A-20s from the 5th Air Force visited Aitape, a small town on the north coast of Papua New Guinea between Wewak and Hollandia (Jayapura) that the Japanese were building up into a base, and sank the 872-ton cargo ship *Yoshino Maru* and a motorized sailboat she was towing.[296]

On the morning of February 14, 1944, Japanese reconnaissance planes found a convoy of some 30 transports escorted by some 15 cruisers and destroyers west of Bougainville headed north. The Japanese astutely determined this was "apparently a new enemy landing force."[297] Where was it going?

Japanese reconnaissance planes kept the convoy under surveillance throughout the day, the night, and into the next morning, February 15. That night, Base Air Force sent up a total of 32 planes (six Type 1 land attack planes, ten Nakajima carrier attack planes, 15 Aichi carrier bombers, and one "reconnaissance seaplane") to make multiple attacks on the convoy. Ten carrier bombers attacked one of the covering groups and managed one hit and three near misses on the light cruiser *St Louis*, freshly repaired after getting her bow blown off at the Battle of Kolombangara.[298] This time, she took a bomb hit near her Number Six 40mm mount at about frame 100 that started a significant fire that was under control in three minutes; and two near misses off the port quarter near the Number Five main turret. The crew had to put out a fire, mourn the deaths of one officer and 22 of her crew and treat 28 others who were wounded.[299] That was all Base Air Force could get that night, but it reported sinking one transport and damaging three transports, two cruisers, and one destroyer in exchange for three of the Type 1s, two carrier attack planes, six Aichis, and that "reconnaissance seaplane" failing to return.[300]

Daylight on February 15 revealed a lot more about the convoy and its destination. This was not one of General MacArthur's and Admiral Barbey's amphibious invasion forces; it was Admiral Halsey's and Admiral Wilkinson's amphibious invasion force. It consisted of eight of those fast destroyer transports (*Stringham*, *Talbot*, *Waters*, *Noa*, *Kilty*, *Crosby*, *Ward*, and *Dickerson*), seven tank landing ships, six tank landing craft, and 13 infantry landing craft shepherded by 17 destroyers (Wilkinson's flagship *Halford*, *Fullam*, *Guest*, *Bennett*, *Hudson*, *Waller*, *Pringle*, *Saufley*, *Philip*, *Renshaw*, *Sigourney*, *Conway*, *Eaton*, *Anthony*, *Wadsworth*, *Terry*, and *Braine*). They were covered by Admiral Ainsworth's freshly repaired task force with the light cruiser flagship *Honolulu* and sister ship *St Louis* and destroyers *Farenholt*, *Buchanan*, *Woodworth*, *Lansdowne*, and *Lardner*.[301] There was also Admiral Merrill's force with light cruiser flagship *Montpelier* and sister ships *Cleveland* and *Columbia* with Captain Burke's destroyers *Charles Ausburne*, *Dyson*, *Converse*, *Stanly*, and *Spence*.[302]

The Allies were driven to take Nissan and the other Green Islands because of those three most important things in real estate: location, location, and location. After the Bougainville and Cape Gloucester landings, Admiral Halsey's fleet didn't have much to do. Most of what they needed for amphibious landings was in the central Pacific. They had to wait a long time – until at least April 1944 – before they could land again. But Halsey was not one to sit around twiddling his thumbs for any significant length of time.

And not only did Admiral Halsey want to continue the advance, but to get a new airfield. As Halsey himself later explained:

> Commanding the eastern approach to Rabaul was Green Island, 120 miles away; commanding the northern approach to Kavieng was Emirau, 90 miles away; and commanding the western approaches to both Rabaul and Kavieng was Manus, 220 miles from Kavieng. All three islands were push-overs, and when they fell, Japan's South Pacific campaign would fall with them.[303]

In fact, the Green Islands were 37 miles northwest of Buka and 55 miles east of East Cape, New Ireland. Nissan was useful to the Japanese as a relay station for their beloved barges. An airfield built there would be 220 miles from Kavieng, 115 miles from Rabaul and 720 miles from Truk, and thus useful for air attacks on those bases. And eight-mile-long

Nissan, the largest of the Green Islands, was near enough to Torokina to permit AirSols fighters to cover the landing.[304]

So off the invasion convoy went in what was called Operation *Squarepeg*. Admiral Wilkinson led the naval force, and New Zealand Major General Harold E. Barrowclough led the land forces, who were on the transports. The centerpiece of the invasion was the 4,242 Kiwis of the 3rd New Zealand Division's 14th Brigade under the command of Brigadier Leslie Potter, who were new veterans from their landing on Vella Lavella during the New Georgia campaign. There were also 1,564 Americans in support functions.[305] With 32 fighters from AirSols already overhead by 6:30am, everyone felt relatively safe.[306] Base Air Force tried to test that with four land attack planes, four carrier attack planes, and nine carrier bombers, who were so ineffective that, with the loss of one G4M, the Japanese even admitted, "Although an attack was made at the enemy landing point, little damage was inflicted because of interference by enemy planes."[307]

There was no bombardment of Nissan by ships or aircraft. After a reconnaissance visit by Kiwi troops and US Navy scouts, intelligence analysts, "by some mysterious method of computation that is their trade secret," estimated that the Japanese defense force numbered no more than a hundred. Actually, there seem to have been 102 naval infantry, so that mysterious method of computation needed work. The scouts also found the Green Islands to be inhabited by some 1,200 Melanesians, who were so friendly to the Allies and so hostile to the Japanese that the naval and air bombardment was omitted.[308]

The landing itself came off smooth as glass. According to Morison:

This operation was planned to the last detail and executed with the precision, enthusiasm and smooth team play that characterized everything that Admiral Wilkinson undertook. When "Ping" (Wilkinson) led, every man jack knew exactly what he had to do, which was the best means to ensure that he did it. He himself regarded this as the neatest landing that III [Amphibious Force] ever pulled off.[309]

Everyone landed just fine and the ships quickly left. And the Kiwis got to work on Nissan, completing their mission very quickly. At 6:20am on February 19, Rabaul received a message from the garrison. "We are charging the enemy and beginning radio silence," it said. There was no more communication from the Japanese on Nissan.[310] Ten New Zealanders and three Americans had been killed; 21 New Zealanders and three Americans wounded.[311]

February 15 brought *some* good news to the Japanese: light cruiser *Agano*, damaged in Simpson Harbor during the air attacks of last November, hunted by submarine USS *Albacore*, and under emergency repair ever since, was finally ready to go home.[312] Not ready to fight, but ready to go home. Repaired just enough to enable her to get back to the Home Islands without sinking. As it was, she was using only two of her four propellers. Even so, at 10:00pm, she sailed out of Truk Harbor, escorted by ancient destroyer *Oite* and subchaser *Ch-28*.

Shortly before 6:00pm the next day, when she was maybe 160 miles north of Truk, the *Agano* was hit on her starboard side by two Mark 14 torpedoes that actually detonated. They were compliments of the submarine USS *Skate* and her new skipper Lieutenant Commander William P. Gruner. The *Agano* suffered flooding in two of her boiler rooms and could not move. It seems the subchaser *Ch-28* went to chase the submarine down with, as Gruner described the, "the gentle patter of depth charges." As that was going on, attempts to save the new cruiser were ongoing. But by 9:30 that night, five of her boiler rooms were flooded and one of those was on fire; the flooding was getting worse, reaching the main deck, and she had a 10-degree list. She requested a tow, reporting "navigation impossible [...] Although there is a degree of buoyancy, the situation verges on the dangerous."

It was well beyond that. The escorts stopped looking for the submarine and went back to looking for survivors. The *Oite* rescued 523, including the cruiser's skipper, Captain Matsuda Takatomo, who had assumed command while the *Agano* was under repair at Rabaul. The *Ch-28* took in 125. As they did so, the *Skate* tried to maneuver into position to finish the cruiser off, but there was no need. With one final explosion at 2:47am on February 17, the *Agano* went to the depths. The *Oite* headed back to Truk. Big mistake.

The AirSols attack on Keravia Bay that February 17 was followed by others from more unexpected directions. That night, it was no air attack, but US Navy destroyers. Captain Simpson was coming to the Rabaul area to destroy all its privies. And he was coming with his Destroyer Squadron 12, with destroyers *Farenholt*, *Buchanan*, *Lansdowne*, *Lardner*, and *Woodworth*. Veterans all. Simpson, too, was willing to borrow Japanese tactics, and let loose with a smoke screen behind his ships to confound Japanese lookouts and neutralize illumination rounds. Around 1:00am on February 18, the destroyers began bombarding gun batteries, supply caches, and, particularly, privies near Praed Point. The Japanese turned on their search lights but aimed them at the sky; they thought they were under a nocturnal air attack. That made Simpson's job all the easier. When shore defense guns near Cape Gazelle finally figured out who was attacking, it did not take long to silence them, at least temporarily. Vunapope (or, as the *Farenholt* called it, Vunapopo) took some blasting as well. Torpedoes launched through the minefield across the entrance to Keravia Bay neutralized mines and privies, but also attracted some return torpedoes from the shipping there. The Cape Gazelle battery made itself known again, but scored no hits and all the destroyers escaped about an hour later with nary a scratch. From the Japanese, anyway.[313]

Dawn on February 18 would bring Rabaul no relief. A lot of bombers, including six Avengers from Marine Torpedo 134 and 17 more from 143, joined maybe 48 SBD Dauntlesses and a lot of fighters, including about 20 P-40 Kittyhawks, 12 Corsairs from Marine Fighting 217 and 26 more from Fighting 17. Base Air Force scrambled 36 Zeros, including 26 under Warrant Officer Iwamoto from the 253 Air Group, but the intercept was strangely listless and hardly pressed at all, though Iwamoto would disagree with that assertion. As he wrote in his diary, "Our fighters were already engaged with the escort fighters. The bomber group was now trying to retreat. This was the opportunity we had been waiting for. We dove from 9,000 meters; the main force attacked the bombers while a few of us attacked the F4Us above." You love it when a plan comes together. The Japanese were rewarded by shooting down 31 Allied aircraft. Or so they said. The real total was, roughly, one Corsair from Marine Fighting 222 whose pilot, Lieutenant R. A. Schaeffer, was rescued. In turn, the Americans claimed to have shot down 21 Zeros. The 253 Air Group is known to have lost five. While the bombers set fire to a fuel dump near Lakunai, this was going to be a marathon of air attacks. For as this strike was leaving, the next one was coming in: six B-24 Liberators hitting Lakunai again. And after that, 14 B-24s with 35 Corsairs and Lightnings for escorts hit Tobera. The escorts would claim two fighters shot down. The damage at Lakunai and Tobera forced the Japanese defenders to land at Vunakanau.[314]

But this was not the big news of the day.[315] An exhausted Warrant Officer Iwamoto was able to fly to Tobera after dark, when its runway had been repaired. After rest that was all too brief, he was called into a secret conference at air group headquarters. Commander Fukuda Taro, commanding officer of the 253 Air Group, looked solemnly at Iwamoto, assembled officers, and the chief of the ground crews. Then again, while on duty, Japanese officers always looked solemn, and frequently had a black scowl. Nevertheless, this was the real thing. Taro gave the news.

Truk had been attacked.

The great Japanese base at Truk in the Caroline Islands had been attacked. Not just attacked. Smashed. The damage was catastrophic. The Japanese air defenses were completely ineffective. US Navy carrier planes had sunk ships left and right inside and outside Truk Harbor. Carrier planes sank both veteran light cruiser *Naka* west of Truk and destroyer *Oite*, still carrying survivors of the *Agano*, north of Truk, and the destroyer *Tachikaze*. Damaged in the air attacks were destroyers *Shigure* and *Matsukaze*, submarines *I-10* and *Ro-37*, target ship *Hakachi*, repair ship *Akashi*, ammunition ship *Soya*, seaplane tender *Akitsushima*, and auxiliary submarine chaser *Cha-20*. Additionally, the surface escorts for the US Navy carriers sank the training cruiser (not the *Natori*) *Katori*, destroyer *Maikaze*, and submarine chaser *Ch-24*.

But those warships and support ships were nothing compared to the supply ships, freighters, tankers, and other ships. They included the 7,389-ton armed merchant cruiser *Akagi Maru*, 11,614-ton auxiliary submarine depot ship *Heian Maru*; 6,938-ton aircraft transport *Fujikawa Maru*; transports *Rio de Janeiro Maru* (9,626 tons), *Kiyozumi* (or *Kiyosumi*) *Maru* (8,613 tons), *Aikoku Maru* (10,437 tons), *Gosei Maru* (1,931 tons), *Hanagawa* (or *Hanakawa*) *Maru* (4,739 tons), *Hokuyo Maru* (4,216 tons), *Amagisan Maru* (7,620 tons), *Kensho Maru* (4,862 tons), *Matsutan* (or *Matsutani* or *Shotan*) *Maru* (1,999 tons), *Momokawa* (or *Momogawa*) *Maru* (3,829 tons), *Reiyo Maru* (5,445 tons), *San Francisco Maru* (5,831 tons), *Seiko Maru* (5,385 tons), *Taiho Maru* (2,829 tons); *Zuikai Maru* (2,827 tons), *No.6 Unkai Maru* (3,220 tons); *Yamagiri Maru* (6,438 tons); fleet tankers *Fujisan Maru* (9,524 tons), *Hoyo Maru* (8,691 tons), *Shinkoku Maru* (10,020 tons), and *No.3 Tonan Maru* (19,209 tons); 3,763-ton water carrier *Nippo Maru*; and army cargo ships *Nagano Maru* (3,824 tons) and *Yubai Maru* (3,217 tons).[316]

Admiral Koga had ordered a stunned Admiral Kusaka to send all his available aircraft, promising they would eventually be returned. Kusaka, in turn, ordered Commander Fukuda to prepare for immediate withdrawal. Fukuda admonished everyone to keep this a secret for now.

Admiral Kusaka arrived at Lakunai Airfield on February 20, 1944, with his staff to watch the departure. Turning to Captain Sanagi Takeshi and Commander Hori Tomoyoshi, Kusaka sighed sadly, "They're never coming back. Never! But it can't be helped. We'll just have to do the best we can with what we have." He felt certain that Tokyo had abandoned Rabaul to its fate.

So it began. The withdrawal of all usable air power from Rabaul. It continued until the evening of February 24–25. The aircraft that would be leaving: 30 Zeros, six Mitsubishi G4M Type 1 land attack planes, eight Aichi D3 Type 99 carrier bombers, and five or six Nakajima B5N Type 97 carrier attack planes. This was all that was left of the great 11th Air Fleet – Base Air Force – that had Henderson Field shaking in its boots only 18 months earlier.

The air campaign for the Solomon Islands was over.

But don't tell that to the 22nd Naval Construction Regiment, who was working on Green Island. By February 17, a PT boat base had been opened. The Americans did love their PT boats; the Japanese didn't. Perhaps a curious juxtaposition considering the PTs seemed to damage US Navy ships more often than Japanese ones. In any case, by March 4, a 5,000-foot fighter field was ready; later that same month a 6,000-foot bomber field was opened. And by March 17, 16,448 men and 43,088 tons of supplies had been sent to the Green Islands.[317]

But if the Japanese did not like that landing, well, there would be others.

This next particular tale begins on or about (it's disputed) February 23, 1944. In January and February 1944, General Kenney's 5th Air Force made several bombing attacks on the Admiralty Islands in the Bismarck Sea, where the Japanese had air bases at Lorengau on Manus, the main island of the Admiralties; and Momote on Los Negros, the third largest island of the Admiralties, just northeast of Manus. In theory, anyway. The Admiralties' supply situation had been very iffy of late, and the runways seemed to be hardly used and maybe unusable. Nevertheless, the Momote air base – 5,000-by-300-foot runway, with dispersal bays nearly all around it – had a lot of potential.[318] General Kenney said of the Momote airdrome, "That coral strip on Los Negros, a little over 200 miles from Kavieng, was the most important piece of real estate in the theater."[319]

More than that, as one US Army history explained it:

Capture of the Admiralties would represent a strategic gain of the greatest importance. Three hundred and sixty miles west of Rabaul and two hundred miles from the Wewak-Madang coastal area, the islands were not only near the center of the great semicircle formed by the main enemy defenses on New Guinea and the Bismarcks, but were on the Japanese side of this crescent. Developed as an offensive base for Allied air and naval power, they would control the western approaches to the Bismarck Sea, flank Japanese strongholds on the New Guinea coast, and protect Allied advance into the open waters leading toward the Philippines.[320]

This was why the Admiralties were already on the agenda for *Cartwheel*. But they were not to be invaded yet. Should that be changed? Should their seizure be moved up?

In January and February 1944, the 5th Bomber Command made bombing the Admiralties a priority. On the evening of February 23, General Kenney received a report from a B-25 flying a reconnaissance mission over the Admiralties. It included the note "Momote and Lorengau strips appeared unserviceable. Nil activity. Nil new aircraft. Nil unusual signs of activity in entire Admiralty Islands."[321] Kenney was almost giddy. "[T]he Jap might be withdrawing his troops from Los Negros back to Manus," he later wrote. "There was nothing for him to stay for. The airdrome installations had been taken out, the last airplane destroyed, and his fuel supplies burned. Even his anti-aircraft guns had been knocked out of action."[322] Well, OK, then.

The report the next evening, February 24, included "Aircraft flew low but nil A/A (antiaircraft) fire encountered. Nil signs of enemy activity. The island [Lorengau] appears deserted."[323] General Kenney had a few more details. "It said that the reconnaissance plane had flown at low-altitude all over the island for half an hour. No one had fired a shot at it." That was important, but there was more. "There was still a heap of dirt in front of the Jap field hospital door that had been piled there two days before by the bombing. There had been no washing on the lines for three days." The 5th Air Force commander spelled it out: "Los Negros was ripe for the picking."[324]

General Kenney bolted upstairs to General MacArthur's office and suggested immediately seizing the Momote air base. He just needed a few hundred troops and some engineers, who would quickly put the runways in shape so that it could be supplied by air. With nobody left there, taking it would actually be quite easy, barely an inconvenience. As part of his lengthy spiel, Kenney pointed out that with Momote, "The whole Jap force in New Britain and New Ireland could be cut off and left to die on the vine. With Manus in our hands, we could jump the next show up the New Guinea coast."[325]

General MacArthur listened, pacing back and forth as General Kenney kept talking, nodding here and there. Then, he suddenly stopped and said, "That will put the cork in the bottle."[326]

An odd choice of words for General MacArthur, considering he had considered Bataan and Corregidor the cork in the bottle of Manila Bay, and perhaps an ominous choice. Be that as it may, on February 24, he radioed orders to General Krueger, General Whitehead, and Admiral Barbey to "prepare for immediate reconnaissance in force." Some 800 men of Major General Innis Swift's 1st Cavalry Division and other units were to ride those fast destroyer transports to Momote no later than February 29. If successful the cavalrymen were to prepare the airfield for transport aircraft and hold their positions pending arrival of reinforcements.[327]

Organizing amphibious operations on short notice is tricky. It did help that the February 25 scouting report included "No signs of enemy activity on Manus and Los Negros Islands. All crews claim these islands have been evacuated. Grass growing thickly on Momote and Lorengau strips. Runways unserviceable, and badly pitted. No A/A fire, even at low altitude." (The B-25s flew over Momote strip at 20 feet.)[328] The report for the next evening included, "Both Lorengau and Momote strips are unserviceable. The wrecked aircraft and trucks on Momote are untouched and bomb craters still unfilled. Villages on Los Negros Island appeared deserted and roads have not been used lately. Damage in Lorengau town has not been repaired. No activity of any kind observed."[329] General Whitehead, whose 5th Bomber Command was providing the reconnaissance planes, estimated the number of Japanese on the island was, "not over 300 combat troops."[330]

Although there were discouraging words here and there. General Willoughby, General MacArthur's intelligence chief, said that, on the basis of intercepted information and ground reports over a long period of time, he determined "cumulative intelligence does not support air observer reports that the islands have been evacuated." As of February 15, there were about 3,250 enemy combatants in the Admiralties. On February 24, Willoughby revised that figure upward to 4,000. He added that the lack of antiaircraft fire was due to the compromised Japanese supply situation, and that "the enemy will hold his fire until the final defense of the Admiralties is imminent."[331] But Willoughby was also called "likely the worst intelligence chief the US Army has ever had."[332] So what did he know?

While Generals Kenney and Whitehead were arranging the air support and Admirals Kinkaid and Barbey were organizing the ships needed for the invasion of the Admiralties, designated Operation *Brewer*, General Krueger had an idea. His own intelligence chief estimated that the Japanese had about 4,500 troops in the Admiralties.[333] If they are gone, what happened to them? There's no evidence ships picked them up. They weren't going to swim from the Admiralties to Kavieng. Where are these people? What if we sent actual people to Los Negros to look under the treetops and inside the buildings to see if any Japanese were on the island? A reconnaissance not in force just before reconnaissance in force. It was an idea so crazy it just might work.

The morning of February 27, 2nd Lieutenant John R. McGowen of the 158th Infantry Regiment and five enlisted men were dropped by a PBY Catalina flying boat some 500 yards off the southeastern shore of Los Negros at 6:45am. They went ashore in a rubber boat, pushed halfway across the island, and at 4:00pm radioed "Could not get to river. Lousy with Japs." McGowan and his men were picked up and flown back to safety.[334]

Well, now what? Rear Admiral William M. Fechteler, who had been tabbed to lead the naval attack group, said the report "laid the previous intelligence information from air reconnaissance open to suspicion."[335] General Kenney responded that the scouts had seen only one spot on the south end of the island where they would expect the Japanese to be, to keep away from areas which were being bombed. Plus, if there were even 25 Japs in those woods at night, the scouts would think that the place really was "lousy with Japs." "I was sure the scheme would work," Kenney reassured. "[T]hat in a few days we would be landing airplanes at Los Negros."[336] Everyone except Kenney was very concerned. The operation may have been brewed under false information.[337]

So this was the best force, the best operation they could slap together. Under the command of Admiral Fechteler, the destroyers *Reid*, *Flusser*, *Mahan*, *Drayton*, *Smith*, *Bush*, *Welles*, *Stockton*, and *Stevenson* and the fast destroyer transports *Humphreys*, *Brooks*, and *Sands*, would carry the reinforced 2nd Squadron of the 5th Cavalry Regiment of the 1st Cavalry Brigade of the 1st Cavalry Division, and 1st Cavalry Brigade's commanding officer Brigadier General William C. Chase to serve as operational commander on land.[338] They would be covered by the light cruisers *Phoenix* and *Nashville*; and destroyers *Beale*, *Bache*, *Hutchins*, and *Daly*.[339] The *Phoenix* would carry General MacArthur and Admiral Kinkaid. General Krueger had opposed MacArthur going on this operation; MacArthur had listened to Krueger's objections attentively and thanked him, but added, "I have to go."[340] The Southwest Pacific commander wanted to be personally involved because of the slap-dash nature of this risky operation that was taking place on his authority and the possibility that quick decisions would be needed on site; such as whether the invading troops would stay and fight or withdraw.

After a bombardment by the covering cruiser forces that was extended a bit because overcast weather and a very low cloud ceiling had prevented most of the air support from even finding the beach, let alone attacking it, came the landing itself. It took place on the east side of Los Negros in the small Hyane Harbor, whose entrance consisted of a 50-yard gap between two high points of land that descend into coral reefs and whose south shore was at the literal end of Momote's runway.[341]

The first sign of trouble was when the first wave got through the narrow entrance to the harbor. The landing craft started getting hit by machine-gun fire. Shells started splashing near the destroyers and even the *Phoenix*.[342] The men started to wonder if maybe this island was not quite as abandoned as they had thought.

It wasn't. For all of General Willoughby's incompetence, of which General MacArthur was aware but about which he did not seem to care (because Willoughby had what MacArthur considered the single most important quality: sycophancy), had actually – for once – developed a decent picture of the Japanese troops in the Admiralties. The bulk of them were from the Imperial Army's 51st Transportation Regiment, but the Imperial Navy was represented here, too, with elements of the 14th Base Force, specifically the 88th Guard Unit and possibly the 81st Guard Unit.[343] With extreme difficulty, General Inamura had recently been able to send the 2nd Battalion of the 1st Mixed Independent Regiment, and the 1st Battalion of the 229th Infantry Regiment of the 38th Division. This totaled 3,646 men, all under the command of Colonel Ezaki Yoshio, commander of the 51st.[344]

Colonel Ezaki was cunning. He had managed to hide his almost 4,000 fighting men from aerial eyes by ordering his forces not to fire at aircraft or otherwise disclose their presence. It sounds ridiculous, but it fooled General Kenney. So Ezaki had something of the element of surprise, but this was not a true ambush because, though Ezaki had expected an invasion, he had expected it on the other side of the island at Seeadler Harbor, which was much larger and more accessible than Hyane.[345] So Ezaki was fooled, too. When the cavalry troopers landed at Hyane Harbor, Ezaki had to redeploy his troops and the heavy guns had to be repositioned or turned around.

For that reason, though there was gunfire from the Japanese, it was relatively inaccurate, and almost nonexistent at the beach itself. The incoming landing boats had problems from some 25mm guns. Two soldiers and the coxswain died before the counterbattery fire from the US Navy ships silenced the remaining guns. For now.

Due to the relative lack of resistance at the beach, the Momote air base was taken before 10:00am – just 90 minutes after landing. The cavalry troopers deployed antiaircraft guns on the beach, unloaded supplies, set up communications, and began a probing patrol inland. Two soldiers had been killed and three wounded. General Chase came ashore to take charge of the situation. For now, because at 4:00pm, it was deemed safe enough for General MacArthur and Admiral Kinkaid to come ashore and see how things were going. Or not.

Anguished aides tried to persuade him not to expose himself. One senior officer warned him that he was in "very intimate danger." General MacArthur looked very conspicuous in his trench coat and cap, but he nevertheless awarded a Distinguished Service Cross to the man who had led the first wave, Lieutenant Marvin J. Henshaw.[346] He also extolled General Chase: "You have all performed marvelously. Hold what you have taken, no matter against what odds. You have your teeth in him now – don't let go."[347] Then, to the amazement (and horror) of his party, he strolled casually inland.

The Southwest Pacific commander lit up his corncob pipe, waved out the match, and explained that he wanted to get "a sense of the situation." It was more – a lot more – than he had done at Buna or, for that matter, Bataan. A lieutenant pointed at a path and said, "Excuse me, sir, but we killed a Jap sniper in there just a few minutes ago."

General MacArthur nodded. "Fine," he said. "That's the best thing to do with them." Then he walked in that direction. Stumbling over two enemy corpses, soldiers who had been slain a few minutes earlier, he continued on, merely remarking, "That's the way I like to see them." A soldier called, "You are beyond the perimeter, sir!" MacArthur courteously thanked him for the information, but he kept going until he came to a wounded American infantryman, with whom he spoke for a few minutes. For a while, the general had abandoned his traditional aloofness.[348]

Dr Roger O. Egeberg, MacArthur's new physician, had joined his staff the month before. Other aides, he remembered, had told him that accompanying MacArthur within range of enemy riflemen was to be avoided if at all possible. Now, Egeberg was terrified. He later remembered, "All of the officers with MacArthur were uneasy at Los Negros – uneasy about MacArthur's safety and, more vital to them, about their own safety."[349] So much for that whole "Dugout Doug" thing, which was an inaccurate, if understandable, slur in the first place.[350] Maybe that was part of his motivation to come ashore.

In any event, after examining the runways of the Momote air base, General MacArthur decided the operation would continue. He and Admiral Kinkaid returned to the *Phoenix*, and, with everyone landed and their supplies offloaded, the US Navy ships departed at about 5:30pm. Except for the destroyers *Bush* and *Stockton*, who could be called on to provide artillery support if needed.[351]

But this wasn't over, and General Chase knew it. Because he had few ways to physically fortify his position, Chase actually pulled back, abandoned the airfield, and shortened his lines along the beach in order to thicken them. He knew what was coming.

Colonel Ezaki believed that the main enemy effort would come at Seeadler Harbor, so he kept most of his forces where they were, but he sent orders to the 1st Battalion of the 229th Infantry Regiment, who was responsible for defending the Momote air field. "Tonight the battalion under Captain Baba will annihilate the enemy who have landed," he said. "This is not a delaying action. Be resolute to sacrifice your life for the Emperor and commit suicide in case capture is imminent ... We must carry out our mission and annihilate the enemy on the spot. I am highly indignant about the enemy's arrogant attitude. Remember to kill or capture all ranking officers for intelligence purposes."[352]

Colonel Ezaki had already established himself as a dangerous foe by hiding his men so effectively, but he had also hamstrung himself with his belief the main effort would come at Seeadler, requiring him to keep most of his units where they were. So he could only attack with Captain Baba's battalion. That first night, February 29, small numbers of Japanese attempted to infiltrate the American lines and were beaten back. Same thing the following evening and night, during which Captain Baba was killed. On March 2, Chase got some reinforcements in the form of about 1,500 combat troops, mostly from the 1st Squadron of the 5th Cavalry Regiment; and 534 naval construction men, mostly from 40th Naval Construction Battalion. Coincidentally, that same day, Chase reoccupied the airfield and began reinforcing it. Now land mines were laid, automatic weapons positions were prepared, protected by dugouts at their flanks and rear, and artillery was positioned to sweep the front.[353]

It would be needed, because the Japanese attacks continued. Spurred on by orders from General Inamura, Colonel Ezaki finally prepared his all-out attack. And he had a secret weapon up his sleeve. The night of March 3–4 the 1st Mixed Independent Battalion made its big attack on the now-reinforced American lines at the north end of the perimeter. Not only did the Imperial Army troops use their traditional banzai charges, but an hour before daylight, one column of Japanese charged while singing "Deep in the Heart of Texas." How the cavalry troopers were able to resist the nightmare of such horrific tactics is unknown, but resist it they did. A "Deep in the Heart of Texas" charge was not as effective as a banzai charge. They were killed by antipersonnel mines and crossfire from machine guns and small arms fire.[354]

So began the month-long slog to clear the Admiralties, but mostly Los Negros and Manus, of Japanese. That was a long time to capture an abandoned set of islands. But capture them the Americans did. The Greater East Asia Co-prosperity Sphere had gotten a little smaller.

But if the Japanese did not like that landing, well, there were others.

On March 20, 1944, some 4,000 US Marines, mostly from the 4th Marine Regiment of the 3rd Marine Division, occupied Emirau Island. Well, if the Japanese did not like that landing, they couldn't do much about it, because there were no Japanese on Emirau. Not that they did not respond: the Japanese commander in Kavieng murdered all his European prisoners. The Allies would still build their air base.

That was it. Rabaul was now surrounded.

During the Java Sea Campaign, the Japanese had been very careful in their approach to the Netherlands East Indies and especially Java. They approached from the north and from the flanks. Malaya to the west, Celebes to the east. They brought Java into bomber range with the airfield at Kendari II. They shattered the western flank of Java by taking Singapore, then Palembang and its air bases. They shattered the eastern flank by taking Bali, with an air base that allowed Japanese air power to reach into the Indian Ocean south of Java. Java was cut off. Finished. Before a single Japanese soldier set foot on it. Before General Inamura had set foot on it.

Now the situation was reversed. From the southeast, Admiral Halsey had moved up the Solomon Islands and built a beachhead on Bougainville that they turned into an air base and cut off all the Japanese troops on that island. General MacArthur had taken Cape Gloucester on New Britain itself. He had just taken the Admiralties, putting him behind the barrier of the Bismarck Islands. Halsey had moved right up to Rabaul by taking the Green Islands, then be broke the Bismarcks Barrier himself by taking Emirau.

Rabaul was surrounded. Cut off. Just like Java had been.

All that was left for the Allies was to take Rabaul. And Kavieng, but mostly Rabaul. Admiral Kusaka and General Inamura had been determined that this would not be a repeat of Java. They had prepared for this. Stockpiled supplies. Dug tunnels and bunkers deep into the surrounding hills, albeit not so deep that they would run into the magma beneath the Rabaul caldera.

The Japanese were ready. The Allies were in for a big surprise.

Because they were going to try to take Rabaul.

Right?

CHAPTER 10

ANTICLIMAX

Meetings. The practical alternative to work. So the meme goes. And, to be sure, that description is usually pretty accurate.

But there is an exception to the meme. That is the meeting in which important decisions must be made.

That is how the Pacific War began. On multiple fronts. A few hours into the Japanese invasion of Malaya at Kota Bharu, the commander of the British Eastern Fleet, Admiral Sir Thomas Phillips, called a meeting deep in the bowels of the Singapore Naval Base to determine what to do – more accurately, get political backing to do what he had already decided to do – with the battleship *Prince of Wales* and the battlecruiser *Repulse* in response to the Japanese landings. This meeting was called in part because the Admiralty was still meeting in London to determine what to do with the *Prince of Wales* and *Repulse* and thus had sent no instructions – they had adjourned the meeting and gone to bed while the *Prince of Wales* and *Repulse* were on their ill-fated sortie.

About two weeks after Pearl Harbor as Japan swept across Southeast Asia and the Pacific, President Roosevelt and Prime Minister Churchill were having their first secret conference, code-named "Arcadia." It was at Arcadia that it was decided that because the Empire of Japan had attacked the United States, the United States would attack Nazi Germany.

Thus, the "Europe First" policy was firmly established by the US and Britain. Nevertheless, the Pacific was not to be neglected, and the Allies were not to remain passive in defense of this theater. It was at Arcadia where the ill-fated organization known as ABDACOM (American-British-Dutch-Australian Command) was formed to pool Allied resources in the defense of Malaya and the Netherlands East Indies in what has been called the Java Sea Campaign.

Also in attendance at the Arcadia meeting was Admiral Ernest J. King, the commander-in-chief of the US Fleet and, a short time later, also the chief of naval operations. King's presence might be considered something of an accomplishment since it would later be revealed that he was hated by such a distinguished cast of characters as

Secretary of War Henry Stimson; General Dwight Eisenhower; British Prime Minister Winston Churchill; Chief of the Imperial General Staff Field Marshal Sir Alan Brooke; and Royal Navy Admiral Sir Andrew Cunningham.[1] Official US Navy historian Samuel Eliot Morison described King as "a hard man with little sense of humor" who had made few friends ascending the ranks, but had done enough to be noticed by the right people.[2] A trained aviator, the 63-year-old King was brilliant, determined – and arrogant. Historian William Tuohy would say King "believed he could do any job in the US Navy better than anyone else," and would run the Navy "with an iron fist and no velvet glove."[3]

Although he may have been dark and humorless, Admiral King had a can-do philosophy. He approached the Pacific War with the idea of "Make the best of what you have":

> There must be no tendency to excuse incomplete readiness for war on the premise of future acquisition of trained personnel or modernized material ... personnel shall be trained and rendered competent ... existing material shall be maintained and utilized at its maximum effectiveness at all times.[4]

It was from Arcadia that, on December 31, 1941, Admiral King issued his first substantive orders, in the stilted language of the wireless telegraph, to the new commander-in-chief of the Pacific Fleet, Admiral Chester Nimitz:

> CONSIDER TASKS ASSIGNED YOU SUMMARIZE[D] INTO TWO PRIMARY TASKS[.] IN ORDER OF PRIORITY FIRST COVERING AND HOLDING LINE HAWAII[-]MIDWAY AND MAINTAINING ITS COMMUNICATIONS WITH WEST COAST[.] SECOND AND ONLY IN SMALL DEGREE LESS IMPORTANT MAINTENANCE OF COMMUNICATION WEST COAST AUSTRALIA CHIEFLY BY COVERING SECURING AND HOLDING LINE HAWAII[-]SAMOA WHICH SHOULD BE EXTENDED TO INCLUDE FIJI AT EARLIEST PRACTICABLE DATE[.][5]

That wasn't all. Even though the agreement out of Arcadia was very clearly "Europe First" for resources and efforts, Admiral King got in a few helpful lines about the war against Japan. The carefully worded and intentionally vague declaration said efforts in the Pacific would involve "[m]aintaining only such positions in the [Pacific] theatre as will safeguard vital interests and deny to Japan access to raw materials vital to her continuous war effort while we are concentrating on the defeat of Germany."[6] King managed to slip in some critical language in a small section called "THE SAFEGUARDING OF VITAL INTERESTS IN THE EASTERN THEATRE."

> 18. The security of Australia, New Zealand, and India must be maintained, and the Chinese war effort supported. Secondly, points of vantage from which an offensive against Japan can eventually be developed must be secured.

This particular line was added at Admiral King's insistence.[7]

Our immediate object must therefore be to hold:

a. Hawaii and Alaska.
b. Singapore, the East Indies Barrier, and the Philippines.
c. Rangoon and the route to China.
d. The Maritime Provinces of Russia.

The minimum forces required to hold the above will have to be a matter of mutual discussion.

Ay, there's the rub. And that would require more of those meetings, the practical alternative to work.

The Arcadia declaration also identified "main sea routes which must be secured," including "the Pacific routes from United States and the Panama Canal to Alaska, Hawaii, Australia, and the Far East." Securing those routes required holding and capturing "essential sea bases," which included Hawaii and Samoa. There were also "main air routes which must be secured," which included "the U.S. to Australia via Hawaii, Christmas Island, Canton, Palmyra, Samoa, Fiji, [and] New Caledonia." This required securing "essential air bases," including Hawaii, Christmas Island, Palmyra, Canton, Samoa, Fiji, New Caledonia, and Townsville.[8]

Allied action in the Pacific seemed to be severely limited by this document. But Admiral King had a lawyer's eye. For instance, Australia was some 7,000 miles from San Francisco. As Vice Admiral George Dyer pointed out in discussing King's seemingly limited options:

A straight line on a Mercator chart from San Francisco in California to Townsville [...] passes just south of the island of Hawaii and just south of Guadalcanal Island in the Solomons. In Admiral King's belief, the Japanese should not be permitted to impinge on this line, if the line of communications from Hawaii to Australia through Samoa, Fiji, and the New Hebrides was to be secure.[9]

Guadalcanal would come up again, to put it mildly.

Admiral King looked for ways to wedge his allowances under the Arcadia declaration ever wider to position US forces in the Pacific for not just defense but offensive operations as well. Under pre-existing defense plans, he was able to send small garrisons to Palmyra and American Samoa, while under the Arcadia declaration, the US Army garrisoned Canton and Christmas Islands. New Caledonia was specifically listed in the Arcadia declaration, but neither the Free French nor the Australians had the manpower to effectively garrison it, so King forced the Army to scrape up some 17,000 troops, including the Army Air Force's 67th Pursuit Squadron, and sent them to Nouméa.

At a March 2, 1942 meeting of the newly formed Joint Chiefs of Staff, Admiral King was the man with a plan, which was more than anyone else had at that time. King handed out a memorandum detailing his proposal, which summarized his proposal with nine words: "Hold Hawaii; Support Australasia; Drive northwestward from New Hebrides."[10] "The general scheme or concept of operations is not only to protect the lines of communication with Australia," he wrote, "but in so doing to set up 'strong points' from which a step-by-step general advance can be made through the New Hebrides, Solomons, and Bismarck Archipelago."[11] For this proposal, King said he needed two, maybe three, Army divisions and maybe eight groups of aircraft. By this time, Singapore had fallen only a few weeks earlier; defeat in the Battle of the Java Sea had spelled the end of the Allies in the Netherlands East Indies. President Roosevelt needed something, anything, on which to hang some hope. Admiral King's proposal did just that. Roosevelt gave his tacit approval.[12]

However, by this time the Joint Chiefs could not even agree if keeping the lines of communication open to Australia was necessary, as had been contemplated in the Arcadia declaration. On February 28, 1942, General Eisenhower told General Marshall:

> The United States' interest in maintaining contact with Australia and in preventing further Japanese expansion to the Southeastward is apparent … but … they are not immediately vital to the successful outcome of the war. The problem is one of determining what we can spare for the effort in that region, without seriously impairing performance of our mandatory tasks.[13]

This comment was not to Eisenhower's credit, and probably reflected an institutional myopia on the part of the US Army that would reveal itself again and again. The result was that Admiral King would often end up going on his own, leveraging the lawyerly language he had put in the Arcadia declaration to reinforce and begin to attack in the Pacific – over the explicit objections of General Marshall and especially General Arnold. Touring the Pacific, General Arnold later said, "it was impossible not to get the impression that the Navy was determined to carry on the campaign in that theater, and determined to do it with as little help from the Army as possible."[14] It was a dishonest deflection of the real issue, which was the opposition by the Army and especially Arnold to provide additional units to the Pacific or to agree to offensive action.

But that opposition strangely softened when General Douglas MacArthur was rescued from the fall of the Philippines in March 1942. When the Japanese first attacked the Philippines on December 8, 1941, MacArthur, already a national hero, "demonstrated his unique leadership style: when he was good, he was very, very good[;] when he was bad, he was horrid."[15] MacArthur's performance in the Philippines in 1941–42 was much closer to the "horrid" side of that limited spectrum.

Nevertheless, MacArthur was still a national hero, with a formidable public relations machine that covered up much of his horrid performance – and made him a domestic political threat to Roosevelt. Keeping him on the sidelines was out of the question. Now the Army was interested in reinforcing the Pacific – for an offensive led by Douglas MacArthur. Which brought up the question of whether the Pacific needed to be like Europe under General Eisenhower and have one theater commander. Douglas MacArthur was the obvious choice. To the Army, at any rate.

To the Navy leadership, MacArthur was the one who had constantly berated the Asiatic Fleet and its commander Admiral Hart as not being worthy of the name; allowed the Japanese to completely destroy their main Far East base at Cavite; then, to top it off, blamed the fleet for the collapsing situation in the Philippines. Finding MacArthur's performance in the Philippines horrid and believing MacArthur knew nothing about sea power – he didn't – Admiral King, with the full backing of the Navy leadership, vowed that MacArthur would never have operational command of the Pacific Fleet.[16]

"[General Marshall's] basic trouble," Admiral King later said, "was that like all Army officers he knew nothing about sea power and very little about air power."[17] This was the absolute truth. The biggest example was the insistence of the Army Air Force to always bomb from high altitude (as in, 20,000 feet altitude) regardless of whether the target was a big stationary German munitions plant or a small ship moving at sea. The latter reduced Army Air Force bombing of targets at sea to almost complete ineffectiveness until Pappy Gunn – over the objections of the Army Air Force brass except for General Kenney – developed the B-25 gunship and experimented with low-level bombing, with the proof being the so-called "Battle of the Bismarck Sea."

Admiral King told General Marshall that he had agreed to have an Army general in command of the European theater – "unity of command" – because it would be fought primarily by the Army. The Pacific was being fought primarily by the Navy and Marine Corps; hence it made more sense to have a Navy admiral in charge. The offensive "must be conducted under the direction of [the Commander-in-Chief of the Pacific Fleet] and cannot be conducted in any other way."[18] Europe was a land war, so put the Army in charge. The Pacific was a sea war, so put the Navy in charge. But in the face of this undeniable logic the Army still believed that Douglas MacArthur should be in charge of the Pacific. The Army believed MacArthur bore no responsibility for the disaster in the Philippines – that public relations machine at work – and would not agree to command by a Navy admiral.

Moreover, it was that same institutional arrogance and myopia that was behind the relentless drive to put Douglas MacArthur in that role of Pacific supreme commander. MacArthur's performance in the 1941–42 Philippines Campaign was so wracked with ineptitude, arrogance, and willful violation of orders that investigation and possible court martial were warranted. That such steps were impossible due to MacArthur's reputation is perhaps understandable, but that does not excuse the refusal by Generals Marshall and Arnold to acknowledge even privately that MacArthur's performance in the Philippines was perhaps below his usual standards, or to understand why the US Navy, slandered, abused, and blamed by MacArthur for the loss of the Philippines, did not want to serve under him or cater to his inability to accept being under anyone else's command. The possibility that Generals Marshall and Arnold would be able to ram a unified Pacific command under MacArthur down the Navy's throat hung over everything Admiral Nimitz and the Pacific Fleet did.

To break the impasse, on March 9, the Joint Chiefs created two command areas of the Pacific theater. One, a "Southwest Pacific Command," encompassed the Philippines, the Netherlands East Indies, Australia, the Solomon Islands, and adjoining ocean areas. Most of these were not currently under Allied control. It would be up to its commander, General MacArthur, to retake them. As part of the command, MacArthur even got his own little navy to abuse just as he had Admiral Hart and the Asiatic Fleet. And he did. At his new headquarters in Melbourne, MacArthur told a reporter, "[T]he best navy in the world is the Japanese navy. A first-class navy. Then comes the British navy. The US Navy is a fourth-class navy, not even as good as the Italian navy."[19] And to think the US Navy did not want to work under him.

Admiral Nimitz got the rest as part of a "Pacific Ocean Area," and, like General MacArthur, he reported to his respective service chief on the Joint Chiefs of Staff, who would be conducting this Pacific War by committee. Nimitz's Pacific Ocean Area was further divided into three regions: North, Central, and South. Nimitz could directly command the first two, but the new South Pacific Command for the area south of the equator would have to be handed off to a subordinate, with Vice Admiral Robert L. Ghormley eventually selected.

During this period of planning, the basic plan for the Pacific War was formally birthed on April 16, 1942, when Admiral King's assistant chief of staff for planning, Rear Admiral Richmond Kelly Turner, presented him with the cleverly named "Pacific Ocean Campaign Plan." It consisted of four phases. Phase One was the buildup of forces and bases in the South Pacific to secure the area and position for an offensive against the Japanese. Phase Two was an offensive up through the Solomons and New Guinea to seize the Bismarck and Admiralty Islands. Phase Three would extend that offensive to the central Pacific, such as the Marshall and especially the Caroline Islands. Phase Four would involve a drive into the Philippines or the Netherlands East Indies, "whichever offers the more promising and enduring results."[20] To make this plan work, earlier Admiral Turner had also recommended the establishment of an amphibious assault force in the South Pacific. King agreed and ordered Admiral Nimitz to create it and put Turner in charge of it. Turner, very uncharacteristically, admitted that he knew little of the subject. King responded, "Kelly, you will learn."[21] It was a new war, with new weapons, new tactics, and new ways of thinking. How this all interacted, no one knew. They would have to learn on the fly, something that American officers would later call "makee learnee."[22]

Admiral King started to put this plan into motion, both materially and within the bureaucracy of the War Department, meaning he had to fight with Generals Marshall, Arnold, and MacArthur. During more of those meetings in the last two days of June, Marshall and King hammered out the "Joint Directive for Offensive Operations in the

Southwest Pacific Area Agreed on by the United States Chiefs of Staff" that consisted of three phases. Phase One, already given its own code name of "Watchtower," would ultimately involve the seizure of Guadalcanal and Tulagi. This task would be completed by the Pacific Fleet. Phase Two would be the capture of Lae, Salamaua, the rest of the northeast coast of New Guinea, and the central Solomons. Phase Three would involve the reduction and capture of Rabaul. Phases Two and Three would be under the command of General MacArthur. This three-part plan was given the cheerful name of "Pestilence."

Admiral Turner assembled the force that landed General Vandegrift and the 1st Marine Division on Guadalcanal and Tulagi as part of *Watchtower*. But while Turner and Vandegrift were all about doing, in particular this whole Guadalcanal thing, Admiral Ghormley was all about meetings. He later claimed he was too busy to visit Guadalcanal, despite Admiral Nimitz having ordered him to do so, to see the conditions there. In fact, Ghormley was too busy to visit Nouméa, which is saying something because his flagship, the converted cargo ship and submarine tender and now command ship *Argonne*, was in Nouméa's harbor. While Admiral Fletcher had come into the Guadalcanal Campaign believing it would fail, Ghormley came in believing it had already failed, and starved General Vandegrift and the Marines of reinforcements and supplies so he could hoard them in rear areas he believed would be threatened. When Ghormley responded to the bombardment of Henderson Field by the *Kongo* and *Haruna* with panic, Admiral Nimitz sacked him and replaced him with Halsey. And the foundering campaign started turning for the better.

Ultimately, the Guadalcanal Campaign was successfully concluded, and at around the same time General MacArthur captured Buna, Gona, and Sanananda. And then MacArthur, thanks to General Kenney and Pappy Gunn, massacred that big Japanese convoy in the "Battle of the Bismarck Sea," which basically cut the Japanese 18th Army off from any significant troop reinforcements. That left MacArthur time to devote to his next project. On February 12, he completed development of a strategic framework he called "Elkton."

Elkton was basically a reworking of Phases Two and Three of *Pestilence*. Phase Two would involve capture of the central and upper Solomons concurrent with movements along the north coast of New Guinea to capture both Lae and Madang. Both advances would converge in the climactic Phase Three: the capture of Rabaul. Completion of these objectives would be in 1943 in order for MacArthur to proceed with his real objective: a return to the Philippines, which he called Operation *Reno*.

General MacArthur wanted to advance against Rabaul with both axes in one continuous movement. In order to do so, MacArthur wanted to assemble all the necessary forces beforehand. That would be a tall order, because he had nowhere near the forces that he believed he needed. On March 12, Admiral King convened a set of meetings with representatives of General MacArthur, Admiral Nimitz, and Admiral Halsey that would become known as the Pacific Military Conference. Army historian John Miller, Jr would describe this conference as "an excellent example of the detailed and undramatic, but absolutely essential, spadework that had to precede major decisions affecting the course of the war in the Pacific."[23] And indeed they did. The acrimony, the arrogance, the suspicion that overshadowed earlier discussions was mostly gone, perhaps the reality of warfare having pushed everyone onto the same side.

General Sutherland, MacArthur's chief of staff, presented a revised *Elkton* plan. MacArthur had prepared it on the assumption that he would control both the Southwest and South Pacific forces for Phases Two and Three of *Pestilence*. That was the original plan, and Admiral Halsey, according to MacArthur, had already assented to *Elkton*.

Between 79,000 and 94,000 Japanese troops were thought to be stationed in the New Guinea-Bismarck Archipelago-Solomons area. Enemy air strength was estimated at 383 land-based planes, while four battleships, two aircraft carriers, 14 cruisers, 11 seaplane tenders, about 40 destroyers, numerous auxiliaries, and about 50 merchant ships of 3,000 tons or over were on hand for operations. It was expected that the Japanese, if attacked, could be immediately reinforced by 10,000 to 12,000 troops and about 250 planes as well as major portions of the Combined Fleet from the Netherlands Indies, Japanese home waters, and the Philippine Islands. In six months, 615 more aircraft could be committed, and ten or 15 divisions might be dispatched if shipping was available.

The execution of Phases Two and Three would require mutually supporting, coordinated advances along two lines: one, by Southwest Pacific forces in the west, from New Guinea to New Britain; the other, by South Pacific forces in the east, through the Solomons. The timing of these missions was not rigidly fixed, nor was there an estimate of the time required to carry them out. The operations were intended to inflict losses on the Japanese, to deny the target areas to the enemy, to contain Japanese forces in the Pacific by retaining the initiative, and to prepare for the ultimate seizure of the Bismarck Archipelago. The operations were to be under MacArthur's command. The advances in the Solomons were to be under the direct command of Halsey, who would operate under MacArthur's "strategic direction." Except for those units assigned by the Joint Chiefs of Staff to task forces engaged in these campaigns, all elements of the Pacific Ocean Areas would remain under Nimitz.

In essence, however, General MacArthur's direction over the Solomons Campaign would be nominal. He had his hands full in New Guinea, and he recognized that reality. To discuss their plans, Admiral Halsey requested an appointment with General MacArthur in Brisbane. Many waited for the fireworks to start. These were two strong-willed personalities used to getting their way.

But those looking for a spectacular display of verbal combat were to be disappointed. In Admiral Halsey's words:

Five minutes after I reported, I felt as if we were lifelong friends. I have seldom seen a man who makes a quicker, stronger, more favorable impression. He was then sixty-three years old, but he could have passed as fifty. His hair was jet black; his eyes were clear; his carriage was erect. If he had been wearing civilian clothes, I still would have known at once that he was a soldier.

The respect that I conceived for him that afternoon grew steadily during the war and continues to grow as I watch his masterly administration of surrendered Japan. I can recall no flaw in our relationship. We had arguments, but they always ended pleasantly. Not once did he, my superior officer, ever force his decisions upon me. On the few occasions when I disagreed with him, I told him so, and we discussed the issue until one of us changed his mind. My mental picture poses him against the background of these discussions; he is pacing his office, almost wearing a groove between his large, bare desk and the portrait of George Washington that faced it; his corncob pipe is in his hand (I rarely saw him smoke it); and he is making his points in a diction I have never heard surpassed.[24]

The respect was mutual. As General MacArthur later wrote:

William Halsey was one of our great sailors. He was a graduate of the Naval Academy in the class of 1904. While I had never known him personally, I was familiar with him as the fullback of the Navy eleven in its contests with West Point. Blunt, outspoken, dynamic, he had already proven himself to be a battle commander of the highest order. A strong advocate of unity of command in the Pacific, there seemed always to be an undercurrent opposed to him in the Navy Department. He was of the same aggressive type as John Paul Jones, David Farragut, and George Dewey. His one thought was to close with the enemy and fight him to the death. The bugaboo of many sailors, the fear of losing ships, was completely alien to his conception of sea action. I liked him from the moment we met, and my respect and admiration increased with time. His loyalty was undeviating, and I placed the greatest confidence in his judgment. No name rates higher in the annals of our country's naval history.[25]

It was in this positive atmosphere that the name of the overall operation would be changed from *Elkton* to something that would be, well, a little more famous: *Cartwheel*. And it was in this positive atmosphere that *Cartwheel* began. The seizure of the Woodlark and Trobriand islands in *Chronicle*. The landings on the New Georgia islands in *Toenails*. The landings near Lae in *Postern*.

But things were going on behind the scenes, as there usually were. It was at the famous Casablanca Conference that the decision was made to advance through the Central Pacific. General MacArthur was not happy about it, and understandably so. *Cartwheel* had faithfully followed Phase Two of Admiral Turner's plan to prosecute the Pacific War. But the Joint Chiefs had decided to start the Central Pacific phase – Phase Three – before Phase Two was even completed. It does beg the question of why did the US Navy not pursue the Central Pacific route in the first place in lieu of the Solomon Islands and Papua New Guinea route. The obvious explanation was the Pacific Fleet's lack of aircraft carriers in 1942. Amphibious landings require air support, but without an adequate number of carriers, any such landings would depend on land-based air. The Allies had no air bases in the Central Pacific, but the Allies did have New Zealand, New Caledonia, and the New

Hebrides. That last one was where Espiritu Santo was located, and the Allies constructed an air base there. And while aircraft based at Espiritu Santo played only a limited role in the landings on Guadalcanal and Tulagi, they were able to support the Pacific Fleet carriers during and after *Watchtower*. There was no equivalent base in the Central Pacific and, with so few carriers available, Admiral Nimitz could not afford to risk them in an area with no other air support.

Now, more carriers were available. Many more carriers were available. Not only that, Japanese air power had been worn down by the war at Rabaul. So Admiral Nimitz could afford to risk them to strike at small, vulnerable islands too widely separated for mutual support. Island hopping. To be sure, Admiral King and the US Navy leadership preferred the Central Pacific route for the main effort because it was shorter than the South and Southwest Pacific route. It was also not riddled with pestilence like the Solomons and Papua New Guinea. The Central Pacific would allegedly require fewer ships, troops, and supplies. And success in the Central Pacific would cut off Japan from her overseas empire, including the South Pacific area. Destruction of the Japanese Combined Fleet in defense of the Central Pacific would be the icing on the proverbial cake. Twin drives, coordinated and timed for mutual support, would give Allied forces great strategic advantages in the Japanese never knowing where the next blow would fall.[26]

This did pose a problem of how to support, supply, and coordinate both operations. General MacArthur did not like the idea of giving up any of his combat power to the Central Pacific drive. MacArthur emphasized that losing too many of his units might negatively impact the ability to capture Rabaul. On June 22, Admiral Halsey protested at the proposed removal of the 2nd Marine Division and most of his ships to take part in the Central Pacific offensive. No one knows where the solution eventually came from, or who suggested it, or when. And no one knows where it went or bounced around in discussions before it ended up in the final orders to General MacArthur.

When President Roosevelt and Prime Minister Churchill met at the Quadrant conference in Québec City in August 1943, the Combined Chiefs met as well. Here was where the British and Americans duked it out (almost literally) over what resources should be sent to Europe and thus to the Pacific. Their solution was one that MacArthur had perhaps not anticipated: if taking assets from MacArthur to use in the Central Pacific impaired his ability to capture Rabaul, then he should not capture Rabaul. Instead, he should cut it off, neutralize it, and bypass it. The Combined Chiefs also agreed that after *Cartwheel* MacArthur and Halsey should neutralize New Guinea as far west as Wewak, and should capture Manus and Kavieng to use as naval bases for supporting additional advances westward, eventually reaching the Vogelkop Peninsula. The sop for MacArthur was that once these operations were concluded successfully, the Philippine Islands and specifically Mindanao would be open to him.[27]

General Marshall radioed General MacArthur with this news, but the formal written orders for same reached the Southwest Pacific commander only on September 17.[28] As historian John Miller described it:

From then on MacArthur did not raise the question of Rabaul with the Joint Chiefs; his radiograms dealt instead with broader questions relating to the Philippines and the relative importance of the Central and Southwest Pacific offensives. Although the evidence is not conclusive, the general course of events and certain opinions MacArthur gave during the planning for Bougainville seem to indicate that he knew of the decision to neutralize rather than capture Rabaul, or else had reached the same decision independently, some time before [the new orders] reached the Southwest Pacific.[29]

There is a lot that is mysterious about how this whole thing came about. After the war, even the United States Strategic Bombing Survey was a bit nebulous:

By July 1944 it was clear that Rabaul's position was irrevocably lost. *It was apparently decided, therefore, that an invasion of the base was unnecessary*; and the Allied offensive in the area bypassed Rabaul completely. [Emphasis added.] For the remainder of the war, however, a rigid aerial and naval blockade was enforced over New Britain and systematic bombing of Rabaul continued with the *two-fold purpose of maintaining its neutralization and weakening the will of its garrison.* [Emphasis in original.][30]

Certainly, Douglas MacArthur took credit for the idea. "My primary goal in 1943 was to cut off the major Japanese naval staging area, the menacing airfields, and the bulging supply bases at Rabaul," he later wrote. He went on:

To push back the Japanese perimeter of conquest by direct pressure against the mass of enemy-occupied islands would be a long and costly effort. My staff worried about Rabaul and other strongpoints. They were skeptical of the possibility of its capture unless the number of our troops and planes was increased tremendously, and predicted losses in men and matériel that would make those we had suffered in capturing Buna, or in holding Guadalcanal, seem minor. Replacements were trickling in slowly, providing only the minimum essentials with which to conduct immediate operations. At a staff meeting, one of them said, "General, I know your peculiar genius for slaughtering large masses of the enemy at little cost in the lives of your own men, but I just don't see how we can take these strongpoints with our limited forces." I thoroughly agreed with him, but said I did not intend to take them – I intended to envelop them, incapacitate them, apply the "hit 'em where they ain't – let 'em die on the vine" philosophy. I explained that this was the very opposite of what was termed "island-hopping," which is the gradual pushing back of the enemy by direct frontal pressure, with the consequent heavy casualties which would certainly be involved. There would be no need for storming the mass of islands held by the enemy. "Island-hopping," I said, "with extravagant losses and slow progress, is not my idea of how to end the war as soon and as cheaply as possible. New conditions and new weapons require new and imaginative methods for solution and application. Wars are never won in the past.

To successfully envelop the enemy called for the careful selection of key points as objectives and the choosing of the most opportune moment to strike. I accordingly applied my major efforts to the seizure of areas which were suitable for airfields and base development, but which were only lightly defended by the enemy. Thus, by daring forward strikes, by neutralizing and by-passing enemy centers of strength, and by the judicious use of my air forces to cover each movement, I intended to destroy Japanese power in New Guinea and adjacent islands, and to clear the way for a drive to the Philippines.[31]

To MacArthur, everything was about getting back to the Philippines.

MacArthur biographer William Manchester admits, "Exactly who first suggested the stratagem is unclear." Manchester traces the genesis of the idea to bypass Rabaul to March 1943 meetings in Washington with General Sutherland, General Kenney, and Brigadier General Stephen J. Chamberlin, MacArthur's operations officer.[32] Perhaps that was the first mention of bypassing Rabaul by itself, but the idea of bypassing Rabaul at all had been broached by Admiral King, who on November 30, 1942, suggested to Admiral Nimitz going around both the Solomons and Rabaul to take the Admiralties.[33] This at a time before MacArthur had even captured Buna, Gona, and Sanananda. Nimitz, understandably, found it to be an island too far. At least. Anyway, if Sutherland and company even mentioned it to MacArthur, he was unimpressed and did not mention it at all at this time. Later, when the Joint Chiefs ordered MacArthur to take Rabaul and Kavieng, he did not protest. When the Joint Chiefs in June even brought the idea of bypassing Rabaul, MacArthur objected, claiming he needed "an adequate forward naval base" at Rabaul to protect his right flank. Without it, he said, any westward drive along the north coast of New Guinea "would involve hazards rendering success doubtful."[34]

Finally, the Quadrant Declaration contained repeated statements, including "Annex 'II' Specific Operations Approved in The Pacific Theater 1943–44, Including the Development of the Air Route Into China," specifically Point 7 of "Operations in the New Guinea-Bismarcks-Admiralty Islands Subsequent to Cartwheel" to the effect that "Rabaul is to be neutralized rather than captured."[35]

None of this is to say General MacArthur did not independently come up with the idea of bypassing Rabaul. In all likelihood, he did. The catalyst was the brutal campaign to take Buna, Gona, and Sanananda, which was itself the result of another of MacArthur's mistakes. After the capture of Buna, the general rather (in)famously said, "The utmost care was taken for the conservation of our forces, with the result that probably no campaign in history against a thoroughly prepared and trained army produced such complete and decisive results with so low an expenditure of life and resources."[36] His troops, who were still concluding that campaign, were shocked and outraged. The cost in blood had been tremendous. And MacArthur knew it. After all, he had told General Robert Eichelberger, "I want you to take Buna, or not come back alive." Far from a one-off, he added, "And that goes for your chief of staff too."[37] Yup, the utmost care was taken for the conservation of forces to achieve the objective with such a low expenditure of life and resources.

General MacArthur may have privately chastened himself for the conduct of the Buna campaign and his mistakes, however, not that he'd admit those mistakes to anyone. He promised "No more Bunas." Indeed, MacArthur learned a lot from the campaign in Papua. As historian Alan Rems opined:

> Like a stereotypical World War I general seated far to the rear, he disparaged commanders and repeatedly ordered costly frontal attacks without full firsthand knowledge of battlefield conditions and regard for casualties. He would later avoid heavy enemy concentrations and protracted static fighting and would not initiate operations before establishing sound logistics. Also […] he gained an appreciation of the need for thorough troop training under realistic jungle conditions.[38]

Recall that MacArthur did not attack Lae and Salamaua directly. He outflanked both, compelling the Japanese to retreat from both.

With orders to bypass Rabaul and ultimately Kavieng, *Cartwheel* became one big outflanking operation, or, more accurately, multiple little operations to outflank Rabaul. The capture of the Treasury Islands in *Goodtime*. The landing at Torokina in *Cherryblossom*. Arawe and Cape Gloucester on New Britain and Saidor on New Guinea in the three-part *Dexterity*. Taking the Green Islands in *Squarepeg*. The Admiralties in *Brewer*.

The result was a noose tightened around Rabaul and Kavieng, with a minimum of casualties. The response from his men was more complicated than one might imagine. They belittled and denigrated General MacArthur, or, more accurately, the image of himself he had created. The bloody Buna campaign and MacArthur's comments immediately afterward were remembered. Even so, there were plenty of troops who wanted to fight, who wanted to take the fight to the great fortress of Rabaul that had been torturing them for almost two years, and who did not like going around it. MacArthur couldn't win. No general can. But, as Manchester explained it:

> [H]ad his bitter men understood the consequences of the General's strategy they would have taken a very different view. For every Allied serviceman killed, the General killed ten Japanese. Never in history, John Gunther wrote, had there been a commander so economical in the expenditure of his men's blood. In this respect certain comparisons with ETO campaigns are staggering. During the single Battle of Anzio, 72,306 GIs fell. In the Battle of Normandy, Eisenhower lost 28,366. Between MacArthur's arrival in Australia and his return to Philippine waters over two years later, his troops suffered just 27,684 casualties – and that includes Buna.[39]

Douglas MacArthur had learned his lesson. For now, anyway. Had the Japanese?

The beleaguered Japanese troops now cooped up inside the Rabaul caldera did get a reinforcement of sorts. The prime minister, General Hideki Tojo, paid Rabaul a visit, accompanied by Admiral Nagano Osami, chief of the naval general staff, and Admiral Shibata Yaichiro, the navy minister. What they talked about in meetings with Admiral Kusaka and General Inamura is not recorded. "Tojo presumably implored the two commanders to hold Rabaul at all cost," speculated South Pacific historian Bruce Gamble.[40] Yup, that'll fire up the troops.

But if there was any doubt as to just how isolated Rabaul truly was, that doubt was eliminated on February 21. On February 20, Convoy O-003 had left Simpson Harbor headed for Palau. The convoy consisted of the tug *Nagaura*, a veteran in these waters, the 1,106-ton gunboat *Kowa Maru*, and the 3,871-ton transport *Kokai Maru*, escorted by subchasers *Ch-37* and *-38*, and auxiliary subchaser *Cha-48*. What made this convoy especially important was the passenger manifest of the *Kowa* and *Kokai Maru*s: the ground echelon of the 751 Air Group. Combined Fleet knew these were 400 experienced aviation maintenance personnel that Japan badly needed right now.[41]

Somone else may have known about them as well. By noon on February 21, they were west of New Hanover, using overcast skies and drizzle to their advantage. Or not. B-25 gunships of the 500th and 501st Bombardment Squadrons (seven from the former, as one had to abort, and eight from the latter) of the 345th Bombardment Group found them anyway, though it seems elements of the 38th Bombardment Group, who were also supposed to be part of the attack, could not. No matter. The *Kokai Maru* was hit by multiple bombs and left "listing and burning fiercely." The *Kowa Maru* was left in a similar state. Neither would survive the afternoon, the *Kokai Maru* taking 19 crew and seven passengers with her and the *Kowa Maru* 22 crew. The auxiliary subchaser *Cha-48* was also sunk and the *Ch-38* suffered heavy damage. The Japanese put up a fight, however, damaging eight of the B-25s, one so badly that it ultimately had to ditch off Finschhafen, its crew rescued. The *Nagaura* made some repairs to the *Ch-38* and picked up as many of the valuable aviation personnel as she could, then everyone headed toward Truk as fast as they could.[42]

But not fast enough. Captain Burke and the Little Beavers of Destroyer Squadron 23 – this time with command ship *Charles Ausburne* leading the *Dyson, Stanly, Conway*, and *Spence* – were on an antishipping sweep around Kavieng. Midmorning on February 22, they found the *Nagaura*, apparently alone some 160 miles northwest of Kavieng, and sank her with gunfire. About 100 survivors were spotted in the water. Maybe 73 were rescued, but the rest refused. The *Ch-37* and *Ch-38* scampered their way to Truk, while Burke's ships went on to sink the minelayer *Natsushima*. So ended Convoy O-003, which now had the distinction of being the last convoy to leave Rabaul.[43]

Rabaul was now truly isolated. And alone.

As the noose tightened on Rabaul, as the Allied troops moved around and got closer, desperation set in among General Inamura and his 8th Area Army staff. The invasion was coming, they knew. Who still anticipated an invasion? After the withdrawal of the Imperial Navy's warships and aircraft, Imamura and the army pledged to resist alone. "All the troops," he added later, "made up their minds to fight to the end."[44] Well, of course they did. That's what the Japanese did. That was Bushido. But what would the end be?

At the beginning of March, a senior member of Inamura's staff Major General Kimihira Masatake attended a conference with personnel from the 38th Division personnel regarding the defense of the Rabaul caldera. "It is evident," Kimihira concluded, "that it will be extremely difficult to hold Rabaul." Similar meetings in which little was heard but a discouraging word were held at practically every headquarters.[45]

It would get worse. Much worse. AirSols and the 13th Air Force had settled on the complete destruction of Rabaul, far worse than anything Tavurvur, Vulcan, or Tavurvur and Vulcan together had done, could do, or would do. As Admiral Halsey described it, "The town was divided into 14 target areas, each further subdivided into two or three parts. One by one they were rubbed out."[46] Starting on February 28, constant air attacks systematically destroyed every manmade structure standing in Rabaul. By the middle of March, two thirds of Rabaul was rubble. On April 20 – Hitler's birthday – it was announced that Rabaul was 90 percent destroyed.[47]

Not to worry, though. The Japanese had prepared for this. The soil of the Rabaul caldera was volcanic, and thus soft. Perfect for digging tunnels, as in, the 300 miles of tunnels and storage caves the Japanese dug between late 1943 and early 1945. Barracks, headquarters, and hospitals were dug out, reinforced against cave-ins, and finished for habitability, including electricity. So the Japanese made a veritable Moria, always keeping lookout for the Balrog in the form of the magma ever present under the Rabaul caldera. Any movement above ground drew an air attack, but they could move below ground. They had all the supplies they needed. They were safe.[48] Let those decadent American, Australian, and New Zealand troops come *now*.

Except …

Day after day went by, the Allied air attacks continued. The Japanese lookout posts gripped their rifles tighter, waiting for those dastardly Americans and Australians to emerge from the jungle to begin the final battle for Rabaul. And they waited …

And waited … And waited …

The senior intelligence officer of the 8th Area Army, Colonel Juio Matsuichi, later explained it:

This was the type of strategy we hated most. The Americans, with minimum losses, attacked and seized a relatively weak area, constructed airfields and then proceeded to cut the supply lines to troops in that area. Without engaging in a large-scale operation, our strongpoints were gradually starved out. The Japanese Army preferred direct assault, after the German fashion, but the Americans flowed into our weaker points and submerged us, just as water seeks the weakest entry to sink a ship. We respected this type of strategy for its brilliance because it gained the most while losing the least.[49]

They respected it, but, oh, yes, they hated it. MacArthur biographer William Manchester described the plight of the Japanese trapped in the Rabaul caldera so eloquently: All they wanted was an opportunity to sell their lives dearly before they were killed or eviscerated themselves in honorable seppuku …

> Their officers' war diaries leave the impression that they felt themselves the victims of a monstrous injustice. Here they were, commanding an army larger than Napoleon's at Waterloo or Lee's at Gettysburg – or Wellington's or Meade's, for that matter – which was spoiling for a fight. Their sappers had thrown up ramparts, revetments, parapets, barbicans, and ravelins. Hull-down tanks were in position. Mines had been laid, Hotchkiss-type guns sited, Nambus cunningly camouflaged. Mortarmen had calculated precise ranges. Crack troops, designated to launch counterattacks, lurked in huge bunkers behind concertinas of barbwire. And there they remained, in an agony of frustration, for the rest of the war. Their loss of face was incalculable, and when they finally received Hirohito's imperial rescript, ordering them to surrender, many of them, unable to bear the humiliation, faded into New Britain's rain forests to live out the rest of their wretched days as tropical animals. The Japanese equivalent of "It never rains but it pours" is "When crying, stung by bee." Never in the empire's long martial history – Dai Nippon hadn't lost a war since 1598 – had so many warriors been tormented by such a hive.
>
> This phenomenon was not confined to Rabaul, but Rabaul is the most dramatic illustration of what happened to the enemy legions MacArthur bypassed.[50]

There would be no forgiving for a war they started, a war they had conducted so brutally, mindlessly so. Not when their victims knew the truth. That favor would not be granted.

The Japanese in the Rabaul caldera would not, staring down a bullet, make their final stand.

The Japanese would not be shot down in a blaze of glory, though many of the prisoners of war they still held would die in the infamous Tunnel Hill Massacre.

The Japanese would not go out in a blaze of glory, but in a whimper. Quietly surrendering in 1945.

NOTES

Prologue

1 For a full critique of Ghormley's actions, see the previous three titles by this author on the Guadalcanal-Solomons campaign: *Morning Star, Midnight Sun; Blazing Star, Setting Sun;* and *Dark Waters, Starry* Skies, all published by Osprey Publishing.

2 The political entity called "The Solomon Islands" contains islands, such as the Santa Cruz, that are not part of the geographic entity called "The Solomon Islands" and excludes islands such as Bougainville that are part of the Solomon Islands. The border between the Solomon Islands political entity and the Bougainville autonomous region of Papua New Guinea runs between the Shortland Islands and Bougainville.

3 John Miller, *Cartwheel: The Reduction of Rabaul*, Office of the Chief of Military History, Dept. of the Army, 1959, 234; Major John N. Rentz, *Bougainville and the Northern Solomons* (Washington, DC: Historical Branch, Headquarters, US Marine Corps, 1946), 148. Admiral Halsey called Empress Augusta Bay "Emperor Augustus Bay."

4 Miller, *Cartwheel*, 234; "Empress Augusta Bay," *Pacific Wrecks* (www.pacificwrecks.com); Rentz, *Bougainville*, 151.

5 Alan Rems, *South Pacific Cauldron: World War II's Great Forgotten Battlegrounds* (Annapolis: Naval Institute Press, 2014), 2291–92.

6 Robert Sherrod, *History of Marine Corps Aviation in World War II* (Washington, DC: Combat Forces Press, 1952), 171.

7 Or Hyakutake Haruyoshi. Or Hyakutake Seikichi.

8 Miller, *Cartwheel*, 235.

Chapter 1

1 Or Dionysius I. Or Dionysius II. Or Dionysius the Elder. Or Dionysius the Younger.

2 "Dionysius," *Encyclopædia Britannica. Vol. 8*, ed. Hugh Chisholm, 11th edn (Cambridge: Cambridge University Press, 1911), 284.

3 *Ro-108* TROM, *USS Henley* (391) Loss of Ship in New Guinea Area on 3 October 1943, Report of circumstances, 1–2.

4 Ikuhiko Hata, Yasuho Izawa, and Christopher Shores, *Japanese Naval Air Force Units and Their Aces, 1931–1945* (London: Grub Street, 2002), 1569.

5 Mark Lardas, *Rabaul 1943–44: Reducing Japan's Great Island Fortress* (Oxford: Osprey, 2018), 828; Bruce Gamble, *Target: Rabaul: The Allied Siege of Japan's Most Infamous Stronghold, March 1943–August 1945* (Minneapolis, MN: Zenith Press, 2013), 136–37.

6 Gamble, *Target: Rabaul*, 136–37.

7 Gamble, *Target: Rabaul*, 136–38.

8 Gamble, *Target: Rabaul*, 138.

9 Gamble, *Target: Rabaul*, 136–37.

10   Gamble, *Target: Rabaul*, 136–37.

11   Gamble, *Target: Rabaul*, 139; Japanese Monograph No. 140, *Outline of Southeast Area Naval Air Operations, Part IV, Jul.–Nov. 1943* (US Armed Forces Far East, History Division), 41 (hereinafter "Monograph 140").

12   Lex McAulay, *Into The Dragon's Jaws – The US 5th Air Force at Rabaul October–November 1943* (Maryborough, Queensland: Banner Books, 2012), 1346–64; Hata, Izawa, and Shores, *Japanese Naval Air Force*, 6057–64; Lawrence J. Hickey, *Warpath Across the Pacific: The Illustrated History of the 345th Bombardment Group During World War II* (Boulder, CO: International Historical Research Associates, 2008), 54–55.

13   Gamble, *Target: Rabaul*, 140; Hata, Izawa, and Shores, *Japanese Naval Air Force*, 133; Monograph 140, 41. The time given for the 253 Air Group's scramble is 8:25am and the 204's is 8:35am, but that's presumably Japan Standard Time, which the Japanese usually used, which is one hour behind Rabaul. Otherwise, they would have been in the air before the air strike arrived, and all sources agree the Japanese were taken completely by surprise.

14   Gamble, *Target: Rabaul*, 140; Hickey, *Warpath*, 56–58. Hickey says Kawato briefly considered ramming the B-25 but instead ducked under it. Hata, Izawa, and Shores (*Japanese Naval Air Force*, 6064) have Kawato ducking under the B-25 to avoid P-38s and either rammed or collided with it, but says it took place on November 2, calling it "[h]is first ramming attack."

15   Gamble, *Target: Rabaul*, 136, 141; Jim Turner, "October 12, 1943 Big Raid on Rabual" [sic] *Beaufighter – 30 Squadron RAAF* (https://beaufighter30squadronraaf.com.au). Back at base, the pilot who fired at the Beaufighters, Captain Martin Radnik, was reprimanded by Colonel Hall, but over drinks the Australians forgave him and said, "it was a bloody good show, mate." McAuley, *Dragon's Jaws*, 1761–69. Jay A. Stout (*Air Apaches: The True Story of the 345th Bomb Group and Its Low, Fast, and Deadly Missions in World War II* (Guilford, CN: Stackpole Books, 2019), 1199) says the squadrons were "unnamed but probably from the 345th (Bombardment Group)."

16   Gamble, *Target: Rabaul*, 141; McAulay, *Dragon's Jaws*, 1390, 1461; George Odgers, *Australia in the War of 1939–1945: Series Three (Air) Volume II – Air War Against Japan, 1943–1945* (Canberra: Australian War Memorial, 1968), 91–92; Michael Claringbould, *Pacific Adversaries Three: Imperial Japanese Navy vs The Allies, New Guinea & the Solomons 1942–1944* (Kent Town, Australia: Avonmore Books, 2020), 85–86; Jim Turner, "October 1943 30 Squadron Daily Combat Mission Reports Photos and Eyewitness Accounts," *Beaufighter – 30 Squadron RAAF* (https://beaufighter30squadronraaf.com.au); Jim Turner, "30 Squadron Aircrew 1942–1945," *Beaufighter – 30 Squadron RAAF* (https://beaufighter30squadronraaf.com.au); Turner, "October 12, 1943 Big Raid on Rabual"; Richard L. Dunn, "Shootout at Rabaul," *Air Power History*, Vol. 59, No. 3 (Fall 2012), 14–27, 19. The narrative presented here is an amalgamation of these sources. Curiously, only Richard Dunn in his 2012 article (69 years after the attack) says that the Beaufighters "aborted their strafing attack." None of the other available sources, including all the contemporary sources and all the official sources, say whether No. 30 Squadron actually carried out its strafing mission at Tobera or not.

17   Gamble, *Target: Rabaul*, 141–43.

18   Gamble, *Target: Rabaul*, 142.

19   Gamble, *Target: Rabaul*, 143.

20   Gamble, *Target: Rabaul*, 143.

21   Gamble, *Target: Rabaul*, 143–44.

22   Gamble, *Target: Rabaul*, 144.

23   Gamble, *Target: Rabaul*, 144–45.

24   Gamble, *Target: Rabaul*, 145.

25   Gamble, *Target: Rabaul*, 145.

26   General George C. Kenney, *Air War in the Pacific: The Journal of General George Kenney, Commander of the Fifth U.S. Air Force* (Los Angeles: P-47 Press, 2018), Kindle edition, 203.

27   Monograph 140, 72; John Prados, *Islands of Destiny: The Solomons Campaign and the Eclipse of the Rising Sun* (New York: NAL Caliber, 2012), 317–18.

28   Gamble, *Target: Rabaul*, 147.

29   Gamble, *Target: Rabaul*, 147.

30 Gamble, *Target: Rabaul*, 147; Odgers, *Air War Against Japan*, 92.

31 Tameichi Hara, Fred Saito, and Roger Pineau, *Japanese Destroyer Captain: Pearl Harbor, Guadalcanal, Midway – The Great Naval Battles as Seen Through Japanese Eyes* (Annapolis: Naval Institute Press, 1967), 215; 244n.

32 *Keisho Maru, Mochizuki, Minazuki*, and *Tachikaze* TROMs.

33 Gamble, *Target: Rabaul*, 147; Odgers, *Air War Against Japan*, 92.

34 Samuel Eliot Morison, *History of United States Naval Operations in World War II, Vol VI: Breaking the Bismarcks Barrier 22 July 1942–1 May 1944* (Edison, NJ: Castle, 1950), 286.

35 Odgers, *Air War Against Japan*, 92. The Bristol Beaufort must not be confused with the Bristol Beaufighter.

36 Hara, Saito, and Pineau, *Destroyer Captain*, 215.

37 The night of March 22–23, a B-17 from the 5th Bomber Command dropped two 2,000lb bombs into the crater of the dormant Rabalanakaia volcano next to the Lakunai air base hoping to cause an eruption. It didn't.

38 Monograph 140, 73; Hata, Izawa, and Shores, *Japanese Naval Air Force*, 133–34; William Wolf, *The 5th Fighter Command in World War II: Vol.1: Pearl Harbor to the Reduction of Rabaul* (Atglen, PA: Schiffer, 2011), 396–401; "Unit History," *475th Fighter Group Historical Foundation* (https://475th.org/); Kenney, *Air War*, 203.

39 Gamble, *Target: Rabaul*, 151; Hata, Izawa, and Shores, *Japanese Naval Air Force*, 134; Wolf, *5th Fighter Command*, 404–07.

40 W. F. Craven and J. L. Cate (eds.), *Army Air Forces in World War II, Vol. IV: The Pacific: Guadalcanal to Saipan August 1942 to July 1944* (Washington, DC: Office of Air Force History, 1983), 321.

41 Craven and Cate, *Guadalcanal*, 322; Gamble, *Target: Rabaul*, 152–53.

42 Gamble, *Target: Rabaul*, 154.

43 Gamble, *Target: Rabaul*, 155; *Ch-23* TROM.

44 Gamble, *Target: Rabaul*, 155–58.

45 Gamble, *Target: Rabaul*, 158–60; Hata, Izawa, and Shores, *Japanese Naval Air Force*, 793–94.

46 Gamble, *Target: Rabaul*, 160.

47 Craven and Cate, *Guadalcanal*, 323; McAulay, *Dragon's Jaws*, 2678–86; "P-38H-5-LO Lightning Serial Number 42-66849," *Pacific Wrecks* (www.pacificwrecks.com); Hata, Izawa, and Shores, *Japanese Naval Air Force*, 134; Dunn, 14–27, 21. Dunn says, "Available Japanese records for Air Groups 201 and 204 are contradictory, but they apparently scrambled twenty fighters." Hata says the 201 Air Group sent up 15 Zeros but does not say how many fighters the 204 Air Group sent up.

48 Monograph 140, 75; Dunn, "Shootout at Rabaul," 21.

49 Craven and Cate, *Guadalcanal*, 323; McAulay, *Dragon's Jaws*, 2843–51.

50 Gamble, *Target: Rabaul*, 165.

51 Hata, Izawa, and Shores, *Japanese Naval Air Force*, 134, 795–96; Gamble, *Target: Rabaul*, 166–67; Craven and Cate, *Guadalcanal*, 323; Monograph 140, 75.

52 Gamble, *Target: Rabaul*, 167.

53 McAulay, *Dragon's Jaws*, 2843–51.

54 Craven and Cate, *Guadalcanal*, 323–24.

55 Craven and Cate, *Guadalcanal*, 324; Gamble, *Target: Rabaul*, 168.

56 Gamble, *Target: Rabaul*, 168; Monograph 140, 76.

57 Gamble, *Target: Rabaul*, 168–69; *Myoko, Haguro, Shigure, Samidare*, and *Shiratsuyu* TROMs.

58 Gamble, *Target: Rabaul*, 168; Hata, Izawa, and Shores, *Japanese Naval Air Force*, 134, 795–96. Hata mistakenly says the attacking bombers on October 25 were B-25s.

59 Gamble, *Target: Rabaul*, 169.

60 Gamble, *Target: Rabaul*, 169; Monograph 140, 76.

61 Gamble, *Target: Rabaul*, 169–70.

62 Gamble, *Target: Rabaul*, 171–72; Craven and Cate, *Guadalcanal*, 324–25; Monograph 140, 77.

63 Craven and Cate, *Guadalcanal*, 324.

64 Eric M. Bergerud, *Fire in the Sky: The Air War in the South Pacific* (Boulder, CO: Westview Press, 2000), 9556–58.

65   Hata, Izawa, and Shores, *Japanese Naval Air Force*, 130.

66   Office of Naval Intelligence, *Combat Narratives Solomon Islands Campaign: XII The Bougainville Landing and the Battle of Empress Augusta Bay 27 October–1 November 1943*. Washington, DC: Publications Branch, Office of Naval Intelligence, United States Navy, 1945 (hereinafter "ONI Narrative"), 77; Hata, Izawa, and Shores, *Japanese Naval Air Force*, 131, 793–94; Monograph 140, 73; William Wolf, *13th Fighter Command in World War II: Air Combat Over Guadalcanal and the Solomons* (Atglen, PA: Schiffer, 2004), 217. Monograph 140 says one fighter failed to return but Hata, Izawa, and Shores, *Japanese Naval Air Force*, say that two more fighters, those of Petty Officer 1st Class Adachi Shigenobu and Petty Officer 2nd Class Tanaka Kisaku, were also killed over Buin.

67   ONI Narrative, 77; Eric Hammel, *Air War Pacific Chronology: America's Air War Against Japan in East Asia and the Pacific 1941–1945* (Pacifica, CA: Pacifica Military History, 1998), 7629; ComAirSoPacFor War Diary.

68   ONI Narrative, 77; ComAirSoPacFor War Diary; Wolf, *13th Fighter Command*, 217.

69   ONI Narrative, 77; ComAirSoPacFor War Diary; Hammel, *Air War*, 7667; Monograph 140, 73; Hata, Izawa, and Shores, *Japanese Naval Air Force*, 793–94.

70   ONI Narrative, 77; Monograph 140, 73.

71   ONI Narrative, 77; ComAirSoPacFor War Diary; Hata, Izawa, and Shores, *Japanese Naval Air Force*, 1575, 793–94; Monograph 140, 73; Wolf, *13th Fighter Command*, 217.

72   ONI Narrative, 77; ComAirSoPacFor War Diary. The ONI Narrative's table describes the fighters that escorted the TBFs and SBDs to Kara as "20 VF." "VF" is the abbreviation for a US Navy fighter squadron. The ComSoPacFor War Diary only calls them "fighters."

73   ONI Narrative, 77; ComAirSoPacFor War Diary; Monograph 140, 74.

74   ONI Narrative, 77; ComAirSoPacFor War Diary.

75   ONI Narrative, 77; Wolf, *13th Fighter Command*, 217; Monograph 140, 74; Hata, Izawa, and Shores, *Japanese Naval Air Force*, 1575; ComAirSoPacFor War Diary.

76   ONI Narrative, 77; ComAirSoPacFor War Diary. The ONI Narrative mistakenly says the attack on Pora Pora was performed by B-29s.

77   ONI Narrative, 77.

78   ComAirSoPacFor War Diary; Hammel, *Air War*, 7774.

79   ComAirSoPacFor War Diary.

80   ComAirSoPacFor War Diary.

81   ComAirSoPacFor War Diary; Wolf, *13th Fighter Command*, 217.

82   ComAirSoPacFor War Diary.

83   Japanese Monograph No. 100, *Southeast Naval Operations, Part III* (US Armed Forces Far East, History Division), 9 (hereinafter "Monograph 100").

84   Miller, *Cartwheel*, 238; Monograph 100, 7.

85   Monograph 100, 7.

86   Monograph 100, 7–8.

87   Monograph 100, 8; Miller, *Cartwheel*, 238; Japanese Monograph No. 35, *Southeast Area Operations Record 17th Army Operations Volume II (February 1943–August 1945)* (US Armed Forces Far East, History Division), 93 (hereinafter "Monograph 35").

88   Monograph 100, 8. Gazelle Harbor must not be confused with the Gazelle Peninsula, which must not be confused with Cape Gazelle. As Samuel Eliot Morison put it, "The historian wishes that the exploring captains of HMS *Blanche*, *Renard*, and *Gazelle* had not been so fond of their ships as to name several harbors, channels, and sounds after each one." *Bismarcks Barrier*, 293, n1.

89   Miller, *Cartwheel*, 229, 239; Morison, *Bismarcks Barrier*, 296.

90   Miller, *Cartwheel*, 239; Monograph 35, 95.

91   *Kiso*, *Tama*, *Uzuki*, and *Samidare* TROMs; Odgers, *Air War Against Japan*, 93; "DAP Beaufort Mark VIII Serial Number A9-244," *Pacific Wrecks* (www.pacificwrecks.com).

92   Hara, Saito, and Pineau, *Destroyer Captain*, 216; *Hakusan Maru* TROM; Robert J. Cressman, *The Official Chronology of the U.S. Navy in World War II* (Washington, DC: Contemporary History Branch, Naval Historical Center, 1999); Alan C. Carey, *We Flew Alone: Men and Missions of the United States*

Navy's B-24 Liberator Squadrons Pacific Operations: February 1943–September 1944 (Atglen, PA: Schieffer Military History, 2017), 36–37.

93   Hara, Saito, and Pineau, *Destroyer Captain*, 216.

94   *Uzuki* and *Mochizuki* TROMs; Hammel, *Air War*, 7767; "Patrol Squadron 101 (VP-101)," *Pacific Wrecks* (www.pacificwrecks.com). Almost all sources indicate the *Mochizuki* was sunk by a US Navy plane, though Cressman (*Official Chronology*) has a double entry that gives US Marine aircraft credit in the other entry. Hammel alone identifies the Black Cat unit involved as US Navy Patrol Squadron 101. Curiously, Hammel has the sinking taking place a day later – the night of October 24–25 – than most sources do. What is more interesting is that ComAirSoPacFor War Diary says that at 3:03am on October 25: "A search plane, 20V26, made a direct hit on one of two destroyers in position 05-32S, 155-20E. An explosion and fire were observed and the ship was believed to have sunk."

What makes this so curious is how similar this account is to the attack on the *Uzuki* and the sinking of the *Mochizuki* except for the date and the location of the attack, which was east of Bougainville. There was no attack on October 25 that fits the scenario of the attack on the *Uzuki* and *Mochizuki*. This entry sounds like a reference to the attack on the *Uzuki* and *Mochizuki*. The problem is that the unit given credit for the sinking, VP-101, was not part of the South Pacific command, but was part of MacArthur's South-West Pacific command. Unless the wrong unit has been credited, there is no reason for the attack on the *Uzuki* and *Mochizuki* to be in the ComAirSoPacFor diary.

95   ComAirSoPacFor War Diary; Cressman, *Official Chronology*.

96   *Shigure*, *Samidare*, and *Shiratsuyu* TROMs; Hara, Saito, and Pineau, *Destroyer Captain*, 216. The TROMs for *Shigure*, *Samidare*, and *Shiratsuyu* have all three ships going to Garove Island and Iboki on October 23 and Qavuvu on October 26, but only the *Shigure* and *Shiratsuyu* making that same run to Qavuvu on October 29. Hara says that on October 23 the *Shigure*, *Samidare*, and *Shiratsuyu* went to Iboki and on October 29 all three went to Garove Island. Hara does not mention a mission for October 26. It seems likely that Hara has garbled some of the mission elements while there might be a double mission misprint in the TROMs. The narrative here goes with the *Shigure*, *Samidare*, and *Shiratsuyu* going to Iboki on October 23; the *Shigure*, *Samidare*, and *Shiratsuyu* going to Qavuvu on October 26; and the *Shigure* and *Shiratsuyu* going to Garove Island on October 29.

97   Monograph 100, 9–10; Monograph 140, 41, 44; Wolf, *13th Fighter Command*, 221; Prados, *Islands of Destiny*, 321.

98   Monograph 100, 10; Miller, *Cartwheel*, 240.

99   ONI Narrative, 15, 79. Blanche Harbor must not be confused with Blanche Channel, which must not be confused with Blanche Bay.

100 ONI Narrative, 15.

101 ONI Narrative, 15–16, 79.

102 ONI Narrative, 15–16.

103 ONI Narrative, 15–16.

104 ONI Narrative, 16–17, 79.

105 ONI Narrative, 18.

106 ONI Narrative, 18.

107 ONI Narrative, 18–19.

108 ONI Narrative, 13; Miller, *Cartwheel*, 240–41.

109 Miller, *Cartwheel*, 240–41.

110 Miller, *Cartwheel*, 240.

111 Monograph 100, 10; *Nagara* TROM.

112 Monograph 140, 41, 44.

113 Monograph 140, 10.

114 ONI Narrative, 22; Monograph 140, 44, 76. Monograph 140 says on page 44 that one fighter and five carrier dive bombers were lost, but on page 76 says one Zero and four bombers failed to return.

115 Hata, Izawa, and Shores, *Japanese Naval Air Force*, 135; ComAirSoPacFor War Diary; ONI Narrative, 22–23.

116 ONI Narrative, 18–19.

117 ONI Narrative, 23; Monograph 140, 76.

118 ONI Narrative, 24; Monograph 140, 76; Monograph 100, 10. The American force heading for Choiseul reported being bombed twice, the second of which was by "a Japanese twin-float observation seaplane of the Jake type." The Japanese reported that on October 28, "[indecipherable] reconnaissance plane reconnoitered the central Solomons." This probably references a single scout plane, but that is not definite. The Japanese also reported, "As air reconnaissance of the central Solomons before dawn on the 28th revealed no signs of enemy activity, the commander of the Southeast Area Fleet cancelled his Solomons interception assignments and once again began to concentrate on the attack in (the) New Guinea area." From these three pieces of information, it can be deduced that during the night of October 27–28, the Japanese launched one Aichi E13A Type 0 Reconnaissance Seaplane ("Jake"), which must not be confused with the Mitsubishi F1M Type 0 Observation Seaplane ("Pete"). That reconnaissance seaplane flew over the US Navy ships headed for Choiseul, making one and possibly two unsuccessful bombing attacks. After its bombing attack(s), the reconnaissance seaplane reported "no signs of enemy activity" or words to that effect.

119 Prados, *Islands of Destiny*, 322; Monograph 100, 10–11.

120 The Japanese mindset might be better shown than explained. This tidbit from Monograph 100 (10) describing the strength of Base Air Force (11th Air Fleet) is unintentionally revealing:

> 11 Air Fleet (25 Air Squadron, 26 Air Squadron) – 312 fighters, 96 bombers, 144 medium land attack planes, 24 attack planes, 24 reconnaissance planes. Total: 600 planes. The figures given for the 11th Air Fleet represent *authorized strength*. As a result of heavy losses in successive air operations, its actual operational strength at that time had declined to approximately 200 planes. (Emphasis added.)

The authorized strength of Base Air Force was irrelevant for purposes of *Ro-Go*. The authorized strength might as well have been 10,000 planes. It did not matter. Base Air Force did not have 10,000 planes just as it did not have 600 planes; it had barely a third of that figure in about 200 planes. But that 600-plane figure was something nice to quote so the Japanese could convince themselves that the situation with Base Air Force was not as grim as it actually was.

121 ComAirSoPacFor War Diary.

122 ComAirSoPacFor War Diary.

123 Miller, *Cartwheel*, 241; ONI Narrative, 24; ComAirSoPacFor War Diary.

124 ComAirSoPacFor War Diary; J. M. S. Ross, *Official History of New Zealand in the Second World War 1939–45: Royal New Zealand Air Force* (Wellington: War History Branch, Department of Internal Affairs, 1955), 216–17; Wolf, *13th Fighter Command*, 220; Cressman, *Official Chronology*. Wolf says the fighters in the Kieta attack were from the Army Air Force's 44th Fighter Squadron, but the ComAirSoPacFor War Diary specifically says all 32 of the fighters were "F4Us." The Army Air Force did not use F4Us. The ComAirSoPacFor and AirSols Strike Command's war diaries disagree on the Kieta attack. AirSols Strike Command does not mention the attack by the B-25s and F4Us and has the second attack (probably the P-39s) strafing "a moving truck near the mouth of the Aropa River." ComAirSoPacFor has the F4Us in the first attack strafing "four small AKs" off the coast. It does not have the second attack taking any action against shipping.

125 ComAirSoPacFor War Diary

126 Monograph 140, 77; Monograph 100, 11.

127 Monograph 100, 11.

128 Monograph 100, 12; Monograph 140, 77.

129 Monograph 100, 12; Monograph 140, 77.

130 Monograph 100, 12.

131 *United States Strategic Bombing Survey Report 69: The Thirteenth Air Force in the War Against Japan, 30 September 1946* (Washington, DC: Military Analysis Division, 1946), 7.

132 Omori Interrogation Nav No. 78 USSBS No. 889 Interrogation of: Vice Admiral Omori, S. IJN, 16 November 1945 (hereinafter "Omori Interrogation"), 337; *Samidare* and *Minazuki* TROMs. None of the TROMs for the ships involved mention anything about this particular sortie, but Omori is very specific about it. Omori identifies by name the *Myoko*, *Haguro*, *Sendai*, and *Nagara* as participating, along with "Rear Admiral Ijuiene, S.," likely a reference to Rear Admiral Baron Ijuin Matsuji. Captain Hara makes no mention of this sortie, either, despite talking to Admiral Ijuin at the conference

between this sortie and the sortie that resulted in the Battle of Empress Augusta Bay. The identification of the *Nagara* is a continuing problem, as her TROM says she left Rabaul on October 27 and arrived at Truk on October 29, where on November 1 she was made the flagship of the 4th Fleet. However, this is the second identification of the *Nagara* with the early response to late October 1943 Allied moves in the Solomons, the other being Monograph 100 (10). Moreover, there is no other light cruiser which could have been in Rabaul or even "the Rabaul area" and available for this mission. Omori does not identify the two destroyers involved. The suggestion of the *Samidare* and *Minazuki* being the destroyers is based on their probable presence in Rabaul – the *Samidare* through her unexplained omission from Captain Hara's run to Garove Island – and availability. According to their TROMs, the other Japanese participants in the Battle of Empress Augusta Bay (light cruiser *Agano*, antiaircraft destroyer *Wakatsuki*, and destroyers *Hatsukaze* and *Naganami*) did not arrive in Rabaul until November 1.

133 Monograph 100, 12; ComTF39 Action Reports – Task Force Thirty-Nine covering operations for Empress Augusta Bay and Treasury Island Echelons – Period 31 October to 3 November 1943, including: (1) Night Bombardment of Buka-Bonis Area. (2) Day Bombardment of Shortlands Area. (3) Battle of Empress Augusta Bay. (4) Day anti-aircraft action off Empress Augusta Bay (hereinafter "Merrill Report"), 7; ComDesron 23 Report of the Bombardments of Buka and Bonis Airfields, and of the Shortland Islands, October 31–November 1, 1943 (hereinafter "Burke Bombardment Report"), 4.

134 Merrill Report, 7–8; Burke Bombardment Report, 4.

135 Merrill Report, 7–8; Burke Bombardment Report, 6.

136 Omori Interrogation, 337.

137 Merrill Report, 10; ONI Narrative, 30–31. The times used here start to get confusing. As a reminder, the Japanese typically used only Japan Standard Time in their reports, which was two hours behind Solomon Islands time and one hour behind Rabaul time. Bougainville, Buka, and the Shortlands are on Rabaul time. However, US commanders seem to have been using Solomon Islands time in their reports, not Rabaul time.

138 Burke Bombardment Report, 8; Merrill Report, 10; ONI Narrative, 32.

139 Burke Bombardment Report, 8; ONI Narrative, 32.

140 Merrill Report, 11; Burke Bombardment Report, 8.

141 Merrill Report, 11.

142 Burke Bombardment Report, 8; Merrill Report, 11, 75.

143 Burke Bombardment Report, 8; Merrill Report, 11.

144 Merrill Report, 11; Tony DiGiulian, "5.5"/50 (14 cm) 3rd Year Type; 14 cm/50 (5.5") 3rd Year Type; Official Designation: 50 caliber 3rd Year Type 14 cm Gun," NavWeaps: Naval Weapons, Naval Technology and Naval Reunions (http://www.navweaps.com/).

145 Burke Bombardment Report, 8; Merrill Report, 11–12; *USS Dyson* Action Report of Night Bombardment of Buka Airdrome – Sohana Island Area and the Day Bombardment of Islands in the Shortlands Group – Nov. 1, 1943, 2, 4; "Nila," *Pacific Wrecks* (www.pacificwrecks.com).

146 Burke Bombardment Report, 9; Merrill Report, 11–12. Two of the 14cm guns on Poporang were still present at the end of the war. "Nila."

147 Monograph 100, 12.

Chapter 2

1 Miller, *Cartwheel*, 235.

2 Miller, *Cartwheel*, 225–26.

3 Miller, *Cartwheel*, 226.

4 Miller, *Cartwheel*, 226.

5 Miller, *Cartwheel*, 226–27.

6 Rentz, *Bougainville*, 8–9; Miller, *Cartwheel*, 227.

7 Rentz, *Bougainville*, 9.

8 Or Tenekau. Or Tenekow. Or Tenekai. Rentz, *Bougainville*, 10; Miller, *Cartwheel*, 228–29; "Tenakau Airfield (Tenekow) Autonomous Region of Bougainville Papua New Guinea (PNG)," *Pacific Wrecks* (www.pacificwrecks.com).

9   Rems, *South Pacific Cauldron*, 2063–64; William F. Halsey, *Admiral Halsey's Story* (Pickle Partners Publishing, 2013), 3679.

10   Miller, *Cartwheel*, 229.

11   David C. Fuquea, "Bougainville: The Amphibious Assault Enters Maturity," *Naval War College Review*, Vol. 50, No. 1 (Winter 1997), Article 7, 104–21, 108.

12   Commander Third Fleet (formerly Commander South Pacific Force and Area), South Pacific Campaign – Narrative account (hereinafter "ComSoPac Narrative"), 8.

13   Miller, *Cartwheel*, 235.

14   ONI Narrative, 34.

15   Rentz, *Bougainville*, 21.

16   General Barrett died after he fell from a second story window at the I Marine Amphibious Corps headquarters building in Nouméa. At the time and for decades afterwards, Barrett's death was treated as accidental, even the result of a cerebral hemorrhage. It is now believed that Barrett committed suicide after finding out Admiral Halsey planned to replace him as corps commander. The exact nature of his death was covered up for multiple reasons: to preserve Marine Corps morale, as Barrett was a very respected commander, on the eve of a major operation; to avoid giving the Japanese a propaganda coup, and to preserve the reputations of Barrett and Halsey. Alan P. Rems, "Halsey Knows the Straight Story," *Naval History Magazine*, Vol. 22, No. 4 (August 2008). It was a sad and tragic end to a storied career, of which Barrett and his family should be proud. Barrett had played a leading part in formulating amphibious operation doctrine and once served as assistant to the Marine Corps Commandant. Barrett also had formed and trained the 3rd Marine Division. (Rems, *South Pacific Cauldron*, 2038–40). "There was hardly an area of Marine Corps activity … that [Barrett] did not play a role in or contribute to in some notable way." (Rems, "Straight Story" (quoting Barrett biographer Tom FitzPatrick.)

17   Halsey, *Story*, 3679–86.

18   Miller, *Cartwheel*, 236; Halsey, *Story*, 3686.

19   Fuquea, "Bougainville," 105.

20   ONI Narrative, 38; Halsey, *Story*, 3695.

21   Miller, *Cartwheel*, 236–27; Rentz, *Bougainville*, 12.

22   Morison, *Bismarcks Barrier*, 290; Prados, *Islands of Destiny*, 325–26.

23   ONI Narrative, 23–24.

24   Miller, *Cartwheel*, 241; Rems, *South Pacific Cauldron*, 2220–29; Action Report, *USS Conway*, Initial Landing of Marine Paratroops on Choiseul Island, Solomon Islands, Night of October 27–28 1943 (hereinafter "*Conway* Choiseul Report"), 1–2.

25   Transport Division 22 War Diary.

26   Rentz, *Bougainville*, 106–07.

27   *Conway* Choiseul Report, 2; Rentz, *Bougainville*, 107.

28   *Conway* Choiseul Report, 3.

29   Rems, *South Pacific Cauldron*, 2219–21, 2229–30.

30   Rentz, *Bougainville*, 109–10; Harry A. Gailey, *Bougainville, 1943–1945: The Forgotten Campaign* (Lexington, KY: University Press of Kentucky, 1991, Kindle edition), 682–84. Sangigai is also known as Sanggighae, Sagigai, and Sanggigae. "Sangigai (Sanggighae, Sagigai, Sanggigae)," *Pacific Wrecks* (www.pacificwrecks.com).

31   Gailey, *Bougainville*, 677–78; Rentz, *Bougainville*, 114.

32   Gailey, *Bougainville*, 690–94. This is apparently a reference to a minelaying mission performed the night of November 12 – just after the Torokina landings – involving the converted destroyer minelayers *Tracy* and *Pruitt*, which, while covered by the destroyer *Eaton*, laid a two-row minefield across the eastern entrance to the Shortlands. The identities of the ships that were sunk or when they were sunk remains unclear. On November 25, the Japanese submarine *I-100* hit a mine, but it was reportedly while trying to navigate the northern channel to Buin. The submarine sank almost immediately, with only 12 survivors. *I-100* TROM.

33   Rentz, *Bougainville*, 110; Gailey, *Bougainville*, 694–95.

34   Miller, *Cartwheel*, 241; Rentz, *Bougainville*, 113–14.

35   Miller, *Cartwheel*, 241.

36 ONI Narrative, 38.

37 ONI Narrative, 38; Halsey, *Story*, 3723; Fuquea, "Bougainville," 110.

38 ONI Narrative, 38; Halsey, *Story*, 3723.

39 Admiral Merrill called Camp Crocodile "Camp Alligator." Merrill Report, 5.

40 ONI Narrative, 37, 39, 81–82; Miller, *Cartwheel*, 244.

41 ONI Narrative, 37, 39, 81–82; Miller, *Cartwheel*, 244.

42 ONI Narrative, 39.

43 Merrill Report, 6.

44 Monograph 140, 77.

45 Mark L. Evans and Roy A. Grossnick, *United States Naval Aviation 1910–2010, Volume I: Chronology* (Washington, DC: Naval History and Heritage Command, Department of the Navy, 2015), 183; Hammel, *Air War*, 7895; Michael J. Claringbould, *Operation Ro-Go 1943: Japanese Air Power Tackles the Bougainville Landings* (Oxford: Osprey, 2023), Kindle edition, 65, 67, 70; VF(N)-75 history; Richard L. Dunn, *South Pacific Air War: The Role of Air Power in the New Guinea and Solomon Island Campaigns, January 1943 to February 1944* (Atglen, PA: Schiffer Publishing, 2024), 464–65. Japanese Monograph 140 does not mention this attack per se, but does say (45) on the afternoon of October 31, "[U]ntil nightfall, land medium bomber and reconnaissance planes flew over the area on search and contact missions."

46 Claringbould, *Ro-Go*, 65, 67, 70; VF(N)-75 history; VMF-211 and -212 war diaries.

47 ONI Narrative, 40; Rems, *South Pacific Cauldron*, 2314–15; Miller, *Cartwheel*, 244.

48 ONI Narrative, 40.

49 ONI Narrative, 40.

50 ONI Narrative, 40.

51 ONI Narrative, 40–41; Rentz, *Bougainville*, 24.

52 Miller, *Cartwheel*, 244; Rentz, *Bougainville*, 18; Halsey, *Story*, 3716–31; ComTran, 8; Morison, *Bismarcks Barrier*, 298–99.

53 Rentz, *Bougainville*, 24; Morison, *Bismarcks Barrier*, 302–03.

54 Rentz, *Bougainville*, 24.

55 Miller, *Cartwheel*, 244–45; Rentz, *Bougainville*, 24; Morison, *Bismarcks Barrier*, 303.

56 ONI Narrative, 46; Monograph 100, 13; Monograph 140, 77; Wolf, *13th Fighter Command*, 221; Claringbould, *Ro-Go*, 74. The presence of the lone Yokosuka D4Y "Suisei" is attested in Monograph 140, which notes that the first attack on November 1 consisted of "44 fighters and 9 dive bombers (1 SUISEI)."

57 Rentz, *Bougainville*, 25, ComAirSoPacFor War Diary; Sherrod, *Marine Corps Aviation*, 181 and n12; Rems, *South Pacific Cauldron*, 2356–57. For most Navy and Marine air squadrons, the narrative has dispensed with the military abbreviations like VF-8, VT-8, or VMSB-211, too many of which can be off-putting to the uninitiated or newcomers to military history, and gone with nicknames like "Fighting 8," "Torpedo 8," or "Marine Scout Bombing 211" respectively, which were commonly used during the war. However, for the squadron with the abbreviation "VC-38," the closest thing to a comparable nickname was "Composite 38" or "Compositing 38."

58 Rentz, *Bougainville*, 25, ComAirSoPacFor War Diary; Sherrod, *Marine Corps Aviation*, 181 and n12.

59 Miller, *Cartwheel*, 247; Ross, *Royal New Zealand Air Force*, 207–08; Morison, *Bismarcks Barrier*, 303; Wolf, *13th Fighter Command*, 221; Claringbould, *Ro-Go*, 74–75; Dunn, *South Pacific Air War*, 467. Claringbould has 16 P-38s from the 339th. Wolf has 16 P-38s at 20,000–25,000 feet and does not identify the unit, but later says eight P-38s of the 339th engaged the Zeros. The narrative is an amalgamation of Claringbould and Wolf.

60 Sherrod, *Marine Corps Aviation*, 181 n12, 182; VF-17 War Diary. Curiously, the Marine Fighting 221 War Diary does not mention an early morning mission. Citing the VF-221 War Diary, Sherrod had Captain James E. Swett claiming two Vals shot down and one "Tony" probable. Swett's claim form does indeed give the date of November 1, but the war diary's narrative has the combat in which those shootdowns took place on November 2.

61 ONI Narrative, 46; Hata, Izawa, and Shores, *Japanese Naval Air Force*, 135; Monograph 140, 46, 77; Sherrod, *Marine Corps Aviation*, 182; Claringbould, *Ro-Go*, 75. Monograph 140 says 12 fighters "failed

to return" to Rabaul, while Hata, Izawa, and Shores also say "no less than 12 Zeros failed to return and two more force-landed."

62   Monograph 140, 46, 77; Hata, Izawa, and Shores, *Japanese Naval Air Force*, 135; Craven and Cate, *Guadalcanal*, 256–57. In point of fact, the ComAirSoPac War Diary shows no activity around 9:00am over or near the invasion beaches, and Claringbould (*Ro-Go*) also does not mention an attack at this time. Craven and Cate say, "Shortly before 0900, eight F-4Us stopped another thrust, sending down five fighters and turning back the bombers [...]," thus counting this as "another thrust" of the first attack. However, the Japanese are insistent that these were two separate attacks, the first making contact at 8:05am, the second at 8:55. Moreover, the 8:55 attack faced fighter opposition, and claimed to have shot down one Allied fighter with a second probable. The initial Allied fighter cover that faced the 8:05 Japanese attack consisted of 16 P-38 Lightnings and 16 P-40s (Wolf, *13th Fighter Command*, 221). Fighting 17, and Marine Fighting 215 and 221 had been on hand to cover the air attack on the invasion beaches. All of Marine Fighting 215's Corsairs that engaged the Japanese returned before the second strike arrived except for two: one had crashed in an operational accident, the second was that of 2nd Lieutenant George Kross, who landed at 9:25 (VMF-215 War Diary). The ComAirSoPac War Diary does not mention Fighting 17 in action at this time, but the Fighting 17 War Diary claims five Zeros – but no Vals – shot down in combat against Zeros and Vals at this time, thus matching Craven and Cate. The Fighting 17 War Diary does not give a return time for this flight, which leaves an opening for Fighting 17 to have stayed over the landing beaches long enough to engage this second wave of Zeros and thus makes it the most likely candidate. Prados (*Islands of Destiny*, 326) calls this a "pure fighter sweep," but Monograph 140 says the targets were on the ground, either "small craft in the vicinity of Torokina"(46) or "transport group at the mouth of (the) Mutupina River"(77). In external racks, the Zero could carry two 60kg (132lb) bombs, which were ineffective against shipping. It was used as a fighter bomber for a June 7, 1943 attack on the Russell Islands, but suffered heavy losses, so it was extremely rare for it to be used as a fighter bomber and not when aerial opposition was expected, until the advent of the Kamikaze Corps in late 1944. Monograph 140 says 18 Zeros were involved in this attack, as does Dunn (*South Pacific Air War*, 468), who adds that "[a]vailable evidence points to Air Group 253," but all other sources including Hata, Izawa, and Shores, give a count of 16, which the narrative is interpreting as 18 Zeros, which Hata, Izawa, and Shores specifically, came from the 204 Air Group, were launched but only 16 attacked, which in turn suggests two turned back before the attack.

63   ONI Narrative, 43; ComSoPac Narrative, 9.

64   ONI Narrative, 43–44; ComSoPac Narrative, 9.

65   Miller, *Cartwheel*, 246; ONI Narrative, 45; ComTrans, 4.

66   Miller, *Cartwheel*, 246; Rentz, *Bougainville*, 30; Gailey, *Bougainville*, 954–55.

67   Miller, *Cartwheel*, 246; ComTrans, 22.

68   ONI Narrative, 46; Hata, Izawa, and Shores, *Japanese Naval Air Force*, 1623; Monograph 140, 46, 77; Claringbould, *Ro-Go*, 77. Japanese numbers for the fighters involved in this attack are all over the place. Monograph 140 says on page 46 that 42 Zeros escorted seven carrier dive bombers in the 1:45pm attack, but on page 77 says that that same attack involved only 17 Zeros. Meanwhile, Hata, Izawa, and Shores say, "[O]n the third attack, a dozen 201 Ku aircraft again escorted dive-bombers [...]." This figure may be the result of a misread of Monograph 140 (46), which is difficult to read in places. Monograph 100 (13) says that during the day a total of 104 Zeros and 16 carrier bombers attacked. This number is consistent with Monograph 140 if the third attack involved 42 Zeros (44 in first attack plus 18 from second attack plus 42 in third attack equals 104). However, Monograph 140 was completed after Monograph 100, and may have been relying on Monograph 100 to complete its numbers. The narrative here treats "a dozen 201 Ku aircraft" as non-exclusive, meaning other aircraft and other squadrons could have been involved. Additionally, the narrative takes the number of 42 Zeros from the third attack as accurate simply because sending 12 or 17 against the numbers Admiral Kusaka knew they were facing would have been suicide.

69   ONI Narrative, 46–47.

70   Monograph 140, 46, 77. The time of the Japanese attack given by the ONI Narrative (46–47) as 1:16pm is treated as erroneous. It would have meant that the Japanese had almost a half hour to attack the invasion force and landing beaches with no aerial interference. There is no indication that this was

the case. Furthermore, all of the air reports (including that by the Japanese themselves) gives a contact time of 1:45pm or thereabouts. None of the times reported by the air crews is anywhere close to 1:16pm.

71 Monograph 140, 46, 77; VMF 215 and 221, and VF-17 war diaries; Hata, Izawa, and Shores, *Japanese Naval Air Force*, 135; Claringbould, *Ro-Go*, 77–78. Claringbould has two Vals shot down by antiaircraft fire, but Monograph 140 does not say any of the carrier dive bombers "failed to return" in its usual parlance, only that two were "seriously damaged" and two were "hit." The narrative tries to give effect to both sources. Claringbould says the Japanese fighter losses from the last attack all came from the 253 Air Group. Hata, Izawa, and Shores only mention the 201 Air Group as taking part in the last attack and say all four Zeros shot down came from this unit. Moreover, their breakdown of "Key Fighter Pilots Killed in Action" has five pilots from the 201 killed on November 1 and none from the 253. However, their chart does not appear to be exhaustive, as its numbers do not match the numbers given in their narrative for the total losses for the day. Furthermore, their numbers for the last attack do not match the numbers from Monograph 140. For these reasons, the narrative here goes with Monograph 140 and Claringbould.

72 ComAirSoPac War Diary.

73 The Type 0 Reconnaissance Seaplane must not be confused with the Type 0 Observation Seaplane.

74 Claringbould, *Ro-Go*, 72–73.

75 ComAirSoPac War Diary; Wolf, *13th Fighter Command*, 222; Claringbould, *Ro-Go*, 70; Hammel, *Air War*, 7899–910.

76 Rear Admiral Frederick C. Sherman, who had skippered an aircraft carrier until it was sunk out from under him in the South Pacific, must not be confused with Rear Admiral Forrest P. Sherman, who had skippered an aircraft carrier until it was sunk out from under him in the South Pacific. There remains heated debate as to which should be considered "the other Admiral Sherman."

77 Frederick C. Sherman, *Combat Command* (Toronto, New York, London, and Sydney: Bantam Books, 1982).

78 Sherman, *Combat Command*, 166.

79 Halsey, *Story*, 3745–55.

80 Sherman, *Combat Command*, 166; ONI Narrative, 35; ComTF38 Action Report, Buka-Bonis Strikes, November 1 and 2, 1943.

81 ONI Narrative, 35; ComTF38 Action Report, Buka-Bonis Strikes, November 1 and 2, 1943, 2; Air Group 23 Aircraft Action Report No. 1 (Nov. 1, 1943).

82 ONI Narrative, 35; ComTF38 Action Report, Buka-Bonis Strikes, November 1 and 2, 1943, 2; Air Group 23 Aircraft Action Report No. 1 (Nov. 1, 1943).

83 ONI Narrative, 35; ComTF38 Action Report, Buka-Bonis Strikes, November 1 and 2, 1943, 2; Air Group 23 Aircraft Action Report No. 1 (Nov. 1, 1943).

84 Morison, *Bismarcks Barrier*, 302.

85 Morison, *Bismarcks Barrier*, 302–03.

86 Miller, *Cartwheel*, 249–50.

87 Miller, *Cartwheel*, 249–50.

88 Miller, *Cartwheel*, 249–50.

89 Morison, *Bismarcks Barrier*, 302; Rems, *South Pacific Cauldron*, 2408–11.

90 ONI Narrative, 5; ComSoPac Narrative, 8.

91 Miller, *Cartwheel*, 246.

92 Just after the start of the "Spartacus Revolt" (Third Servile War) in 73 BC, Spartacus and the escaped slaves camped on Mount Vesuvius, apparently in the crater.

93 ONI Narrative, 49; Task Group 31.8 War Diary.

94 Cape Moltke was named after the Prussian General Moltke, but not the Prussian General Moltke you're thinking of, whichever Prussian General Moltke that is. This was the other Prussian General Moltke.

95 ONI Narrative, 49.

96 Miller, *Cartwheel*, 248.

97 Miller, *Cartwheel*, 248.

98 Claringbould, *Ro-Go*, 61–62. Eric Lacroix and Linton Wells II (*Japanese Cruisers of the Pacific War* (Annapolis: Naval Institute Press, 1997), 595) have the light cruiser *Agano* escorting the *Shokaku*,

Zuikaku, and *Zuiho* to a point 200 miles south of Truk, where they launched their planes for the trip to Rabaul, after which the carriers returned to Truk. The TROMS of all four ships fail to mention such a sortie; in fact, the TROMs of the *Shokaku* and *Zuikaku* specifically say their aircraft were transferred to land bases at Truk from where they would take off for Rabaul. Given that US Navy submarines were known to be operating between Truk and Rabaul, such a sortie would have been exceedingly dangerous.

99 Claringbould, *Ro-Go*, 78.

100 Claringbould, *Ro-Go*, 78–79.

101 Monograph 140, 53.

102 Monograph 100, 12.

103 Monograph 100, 13.

104 US Armed Forces Far East, History Division, *Southeast Naval Operations, Part III*, 13.

105 Except where noted otherwise, the account of Admiral Omori's conference and its aftermath aboard the *Myoko* comes from Hara, Saito, and Pineau, *Destroyer Captain*, 217–18.

106 The exchange between Hara Tameichi and Baron Ijuin Matsuji is included here to show the mindset of the Japanese commanders before going to Empress Augusta Bay, but the conversation as related by Hara includes several factual inaccuracies, the reasons for which remain unclear. The light cruiser *Sendai* was commissioned in 1924, therefore in 1943 she should have been 19 years old, not nine. Even if the *Sendai* was nine years old in 1943, the destroyer *Shigure* was commissioned in 1936, so in 1943 she would have been seven years old and thus younger than the *Sendai*.

107 Kent G. Budge, "Ijuin Matsuji (1893–1944)," *The Pacific War Online Encyclopedia* (http://pwencycl .kgbudge.com).

108 Prados, *Islands of Destiny*, 325.

109 The account of Admiral Omori's conference aboard the *Myoko* comes from Hara, Saito, and Pineau, *Destroyer Captain*, 217–18.

Chapter 3

1 Ian W. Toll, *The Conquering Tide: War in the Pacific Islands 1942–1944* (New York; London: Norton, 2016, Kindle edition), 257; Arthur J. Marder, Mark Jacobsen, and John Horsfield, *Old Friends, New Enemies: The Royal Navy and the Imperial Japanese Navy, Vol. 2: The Pacific War 1942–1945* (Oxford: Clarendon Press, 1990), 13–14.

2 The narrative is aware of the 2019 article by P. C. Boer and R. Enthoven titled, "Rear Admiral Doorman and the Java Sea Campaign: A case of a persistent reputation building?" published in the Dutch magazine *Militaire Spectator* 188 (3-2019) that appears to question the courage of Admiral Doorman. A full discussion of the article is beyond the scope of this book, but a few points should be noted in response. First, Karel Doorman became a naval air force pilot in 1915. With flight still in its infancy, the young Karel Doorman would be on the cutting edge of aviation for the Royal Netherlands Navy – so much so that he would survive 33 emergency landings, in part a reflection of his duties as a flight instructor, one of the first in the Royal Netherlands Navy. Anyone who was a pilot during this time period and especially a pilot who navigates through so many emergency situations is not lacking in courage. Second, Doorman was the only aviator in the leadership of ABDAFloat. Doorman knew the effect of air power and lack thereof. The Japanese air attack in the Flores Sea on February 4, 1942, that nearly sank the light cruiser *Marblehead*, disabled the aft turret on the heavy cruiser *Houston*, and damaged Doorman's flagship light cruiser *De Ruyter* is generally seen as the point at which Doorman's courage started to falter, but that is a misread of his feelings. The Flores Sea attack killed men under Doorman's command, which he took very hard, but also convinced him that the Java Sea Campaign was unwinnable against overwhelming Japanese air supremacy, and, as such, continuing to fight under these conditions would just cost the lives of his men for no gain. Not surprisingly, the effect on Doorman's mood was not good, but it was not a lack of courage, but a lack of hope. Third, if everything Doorman did after the Flores Sea attack is read in this light, then it becomes clear he was trying to carry out orders he knew to be hopeless while preserving the lives of his men as best he could. His conduct during combat, especially the Battle of the Java Sea, exemplifies his thinking. Doorman used every opportunity to send ships back to Soerabaja, even ones that were still arguably capable of combat; and when the *De Ruyter* was fatally torpedoed, he ordered his two surviving ships, the HMAS *Perth* and the USS *Houston*, to save themselves by going to Tandjoeng Priok

instead of stopping for survivors – including Doorman himself. These are not the actions of a coward, but of someone who cared deeply about the men under his command and was trying to avoid their deaths in combat that even if it was successful tactically would not change the outcome of the Java Sea Campaign.

3   No, the *Maya* was not named after the Central American Indian people. The *Maya* was named after a mountain in Hyogo Prefecture. All heavy cruisers in the Imperial Japanese Navy were named after mountains.

4   Or at least the best educated.

5   Kent G. Budge, "Omori Sentaro (1894–1974)," *The Pacific War Online Encyclopedia* (http://pwencycl. kgbudge.com); Prados, *Islands of Destiny*, 327.

6   Hara, Saito, and Pineau, *Destroyer Captain*, 218.

7   Hara, Saito, and Pineau, *Destroyer Captain*, 218.

8   Prados, *Islands of Destiny*, 327.

9   Hara, Saito, and Pineau, *Destroyer Captain*, 218; *Myoko* TROM. Omori (Interrogation, 337) has the time of departure as 4:00pm. Monograph 100 says the time of departure was 4:30pm. Note that the Japanese generally give all times as Tokyo time (UTC+9). Rabaul was one hour ahead of Tokyo, and Bougainville was one hour ahead of Rabaul. This narrative tries to use local times wherever possible.

10   Hara (Saito, and Pineau, *Destroyer Captain*, 217) says the commander of the 10th Destroyer Flotilla at this time was Rear Admiral Matsubara Hiroshi. Hara's memory appears to be in error. Most other sources identify the commander of the 10th as Rear Admiral Osugi Morikazu. At this time, Matsubara Hiroshi was a captain and skipper of the light cruiser *Agano* (*Agano* TROM). Hara's faulty recollection is understandable here inasmuch as Matsubara was present for the Empress Augusta Bay action commanding the flagship of the 10th and was promoted to rear admiral some 11 months later.

11   Monograph 100, 14; *Myoko, Haguro, Sendai, Agano, Amagiri, Yunagi, Uzuki, Yuzuki, Fumizuki*, and *Minazuki* TROMs; Miller, *Cartwheel*, 248 n47. There seems to be some confusion over the number and identities of the destroyer transports. Most sources say there were five, but do not identify them. Monograph 100 says six, but, again, does not identify them. Miller (probably based on Monograph 100) says six, but does not identify them. The TROMs for the *Myoko, Haguro*, and *Agano* say the transport destroyers were the *Amagiri, Yunagi, Uzuki*, and *Yuzuki*. The *Yuzuki*'s TROM does not mention a run to Bougainville, and indicates she was during this time a part of the 4th Fleet's 2nd Surface Escort Division. The *Sendai*'s TROM does not include the *Yuzuki* among the destroyer transports, replacing it with a ship called the "*Fuzuki*." There was no destroyer *Fuzuki*, but the name *Fuzuki* suggests these are typos for *Fumizuki*, a sister ship of the *Yuzuki* and *Uzuki* whose TROM does list the aborted reinforcement mission. Another sister ship of the *Fumizuki, Yuzuki*, and *Uzuki* was the *Minazuki*, whose TROM also lists the aborted reinforcement mission, but adds that the *Minazuki* was instead directed to reinforce Buka.

12   Monograph 100, 14.

13   Hara, Saito, and Pineau, *Destroyer Captain*, 218. Hara actually says, "The convoy of five troop-filled transports and their five destroyer escorts followed at a distance of several miles." There is no indication that the five destroyer transports had another five destroyers as escort. Omori (Omori Interrogation, 337) says there were only the five destroyer transports.

14   Omori Interrogation, 337–38.

15   Hara, Saito, and Pineau, *Destroyer Captain*, 218.

16   Omori Interrogation, 338.

17   *Myoko, Haguro, Agano*, and *Sendai* TROMs; Kent G. Budge, "Type 21 General Purpose Radar," *The Pacific War Online Encyclopedia* (http://pwencycl.kgbudge.com); Omori Interrogation, 340. Though Budge calls the Type 21 a "general purpose radar" because it was used for surface searches as well, he admits it was "nominally an air search radar." Therefore, the narrative goes with *The Imperial Japanese Navy Page* in calling it an "air search radar."

18   Omori Interrogation, 338; Hara, Saito, and Pineau, *Destroyer Captain*, 218.

19   Omori Interrogation, 338; Hara, Saito, and Pineau, *Destroyer Captain*, 218, 244n; Hammel, *Air War*, 7944.

20   Omori Interrogation, 338.

21 Omori Interrogation, 338. Omori gives 7:20pm (8:20pm Rabaul time) as the time when the bombing attack on the *Sendai* took place. In that same entry, however, he gives his justifications for recommending canceling the counterlanding that night, which include the enemy planes finding him but include neither the bombing attack nor the scouting report. Because multiple sources give 7:45pm (8:45 Rabaul time) as the time of the attack on the *Sendai*, the narrative here considers 7:45 to be the accurate time of the bombing attack and believes 7:20 was the time Omori sent his request to Rabaul while rolling the bombing attack into that time entry.

22 Hara, Saito, and Pineau, *Destroyer Captain*, 219. Hara says, "By this time" the Japanese scout planes were reporting in, a reference to the 7:45pm time he gives for the attack on the *Sendai*. Because Hara says this information came in before the 7:45 attack, while Omori does not use the scouting report as a reason for his recommendation to cancel the counterlanding operation, the narrative timeline here has Omori making his recommendation to Rabaul at 7:20pm, the scouting report coming in shortly thereafter, but before the bombing attack on the *Sendai* took place at 7:45pm.

23 Hara, Saito, and Pineau, *Destroyer Captain*, 218.

24 Omori Interrogation, 338.

25 Monograph 100, 14. Note that the original source had two spelling mistakes that have been corrected here for ease of reading.

26 Hara, Saito, and Pineau, *Destroyer Captain*, 219.

27 Vincent P. O'Hara, "Battle of Empress Augusta Bay – November 2, 1943," *The Thunder of the Guns: Battles of the Pacific War* (http://www.microworks.net/pacific/battles/); *Minazuki* TROM.

28 Omori Interrogation, 338; Hara, Saito, and Pineau, *Destroyer Captain*, 219. There is considerable uncertainty surrounding the SB-24's attack on the *Haguro* at this time. Omori gives the time of the attack as 11:30pm; Hara says 11:24. It's not clear where the Combined Assault Force was, but there is a two-hour differential between the Japanese accounts and many of the American accounts. That Bougainville is in the same time zone as Rabaul seems to have been ignored in American accounts, which continue to use Solomon Islands time, which is two hours ahead of Japan Standard Time. A problem more difficult to address is the result of the SB-24's attack. Because Omori was in direct command of the 5th Cruiser Division, this narrative treats as binding his statement that the bomb hit the *Haguro* amidships, opened up hull plating, and reducing her top speed to 30 knots. However, Hara (Saito, and Pineau, *Destroyer Captain*, 219) says the *Haguro* was not hit at all. Hara may have been supplementing his recollection with Monograph 100, 14), which also has the *Haguro* receiving no damage from this attack. The rather disconcerting part about trusting Omori's version of events here is that the TROM of neither the *Haguro* nor any other Japanese ship involved in the Empress Augusta Bay action mentions the attack even taking place, let alone the *Haguro* receiving damage. There is no way to resolve the contradiction. The *Haguro* was either damaged or not. While the narrative goes with Omori, readers should be aware of the disagreement and make their own conclusions.

29 Hara, Saito, and Pineau, *Destroyer Captain*, 219; Monograph 100, 14.

30 Hara, Saito, and Pineau, *Destroyer Captain*, 219; Omori Interrogation, 338.

31 Hara, Saito, and Pineau, *Destroyer Captain*, 219.

32 Hara, Saito, and Pineau, *Destroyer Captain*, 219.

33 Hara, Saito, and Pineau, *Destroyer Captain*, 219.

34 Hara, Saito, and Pineau, *Destroyer Captain*, 220.

35 Hara, Saito, and Pineau, *Destroyer Captain*, 220.

36 Hara, Saito, and Pineau, *Destroyer Captain*, 220.

37 Hara, Saito, and Pineau, *Destroyer Captain*, 220.

38 Lacroix and Wells, *Japanese Cruisers*, 428.

39 Hara, Saito, and Pineau, *Destroyer Captain*, 220.

40 Hara, Saito, and Pineau, *Destroyer Captain*, 220.

41 Hara, Saito, and Pineau, *Destroyer Captain*, 220–22.

42 Hara, Saito, and Pineau, *Destroyer Captain*, 220–22; *Samidare* and *Shiratsuyu* TROMs. Hara's explanation of the cause and timing of the collision between the *Samidare* and *Shiratsuyu* is at variance with that of, among others, Omori (Omori Interrogation, 338), who says, "In avoiding fire of U.S. ships, the destroyers *Samidare* and *Shiratsuyu*, which were with the *Sendai*, collided. The

collision occurred while in a turn just after firing torpedoes." The narrative goes with Hara's explanation because he was the destroyer division commander and thus was closer in the chain of command than Omori to both destroyers. Moreover, Hara personally witnessed the collision, while Omori did not – the collision would have occurred behind him and he did not know to look for it, while Hara did – and is relying on, at best, secondhand information. Finally, Omori's statement that "The collision occurred while in a turn just after firing torpedoes" is slightly misleading inasmuch as the *Samidare* fired torpedoes but the *Shiratsuyu* apparently did not, suggesting the *Shiratsuyu* was unable to fire torpedoes, which is in line with the *Shiratsuyu*'s damage to her torpedo tubes from the collision.

43 Hara, Saito, and Pineau, *Destroyer Captain*, 220–22.
44 Omori Interrogation, 338.
45 Hara, Saito, and Pineau, *Destroyer Captain*, 222.
46 Hara, Saito, and Pineau, *Destroyer Captain*, 222–23.
47 Hara, Saito, and Pineau, *Destroyer Captain*, 222.
48 Lacroix and Wells, *Japanese Cruisers*, 428.
49 Amalgamation of Lacroix and Wells, *Japanese Cruisers*, 428; and Hara, Saito, and Pineau, *Destroyer Captain*, 222.
50 Hara, Saito, and Pineau, *Destroyer Captain*, 222.
51 Hara, Saito, and Pineau, *Destroyer Captain*, 222.
52 Hara, Saito, and Pineau, *Destroyer Captain*, 223.
53 Hara, Saito, and Pineau, *Destroyer Captain*, 223.
54 Morison, *Bismarcks Barrier*, 311.
55 Hara, Saito, and Pineau, *Destroyer Captain*, 218; Monograph 100, 14.
56 "Tip" was short for Tippecanoe. A great-grandfather of Merrill's fought in the 1811 Battle of Tippecanoe, near the appropriately named town of Battle Ground, Indiana. Kent G. Budge, "Merrill, Aaron Stanton (1890–1961)," *The Pacific War Online Encyclopedia* (http://pwencycl.kgbudge.com).
57 William Tuohy, *America's Fighting Admirals: Winning the War at Sea in World War II* (St Paul, MN: Zenith Press, 2007), Kindle edition.
58 Tuohy, *America's Fighting Admirals*, 1874.
59 Tuohy, *America's Fighting Admirals*, 1874–76. When Admiral Merrill received word that the son of Mick Carney, now Halsey's chief of staff, was going to marry the daughter of General Sutherland, MacArthur's chief of staff, he messaged Carney: "Wedding announcement noted. Paragraph. Jesus Christ! Intertheater solidarity is very much to be desired, but is it necessary to go this far?" Tuohy, *America's Fighting Admirals*, 2936–41.
60 Tuohy, *America's Fighting Admirals*, 1877.
61 Crenshaw, *Tassafaronga*, 76; Tuohy, *America's Fighting Admirals*, 1872–73.
62 Tuohy, *America's Fighting Admirals*, 1890–91. Of all the major surface combat actions at this point in the Pacific War, only the daylight portion of the Battle of the Java Sea, the so-called Second Battle of the Java Sea, which involved Japanese sinking of the heavy cruiser *HMS Exeter* and destroyers *HMS Encounter* and *USS Pope*; and the frigid Battle of the Komandorski Islands in the Aleutians campaign in March 1943 had taken place when the sun was up. All of the other surface actions (Balikpapan, Endau, Badoeng Strait, nighttime portion of the Battle of the Java Sea, Soenda Strait, Savo Island, Cape Esperance, Friday the 13th (Guadalcanal I), Guadalcanal II, Tassafaronga, Vila-Stanmore, Kula Gulf (twice), Kolombangara, Vella Gulf, Horaniu, and Vella Lavella) had taken place at night.
63 Ken Jones, *Destroyer Squadron 23: Combat Exploits of Arleigh Burke's Gallant Force* (Uncommon Valor Press, 2016), Kindle edition, 171–72.
64 E. B. Potter, *Admiral Arleigh Burke* (Annapolis: Naval Institute Press, 1990), 77.
65 Tuohy, *America's Fighting Admirals*, 2860–62.
66 Potter, *Burke*, 73.
67 Jones, *Destroyer Squadron 23*, 25.
68 The Office of Naval Intelligence's narrative (ONI Narrative, 52) says, "Our destroyer attack doctrine under conditions of low visibility envisioned an undetected approach to torpedo-firing position." This statement is misleading at best. The only times even an attempt was made to follow the doctrine were at

Balikpapan, Kolombangara, Vella Gulf, and Horaniu. At Balikpapan, the four destroyers were penetrating in a Japanese-held harbor at night and were badly outnumbered and outgunned, so firing torpedoes first was less doctrine and more necessity to preserve their camouflage among the darkened Japanese invasion transports. At Kolombangara, Admiral Ainsworth had given his destroyers permission to make such an attack, but the Japanese had already detected Ainsworth's force and maneuvered to evade any torpedo attack while launching a torpedo attack of their own. Moreover, as Arleigh Burke would later hold, the necessity of getting such permission in the first place helped to short-circuit these torpedo attacks. At Vella Gulf it was indeed followed with spectacular and complete success. At Horaniu a Japanese search plane dropped a flare over the US Navy destroyers, ruining any attempt at remaining undetected. Torpedoes were launched before gunfire was opened at both Vila-Stanmore and Vella Lavella, but because gunfire was opened before the torpedoes could have hit their targets, they do not seem like efforts at following the doctrine.

69   Though, to be sure, there was a flash. See, e.g., the destroyer *Takinami* at Tasssafaronga; the only Japanese ship to open fire with her guns became the only Japanese ship sunk in that engagement because her gunfire gave the gunners of the US Navy cruisers a point of aim.

70   Potter, *Burke*, 72.

71   Tuohy, *America's Fighting Admirals*, 1903–01.

72   Merrill Report, 13.

73   Merrill Report, 13; ComDesRon23 "Action Report of Night Engagement off Cape Moltke the Night of November 1st–2nd, 1943" (hereinafter "Burke Report" or "Burke Empress Augusta Bay Report"), 5.

74   *Charles Ausburne* Empress Augusta Bay Report, 2.

75   *Charles Ausburne* Empress Augusta Bay Report, 2; *Claxton* War Diary.

76   Jones, *Destroyer Squadron 23*, 207.

77   Jones, *Destroyer Squadron 23*, 208.

78   Jones, *Destroyer Squadron 23*, 207. In January, 1944, Captain Simpson ordered: "Unless emergency demands, vessels of this Squadron will not use speeds in excess of 25 knots in Blackett Strait. It has been observed that wakes from this speed give Army privies built over the water a good flushing without damaging them. A hashmark under the picture of a privy on the bridge for each one knocked down will be discontinued."

79   ONI Narrative, 51; Merrill Report, 14.

80   Odgers, *Air War Against Japan*, 96; Merrill Report, 14.

81   Burke Empress Augusta Bay Report, 5–6.

82   *Claxton* War Diary.

83   Burke Empress Augusta Bay Report, 6.

84   Burke Empress Augusta Bay Report, 6.

85   Burke Empress Augusta Bay Report, 6; *Stanly* Empress Augusta Bay Report, 5.

86   Burke Empress Augusta Bay Report, 6.

87   Burke Empress Augusta Bay Report, 6.

88   ONI Narrative, 51; Burke Empress Augusta Bay Report, 6; Merrill Report, 15.

89   Burke Empress Augusta Bay Report, 7.

90   Burke Empress Augusta Bay Report, 7.

91   Burke Empress Augusta Bay Report, 7.

92   Burke Empress Augusta Bay Report, 8.

93   Merrill Report, 12.

94   Merrill Report, 76.

95   Burke Report, 9.

96   Merrill Report, 76. The order of the ships in the minelaying group is from the USS *Breese* War Diary.

97   Merrill Report, 76.

98   Omori Interrogation, 338.

99   Merrill Report, 76. This is from the voice radio ("Talk Between Ships" or "TBS") log. In the narrative of Merrill's Report (17), Admiral Merrill says the initial radar contact was at 2:27am, with a bearing of 308 degrees and a range of 38,000 yards, or more than 21 miles. In the timeline to that report (22), he says the initial contact was at 2:27am, bearing 308, range 35,900 yards, or more than

20 miles. Merrill does not say which ship made the initial detection, but it's generally assumed to have been the *Montpelier*. That same timeline says at 2:30am, Destroyer Division 45 (Captain Burke's division) detected the enemy bearing 306 degrees True distance 32,800 yards, or more than 18 miles, from the *Montpelier*. In his own report, Burke (9) says at 2:30am, Merrill reported a radar contact bearing 306 degrees, distance 16 miles. One minute later, according to Burke, the *Charles Ausburne*'s radar picked up the same contact bearing 291 degrees, distance 30,100 yards. For his part, Austin ("Action Report of Night Engagement off Cape Moltke the Night of November 1st–2nd, 1943" (hereinafter "Austin Report"), 7) also says that at 2:30am, Merrill reported a radar contact bearing 306 degrees, distance 16 miles. The narrative goes with Merrill's voice radio log because that figure was corroborated by Burke and Austin, though, to be sure, some corroboration on Burke's and Austin's parts is likely given the identical titles for their reports. It may be that Merrill made the initial contact at 2:27am at a bearing of 308 but did not announce it as he watched to see if the contact firmed up. When it did, the bearing and distance had changed and that is what he reported. It does not explain why his initial contact had significantly different distances in the narrative and the timeline, however.

100 Burke Report, 9.
101 Merrill Report, 76; Burke Report, 9.
102 Merrill Report, 17.
103 Merrill Report, 17.
104 Vincent O'Hara, *The US Navy Against the Axis: Surface Combat 1941–1945* (Annapolis: Naval Institute Press, 2007), Kindle edition, 4529.
105 Merrill Report, 16
106 Merrill Report, 16.
107 Merrill Report, 16.
108 Merrill Report, 16.
109 Merrill Report, 16.
110 Merrill Report, 76; "Action Report of Night Surface Engagement on November 1–2, 1943, to Westward of Emperess (sic) Augusta Bay, Bougainville Island" (hereinafter "*Spence* Report"), 7
111 This exchange is an amalgamation of both Merrill Report, 76; and *Spence* Report, 8. Merrill actually has Commander Austin's question as, "Am making countermarch 180, is that correct?." The *Spence* has it as "Just to clear up we are to stay in column." Though lacking the punctuation of a question, the *Spence*'s version is taken as true because 1. It makes more sense in the context than Merrill's version; and 2. The *Spence*'s version of Austin's question is more likely to be accurate because Austin was physically on the *Spence*.
112 O'Hara, *US Navy*, 4641.
113 *Spence* Report, 2.
114 Austin Report, 7.
115 Merrill Report, 77; *Spence* Report, 8.
116 Burke Report, 9–10.
117 Burke Report, 10; Merrill Report, 77.
118 Merrill Report, 77; "Action report of Engagement off Bougainville Island on 1 and 2 November, 1943" (hereinafter "*Claxton* Report"), 2 and 5. At one point (2), Commander Stout says he launched the second half salvo of torpedoes after the *Claxton* turned away; at a second point (5), he indicates he fired either before or as the *Claxton* turned away. The *Stanly* Report (3) indicates the *Claxton* turned late in order to fire the second salvo of torpedoes, with the result that the *Claxton* was in the *Stanly*'s line of fire for her guns. The narrative goes with the *Stanly*'s interpretation.
119 Jones, *Destroyer Squadron 23*, 224–25.
120 Burke Report, 10–11. Jones (*Destroyer Squadron 23*, 224–25) says Captain Burke knew the torpedoes were going to miss when the *Spence*'s combat information center reported, "The enemy is altering course to the south." However, Burke's report says he did not find out when the Japanese had changed course until after Admiral Merrill's cruisers had opened fire.
121 Burke Report, 11.
122 Burke Report, 11.

123 Prados, *Islands of Destiny*, 329.

124 Merrill Report, 77; "Action Report USS Denver – the Night Engagement off Empress Augusta Bay, 1 November, 1943" (hereinafter "*Denver* Report"), 2.

125 Morison, *Bismarcks Barrier*, 311.

126 Merrill Report, 17.

127 *Spence* Report, 2.

128 *Spence* Report, 2; *Foote* Report, 9; Merrill Report, 78.

129 *Foote* Report, 9.

130 Merrill Report, 78.

131 Merrill Report, 78.

132 *Claxton* Report, 9; Merrill Report, 78.

133 Merrill Report, 78.

134 O'Hara, *US Navy*, 4589; Merrill Report, 21.

135 *Spence* Report, 2; *Thatcher* Report, 2.

136 Merrill Report, 78.

137 *Foote* Report, 2.

138 Merrill Report, 20; *Foote* Report, 4.

139 *Claxton* Report, 9.

140 Merrill Report, 78.

141 Merrill Report, 78.

142 Morison, *Bismarcks Barrier*, 316; *Foote* Report, 5.

143 *Samidare* TROM.

144 *Foote* Report, 5; Merrill Report, 20–21.

145 USS *Cleveland* Action Report – Engagement with Japanese Surface Force off the West Coast of Bougainville Island During the Night of 1–2 November 1943 (hereinafter "*Cleveland* Report"), 2–3, 19.

146 Amalgamation of Merrill Report, 78; *Cleveland* Report, 19; *Stanly* Report, 6. The voice radio log entries for the *Foote*'s message about being hit and disabled are usually slightly different from each other. The narrative has gone with the wording from the *Cleveland* Report because the *Stanly* Report corroborates that the hit was described in "the steering engine room." That probably would not happen today, since the "Talk Between Ships" voice radio system had been largely superseded by a type of "Texting Between Ships," which is as it sounds.

147 Burke Report, 11.

148 Burke Report, 11–12; Merrill Report, 78.

149 *Claxton* Report, 9.

150 *Cleveland* Report, 19.

151 *Claxton* Report, 10; *Charles Ausburne* Report, 18.

152 Merrill Report, 78.

153 O'Hara, *US Navy*, 4596.

154 Merrill Report, 78; *Charles Ausburne* Report, 18–19.

155 Burke Report, 12.

156 *Stanly* Report, 5.

157 Burke Report, 12.

158 O'Hara, *US Navy*, 4656; Hara, Saito, and Pineau, *Destroyer Captain*, 223–24.

159 Lacroix and Wells, *Japanese Cruisers*, 428.

160 Hara, Saito, and Pineau, *Destroyer Captain*, 223.

161 The signal from the *Sendai* and the exchange on the bridge of the *Shigure* come from Hara, Saito, and Pineau, *Destroyer Captain*, 223–24.

162 Omori Interrogation, 338.

163 Omori Interrogation, 338; O'Hara, *US Navy*, 4573.

164 O'Hara, *US Navy*, 4581; Hara, Saito, and Pineau, *Destroyer Captain*, 222.

165 USS *Columbia* Report on Surface Engagement with Japanese Imperial Force Approximately Forty Miles West of Cape Torokina, Bougainville Ialand on 2 November, 1943, 3 (hereinafter "*Columbia* Report"). Merrill Report, 24.

166 Omori Interrogation, 339.

167 Inference based on the *Hatsukaze* taking evasive action and that the remainder of the 10th Destroyer Flotilla suffered no damage despite being under fire. Omori Interrogation, 338, 340.

168 Hara, Saito, and Pineau, *Destroyer Captain*, 223.

169 Omori Interrogation, 340; *Hatsukaze* TROM.

170 Omori Interrogation, 338.

171 Hara, Saito, and Pineau, *Destroyer Captain*, 223.

172 Hara (Saito, and Pineau, *Destroyer Captain*, 223) says Admiral Osugi's column crossed the path of Admiral Omori's column "at a right angle."

173 Omori Interrogation, 338.

174 Morison, *Bismarcks Barrier*, 312.

175 Omori Interrogation, 338. Morison (*Bismarcks Barrier*, 312) has the two torpedo tubes torn off the *Hatsukaze*, but Omori is clear in his interrogation that they were from the *Myoko*.

176 An amalgamation of Hara, Saito, and Pineau, *Destroyer Captain*, 222–23 (after making allowances for Hara misidentifying Admiral Osugi as Admiral Matsubara); Omori Interrogation, 340; and *Hatsukaze* TROM. Hara says that the 10th Destroyer Flotilla turned around to get back to the damaged *Hatsukaze* and found her, but quickly determined nothing could be done for her during battle, so they fell in with the *Myoko* and *Haguro*. But a note to the *Hatsukaze*'s TROM says of the destroyer "The Japanese did not see her again after the collision." Furthermore, Omori told his interrogator that the *Hatsukaze* had sunk as a result of the collision, which indicates that Osugi did not tell him about finding the crippled *Hatsukaze*. Hara might not be the best of sources on this collision because 1. He was not present on the *Agano*'s bridge during this time and thus got his information secondhand, and 2. Hara himself had left the *Sendai* disabled and burning without giving her aid despite an order from Admiral Ijuin to approach the light cruiser and despite a major argument with the *Shigure*'s skipper, Lieutenant Commander Yamagami Kamesaburou. Having an admiral do the same thing Hara had done, however justified it was (and it was in both instances), helps bolster Hara's case.

177 Merrill Report, 24; Morison, *Bismarcks Barrier*, 312; Omori Interrogation, 338.

178 Merrill Report, 25.

179 Burke Report, 12.

180 Merrill Report, 24; *Sendai* TROM.

181 Merrill Report, 24; *Sendai* TROM.

182 Hara, Saito, and Pineau, *Destroyer Captain*, 223.

183 Hara, Saito, and Pineau, *Destroyer Captain*, 222. Omori (Interrogation, 338) has them both at 3:20am, but many of the times he gives appear to be rounded to the nearest five or ten, so the narrative goes with Hara here.

184 Hara, Saito, and Pineau, *Destroyer Captain*, 223. Hara actually says, "In the next few minutes [after 3:15am] they [the *Myoko* and *Haguro*] also released a total of 24 torpedoes which were entirely wasted." While the narrative has gone with Hara on the times of these launches because many of the times Omori gives appear to be rounded to the nearest five or ten, as to the numbers of torpedoes launched, the narrative goes with Omori (Interrogation, 338), who is specific that the *Myoko* fired four torpedoes and the *Haguro* six.

185 *Spence* Report, 3; Hara, Saito, and Pineau, *Destroyer Captain*, 224. Identifying this ship as the *Shigure* is a deduction based on the two aforementioned sources. The *Spence* Report is the only source to mention this incident, as neither Admiral Merrill, Captain Burke, nor Commander Austin mention it, nor, for that matter, does Captain Hara. However, the *Spence* Report is difficult to follow. She was headed almost directly for the *Myoko* and *Haguro*, though she did not know their identity at the time. Commander Armstrong laments that they mistook this one ship for a friendly ship, but instead turned off and attacked a ship to the north that appeared to be "slowly turning, as though crippled." That ship was the *Sendai*. Armstrong implies that the one ship that passed down his port side was one of the big heavy cruisers *Myoko* and *Haguro*. The problem with that interpretation, however, is that 1. They had been tracking the *Myoko* and *Haguro* for some time to develop the torpedo firing solution and were aware of their position. It does not seem possible that the *Spence* would be approaching two targets as she passed one of those same targets. 2. The Japanese cruisers were together throughout the engagement. The only

Japanese ships which were by themselves at this time were the *Shigure*, which was headed south; and the *Hatsukaze*, which was limping away toward the west. The *Spence*'s quartermaster's log (18) has this entry for 3:14am: "Enemy off port hand." For 3:15am: "Passed possible Jap Cruiser on port bow – being fired at – in middle of Jap formation – came right to course 30 [degrees True]." It's not clear if both of these entries are referring to the same ship, or if either is the same ship Commander Armstrong reported, in part because a lot of Armstrong's times seem to be off. That the "possible [Japanese] cruiser" was "being fired at" would seem to be two rather important details Armstrong left out of his report. Moreover, by this time the *Myoko* and *Haguro* were not in the "middle of [the Japanese] formation," as by this time they had no Japanese ships south of them, except for possibly the *Shigure*.

186 Merrill Report, 24–25.
187 Austin Report, 13; *Spence* Report, 3.
188 *Spence* Report, 3.
189 *Spence* Report, 3.
190 O'Hara, *US Navy*, 4606.
191 "USS *Spence* DD 512"/"Heinie Armstrong," *Destroyer History Foundation* (www.destroyerhistory.org).
192 *Spence* Report, 3.
193 *Spence* Report, 3.
194 Merrill Report, 21.
195 Merrill Report, 21.
196 *Thatcher* Report, 3. The identification of these three ships as the *Agano*, *Naganami*, and *Wakatsuki* is another deduction. Commander Austin's destroyers had passed the *Myoko* and *Haguro* in the mistaken belief that they were friendly ships and instead headed north toward the *Sendai*. It was during this time that the three ships were seen passing down the port side. It is consistent with the 10th Destroyer Flotilla's position behind and to starboard of the 5th Cruiser Division. Furthermore, by this time, the only Japanese unit operating with three ambulatory ships was the 10th with the *Agano*, *Naganami*, and *Wakatsuki*. The *Thatcher* was the only US Navy ship to report sighting this group at or around this time.
197 Austin Report, 7.
198 Jones, *Destroyer Squadron 23*, 233.
199 Merrill Report, 21; Austin Report, 7.
200 Austin Report, 7.
201 Merrill Report, 33.
202 Merrill Report, 79.
203 Merrill Report, 24.
204 Merrill Report, 79.
205 *Cleveland* Report, 9.
206 Merrill Report, 25.
207 *Cleveland* Report, 9; Merrill Report, 25.
208 *Denver* Report, 7, 15–16.
209 Merrill Report, 18.
210 Merrill Report, 18, 79.
211 Merrill Report, 25, 79.
212 Omori Interrogation, 338.
213 Omori Interrogation, 338.
214 Omori Interrogation, 340.
215 Omori Interrogation, 340.
216 Omori Interrogation, 340; Hara, Saito, and Pineau, *Destroyer Captain*, 222.
217 *Thatcher* Report, 3.
218 Austin Report, 7; *Thatcher* Report, 3; USS *Converse* Report of Action, 2 (hereinafter "*Converse* Empress Augusta Bay Report").
219 *Thatcher* Report, 3; *Spence* Report, 3–4; *Converse* Report, 2.
220 Austin Report, 7–8.
221 Hara, Saito, and Pineau, *Destroyer Captain*, 222; Austin Report, 8. The time of *Samidare*'s launch of torpedoes at Commander Austin's pursuing destroyers comes from a detail in Hara's map.

222 Hara, Saito, and Pineau, *Destroyer Captain*, 222.

223 *Spence* Report, 10–11; *Converse* Report, 2. According to Ken Jones (*Destroyer Squadron 23*, 232): In broad terms suction is used to supply fresh water to the boilers. This is converted into superheated steam, which passes through the tubes at a tremendous speed. The fire boxes are so hot that, if there is an interruption of this flow of steam, the tubes will melt. Lost suction, then, requires that all engines must be secured for as long as it may take to correct the situation. This is sometimes accomplished in minutes; on other occasions it may take from 4 to 6 hours.

224 Burke Report, 12–13.

225 Burke Report, 13.

226 Burke Report, 13.

227 Burke Report, 13.

228 Jones, *Destroyer Squadron 23*, 233.

229 Lacroix and Wells, *Japanese Cruisers*, 428.

230 Jones, *Destroyer Squadron 23*, 233.

231 Burke Report, 13–14.

232 Amalgamation of Burke Report, 14; and *Spence* Report, 11.

233 Merrill Report, 82; ONI Narrative, 68.

234 Amalgamation of Merrill Report, 83; *Spence* Report, 11; and *Cleveland* Report, 30.

235 Burke Report, 14.

236 Morison, *Bismarcks Barrier*, 316; ONI Narrative, 68; *Converse* Report, 2.

237 ONI Narrative, 68.

238 Jones, *Destroyer Squadron 23*, 234.

239 *Charles Ausburne* Report, 26–27.

240 Jones, *Destroyer Squadron 23*, 234.

241 *Columbia* Report, 7, 10, 12.

242 Merrill Report, 25.

243 *Cleveland* Report, 34; Merrill Report, 84.

244 *Cleveland* Report, 34; Merrill Report, 85.

245 *Montpelier* Report, 3.

246 *Montpelier* Report, 3; C. W. Kilpatrick, *The Night Naval Battles in the Solomons* (Pompano Beach, FL: Exposition-Banner, 1987), 252; Merrill Report, 87.

247 *Charles Ausburne* Report, 4.

248 *Spence* Report, 4; Merrill Report, 28.

249 *Hatsukaze* TROM; Merrill Report, 28.

250 Merrill Report, 28; *Hatsukaze* TROM.

251 *Hatsukaze* TROM.

252 First salvo hits never happen. Except on November 2, 1943, when it happened twice.

253 *Spence* Report, 13.

254 Austin Report, 14.

255 *Hatsukaze* TROM; *Spence* Report, 14.

256 Burke Report, 14–15; *Spence* Report, 4.

257 *Spence* Report, 5; Merrill Report, 89; Burke Empress Augusta Bay Report, 15; *Hatsukaze* TROM.

258 Merrill Report, 28; Monograph 140, 48; Claringbould, *Ro-Go*, 80. Reporting time differentials are due to use of different time zones in reporting. Imperial Japanese Navy ships usually used Japan Standard Time, which was one hour behind Rabaul and Bougainville and two hours behind the Solomons. Admiral Merrill does not seem to have changed his ships' clocks after leaving their rendezvous.

259 Lacroix and Wells, *Japanese Cruisers*, 428; *Sendai* TROM. Omori (Interrogation, 340) has the *Sendai*'s sinking as 4:00am (2:00am Japan Standard Time), but that appears to be too early and may have been confused with the time she was abandoned, which Lacroix and Wells give as "0400." Lacroix and Wells also have the sinking at "0530" while the *Sendai* TROM has the time as "0430."

260 "Hull-down" means their hulls were below the horizon and thus not visible, but their superstructures were visible above the horizon.

261 Merrill Report, 29. The ONI Narrative (72) says the four fighters were P-38s.

262 Morison, *Bismarcks Barrier*, 319; Hammel, *Air War*, 7938, 7972; VF-40 War Diary; Hata, Izawa, and Shores, *Japanese Naval Air Force*, 1629; Claringbould, *Ro-Go*, 81–83. Hammel specified that there were only three Navy squadrons flying F6F Hellcats in the Solomons: VF-33, VF-38, and VF-40, all out of Segi. He lists VF-33 as fighting in the early morning operations of November 2 while, according the VF-40 War Diary, VF-40 did not. Whether VF-38 did is unclear. Claringbould gives the breakdown of attackers from *Kido Butai*, but does not mention any attackers from Base Air Force. Monograph 140 (50) specifies 89 attacking fighters, but does not give a breakdown of units.

263 Merrill Report, 30.

264 Merrill Report, 31; ONI Narrative, 74.

265 Merrill Report, 31; USS *Denver* Report of Anti-Aircraft Action, 2 November, 1943, 3; Claringbould, *Ro-Go*, 84.

266 Merrill Report, 31; ONI Narrative, 73–74; Claringbould, *Ro-Go*, 85.

267 Merrill Report, 31; Claringbould, *Ro-Go*, 85–87.

268 Jones, *Destroyer Squadron 23*, 235–36.

269 Monograph 100, 15; Monograph 140, 78; Claringbould, *Ro-Go*, 85–87.

Chapter 4

1 Trying to determine exactly when all of the surviving elements of the Combined Assault Force returned to Rabaul is an exercise in futility. Omori (Interrogation, 340) has them arriving at "1300." Because Omori gives his other times for the Battle of Empress Augusta Bay in Japan Standard Time, it is reasonable to interpret "1300" as 1:00pm Japan Standard Time, 2:00pm Rabaul time, and 3:00pm Solomon Islands time. The problem is that this pushes the 5th Air Force's attack to late afternoon – Omori gives the time of the attack as "1500" – which was clearly not the case. Hara (Saito, and Pineau, *Destroyer Captain*, 226) has the force returning at 8:00 Japan Standard Time on November 2, with the air attack taking place on November 3. There was no 5th Air Force attack on Rabaul on November 3 as a result of bad weather. Gamble (*Target: Rabaul*, 182) has them coming in at "0917 Tokyo time, seven hours after withdrawing in defeat …" That would be 9:17am Japan Standard Time, 10:17am Rabaul time, and 11:17am Solomon Islands time. This would seem to be the most reasonable time, and is the basis for the time used in the narrative. Unfortunately, Gamble does not list his source.

2 Hara, Saito, and Pineau, *Destroyer Captain*, 226.

3 Hara, Saito, and Pineau, *Destroyer Captain*, 226.

4 Hara, Saito, and Pineau, *Destroyer Captain*, 226–27.

5 Hara, Saito, and Pineau, *Destroyer Captain*, 227.

6 Lacroix and Wells, *Japanese Cruisers*, 428; *Sendai* and *Hatsukaze* TROMs. Hara, Saito, and Pineau, *Destroyer Captain* (229) says 335 were killed aboard the *Sendai*.

7 Hara, Saito, and Pineau, *Destroyer Captain*, 227.

8 *Haguro* TROM; Prados, *Islands of Destiny*, 334.

9 Monograph 100, 11.

10 Monograph 140, 41–42. McAulay, *Dragon's Jaws*, 3748. The identifications of the units based at Lakunai are based on Monograph 140, which calls Lakunai "RABAUL."

11 McAulay, *Dragon's Jaws*, 3806–16; Gamble, *Fortress Rabaul*, 178.

12 McAulay, *Dragon's Jaws*, 3806–16; Gamble, *Fortress Rabaul*, 178. Commander Nakano Chujiro was the commander of the 201 Air Group between March 1943 and July 1944. Commander Shibata Takeo commanded the 204 Air Group from September 1943 to March 1944, at which time it was disbanded. (Hata, Izawa, and Shores, *Japanese Naval Air Force*, 4159, 4274). According to McAulay, Shibata was commanding both the 201 and 204 Air Groups at this time. It is difficult to reconcile that with Hata et al., who say that Nakano was commander of the 201 from March 1943 to July 1944 with no apparent interruptions. It may simply be that with both air groups at one base it was easier to have one commander.

13 Claringbould, *Ro-Go*, 90–92; Gamble, *Fortress Rabaul*, 178; Dunn, "Shootout at Rabaul," 23, 25; Hickey, *Warpath*, 81; McAulay, *Dragon's Jaws*, 3903; Hata, Izawa, and Shores, *Japanese Naval Air Force*, 6057–64, 7398. McAulay has Tanimizu taking off from Tobera with the 253 Air Group, but Hata et al. have him as a member of the *Shokaku*'s air group who had just arrived in Rabaul. Dunn includes

Tanimizu (rendered as "Tanimuzu") in his description of the performance of *Shokaku* pilots. This makes sense because it is widely acknowledged that November 2, 1943 was Tanimizu's first combat, which would not have been the case if he had been with the 253 Air Group in Rabaul. However, while the *Shokaku*'s air group was at Vunakanau, it seems that Tanimizu was sent to Tobera, which means he was attached to the 253. The major volcanoes in the Rabaul caldera are not limited to Tavurvur and Vulcan. They include Kombiu (The Mother), which is flanked by Toyanumbatir and Turanguna (North and South Daughters), and Rabalanakaia, which the Americans for some reason called "Rabatana," located just north of Lakunai. The US 5th Air Force bombed Rabalanakaia in early 1943 in a ludicrously futile effort to cause the dormant volcano to erupt and wipe out Lakunai.

14   Craven and Cate, *Guadalcanal*, 325. Special Intelligence Bulletin (SIB; based on *Magic*) Number 181 for October 31, 1943, and issued November 2, 1943, warned that a new fighter unit, the 231 Air Group, might have joined Base Air Force in Rabaul (McAulay, *Dragon's Jaws*, 3755). There was no 231 Air Group.

15   Craven and Cate, *Guadalcanal*, 325.

16   William H. Webster, "November 2, 1943 William H. Webster," (3rd Bombardment Group) *Stories* (http://3rdstories.yolasite.com/), 3.

17   Peter Dunn, "Raid on Rabaul on 2 November 1943 as told by Dick Walker," *Australia@War* (www.ozatwar.com).

18   John P. Henebry, *The Grim Reapers at Work in the Pacific Theater: The Third Attack Group of the US Fifth Air Force* (Missoula, MT: Pictorial Histories Publishing Company, 2002), 114–15.

19   In the local Tolai language, "Turangunan" means "the peak." R. W. Johnson and N. A. Threlfall, *Volcano Town: The 1937–43 Eruptions at Rabaul* (Bathurst, Australia: Robert Brown & Associates, 1985), 2.

20   In the local Tolai language, "Tavurvur" means "the hornet's nest." Johnson and Threlfall, *Volcano Town*, 2.

21   In the local Tolai language, "Kabiu" means "the pair of breasts." Johnson and Threlfall, *Volcano Town*, 1–2.

22   In the local Tolai language, "Rabalanakaia" means "the heart of the volcano." Like Mount Vesuvius, Rabalanakaia is in the breached crater of an older volcano, called Palangiangia, the name of a type of seashell. Between Rabalanakaia and Simpson Harbor are three other, small craters. Into the midst of these craters runs Sulphur Creek. Johnson and Threlfall, *Volcano Town*, 2.

23   Gamble, *Fortress Rabaul*, 177, 179; Henebry, *Grim Reapers*, 114; Webster, "November 2, 1943," 1–2.

24   Gamble, *Fortress Rabaul*, 177.

25   Gamble, *Fortress Rabaul*, 173; Craven and Cate, *Guadalcanal*, 325; Thomas McKelvey Cleaver, *Under the Southern Cross: The South Pacific Air Campaign Against Rabaul* (Oxford: Osprey, 2021), Kindle edition, 191; Webster, "November 2, 1943," 1; McAulay, *Dragon's Jaws*, 3674.

26   Mark E. Stille, *The Imperial Japanese Navy in the Pacific War* (Oxford: Osprey, 2014), Kindle edition, 2481–91.

27   *Agano* TROM; Stille, *Imperial Japanese Navy*, 3790–98.

28   Kenney, *Air War*, 205–06; McAulay, *Dragon's Jaws*, 3735.

29   McAulay, *Dragon's Jaws*, 3735, 3795.

30   Henebry, *Grim Reapers*, 114.

31   Gamble, *Fortress Rabaul*, 176.

32   Gamble, *Target Rabaul*, 178; Cleaver, *Southern Cross*, 193; McAulay, *Dragon's Jaws*, 3836; Henebry, *Grim Reapers*, 118; Monograph 100, 15–16. Hata, Izawa, and Shores (*Japanese Naval Air Force*, 1623–33) say the number of Zeros was 74 from Base Air Force and 38 from *Kido Butai*.

33   McAulay, *Dragon's Jaws*, 3836.

34   McAulay, *Dragon's Jaws*, 3836.

35   McAulay, *Dragon's Jaws*, 3879–90.

36   McAulay, *Dragon's Jaws*, 4380; Gamble, *Target: Rabaul*, 178; "P-38G-13-LO Lightning Serial Number 43-2203," *Pacific Wrecks* (www.pacificwrecks.com).

37   Gamble, *Target: Rabaul*, 179.

38   Hickey, *Warpath*, 81.

39   Stout, *Air Apaches*, 1761.

40 Gamble, *Target: Rabaul*, 180; "B-25D-1 'Miss Ellen' Serial Number 41-30039," *Pacific Wrecks* (www.pacificwrecks.com).

41 Gamble, *Target: Rabaul*, 181; Stout, *Air Apaches*, 1779–87.

42 McAulay, *Dragon's Jaws*, 3792–801, 3966; Hata, Izawa, and Shores, *Japanese Naval Air Force*, 5632; Gamble, *Target: Rabaul*, 181–82; Cleaver, *Southern Cross*, 194; "B-25D-1 'Hellzapoppin' Serial Number 41-30094," *Pacific Wrecks* (www.pacificwrecks.com). For some reason, McAulay says the B-25 defended by Lieutenant Kirby and friends was flown by Robert Fox (*Dragon's Jaws*, 3958–66).

43 Gamble, *Target: Rabaul*, 182.

44 McAulay, *Dragon's Jaws*, 3974; "P-38G-15-LO Lightning Serial Number 43-2387," *Pacific Wrecks* (www.pacificwrecks.com); Missing Air Crew Report (MACR) 1315; "P-38G-5-LO Lightning Serial Number 42-12848," *Pacific Wrecks* (www.pacificwrecks.com).

45 McAulay, *Dragon's Jaws*, 3996–4006, 4038, 4388; MACR 1263; "P-38H-5-LO Lightning Serial Number 42-66747," *Pacific Wrecks* (www.pacificwrecks.com).

46 McAulay, *Dragon's Jaws*, 3900.

47 McAulay, *Dragon's Jaws*, 3996.

48 MACR 1951.

49 Prados, *Islands of Destiny*, 334; Hara, Saito, and Pineau, *Destroyer Captain*, 227.

50 Hara, Saito, and Pineau, *Destroyer Captain*, 227–28.

51 Gamble, *Target: Rabaul*, 183.

52 McAulay, *Dragon's Jaws*, 3792, 3826–32. *Seabiscuit* was named after the famous race horse.

53 Craven and Cate, *Guadalcanal*, 326.

54 McAulay, *Dragon's Jaws*, 3827.

55 38th Bombardment Group History, 207; USSBS 75 *Campaign Against Rabaul*, 48; Gamble (*Target: Rabaul*, 185) is uncertain but says Cecil "apparently" bombed the 1,500-ton *Manko Maru*. McAulay (*Dragon's Jaws*, 4536) credits the *Manko Maru* to Howe.

56 Gamble, *Target: Rabaul*, 366; MACR 1246; "B-25D-10 Mitchell Serial Number 41-30240," *Pacific Wrecks* (www.pacificwrecks.com).

57 Gamble, *Target: Rabaul*, 185; 38th Bombardment Group History, 209.

58 Gamble, *Target: Rabaul*, 185; MACR 1218; *W-26* TROM.

59 38th Bombardment Group History, 209; McAulay, *Dragon's Jaws*, 4207–18.

60 Gamble, *Target: Rabaul*, 185–86; MACR 1086. Lieutenant Fox's B-25 had Serial Number 41-30433. Gamble erroneously has Fox's given name as "Roger."

61 Webster, "November 2, 1943," 5.

62 Henebry, *Grim Reapers*, 116.

63 McAulay, *Dragon's Jaws*, 3986.

64 Gamble, *Target: Rabaul*, 186.

65 Gamble, *Target: Rabaul*, 186; Henebry, *Grim Reapers*, 116–17; *Hakusan Maru* TROM.

66 Henebry, *Grim Reapers*, 117, 120.

67 McAulay, *Dragon's Jaws*, 4017; *Chogei* TROM.

68 McAulay, *Dragon's Jaws*, 4017–27.

69 McAulay, *Dragon's Jaws*, 4049.

70 McAulay, *Dragon's Jaws*, 4049–60.

71 McAulay, *Dragon's Jaws*, 4023, 4095, 4538; *Manko Maru* TROM; USSBS 75 *Campaign Against Rabaul*, 59; Gamble, *Target: Rabaul*, 187. Admiral Kusaka said that skip bombing was never used in enemy attacks on Simpson Harbor.

72 No, the squadrons did not fly in numerical order.

73 Webster, "November 2, 1943," 5.

74 Dunn, "Raid on Rabaul on 2 November 1943 as told by Dick Walker"; "B-25D-10 Mitchell Serial Number 41-30213," *Pacific Wrecks* (www.pacificwrecks.com).

75 Dunn, "Raid on Rabaul on 2 November 1943 as told by Dick Walker."

76 Gamble, *Target: Rabaul*, 188.

77 Webster, "November 2, 1943," 5.

78 Gamble, *Target: Rabaul*, 136; McAulay, *Dragon's Jaws*, 820–31; 3700-11; John L. Frisbee, "Raid on Rabaul," *Air Force Magazine*, November 1987, 112.

79 Webster, "November 2, 1943," 5, 7.

80 Webster, "November 2, 1943," 6. MACR 1459 has an undated witness statement signed by both Flight Officers Trout and Keyes. Trout's signature is above that of Keyes, but Trout's signature caption says "Co-pilot" while Keyes' caption says "Pilot." Webster's letter consistently refers to the aircraft as Trout's.

81 Webster, "November 2, 1943," 6.

82 Webster, "November 2, 1943," 6; Gamble, *Target: Rabaul*, 188–89.

83 Webster, "November 2, 1943," 6.

84 Gamble, *Target: Rabaul*, 189. Henebry (*Grim Reapers*, 119) has a map diagramming the position of the ships in Simpson Harbor during the attack. One of the marks on the diagram is marked "25. H'VY CRUISER NACHI CLASS 10,000 TONS DAMAGED." This is accepted, especially based on photographic evidence, as the *Haguro*. There is nothing else on the diagram as marked that could be the *Agano*, though the light cruiser is believed to have been in Simpson Harbor, or the *Myoko*.

85 Webster, "November 2, 1943," 6.

86 Webster, "November 2, 1943," 6.

87 Webster, "November 2, 1943," 7. "[T]he Beehive rock formations in the middle of [Simpson] Harbor" are generally called "The Beehives" or "Dawapia Rocks."

88 Webster, "November 2, 1943," 7.

89 Webster, "November 2, 1943," 7–8.

90 Webster, "November 2, 1943," 7–8; Gamble, *Target: Rabaul*, 190.

91 MACR 1459; Gamble, *Target: Rabaul*, 189.

92 MACR 1459. For some reason, McAulay (*Dragon's Jaws*, 4164) only says of Major Wilkins' crash, "The only man to report seeing what happened to Wilkins was one of the pilots, Flight Officer 'Woody' Keyes, flying with Lee Trout, who said he saw one wing of the B-25 'fold up.'" In fact, MACR 1459, which deals with the loss of the aircraft of Major Wilkins and his crew, has two signed witness statements, one by Lieutenant Clarence Martindale, the second by Flight Officers Lee Trout and Woody Keyes. It also lists three possible witnesses to the crash, though, curiously, Trout is not among them. The quotes in the preceding paragraph are taken directly from Keyes' and Trout's statement.

93 Webster, "November 2, 1943," 8.

94 MACR 1633; "B-25C 'Tugboat Annie' Serial Number 41-12998," *Pacific Wrecks* (www.pacificwrecks.com).

95 McAulay, *Dragon's Jaws*, 3950–58, 4356.

96 The creativity of the aviators in naming their aircraft is as impressive as any book. Fiction, at least.

97 Henebry, *Grim Reapers*, 125–28; McAulay, *Dragon's Jaws*, 4356. Henebry had named the B-25 *Notre Dame de Victoire* at the suggestion of the 3rd Bombardment Group's chaplain, Father John Wood, on account of Henebry being a graduate of Notre Dame and the aircraft then having a name and nose art "of a lurid nature." Father John brought over the 5th Air Force's chief of chaplains, Colonel Father Augustus Gearhard, to christen the plane and bless it with holy water. When General Kenney and Father Gearhard reviewed the reports from the November 2 attack on Rabaul, Gearhard commented that he had blessed the fallen *Notre Dame de Victoire*. Kenney reacted with, "Good enough, but the plane was shot down." The 5th Air Force commander threatened to keep Father Gearhard and his holy water away from Henebry's next aircraft. Father Gearhard responded, "Nobody was hurt. That sounds like a blessing to me." Henebry, *Grim Reapers*, 123–24, 128. Henebry calls the chaplain "Father Gerhardt" but the Air Force history specifies the chaplain's surname is "Gearhard." "Chaplain (Brig. Gen.) Augustus F. Gearhard," *Air Force* (www.af.mil).

98 McAulay, *Dragon's Jaws*, 4398–409.

99 McAulay, *Dragon's Jaws*, 4398–409. What became of Captain Hearn is unclear, but a photo spread of the officers of the 13th Bombardment Squadron dated December 17, 1943 does not show him.

100 MACR 1262; "P-38H-5-LO Lightning Serial Number 42-66821," *Pacific Wrecks* (www.pacificwrecks.com).

101 Kenney, *Air War*, 207–08.

102 Kenney, *Air War*, 206.

103 Craven and Cate, *Guadalcanal*, 326 (citing USSBS Rabaul, Table 6).

104 Kenney, *Air War*, 208.

105 Monograph 100, 15–16; Monograph 140, 78; Hata, Izawa, and Shores, *Japanese Naval Air Force*, 1626.

106 Hata, Izawa, and Shores, *Japanese Naval Air Force*, 1626.

107 Monograph 100, 15–16; Monograph 140, 78; McAulay, *Dragon's Jaws*, 4462–73.

108 USSBS 75 *Campaign Against Rabaul*, 258.

109 McAulay, *Dragon's Jaws*, 5830–96; *Yamabiko Maru*, *Onoe Maru*, and *Chogei* TROMs. *Onoe* is sometimes rendered as "*Onoue*."

110 Prados, *Islands of Destiny*, 334; *Myoko* and *Haguro* TROMs; McAulay, *Dragon's Jaws*, 5842; Monograph 140, 78; Claringbould, *Ro-Go*, 90-2; Hata, Izawa, and Shores, *Japanese Naval Air Force*, 795–96. The figures given in Hata et al. do not match those given by Claringbould, nor do either match those given by Monograph 140. The narrative goes with Hata et al., where the pilots' names are specifically listed in the chart "Key Fighter Pilots Killed in Action." The difference may simply be the Zeros lost in takeoff accidents, as Hata's chart does not include the causes of the pilots' deaths. One interesting note is that Hata et al. lists Lieutenant (jg) Miyabe as being killed on November 3, which is when he died from his wounds received on November 2, although they do have a note about this discrepancy.

111 Dunn, "Shootout at Rabaul," 25.

112 Gamble, *Target: Rabaul*, 192.

113 ONI Narrative, 76; Halsey, *Story*, 3773–84.

114 ONI Narrative, 48.

115 Hara, Saito, and Pineau, *Destroyer Captain*, 226.

116 Omori Interrogation, 340.

117 Hara, Saito, and Pineau, *Destroyer Captain*, 228; Omori Interrogation, 338–40; Monograph 100, 15. It is not entirely clear how many US Navy ships Admiral Omori and the Japanese believed they sank at Empress Augusta Bay. In his postwar interrogation, Omori said, "The definite composition of the US Forces was never established. The analysis of reports indicated that there were at least 7 heavy cruisers and 12 destroyers opposing us." He also said, "Received report that 1 torpedo hit leading US cruiser, 2 torpedo hits on second US cruiser, 2 torpedo hits on third US cruiser. Shell fire hits also reported on US Force." He does not say how many he thought he actually sank. Meanwhile, Monograph 100 says in relevant part exactly the following:
The general outcome of this night action, known as the Battle off BOUGAINVILLE, was as follows:
a. Damage inflicted
(1) heavy cruiser – sunk
(2) large destroyers – sunk
(3) heavy cruisers – sinking fairly certain
(4) 1 heavy cruiser or destroyer – sinking fairly certain.
If you can figure out what this means, please call. Maybe something got lost in the translation. Is it supposed to mean, "One heavy cruiser was sunk, two large destroyers were sunk, three heavy cruisers were fairly certainly sunk, and four ..." why is that "1" there? Or does it mean, "(1) heavy cruiser – sunk; (2) large destroyers ..." but then how many large destroyers? Hence the uncertainty here in what the Japanese thought they had accomplished.

118 Hara, Saito, and Pineau, *Destroyer Captain*, 228.

119 Claringbould, *Ro-Go*, 93; Monograph 140, 53, 78. Claringbould and Monograph 140 give slightly different timeframes, but refer to the same attack. Oddly, Monograph 140 does not directly reference the lost attack plane.

120 Odgers, *Air War Against Japan*, 97; Claringbould, *Ro-Go*, 93.

121 *Yamabiko Maru* TROM; Hara, Saito, and Pineau, *Destroyer Captain*, 229.

122 *Myoko* and *Haguro* TROMs; Budge, "Omori Sentaro (1894–1974)"; Kent G. Budge, "Osugi Morikazu (1892–1948)," *The Pacific War Online Encyclopedia* (http://pwencycl.kgbudge.com); O'Hara, *US Navy*, 4647; Budge, "Ijuin Matsuji (1893–1944)."

123 *Myoko* and *Haguro* TROMs.

124 ONI Narrative, 36; Air Group 23 Aircraft Action Report 3 (Nov. 2, 1943); ComTF38 Action Report, Buka-Bonis Strikes, November 1 and 2, 1943, 3.

125 ComAirSoPacFor War Diary, AirSols Strike Command War Diary.

126 ONI Narrative, 36; "F6F-3 Hellcat Bureau Number 66021," *Pacific Wrecks* (www.pacificwrecks.com); Air Group 23 Aircraft Action Report 4 (Nov. 2, 1943). *Pacific Wrecks* has Ensign Keener disappearing on November 1; Air Group 23's Aircraft Action Report No. 4 makes it clear Keener did not return from the second mission on November 2.

127 Halsey, *Story*, 3758; Prados, *Islands of Destiny*, 336; ComTF38 Action Report, Buka-Bonis Strikes, November 1 and 2, 1943, 2–4.

128 Hata, Izawa, and Shores, *Japanese Naval Air Force*, 1626–36; Monograph 100, 116; Monograph 140, 53, 78; Claringbould, *Ro-Go*, 94; VMF-211 War Diary. Monograph 140 gives two different figures for the number of enemy fighters engaged. Claringbould points out that none of the returning Marine pilots reported engaging the Vals and suggests that Moffat and Hatfield may have done so. However, Moffat was last seen under attack by three Zeros and his wingman, Lieutenant H. W. Mosley, did not report engaging any Vals, either. No one saw what happened to Hatfield at all, suggesting Hatfield had split off and gone after the Vals himself.

129 Prados, *Islands of Destiny*, 335–36.

130 ComSoPac Narrative, 10.

131 Halsey, *Story*, 3784–95.

132 Carey, *We Flew Alone*, 41; *Gogoku Maru, Naka, Isuzu*, and *Yamagumo* TROMs.

133 *Gogoku Maru* TROM; USS *Shad* Report of Sixth War Patrol.

134 *Naka, Isokaze*, and *Urakaze* TROMs; MACR 1176.

135 *Kiyosumi Maru* and *Urakaze* TROMs.

136 Carey, *We Flew Alone*, 40; Monograph 100, 16; *Nissho Maru, Nichiei Maru, Shimakaze*, and *Amatsukaze* TROMs. Japanese sources don't agree on whether the *Amatsukaze* was with the *Shimakaze* in escorting the *Nissho* and *Nichiei Maru*s or not. The *Shimakaze* and the *Nissho* and *Nichiei Maru*s had left Truk on November 2 on a run to Rabaul. The *Amatsukaze* also left Truk on November 2 on a run to Rabaul, but she was transporting aircrew. In all likelihood, though she was on an independent mission, she ran with the *Shimakaze* and the *Nissho* and *Nichiei Maru*s to serve as an escort for them.

137 Jonathan Parshall, "Shimakaze Class," *The Imperial Japanese Navy Page* (www.combinedfleet.com); Allyn Nevitt, "*Shimakaze* Class Notes," *The Imperial Japanese Navy Page* (www.combinedfleet.com); Stille, *Imperial Japanese Navy*, 5740–67.

138 Carey, *We Flew Alone*, 40; *Nissho Maru* TROM.

139 Carey, *We Flew Alone*, 40; *Nissho Maru* TROM.

140 Carey, *We Flew Alone*, 40; *Nissho Maru, Shimakaze*, and *Amatsukaze*'s TROMs.

141 ComAirSoPacFor, ComAirSols Strike Command, VMSB-244, VF-17, VMF-212, VMF-215, and VMTB-143 war diaries; "John W. Tunnell," *Missing Marines* (www.missingmarines.com); Sam S. Britt, *The Long Rangers: A Diary of The 307th Bombardment Group (H)* (Spartanburg, SC: Reprint Company Publishers, 1990), 68–69. AirSols Strike Command says 36 fighters accompanied the SBDs and TBFs, but the VF-17 War Diary says 28.

142 Gamble, *Target: Rabaul*, 200; Rems, *South Pacific Cauldron*, 2576; ComAirSoPacFor War Diary.

143 Prados, *Islands of Destiny*, 335.

144 Prados, *Islands of Destiny*, 335; CINCPAC War Diary.

145 Prados, *Islands of Destiny*, 335–36.

Chapter 5

1 Hara, Saito, and Pineau, *Destroyer Captain*, 231.

2 Hara, Saito, and Pineau, *Destroyer Captain*, 230; Prados, *Islands of Destiny*, 334.

3 *Gogoku* and *Kiyosumi Maru* TROMs; Monograph 100, 16. The *Gogoku Maru* TROM says the ship was not damaged, but Monograph 100 says she was.

4 *Kiyosumi Maru* and *Urakaze* TROMs.

5 *Kiyosumi Maru, Naka, Yubari, Isokaze*, and *Minazuki* TROMs. The *Yubari* and *Minazuki* TROMs say they came from Rabaul.

6   *Kiyosumi Maru, Isuzu, Isokaze,* and *Tsukushi* TROMs; RAAF Historical Section, *Units of the Royal Australian Air Force – A Concise History: Volume 4 Maritime and Transport Units* (Canberra: Australian Government Publishing Service, 1995), 20; USS *Silversides* Report of Fifth War Patrol. Most accounts credit the *Silversides* with laying the minefield that sank the *Ryuosan Maru* and *Tsukushi* and damaged the *Isuzu* and *Isokaze.* The narrative goes with the *Tsukushi* TROM, which says RAAF Catalinas laid the minefield, because the *Silversides* laid her minefield in the Steffen (or Steffan) Strait on June 4. That no one would hit any of her mines between June 4 and November 4 and then four hit mines in the same day is not credible. No. 11 Squadron repeatedly laid mines in the Kavieng area, so it's likely that she had just finished laying a new one on or just before November 4. As Allyn Nevitt and Anthony Tully point out on the TROM of the destroyer *Isokaze,* what the Japanese called "medium damage" consisted of: turbine damage that would require two days of repair; transmitter and steering engine badly damaged; upper deck buckled and both sides of ship wrinkled between frames 110 and 111; #24 fuel oil tank ruptured; main battery, compass, telephone system all damaged; and the destroyer's maximum speed cut to 16 knots. They comment, "Yet curiously all this is termed officially merely as "*Medium Damage*" [sic] Something to bear in mind when encountering this phrase."

7   *Gokoku Maru, Urakaze, Yamagumo Yubari, Kiyosumi Maru, Naka, Minazuki, Isokaze,* and *Isuzu* TROMs. For an example of the difficulty in sorting out what happened with this convoy, compare the *Naka* TROM (quoted in relevant part: "4 November 1943 […] At 1700, *Naka* arrives at Kavieng. Disembarks troops," and the *Kiyosumi Maru* TROM (quoted in relevant part: "4 November 1943 […] All the troops are landed at Rabaul") with the *Urakaze* TROM (quoted in relevant part: "1–4 November […] On 3 November air attacks left *Kiyozumi Maru* dead in the water. *Gokoku Maru* and *Urakaze* continued on to Rabaul while remainder diverted to Kavieng.")

8   Or the *Ryosan Maru.* Or *Ryuozan Maru.* Or *Ryozan Maru.*

9   *Tsukushi* TROM. The *Tsukushi* was armed with four 4.7-inch .45-cal. antiaircraft guns. Jonathan Parshall, "*Tsukushi* Class Survey Vessel," *Imperial Japanese Navy Page* (www.combinedfleet.com).

10   *Nissho Maru, Nichiei Maru, Shimakaze, Amatsukaze, Chokai,* and *Suzunami* TROMs. The *Amatsukaze* and *Suzunami* TROMs do not say when – or in the *Amatsukaze's* case, if – they arrived at Truk. But they did not say that either arrived in Rabaul in this time period (while the *Shimakaze's* TROM does) and they were assigned to assist the two tankers, so it is assumed the two destroyers arrived at Truk on November 6 like the tankers and the *Chokai* did.

11   Monograph 100, 18; Hara, Saito, and Pineau, *Destroyer Captain,* 231; Claringbould, *Ro-Go,* 99. The identification of the plane and commander come from Claringbould, who says the carriers were reported as battleships. Monograph 100 and Hara say the report was of transports, not cruisers, but otherwise their timeline of the contact report matches up with Claringbould's description. Monograph 100 is specific that the initial report of transports came in at 0700, but "[a]fter the search plane returned, however, further investigation revealed that two large transports were definitely aircraft carriers." The US attack came in at 0915. Both times are Japan Standard, which the Japanese typically used in their reports regardless of the local time zone. Claringbould says Kibayashi reported the carriers as battleships at 0855, and the *Zuikaku* scout's correction was at 0900, but agrees with Monograph 100 and Hara that the attack arrived at 0915. Rabaul was one hour ahead and the Solomon Islands two hours ahead of Japan Standard Time. The timeline is consistent with Kibayashi reporting the "large transports" by wireless, returning to Vukananau, and then being corrected by the *Zuikaku* scout. The narrative accepts this scenario and timeline. Whether the *Zuikaku* scout reported the presence of the carriers by wireless or in person is not clear but is irrelevant for this scenario.

12   Prados, *Islands of Destiny,* 337.

13   Claringbould, *Ro-Go,* 99, 102.

14   Claringbould, *Ro-Go,* 102; Monograph 100, 18; Morison, *Bismarcks Barrier,* 326; Prados, *Islands of Destiny,* 337. The timeline here may be especially confusing because it involves at least three different time zones. Admiral Sherman's task force was coming from the Solomon Islands and generally used local time, sometimes with Greenwich Mean Time, in its reports. The target, Rabaul, was one time zone to the west, meaning one hour earlier than Solomons time, but Sherman's forces generally kept Solomons time throughout. Meanwhile, Rabaul was occupied by the Japanese, who always used in their reports Japan Standard Time, which was one hour behind Rabaul and two hours behind the Solomons. For the

convenience and sanity of readers, the narrative here will describe the attack using only Solomons Islands time, but readers should be aware of the time zone issues when comparing sources.

15 Monographs 100 (16) and 140 (78) say 59 fighters "intercept"[ed] the enemy. Hata (Izawa, and Shores, *Japanese Naval Air Force*, 136) has the number as 71. Claringbould (*Ro-Go*, 103) has the number as 86.

16 Morison (*Bismarcks Barrier*, 326) says 70 aircraft were in the air when the warning was issued. This is an unrealistic number to have been in the air on a regular combat air patrol, as is 71 or 59, but the difference in those figures (11 or 12) is a reasonable figure for a regular combat air patrol over the Rabaul caldera to serve as early warning and a trip wire. This patrol was likely from Base Air Force due to its familiarity with the local layout and the plan to have the aviators from *Kido Butai* attack enemy ships and bases. Morison is also clear that Rabaul headquarters was first warned of the incoming strike by an aircraft, meaning a Japanese plane with a radio. Zeros typically did not have radios, but their squadron leaders did. Gamble theorized that of the defending fighters, "probably less than twenty were launched by the Eleventh Air Fleet," which is consistent with the above theory. Gamble has the Judys taking off from Lakunai air base.

17 Lardas, *Rabaul 1943–44*, 55; Gamble, *Target: Rabaul*, 206.
18 Gamble, *Target: Rabaul*, 206.
19 Gamble, *Target: Rabaul*, 200–01.
20 Gamble, *Target: Rabaul*, 200.
21 Gamble, *Target: Rabaul*, 201; Bruce Gamble, "The 'Reluctant Dragon' awakens: Saratoga's brave raid on Rabaul," www.navytimes.com (Nov. 1, 2019); Halsey, *Story*, 3795.
22 Halsey, *Story*, 3795–808.
23 Halsey, *Story*, 3795.
24 Gamble, *Target: Rabaul*, 201.
25 Gamble, *Target: Rabaul*, 202; Sherman, *Combat Command*, 169–70.
26 Gamble, *Target: Rabaul*, 202.
27 Gamble, *Target: Rabaul*, 202–03; Sherman, *Combat Command*, 169–70.
28 "Joseph Clinton Clifton 31 October 1908–24 December 1967," *Naval History and Heritage Command* (www.history.navy.mil).
29 Gamble, *Target: Rabaul*, 196.
30 Gamble, *Target: Rabaul*, 196.
31 Gamble, *Target: Rabaul*, 196.
32 Reynolds, *Fast Carriers*, 132.
33 Gamble, *Target: Rabaul*, 204, 216.
34 Gamble, *Target: Rabaul*, 203; Sherman, *Combat Command*, 170; ComTaskFor38 "First Rabaul Strike, November 5, 1943," 1.
35 USS *Saratoga* "Action Reports U.S.S. Saratoga (CV-3) – Period 1–5 November, 1943," 8; Gamble, *Target: Rabaul*, 203.
36 Gamble, *Target: Rabaul*, 205.
37 Gamble, *Target: Rabaul*, 205.
38 Prados, *Islands of Destiny*, 337.
39 Prados, *Islands of Destiny*, 337; USSBS 75 *Campaign Against Rabaul*, 15–16, 72; Lardas, *Rabaul*, 587.
40 Gamble, "Reluctant Dragon"; Hara, Saito, and Pineau, *Destroyer Captain*, 231.
41 Gamble, *Target: Rabaul*, 206.
42 Gamble, *Target: Rabaul*, 206.
43 Reynolds, *Fast Carriers*, 133. Dive bombing varied from 60 to 90 degrees, glide bombing 30 to 55 degrees, skip or masthead bombing was at 20 degrees, horizontal bombing below that. Reynolds, *Fast Carriers*, 613 (citing Aviation Training Division, *Introduction to Naval Aviation* (NavAer-80R-19, January 1946)).
44 Prados, *Islands of Destiny*, 338; *Atago* TROM. Prados says the *Atago* suffered from four near misses. The *Atago* TROM says there were three near misses, but all were from 500lb bombs.
45 Prados, *Islands of Destiny*, 339; *Maya* TROM; Gamble, *Target: Rabaul*, 207.
46 Prados, *Islands of Destiny*, 339; Gamble, *Target: Rabaul*, 207; *Takao* TROM. For some reason, the *Takao*'s TROM does not mention the damage to her Number 1 and 2 8-inch turrets.

47 Gamble, *Target: Rabaul*, 207.
48 Gamble, *Target: Rabaul*, 207.
49 Gamble, *Target: Rabaul*, 207; Prados, *Islands of Destiny*, 339; *Chikuma* TROM.
50 Gamble, *Target: Rabaul*, 208.
51 Gamble, "Reluctant Dragon."
52 Gamble, *Target: Rabaul*, 208; *Noshiro* TROM.
53 Prados, *Islands of Destiny*, 339; *Mogami* TROM.
54 Lardas, *Rabaul*, 996–1011; *Fujinami* TROM.
55 *Agano* TROM.
56 *Amagiri* TROM.
57 *Wakatsuki* TROM.
58 Gamble, *Target: Rabaul*, 209.
59 Gamble, *Target: Rabaul*, 209, 212.
60 Prados, *Islands of Destiny*, 340.
61 Gamble, *Target: Rabaul*, 210; Claringbould, *Ro-Go*, 105. Pilot is from Gamble. Unit and base are from Claringbould. Gamble has the Sally taking off from Tobera, but Tobera was specifically designed for fighters and was too small to handle heavy bombers. Furthermore, Rapopo was a Japanese Army Air Force base.
62 Gamble, *Target: Rabaul*, 210.
63 Murray Head, "One Night in Bangkok," Disc 2, Track 1 on *Chess*, RCA Records, 1984, CD.
64 "Princeton IV (CV-23) 1943–1944," *Dictionary of American Naval Fighting Ships* (hereinafter "*DANFS*"), https://www.history.navy.mil/research/histories/ship-histories/danfs.html.
65 Gamble, *Target: Rabaul*, 211–12.
66 Gamble, *Target: Rabaul*, 212, 216; Eugene Burns, "We Avenge Pearl Harbor," *Saturday Evening Post*, Vol. 216, No. 4 (July 22, 1944) 18–19, 73–75, 73.
67 Gamble, *Target: Rabaul*, 212.
68 Gamble, *Target: Rabaul*, 212.
69 Gamble, *Target: Rabaul*, 212, 218; Lawrence J. Hickey and James T. Pettus, *Ken's Men Against the Empire: The Illustrated History of the 43rd Bombardment Group During World War II, Volume II: The B-24 Era* (Boulder, CO: International Historical Research Associates, 2019), 31–33; Wolf, *5th Fighter Command*, 432; Kenney, *Air War*, 208–09; MACR 1074; Prados, *Islands of Destiny*, 342.
70 Halsey, *Story*, 3818.
71 Kenney, *Air War*, 208.
72 Reynolds, *Fast Carriers*, 133.
73 Halsey, *Story*, 3808.
74 Gamble, "Reluctant Dragon."
75 Hara, Saito, and Pineau, *Destroyer Captain*, 231–32.
76 Prados, *Islands of Destiny*, 338.
77 Prados, *Islands of Destiny*, 340; *Mogami* TROM; Gamble, *Target: Rabaul*, 208.
78 *Maya* TROM.
79 Prados, *Islands of Destiny*, 339; *Atago* TROM.
80 Hata, Izawa, and Shores, *Japanese Naval Air Force*, 136, 795–96; Claringbould, *Ro-Go*, 103–04. Hata et al. has a typo and calls the 201 Air Group the "291 Ku (Air Group)" and, curiously, does not mention the loss of a *Zuiho* pilot in the narrative even though Minato is listed in the table of "Key Fighter Pilots Killed in Action."
81 Claringbould, *Ro-Go*, 109.
82 Or Hagane.
83 Claringbould, *Ro-Go*, 109–11.
84 Amalgamation of Claringbould, *Ro-Go*, 109–11; Monograph 100, 18; Monograph 140, 55; and Gamble, *Target: Rabaul*, 213. The accounts are not completely consistent with each other. Claringbould, the most recent scholarship, says in the relevant part:
    Kiyomiya sent two separate pairs of *Zuikaku* and *Zuiho* Kates on a "search and destroy" mission. These were divided into two pairs, and at 1617hrs team *Zuikaku* launched two Kates commanded

by observers Leading Aircraftsman Itokawa Morio and FPO2c Yamazaki Saburo. They split up and separately reported *PT-167*'s collective of three vessels 175 nautical miles distant, then, ten minutes later, a larger flotilla 200 nautical miles distant, being TF38. This pair returned to Vunakanau in the dark at 2150hrs. The second pair of Kates from *Zuiho* launched half an hour after the first, finding the smaller flotilla at 2000hrs, then diverting to Kavieng in pitch darkness, where they touched down at 2345hrs. None of these Kates conducted attacks.

At 1815hrs an unidentified aircraft flew eastwards past *PT-167* and friends, about two miles shy of them. It flashed a red light only once but maintained course before disappearing to the east. This was Itokawa in the first *Zuikaku* Kate, whose radio operator transmitted the small flotilla's location five minutes later at 1820hrs. [...]

Finally, at 1910hrs Kiyomiya had a confirmed sighting and descended his 15 Kates rapidly for an attack position. Below, *PT-167*'s log notes that by 1915hrs the supply flotilla had steadied course and was well under way.

Gamble says in the relevant part:

Late that afternoon, four Type 97 carrier attack aircraft (Nakajima B5N2 "Kates") from *Zuikaku* and *Zuiho*, temporarily based at Rabaul for Operation *Ro-Go*, took off to conduct vector searches for the American fleet. At 1515 Tokyo time, approximately an hour after the first pathfinder departed, Lt Hagane Kiyomiya led fourteen Kates aloft. Armed with torpedoes, they headed southwest. Eighty minutes later, Kiyomiya received a report from the second sector patrol, which had sighted four cruisers, five destroyers, and "two transports resembling carriers" three hundred statute miles from Rabaul, bearing 130 degrees. At 1640, the first sector plane confirmed the sighting. This was undoubtedly Task Force 38. During the next forty-five minutes, Sherman's warships slipped away into the dusk. The strike force flew a heading of 138 degrees from Rabaul until 1702, when the first sector plane transmitted a homing signal and Kiyomiya turned his force left to a heading of 120 degrees. At 1710, the torpedo bombers made visual contact with the targets.

The Japanese record of naval air operations in the South Pacific during this time period, Monograph 140, states in the relevant part:

At 1255 hours, our reconnaissance planes sighted the enemy, bearing 145 degrees, distance 235 nautical miles from Rabaul. At 1445 hours, four carrier attack planes were dispatched on search and contact missions. At 1515 hours, 14 carrier attack planes (of the 1 Carrier Division, carrying torpedoes) were dispatched. At 1715 hours, the attacking units contacted the enemy (the search planes also sighted the enemy at the same time) and conducted the attack.

For its part, the Japanese record of naval operations in the South Pacific during this time period, Monograph 100 (18), is largely the same as Monograph 140:

Directly after the air interception battle at Rabaul, a search for the enemy was begun, our search planes establishing contact at 1255 hours at point 145 degrees and 235 nautical miles off Rabaul. Four carrier attack planes were sent out at 1445 hours for tracking purposes, followed by 14 carrier attack planes from the carrier air force at 1515 hours. At 1715 hours the attack unit found and attacked the enemy [...]

While many of these conflicting times can be resolved by adjusting for different time zones (Claringbould uses Rabaul local time while the other three use Japan Standard Time, as was typical of Japanese reports), it is impossible to give effect to all these reports. The narrative goes with Claringbould as the most recent scholarship, but fits in as much of Gamble and Monograph 140 as possible where applicable.

85 Claringbould (*Ro-Go*, 111) has Lieutenant Kiyomiya leading 15 Kates, but Monograph 140 (55) and 100 (18) have only 14 Kates in this attack, suggesting one of the attack planes had to turn back, either because of mechanical trouble or getting lost in the dark and having to return.

86 Monograph 140, 55; Claringbould, *Ro-Go*, 111; Gamble, *Target: Rabaul*, 213–14.

87 Monograph 140, 55; Gamble, *Target: Rabaul*, 214.

88 Robert J. Bulkley, Jr, *At Close Quarters: PT Boats in the United States Navy* (Washington: Naval History Division, 1962), 132; Gamble, *Target: Rabaul*, 214.

89 Bulkley, *At Close Quarters*, 132; Claringbould, *Ro-Go*, 111–12. As Claringbould notes, "As proven over the years in times of both conflict and peace, the enemy of every aviator is an invisible wire strung between two objects."

90   Bulkley, *At Close Quarters*, 132; Claringbould, *Ro-Go*, 112.
91   Bulkley, *At Close Quarters*, 132; Gamble, *Target: Rabaul*, 214; Claringbould, *Ro-Go*, 114.
92   Bulkley, *At Close Quarters*, 132–33.
93   Claringbould, *Ro-Go*, 115; Odgers, *Royal Australian Air Force*, 99–100.
94   Monograph 140, 55; Gamble, *Target: Rabaul*, 214; Prados, *Islands of Destiny*, 342; Monograph 100, 18.
95   Hara, Saito, and Pineau, *Destroyer Captain*, 232.
96   Hara, Saito, and Pineau, *Destroyer Captain*, 232.
97   Monograph 100, 17.
98   *Atago, Takao, Chikuma, Mogami, Suzuya,* and *Maya* TROMs; Prados, *Islands of Destiny*, 342.
99   Hara, Saito, and Pineau, *Destroyer Captain*, 232.

Chapter 6

1   Henry I. Shaw and Douglas E. Kane, *History of U.S. Marine Corps Operations in World War II Volume II: Isolation of Rabaul* (Washington, DC: Historical Branch, G-3 Division, Headquarters, US Marine Corps, 1963), 225–28.
2   Hara, Saito, and Pineau, *Destroyer Captain*, 232–33.
3   Hara, Saito, and Pineau, *Destroyer Captain*, 223; *Yubari* TROM; Monograph 100, 21.
4   Hara, Saito, and Pineau, *Destroyer Captain*, 233.
5   Hara, Saito, and Pineau, *Destroyer Captain*, 233–34.
6   Monograph 140, 55; Claringbould, *Ro-Go*, 117.
7   Claringbould, *Ro-Go*, 117–18. Time zone adjusted.
8   *Amagiri* TROM. Only *The Imperial Japanese Navy Page*'s TROMs for the *Amagiri* and *Uzuki* list all the ships that took part in the Torokina counterlanding. Monograph 100 (19) has a transport division of four destroyers, a screening unit of two destroyers, and a support unit of one light cruiser and five or six destroyers under the 10th Destroyer Flotilla. Morison (*Bismarcks Barrier*, 341) has Admiral Osugi "who had played an inactive part in the Battle of Empress Augusta Bay," commanding a force of light cruiser *Agano* and destroyers *Naganami, Wakatsuki, Shigure, Samidare, Shiratsuyu,* and *Amagiri* to cover landings at both Torokina and Buka.
9   Shaw and Kane, *Isolation of Rabaul*, 230; Monograph 100, 20.
10   Shaw and Kane, *Isolation of Rabaul*, 230.
11   Curt Clark, *The Famed Green Dragons: The Four Stack APDs, The APD Destroyer Sailors of WWII* (Paducah, KY: Turner Publishing, 2003), 32; Miller, *Cartwheel*, 255–56; Shaw and Kane, *Isolation of Rabaul*, 229–30; William L. McGee, *The Solomons Campaigns, 1942–1943: From Guadalcanal to Bougainville, Pacific War Turning Point* (Tiburon, CA: BMC Publications, 2001), 515.
12   Shaw and Kane, *Isolation of Rabaul*, 235.
13   Rentz, *Bougainville*, 46–47.
14   Rentz, *Bougainville*, 47.
15   United States Army Air Forces, "The Crusaders: A History of the 42nd Bombardment Group (M)" (1946), *World War Regimental Histories*, 113, 53; Cressman, *Official Chronology*; Claringbould, *Ro-Go*,117; Hammel, *Air War*, 8026–36; ComAirSoPacFor War Diary, *Ch-11* and *Asayama Maru* TROMs. The *Asayama Maru* was also known as the *Chozan Maru*. Or the *Chosan Maru*.
16   Cressman, *Official Chronology*.
17   VF-17 War Diary; Tom Blackburn, *Jolly Rogers* (New York: Pocket Books, 1989), 137; Claringbould, *Ro-Go*, 117; Monograph 140, 55, 78. Rather curiously, USSBS 75 *Campaign Against Rabaul* (19) has Fighting 17 flying F6Fs, but the VF-17 War Diary specifically identifies the fighter flown as the F4U.
18   VMSB-244, VMTB-233, VMF-212, and ComAirSols Strike Command War Diaries; USAAF, "Crusaders," 1434. According to the VC-40 War Diary, seven of its SBDs and five of its TBFs were borrowed by other squadrons for this attack. Curiously, the ComAirSoPacFor War Diary says the attack by the SBDs and TBFs was on Bonis, not Kara. Even more curiously, the Japanese Monograph 140 (78–79) records two attacks on Buka by heavy bombers but none on Kara, though it does have an attack on Buin that might actually be on Kara.
19   Kit C. Carter and Robert Mueller, *US Army Air Forces in World War II Combat Chronology 1941–1945* (Washington, DC: Center for Air Force History, 1991); Monograph 140, 55, 79; Claringbould, *Ro-Go*, 118.

20 Carter and Mueller, *Combat Chronology*; Monograph 140, 55, 79; Claringbould, *Ro-Go*, 118–19.

21 Monograph 100, 20; Miller, *Cartwheel*, 259–60.

22 Monograph 100, 20; Miller, *Cartwheel*, 259–60; Shaw and Kane, *Isolation of Rabaul*, 234; Hara, Saito, and Pineau, *Destroyer Captain*, 230.

23 Monograph 100, 20; Miller, *Cartwheel*, 259–60; Bulkley, *At Close Quarters*, 131; Shaw and Kane, *Isolation of Rabaul*, 234.

24 Monograph 140, 55, 79; Monograph 100, 21; Claringbould, *Ro-Go*, 122. Oddly, Claringbould does not mention the support mission by the 13 carrier bombers and 13 carrier attack planes, but Monographs 100 and 140 insist there was such a mission. 0700 Japan Time is 0800 Rabaul time.

25 McAulay, *Dragon's Jaws*, 4871–935; Wolf, *5th Fighter Command*, 433; Steve W. Ferguson and William K. Pascalis, *Protect & Avenge: The 49th Fighter Group in World War II* (Atglen, PA: Schiffer Publishing, 1996), 214; Monograph 140, 56, 79; Hata, Izawa, and Shores, *Japanese Naval Air Force*, 136; Claringbould, *Ro-Go*, 123–24.

26 Gamble, *Target: Rabaul*, 218.

27 MACR 1075, MACR 1202; Ferguson and Pascalis, *Protect & Avenge*, 214. Apologies for efforts at identifying the third pilot shot down coming up short.

28 Kenney, *Air War*, 209.

29 Monograph 140, 79; Hata, Izawa, and Shores, *Japanese Naval Air Force*, 136.

30 Dunn, "Shootout at Rabaul," 26

31 Monograph 140, 56.

32 Claringbould, *Ro-Go*, 125.

33 Wolf, *5th Fighter Command*, 435–36; Kenney, *Air War*, 210; Richard L. Dunn, "248th Hiko Sentai: A Japanese 'Hard luck' Fighter Unit," *j-aircraft.com: Japanese Aircraft, Ships, & Historical Research* (www.j-aircraft.com); "Missions against Nadzab," *Pacific Wrecks* (www.pacificwrecks.com).

34 Wolf, *5th Fighter Command*, 435–36; Dunn, "248th Hiko Sentai"; Michael Claringbould, *Pacific Adversaries Volume One: Japanese Army Air Force vs The Allies, New Guinea 1942–1944* (Kent Town, Australia: Avonmore Books, 2019), 71.

35 Wolf, *5th Fighter Command*, 435–36; Kenney, *Air War*, Dunn, "248th Hiko Sentai"; *Tencho Maru* TROM; "Missions against Nadzab"; Lex McAulay, *A Clean Sweep: The Destruction of the Japanese Army Air Force Fighter Arm Over New Guinea 1943–44* (Maryborough, Qld.: Banner Books, 2016), Kindle edition, 753. Dunn says 186 of 191 members of the 248's ground echelon were killed when the *Delagoa Maru* was sunk. Claringbould (*Pacific Adversaries Volume One*, 72–73) says one Ki-21 ditched and one force-landed.

36 Dunn, "248th Hiko Sentai"; "Missions against Nadzab"; Wolf, *5th Fighter Command*, 434; 38th Bombardment Group History, 212; 13th Bombardment Squadron Combat Log. Carter and Mueller, *Combat Chronology* say that on November 7, "9 B-25s bomb Wewak and more than 40 others turn back when ftr escort is intercepted by airplanes over Nadzab." Other histories say something similar. However, the full story appears to be more complicated and ambiguous. The records of the 38th Bombardment Group state that all four of its squadrons were to participate in the attack on Wewak's Boram airfield, with nine each from the 71st and 823rd, eight from the 822nd, and, apparently, ten from the 405th for a total of 36 B-25s, a number that consistently appears in the records of the 38th. When the rendezvous with the fighter escort failed because of the Japanese attack on Nadzab, "the formation returned to base without completing their [sic] mission for the second day in a row." The 71st Squadron's history says that the 405th "was radioed" to turn back; when the 405th did so, the 71st followed. The 822nd reportedly was briefly engaged by the attacking Japanese fighters. There is no reference to anyone in the 38th continuing onward to Wewak. The 38th's records consistently state the attack was to consist of 36 B-25s and lists only its four squadrons as participating, but the 13th's combat logs insist that it was to contribute nine B-25s to the Wewak attack as well, which would have made a total of 45 B-25s attacking Wewak. But the 13th also aborted its attack, saying, "All aircraft returned to base on instructions from fighter control at Nadzab due to enemy aircraft in the area." The remainder of the 3rd Bombardment Group was in the midst of transitioning to A-20 Havocs, so the nine B-25s that reportedly attacked Wewak could not have been them. There does not appear to be a record of anyone from the 345th Bombardment

Group attacking Wewak on this day. Finally, General Kenney, in his memoirs, mentions the Japanese November 7 raid on Nadzab and the fighter interception of that attack, but does not mention the planned attack on Wewak, the scrubbing of that attack due to the Japanese raid, or, most curiously of all given Kenney's personality, any of the B-25s going on to attack heavily defended Wewak with no fighter escort. Thus, unclear is the identity of the nine B-25s who reportedly attacked Wewak, or even if such an attack took place at all.

37 ComAirSoPacFor, ComSoPac, AirSols Strike Command, VMTB-233, VC-40, VMF-212 and -215 war diaries. The ComAirSoPacFor has the aircraft attacking Buka as B-25s.

38 ComAirSoPacFor and VF-17 war diaries. ComAirSoPacFor war diary says 24 fighters escorted the Venturas in, followed by the Mitchells. VF-17's war diary says 16 of its F4US escorted "B-25s [sic] and PV-1s [sic]" and makes no mention of aircraft from other squadrons being involved.

39 Rentz, *Bougainville*, 47.

40 Shaw and Kane, *Isolation of Rabaul*, 234.

41 Rentz, *Bougainville*, 48.

42 Shaw and Kane, *Isolation of Rabaul*, 234–35.

43 Bulkley, *At Close Quarters*, 133.

44 Bulkley, *At Close Quarters*, 133.

45 Bulkley, *At Close Quarters*, 133.

46 Naval Advance Base Torokina War Diary; Morison, *Bismarcks Barrier*, 342–43; Bulkley, *At Close Quarters*, 134.

47 Morison, *Bismarcks Barrier*, 342–43.

48 Bulkley, *At Close Quarters*, 134.

49 Morison, *Bismarcks Barrier*, 343–44; Task Force 31 and Task Group 31.6 war diaries.

50 Bulkley, *At Close Quarters*, 133; Task Force 31 War Diary.

51 Bulkley, *At Close Quarters*, 134.

52 ComSoPac and VF-17 war diaries; Blackburn, *Jolly Rogers*, 140–42; Claringbould, *Ro-Go*, 126.

53 TF 31 War Diary.

54 Task Unit 31.5.4 Report of action against Japanese aircraft at Cape Torokina, Empress Augusta Bay, Bougainville, Solomon Islands, on 8 November 1943 (hereinafter "Anderson Report)," 3–4.

55 VF-17, VF-40, and VMF-212 war diaries; Blackburn, *Jolly Rogers*, 144; Hammel, *Air War*, 8066; Wolf, *13th Fighter Command*, 223–24.

56 Monograph 100, 21; Monograph 140, 57; Claringbould, *Ro-Go*, 127. Monograph 140 has 71 Zeros in the attack while Claringbould has 74 taking off; the obvious deductive resolution to this contradiction is three of the Zeros took off but had to abort. Reminder here that the different time zones can lead to seemingly inconsistent times.

57 Flying a defensive circle over a target you are trying to protect was very common, but forming a defensive circle for mutual protection while in combat, as was done here, was not. This type of defensive circle is known as a Lufbury (or Lufberry or Lufbery or Luffberry) Circle (or Wheel). It is named after World War I French fighter ace Gervais Raoul Lufbery, who neither invented the Lufbery Circle nor used it.

58 Blackburn, *Jolly Rogers*, 145–48; Wolf, *13th Fighter Command*, 224; William H. Starke, *Vampire Squadron!: The Saga of the 44th Fighter Squadron in the South and Southwest Pacific* (Anaheim, CA: Robinson Typographics, 1985), 70; Claringbould, *Ro-Go*, 127–31. Starke says the 12th Fighter Squadron, also from the 18th Fighter Group, took part in the interception as well.

59 USS *President Jackson* Report of Action against Japanese Aircraft off Northern Empress Augusta Bay, Bougainville Island, on 8 November 1943 (hereinafter "*President Jackson* Report"), 1–3.

60 Action Report, USS *Fuller* (APA-7), 8 November 1943 (hereinafter "*Fuller* Report"), 2.

61 *Fuller* Report, 2–3.

62 MACR 1088.

63 VMF-212 War Diary.

64 MACR 1089.

65 ComAirSoPacFor and NAS Segi War Diaries; Claringbould, *Ro-Go*, 133–34.

66 Or Nobutaka.

67 Hata, Izawa, and Shores, *Japanese Naval Air Force*, 136; Monograph 100, 21; Monograph 140, 58; Claringbould, *Ro-Go*, 131–32. Monograph 140 and Hata et al. say ten carrier bombers failed to return, but Claringbould's figures add up to 11. Monograph 140 and Hata et al. also say five Zeros failed to return, but Claringbould has only four.

68 Monograph 140, 59; Claringbould, *Ro-Go*, 134–35, 137.

69 Monograph 140, 59; Claringbould, *Ro-Go*, 134–35, 137. Times are from Monograph 140; units from Claringbould. Monograph 140 specifically says that all nine of the B5Ns and all the G4Ms were armed with torpedoes. That leaves open the likelihood that the B5Ns sent as scouts were armed with bombs.

70 Action Report, Cruiser Division Thirteen, 8–9 November, 1943 (hereinafter "DuBose Report"), 1–2. The namesake of the cruiser *Portland* is not the Portland you're thinking of. You're thinking of Portland, Oregon. The *Portland* was actually named after Portland, Maine.

71 DuBose Report, 2; Morison. *Bismarcks Barrier*, 344.

72 DuBose Report, 2.

73 Monograph 100, 21.

74 DuBose Report, 3, 6.

75 VMF(N)-531 War Diary.

76 War Damage Report Number 48: USS BIRMINGHAM (CL62) Torpedo and Bomb Damage, Solomon Islands, 8 November, 1943 (hereinafter "*Birmingham* Damage Report"), 2; *Santa Fe* Action Report – Night Anti-aircraft Action, 8 November 1943 (hereinafter "*Santa Fe* Report"), 2.

77 DuBose Report, 3.

78 *Birmingham* Action Report – Night Air Attack – 8–9 November 1943 (hereinafter "*Birmingham* Report"), 1–2.

79 *Birmingham* Damage Report, 2; *Birmingham* Report, 1–2.

80 *Birmingham* Damage Report, 2; *Birmingham* Report, 2.

81 *Birmingham* Damage Report, 2; *Birmingham* Report, 10.

82 DuBose Report, 9.

83 DuBose Report, 8–9; *Birmingham* Damage Report, 3.

84 DuBose Report, 9.

85 DuBose Report, 9.

86 See, e.g., DuBose Report, 4 ("1919 – *Birmingham* hit forward, probably by torpedo"); *Birmingham* Report, 2 ("[T]he ship was jarred again and water came over the open bridge. An explosion had occurred on the port bow at frame 20"), 7 ("Hit 2 was probably a torpedo hit at frame 20 port"); ComSoPac War Diary ("The Blue CL *Birmingham* sustained 3 bomb hits [...] and a third on the port bow"); Merrill Report, 1 ("[T]he *Birmingham* received three bomb (or torpedo) hits").

87 Monograph 140, 59–60; Monograph 100, 22; Osamu Tagaya and Mark Styling, *Mitsubishi Type 1 Rikko "Betty" Units of World War 2* (Oxford: Osprey, 2001), Kindle edition, 1430. Tagaya credits a G4M *rikko* for torpedoing the *Birmingham*. If the Japanese timeline for the attack as given in Monograph 140 (carrier attack planes from 1712 to 1720; land attack planes from 1725 until 1800 Japan Standard Time) is accepted as true, then the credit for the torpedo hit should go to a B5N *kanko*. But there is more evidence that credit should go to the *rikko*. Morison (*Bismarcks Barrier*, 344) says each bomb came from a "Val" but the torpedo came from a "Betty." It's not clear how Morison came to this conclusion, but it does make sense. In point of fact, no one saw or heard the aircraft that launched the torpedo that hit the *Birmingham*. That by itself suggests the aircraft came from some place other than the west, which was still showing some light that would later reveal by silhouette another attacker. The *Birmingham* appears to have been heading southwest or south when the torpedo hit her port bow. A torpedo attack from the dark side of the enemy at twilight suggests the attacking aircraft was a G4M Betty, the same type of aircraft that took part in the Rennell Island attack, which also involved a twilight attack from the dark side of the enemy and with which the aircrews of the G4Ms at Rabaul would have been more familiar than the aviators of *Kido Butai*. The source of each bomb hit on the *Birmingham* was likely a Kate. The first bomber was seen and identified as a "Val with retractable landing gear," which did not exist, and was almost certainly a B5N "Kate." The third attacker was seen against the last twilight, but was not identified. Nevertheless, that it dropped only one bomb also suggests it was a Kate, as a Betty would likely have had more than one general-purpose bomb.

88 *Birmingham* Damage Report, 1, 3–4, 7; Captain Thomas B. Inglis, "The Mighty 'B,'" *Shipmate*, June 1945 Fleet Issue, 124 (posted in "Mister Mac," "The Mighty "B" – Don't Give Up The Ship… The Story Of The USS Birmingham CL-62," *THELEANSUBMARINER: Steel Boats, Iron Men and their stories (plus a bit more)* (www.theleansubmariner.com)).

89 *Birmingham* Report, 2–3; Inglis, "The Mighty 'B'"; *Birmingham* Damage Report, 6–7.

90 *Birmingham* Damage Report, 6–7.

91 DuBose Report, 3; *Birmingham* Report, 7.

92 *Birmingham* Report, 2–3; *Birmingham* Damage Report, 6–7.

93 Monograph 140, 59; Monograph 100, 22.

94 Monograph 140, 59–60; Monograph 100, 22; Tagaya and Styling, *Rikko*, 1430; Claringbould, *Ro-Go*, 137–38, 140. While the monographs say six G4Ms "failed to return," Tagaya says seven were "lost." The difference might be that one G4M attack plane returned to base but was so badly damaged as to be written off. Claringbould does not specify in which attack Nozaka and his crew were killed; that he was killed in the first attack by the 751 and not the later one is a deduction based on the timing of the return of the first 751 strike and the launch of the second.

95 Claringbould, *Ro-Go*, 134.

96 DuBose Report, 3–4; Monograph 140, 79–80; Claringbould, *Ro-Go*, 140.

97 Anderson Report, 2, 6.

98 Anderson Report, 34; VMF(N)-531 War Diary.

99 Odgers, *Royal Australian Air Force*, 100–01.

100 Claringbould, *Ro-Go*, 143; Odgers, *Royal Australian Air Force*, 100–01; "Honours and Awards: Lloyd Russell Greentree," *Australian War Memorial* (www.awm.gov.au); "Wing Commander Geoffrey Dimmock Nicoll," *Australian War Memorial* (www.awm.gov.au).

101 Odgers, *Royal Australian Air Force*, 100–01; Claringbould, *Ro-Go*, 143.

102 Odgers, *Royal Australian Air Force*, 100–01; Claringbould, *Ro-Go*, 144.

103 Odgers, *Royal Australian Air Force*, 101; Claringbould, *Ro-Go*, 144.

104 Odgers, *Royal Australian Air Force*, 101; Claringbould, *Ro-Go*, 144; "Wing Commander Noel Thomas Quinn," *Australian War Memorial* (www.awm.gov.au).

105 Odgers, *Royal Australian Air Force*, 101; Claringbould, *Ro-Go*, 144.

106 Odgers, *Royal Australian Air Force*, 101; Claringbould, *Ro-Go*, 143.

107 Odgers, *Royal Australian Air Force*, 101; Claringbould, *Ro-Go*, 144.

108 Odgers, *Royal Australian Air Force*, 102.

109 Odgers, *Royal Australian Air Force*, 18, 102–03; Stephens, *Royal Australian Air Force: A History*, 122–23.

110 Morison, *Bismarcks Barrier*, 345.

111 Inglis, "The Mighty 'B.'"

112 See Anthony P. Tully, "The Loss of Battleship KONGO" (in "Mysteries/Untold Sagas of the Imperial Japanese Navy," *The Imperial Japanese Navy Page* (www.combinedfleet.com)) for an example of how difficult it is.

113 *Ro-104* TROM.

114 ComSoPac, ComAirSoPacFor, VMTB-233 and -143, VMSB-244.

115 ComAirSoPacFor War Diary.

116 ComAirSols Strike Command, VC-24, VC-40, VF-17, VF-40, VMF-212, VMF-221 war diaries.

117 ComAirSols Strike Command and VC-40 war diaries. It was later determined that after Lieutenant McIntire's bomb was released and detonated, the concussion from the explosion caused the Dauntless to go out of control and crash near the runway. See "SBD-5 Dauntless Bureau Number 35931," *Pacific Wrecks* (www.pacificwrecks.com).

118 Rentz, *Bougainville*, 49.

119 Rentz, *Bougainville*, 49–50.

120 Sherrod, *Marine Corps Aviation*, 189–90.

121 Sherrod, *Marine Corps Aviation*, 190.

122 Shaw and Kane, *Isolation of Rabaul*, 240.

123 Rentz, *Bougainville*, 50.

124 Sherrod, *Marine Corps Aviation*, 190; Shaw and Kane, *Isolation of Rabaul*, 240.

125 Shaw and Kane, *Isolation of Rabaul*, 240; Rentz, *Bougainville*, 50.

126 Shaw and Kane, *Isolation of Rabaul*, 240.

127 Monograph 100, 30.

128 Sherrod, *Marine Corps Aviation*, 189.

129 ComSoPac and ComAirSoPacFor war diaries; Cressman, *Chronology*; R. H. Cohn, *The Crusaders: A History of the 42nd Bombardment Group (M)* (Baton Rouge, LA: Army & Navy Pictorial Publications, 2013), 1440–54.

130 Monograph 140, 61, 80.

131 Monograph 140, 61, 80; Claringbould, *Ro-Go*, 145.

132 Monograph 140, 61, 80; Claringbould, *Ro-Go*, 145.

133 Monograph 140, 61, 80; Claringbould, *Ro-Go*, 145. Admiral Merrill (2) wrote, "For a Task Force that has trained as diligently at anti-aircraft firing as has Task Force THIRTY-NINE, and one which has performed so satisfactorily at towed sleeves and enemy planes during daylight, our snooper shooting at night has been disappointing." Merrill glossed over some rather significant differences between day and night, especially one in particular. Go outside during the day, then go outside at night and see if you notice a difference.

134 Monograph 140, 61, 80; Claringbould, *Ro-Go*, 145–46.

135 Claringbould, *Ro-Go*, 156. Monograph 140 does not mention this report, though it mentions Masaki's previous report of the transport on fire.

136 Hickey and Pettus, *Ken's Men, Vol. II*, 36; Craven and Cate, *Guadalcanal*, 327–28. There seems to have been a lot of confusion as to the 5th Air Force's activities concerning Rabaul on this day, with many claiming that either one big attack was launched, but only the Liberators got through the stormy weather, or there was one attack and it had to be aborted because of the weather.

137 Monograph 140, 61; Claringbould, *Ro-Go*, 156.

138 Monograph 140, 62; Claringbould, *Ro-Go*, 156–57.

139 ComSoPac, VMF-215, and *Princeton* war diaries; USS *Saratoga* Air Attack on Rabaul Shipping, 11 November, 1943 (hereinafter "*Saratoga* November 11 Report"), 1–2; USS *Essex* Operations in Rabaul area, 11 November 1943 (hereinafter "*Essex* Report"), 2; Monograph 140, 63; Hata, Izawa, and Shores, *Japanese Naval Air Force*, 136–37; Gamble, *Target Rabaul*, 223; Claringbould, *Ro-Go*, 157. Marine Fighting 215's war diary has two four-plane divisions taking off "to patrol over a task force of aircraft carriers whose planes were to hit Rabaul Harbor." The task force of aircraft carriers is not specified. For that matter, neither the war diary of VMF-212 nor VMF-215 specifies which carrier force they covered. VMF-221's war diary does not give the numerical designation, but mentions, "The *Essex* was hit by four waves of dive bombers but we missed the show." Because VMF-212 and VMF-221 have been credited with covering Admiral Montgomery's carrier task force, with VMF-215 not even mentioned, process of elimination leaves Admiral Sherman's as the only candidate for the task force of aircraft carriers covered by VMF-215. However, VMF-212 did cover Admiral Sherman's carriers later that day and may have done so that morning as well. Halsey has 55 F6Fs, 21 SBDs, and 25 TBFs in this attack by Task Force 38. According to the *Saratoga*'s report, she launched 36 F6Fs, 23 SBDs, and 15 TBFs by herself. The *Princeton*'s War Diary has her launching 22 F6Fs and nine TBFs. Both Japanese Monographs 100 (23) and 140 (63) use the 68 figure; 140 says the 68 represents "Japanese Air Strength" while 100 says the Japanese "sent up" 68. Hata et al. say 78 (35 *Kido Butai*, 19 201 Air Group, and 24 204) "intercepted" the attack. Gamble has 107 (68 from Base Air Force and 39 from *Kido Butai*), but says they were not all airborne until Admiral Montgomery's attack arrived. This partially agrees with Claringbould, the most recent scholarship, who says 107 (15 *Shokaku*, 12 *Zuikaku*, 12 *Zuiho*, 19 201 Air Group, 24 204, and 25 253), but Claringbould specifies they "scrambled at exactly 0900" and made "first contact" ten minutes later.

140 ComSoPac; *Saratoga* November 11 Report, 2, 5; *Saratoga* and *Princeton* war diaries; "TBF-1 Avenger Bureau Number 23973," *Pacific Wrecks* (https://pacificwrecks.com/).

141 Halsey, *Story*, 3829.

142 Sherrod, *Marine Corps Aviation*, 186.

143 Gailey, *Bougainville*, 1177.

144 Morison, *Bismarcks Barrier*, 330–31.

145 The USS *Bunker Hill* was named after the American Revolutionary War Battle of Bunker Hill, which did not actually take place on Bunker Hill but on nearby Breed's Hill. Nevertheless, the engagement is known as the Battle of Bunker Hill.

146 Morison, *Bismarcks Barrier*, 332–33; Blackburn, *Jolly Rogers*, 159, 164–65, VMF-212 and VMF-221 war diaries.

147 ComSoPac War Diary; *Essex* Report, 2; USS *Bunker Hill* Report of Action on November 11, 1943 (hereinafter "*Bunker Hill* Rabaul Report"), 11; Action Report – Attack on Enemy Surface Forces at Rabaul and Attack by Japanese Aircraft on this Task Force on November 11, 1943 – USS *Independence* (hereinafter "*Independence* Report"), 3; Robert F. Dorr, "The Curtiss SB2C Helldiver: An Unpopular and Flawed Allied War Machine," *Warfare History Network* (www.warfarehistorynetwork.com).

148 *Bunker Hill* Rabaul Report, 11; Gamble, *Target: Rabaul*, 222; Robert Guttman, "Curtiss SB2C Helldiver: The Last Dive Bomber," *HistoryNet* (www.historynet.com); Dorr, "The Curtiss SB2C Helldiver." For some reason, the *Bunker Hill*'s action report calls Lieutenant (jg) Ralph Gunville "Ensign C.L. Gunville." The list of war deaths in the USS *Bunker Hill* Cruise Book Nov 1943–Nov 1944 (229) has Gunville's correct name. Curtiss had to make more than 880 changes to the SB2C's design before the US Navy would accept the aircraft. Aviation historian Stephen Sherman summarized the criticisms of the Helldiver: "weak structure," "poor handling," "inadequate stability," "unacceptable stall characteristics," "severe buffeting in dives," and "sluggish ailerons." Stephen Sherman, "SB2C Helldiver Curtiss dive bomber," *AcePilots.com* (www.acepilots.com). Most of these defects were corrected by the end of the war, but the Helldiver has always been seen as a disappointment and overall not much of an improvement over the SBD Dauntless.

149 *Essex* Report, 34.

150 *Essex* Report, 2.

151 *Bunker Hill* Report, 12.

152 *Essex* Report, 28.

153 *Bunker Hill* Report, 21.

154 *Bunker Hill* Rabaul Report, 13; Morison, *Bismarcks Barrier*, 332; *Suzunami* TROM.

155 *Bunker Hill* Report, 14–15.

156 Gamble, *Target: Rabaul*, 220; Guttman, "The Last Dive Bomber."

157 From Guttman, "The Last Dive Bomber." Commander Herbert D. Riley, who served on the staff of the deputy chief of Naval Operations (Air) during that period, was one of the officers responsible for procuring new aircraft for the Navy. He later recalled that "the SB2C was so tricky to fly, compared to the SBD, and so hard to maintain that the skippers of the new carriers preferred to have the old SBDs. We had quite a battle forcing the SB2C down their respective throats."

158 *Essex* Report, 55.

159 *Independence* Report, 17.

160 *Bunker Hill* Report, 10.

161 ComSoPac War Diary; *Essex* Report, 20.

162 ComSoPac War Diary; *Independence* Report, 5; *Essex* Report, 20; *Bunker Hill* Report, 15–17; Lisa Land Cooper, "The Carby Family Sacrifice," *The Story Behind the History* (www.LisaLandCooper.com), and Gamble, *Target: Rabaul*, 220, 224–5; 231–2; 248–50.

163 Headquarters 307th Bombardment Group (H) "Historical Data" Report – 1 October 1943 to 31 December 1943, Periodic Activities Summary 1 November 1943 to 30 November 1943, 1–2; ComTasFor39 Action Report – Task Force Thirty-Nine covering operations for Empress Augusta Bay and Treasury Island Echelons – Period from 8 November 1943 to 14 November 1943 (hereinafter "Merrill November Report"), 3–4; 5th Bombardment Group Association, *Bomber Barons*, 497; 13th Air Force, USAAF, *Fifth Bombardment Group Heavy) in World War II* (Hoosick Falls, NY: Merriam Press, 2012), 53; Britt, *Long Rangers*, 69–71; ComSoPac War Diary.

164 ComSoPac Narrative, 10.

165 Morison, *Bismarcks Barrier*, 332.

166 Monograph 100, 23; *Agano* and *Naganami* TROMs; Morison, *Bismarcks Barrier*, 332; Lacroix and Wells, *Japanese Cruisers*, 595.

167 Monograph 140, 62.

168 Monograph 100, 23; *Noshiro* TROM. Monograph 100 has three destroyers leaving for Truk, not five as indicated here, and does not identify the destroyers.

169 *Essex* Report, 29.

170 *Essex* Report, 29.

171 Hata, Izawa, and Shores, *Japanese Naval Air Force*, 136–37, 795–96; Claringbould, *Ro-Go*, 157, 164–65.

172 Monograph 100, 23; Monograph 140, 64; Gamble, *Target: Rabaul*, 227–28; Claringbould, *Ro-Go*, 161–62; Hata, Izawa, and Shores, *Japanese Naval Air Force*, 137. Monograph 140 has 69 Zeros in the attack, but does not give a breakdown. Hata et al. say the attack consisted of 67 Zeros, 27 dive bombers and 14 torpedo bombers, but, again, does not give a breakdown. Gamble has 23 Vals, 14 Kates, and 33 Zeros from *Kido Butai* and four Judys and 32 Zeros from Base Air Force, for a total of 65 Zeros. Claringbould says "69 Zero-sen from various units headed off to find the carriers." He does give a breakdown: 32 from the 204 Air Group, then "15 more land-based Zero-sen took off," consisting of "a dozen 201 Ku fighters led by a 204 Ku flight headed by Ens Katayama"; nine *Zuikaku*, 15 *Shokaku*, and nine *Zuiho*. The narrative uses Claringbould's breakdown. However, Claringbould's breakdown adds up to 80 fighters. Claringbould's is the only history that references Ensign Katayama's flight, but even subtracting the 15 leads to a total of 65. For that reason, the narrative uses the figure of 80 Zeros.

173 Monograph 140, 64; Monograph 100, 23–24; Hata, Izawa, and Shores, *Japanese Naval Air Force*, 137; Claringbould, *Ro-Go*, 162. Monograph 140 has seven Vals turning back because of mechanical issues, but gives no breakdown; Gamble has only three Vals turning back but does not give a breakdown; while Claringbould has six turning back but does give a breakdown. Monograph 140 does not have the 15 Zeros under Ensign Katayama turning back – or accounted for at all – but Claringbould does. Monograph 100 (24) cited "the impossibility of assembling planes [referring to the air strike] in the air (caused by imperfect co-ordination between the carrier air force and the base air force) forced some pilots to turn back [...]"; recall that the D4Y reconnaissance planes used here all came from *Kido Butai* and thus had better communication with other units of *Kido Butai* than those of Base Air Force. Gamble (*Target: Rabaul*, 227) says the land-based fighters were "led by a young officer with little combat experience" who "failed to rendezvous with the main strike force and returned." Again, this is not inconsistent with the deduction posited above for the reasons posited above.

174 ComCarDiv12 War Diary; *Bunker Hill* Report, 25.

175 *Independence* Report, 27; *Bunker Hill* Report, 25; Monograph 100, 23–24.

176 *Essex* Report, 3.

177 USS *Kidd* Report of action off Rabaul –11 November 1943 (hereinafter "*Kidd* Report"), 4.

178 ComCarDiv12 War Diary.

179 *Essex* Report, 3, 20, 70, 72.

180 *Bunker Hill* Report, 22.

181 *Independence* Report, 3.

182 *Essex* Report, 11.

183 *Essex* Report, 11.

184 *Essex* Report, 5.

185 *Essex* Report, 91; Morison, *Bismarcks Barrier*, 333.

186 Blackburn, *Jolly Rogers*, 164–66.

187 *Essex* Report, 3.

188 *Independence* Report, 30.

189 *Bunker Hill* Report, 26.

190 Montgomery Report, 2. It is interesting to note that a US Navy flag officer continues to refer to the "clipped-wing" Zeros as "Haps," a reporting name that was changed to "Hamp" upon the objection of Army Air Force head General Henry "Hap" Arnold. Evidently, the hard feelings toward Arnold regarding his throttling the Pacific of reinforcements continued.

191 *Bunker Hill* Report, 10.

192 Morison, *Bismarcks Barrier*, 333.

193 *Bunker Hill* Report, 43.

194 Commander Task Group Fifty Point Three Attack on Enemy Ships at Rabaul and Subsequent Enemy Aircraft Raid on Task Group Fifty Point Three, Action report of (hereinafter "Montgomery Report"), 4; *Essex* Report, 30; *Bunker Hill* Report, 26.

195 *Essex* Report, 45, 83; Morison, *Bismarcks Barrier*, 333.

196 *Bunker Hill* Report, 42.

197 Amalgamation of *Bunker Hill* Report, 3, and *Independence* Report, 41.

198 Montgomery Report, 4.

199 *Essex* Report, 83; *Bunker Hill* Report, 10.

200 Montgomery Report, 4.

201 *Bunker Hill* Report, 22. This is a deduction based on: 1. A carrier generally would not be launching aircraft while it was under air attack and certainly not while dive bombers were releasing bombs overhead, which would be extremely dangerous for the carrier and the plane taking off; 2. If a dive bomber pulled out of its dive near the *Bunker Hill*, it was most certainly after diving on the *Essex*, because the *Independence* was on the opposite site of the triangle formation of the carriers from the *Bunker Hill*, with the *Essex* between and ahead of both; 3. The Vals attacked the *Essex* from 40 degrees relative, 50 degrees True (*Essex* Report, 83), which would take them in the direction of the *Bunker Hill* off the *Essex* port quarter; and 4. Commander Emrick, heading the *Essex* air group in a command TBF Avenger, mentions that at the beginning of the Japanese attack, he saw ten Vals diving and chased one on its pullout, but a US Navy fighter cut in and shot it down (*Essex* Report, 28), a description that sounds very similar to Ensign Watts' encounter. That said, readers should be aware that this is only the most likely time of Watts' takeoff and shootdown of the Val, but other times are possible.

202 *Essex* Report, 4, 11–12. This is another deduction based on: 1. The *Essex*'s main encounter with the Vals was during the first wave; and 2. The various descriptions of the near miss in the *Essex* Report, while not saying exactly when the near miss took place, imply that it was early in the Japanese attack, with little in the way of description of combat taking place before the near miss. Again, this is considered only the most likely scenario; others are possible.

203 *Independence Report*, 10, 20, 33.

204 *Bunker Hill* Report, 26.

205 *Bunker Hill* Report, 31, 35.

206 *Essex* Report, 6.

207 *Bunker Hill* Report, 37.

208 *Bunker Hill* Report, 37.

209 *Essex* Report, 5.

210 *Essex* Report, 9; *Bunker Hill* Report, 42.

211 Montgomery Report, 3.

212 *Essex* Report, 72–73.

213 *Essex* Report, 30.

214 *Essex* Report, 73.

215 Montgomery Report, 3.

216 *Bunker Hill* Report, 31.

217 Montgomery Report, 3; *Bunker Hill* Report, 31.

218 Monograph 100, 24; Monograph 140, 65.

219 Blackburn, *Jolly Rogers*, 169–70.

220 *Independence* Report, 20; Montgomery Report, 3; Monograph 100, 24; Monograph 140, 65.

221 Monograph 100, 24.

222 Monograph 140, 64.

223 Monograph 100, 24; Monograph 140, 65.

224 Hata, Izawa, and Shores, *Japanese Naval Air Force*, 137.

225 Claringbould, *Ro-Go*, 164.

226 Monograph 100, 24; Monograph 140, 65.

227 Montgomery Report, 4.

228 Gamble, *Target: Rabaul*, 227; Hata, Izawa, and Shores, *Japanese Naval Air Force*, 7794; Claringbould, *Ro-Go*, 165.

229 Gamble, *Target: Rabaul*, 229.
230 Morison, *Bismarcks Barrier*, 335.
231 *Essex* Report, 4.
232 Morison, *Bismarcks Barrier*, 335.
233 There was actually an episode of *Seinfeld* about this.
234 The account of Ensign Kepford's pit stop on the *Bunker Hill* comes from Blackburn, *Jolly Rogers*, 173–74.
235 Montgomery Report, 3.
236 *Essex* Report, 96.
237 *Essex* Report, 96. Fitzhugh Lee III was a grandson of former Confederate general and later Virginia governor Fitzhugh Lee, great-grandnephew of former Confederate General Robert E. Lee, great-grandson of Admiral Sydney Smith Lee, and great-great-grandson of American Revolutionary War General Henry "Light Horse Harry" Lee III.
238 This is where time zones become an issue again. Japanese reports always use Japan Standard Time, which is UTC+9. Rabaul is Papua New Guinea Standard Time: UTC+10. Bougainville is Bougainville Standard Time: UTC+11.
239 Monograph 100, 24; Monograph 140, 66, 81; Claringbould, *Ro-Go*, 165. Monograph 100 (25) says the 702 Air Group's attack took off at 5:30pm. The narrative of Monograph 140 (66) says two G4Ms were sent up to search for the American carriers, but Monograph 140's chart (81) says there were two search missions, one of five and one of 11.
240 Monograph 100, 25; Monograph 140, 66.
241 ComTasFor31 War Diary.
242 ComTasFor31 and USS *Stringham* war diaries.
243 Merrill Report, 4, 6; *Eaton* War Diary.
244 Merrill Report, 4.
245 Merrill Report, 4–5.
246 Merrill Report, 5.
247 Merrill Report, 8.
248 Merrill Report, 5.
249 Monograph 100, 24–25; Monograph 140, 66.
250 Merrill Report, 6; *Saufley* War Diary.
251 Merrill Report, 7.
252 Merrill Report, 7; USS *Columbia* Action Reports [sic] Against Enemy Aircraft during period from 1945 on 11 November, 1943, until 2250 on 12 November, 1943 (hereinafter "*Columbia* AA Report"), 3, 5. Admiral Merrill's report says the *Columbia* was firing to starboard, but the *Columbia*'s own report says she was firing to port. It is rather disconcerting to see that the US Navy thought it necessary to start its directions on how to fill out the form "Revised Form for Reporting AA Action by Surface Ships," which the *Columbia* used to report her antiaircraft activities, with "(a) REPEL ATTACK FIRST – then collect data for this report." (Emphasis in original.)
253 Merrill Report, 4, 7–8.
254 Monograph 140, 66; Merrill Report, 8.
255 Monograph 100, 25; Monograph 140, 66.
256 Monograph 100, 24–25; Monograph 140, 66.
257 *Essex* Report, 96.
258 Claringbould, *Ro-Go*, 167. Oddly, Monograph 140 makes no mention of this mission.
259 *Essex* Report, 4.

Chapter 7

1 Hara, Saito, and Pineau, *Destroyer Captain*, 238. Hara gives the time as noon.
2 Hara, Saito, and Pineau, *Destroyer Captain*, 234.
3 Hara, Saito, and Pineau, *Destroyer Captain*, 234.
4 Except where noted otherwise, the account of the air attack on the *Shigure* comes from Hara, Saito, and Pineau, *Destroyer Captain*, 234–36.

5   Hickey and Pettus, *Ken's Men, Vol. II*, 34. Another possibility is a Royal Australian Air Force PBY
     Catalina. The Consolidated Catalinas of Nos. 11, 20, and 43 Squadrons had just completed a week-long
     campaign of night bombing attacks against Kavieng, but that campaign was directed at Kavieng's airfield
     and ended at the beginning of November (Odgers, *Royal Australian Air Force*, 95.) However, Australian
     Catalinas had been known to prowl the nights around New Britain and New Ireland since the previous
     summer. To complicate matters further, submarine historians John D. Alden and Craig R. McDonald,
     in their highly respected work *United States and Allied Submarine Successes in the Pacific and Far East
     During World War II* (4th ed.) (Jefferson, NC: McFarland, 2009), 111, cite respected researcher William
     G. Somerville's translation of Japanese records as revealing the *Tokyo Maru* was attacked at 0925 on
     November 9 by B-17s, which caused "slight damage." This may have been a separate air attack. It could
     also be a garbled reference to the attacks by either *Art's Cart* or *Who's Next*. Hara's recollection was that
     the air attack took place at night. In what seems to be a minority position, the narrative goes with Hara,
     who was an eyewitness in command of the convoy, but readers should be aware of the disagreement
     between the narrative and some very respected historians.

6   Hara, Saito, and Pineau, *Destroyer Captain*, 236.

7   Hara, Saito, and Pineau, *Destroyer Captain*, 236.

8   USS *Scamp* Report of Fifth War Patrol. Hara wrote his account almost entirely from memory, while the
     Scamp's account is, like most US submarine patrol reports, meticulously and contemporaneously
     documented. So where there is a conflict between the eyewitness accounts of Hara and the *Scamp*, the
     narrative goes with the *Scamp*'s version.

9   Hara, Saito, and Pineau, *Destroyer Captain*, 237.

10   Alden and McDonald, *United States and Allied Submarine Successes*, 111.

11   USS *Scamp* Report of Fifth War Patrol.

12   USS *Scamp* Report of Fifth War Patrol.

13   Hara, Saito, and Pineau, *Destroyer Captain*, 237. According to The Joint Army–Navy Assessment
     Committee (JANAC) (*Japanese Naval and Merchant Shipping Losses During World War II by All
     Causes*, NAVEXOS P-468 (Washington, DC: Government Printing Office, 1947)), the *Tokyo Maru*
     sank on November 10. Esteemed submarine historians Alden and McDonald, in their widely
     respected *United States and Allied Submarine Successes*, say that messages intercepted by *Magic*
     reported that it sank on November 12. Alden and McDonald go on to say renowned researcher
     William G. Somerville's translation of Japanese records reveal that the *Tokyo Maru* was torpedoed in
     the engine room and No. 4 hold the morning of November 10, and sank on November 12. They also
     cite historian Erich Mühlthaler, who focuses on the wartime activities of Japanese shipping, for
     indicating the *Tokyo Maru* was damaged during the November 2 attack on Rabaul by the 5th Air
     Force and that the *Scamp*'s torpedo hit in the damaged area. However, Captain Hara has a timeline
     that disagrees with Alden et al. According to Hara, he took survivors off the *Tokyo Maru* just before
     she sank, and the *Shigure* and *Mitakesan Maru* went on to enter Truk Harbor on November 11. The
     major point to take away is that the *Tokyo Maru* sank before Hara entered Truk Harbor. Additionally,
     when Hara went to report on his mission, he was told that Rabaul had been hit with a strong attack
     that morning, which left him stunned and which places his arrival on November 11. While eyewitness
     accounts are usually the least reliable form of testimony, and Hara's account was written almost
     entirely from memory, the narrative here goes with Hara. Even if Hara's dates and times are off, the
     timeline of events is simply not consistent with the idea that the *Tokyo Maru* sank on November 12.
     Because Hara was not only an on-site eyewitness but the commander of the convoy, his statements are
     considered more reliable here than the research compiled by Alden et al., which relied on reports sent
     to Japan from Truk. However, this appears to be a minority position. Readers should be aware that
     the narrative respectfully disagrees with the scenario put forth by some very renowned researchers and
     make their own judgments.

14   Hara, Saito, and Pineau, *Destroyer Captain*, 237–38.

15   Except where noted otherwise, the account of Hara's stop at Truk comes from Hara, Saito, and Pineau,
     Destroyer Captain, 238–39.

16   Budge, "Omori Sentaro (1894–1974)"; Richard Fuller, *Shokan: Hirohito's Samurai* (London: Arms and
     Armour Press, 1992), 279–80.

17 Except where noted otherwise, the account of the *Scamp*'s attack on the *Agano* comes from USS *Scamp* Report of Fifth War Patrol.
18 USS *Albacore* Report of Seventh War Patrol.
19 David Jones and Peter Nunan, *U.S. Subs Down Under: Brisbane 1942–1945* (Annapolis: Naval Institute Press, 2005), 197.
20 *Agano* TROM.
21 *Agano*, *Noshiro*, and *Nagara* TROMs; Alden and McDonald, *United States and Allied Submarine Successes*, 112; Lacroix and Wells, *Japanese Cruisers*, 595.
22 *Agano*, *Noshiro*, *Nagara*, and *Urakaze* TROMs.
23 *Agano*, *Noshiro*, *Nagara*, and *Urakaze* TROMs.
24 *Agano*, *Noshiro*, *Nagara*, and *Urakaze* TROMs; Alden and McDonald, *United States and Allied Submarine Successes*, 112.
25 Monograph 100, 25.
26 Monograph 100, 25; Monograph 140, 68.
27 Prados, *Islands of Destiny*, 345.
28 Monograph 100, 26; Monograph 140, 67.
29 R. J. Francillon, *Japanese Aircraft of the Pacific War* (1st ed.) (New York: Funk & Wagnalls, 1970), 456.
30 Monograph 100, 26; Monograph 140, 67.
31 David C. Evans, *The Japanese Navy in World War II in the Words of Former Japanese Naval Officers* (2nd ed.) (Annapolis: Naval Institute Press, 1986), Kindle edition, 4639–46.
32 Monograph 140, 68.
33 Monograph 100, 26; Monograph 140, 68.
34 Monograph 100, 26; Monograph 140, 68; Tagaya, *Rikko*, 1433. The identification of the G4Ms' air groups is a deduction. Tagaya says, "Lt(jg) Hidezumi Maruyama (No 321) of 702 *Ku* put a torpedo into the light cruiser USS *Denver*." Monograph 100 says the first group of land attack planes found the US Navy task force and attacked, but the second group did not. Since Lieutenant (jg) Maruyama of the 702 Air Group was credited with hitting the *Denver*, this means the six bombers that launched first were from the 702 Air Group and the five that launched later were from the 751.
35 Francillon, *Japanese Aircraft*, 420–21.
36 Monograph 100, 26; Monograph 140, 68.
37 Monograph 140, 68.
38 ComTaskFor31 War Diary.
39 Monograph 140, 68.
40 USS *Columbia* Action Reports against Enemy Aircraft [sic] during the Early Morning of 13 November, 1943 (hereinafter "*Columbia* AA Report"), 1.
41 Merrill Report, 9; VMF(N)-531 War Diary.
42 Merrill Report, 9; VMF(N)-531 War Diary; *Columbia* AA Report, 3–4.
43 VMF(N)-531 War Diary.
44 *Columbia* AA Report, 3–4.
45 *Columbia* AA Report, 4.
46 Merrill Report, 9.
47 Hammel, *Air War*, 8172.
48 Merrill Report, 10.
49 Action Report – U.S.S. DENVER – 13 November 1943 (hereinafter "*Denver* AA Report"), 3.
50 *Denver* AA Report, 3.
51 *Denver* AA Report, 3.
52 *Denver* AA Report, 3–4; War Damage Report Number 52: U.S.S. INDEPENDENCE (CVL22) & U.S.S. DENVER (CL58) Torpedo Damage Tarawa 20 November 1943 & Treasury Islands 13 November 1943 (hereinafter "*Independence* Damage Report" or "*Denver* Damage Report"), 10.
53 *Denver* AA Report, 4–5.
54 *Denver* Damage Report, 14.
55 ComTaskUnit 31.5.5 Action Reports and report of operations of the Fourth Echelon carrying reinforcements to our position on Bougainville Island – 11–14 November 1943 (hereinafter "Reifsnider

Report"), 3; VF-17, VMF-211, -212, and -221 war diaries; Denver AA Report, 4–5; Monograph 140, 68; Merrill Report, 13.

56 Monograph 100, 26–27; Monograph 140, 68.

57 Tagaya, *Rikko*, 1433.

58 Monograph 100, 26; Monograph 140, 68.

59 *Columbia* AA Report, 2.

60 *Columbia* AA Report, 5.

61 Merrill Report, 14.

62 Reifsnider Report, 4.

63 USS *Eaton* Action Report Anti-Aircraft Engagements; 7, 10, and 13 November 1943 (hereinafter "*Eaton* AA Report"), 6.

64 Shaw and Kane, *Isolation of Rabaul*, 241.

65 Shaw and Kane, *Isolation of Rabaul*, 242; Gailey, *Bougainville*, 1374.

66 Gailey, *Bougainville*, 1377–78.

67 Gailey, *Bougainville*, 1379–84; Shaw and Kane, *Isolation of Rabaul*, 242–43; Rentz, *Bougainville*, 55–57.

68 Gailey, *Bougainville*, 1379–84; Shaw and Kane, *Isolation of Rabaul*, 243–44; Rentz, *Bougainville*, 57–58; VC-40 War Diary.

69 Gailey, *Bougainville*, 1389; Shaw and Kane, *Isolation of Rabaul*, 244; Rentz, *Bougainville*, 58.

70 Gailey, *Bougainville*, 1389; Shaw and Kane, *Isolation of Rabaul*, 244; Rentz, *Bougainville*, 58–59.

71 Hata, Izawa, and Shores, *Japanese Naval Air Force*, 1661. Sakaida (*The Siege of Rabaul* (St Paul, MN: Phalanx, 1996), 10) has the flight led by Chief Petty Officer Iwamoto Tetsuzo, who would go on to become the Imperial Japanese Navy's top fighter ace, and landing at Tobera. Hata et al. has Iwamoto as part of this flight, but not leading it.

72 Monograph 100, 25; Monograph 140, 68; Sherrod, *Marine Corps Aviation*, 188; Claringbould, *Ro-Go*, 169; "Kerevat Airfield (Keravat, Karavat, Tavelo,)" *Pacific Wrecks* (www.pacificwrecks.com). Neither monograph identifies the carrier bombers involved. Hammel (*Air War*, 8245) has D4Ys "diverted from land-based duty in the Marshall Islands," but does not say when.

73 Monograph 140, 69.

74 Monograph 140, 69.

75 Mark Chambers and Tony Holmes, *Nakajima B5N "Kate" and B6N "Jill" Units* (Oxford: Osprey, 2017), Kindle edition, 96.

76 ComTaskFor31 War Diary; Miller, *Cartwheel*, 257.

77 ComTaskGr31.6 Action Fifth Echelon Northern Force – Empress Augusta Bay, Bougainville, B.S.I. Task Group 31.6 – November 15th – 21st 1943 inclusive (hereinafter "Carter Report"), 2; USS *McKean* Action report involving the loss of the USS *McKean* as a result of enemy action on November 17, 1943 – Forwarding of (hereinafter "*McKean* Report"), 2, 5; USS *Pringle* Action Report, 2.

78 Monograph 100, 27; Monograph 140, 69.

79 USS *Pringle* Action Report, 1.

80 ComTransDiv12 Report of Action with Japanese Torpedo Planes, Morning of 17 November 1943, during which USS *McKean* was sunk off Bougainville (hereinafter "Sweeney Report"), 2.

81 Sweeney Report, 2.

82 ComDesron22 Report of Action 17, November 1943 (hereinafter "Hurff Report"), 1.

83 USS *Sigourney* Anti-Aircraft Action Report – forwarding of (hereinafter "*Sigourney* Report"), 4.

84 Hurff Report, 2.

85 *McKean* Report, 2, 6.

86 *McKean* Report, 2.

87 *McKean* Report, 2–3; *Talbot* War Diary. There is considerable confusion as to when the torpedo hit the *McKean*. Lieutenant Commander Ramey gives the time as 3:50, as does the *Talbot*. But Captain Hurff's report (1) gives the time as 3:40. So does Captain Carter (3). The *Pringle* has "*McKean* torpedoed" at 3:50 but at 3:40 has "Hear bomb explosion on sound gear." The *Sigourney* (4) reported that at 3:39, "Underwater explosion felt, flames observed in rear of formation." Commander James R. Pahl, head of Destroyer Division 44 (including the *Sigourney* and *Conway*) (2), has the time of the *McKean*'s hit even earlier at 3:37. Though Ramey probably did not have access to all his ship's documentation when he filed his report, the narrative

here goes with Ramey's time of 3:50am or slightly before. First, as commanding officer of the *McKean*, Ramey probably knew better than anyone at what time the *McKean* received her fatal hit. Second, the *Talbot*'s warning message "Believe that last one got *McKean*" is generally cited as made at 3:50am. A time of 3:40am for the *McKean*'s hit would leave an uncomfortable ten-minute period when she was burning fiercely and exploding with no one calling any attention to her plight. That is simply not realistic under the circumstances. Readers are advised to make their own conclusions.

88   *McKean* Report, 6; Sweeney Report, 2.
89   *McKean* Report, 3; Sweeney Report, 2–3; ComSoPac War Diary. In his report, Commander Sweeney commented, "Discipline was perfect," then went on to explain the Marines disregarded orders.
90   *McKean* Report, 3.
91   *McKean* Report, 3.
92   Hurff Report, 2.
93   Hurff Report, 7; ComDesDiv44 Action Report for 17 November 1943 – Air Attacks on Task Group 31.6 at Torokino (sic), Bougainville, Solomon Islands, and Bombardment of Shore Targets (hereinafter "Pahl Report"), 2.
94   *Sigourney* AA Report, 5; Pahl Report, 2.
95   Hurff Report, 3.
96   *Sigourney* AA Report, 5; Hurff Report, 3.
97   Pahl Report, 2.
98   USS *Renshaw* Report of Action, 17 November, 1943; *McKean* Report, 5; Carter Report, 6.
99   Hurff Report, 7; *Sigourney* AA Report, 5–6.
100 *Talbot* War Diary; *McKean* Report, 14; "McKean I (Destroyer No. 90)," *DANFS*.
101 *McKean* Report, 4.
102 Sweeney Report, 5.
103 *McKean* Report, 18.
104 Sweeney Report, 5.
105 VMF(N)-531 War Diary; ComDesRon 23 Action Report of the Bombardment of Buka Airfield, Anti-submarine Action, and Miscellaneous Anti-aircraft Actions, November 16–17, 1943 (hereinafter "Burke Buka Report"), 3.
106 Burke Buka Report, 11–12, 17; *Ro-104* and *-109* TROMs.
107 Burke Buka Report, 5; ComAirSoPacFor War Diary; VB-140, VMTB-143, and VMTB-233 war diaries. There is a curious lack of information about this particular air attack, and what information is available is often contradictory. The most curious detail is that Admiral Halsey's and Admiral Fitch's reports only refer generally to a mining mission (or, as Fitch calls it, a "mine sewing" mission). The bombing by the B-25s was to support or cover the mining mission. Aside from the mining being aerial, there is no indication of who or what is performing the mining. More confusingly, there were multiple nights of aerial mining operations in Buka Passage, which also was not mentioned in Halsey's or Fitch's reports. The night of November 15–16, 39 TBF Avengers, including 11 from Marine Torpedo Bombing 143 and 17 from Marine Torpedo Bombing 233, each dropped one mine in Buka Passage, but this was off Madehas Island, closer to the western end. This was not mentioned at all in Halsey's or Fitch's war diaries. Confusing matters even further is disagreement as to the number of B-25s involved. Captain Burke says it was to be 33 aircraft, but, not surprisingly, does not break that figure down. Halsey has two flights of eight B-25s bombing both Buka and Bonis in support of the mining mission, followed by a flight of three B-25s that bombed only Buka. Fitch says eight bombed Buka and eight bombed Bonis, but does not indicate if they were the same eight or two different eights. The honor of the mysterious mining mission on the night of November 16–17 goes to Navy Bombing 140 (VB-140), who sent up eight PV-1 Venturas to each drop one mine. They were escorted by eight B-25s of the 42nd Bombardment Group, whose job was to bomb both Buka and Bonis and thus hopefully confuse the Japanese defenders. In the event, two of the Venturas were unable to release their mines. All returned to base safely. This attack was followed by yet another raid by eight B-25s on Buka and Bonis, then one last attack on Buka by three B-25s.
108 VMF(N)-531 War Diary; Burke Buka Report, 14.
109 Burke Buka Report, 16–17.

110 VB-140 War Diary.

111 ComSoPac War Diary.

112 Sweeney Report, 3.

113 For reasons known only to the Japanese, *Mutsu* is pronounced "moot-seh."

114 *Mutsu* TROM.

115 *Mutsu* TROM. Then again, maybe that's what he wanted everyone to think.

116 Monograph 100, 27; Monograph 140, 69; Tagaya, *Rikko*, 1452.

117 *Pringle* Action Report, 2.

118 Monograph 100, 27–28; Monograph 140, 69–70; VMF-221 War Diary. The VMF-221 war diary calls these strike aircraft "dive bombers," which is usually a reference to the Aichi D3A Type 99 Vals. However, the pilots described them as "small, low mid-wing monoplanes with an in-line engine having a pronounced scoop under the nose." This is an apt description of the Yokosuka D4Y Judy.

119 VF-17, VMF-215, and VMF-221 war diaries.

120 Blackburn, *Jolly Rogers*, 189–90.

121 VF-17, VMF-215, and VMF-221 war diaries.

122 Carter Report, 5.

123 Monograph 100, 27–28; Monograph 140, 69.

124 ComSoPac, VMTB-233, VF-17, VMF-212, and VMF-221 war diaries.

125 Monograph 100, 28; Monograph 140, 69.

126 VF-17 War Diary; Blackburn, *Jolly Rogers*, 190.

127 ComAirSoPacFor War Diary; VF-221 War Diary; Monograph 100, 28; Monograph 140, 69; Hata, Izawa, and Shores, *Japanese Naval Air Force*, 7795.

128 Carter Report, 3.

129 Monograph 140, 69, 82.

130 ComSoPac War Diary.

131 ComSoPac and ComAirSoPacFor war diaries.

132 Monograph 140, 69, 82.

133 ComSoPac, ComTaskFor31, ComDesRon45, and VMF(N)-531 war diaries.

134 ComSoPac, ComAirSoPacFor, AirSols Strike Command, VMF-244, VC-24, VMTB-233, and VMF-222 war diaries.

135 Rentz, *Bougainville*, 60.

136 Shaw and Kane, *Isolation of Rabaul*, 248–51; Rems, *South Pacific Cauldron*, 2927–28.

137 Rentz, *Bougainville*, 63; Shaw and Kane, *Isolation of Rabaul*, 255–56.

138 It's pronounced "Chibik."

139 Shaw and Kane, *Isolation of Rabaul*, 264; Morison, *Bismarcks Barrier*, 352; Rentz, *Bougainville*, 68. In a footnote (163), however, Rentz says, "Personal reports submitted later by officers engaged in this action, [sic] state this figure (of Japanese dead) is greatly exaggerated."

140 Morison, *Bismarcks Barrier*, 352.

141 Rems, *South Pacific Cauldron*, 2933.

142 Vandegrift, *Once a Marine*, 230.

143 Vandegrift, *Once a Marine*, 230.

144 Jeter A. Isely and Philip A. Crowl, *US Marines and Amphibious Warfare: Its Theory, and Its Practice in the Pacific* (Pickle Partners Publishing, 2016), Kindle edition, 299.

145 Isely and Crowl, *Amphibious Warfare*, 300–01.

Chapter 8

1 Shaw and Kane, *Isolation of Rabaul*, 247.

2 *Yubari* TROM; Lacroix and Wells, *Japanese Cruisers*, 368.

3 Monograph 161, 79 (115); Monograph 173, 29-a.

4 Monograph 161, 79 (115).

5 The identification of the unit as the 752 Air Group is a deduction based on Monograph 100 (28), Monograph 140 (69), Tagaya (*Rikko*, 1498), Monograph 161 (actual page 79 (marked page 115), 84 (118), 86 (120), 98 (132); and Monograph 173: Inner South Seas Islands Area Naval Operations, Part

II: Marshall Islands Operations (Headquarters, Army Forces, Far East, Military History Section, Japanese Research Division, 1951) (hereinafter "Monograph 173").

6 Monograph 161, 79 (115)–82 (116).

7 VB-138, VMTB-143, VMTB-233.

8 Cressman, *Chronology*; Hammel, *Air War*, 8308; *Ch-17* and *-18* TROMs. There is little specific information about this attack; the narrative version was pieced together from several sources. Hammel identifies the unit involved and says the aircraft were Black Cats, but says the ship, which is not identified, was sunk in "Rabaul Harbor." The *Ch-17*'s TROM says multiple Catalinas attacked but the *Ch-18*'s TROM says it was a single Catalina. Both TROMs say the attack took place north of New Ireland, but the coordinates they give, which are close to those cited by Cressman, are actually south of New Ireland. Both TROMs also imply that the attack took place during the day. This attack is actually a fairly typical Black Cat night attack.

9 Japanese sources consistently have the date for the *Galvanic* landings on Tarawa and Makin as November 21. American sources consistently have the date for the landings on Tarawa and Makin as November 20. The issue is the International Date Line. Pearl Harbor, where much of the US invasion force was based, is on the West Longitude Date while the Gilbert Islands are on the East Longitude Date, or a day ahead of Pearl Harbor. Most of the US Navy records either use November 20 as the invasion date or don't reference the specific date but use a day relative to D-Day in the Gilberts (such as D minus 1). An exception to the US rule is Admiral Halsey (*Story*, 3829). Halsey has the date of the *Galvanic* landings as November 21, because Nouméa, French New Caledonia, where Halsey was based, like the Gilberts was west of the International Date Line. The Solomon Islands, the Bismarck Archipelago, and Papua New Guinea were and are all west of the International Date Line. For this reason, the narrative here uses the East Longitude Date of November 21 for the *Galvanic* landings.

10 The invasion of Tarawa and Makin as Operation *Galvanic* was conducted by the V Amphibious Corps under US Marine Lieutenant General Holland M. Smith, with the 2nd Marine Division under Major General Julian C. Smith, and the US Army's 27th Infantry Division under Major General Ralph C. Smith.

11 Monograph 161, 83 (117). *Hei* should not be confused with *Hiei*.

12 Interrogation Nav No. 115; USSBS No. 503 Interrogation of Vice Admiral Fukudome, Shigeru, IJN (hereinafter "Fukudome Interrogation"), 516.

13 Fukudome Interrogation, 516.

14 Fukudome Interrogation, 514.

15 Fukudome Interrogation, 514.

16 Interrogation Nav No. 38; USSBS No. 160 Interrogation of: Captain Ohmae, Toshikazu, IJN (hereinafter "Ohmae Interrogation"), 165.

17 Monograph 161, 84 (118).

18 Monograph 161, 83–84 (117–18); ComAirSoPacFor War Diary; Britt, *Long Rangers*, 72; *Fifth Bombardment Group (Heavy) in World War II*, 53; Britt, *Long Rangers*, 69–71; ComSoPac War Diary; Headquarters 307th Bombardment Group (H) "Historical Data" Report – 1 October 1943 to 31 December 1943, Periodic Activities Summary 1 November 1943 to 30 November 1943, 2.

19 Monograph 161, 84 (118).

20 Monograph 161, 84 (118); *Independence* Damage Report, 4.

21 *Independence* Damage Report, 1–2. The Bureau of Ships gave the following explanation for the very unusual move of combining the damage to the *Denver* and *Independence* into one report:

      1. In November, 1943, both *Independence* and *Denver* were damaged by Japanese aircraft torpedoes. Each ship was struck by a single torpedo on the starboard side in the vicinity of the after bulkhead of the after engine room. The resultant structural damage, flooding and engineering casualties were quite similar in each case as were the damage control problems with which each ship was confronted.

      2. The two vessels have almost identical engineering plants. The hulls initially were identical, but in converting *Independence* to a CVL [light carrier] the side armor was omitted and blisters were added. The interior arrangement aft of the machinery spaces in *Independence* also is quite different from that in *Denver*. For cruiser type hulls, however, both cases present typical

examples of the effects of a single torpedo detonating in the vicinity of the after end of the machinery spaces. It thus has been convenient to issue a combined report for the two vessels.

22   Monograph 161, 84 (118). Curiously, Monograph 161 describes the two land attack planes taking off at 9:17am and the follow-up strike taking off at 10:01. Both times are assumed to be Japan Standard Time, which was three hours behind the Gilbert Islands and one hour behind Truk. Even more curiously, the Japanese attack is consistently described as a "night" attack. In fact, the *Independence* was hit at 6:07pm. Sunset was at 6:15pm.

23   Monograph 100, 29; Monograph 140, 60.

24   ComSoPac, ComAirSoPacFor, and VF-17 war diaries; Wolf, *13th Fighter Command*, 228; Monograph 140, 83; Hata, Izawa, and Shores, *Japanese Naval Air Force*, 7795.

25   ComAirSoPacFor, VMF-212 and -215; VMSB-243 and -244; and VMTB-233 war diaries.

26   VF-17 War Diary; Blackburn, *Jolly Rogers*, 200; "F4U-1A Corsair Bureau Number 17804," *Pacific Wrecks*, (www.pacificwrecks.com).

27   Monograph 140, 83; ComSoPac War Diary.

28   Monograph 140, 83; MAG 14, ComSoPac, ComAirSoPacFor war diaries; Hata, Izawa, and Shores, *Japanese Naval Air Force*, 7795.

29   ComAirSoPacFor, ComSoPac, VB-138 and VMF-211 war diaries; Carter and Mueller, *Combat Chronology*. Admiral Fitch's diary has eight Venturas in the attack, but the only American units in AirSols equipped with Venturas were Navy Bombing 138 and 140. Bombing 138 has five of its own taking part in the attack, while Bombing 140 says it did not take part.

30   VC-24 VMTB-143, VF-17.

31   Cohn, *Crusaders*, 1463; MACR 1217, "B-25C-10 Mitchell Serial Number 42-32255," *Pacific Wrecks*, (www.pacificwrecks.com); VB-138, VF-17, and VMF-222 war diaries.

32   Determined by process of elimination. Headquarters 307th Bombardment Group (H) "Historical Data" Report – 1 October 1943 to 31 December 1943, Periodic Activities Summary 1 November 1943 to 30 November 1943, 2, lists no mission for the 307th on November 23.

33   VMSB-244, VMTB-143, and VF-17 war diaries.

34   The B-25 Mitchell has been christened *Careless*.

35   ComAirSoPacFor War Diary, Cohn, *Crusaders*, 54. Again, the identification of the group as the 5th is determined by process of elimination. Headquarters 307th Bombardment Group (H) "Historical Data" Report – 1 October 1943 to 31 December 1943, Periodic Activities Summary 1 November 1943 to 30 November 1943, 2, lists no mission for the 307th on November 24.

36   Mel Crocker, *Black Cats and Dumbos: WW II's Fighting PBYs* (2nd ed.) (Huntington Beach, CA: Crocker Media Expressions, 2002), 253; Cohn, *Crusaders*, 54.

37   Crocker, *Black Cats and Dumbos*, 253.

38   Morison, *Bismarcks Barrier*, 354.

39   Monograph 100, 32.

40   Bulkley, *At Close Quarters*, 134.

41   O'Hara, *US Navy*, 4682; Monograph 100, 32.

42   Bulkley, *At Close Quarters*, 134.

43   Monograph 100, 31.

44   Monograph 100, 31.

45   Monograph 100, 31.

46   Monograph 100, 31.

47   Monograph 100, 32; Hara, Saito, and Pineau, *Destroyer Captain*, 241; O'Hara, "Battle of Cape St George – November 25, 1943," *Thunder of the Guns: Battles of the Pacific War* (http://www.microworks.net/pacific/battles/).

48   Hara, Saito, and Pineau, *Destroyer Captain*, 241–42; Commander Destroyer Squadron 23, "Action Report of Night Engagement off Cape St George on the night of November 24th–25th, 1943" (hereinafter "Burke St George Report"), 4.

49   Hara, Saito, and Pineau, *Destroyer Captain*, 241.

50   Monograph 100, 32.

51   O'Hara, *US Navy*, 4682; Monograph 100, 32; Hara, Saito, and Pineau, *Destroyer Captain*, 242.

52 Of the Type 22 radar, *The Pacific War Online Encyclopedia* notes, "Quality control during production was a serious problem: Of the first [60] sets built, only about six actually worked." Kent G. Budge, "Type 22 General Purpose Radar," *The Pacific War Online Encyclopedia* (http://pwencycl.kgbudge.com/).

53 Monograph 100, 32.

54 Burke St George Report, 9–10.

55 Prados, *Islands of Destiny*, 346.

56 Arleigh Burke, "Spirit of the Spence: 'We want to do our share … and more!,'" *Destroyer History Foundation*, (www.destroyerhistory.org); Burke St George Report, 4; Jones, *Destroyer Squadron 23*, 244.

57 Burke, "Spirit of the Spence"; Burke St George Report, 4; Jones, *Destroyer Squadron 23*, 244.

58 Jones, *Destroyer Squadron 23*, 244–45.

59 Burke St George Report, 8; Jones, *Destroyer Squadron 23*, 244–45.

60 Potter, *Burke*, 102; Burke St George Report, 4.

61 Burke St George Report, 8; Potter, *Arleigh Burke*, 101; Arleigh Burke, "Spirit of the Spence."

62 Burke, "Spirit of the Spence."

63 Jones, *Destroyer Squadron 23*, 245.

64 Burke St George Report, 5; Jones, *Destroyer Squadron 23*, 245.

65 Jones, *Destroyer Squadron 23*, 245; Burke St George Report, 4; Mark Stille, *The United States Navy in World War II: From Pearl Harbor to Okinawa* (Oxford: Osprey, 2021), Kindle edition, 386; Potter, *Burke*, 102.

66 Jones, *Destroyer Squadron 23*, 246; Burke St George Report, 4.

67 Jones, *Destroyer Squadron 23*, 246; Burke St George Report, 4. There is an alternative story of the origin of the "31-Knot" Burke moniker. In this version, Burke mistakenly led his destroyer squadron into a Japanese minefield. Admiral Halsey radioed to ask Burke what he was doing in a Japanese minefield. "Thirty-one knots," Burke answered (Jean Edward Smith, *Eisenhower in War and Peace* (New York: Random House, 2012), Kindle edition, 836). That version is widely considered apocryphal, and for good reason. Logistically speaking, it would be extremely difficult for Halsey to know exactly when Burke and his destroyers had entered a Japanese minefield in real time. It would be even more difficult for Halsey to send Burke a message via the wireless telegraph that would be decoded and reach him while he was still in the minefield. Finally, given how Burke responded to the distraction posed by a communications officer when he was trying to fire torpedoes, Burke would likely not respond to any wireless telegraph message while he was navigating said minefield.

68 Jones, *Destroyer Squadron 23*, 246; Burke St George Report, 4.

69 Burke St George Report, 5.

70 Burke St George Report, 7.

71 Burke St George Report, 7, 8; Commander Destroyer Division Forty-Six, "Report of Surface Action off Buka on the Night of 24–25 November, 1943" (hereinafter "Austin St George Report"), 2; Except where noted otherwise, the account of the conference comes from Jones, *Destroyer Squadron 23*, 247–48.

72 Burke St George Report, 7.

73 Jones, *Destroyer Squadron 23*, 249.

74 Burke St George Report, 8.

75 Burke St George Report, 8.

76 Jones, *Destroyer Squadron 23*, 251–52; Burke St George Report, 9, 24. Jones credits the "Hello, DesRon-23!" remark to Commander Stout, but Captain Burke's TBS log has Burke himself saying it.

77 Burke St George Report, 24; Jones, *Destroyer Squadron 23*, 252.

78 Burke St George Report, 10.

79 Jones, *Destroyer Squadron 23*, 252; Burke St George Report, 10.

80 Burke St George Report, 24.

81 Morison (*Bismarcks Barrier*, 355–56) has Captain Burke responding with one word later made famous for its alleged utterance during the Siege of Bastogne: "Nuts!" The TBS Log (Burke St George Report, 24–25 covers the relevant time period) does not support his assertion.

82 Amalgamation of Jones, *Destroyer Squadron 23*, 253; and Burke St George Report, 10. Jones has Burke's response as, "Well, you can throw it overboard! After all, we know where the enemy is now. Those guys upstairs are just a little bit late!"

83 Morison, *Bismarcks Barrier*, 356; Burke St George Report, 10, 40; *Onami* TROM.
84 *Makinami* TROM; Potter, *Burke*, 104–05; Morison, *Bismarcks Barrier*, 356; Burke St George Report, 10; Jones, *Destroyer Squadron 23*, 254; Kilpatrick, *Naval Night Battles*, 262. USS *Dyson* Report of Surface Action off St George Channel on the night of November 24–25, 1943 (hereinafter "*Dyson* St George Report"), 2, says its lookouts "reported two sets of violent explosions […]." Evidently, it was important to clarify that these were violent explosions so they would not be confused with the usual nonviolent explosions.
85 Burke St George Report, 25.
86 Burke St George Report, 25.
87 Monograph 100, 32.
88 Jones, *Destroyer Squadron 23*, 254; *Amagiri*, *Yugiri*, and *Uzuki* TROMs.
89 Burke St George Report, 11, 25; Jones, *Destroyer Squadron 23*, 254.
90 Potter, *Burke*, 105.
91 Burke St George Report, 26.
92 Burke St George Report, 26.
93 Burke St George Report, 12; Jones, *Destroyer Squadron 23*, 255.
94 Burke St George Report, 12.
95 *Claxton* St George Report, 4; Monograph 100, 32. That the *Yugiri* had slowed down to allow the *Amagiri* to clear her line of fire before launching torpedoes is a deduction based on the track chart in Burke St George Report, 22.
96 Burke St George Report, 12.
97 Jones, *Destroyer Squadron 23*, 255.
98 Burke St George Report, 26.
99 Burke St George Report, 26.
100 Burke St George Report, 27.
101 *Converse* St George Report, 2; Austin St George Report, 4.
102 Austin St George Report, 4.
103 Burke St George Report, 27.
104 Burke St George Report, 12, 27, 43. Curiously, Burke's narrative has the time of his giving the order to open fire with guns at 2:22, but both his TBS Log and his timeline give the time as 2:21.
105 Burke St George Report, 27.
106 *Claxton* St George Report, 4; Burke St George Report, 12.
107 Burke St George Report, 12.
108 Burke St George Report, 18.
109 *Uzuki* TROM; Stille, *Imperial Japanese Navy*, 4544.
110 Stille, *United States Navy*, 386.
111 Burke St George Report, 11.
112 *Claxton* St George Report, 4.
113 Deduction based on Captain Burke's track chart of the engagement (Burke St George Report, 22).
114 Burke St George Report, 43; Office of Naval Intelligence, US Navy – *Solomon Islands Campaign (XIII): Bougainville Operations and the Battle of Cape St George, 3–25 November 1943*, 57–58.
115 Burke St George Report, 22.
116 The scenario in the narrative comes from Jones, *Destroyer Squadron 23*, 252, 256 (Captain Yamashiro's reported dialogue here is considered apocryphal) but there are other potential scenarios as well. O'Hara (*US Navy*, 4716–27) says, "The *Amagiri* went northwest, the *Yugiri* went north, and the *Uzuki* went north northwest." The problem with this scenario is that, whether the formation is the one presented in the narrative, or the column formation with the *Yugiri* and *Uzuki* reversed (which Hara Tameichi appears to believe) or line abreast (which Kilpatrick appears to favor) with the order from port to starboard *Amagiri*, *Yugiri*, and *Uzuki*, it would have, at the very least, the *Uzuki* crossing the path of the *Amagiri* and possibly crossing the path of the *Yugiri* as well. At night, at high speed, and with enemy ships at their heels, the risk of collision between the Japanese destroyers was high. The only way O'Hara's scenario works is if the destroyers were abreast in the order *Amagiri*, *Uzuki*, and *Yugiri*.

117 Winston S. Churchill, *The Second World War, Vol. IV: The Hinge of Fate.* (New York: Rosetta Books, 2010), Kindle edition, 4541.

118 David H. Lippman, "'Convoy is to Scatter': Arctic Convoy Disaster," *Warfare History Network* (www.warfarehistorynetwork.com).

119 *Charles Ausburne* St George Report, 6; Burke St George Report, 13; *Claxton* St George Report, 4.

120 Burke St George Report, 13, 27.

121 Burke St George Report, 11.

122 Burke St George Report, 13, 22.

123 Burke St George Report, 27.

124 Austin St George Report, 4, *Converse* St George Report, 2.

125 Burke St George Report, 27; Jones, *Destroyer Squadron 23*, 258.

126 Jones, *Destroyer Squadron 23*, 259.

127 Burke St George Report, 13.

128 *Claxton* St George Report, 4–5, 46; Burke St George Report, 13, 22; *Dyson* St George Report, 3; O'Hara, *US Navy*, 4727.

129 Burke St George Report, 27–28.

130 Burke St George Report, 28.

131 *Claxton* Report, 5; Burke St George Report, 22.

132 Burke St George Report, 28.

133 *Yugiri* TROM.

134 Burke St George Report, 28.

135 Jones, *Destroyer Squadron 23*, 261.

136 Burke St George Report, 28; Austin St George Report, 4; *Converse* St George Report, 2.

137 Hara, Saito, and Pineau, *Destroyer Captain*, 242.

138 *Converse* St George Report, 2; O'Hara, *US Navy*, 349–50.

139 *Makinami* TROM.

140 Burke St George Report, 28.

141 Burke St George Report, 46–47.

142 Burke St George Report, 14; Jones, *Destroyer Squadron 23*, 261.

143 Burke St George Report, 47–48.

144 Burke St George Report, 29.

145 Jones, *Destroyer Squadron 23*, 261.

146 Burke St George Report, 15, 29.

147 Burke St George Report, 15.

148 Burke St George Report, 29; *Claxton* St George Report, 5.

149 Burke St George Report, 29.

150 *Dyson* St George Report, 3.

151 Jones, *Destroyer Squadron 23*, 261–62.

152 *Dyson* St George Report, 3.

153 Burke St George Report, 15, 30.

154 Burke St George Report, 30.

155 ONI Narrative, 61; Burke St George Report, 16.

156 Jones, *Destroyer Squadron 23*, 262–63.

157 Captain Burke's TBS log has Commander Gano actually saying, "I think I see the southern tip of that Island over there on our SG." "[T]hat Island" does not make a lot of sense and is open to multiple interpretations. Jones (*Destroyer Squadron 23*, 263) has the quote as referencing New Britain, as well as coming from the *Converse*'s Commander Hamberger. However, both Gano's (*Dyson* St George Report, 4) and Hamberger's (*Converse* St George Report, 2) reports mention approaching New Ireland, not New Britain. It's also easy to hear how "New Ireland" could turn into "that Island" to a human ear. For that reason, the narrative assumes that Gano said "New Ireland" and not "that Island."

158 Captain Burke's TBS log has "boys" in the singular, not plural. The narrative assumes that is a typo, as calling one of his skippers "boy" is at the very least mildly insulting, especially over an open channel, and Burke is highly unlikely to have done so.

159 Burke St George Report, 16.
160 Jones, *Destroyer Squadron 23*, 264.
161 Burke St George Report, 20.
162 Burke St George Report, 18–19.
163 Monograph 100, 32; *Yugiri* and *I-177* TROMs. Monograph 100 says, "The crew of the *Yugiri* and 278 of the troops aboard her were rescued on the 26th by the submarine *I-177*." It's likely a mistranslation, with the intended meaning being *I-177* recovered a total of 278 survivors from the *Yugiri*, but the wording does leave the possibility that the 278 who were recovered by the *I-177* were all passengers. The *Yugiri*'s TROM says, "278 survivors rescued by *I-177* and 11 by *I-181*; Lieutenant Commander Otsuji killed in action."
164 Tuohy, *America's Fighting Admirals*, 2899–901.
165 O'Hara, *US Navy*, 4735–41.
166 Burke St George Report, 20.

Chapter 9

1 United States Army Center of Military History, *American Forces in Action: The Capture of Makin (20–24 November 1943)* (Washington, DC: Office of the Chief of Military History, Department of the Army, 1990), 124.
2 Leland Ness, *Rikugun: Guide to Japanese Ground Forces 1937–1945: Volume 1: Tactical Organization of Imperial Japanese Army & Navy Ground Forces* (Solihull, UK: Helion and Company, 2014), Kindle edition, 6143–56.
3 Philip A. Crowl and Edmund G. Love, *United States Army in World War II – The War in the Pacific – "Seizure of the Gilberts and Marshalls"* (Washington, DC: Office of the Chief of Military History, Department of the Army, 1955), 70–71.
4 Army Center of Military History, *Capture of Makin*, 124.
5 Crowl and Love, *Seizure of the Gilberts and Marshalls*, 125.
6 Molly Moore, "USS *Iowa* Investigation Focuses on Gunpowder," *The Washington Post*, May 2, 1989.
7 James Noles, *Twenty-Three Minutes to Eternity: The Final Voyage of the Escort Carrier USS Liscome Bay* (Tuscaloosa, AL: University of Alabama Press, 2010), Kindle edition, 113.
8 Joseph H. Alexander, *Utmost Savagery: The Three Days of Tarawa* (Annapolis: Naval Institute Press, 1995), Kindle edition, 74. For a different view, see Alexander (*Utmost Savagery*, 74):

> I personally doubt that Shibasaki intended those words to be his eternal epitaph. More likely, he used the expression to bolster the courage of his troops, a garrison of forty-five hundred men, far from home, sweltering on the equator, fearfully aware that an enormous American fleet was heading their way. As a professional naval officer, he probably knew his chances of prevailing against such a gathering storm were slim. His one hope may have been that the garrison could hold on, endure the inevitable shelling, and inflict such heavy casualties on the attackers that he could, in fact, give Koga his "three to seven days" to deploy the Combined Fleet.
>
> While most Japanese naval officers did not like to admit it, there was the 1941 example of the American defense of Wake Island to consider, wherein the US Marines, sailors, and civilians kept the invading force at bay for two weeks. Shibasaki had bigger guns, more men, and a coral reef. His garrison might hold on.

This well-presented argument would be more compelling if the Imperial Japanese military did not have a history of making such bombastic, hyperbolic statements and actually believing them, even acting on them. Even without that history, Shibasaki had plenty of options to drag out the defense to that "three to seven days," such as constructing fortifications in depth for the naval infantry to occupy if they needed to retreat from the beaches. Indeed, the Japanese could have held on with their formidable defenses, but those defenses were thin because Shibasaki had put very little behind them.
9 Crowl and Love, *Seizure of the Gilberts and Marshalls*, 154.
10 Capt. James R. Stockman, USMC, *Marines in World War II Historical Monograph: The Battle for Tarawa* (Washington, DC: Historical Section, Division of Public Information, Headquarters, US Marine Corps, 1947), 59.

11   The account of the sinking of the *Ro-100* comes from Cressman, *Official Chronology*, and the *Ro-100* TROM.

12   Morison, *Bismarcks Barrier*, 360.

13   Commander Destroyer Squadron 23, "Anti-aircraft action by Destroyer Squadron 23 during the period 30 November to 6 December 1943" (hereinafter "Burke Anti-aircraft Report"), 2.

14   Monograph 100, 34.

15   Commander Destroyer Squadron Forty-Five, "Action Report" (hereinafter "ComDesRon 45 Action Report"), 1.

16   Tagaya, *Rikko*, 1467; Monograph 100, 34.

17   ComDesRon 45 Action Report, 2.

18   Monograph 100, 34.

19   ComDesRon 45 Action Report, 1; Burke Anti-aircraft Report, 20.

20   Monograph 100, 34.

21   Burke Anti-aircraft Report, 1.

22   Monograph 100, 34.

23   Sherrod, *History*, 194–95.

24   Shaw and Kane, *Isolation of Rabaul*, 283-4; "Torokina Airfield," *Pacific Wrecks* (www.pacificwrecks.com).

25   One Marine history dryly notes, "There is no official record of the subsequent proceedings of this Japanese officer." Rentz, *Bougainville*, 75 n.183.

26   Rentz, *Bougainville*, 75.

27   Shaw and Kane, *Isolation of Rabaul*, 272.

28   The account of the sinking of the *Buenos Aires Maru* comes from the *Buenos Aires Maru* TROM, USS *Runner* "Report of Second War Patrol"; and "The Hospital Ships Buenos Aires Maruand [sic] Wah Sui," Naval Historical Society of Australia (www.navyhistory.au).

29   *Himalaya Maru* TROM; Cressman, *Chronology*. The *Himalaya Maru*'s TROM is confusing. Using Japan Standard Time (one hour behind Rabaul), it reads, "At 2333, the convoy is attacked by a USN Consolidated PBY 'Catalina' floatplane. HIMALAYA MARU is hit by one of three incendiary bombs and set afire. At 2315, Abandon Ship is ordered. At 2334, HIMALAYA MARU sinks." Abandon ship could not have been ordered before the attack was even made, and fire by itself is not likely to sink a 5,229-ton ship in one minute. It's not clear where the typo is, so the narrative here has deliberately left the time of the attack and sinking vague. Interestingly, the JANAC compilation of Japanese ships sunk has the *Himalaya Maru* sinking on December 2.

30   Hickey and Pettus, *Ken's Men, Vol. II*, 44; Thomas A. Baker, *It Wasn't so Jolly: The Story of the Jolly Rogers and the James Horner Crew* (Tijeras, NM: Thomas A. Baker, 2018), 347; Alcorn, *Jolly Rogers*, 107–08; Wolf, *5th Fighter Command, Vol.2*, 477–78.

31   McAulay, *Clean Sweep*, 938–83.

32   The Nakajima Ki-43 Army Type 1 Fighter was not just a Falcon, but a Peregrine Falcon.

33   Baker, *It Wasn't so Jolly*, 348; "Dagua Airfield (But East)," *Pacific Wrecks*, (www.pacificwrecks.com).

34   Hickey and Pettus, *Ken's Men, Vol. II*, 45.

35   Cressman, *Chronology*, JANAC.

36   Baker, *It Wasn't so Jolly*, 348–60.

37   McAulay, *Clean Sweep*, 938–83. McAulay notes the Japanese Army Air Force's 24 Air Group reported losing seven fighters over Wewak this day – except the 24th had been withdrawn in October. McAulay says, "This report is perhaps wrongly dated or the report was found and logged late; another example of poor record keeping. The loss of eight pilots could be for the period in combat, May–October, in addition to those already listed."

38   Or Hoskins. Or Gavuvu. Or Gabubu. "Cape Hoskins (Hoskins)," *Pacific Wrecks*, (www.pacificwrecks.com); "Gavuvu (Gabubu)," *Pacific Wrecks* (www.pacificwrecks.com).

39   Craven and Cate, *Guadalcanal*, 334–35; AAFHS-43, 29, 140–41 n.41.

40   Craven and Cate, *Guadalcanal*, 334–35; AAFHS-43, 29–30.

41   Don L. Evans, Walter Gaylor, Harry A. Nelson, and Lawrence J. Hickey, *Revenge of the Red Raiders: The Illustrated History of the 22nd Bombardment Group During World War II: Complete Volume Two* (Boulder, CO: International Research and Publishing Corporation, 2006), Kindle edition, 2221.

42 AAFHS-43, 30, 140–41 n.41; "December 14, 1943," *Pacific Wrecks* (www.pacificwrecks.com).

43 VP-52 War Diary; Cressman, *Chronology*; JANAC.

44 Cressman, *Chronology*; JANAC; *Alaska Maru, Kaika Maru*, and *Ch-38* TROMs.

45 It seems no one passed the lessons of this amphibious operation by paratroopers to the US Army's 82nd Airborne Division.

46 The *Ro-105*'s Tabular Record of Movement says on the evening of November 6, "*Ro-105* rescue[d] two downed pilots from an inflatable boat." What the inflatable boat was doing to the downed pilots that required rescue from it is not stated.

47 Sarmi is named from an acronym of the five main Papuan tribes in the area: Sobey, Armati, Rumbuai, Manirem, and Isirawa. The area actually has 87 tribes, each with its own language, but no one wanted to make an 87-letter acronym. Someone always gets left out.

48 Or Merkus Cape.

49 *Ro-105* TROM; Morison, *Bismarcks Barrier*, 374.

50 Dunn, *South Pacific*, 492; Monograph 100, 40.

51 Or Arawee. Pronounced "Arawee." "Arawe (Merkus, Cape Merkus)," *Pacific Wrecks* (www.pacificwrecks.com).

52 Monograph 100, 40.

53 William Shakespeare, *Julius Caesar*, III, 1.

54 Dunn, *South Pacific*, 492; Monograph 100, 40.

55 Monograph 100, 40.

56 Dunn, "Tuluvu's Air War," *J-Aircraft* (https://j-aircraft.com/); Dunn, *South Pacific*, 492–93; Hata, Izawa, and Shores, *Japanese Naval Air Force*, 138; Wolf, *5th Fighter Command, Vol. 2*, 482; Odgers, *Air War Against Japan, 1943–45*, 127; Martin Caidin, *Fork-Tailed Devil: The P-38* (Dering Harbor, NY: iBooks, 2001), Kindle edition, 4832; Monograph 100, 40–41; AAFHS-43, 34, 38; Monograph 142, 8. Monograph 100 says, "Two Zeros and two carrier bombers failed to return." Hata et al. say:

> 54 Zeros at once provided escort to eight dive-bombers, 15 of these also carrying out strafing attacks. Led by Wt Off Tadao Yamanaka, who had recently joined 204 Ku from 202 Ku, all the strafing fighters were hit by AA fire, and while two pilots had to force-land, all crews ultimately returned safely to Rabaul.

It is not clear whether "all crews" refers to just the strafing fighters or the overall strike, but Hata's "Appendix B Key Fighter Pilots Killed In Action (by date)," while not exhaustive, shows no Zero pilots killed on December 15, 1943. If both Hata et al. and Monograph 100 are taken to be accurate, then "all crews" must be interpreted to refer only to the strafing fighters. A second Base Air Force attack was attempted the afternoon of December 15, says Monograph 142, "but because of bad weather conditions with great regret, it was suspended." It is unclear what constitutes "bad weather conditions with great regret."

57 Miller, *Cartwheel*, 285–86; Shaw and Kane, *Isolation of Rabaul*, 339; Daniel E. Barbey, *MacArthur's Amphibious Navy: Seventh Amphibious Force Operations, 1943–1945* (Annapolis: Naval Institute Press, 1969), 106–07.

58 Dunn, *South Pacific*, 493.

59 Whether it was an African or European swallow is not specified.

60 Craven and Cate, *Guadalcanal*, 336; Wolf, *5th Fighter Command, Vol. 2*, 482; Ronald W. Yoshino, *Lightning Strikes: The 475th Fighter Group in the Pacific War, 1943–1945* (Manhattan, KN: Sunflower University Press, 1988), 55; Henry Sakaida, *Japanese Army Air Force Aces 1937–45* (Oxford: Osprey, 2012), Kindle edition, 114.

61 Monograph 100, 41.

62 MTB Ron 7 "Combat Report as told by Lieut E. W. Roberts O.T.C, Lieut. J Ellicott and Lieut. R. R. Read, to Lieut. J. H. DeCourey, Intelligence Officer Squadron Seven" (hereinafter "Combat Report"), 1–4.

63 MACR 1417; "B-24D-125-CO Liberator Serial Number 42-41043," *Pacific Wrecks* (www.pacificwrecks.com); Dunn, *South Pacific*, 493; ComTaskGr 70.1 War Diary.

64 The VP-52 War Diary says that at 1215 on December 16 "two enemy patrol craft" opened fire on Lieutenant (jg) DeGuzman. DeGuzman had taken off at 6:01pm on December 15 and landed at

8:45am on December 16, so he could not have taken fire at 12:15pm on December 16. The narrative treats "1215" as containing a typo, with the actual time likely 2:15am.

65   VP-52 War Diary.

66   VP-52 War Diary.

67   Dunn, *South Pacific*, 493; ComTaskGr 70.1 War Diary. Commander Morton C. Mumma, commanding officer of Task Group 70.1, which was the 7th Fleet's PT boats, had this comment to the Combat Report:

> The Commander Task Group 73.1 [Captain Edwin R. Peck, who commanded all of the 7th Fleet's PBY Catalina flying boats] reported by dispatch that a [PBY] Catalina patrol plane [that of Lieutenant (jg) Pattison] on the morning of 16 December, 1943 sighted two patrol boats equipped with I.F.F. [Identification Friend Foe] about 18 miles southwest of Gasmata, and that at 2:30L the Catalina saw a large plane with square wing tips shot down in flames by these patrol boats. While there is a discrepancy of about one hour in the times reported by the Commander Task Group 73.1 and the Commander MTB Squadron 7, it is believed that both reports cover the same action and that the report of the Commander Task Group 73.1 confirms destruction of a large aircraft by PTs 131 and 133.

This statement had been interpreted as confirming that the PT boats shot down Lieutenant Harris's B-24. While that is the most likely scenario here, it is curious that the B-24 is described as "a large plane with square wing tips" when both the B-24 Liberator and the Kawanishi H6K "Type 97 Large Flying Boat" ("Mavis") had rounded wingtips.

68   Hata, Izawa, and Shores, *Japanese Naval Air Force*, 138–39; Monograph 100, 42. Hata et al.'s reference to "CPO Igiya" of the 204 Ku is treated as a typo, as there's no reference to him anywhere else.

69   AAFHS-43, 41–42; Craven and Cate, *Guadalcanal*, 336; Dunn, *South Pacific*, 490; Evans, Gaylor, Nelson, and Hickey; *Revenge of the Red Raiders: Vol. 2*, 2221.

70   Dunn, "Tuluvu's Air War"; "Ki-49-II Helen Manufacture Number 3297," *Pacific Wrecks* (www.pacificwrecks.com).

71   Or Rooke Island. Or Umboi Island.

72   Dunn, "Tuluvu's Air War"; "Ki-49-II Helen Manufacture Number 3297," *Pacific Wrecks* (www.pacificwrecks.com); Hata, Izawa, and Shores, *Japanese Army Air Force*, 95; John Stanaway, *Possum, Clover & Hades: The 475th Fighter Group in World War II* (Atglen, PA: Schiffer Publishing, 2004), 87–88; Wolf, *5th Fighter Command, Vol. 2*, 483; McAulay, *Clean Sweep*, 983–1011. Hata et al. say this:

> A further Allied landing occurred on 15 December 1943, this time at Arawe (Marcus Point) on the southwestern tip of New Britain. Heavy bombers were at once despatched to attack, escorted by the 59th Sentai. Capt Shigeo Nango, leading the fighters, subsequently confided to his diary that it was no longer the day of the Hayabusa, his fighters being overwhelmed by P-38s. Next day Ki 61s and Ki 43s again escorted bombers to the area, but could not defend them against the US interceptors; all five bombers and five of the escorting fighters were shot down.

It's not clear when Captain Nango made the entry into his diary. It can be inferred that Nango made it after the attempted attack on December 15. If so, this timeline does not mesh with the actual results of the 4th Air Army's attacks. Nango's fighters were not overwhelmed by P-38s on December 15 because they faced only two P-38s of the 432nd Fighter Squadron and neither side pressed the issue, so there were no casualties. The next day, December 16, was very different, however, with five bombers and two Peregrine Falcon fighters shot down, a sixth bomber forced landed at Tuluvu and one damaged Peregrine Falcon landing at Gavuvu. Nango's comments were probably made in reference to the December 16 attack.

73   Having to repeatedly differentiate between the 342nd Fighter Squadron (P-47s) and the 432nd Fighter Squadron (P-38s) and the 341st Fighter Squadron (P-47s) and the 431st Fighter Squadron (P-38s) is difficult to say the least.

74   Hata, Izawa, and Shores, *Japanese Naval Air Force*, 138–39, 797; Monograph 100, 42–43; Dunn, "Tuluvu's Air War." Hata et al.'s reference to "CPO Igiya" of the 204 Ku is treated as a typo, as there's no reference to him anywhere else.

75   Dunn, "Tuluvu's Air War."

76   Dunn, "Tuluvu's Air War." Perhaps revealingly, Lieutenant (jg) Oba is not listed in Hata, Izawa, and Shores, *Japanese Naval Air Force*'s Appendix B: "Key Fighter Pilots Killed in Action (by date)."

77 Dunn, "Tuluvu's Air War." Perhaps revealingly, Lieutenant (jg) Oba is not listed in Hata, Izawa, and Shores, *Japanese Naval Air Force*'s Appendix B: "Key Fighter Pilots Killed in Action (by date)."

78 Dunn, "Tuluvu's Air War"; Tagaya, *Rikko*, 1467.

79 Dunn, "Tuluvu's Air War"; Dunn, *South Pacific*, 495; Wolf, *5th Fighter Command, Vol. 2*, 486–87.

80 There were entirely too many "Pappys" in the Pacific War. Though one Pappy was an Army Air Force pilot in the Southwest Pacific and the other Pappy was a Marine pilot in the South Pacific, it was too confusing. There are unconfirmed rumors of fist fights between Army Air Force personnel and Marines, between members of the Southwest Pacific and the South Pacific, on whether Pappy Gunn or Pappy Boyington should be called "The Other Pappy."

81 VF-40 and VMF-214 war diaries.

82 Gamble, *The Black Sheep: The Definitive Account of Marine Fighting Squadron 214 in World War II* (New York: Random House, 1998), Kindle edition, 322; Sakaida, *Siege*, 12–13; Hata, Izawa, and Shores, *Japanese Naval Air Force*, 138.

83 Ross, *Official History*, 213–14.

84 What does "clear as a bell" even mean? Bells are usually opaque and their sound is not always clear.

85 Gamble, *Black Sheep*, 284; Gregory Boyington, *Baa Baa Black Sheep: The True Story of the "Bad Boy" of the Pacific Theatre and His Famous Black Sheep Squadron* (New York: Bantam, 1977), Kindle edition, 147.

86 Gamble, *Black Sheep*, 284; Boyington, *Baa Baa*, 147.

87 Boyington, *Baa Baa*, 147–48.

88 Gamble (*Black Sheep*, 284) says, "The first was a well-known query – 'Major Boyington, what is your position?' – that probably occurred on October 17." While, given the inaccuracies found in both Boyington's memoirs, it may very well have been October 17, 1943, the VMF-214 war diary's description of the missions of October 17 does not fit Boyington's description of the first mission in which the query was initially made.

89 VMF-214 and -221 war diaries.

90 Frank E. Walton, *Once They Were Eagles: The Men of the Black Sheep Squadron* (Lexington, KY: University Press of Kentucky, 1986), Kindle edition, 55.

91 Walton, *Once They Were Eagles*, 55–56.

92 Hata, Izawa, and Shores, *Japanese Naval Air Force*, 132; Sakaida, *Siege*, 12–13; VMF-221 War Diary.

93 VMF-214 War Diary.

94 Gamble, *Black Sheep*, 284.

95 Gamble, *Black Sheep*, 4596; Boyington, *Baa Baa*, 164. According to Sakaida (*Siege*, 12), "The Allied radio transmissions were being monitored by four Niseis (second generation Japanese-Americans) at Rabaul HQ. These civilian translators had learned the American lingo in the good old US of A." He later elaborates (*Siege*, 14.):
> The Japanese Naval Headquarters at Rabaul employed at least four American-born citizens of Japanese descent. It was common for Japanese families in the United States to send their eldest sons back to Japan for a formal Japanese education. When the war broke out, they could not return home. They were conscripted into the military as civilian interpreters. They monitored Allied radio transmissions and helped interrogate captured aviators. [...] The four Niseis were Masayuki Takamoto, Tadashi Mizokawa, Edward Chikaki Honda, and Jun Kawasaki."

96 Gamble, *Black Sheep*, 209; VMF-214 War Diary.

97 VMF-214 War Diary.

98 Gamble, *Black Sheep*, 325–27.

99 VMF-214 War Diary.

100 Sherrod, *History*, 195 (citing ONI, *The Combat Strategy and Tactics of Major Gregory Boyington, USMCR*, 15 February 1944).

101 VMF-214 War Diary.

102 Monograph 100, 43.

103 Hata, Izawa, and Shores, *Japanese Naval Air Force*, 139.

104 Monograph 100, 43.

105 What exactly is a twin-engine light bomber anyway?

106 Dunn, "Tuluvu's Air War"; Dunn, *South Pacific*, 495; Wolf, *5th Fighter Command, Vol. 2*, 487.

107 Monograph 100, 41–42.

108 Dunn, "Tuluvu's Air War"; Dunn, *South Pacific*, 496; AAFHS-43, 45; Craven and Cate, *Guadalcanal*, 337. Dunn says in "Tuluvu's Air War" that the 90th dropped 198 1,000lb bombs, though he does not repeat this claim in *South Pacific*. AAFHS-43, which was prepared by Major Harris J. Warren of the Combat Operational History Division, US Army Air Force Historical Office, also says the 90th dropped 198 1,000lb bombs. Captain Bernhardt L. Mortensen, Air Force Historical Division, who prepared the "Rabaul and Cape Gloucester" chapter in Craven and Cate, says the 90th dropped 80 2,000lb bombs. It should be noted that the forward to AAFHS-43 includes this disclaimer: "Like other AAF Historical studies, the present narrative is subject to revision as additional materials become available."

109 Craven and Cate, *Guadalcanal*, 337; "December 18, 1943," *Pacific Wrecks* (www.pacificwrecks.com).

110 Monograph 32 (map between pages 25–26) has the 68 at Boram, near Wewak. The 248 is shown at Alexishafen's Danip air base and the 59 at Madang. *Pacific Wrecks* (www.pacificwrecks.com) has 68's Ki-61 Flying Swallows detachment staging into Danip on October 15, 1943 ("Danip Airfield (Alexishafen II, Alexishafen No 1)") and all three squadrons also operating out of Madang ("Madang Airfield.")

111 Dunn, "248th Hiko Sentai: A Japanese 'Hard luck' Fighter Unit."

112 "P-38H-5-LO "Regina Coeli" Serial Number 42-66856 Nose 179," *Pacific Wrecks* (www.pacificwrecks.com); Yoshino, *Lightning Strikes*, 56–57.

113 McAulay, *Clean Sweep*, 1011–29; Sakaida, *Japanese Army Air Force Aces*, 114; Hata, Izawa, and Shores, *Japanese Army Air Force*, 577. Dunn (both "248th Hiko Sentai" and "Tuluvu's Air War") says that the 248 Air Group joined the 59 Air Group on the December 18 fighter sweep of Arawe, not mentioning the 68 Air Group, but McAulay has the 433rd Fighter Squadron's Lieutenant Robert Tomberg shooting down Sergeant Major Yamazaki Tamisaku of the 68 during this fighter sweep, indicating the 68 took part. Sakaida says, "By December 1943 the 68th Sentai (Air Group) had only three pilots left[…]," but Dunn says "eight Hiens of 68th [Air Group]" took part in the December 21 attack on Arawe, a figure he reaffirmed in his book (*South Pacific*, 497). Eight is more than three; and note this was after Sergeant Major Yamazaki had been shot down. Sakaida and Dunn are among the gold standards in Imperial Japanese aviation research. Hata et al.'s qualification of "officer pilots" resolves that issue.

114 Royal Australian Air Force Historical Section, *Units of the Royal Australian Air Force: A Concise History Volume 2, Fighter Units* (Canberra: Australian Government Publishing Service, 1995), 70; "No. 79 Squadron," *Australian War Memorial* (www.awm.gov.au). Curiously, the official Australian history by Odgers does not mention this incident, but it is mentioned by the Australian War Memorial and the unit histories by Royal Australian Air Force Historical Section. More curiously, none of these sources provides a given name to "Pilot Officer Barrie."

115 Odgers, *Air War Against Japan, 1943–45*, 127; Dunn, "Tuluvu's Air War"; Dunn, *South Pacific*, 495.

116 Dunn ("Tuluvu's Air War") has the *APc-2* later sinking, but that was not the case; the Navy sold her in 1947. Gary P. Priolo, *USS APc-2, NavSource Naval History* (www.navsource.org).

117 Dunn, "Tuluvu's Air War"; Dunn, *South Pacific*, 495; Monograph 100, 44; Hata, Izawa, and Shores, *Japanese Naval Air Force*, 139; Wolf, *5th Fighter Command*, 489. Monograph 100 says four bombers and one fighter failed to return. Hata et al. say that four fighters were lost.

118 Monograph 142, 9; Dunn, "Tuluvu's Air War"; Dunn, *South Pacific*, 495; Hata, Izawa, and Shores, *Japanese Naval Air Force*, 139; Wolf, *5th Fighter Command*, 490. Dunn says one Thunderbolt was shot down, but that detail is missing in other accounts and is not listed among the Army Air Force's missing and downed aircraft.

119 Dunn, "Tuluvu's Air War"; Dunn, *South Pacific*, 495.

120 Sakaida (*Japanese Army Air Force Aces*, 114) says that on December 21, "Takeuchi escorted light bombers to the enemy landing area, but they were attacked by a large force of P-47s." They were attacked by four P-47s. And the Japanese fighters outnumbered said P-47s five to one.

121 Or Hansa South.

122 Dunn, "Tuluvu's Air War"; Dunn, *South Pacific*, 495; Wolf, *5th Fighter Command*, 490–91; McAulay, *Clean Sweep*, 1029–52; Richard L. Dunn, "Hansa Bay Japanese Army Air Force Activity," *Pacific Wrecks* (www.pacificwrecks.com); "Ki-61-Ia Tony Manufacture Number ???," *Pacific Wrecks* (www.pacificwrecks.com).

com); Sakaida, *Japanese Army Air Force Aces*, 114–15; Hata, Izawa, and Shores, *Japanese Army Air Force*, 577.

123 "December 18, 1943," *Pacific Wrecks* (www.pacificwrecks.com); "December 19, 1943," *Pacific Wrecks* (www.pacificwrecks.com); *History of the 38th Bombardment Group*; "December 20, 1943," *Pacific Wrecks* (www.pacificwrecks.com); "December 20, 1943," "December 21, 1943," *Pacific Wrecks* (www.pacificwrecks.com); *History of the 38th Bombardment Group*; Phil H. Listemann, *The Douglas Boston & Havoc: The Australians. (Squadrons No. 22)*. Philedition, 2017. Kindle edition, 301; Odgers, *Air War Against Japan, 1943–45*, 127–28.

124 "December 22, 1943," *Pacific Wrecks* (www.pacificwrecks.com).

125 Monograph 142, 5a, 9–10.

126 "December 23, 1943," *Pacific Wrecks* (www.pacificwrecks.com).

127 Monograph 142, 5a, 10; "December 24, 1943," *Pacific Wrecks* (www.pacificwrecks.com); "December 24, 1943," *Pacific Wrecks* (www.pacificwrecks.com).

128 "Other than that, how did you like the play, Mrs. Lincoln?"

129 Monograph 142, 11.

130 VMF-214 War Diary; Gamble, *Black Sheep*, 317.

131 Gamble, *Black Sheep*, 318, 321; Hata, Izawa, and Shores, *Japanese Naval Air Force*, 139, 797; VMF-214 War Diary, VF-33 War History.

132 VMF-214 War Diary.

133 Boyington, *Baa Baa*, 202.

134 *W-21* TROM.

135 Monograph 100, 46.

136 Monograph 100, 46.

137 Monograph 100, 47; Morison, *Bismarcks Barrier*, 385.

138 Eric Hammel, *Coral and Blood* (Pacifica, CA: Pacifica Military History, 2009), Kindle edition, 139.

139 Frank O. Hough and John A. Crown, *The Campaign on New Britain* (Washington, DC: Historical Branch, Headquarters, US Marine Corps, 1952), 36.

140 Hough and Crown, *New Britain*, 36 (quoting Fletcher Pratt, *The Marines' War* (New York, 1948), 305).

141 Hough and Crown, *New Britain*, 36.

142 Shaw and Kane, *Isolation of Rabaul*, 317; Morison, *Bismarcks Barrier*, 381–82; USS *Ralph Talbot* and ComDesDiv 48 war diaries. Shaw and Kane say Barbey's invasion force had nine fast destroyer transports, but Morison lists ten. For his part, Morison does not mention the Royal Australian and US Navy destroyers escorting the *Australia* and *Shropshire*.

143 Craven and Cate, *Guadalcanal*, 337–38.

144 Craven and Cate, *Guadalcanal*, 345.

145 Morison, *Bismarcks Barrier*, 385; Craven and Cate, *Guadalcanal*, 339; "B-24D-150-CO Liberator Serial Number 42-41241," *Pacific Wrecks* (www.pacificwrecks.com); *The History of the 380th Bomb Group (H) AAF affectionately known as the Flying Circus, November 1942–September 1945* (New York: Commanday-Roth, Co, NYG), 27-9; Glenn R. Horton, *The Best in the Southwest: The 380th Bombardment Group (H) in World War II, Southwest Pacific Area* (Savage, MN: Mosie Publications, 1995), 133–34; Hickey, *Warpath*, 104; Rems, *South Pacific Cauldron*, 3273–74.

146 Morison, *Bismarcks Barrier*, 385; Rems, *South Pacific Cauldron*, 3288—90.

147 The code name for the fighter director on the *Shaw* was "Duckbutt." Wolf, *5th Fighter Command*, 495.

148 "Brownson I (DD-518)," *DANFS*; Cressman, *Official Chronology*.

149 MACR 3146; Wolf, *5th Fighter Command*, 498.

150 MACR 2026.

151 Hata, Izawa, and Shores, *Japanese Naval Air Force*, 139, 561, 796; Monograph 100, 47.

152 Dunn, "248th Hiko Sentai."

153 Hickey, *Warpath*, 104–07; Wolf, *5th Fighter Command*, 502–03. Wolf says the 342nd was assigned to cover the withdrawal of the ships, but MACR 4474 makes clear their mission was to escort the bombers. In fact, they could have done both.

154 Dunn, "248th Hiko Sentai."

155 Dunn, "248th Hiko Sentai"; McAulay, *Clean Sweep*, 1094.

156 Dunn, "248th Hiko Sentai"; McAulay, *Clean Sweep*, 1094; MACR 4474 and 1847; "P-47D-2-RE Thunderbolt Serial Number 42-8095," *Pacific Wrecks* (www.pacificwrecks.com); Wolf, *5th Fighter Command*, 502–03; "B-25D-1 'Crabb 2nd' Serial Number 41-30517," *Pacific Wrecks*, (www. pacificwrecks.com); "B-25D-1 'Here's Howe' Serial Number 41-30279," *Pacific Wrecks* (www. pacificwrecks.com). Strangely, the Missing Air Crew Reports don't mention the possibility of friendly fire shooting down the aircraft.

157 Rems, *South Pacific Cauldron*, 3305–07.

158 Al Hemingway, "The Incessant Rains of the Green Inferno," *WWII History*, Vol. 9, No. 7 (October 2010), 62 (www.warfarehistorynetwork.com).

159 Morison, *Bismarcks Barrier*, 388.

160 Yoshino, *Lightning Strikes*, 56–57; "William G. Jeakle," *Pacific Wrecks* (www.pacificwrecks.com).

161 Rems, *South Pacific Cauldron*, 3318–20.

162 Hough and Crown, *New Britain*, 41–42.

163 Hough and Crown, *New Britain*, 42.

164 Hough and Crown, *New Britain*, 42.

165 Hough and Crown, *New Britain*, 64.

166 Hough and Crown, *New Britain*, 64.

167 Morison, *Bismarcks Barrier*, 378; Hough and Crown, *New Britain*, 183.

168 Except where otherwise noted, the account of the January 1, 1944 carrier attack on Kavieng is from the *Noshiro*, *Oyodo*, *Akizuki*, and *Yamagumo* TROMs. The *Noshiro*'s TROM, which specifies the arrival time in Kavieng as 0445 (JST), one hour behind local time, erroneously lists the destroyer *Akikaze* in place of the *Akizuki*.

169 USS *Bunker Hill* CV17, "ACA-1 Reports for Strike II, Kavieng, 1 January 1944," 7; *Noshiro* TROM.

170 *Noshiro* TROM.

171 Cressman, *Chronology*; JANAC.

172 Or Gunbi.

173 Morison, *Bismarcks Barrier*, 389–90; Monograph 100, 52.

174 Wolf, *5th Fighter Command*, 510–11; McAulay, *Clean Sweep*, 1113–33; MACR 5375.

175 David Dexter, *The New Guinea Offensives: Australia in the War of 1939–1945, Series 1 – Army, Volume 6* (Canberra: Australian War Memorial, 1961), 736.

176 Walter Krueger, *From Down Under to Nippon: The Story of the Sixth Army In World War II* (Lawrence, KN: Zenger, 1953), Kindle edition, 71.

177 Dexter, *The New Guinea Offensives*, 764.

178 Dexter, *The New Guinea Offensives*, 771.

179 Gamble, *Black Sheep*, 323; Boyington, *Baa Baa*, 202–03.

180 Bruce Gamble, *Black Sheep One: The Life of Gregory "Pappy" Boyington* (New York: Ballantine, 2000), Kindle edition, 334; VMF-214 and 223 war diaries. Gamble says eight Corsairs were from VMF-223, but the VMF-223 War Diary shows only seven. Gamble also says 16 Hellcats came from VF-30, but the VF-30 War History does not show a mission on January 3, 1944. It's probably a typo for VF-33.

181 Gamble, *Black Sheep One*, 334; Hata, Izawa, and Shores, *Japanese Naval Air Force*, 141.

182 Gamble, *Black Sheep*, 364.

183 Boyington, *Baa Baa*, 211–12.

184 Boyington, *Baa Baa*, 211–12.

185 VMF-214 War Diary.

186 Gamble, *Black Sheep One*, 337.

187 *I-181* TROM.

188 Sakaida, *Siege*, 16.

189 John M. Foster, *Hell in the Heavens* (New York: Charter Books, 1961), 234.

190 Sakaida, *Siege*, 16–17; Hata, Izawa, and Shores, *Japanese Naval Air Force*, 141; Wolf, *13th Fighter Command*, 241; VMF-211, 214, 223, and 321, VF-40, and ComSoPac war diaries.

191 Hata, Izawa, and Shores, *Japanese Naval Air Force*, 141.

192 *Fumizuki* and *Satsuki* TROMs; "January 4, 1944," *Pacific Wrecks* (www.pacificwrecks.com); "F6F-3 Hellcat Bureau Number 26100," *Pacific Wrecks* (www.pacificwrecks.com).

193 Wolf, *13th Fighter Command*, 242; VMF-211, 214, and 321, and VF-40 war diaries; VMF-214 ACA Report #20; MACR 2203 and 2204.

194 Or *Kaiga Maru*.

195 *Kaika Maru*, *Choun Maru*, and *Satsuki* TROMs; Cressman, *Chronology*. Cressman has a typo in the coordinates of the *Haguro Maru*'s sinking. It should be 02°43'S, 149°25'E, not 02°43'N, 149°25'E, which would put the convoy well on the way to Guam.

196 *Shunko Maru* and *Ch-24* TROMs. Both the *Shunko Maru* TROM and Cressman (*Official Chronology*) say the subchaser *Ch-29* was also with convoy O-905. The *Ch-24* TROM, however, does not mention *Ch-29* during this period, while the *Ch-29* TROM has her leaving Truk on January 11 headed for the Home Islands with convoy 4111, so she is not included with convoy O-905 here.

197 There are some hints that convoy O-905 may have been ratted out by *Magic*. The VP-34 War Diary is full of single-aircraft scouting missions which sometimes involve single-aircraft attacks, but for the night of January 15–16, 1944, the diary says five PBYs "made a coordinated attack on a Rabaul-bound convoy 30 miles northwest of New Hanover." It gives no explanation as to why on this particular night five Patrolling 34 aircraft decided to congregate off New Hanover. Moreover, most of the usual single-aircraft scouting missions took place in the Bismarck Sea bounded by Papua New Guinea, New Britain, and New Ireland. Going to, let alone beyond, New Hanover, was unusual, and is one of the reasons none of the previous scouting reports had sightings that could explain how VP-34 knew to find convoy O-905 off northwest of New Hanover. Finally, calling the convoy "Rabaul-bound" may be a tell inasmuch as the position of the convoy on its own does not indicate it was headed to Rabaul, as it could have been headed to Kavieng instead. That said, these are just hints that point to the possibility this was an ambush set up with information provided by *Magic*. These are not conclusive proof.

198 Or the *Syunko Maru*. Calling this ship the *Sunko Maru* would be completely inappropriate.

199 Researching the *Kosei Maru* has been a chore. *The Imperial Japanese Navy Page* alone has two listings for a *Kosei Maru*, neither of which were the *Kosei Maru* in convoy O-905. *Imperial Japanese Navy Page* researchers Gilbert Casse and Peter Cundall give the following clarification:

> Numerous ships bore this name [*Kosei Maru*] like auxiliary transports (2,205 GRT [Gross Register Tonnage] '24) and (3,551 GRT '37), auxiliary storeship (8,266 GRT '20), auxiliary small minelayer (1,026 GRT '15), IJA transports No. 889 (1,943 GRT '43) and No. 1031 (865 GRT '40), Okada Shosen cargo ship (3,262 GRT '19) and other smaller vessels.

> But it could be worse. The Macedonian Greek Ptolemaic Dynasty of Egypt, whose last pharaoh was the famous Queen Cleopatra VII, named every one of its male members "Ptolemy."

200 VP-34 War Diary; David Hanson, "Squadron History: VP-34," *Black Cats* (https://www.daveswarbirds. com/blackcat/); Louis B. Dorny, *US Navy PBY Catalina Units of the Pacific War* (Oxford: Osprey, 2013), Kindle edition, 1516; *Shunko Maru* and *Ch-24* TROMs; JANAC. The *Shunko Maru* being the first ship sunk and seen to sink is an educated guess. The VP-34 War Diary says the Liberator "saw the larger [sic] ship sink and the other two burning, exploding and abandoned." The *Shunko Maru* was the largest ship in the convoy. JANAC has the *Shunko Maru* sinking at a different position than the *Hozugawa* and *Meisho Maru*s. That said, JANAC is not always accurate – see the issue with the *Lyons Maru* listed as sinking in a January 17, 1944 air attack when she actually sank in a different air attack a week later, for example – and, though JANAC properly credits Navy Land-Based Aircraft for sinking all three ships, for the *Meisho Maru* it has the curious addition of "Army Aircraft."

201 *Ro-104* and *I-181* TROMs.

202 *I-181* TROM.

203 *I-181* TROM; Henry Sakaida, "Jungle Encounter," *Pacific Wrecks* (www.pacificwrecks.com).

204 *Ro-104* TROM.

205 USS *Ammen*, "Action Report – Bombardment of Gali, British New Guinea, night of 17–18 January, 1944," 1–3; USS *Mullany*, "Night Bombardment of Gali, New Guinea, night of 17 January 1944, and submarine and barge hunt in Gali Area," 1–2.

206 Then again, a cargo of empty drums, old engines, and scrap metal could have been intended to be recycled into steel, of which Japan was critically short and the US made in abundance. On an unrelated note, as the narrative is being written, Nippon Steel is attempting to purchase US Steel.

207 *Kaika Maru, Choun Maru,* and *Oite* TROMs; Cressman, *Chronology*; USS *Blackfish* "Report of War Patrol number seven," 9–10.

208 Wolf, *13th Fighter Command*, 244–45; ComSoPac, ComAirSols Strike Command, VMTB-232, VB-98, VMSB-236, and VMSB-341 war diaries. The Strike Command War Diary mistakenly has VC-40 in place of VMTB-232, but VC-40's war diary makes clear it did not take part in this attack. The *Hakkai Maru's* TROM says that "NZAF Vought F4U 'Corsair' fighter-bombers of No. 15 Fighter Squadron" also acted as escorts for the strike aircraft, "all [taking off] from Cape Torokina, Bougainville." However, 1. The Official History of the Royal New Zealand Air Force shows no such mission, nor does any other source mention the presence of the Kiwis; 2. The Kiwis would not be equipped with F4U Corsairs until later in 1944; and 3. The two Army Air Force fighter squadrons actually took off from Stirling Field in the Treasuries.

209 Wolf, *13th Fighter Command*, 244–45.

210 Wolf, *13th Fighter Command*, 244–45; Hata, Izawa, and Shores, *Japanese Naval Air Force*, 142; "252 Kōkūtai (252 Air Group)," *Pacific Wrecks* (www.pacificwrecks.com); "January 17, 1944," *Pacific Wrecks* (www.pacificwrecks.com). Japanese fighter numbers and unit identification are an amalgamation of Hata et al. and *Pacific Wrecks*. *Pacific Wrecks* and no one else mentions the 252 Air Group being in Rabaul at this time, but *Pacific Wrecks* is specific that the 252 staged into Rabaul in January 1944. It seems to have been a piecemeal commitment, with most of the 252 still operating in the Central Pacific. Or it might be that pilots from the 252 were incorporated into the 204 and 253 air groups, but only *Pacific Wrecks* breaks them out. Hata et al. does not mention the 252 in Rabaul at this time, and Monograph 142 does not list the 252 as part of Base Air Force.

211 Or *Hachikai Maru.*

212 *Hakkai Maru* TROM. The TROM says the *Hakkai Maru* took a torpedo in the engine room, but according to the AirSols Strike Command War Diary, none of the attacking aircraft were carrying torpedoes.

213 Or *Kanshin Maru.*

214 Or *Tanshin Maru.*

215 *Hakkai* and *Lyons Maru* TROMs; "January 17, 1944," *Pacific Wrecks* (www.pacificwrecks.com); "Kanshin Maru (Kenshin)," *Pacific Wrecks* (www.pacificwrecks.com). "Hakkai Maru," *Pacific Wrecks* (www.pacificwrecks.com), JANAC. Rather embarrassingly, JANAC shows the *Hakkai Maru* being sunk on January 17, 1944. The *Hakkai Maru's* TROM makes clear she was not sunk until January 24.

216 VMF-211, VMF-321, and VF-40 war diaries.

217 Or Sterling Field. Or Coronus Strip. Veteran Ralph Joseph "Joe" Deceuster of Marine Bombing 413 (VMB-413) recalled, "The natives from other islands believed that Stirling was like a table top placed on a single pedestal, and if it became unbalanced, it would tip, spilling everything into the sea. They would come and trade with us but they would be gone before nightfall." Before anyone makes any judgment as to this belief, recall that during a March 25, 2010, US House Armed Services Committee hearing on March 25, 2010, US Congressional Representative Hank Johnson (D-Georgia), critical of a proposal to add 8,000 US Marines to Guam, which had a population of 180,000, said to Admiral Robert F. Willard, Commander of US Pacific Command, "My fear is that the whole island will become so overly populated that it will tip over and capsize." Willard replied, "We don't anticipate that." The next day, Johnson's office claimed that it was a facetious metaphor he had deadpanned.

218 Wolf, *13th Fighter Command*, 244–45; "January 17, 1944," *Pacific Wrecks* (www.pacificwrecks.com); MACRs 1772, 1773, 1774, 1775, 1776, 1777, 1778, 1779; "F6F-3 Hellcat Bureau Number 26031," *Pacific Wrecks* (www.pacificwrecks.com); "SBD-5 Dauntless Bureau Number 28316 Plane Number 150," *Pacific Wrecks* (www.pacificwrecks.com); "TBF-1C Avenger Bureau Number 24363," *Pacific Wrecks* (www.pacificwrecks.com); "P-38J-10 Lightning Serial Number 42-67617," *Pacific Wrecks* (www.pacificwrecks.com); "P-38H-5-LO Lightning Serial Number 42-66897," *Pacific Wrecks* (www.pacificwrecks.com); VMTB-232 war diary; Hata, Izawa, and Shores, *Japanese Naval Air Force*, 142.

219 The VMF-321 War Diary says, "Lieutenant [Robert W.] Baker observed two B-25's [sic] crash into the sea, 3-5 mi. off Warangai River." The 42nd's history says only that Lieutenant Williamson's B-25 crashed into the sea. It does not say a second B-25 was lost, nor does the Army Air Force list of downed aircraft

show a B-25 other than Williamson's. What Baker probably saw was Williamson's B-25 and Captain Head's P-38 crashing into the sea, indicating that VMF-321 arrived on scene at around this time.

220 Cohn, *Crusaders*, 1698–705; Wolf, *13th Fighter Command*, 245; VMF-211 and 321 war diaries; MACRs 1802 and 1780; Monograph 142, 58. The location where Lieutenant Williamson's B-25 ditched is given as 4°30'S 152°30'W. It should be 4°30' S 152°30' E, which is in St George's Channel.

221 Wolf, *13th Fighter Command*, 245.

222 Dunn, "248th Hiko Sentai," Lawrence J. Hickey, Michael H. Levy, and Michael J. Claringbould, *Rampage of Roarin' 20's: The Illustrated History of the 312th Bombardment Group during World War II* (Boulder, CO: International Historical Research Associates, 2009), 45–47. Dunn has Captain Kojima Shigeo leading the contingent from the 248 into battle, even though he was the temporary commander of the unit until the arrival of its new commander, Major Kuroda Takefumi. Hickey et al. have Lieutenant Koga leading the contingent from the 248. The narrative goes with Hickey et al. as the more recent scholarship.

223 Dunn, "248th Hiko Sentai," Hickey, Levy, and Claringbould, *Rampage*, 45–51; "P-40N-5-CU Warhawk Serial Number 42-105909," *Pacific Wrecks* (www.pacificwrecks.com).

224 Dunn, "248th Hiko Sentai"; "January 16, 1944," *Pacific Wrecks* (www.pacificwrecks.com).

225 Dunn, "248th Hiko Sentai"; McAulay, *Clean Sweep*, 1181–205; "January 16, 1944," *Pacific Wrecks* (www.pacificwrecks.com); Wolf, *5th Fighter Command*, 514–16; MACR 1690 and 1698; 71st Bombardment Squadron War Diary; "B-25D-1 'Sweet Jeanne' Serial Number 41-30179," *Pacific Wrecks* (www.pacificwrecks.com); "B-25G-5 Mitchell Serial Number 42-64827," *Pacific Wrecks* (www. pacificwrecks.com). Lieutenant Serser's file seems to have been mixed with reports from another missing aircrew. Lieutenant Freek's file does not mention combat, only that when the rest of the squadron turned to make another pass at a target, his plane did not turn but kept going on its original course and never rejoined the formation.

226 Cressman, *Chronology*.

227 Wolf, *5th Fighter Command*, 516–18; Dunn, "248th Hiko Sentai"; MACR 1912, 1913, and 1914; "P-38H-1-LO 'Hot Box Annie' Serial Number 42-66545 Nose 123," *Pacific Wrecks* (www.pacificwrecks. com); "P-38H-1-LO Lightning Serial Number 42-66534 Tail 1??," *Pacific Wrecks* (www.pacificwrecks. com); "P-38H-1-LO Lightning Serial Number 42-66554," *Pacific Wrecks* (www.pacificwrecks.com); McAulay, *Clean Sweep*, 1205–37. The story of Sergeant Aiko comes from McAulay, who says, "Sgt Aiko allegedly shot down his attacker, both baled out, landed near each other, and Aiko then wrestled the US pilot to the ground and captured him. The US version is this P-38 was hit by a jettisoned drop-tank and lost a wing." McAulay's reference is to 2nd Lieutenant Robertson, who was seen to have been hit by a drop tank before combat. A much better candidate for Aiko's prisoner is Lieutenant Ritter, only for his right wing to strike the Tony as he passed the crippled fighter, which set Ritter's plane afire and sent it falling.

228 Cressman, *Chronology*.

229 Or *Tonei Maru*.

230 Bob Hackett and Sander Kingsepp, "Midget Submarines in the Bismarcks 1943–1944," *Imperial Japanese Navy Page* (www.combinedfleet.com); *Ch-17* and *Ch-18* TROMs; ComSoPac and VP-81 war diaries. The VP-81 War Diary only acknowledges the attack obliquely in its tables, which make clear the nature of the mission on January 28. The ComSoPac War Diary mentions an attack in the same area but gets some details wrong.

231 Monograph 142, 20.

232 Monograph 142, 20.

233 Monograph 142, 20.

234 Monograph 142, 18, 57.

235 Monograph 142, 20–21.

236 Wolf, *13th Fighter Command*, 246–47, Cohn, *Crusaders*, 1706–11; ComSoPac, VF-40; VMF-211, 215, and 321 war diaries.

237 Wolf, *13th Fighter Command*, 246–47, Cohn, *Crusaders*, 1706–11; and 321 war diaries.

238 Cohn, *Crusaders*, 1706–11.

239 Cohn, *Crusaders*, 1706–11.

240 Cohn, *Crusaders*, 1734.

241 Cohn, *Crusaders*, 1717–23; MACR 1788; "B-25C-20 'Skilla' Serial Number 42-64570," *Pacific Wrecks* (www.pacificwrecks.com); VMF-321 War Diary.

242 Wolf, *13th Fighter Command*, 246; MACR 16495.

243 Wolf, *13th Fighter Command*, 246–47, Cohn, *Crusaders*, 1706–11.

244 VMF-321 War Diary; "F4U-1 Corsair Bureau Number 02402," *Pacific Wrecks* (www.pacificwrecks.com); "F4U-1 Corsair Bureau Number 55835 Number 900," *Pacific Wrecks* (www.pacificwrecks.com); "F4U-1 Corsair Bureau Number 17914," *Pacific Wrecks* (www.pacificwrecks.com).

245 VP-14 War Diary; Wolf, *13th Fighter Command*, 246; MACR 1781; "P-38J-10-LO 'Hollywood Hep Cat' Serial Number 42-67618," *Pacific Wrecks* (www.pacificwrecks.com).

246 Except where noted otherwise, the account of the encounters between Captain Head, Lieutenant Kelly, and Petty Officer 2nd Class Ishida come from Henry Sakaida, "Jungle Encounter," *Pacific Wrecks* (www.pacificwrecks.com). It should be noted that Sakaida was only able to piece the account together several decades after the fact from the memoirs of veteran Japanese Zero ace Kodaka "Tokkan" Noritsura, a pilot in the 204 Air Group, who mentioned the story of his friend and squadron mate, Petty Officer 2nd Class Ishida Teigo, and Ishida's encounter with two American pilots in the jungles outside Rabaul, and the records of the 204 Air Group. Ishida was killed in air combat over Anami Oshima on April 16, 1945. Sakaida is careful to note that what actually happened is unclear and that the scenario he presents is just what he believes probably happened. The narrative agrees with Sakaida's version of events, but readers should be aware of the uncertainty here.

247 Until Henry Sakaida pieced together this incident, the accepted narrative was that Ishida "encountered two shotdown US pilots, both of whom he knocked unconscious" (Hata, Izawa, and Shores, *Japanese Naval Air Force*, 545.) In identifying the two shotdown US pilots and thus their fates, Sakaida has performed a true service and was able to give Head's sister, who had no knowledge of his fate, closure.

248 Task Unit 35.7.6 "Submarine attack on Task Unit 35.7.6, 22 January 1944; Task Unit Commander and Commanding Officer *Cache*'s Action Report," 1–4, 7; USS *Buchanan* "Action Report – Anti-Submarine Attack, 22 January, 1944," 1–3; USS *Southard* "Action Report," 1–4; *Ro-37* TROM.

249 The FG Corsair was identical to the F4U Corsair, but instead of being manufactured by Vought, it was manufactured by Goodyear under license from Vought.

250 ComSoPac, VF-40, VMF-211, 215, and 321; and VP-14 war diaries; Wolf, *13th Fighter Command*, 247; Cohn, *Crusaders*, 1739; Hata, Izawa, and Shores, *Japanese Naval Air Force*, 142–43, 796; "B-25D-1 Mitchell Serial Number 41-30658," *Pacific Wrecks* (www.pacificwrecks.com); MACR 1782, 1800, 1801, 1803; "P-40N-5-CU Kittyhawk Serial Number NZ3186 Code 81/G," *Pacific Wrecks* (www.pacificwrecks.com); "FG-1A Corsair Bureau Number 14212," *Pacific Wrecks* (www.pacificwrecks.com). Cohn says that Thompson's B-25 went down during the afternoon raid and Snyder's and Eastwood's went down in the evening raid, but the times given in the Missing Air Crew Reports suggest Snyder's went down in the early raid, the others that evening.

251 Or Aikiharu. Wolf, *5th Fighter Command*, 520–23; Hickey and Pettus, *Ken's Men, Vol. II*, 68–69; Dunn, "248th Hiko Sentai"; Sakaida, *Japanese Army Air Force Aces*, 110; MACR 2135, 2136, 2281; McAulay, *Clean Sweep*, 1242–57.

252 "January 23, 1944," *Pacific Wrecks* (www.pacificwrecks.com); ComSoPac, AirSols Strike Command, MAG-14; VMTB-143, VMSB-236 and 341, VB-98, VC-40; VMF-211, 212, 215, and 321; VF-40, and VP-14 war diaries; Wolf, *13th Fighter Command*, 247; Hata, Izawa, and Shores, *Japanese Naval Air Force*, 143; "F4U-1A Corsair Bureau Number 49891," *Pacific Wrecks* (www.pacificwrecks.com). Curiously, Yeilding does not seem to have a Missing Air Crew Report.

253 ComSoPac, VMF-211, 212, and 321 war diaries; Hata, Izawa, and Shores, *Japanese Naval Air Force*, 143, 796.

254 "January 23, 1944," *Pacific Wrecks* (www.pacificwrecks.com); Monograph 132, 56, ComSoPac War Diary.

255 ComSoPac, VMF-211, 215, and 321; VC-40, VMTB-134, VP-14, and USS *Coos Bay* war diaries; *Lyons* and *Koan Maru* TROMs; "P-38H-5-LO Lightning Serial Number 42-66897," *Pacific Wrecks* (www.pacificwrecks.com). The *Koan Maru* TROM says the Royal New Zealand Air Force's No. 1 Squadron, a bomber-reconnaissance unit, was also involved in this attack. No. 1 Squadron was equipped with Vega

PV-1 Venturas. No other source, primary or secondary, mentions the presence of Venturas in this attack. However, one of No. 1 Squadron's missions was to follow behind the air strike and look for downed aviators. The Venturas could drop rubber rafts to such air crews and loiter over the location until a PBY Dumbo could arrive to pick them up. (Ross, *Official History*, 219.) Admiral Halsey mentions that "Venturas" directed PBY Dumbos to downed aviators. No. 1 Squadron may have gotten caught up with the strike craft when the Japanese fighters reached them, which was not unheard of in the course of these duties.

256 Cressman, *Chronology*; "January 24, 1944," *Pacific Wrecks* (www.pacificwrecks.com); Wolf, *5th Fighter Command*, 523; 498th Bombardment Squadron "Narrative report on mission 24-D-1. Performed on the 24th of January, 1944"; 499th Bombardment Squadron "Narrative Report on Mission 24 D-1. Performed on 24 Jan., 44"; 500th Bombardment Squadron "Narrative Report on Mission FFO 24-D-1, Performed by 500th Bombardment Squadron (M) January 24"; 501st Bombardment Squadron "Narrative report on Mission 24-D-1, Performed on 24 January 1944"; *History of the 38th Bombardment Group*.

257 Cressman, *Chronology*; "January 25, 1944," *Pacific Wrecks* (www.pacificwrecks.com); 498th Bombardment Squadron "Narrative report on mission 25-G-1. Performed on 25 January, 1944"; 499th Bombardment Squadron "Narrative Report on Mission FFO 25-G. Performed on 25 Jan., 44"; 500th Bombardment Squadron "Narrative Report on Mission FFO 25-G-1, Performed by 500th Bombardment Squadron (M) January 25"; 501st Bombardment Squadron "Narrative report on Mission 25-G-1, Performed on 25 January 1944"; *History of the 38th Bombardment Group*; "B-25D-1 'Dittum Dattum (II)' Serial Number 41-30312," *Pacific Wrecks* (www.pacificwrecks.com).

258 Or maybe January 26. Or January 24. Hata, Izawa, and Shores, *Japanese Naval Air Force*, 143. Hata et al. say that, after an engagement on January 24, "At this point 204 Ku was ordered to withdraw to recuperate, and on 25 January eight A6Ms led by Lt Yamaguchi departed for Truk." Monograph 132 (16) says:

(1) The bulk of the 2d Carrier Division (air units of Junyo and Hiyo, each consisting of 24 fighters, 18 bombers and 7 carrier attack planes, and Ryuho, 21 fighters and 9 carrier attack planes) advanced to Rabaul on 25 January under the command of the Commander of the said Carrier Division was placed under the command of the base air force.
(2) The 6th Air Attack Force was relieved by the 2d Carrier Division and on 26 January moved to Truk where it was trained to rebuild its fighting power.

259 Monograph 142, 29.

260 Or Joshima. Or Takaji.

261 Hata, Izawa, and Shores, *Japanese Naval Air Force*, 143.

262 Monograph 142, 29.

263 Monograph 142, 16.

264 "January 25, 1944," *Pacific Wrecks* (www.pacificwrecks.com).

265 ComTaskGroup 74.2 "Action Report of bombardment MADANG-ALEXISHAFEN 26 January 1944."

266 ComSoPac, ComAirSols Strike Command, VB-98, VMSB-341, VMTB-143, VF-17, and VMF-215 war diaries; Wolf, *13th Fighter Command*, 247; Hata, Izawa, and Shores, *Japanese Naval Air Force*, 143–44; Blackburn, *Jolly Rogers*, 224–27.

267 Wolf, *13th Fighter Command*, 248; ComSoPac, VF-17; VMF-211, 215, and 217; VMSB-341, VMTB-233, and USS *Guest* war diaries; "F4U-1A Corsair Bureau Number 55927," *Pacific Wrecks* (www.pacificwrecks.com).

268 Hackett and Kingsepp, "Midget Submarines in the Bismarcks 1943–1944," *Imperial Japanese Navy Page* (www.combinedfleet.com).

269 Hackett and Kingsepp, "Midget Submarines in the Bismarcks 1943–1944"; Hickey, *Warpath*, 130–33.

270 Hackett and Kingsepp, "Midget Submarines in the Bismarcks 1943–1944"; Hickey, *Warpath*, 130–33.

271 Hackett and Kingsepp, "Midget Submarines in the Bismarcks 1943–1944"; Hickey, *Warpath*, 130–33.

272 ComSoPac, VF-17, VMF-217, and VMSB-244 war diaries.

273 VMF-217 war diary.

274 VMF-217 war diary.

275 "February 17, 1944," *Pacific Wrecks* (www.pacificwrecks.com).

276 *W-26* TROM; Cressman, *Chronology*.

277 Monograph 100, 60.

278 Monograph 100, 60.

279 Monograph 100, 60.

280 Monograph 100, 60–61.

281 Monograph 100 (60) identifies the submarines as the *I-169* and *I-181*. The *I-181* had been sunk under mysterious circumstances on January 16, 1944. The Japanese garrison at Gali, Papua New Guinea witnessed her sinking after a running battle with an unidentified US destroyer and an identified PT boat. Or, the *I-181* was sunk in St George's Channel by US Navy aircraft. (*I-181* TROM.) The *I-169*'s TROM makes no mention of such an operation, but says that on January 31, 1944 "Departs Rabaul for a supply mission to Buka and Buin." The next entry is for February 12, when a new commanding officer was appointed, after which on February 15, another new commanding officer was appointed. The next entry directly related to the *I-169* is March 11, when she "arrives at Truk." Obviously, there are gaps in this record, and some inaccuracies. Whether the *I-169* was going to Buka and Buin is open to question because the *I-171* had left Rabaul on a supply run to Buka the day before the *I-169* left.

282 Monograph 100, 60–61.

283 Monograph 100, 60–61.

284 *I-171* TROM.

285 The *Talbot* must not be confused with the *Ralph Talbot*.

286 Commander Destroyer Squadron Forty-Five "Action Report, covering operations of Task Group 31.8 from January 28, 1944 to February 1, 1944" (hereinafter "Earle Green Islands Report"), 1; Reginald Newell, "Raiders of the Green Islands," *Naval History* (June 2020).

287 Give the Kiwi aviators serious credit for resourcefulness and quick thinking here.

288 Earle Green Islands Report, 1–2; Newell, "Raiders of the Green Islands."

289 Newell, "Raiders of the Green Islands."

290 Earle Green Islands Report, 3; Newell, "Raiders of the Green Islands."

291 Earle Green Islands Report, 3.

292 Earle Green Islands Report, 3; *I-171* TROM. The TROM says the second message might say she arrived at Buka on February 1 or 2 but it's difficult to read the blurred number. Given the message says she had not been heard from since February 1, it is assumed the message meant February 1.

293 Cressman, *Chronology*; JANAC.

294 Or *Fatsumi Maru*. Cressman, *Chronology*; JANAC; "February 5, 1944," *Pacific Wrecks* (www.pacificwrecks.com).

295 Cressman, *Chronology*; JANAC; "February 6, 1944," *Pacific Wrecks* (www.pacificwrecks.com).

296 Cressman, *Chronology*; JANAC; "February 6, 1944," *Pacific Wrecks* (www.pacificwrecks.com).

297 Monograph 100, 61.

298 Or the Second Battle of Kula Gulf. Or the Third Battle of Kula Gulf.

299 USS *St Louis*, "Action Report, Anti-aircraft on 14–15 February 1944" (hereinafter "*St Louis* Anti-aircraft Report"), 3, 10, 16.

300 Monograph 100, 61; Morison, *Bismarcks Barrier*, 416.

301 *St Louis* Anti-aircraft Report, 1.

302 *St Louis* Anti-aircraft Report, 1; Commander Cruiser Division 12 War Diary; Morison, *Bismarcks Barrier*, 416.

303 Halsey, *Story*, 3915.

304 Morison, *Bismarcks Barrier*, 413.

305 Rems, *South Pacific Cauldron*, 3475–76, 3482–84.

306 Morison, *Bismarcks Barrier*, 416.

307 Monograph 100, 62.

308 Morison, *Bismarcks Barrier*, 414.

309 Morison, *Bismarcks Barrier*, 416.

310 Monograph 100, 62.

311 Miller, *Cartwheel*, 315.

312 The account of the sinking of the *Agano* comes from the *Agano* and *Ch-28* TROMs and USS *Skate* "Report of War Patrol Number Three," 4–5.

313 "February 17, 1944," *Pacific Wrecks* (www.pacificwrecks.com); Cressman, *Chronology*; ComDesRon 12 Report of Torpedo Attack on Enemy Shipping in Keravia Bay and Bombardment of Japanese Shore Installations in the Rabaul–Vunapope Area on February 17–18, 1944; USS *Farenholt* War Diary.

314 February 19, 1944," *Pacific Wrecks* (www.pacificwrecks.com); ComSoPac, VMTB-143, MVF-217, and VF-17 war diaries; Sakaida, *Siege*, 25–27.

315 The account of the withdrawal of Japanese aircraft from Rabaul comes from Sakaida, *Siege*, 25–27.

316 Tonnage is from JANAC.

317 Miller, *Cartwheel*, 315.

318 Krueger, *From Down Under*, 87.

319 Kenney, *Reports*, 359.

320 William C. Frierson, *American Forces in Action: The Admiralties: Operations of the 1st Cavalry Division, 29 February – 18 May 1944* (Washington, DC: Office of the Chief of Military History, Department of the Army, 1990), 7.

321 MacArthur, *Reports of General MacArthur: Japanese Operations in the Southwest Pacific Area* (Washington, DC: United States Government Printing Office, 1966), 137 n.5.

322 Kenney, *Reports*, 358–59.

323 MacArthur, *Reports of General MacArthur*, 137 n.5.

324 Kenney, *Reports*, 359.

325 Kenney, *Reports*, 359–60.

326 Kenney, *Reports*, 360.

327 MacArthur, *Reports of General MacArthur*, 138.

328 MacArthur, *Reports of General MacArthur*, 137 n.5.

329 MacArthur, *Reports of General MacArthur*, 137 n.5.

330 Kenney, *Reports*, 360.

331 MacArthur, *Reports of General MacArthur*, 136–37.

332 Franz-Stefan Gady, "Is This the Worst Intelligence Chief in the US Army's History?" *The Diplomat* (www.thediplomat.com) January 27, 2019.

333 Krueger, *From Down Under*, 88.

334 Morison, *Bismarcks Barrier*, 435.

335 Seventh Amphibious Force, "Admiralty Islands Operation, 29 February, 1944 – Report on," 2.

336 Kenney, *Reports*, 361.

337 Krueger basically admits as much when he later wrote, "The reconnaissance in force was, at best, a risky undertaking. But I felt we would probably outguess the Japanese again as we had done before." Krueger, *From Down Under*, 88.

338 Morison, *Bismarcks Barrier*, 436. For some reason, Morison omits the *Stockton*.

339 USS *Nashville* (CL43), "Report of Bombardment of Manus Island (Admiralty Group) 29 February 1944," 1. USS *Phoenix* "Action Report of Bombardment and Occupation of Momote Airdrome, Los Negros Island, Admiralty Group, on 29 February 1944," 1–2.

340 Krueger, *From Down Under*, 90.

341 Morison, *Bismarcks Barrier*, 436.

342 Miller, *Cartwheel*, 326; Frierson, *The Admiralties*, 23.

343 Ness, *Rikugun I*, 527–28, 547, 553. The 81st Guard Unit, under the 8th Base Force in Rabaul, was on Manus in March 1943 and had a peripheral role in the *Akikaze* Massacre, though it did not conduct the massacre and was probably unaware of it. In December 1943, the 8th Combined Special Naval Landing Force, formed by combining the 6th Kure and 7th Yokosuka Special Naval Landing Forces and which had fought on New Georgia, was disbanded. The 6th Kure was redesignated the 88th Guard Unit and assigned to Manus. The 7th Yokosuka was redesignated the 89th Guard Unit and assigned to Namantai on New Ireland. Together, they would form the core of the newly organized 14th Base Force, headquartered in Kavieng. Other parts of the 8th, though it's not clear which parts, were absorbed into the 87th Guard Unit, formed in September 1943 and assigned to Buka under the 1st Base Force located in Buin, others were assigned to the 1st Base Force itself, and still others were used to form the

headquarters of the 14th Base Force. What happened to the 81st Guard Unit, which was already at Manus, is unclear. It was reportedly disbanded in December 1944, which suggests it was withdrawn to Rabaul to remain under the 8th Base Force, but given the haphazard nature of the organization of the Special Naval Landing Force units, it seems more likely that it was absorbed into the 88th.

344 Rems, *South Pacific Cauldron*, 3987–89; Miller, *Cartwheel*, 319; Edward J. Drea, *MacArthur's ULTRA: Codebreaking and the War against Japan, 1942–1945* (Lawrence, KS: University Press of Kansas, 1992), 102.

345 Rems, *South Pacific Cauldron*, 3993–97.

346 Krueger, *From Down Under*, 92.

347 Frierson, *The Admiralties*, 31.

348 William Manchester, *American Caesar: Douglas MacArthur1880–1964* (New York: Back Bay Books, 1978), Kindle edition, 341.

349 Manchester, *American Caesar*, 341.

350 Rems, *South Pacific Cauldron*, 4032–33.

351 Frierson, *The Admiralties*, 31.

352 Hirrel, Leo, *Bismarck Archipelago: The U.S. Army Campaigns of World War II* (CMH Pub 72-24) (Washington, DC: US Army Center of Military History), 1994.

353 Frierson, *The Admiralties*, 38; Rems, *South Pacific Cauldron*, 4038–41.

354 Frierson, *The Admiralties*, 47; Rems, *South Pacific Cauldron*, 4042–44.

Chapter 10

1 Samuel Eliot Morison, *The Two-Ocean War: A Short History of the United States Navy in the Second World War* (Boston, Toronto; London: Little, Brown, and Company, 1963), 35.

2 Morison, *Two-Ocean War*, 35.

3 William Tuohy, *America's Fighting Admirals: Winning the War at Sea in World War II* (St Paul, MN: Zenith Press, 2007), Kindle edition, 733.

4 Brig Gen Samuel B. Griffith, USMC (ret.), *The Battle for Guadalcanal* (Toronto; New York; London; Sydney: Bantam, 1980), 5.

5 Command Summary of Fleet Admiral Chester W. Nimitz, USN.

6 "Foreign Relations of the United States, The Conferences at Washington, 1941–1942, and Casablanca, 1943 Document 114," Office of the Historian, United States Department of State, (https://history.state.gov/historicaldocuments/frus1941-43/d114).

7 Richard B. Frank, *Guadalcanal: The Definitive Account of the Landmark Battle* (New York: Penguin), 1992, 7–8; Vice Admiral George Carroll Dyer, USN (ret.), *The Amphibians Came to Conquer: The Story of Admiral Richmond Kelly Turner* (Washington, DC: US Government Printing Office, 1971), 234, 239–40.

8 "Foreign Relations of the United States, The Conferences at Washington, 1941–1942, and Casablanca, 1943 Document 114."

9 Dyer, *Amphibians*, 238.

10 Griffith, *Battle for Guadalcanal*, 9–10.

11 Dyer, *Amphibians*, 243.

12 Thomas B. Buell, *Master of Seapower: A Biography of Fleet Admiral Ernest J. King* (Annapolis: Naval Institute Press, 1980), Kindle edition, 3944.

13 Maurice Matloff and Edwin M. Snell, *United States Army in World War II: The War Department, Volume III: Strategic Planning for Coalition Warfare 1941–1942* (Washington: Office of the Chief of Military History, Department of the Army, 1953), 157.

14 Manchester, *American Caesar*, 5591.

15 Williamson Murray and Allan R. Millett, *A War to Be Won: Fighting the Second World War* (Cambridge, MA; London: Belknap Press of Harvard University Press, 2000), Kindle edition, 2606.

16 Manchester, *American Caesar*, 5591; Buell, *Master of Seapower*, 3949.

17 Buell, *Master of Seapower*, 4466.

18 John Toland, *The Rising Sun: The Decline and Fall of the Japanese Empire 1936–1945* (New York: Random House, 1970), Kindle edition, 7676; Frank, *Guadalcanal*, 33; James D. Hornfischer, *Neptune's*

Inferno: The US Navy at Guadalcanal (New York: Bantam, 2011), Kindle edition, 497; Walter R. Borneman, *The Admirals: Nimitz, Halsey, Leahy, and King – The Five-Star Admirals Who Won the War at Sea* (New York; Boston; London: Little, Brown, and Company, 2012), Kindle edition, 284.

19   Borneman, *The Admirals*, 280.

20   Dyer, *Amphibians*, 252–53.

21   Tuohy, *America's Fighting Admirals*, 1156–64.

22   Prados, *Islands of Destiny*, 36.

23   Miller, *Cartwheel*, 12.

24   Halsey, *Story*, 3322–36.

25   MacArthur, Douglas. *Reminiscences*. Annapolis: Naval Institute Press, 2001. Kindle edition, 173–74.

26   Miller, *Cartwheel*, 222–23. Miller calls the planners at the Pentagon the "Washington commanders."

27   Miller, *Cartwheel*, 224–25.

28   Miller, *Cartwheel*, 225.

29   Miller, *Cartwheel*, 225.

30   USSBS Report 75, 19

31   MacArthur, *Reminiscences*, 168–69.

32   Manchester, *American Caesar*, 336–37.

33   Louis Morton, *United States Army in World War II: The War in the Pacific, Strategy and Command – The First Two Years* (Washington: Center of Military History, United States Army, 1962), 370.

34   Manchester, *American Caesar*, 337–38.

35   *Quadrant Conference August 1943, Papers and Minutes of Meetings* (Washington, DC: Office, US Secretary, Office of the Combined Chiefs of Staff, 1943), 246.

36   Manchester, *American Caesar*, 327.

37   Robert L. Eichelberger, *Our Jungle Road to Tokyo* (New York: Viking Press, 1950), Kindle edition, 36.

38   Rems, *South Pacific Cauldron*, 719–23.

39   Manchester, *American Caesar*, 339.

40   Gamble, *Target: Rabaul*, 314.

41   *Nagaura* TROM; Gamble, *Target: Rabaul*, 315; JANAC.

42   *Nagaura, Ch-37*, and *Ch-38* TROMs; 500th and 501st Bombardment Squadron histories.

43   *Nagaura* and *Natsushima* TROMs; Gamble, *Target: Rabaul*, 316; Cressman, *Chronology*; ComDesRon23 "Report of anti-shipping sweep for the period of 21–23 February 1944 and the bombardment of Kavieng and Duke of York Islands on the night of 22–23 February 1944, respectively," 16.

44   Gamble, *Target: Rabaul*, 321.

45   Gamble, *Target: Rabaul*, 321.

46   ComSoPac, "The Reduction of Rabaul, 19 February to 15 May, 1944" (hereinafter "Reduction Report"), 4–5.

47   ComSoPac, "Reduction Report," 5.

48   Gamble, *Target: Rabaul*, 319–20.

49   MacArthur, *Reminiscences*, 167.

50   Manchester, *American Caesar*, 334–36.

SELECT BIBLIOGRAPHY

The 5th Bombardment Group Association, *Bomber Barons: 5th Bombardment Group Heavy*. Paducah, KY: Turner Publishing, 2003. Kindle edition.

13th Air Force, USAAF, *Fifth Bombardment Group (Heavy) in World War II*. Hoosick Falls, NY: Merriam Press, 2012.

Alcorn, John S., *The Jolly Rogers: History of the 90th Bomb Group During World War II*. Temple City, CA: Historical Aviation Album, 1981.

Alden, John D.; and McDonald, Craig R., *United States and Allied Submarine Successes in the Pacific and Far East During World War II* (4th ed.). Jefferson, NC: McFarland, 2009.

Alexander, Joseph H., *Utmost Savagery: The Three Days of Tarawa*. Annapolis: Naval Institute Press, 1995. Kindle edition.

Baker, Thomas A., *It Wasn't so Jolly: The Story of the Jolly Rogers and the James Horner Crew*. Tijeras, NM: Thomas A. Baker, 2018.

Barbey, Daniel E., *MacArthur's Amphibious Navy: Seventh Amphibious Force Operations, 1943–1945*. Annapolis: Naval Institute Press, 1969.

Bergerud, Eric M., *Fire in the Sky: The Air War in the South Pacific*. Boulder, CO: Westview Press, 2000. Kindle edition.

Blackburn, Tom, *Jolly Rogers*. New York: Pocket Books, 1989.

Blair, Clay, Jr, *Silent Victory: The US Submarine War Against Japan*. Annapolis: Naval Institute Press, 1975.

Boehm, Roy; and Sasser, Charles W., *First SEAL*. New York: Atria, 1997.

Borneman, Walter R., *MacArthur at War: World War II in the Pacific*. New York; Boston; London: Little, Brown, and Company, 2016. Kindle edition.

Borneman, Walter R., *The Admirals: Nimitz, Halsey, Leahy, and King – The Five-Star Admirals Who Won the War at Sea*. New York; Boston; London: Little, Brown, and Company, 2012.

Boyd, Carl; and Yoshida, Akihiko, *The Japanese Submarine Force and World War II*. Annapolis: Naval Institute Press, 1995. Kindle edition.

Boyington, Col Gregory "Pappy," USMC (ret.), *Baa baa Black Sheep: The True Story of the "Bad Boy" of the Pacific Theatre and His Famous Black Sheep Squadron*. New York: Bantam, 1977. Kindle edition.

Britt, Sam S., Jr, *The Long Rangers: A Diary of The 307th Bombardment Group (H)*. Spartanburg, SC: Reprint Company Publishers, 1990.

Buell, Thomas B., *Master of Seapower: A Biography of Fleet Admiral Ernest J. King*. Annapolis: Naval Institute Press, 1980. Kindle edition.

Bulkley, Captain Robert J., Jr, USNR (ret.), *At Close Quarters: PT Boats in the United States Navy*. Washington: Naval History Division, 1962.

Bullard, Steven (translator), *Japanese Army Operations in the South Pacific Area: New Britain and Papua Campaigns, 1942–43*. Canberra: Australian War Memorial, 2007.

Burns, Eugene, *Then There Was One*. Pickle Partners Publishing, 2015. Kindle edition.

Caidin, Martin, *Fork-Tailed Devil: The P-38*. Dering Harbor, NY: iBooks, 2001. Kindle edition.

Caidin, Martin, *The B-17: The Flying Forts*. New York: iBooks, 2001. Kindle edition.

Calhoun, C. Raymond, *Tin Can Sailor: Life Aboard the USS Sterett, 1939–1945*. Annapolis: Naval Institute Press, 1993. Kindle edition.

Carey, Alan C., *We Flew Alone: Men and Missions of the United States Navy's B-24 Liberator Squadrons Pacific Operations: February 1943–September 1944*. Atglen, PA: Schiffer Military History, 2017.

Carter, Kit C.; and Mueller, Robert, *U.S. Army Air Forces in World War II Combat Chronology 1941–1945*. Washington, DC: Center for Air Force History, 1991.

Chambers, Mark; and Holmes, Tony, *Nakajima B5N "Kate" and B6N "Jill" Units*. Oxford: Osprey, 2017. Kindle edition.

Chambers, Mark; and Holmes, Tony, *Yokosuka D4Y "Judy" Units*. Oxford: Osprey, 2021. Kindle edition.

Claringbould, Michael John, *A6M2/3 Zero-sen: New Guinea and the Solomons 1942*. Oxford: Osprey, 2023. Kindle edition.

Claringbould, Michael John, *F4U Corsair versus A6M Zero-sen: Rabaul and the Solomons 1943–44 (Duel)*. Oxford: Osprey, 2022.

Claringbould, Michael John, *Operation I-Go: Yamamoto's Last Offensive New Guinea and the Solomons, April 1943*. Kent Town, Australia: Avenmore, 2020.

Claringbould, Michael John, *Operation Ro-Go 1943: Japanese Air Power Tackles the Bougainville Landings*. Oxford: Osprey, 2023. Kindle edition.

Claringbould, Michael John, *Pacific Adversaries Volume Four: Imperial Japanese Navy vs The Allies – The Solomons 1943–1944*. Kent Town, Australia: Avonmore Books, 2021.

Claringbould, Michael John, *Pacific Adversaries Volume One: Japanese Army Air Force vs The Allies, New Guinea 1942–1944*. Kent Town, Australia: Avonmore Books, 2019.

Claringbould, Michael John, *Pacific Adversaries Volume Three: Imperial Japanese Navy vs The Allies, New Guinea & the Solomons 1942–1944*. Kent Town, Australia: Avonmore Books, 2020.

Claringbould, Michael John, *Pacific Adversaries Volume Two: Imperial Japanese Navy vs. The Allies, New Guinea & the Solomons 1942–1944*. Kent Town, Australia: Avonmore Books, 2020.

Clark, Curt, *The Famed Green Dragons: The Four Stack APDs, The APD Destroyer Sailors of WWII*. Paducah, KY: Turner Publishing, 2003.

Clayton, James D., *The Years of MacArthur, Volume Two 1941–1945*. Boston: Houghton Mifflin, 1975.

Cleaver, Thomas McKelvey, *Pacific Thunder: The US Navy's Central Pacific Campaign, August 1943–October 1944*. Oxford: Osprey, 2017. Kindle edition.

Cleaver, Thomas McKelvey, *Under the Southern Cross: The South Pacific Air Campaign Against Rabaul*. Oxford: Osprey, 2021. Kindle edition.

Cohn, Maj R. H., *The Crusaders: A History of the 42nd Bombardment Group (M)*. Baton Rouge, LA: Army & Navy Pictorial Publications, 2013.

Craven, W. F.; and Cate, J. L. (editors), *Army Air Forces in World War II, Vol. IV: The Pacific: Guadalcanal to Saipan August 1942 to July 1944*. Washington, DC: Office of Air Force History, 1983.

Crenshaw, Russell Sydnor, Jr, *The Battle of Tassafaronga*. Annapolis: Naval Institute Press, 1995.

Cressman, Robert J., *The Official Chronology of the U.S. Navy in World War II*. Washington, DC: Contemporary History Branch, Naval Historical Center, 1999.

Crocker, Mel, *Black Cats and Dumbos: WW II's Fighting PBYs*. Huntington Beach, CA: Crocker Media Expressions (2nd ed.), 2002.

Crowl, Philip A.; and Love, Edmund G., *United States Army in World War II – The War in the Pacific – "Seizure of the Gilberts and Marshalls."* Washington, DC: Office of the Chief of Military History, Department of the Army, 1955.

Cuppy, Will, *The Decline and Fall of Practically Everybody*. Boston: David R. Godine, 1950. Kindle edition.

Dean, Peter J., *Australia 1943: The Liberation of New Guinea*. Port Melbourne, Victoria: Cambridge University Press, 2014. Kindle edition.

Dean, Peter J., *MacArthur's Coalition: US and Australian Operations in the Southwest Pacific Area, 1942–1945*. Lawrence: University of Kansas Press, 2018.

Dean, Peter J. (ed.), *Australia 1944–45: Victory in the Pacific*. Port Melbourne, Victoria: Cambridge University Press, 2016. Kindle edition.

DeChant, John A., *Devilbirds: The Story of United States Marine Corps Aviation in World War II*. New York and London: Harper, 1947.

Dexter, David, *Australia in the War of 1939–1945: Series 1 (Army) Volume VI – The New Guinea Offensives*. Canberra: Australian War Memorial, 1961.

Dobson, Carl, *Cleo J. Dobson, U.S. Navy Carrier Pilot World War II: A Personal Account*. [US]: [SI], 2018. Kindle edition.

Dorny, Louis B., *US Navy PBY Catalina Units of the Pacific War*. Oxford: Osprey, 2013. Kindle edition.

Drea, Edward J., *MacArthur's ULTRA: Codebreaking and the War against Japan, 1942–1945*. Lawrence, KS: University Press of Kansas, 1992.

Dull, Paul S., *A Battle History of the Imperial Japanese Navy (1941–1945)*. Annapolis: Naval Institute Press, 1978.

Dunn, Richard L., *South Pacific Air War: The Role of Air Power in the New Guinea and Solomon Island Campaigns, January 1943 to February 1944*. Atglen, PA: Schiffer Publishing, 2024.

Dyer, Vice Admiral George Carroll, USN (ret.), *The Amphibians Came to Conquer: The Story of Admiral Richmond Kelly Turner*. Washington, DC: US Government Printing Office, 1971.

Evans, David C., *The Japanese Navy in World War II in the Words of Former Japanese Naval Officers* (2nd ed.). Annapolis: Naval Institute Press, 1986. Kindle edition.

Evans, David C., and Peattie, Mark R., *Kaigun: Strategy, Tactics, and Technology in the Imperial Japanese Navy 1887–1941*. Annapolis: Naval Institute Press, 1997. Kindle edition.

Evans, Don L.; Gaylor, Walter; Nelson, Harry A.; and Hickey, Lawrence J., *Revenge of the Red Raiders: The Illustrated History of the 22nd Bombardment Group During World War II*, 2 vols. Boulder, CO: International Research and Publishing Corporation, 2006. Kindle edition.

Evans, Mark L.; and Grossnick, Roy A., *United States Naval Aviation 1910–2010, Volume I: Chronology*. Washington, DC: Naval History and Heritage Command, Department of the Navy, 2015.

Fifth Group Historical Officer (ed.), *The Story Of The Fifth Bombardment Group: Heavy*. Whitefish, MT: Kessinger Publishing, 2010.

Foy, David A., *Loyalty First: The Life and Times of Charles A. Willoughby, MacArthur's Chief Intelligence Officer*. Philadelphia and Oxford: Casemate, 2023. Kindle edition.

Francillon, R. J., *Japanese Aircraft of the Pacific War* (1st ed.). New York: Funk & Wagnalls, 1970.

Frank, Richard B., *MacArthur*. New York: Palgrave Macmillan, 2007.

Frierson, Major William C., *American Forces in Action: The Admiralties: Operations of the 1st Cavalry Division, 29 February – 18 May 1944*. Washington, DC: Office of the Chief of Military History, Department of the Army, 1990.

Fuller, Richard, *Shokan: Hirohito's Samurai*. London: Arms and Armour Press, 1992.

Gailey, Harry A., *Bougainville, 1943–1945: The Forgotten Campaign*. Lexington, KY: University Press of Kentucky, 1991. Kindle edition.

Gamble, Bruce, *Black Sheep One: The Life of Gregory "Pappy" Boyington*. New York: Ballantine, 2000. Kindle edition.

Gamble, Bruce, *Fortress Rabaul: The Battle for the Southwest Pacific, January 1942–April 1943*. Minneapolis, MN: Zenith Press, 2013. Kindle edition.

Gamble, Bruce, *Kangaroo Squadron: American Courage in the Darkest Days of World War II*. New York: Da Capo Press, 2018. Kindle edition.

Gamble, Bruce, *Target: Rabaul: The Allied Siege of Japan's Most Infamous Stronghold, March 1943–August 1945*. Minneapolis, MN: Zenith Press, 2013. Kindle edition.

Gamble, Bruce, *The Black Sheep: The Definitive Account of Marine Fighting Squadron 214 in World War II*. New York: Random House, 1998. Kindle edition.

Gann, Maj Timothy, USAF, *Fifth Air Force Light and Medium Bomber Operations During 1942 and 1943: Building Doctrine and Forces that Triumphed in the Battle of the Bismarck Sea and the Wewak Raid*. Maxwell AFB, AL: Air University Press, 1992.

Gillison, Douglas, *Australia in the War of 1939–1945: Series Three (Air) Volume I – Royal Australian Air Force, 1939–1942*. Canberra: Australian War Memorial, 1962.

Goldstein, Donald M.; and Dillon, Katherine V. (ed.), *The Pacific War Papers: Japanese Documents of World War II*. Dulles, VA: Potomac, 2004.

Grider, George; and Sims, Lydel, *War Fish*. New York: Pyramid, 1959.

Halsey, Fleet Admiral William F., USN, *Admiral Halsey's Story*. Pickle Partners Publishing, 2013. Kindle edition.

Hammel, Eric, *Air War Pacific Chronology: America's Air War Against Japan in East Asia and the Pacific 1941–1945*. Pacifica, CA: Pacifica Military History, 1998. Kindle edition.

Hammel, Eric, *Coral and Blood*, Pacifica, CA: Pacifica Military History, 2009. Kindle edition.

Hara, Tameichi; Saito, Fred; and Pineau, Roger, *Japanese Destroyer Captain: Pearl Harbor, Guadalcanal, Midway – The Great Naval Battles as Seen Through Japanese Eyes*. Annapolis: Naval Institute Press, 1967. Kindle edition.

Hashimoto, Lieutenant Commander Mochitsura, *Sunk: The Story of the Japanese Submarine Fleet 1941–1945*. Pickle Partners Publishing, 2015. Kindle edition.

Hata, Ikuhiko; Izawa, Yasuho; and Shores, Christopher, *Japanese Army Air Force Units and Their Aces, 1931–1945*. London: Grub Street, 2002. Kindle edition.

Hata, Ikuhiko; Izawa, Yasuho; and Shores, Christopher, *Japanese Naval Air Force Fighter Units and Their Aces*. London: Grub Street, 2011. Kindle edition.

Henebry, Maj Gen John P. (ret.), *The Grim Reapers at Work in the Pacific Theater: The Third Attack Group of the U.S. Fifth Air Force*. Missoula, MT: Pictorial Histories Publishing Company, 2002.

Hess, William N., *49th Fighter Group: Aces of the Pacific*. Oxford: Osprey, 2013. Kindle edition.

Hickey, Lawrence J., *Ken's Men Against the Empire: The Illustrated History of the 43rd Bombardment Group During World War II, Volume I: Prewar to October 1943 The B-17 Era*. Boulder, CO: International Historical Research Associates, 2016.

Hickey, Lawrence J., *Warpath Across the Pacific: The Illustrated History of the 345th Bombardment Group During World War II*. Boulder, CO: International Historical Research Associates, 2008.

Hickey, Lawrence J.; and Pettus, James T., *Ken's Men Against the Empire: The Illustrated History of the 43rd Bombardment Group During World War II, Volume II: The B-24 Era*. Boulder, CO: International Historical Research Associates, 2019.

Hickey, Lawrence J.; Levy, Michael H.; and Claringbould, Michael J., *Rampage of Roarin' 20's: The Illustrated History of the 312th Bombardment Group during World War II*. Boulder, CO: International Historical Research Associates, 2009.

Hough, Lt Col Frank O.; and Crown, Major John A., *The Campaign on New Britain*. Washington, DC: Historical Branch, Headquarters, US Marine Corps, 1952.

Howarth, Stephen, *The Fighting Ships of the Rising Sun: The Drama of the Imperial Japanese Navy 1895–1945*. New York: Atheneum, 1983.

Hoyt, Edwin P., *How They Won the War in the Pacific: Nimitz and His Admirals*. Guilford, CN: Lyons Press, 2012. Kindle edition.

Huff, Sidney L., *My Fifteen Years with General MacArthur*. New York: Paperback Library, 1964.

Hughes, Thomas Alexander, *Admiral Bill Halsey: A Naval Life*. Cambridge, MA: Harvard University Press, 2016.

Hunt, Frazier, *The Untold Story of Douglas MacArthur*. New York: Manor Books, 1977.

Imparato, Edward T., *General MacArthur: Speeches and Reports 1908–1964*. Paducah, KY: Turner Publishing, 2000.

Isely, Jeter A.; and Crowl, Dr Philip A., *U.S. Marines and Amphibious Warfare: Its Theory, and Its Practice In The Pacific*. Pickle Partners Publishing, 2016. Kindle edition.

Johnson, R. W., and Threlfall, N. A., *Volcano Town: The 193–43 Eruptions at Rabaul*. Bathurst, Australia: Robert Brown & Associates, 1985.

Johnson, William Bruce, *The Pacific Campaign in World War II: From Pearl Harbor to Guadalcanal*. London; New York: Routledge, 2006. Kindle edition.

Joint Army-Navy Assessment Committee (JANAC), *Japanese Naval and Merchant Shipping Losses During World War II by All Causes*, NAVEXOS P-468; Washington, DC: Government Printing Office, 1947.

Jones, David; and Nunan, Peter, *U.S. Subs Down Under: Brisbane 1942–1945*. Annapolis: Naval Institute Press, 2005.

Jones, Ken, *Destroyer Squadron 23: Combat Exploits of Arleigh Burke's Gallant Force*. Uncommon Valor Press, 2016. Kindle edition.

Kenney, George C., *General Kenney Reports: A Personal History of the Pacific War*. Washington, DC: US Government Printing Office, 1997.

Krueger, Walter, *From Down Under to Nippon: The Story of the Sixth Army In World War II*. Lawrence, KN: Zenger, 1953. Kindle edition.

Lacroix, Eric; and Wells, Linton, II, *Japanese Cruisers of the Pacific War*. Annapolis: Naval Institute Press, 1997.

Langelo, Vincent A., *With All Our Might: The WWII History of the* USS Boise *(CL-47)*. Austin, TX; Eakin Press, 2000.

Lardas, Mark; and Postlethwaite, Mark, *Rabaul 1943–44: Reducing Japan's Great Island Fortress*. Oxford: Osprey, 2018. Kindle edition.

Listemann, Phil H., *The Douglas Boston & Havoc: The Australians. (Squadrons No. 22)*. Philedition, 2017. Kindle edition.

Lockwood, Charles A., *Sink 'em All; Submarine Warfare in the Pacific*. New York: E.P. Dutton & Co., 1951. Kindle edition.

MacDougall, Robert, *Leaders in Dangerous Times: Douglas MacArthur and Dwight D. Eisenhower*. Bloomington, IN: Trafford Publishing, 2013. Kindle edition.

Manchester, William, *American Caesar: Douglas MacArthur 1880–1964*. New York: Back Bay Books, 1978. Kindle edition.

Manchester, William, *Goodbye, Darkness: A Memoir of the Pacific War*. New York: Back Bay Books, 1979. Kindle edition.

Matloff, Maurice; and Snell, Edwin M., *United States Army in World War II: The War Department, Volume III: Strategic Planning for Coalition Warfare 1941–1942*, Washington: Office of the Chief of Military History, Department of the Army, 1953.

McAulay, Lex, *A Clean Sweep: The Destruction of the Japanese Army Air Force Fighter Arm Over New Guinea 1943–44*. Maryborough, Qld: Banner Books, 2016. Kindle edition.

McAulay, Lex, *Into The Dragon's Jaws – The US 5th Air Force at Rabaul October–November 1943*. Maryborough, Qld: Banner Books, 2012. Kindle edition.

McAulay, Lex, *MacArthur's Eagles: The U.S. Air War Over New Guinea, 1943–1944*. Annapolis: Naval Institute Press, 2004.

McGee, William L., *The Solomons Campaigns, 1942–1943: From Guadalcanal to Bougainville, Pacific War Turning Point*. Tiburon, CA: BMC Publications, 2001.

McManus, John C., *Fire and Fortitude: The US Army in the Pacific War, 1941–1943*. New York: Penguin Publishing Group, 2019. Kindle edition.

Melson, Maj Charles D. (ret.), "Up the Slot: Marines in the Central Solomons." *World War II Commemorative Series*. Washington, DC: History and Museums Division, Headquarters, US Marine Corps, 1993.

Miller, John, *Cartwheel: The Reduction of Rabaul*, Office of the Chief of Military History, Dept. of the Army, 1959.

Morison, Samuel Eliot, *History of United States Naval Operations in World War II, Vol V: The Struggle for Guadalcanal August 1942–February 1943*. Edison, NJ: Castle, 1949.

Morison, Samuel Eliot, *History of United States Naval Operations in World War II, Vol VI: Breaking the Bismarcks Barrier 22 July 1942–1 May 1944*. Edison, NJ: Castle, 1950.

Morison, Samuel Eliot, *The Two-Ocean War: A Short History of the United States Navy in the Second World War*. Boston, Toronto; London: Little, Brown, and Company, 1963.

Morton, Louis, *United States Army in World War II: The War in the Pacific – Strategy and Command: The First Two Years*. Washington: Center of Military History, United States Army, 1962.

Murphy, James T.; and Feuer, A. B., *Skip Bombing*. Westport, CN: Praeger, 1993.

Murray, Williamson; and Millett, Allan R., *A War To Be Won: Fighting the Second World War*. Cambridge, MA; London: Belknap Press of Harvard University Press, 2000. Kindle edition.

Nelson, Curtis L., *Hunters in the Shallows: A History of the PT Boat*. Washington, DC: Brassey's, 1998.

Ness, Leland, *Rikugun: Guide to Japanese Ground Forces 1937–1945: Volume 1: Tactical Organization of Imperial Japanese Army & Navy Ground Forces*. Solihull, UK: Helion and Company, 2014. Kindle edition.

Noles, James. *Twenty-Three Minutes to Eternity: The Final Voyage of the Escort Carrier USS Liscome Bay*, Tuscaloosa, AL: University of Alabama Press, 2010. Kindle edition.

O'Hara, Vincent P., *The US Navy Against the Axis: Surface Combat 1941–1945*. Annapolis: Naval Institute Press, 2007. Kindle edition.

Odgers, George, *Australia in the War of 1939–1945: Series Three (Air) Volume II – Air War Against Japan, 1943–1945*. Canberra: Australian War Memorial, 1968.

Office of Naval Intelligence, *Combat Narratives Solomon Islands Campaign: XII The Bougainville Landing and the Battle of Empress Augusta Bay 27 October- 1 November 1943*. Washington, DC: Publications Branch, Office of Naval Intelligence, United States Navy, 1945.

Okumiya, Masatake; Horikoshi, Jiro; and Caidin, Martin, *Zero!* Pickle Partners Publishing, 2014. Kindle edition.

Pascalis, William K.; and Ferguson, Steve W., *Protect & Avenge: The 49th Fighter Group in World War II*. Atglen, PA: Schiffer Publishing, 1996.

Perret, Geoffrey, *Old Soldiers Never Die: The Life of Douglas MacArthur*. New York: Random House, 1996.

Porter, R. Bruce; and Hammel, Eric, *Ace! a Marine Night-Fighter Pilot in World War II*. Pacifica, CA: Pacifica Press, 1985.

Potter, E. B., *Admiral Arleigh Burke*. Annapolis: Naval Institute Press, 1990.

Potter, E. B., *Nimitz*. Annapolis: Naval Institute Press, 1976. Kindle edition.

Prados, John, *Islands of Destiny: The Solomons Campaign and the Eclipse of the Rising Sun*. New York: NAL Caliber, 2012. Kindle edition.

RAAF Historical Section, *Units of the Royal Australian Air Force – A Concise History: Volume 4 Maritime and Transport Units*. Canberra: Australian Government Publishing Service, 1995.

Rems, Alan, *South Pacific Cauldron: World War II's Great Forgotten Battlegrounds*. Annapolis: Naval Institute Press, 2014. Kindle edition.

Rentz, Maj John N., *Bougainville and the Northern Solomons*. Washington, DC: Historical Branch, Headquarters, US Marine Corps, 1946.

Reports of General MacArthur: Japanese Operations in the Southwest Pacific Area. Washington, DC: United States Government Printing Office, 1966.

Reynolds, Clark G., *The Fast Carriers: The Forging of an Air Navy*. Annapolis: Naval Institute Press, 2015. Kindle edition.

Rodman, Capt Matthew K., *A War of Their Own: Bombers over the Southwest Pacific*. Maxwell AFB, AL: Air University Press, 2005.

Roscoe, Theodore, *United States Destroyer Operations in World War II*. Annapolis: Naval Institute Press, 1953.

Roscoe, Theodore, *United States Submarine Operations in World War II*. Annapolis: Naval Institute Press, 1949.

Ross, J. M. S., *Official History of New Zealand in the Second World War 1939–45: Royal New Zealand Air Force*. Wellington: War History Branch, Department of Internal Affairs, 1955.

Rottman, Gordon L., *Japanese Army in World War II: The South Pacific and New Guinea, 1942–43*. Oxford and New York: Osprey, 2005.

Sakai, Saburo; Caidin, Martin; and Saito, Fred, *Samurai*. New York: J. Boylston & Company, 2001. Kindle edition.

Sakaida, Henry, *Imperial Japanese Navy Aces 1937–45*. Oxford: Osprey, 1998. Kindle edition.

Sakaida, Henry, *Japanese Army Air Force Aces 1937–45*. Oxford: Osprey, 2012. Kindle edition.

Sakaida, Henry, *The Siege of Rabaul*. St Paul, MN: Phalanx, 1996.

Salecker, Gene Eric, *Fortress Against the Sun: The B-17 Flying Fortress in the Pacific*. Conshocken, PA: Combined Publishing, 2001. Kindle edition.

Samuels, Alfred, *The USS* Ralph Talbot *and her Gallant Men*. Charlottesville, VA: Publishers Syndication International, 1991. Kindle edition.

Shaw, Henry I., Jr; and Kane, Major Douglas T., USMC, *History of U.S. Marine Corps Operations in World War II Volume II: Isolation of Rabaul*. Washington, DC: Historical Branch, G-3 Division, Headquarters, U.S. Marine Corps, 1963.

Sherman, Adm Frederick C. (ret.), *Combat Command*. Toronto, New York, London, and Sydney: Bantam Books, 1982.

Sherrod, Robert, *History of Marine Corps Aviation in World War II*. Washington: Combat Forces Press, 1952.

Spector, Ronald H., *Eagle Against the Sun: The American War With Japan*. New York: Free Press, 1985. Kindle edition.

Stanaway, John C.; and Hickey, Lawrence J., *Attack & Conquer: The 8th Fighter Group in World War II*. Atglen, PA: Schiffer Publishing, 1995.

Stanaway, John, *Kearby's Thunderbolts: The 348th Fighter Group in World War II*. Atglen, PA: Schiffer Publishing, 1997.

Stanaway, John, *P-38 Lightning Aces of the Pacific and CBI*. Oxford: Osprey, 1997. Kindle edition.

Stanaway, John, *Possum, Clover & Hades: The 475th Fighter Group in World War II*. Atglen, PA: Schiffer Publishing, 2004.

Starke, Lt Col William H. (ret.), *Vampire Squadron!: The Saga of the 44th Fighter Squadron in the South and Southwest Pacific.* Anaheim, CA: Robinson Typographics, 1985.

Stephens, Alan, *The Royal Australian Air Force: A History.* Melbourne: Oxford University Press, 2006.

Stille, Mark E., *The Imperial Japanese Navy in the Pacific War.* Oxford: Osprey, 2014. Kindle edition.

Stille, Mark E., *The United States Navy in World War II: From Pearl Harbor to Okinawa.* Oxford: Osprey, 2021. Kindle edition.

Stout, Jay A., *Air Apaches: The True Story of the 345th Bomb Group and Its Low, Fast, and Deadly Missions in World War II.* Guilford, CN: Stackpole Books, 2019. Kindle edition.

Tagaya, Osamu, *Imperial Japanese Naval Aviator 1937–45.* Oxford: Osprey, 1988.

Tagaya, Osamu; and Styling, Mark, *Mitsubishi Type 1 Rikko 'Betty' Units of World War 2.* Oxford: Osprey, 2001. Kindle edition.

Tillman, Barrett, *Corsair: The F4U in World War II and Korea.* Annapolis: Naval Institute Press, 1979. Kindle edition.

Tillman, Barrett, *Enterprise: America's Fightingest Ship and The Men Who Helped Win World War II.* New York: Simon & Schuster, 2012.

Tillman, Barrett, *US Marine Corps Fighter Squadrons of World War II.* Oxford, Osprey, 2014. Kindle edition.

Toland, John, *The Rising Sun: The Decline and Fall of the Japanese Empire 1936–1945.* New York: Random House, 1970. Kindle edition.

Toll, Ian W., *The Conquering Tide: War in the Pacific Islands 1942–1944.* New York; London: Norton, 2016. Kindle edition.

Tuohy, William, *America's Fighting Admirals: Winning the War at Sea in World War II.* St Paul, MN: Zenith Press, 2007. Kindle edition.

United States Army Air Forces, "The Crusaders: A History of the 42nd Bombardment Group (M)," *World War Regimental Histories.* 1946.

United States Army Center of Military History, *American Forces in Action: The Capture of Makin (20–24 November 1943).* Washington, DC: Office of the Chief of Military History, Department of the Army, 1990.

United States Strategic Bombing Survey (Pacific), *Report 75: The Allied Campaign Against Rabaul.* Washington, DC: Naval Analysis Division, Marshalls-Gilberts-New Britain Party, United States Strategic Bombing Survey, 1946.

United States Strategic Bombing Survey, *Report 54: The War Against Japanese Transportation, 1941–45.* Washington, DC: Transportation Division, United States Strategic Bombing Survey, 1947.

Vandegrift, General Alexander A., USMC; and Asprey, Robert B. *Once A Marine: The Memoirs of General A.A. Vandegrift, USMC.* New York: W.W. Norton & Co., 1964.

Walton, Frank E., *Once They Were Eagles: The Men of the Black Sheep Squadron.* Lexington, KY: University Press of Kentucky, 1986. Kindle edition.

Waters, S. D., *The Royal New Zealand Navy.* Wellington: Historical Publications Branch, 1956.

Winton, John, *Ultra in the Pacific: How Breaking Japanese Codes & Ciphers Affected Naval Operations Against Japan.* London: Leo Cooper, 1993.

Wolf, William, *13th Fighter Command in World War II: Air Combat Over Guadalcanal and the Solomons.* Atglen, PA: Schiffer, 2004.

Wolf, William, *The 5th Fighter Command in World War II: Vol.1: Pearl Harbor to the Reduction of Rabaul.* Atglen, PA: Schiffer, 2011.

Wolf, William, *The 5th Fighter Command in World War II: Vol.2: The End in New Guinea, the Philippines to V-J Day.* Atglen, PA: Schiffer, 2012.

Wukovits, John, *Admiral "Bull" Halsey: The Life and Wars of the Navy's Most Controversial Commander.* New York: St Martin's Press; 2010. Kindle edition.

Wukovits, John, *Tin Can Titans: The Heroic Men and Ships of World War II's Most Decorated Navy Destroyer Squadron.* Boston: Da Capo Press, 2017. Kindle edition.

Yoshino, Ronald W., *Lightning Strikes: The 475th Fighter Group in the Pacific War, 1943–1945.* Manhattan, KN: Sunflower University Press, 1988.

Yoshiwara, Kane; and Heath, Doris (trans.), *Southern Cross.* Canberra: Australia-Japan Research Project, Australian War Memorial, 1955.

INDEX